Groupware:
Technology and Applications

Groupware:
Technologies and Applications

David Coleman
and
Raman Khanna

For book and bookstore information

http://www.prenhall.com

Prentice Hall PTR
Upper Saddle River, NJ 07458

Library of Congress Cataloging-in-Publication Data

```
Groupware: technology and applications / David Coleman, Raman Khanna [editors]
      p.  cm,
    Includes bibliographical references and index.
    ISBN 0-13-305194-3
    1. Work groups—Data processing. 2. Business—Data processing.
    3. Information technology. I. Coleman, David 1954-    .
    II. Khanna, Raman
    HD66.E976  1995
    658.4'036'0285—dc20                              95-16552
                                                     CIP
```

Editorial/production supervision: *BooksCraft, Inc., Indianapolis, IN*
Cover design: *DeFranco Design*
Acquisitions editor: *Mary Franz*
Manufacturing manager: *Alexis R. Heydt*

© 1995 by Prentice Hall PTR
Prentice-Hall, Inc.
A Simon & Schuster Company
Upper Saddle River, NJ 07458

The publisher offers discounts on this book when ordered in bulk quantities.
For more information, contact:

  Corporate Sales Department
  Prentice Hall PTR
  One Lake Street
  Upper Saddle River, NJ 07458
  Phone: 800-382-3419 FAX: 201-236-7141
  E-mail: corpsales@prenhall.com.

Printed in the United States of America

10 9 8 7 6 5 4 3 2 1

ISBN: 0-13-305194-3

Prentice-Hall International (UK) Limited, *London*
Prentice-Hall of Australia Pty. Limited, *Sydney*
Prentice-Hall Canada Inc., *Toronto*
Prentice-Hall Hispanoamericana, S.A., *Mexico*
Prentice-Hall of India Private Limited, *New Delhi*
Prentice-Hall of Japan, Inc., *Tokyo*
Simon & Schuster Asia Pte. Ltd., *Singapore*
Editora Prentice-Hall do Brasil, Ltda., *Rio de Janeiro*

Table of Contents

Part I: Technology and Standards

Part II: Vendor Strategies

Part III: Implementation & Management Strategies and Case Studies

Part IV: Groupware Resources

Foreword

Thomas W. Malone
Massachusetts Institute of Technology

It is—by now—boring to talk about the steady improvements in the costs and capabilities of information technologies that we see year after year and decade after decade. For instance, most readers of this book have probably heard more than once how much a Rolls Royce would cost today if progress in the automotive industry had been as rapid in the last 40 years as progress in the computer industry. (The most recent estimate I've heard is about $8.00!) Even though, to the best of my knowledge, this level of sustained, rapid progress has never occurred with any other technology in human history, we now take it for granted with information technology.

If this kind of dramatic progress were to occur for a technology with limited uses (like steel refineries or techniques for constructing buildings), it would revolutionize work in the specific industries that depended on that technology. But computer and communications technologies are far from single-purpose technologies. They completely alter the fundamental economics of whole industries like publishing, television, and advertising. They can dramatically change the capabilities of production processes in various kinds of manufacturing. And, most importantly from the viewpoint of this book, they can be used to change the ways work is coordinated and organized in almost all parts of almost all industries. When a very general-purpose technology like this undergoes the dramatic improvements we have come to take for granted with information technology, we should expect fundamental changes throughout our economy.

That much is easy to predict. The hard part is trying to understand just what kinds of changes to expect and what to do about them. Even though many people would like you to believe that they understand what will happen, I don't think anyone really knows what new kinds of organizations these new technologies will enable.

In fact, I think that one of the most important things we can do today is to imagine new possibilities for how work can be organized. Can we, for instance, figure out how to redesign business processes to radically improve their efficiency and quality? Can we dramatically decrease the time needed to fill orders or design new products? Can we design work organizations that truly engage the intelligence and creativity of thousands or even millions of people? Can we create decentralized networks of people in which no one is really "in charge" but out of which good things emerge? Can we create work organizations that fulfill the emotional as well as the economic needs of the people they employ?

No one knows all the answers to these questions. But the book you are about to read is a good place to start. It provides a comprehensive guide to what is now called "groupware"—one of the most important technologies for businesses to understand today and in the future.

This book brings together in one place the commercial state-of-the-art of groupware as it is actually being used today. You'll hear some of the leading users of these new technologies share their hard-won lessons. You'll hear some of the leading suppliers of groupware systems talk about their current products and their plans for the future. And you'll hear some of the leading commentators on this nascent industry talk about the patterns they see as the industry develops.

You'll still have lots of work to do after you read this book. But at least you'll be able to start where these leaders have left off, rather than having to retrace their steps. Using these new technologies to create the organizations of tomorrow will not be easy, but I believe it is vitally important. The companies that figure out how to use these new technologies wisely will be helping to create a better world for themselves and for the rest of us. Those that don't, probably won't survive to see that world!

Thomas W. Malone

Dr. Malone is the Patrick J. McGovern Professor of Information Systems at MIT's Sloan School of Management. He is also founder and director of the MIT Center for Coordination Science. This research center (and Professor Malone's own research) focuses on (1) how computer and communications technology can help people work together in groups and organizations, and (2) how organizations can be designed to take advantage of the new capabilities provided by information technology. Among other things, Professor Malone is well-known for having led the team at MIT who developed the Information Lens system, a pioneering groupware tool in which intelligent agents help users find, filter, and sort large volumes of electronic information. He also predicted, long before these things became widely believed, that information technology would lead to more electronic buying and selling, to more "outsourcing" of non-core functions in a firm, and to smaller firms.

Professor Malone was a cofounder of two software companies and has consulted and served as a board member for a number of other organizations. He has published over 50 research papers and book chapters and has been quoted frequently in publications such as *Fortune, Scientific American,* and *The Wall Street Journal*. He was also the program chair for the 1994 conference on Computer Support Cooperative Work (CSCW '94). Before joining the MIT faculty, Professor Malone was research scientist at the Xerox Palo Alto Research Center (PARC), where his research involved designing education software and office information systems. His background includes a Ph.D. from Stanford University and degrees in applied mathematics, engineering, and psychology.

Preface

"Groupware" is one of those mysterious and undefinable terms that have the ability to affect all of our lives. This book is an attempt to compile some of the wisdom, knowledge, and experience of technical and business communities that have dealt with groupware since 1989. This book has been written with both the technical and business-oriented reader in mind, and its goal is to enable both audiences to understand the benefits, issues, and methodologies of groupware well enough to determine how to best use groupware in their organizations.

The book is set up in several sections. The first section covers some of the technologies critical to groupware. These include email and messaging, workflow and process management, group calendaring and scheduling, collaborative document and image management, and electronic meeting systems. These are by no means all the technologies or services that fit under the groupware umbrella, but this introductory chapter lays out a functional framework for groupware that can serve as a guideline through the rest of the book.

The second section is also product focused, but from a vendor rather than a technology point of view. This section has executives from the major groupware vendors discussing their products' architecture, history, and future development plans, as well as how the use of these products has affected their and their customers' organizations. Lotus, Microsoft, IBM, DEC, and Novell/WordPerfect are all in this section, and they all provide different views on groupware, including a desktop view, a network view, a messaging view, and a database view. We have encouraged these vendors to write these chapters with the view that they will be read in the second and third quarters of 1995, even though the chapters reflect the state of the art at the end of 1994. Because the groupware market is such a dynamic one, we are sure that by the time you read these chapters some of these vendors will have announced new products, marketing agreements, and distribution channels. The purpose of this section is to provide an overview of the direction in which each company is going with their groupware products rather than a strict product features and benefits description.

The third section focuses on implementation and management strategies for groupware. These chapters are a combination of case studies of groupware implementations, as well as chapters on implementation strategies by experts at various consulting firms. This section also takes a look at some of the organizational aspects of groupware.

The final section of the book is a reference section. This section includes a variety of resources about groupware. Included in this section is a listing of all the 300-plus vendors in the *Groupware Buyer's Guide*, a groupware reading list, and groupware newsletters, events, and newsgroups where information is exchanged.

So in this volume we go from a technical and product focus to a more business and organizational orientation for groupware. The reason for organizing the book this way is to lay a foundation on what groupware technologies are; what products are available; how these products are best used and implemented; and finally, how groupware affects the organization.

This volume addresses a subset of issues related to use of information technology to improve group and organizational productivity. However, we have covered issues such as desktop integration and user experiences with groupware in other volumes. Raman Khanna edited a recently published volume entitled *Integrating Personal Computers in a Distributed Client-Server Environment*. That volume deals with platform integration, application integration, and distributed systems management. David Coleman and Marvin Manheim (author of Chapter 12) are co-authoring a groupware case book. We believe such a book is a necessary follow-on to this volume, and it examines a number of groupware implementations in detail and analyzes the lessons learned in each instance.

We believe that the greatest challenge facing the groupware market (if there is such a thing) today is "education"—educating people, especially business people, about the need and ability to collaborate, and how collaboration can change their organization to be more efficient, more customer-focused, and more profitable.

In a recent discussion with a colleague who is an expert on negotiating with the Japanese, we focused on the role of groupware. He noted that the Japanese have a great deal of interest and curiosity in groupware. And rightly so, as the U.S., the land of rugged individualists, has developed software to help people work as coordinated teams and virtual organizations. This ability, coupled with a knowledge of the Japanese negotiations code (on which my colleague is an expert), we believe will give U.S. negotiators a real competitive advantage with the Japanese.

It is these creative business uses of groupware that will, we believe, drive the groupware market. Although the technology is important, most business people do not care if the technology is called "groupware" or "multimedia" or "remote computing" or whatever, as long as it solves their business problem.

We also believe that groupware, or collaborating over the computer, will radically change the face of business in the next few years. Tom Peter, Peter Drucker, Peter Keen, Don Tapscott, Tom Davenport, and other management gurus are all heralding the changing organization. Groupware is the technology that is enabling these changes. Organizations will begin to decentralize, with contractors and "tiger teams" coming together electronically from all over the world to work on a project or solve a problem. For example, Decathlon Systems of

Colorado has reduced its office space from 6000 square feet to 500 square feet. They only use the office now for occasional meetings and customer visits, and as a site to store and maintain the computers (servers) that tie them all together.

Dr. Thomas Malone of MIT (who wrote the foreword to this book), in an article he wrote in the September 1991 issue of *Scientific American*, looks at the first-, second-, and third-order implications of this technology on our society. He sees sweeping changes in our society, some of which we can already see today, such as an increase in home-based businesses and telecommuting. The largest area of growth in the business community is not in large businesses—they are downsizing—but in the SOHO (small office home office) market. The implications of this trend for home builders is very interesting, and for commercial real estate developers not very bright. However, humans are social animals, so office buildings and cities will not completely disappear. The impact of groupware on businesses is the focus of David's consulting practice and the GroupWare conferences he organizes. It is enlightening to see a Danish hearing aid manufacturer increase its bottom line 500% in two years by using groupware and restructuring its organization.

We have rambled on about the benefits and future of groupware and the text of this volume enough. The first chapter in this book looks at an overview of the groupware technology and its benefits. We hope you will refer to Chapter 1 many times while reading this volume.

David Coleman
Raman Khanna

David Coleman

David Coleman is the founder and conference chairman for the GroupWare '9X Conferences and expositions which are held on an annual basis in Boston, London, and San Jose. He is also the editor of *GroupTalk*, the newsletter of workgroup computing, and of *The GroupWare Products and Services Catalog* and *The Groupware Buyer's Guide*. He is also co-author of a forthcoming groupware book called *Collaborating for Competitive Advantage*, which will be published in 1996.

Mr. Coleman is a frequent author for technical and trade publications, and in the last year has written a groupware supplement for *NetWork World* magazine, a white paper on groupware for *ComputerWorld*, and a special supplement on groupware for *Fortune* magazine. Mr. Coleman has also done work to advance groupware throughout the world by founding G.U.A.V.A. (Groupware Users and Vendors Association).

Mr. Coleman is a principal at Collaborative Strategies, a San Franciso-based consulting firm focused on technology assessment, marketing, and information in the workgroup computing arena. Collaborative Strategies provides business and technology assessment and marketing and business strategies for workgroup products and services. Collaborative Strategies also provides market research, competitive analysis, collateral development, product positioning, and management for increased competitive advantage on a worldwide basis. Collaborative Strategies works with groupware users as well to define groupware projects, examine business processes with an eye toward redesign, and aid in the selection and implementation of pilot or enterprise-wide groupware projects.

Mr. Coleman has an eclectic educational background that covers a wide range from cybernetics to neurobiology. He has held marketing positions at Natural Language and Oracle, and has consulted for many major hardware and software vendors as well as user organizations.

Mr. Coleman can be reached by electronic mail at david121@aol.com or on the World Wide Web at davidc@collaborative.com. He can be reached by phone at (415) 282-9197.

Raman Khanna

Raman Khanna is the director of Distributed Computing and Communication Systems at Stanford University. He is responsible for the design, implementation, and management of the campus-wide data, video, and voice communication facilities and services, the distributed computing infrastructure, the UNIX-based academic computing environment, and software licensing services for the Stanford community of over 25,000 people. Raman has special interest in the design and implementation and management of an enterprise-wide distributed computing infrastructure. Raman also serves on the boards of various networking companies.

Raman holds a B.S. in electrical engineering, an M.S. in computer science, and an M.B.A. in high technology management. He has been working, consulting, and lecturing in computing and data communication fields since 1980. Raman is contributing editor of three technical books, and author and presenter of numerous articles and papers at technical conferences. Raman also teaches courses on computer networks and distributed computing at the UC-Berkeley Extension program.

Acknowledgments

I want to acknowledge an enormous number of people who helped with this project. First I would like to acknowledge my wife, Nancy, who was a patient supporter throughout this process. My assistant, Abby Kutner, was invaluable in dealing with the hundreds of details that a project like this generates; I couldn't have done this book without her! I also want to thank my partners at The Conference Group. Without their initial support I would never have been able to start the GroupWare conferences and would never have met my co-editor, Raman Khanna, and many of the knowledgeable authors that contributed to this volume. I want to acknowledge the GroupWare Conference Advisory Board for the many enlightening discussions we had about groupware and for contributing many of the chapters in this volume. Finally, I want to than all the authors who contributed to this volume for their spirit of sharing and collaboration and for having the patience to go through several iterations of a chapter or for squeezing the writing of a chapter into their already busy schedules. I want to thank you all for your patience with me, my staff, and the process.

David Coleman
Collaborative Strategies

I would like to acknowledge my co-editor, David Coleman, for the key role he played in editing the contents and writing introductions to all chapters. I also want to thank his assistant, Abby Kutner, for her patience and good humor throughout this project. Special thanks to all the contributors for taking time out of their hectic schedules to write the chapters and incorporating suggestions made by David and me. I also want to thank the publishing team: Mary Franz and Noreen Regina of Prentice Hall for their continued support; Don MacLaren of BooksCraft, Inc., for overseeing the production of the volume; and Cathy Kemelmacher for copy-editing the material. Special thanks are due to my wife, Indu, for her indefatigable support, and to my children, Sonal and Sahil, for letting me spend my evenings and weekends working on this project.

Raman Khanna
Stanford University

Technology and Standards

CHAPTER 1

Groupware Technology and Applications: An Overview of Groupware

David Coleman
Collaborative Strategies

1.1 AN INTRODUCTION TO GROUPWARE

Groupware is an umbrella term for the technologies that support person-to-person collaboration. Groupware can be anything from email to electronic meeting systems (EMS) to workflow. It is important to note that groupware is a relatively new term, describing a new market and a new set of technologies. Groupware provides tools to solve collaboration-oriented business problems, and this book is intended to provide readers a broad base of information regarding groupware technologies and strategies.

The trend toward collaboration is a strong one, fueled by changes in technology and business strategy. Technological development, specifically the explosive growth in network infrastructure and capability, is fueled by economic and organizational pressures such as increased global competition and a recession that has been rolling around the world. Furthermore, as businesses strive to become more efficient by taking advantage of these new technologies, they are finding that the old hierarchical organization is not adequate. Many businesses are reinventing or re-engineering themselves using groupware tools.

If you get only one message from this chapter, it is that groupware is not just technology. Groupware is collaborative technology. That means it impacts the way people communicate with each other. Impacting communications results in impacting the way people work and, eventually, the structure of the organization. What I am really saying is that groupware is people! Groupware is a tool that people use. The difficulty most organizations encounter with groupware is not with the technology, because there are many technical alternatives available, but with the relationship between technology and the people in the organization who have to use groupware.

Change management is a group of practices and technologies that evolved out of the field of organizational development and management consulting. Change management is critical with groupware. Planning for change drastically improves the chance of success. Additionally, organizations tend to resist change in proportion to their size. The larger the organization, the greater the resistance (to an exponential degree). Also, the bigger the change, the greater the resistance.

This resistance to change is not unique to groupware. It is true of any new technology or change in business process. The up and down side of groupware is that these technologies have such a great impact on the way people work and communicate, it magnifies the degree of change and can engender strong opinions either for or against the technology.

1.1.1 Why Groupware?

Downsizing and organizational restructuring or redesign and other trends of the '90s are targeted toward increasing productivity (i.e., fewer people doing more with less). These are not the only challenges for business in the '90s. Increased quality, better customer service, lower cost of sales, greater employee autonomy, and more flexible and responsive organizations are all challenges for the current business climate.

Still, many of today's businesses are coping, even thriving, in this dynamic environment of diverse pressures and changing technologies. How do they do it? How do they stay competitive? How do they maintain a focus on increasing customer satisfaction, retaining high quality, and decreasing time to market while reducing costs? What technologies are being introduced to reshape the organization to achieve these goals? The answer to these questions is groupware.

1.1.2 Definitions for Groupware

Groupware is not a panacea, rather a phrase or catch word for a group of technologies that mediate interpersonal collaboration through the computer. Because groupware is a new term for different technologies, it does not really have a specific definition everyone agrees upon. There are as many definitions for groupware as there are people trying to define it. Here are three popular definitions for groupware:

- ☞ "An intentional group process plus software to support them." Peter and Trudy Johnson-Lenz, 1978.
- ☞ "A co-evolving human-tool system." Doug Englebart, 1988.
- ☞ "Computer-mediated collaboration that increases the productivity or functionality of person-to-person processes." David Coleman, 1992.

Rather than debate the best definition of groupware, a more appropriate question is, "Is this definition really important?" The groupware concept intends to foster collaboration and interpersonal productivity by automating many tasks and enhancing the efficiency of others. Whether a product fits into the category of email or workflow, or even if it is not called groupware, does not matter in today's competitive business environment. What matters is whether groupware technology provides a solution to a specific business problem.

1.1.3 Where Does Groupware Technology Sit in the General Scheme of Things?

Where does groupware sit in today's enterprise IT architecture? It lies on a network infrastructure that includes PCs with their operating systems, cabling, network operating systems and administration utilities, or phone lines for a WAN (wide area network). Groupware is part of the networked applications environment. However, not all networked applications are groupware. Access to a corporate database through a network may not be groupware. Interactive or discussion databases may be part of a groupware application (see Figure 1.1). Often, groupware applications are workgroup-oriented and not enterprise-oriented. The issues involved in scaling up these applications for a multinational corporation are not trivial and often require the cooperation of competitive vendors, establishment of standards, and maturation of the supporting infrastructure. Many of the requirements for "enterpriseware" are not yet available today.

Groupware lies at the convergence of a number of technologies. It also rests at the top of a wave made up of a series of smaller waves, composed of technologies

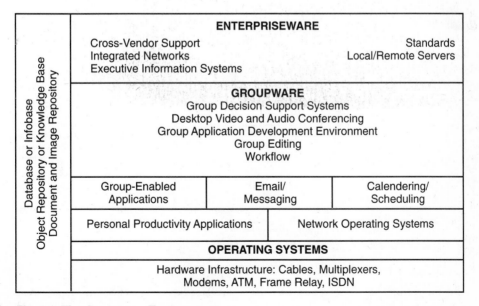

Fig. 1.1 The Groupware Environment

such as client-server, multimedia, document and image management, networked applications, and distributed or mobile/remote computing (see Figure 1.2).

The current trend toward flatter organizations, decentralization, and outsourcing is reflected in the information technologies that businesses employ. The rapid growth of networks and the decline of legacy systems have managers searching for ways to amortize their LANs as well as discover a use for old mainframes that have been paid for and are still functional. The move toward linking companies to their suppliers and/or customers has led to the extension of the organization to include these two groups as well as ad hoc teams that may be project-oriented and cross corporate boundaries.

Many organizations have realized that they cannot be all things to all people. They have discovered the best way to stay competitive is to focus on their primary business and deliver it as efficiently as possible. This specialization means that in order to provide a complete groupware or business solution, many organizations need partners and must enter into new alliances to meet these demands.

The structure of these alliances is often awkward, and the integration of two very different organizations can be painful. There is no set form to follow. However, groupware, because it promotes communication, can often provide a solution.

In essence, groupware is the competitive glue of the '90s. Groupware provides a vehicle for organizations to remain flexible yet be fast on their feet, a way to stay focused on the customer yet support the external salesperson, and a way to provide all employees with greater information and autonomy to be more productive.

1.2 A FRAMEWORK FOR GROUPWARE

Groupware is a broad term for a group of related software technologies that can dramatically affect today's organizations. But how are these technologies classified, and which ones will be most effective for your organization?

There are several classification schemes for groupware. Probably the best known is Dr. Robert Johansen's scheme (see Figure 1.3), which focuses on the

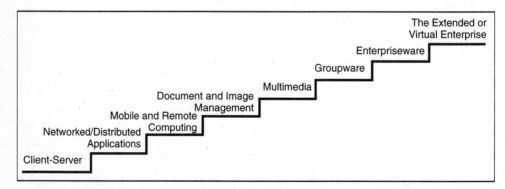

Fig. 1.2 Enabling Technologies for Groupware.

time and place of interaction reference. Less known but also valuable is a classification scheme reference developed by Esther Dyson, which focuses on the locus of control. In her framework, the locus of control can be user-centered, work-or-object-centered, or process-centered, as discussed below.

☞ User-centered

User-centered groupware manages work locally. The user builds his own agent or client. The system is focused on the users, and they receive data and enter commands from the outside. They may not know much about the data or the workflow. Their tools can include email macros, Lotus Agenda, Beyond's Agility Mail Tools, or a user-built view in Lotus Notes. Because the locus of control is centered on the users, they may route work flows themselves.

☞ Work or object-centered

Work or object-centered groupware manages work according to an object, such as a document, that can mail itself, display itself, or update itself. The user writes instructions that follow the work. The problem here is closure. What happens if the document is lost? This locus focuses on work steps, not transaction completion.

☞ Process-centered

Process-centered groupware ensures the work is completed, which may require a transaction or nested transaction model. It checks the state of the

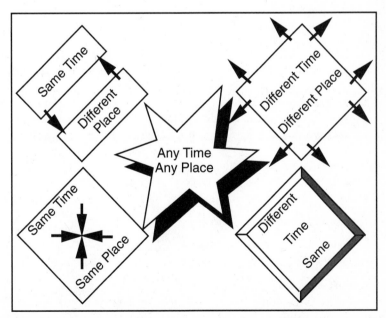

Fig. 1.3 Four-Square Map of Groupware Options. Source: Robert Johansen, et. al., *Leading Business Teams,* Addison Wesley, © 1991. Reprinted by permission of the publisher.

transaction, unlike the work-centered approach, where the object knows its own state. This locus resembles a group agent rather than a user agent. It can be database-oriented and is a more global or enterprise-oriented system. This locus focuses on the work cycle rather than the object or the user.

Another classification scheme for groupware is product-oriented and focuses on product functionality to classify a product in a particular category. This scheme uses ten categories based on product functionality, plus a separate category for groupware services and a new category for groupware applications. These same categories were used at the Groupware Conference in 1994 for the annual Groupware Awards (awarded to the vendor with the best groupware product in each category) and for the 1994 Groupware Buyer's Guide, a catalogue that lists over 300 different groupware products and services. The categories are as follows:

1. Electronic Mail and Messaging (including Group Calendaring and Scheduling)
2. Conferencing
3. Workflow
4. Group Document Handling
5. Workflow
6. Workgroup Utilities and Development Tools
7. Groupware Frameworks
8. Groupware Services
9. Groupware Applications

Associated with each category are names of some sample products. But this listing is neither all-inclusive nor intended to be a catalogue of all the products in each category. The issues identified for each product category are also not exhaustive; rather, they are intended to direct the readers' attention to some of the technical, organizational, and cultural challenges associated with each category. Often, these issues are posed in the form of likely questions one would ask if considering this product category for a specific organization. Please realize that many products fit into more than one category, and products like Lotus Notes may fit into many categories because of the wide variety of functions in the product.

1.2.1 Electronic Mail and Messaging

Includes messaging infrastructures, email systems, and group calendaring and scheduling systems.

Sample products:

cc:Mail—Lotus Development	Futurus Team—Futurus
Microsoft Mail/Exchange	Meeting Maker—On Technologies
Intelligent Mail—Banyan	Network Scheduler—CE Software
MHS—Novell	Time and Place/2—IBM

Issues:

☞ Standards, XAPI, VIM vs. MAPI, X.400, X.500 (directory services).

☞ How is it possible to deal with multiple mail systems in one enterprise?

☞ Proliferation of meetings because they are now easier to schedule.

☞ Privacy for personal calendars (big brother is watching!).

☞ Having enough people in the company use the product to make it worthwhile.

☞ Scheduling across multiple time zones.

1.2.2 Conferencing

Collaborative and Discussion Databases, Electronic Conferencing, and Bulletin Boards. (This is a most controversial category as it includes a wide range of products, but all products in this category store documents or allow others to see and work on documents simultaneously or on each others' screens.)

Sample products:

ShowMe 2.0—Sun Solutions	The Meeting Room—Eden Systems
Aspects—Group Logic, Inc.	LinkWorks—DEC
Lotus Notes—Lotus Development	FirstClass—SoftArc Inc.
Oracle Office—Oracle Systems	Collabra Share—Collabra
TeamTalk—Trax Softworks	Pacer Forum—Pacer Software

Issues:

☞ Management: Who controls the screen? How many people can conference efficiently? What is the role of the facilitator? Is a facilitator needed?

☞ Technical: What are the interaction rate/baud rates? Is your equipment compatible? What is real-time response?

☞ Replication schemes, network topologies, scalability, transaction-based vs. store and forward databases, support for worldwide locations, integration with legacy systems: do they integrate with scheduling systems?

☞ What to do after an electronic meeting? Can you put the resolutions into Notes or other products and track goals and commitments?

1.2.3 Group Decision Support Systems

Electronic Meeting Systems, Audio and Video Conferencing

Sample products:

GroupSystemsV—Ventana	Live PCs 100–200—PictureTel
Person to Person—IBM	Being There—Intelligence at Large
Council—CoVision	Fujitsu Desktop Conferencing
C.A. Facilitator—McCall/Szerdy	
The Virtual Notebook—The Forefront Group	

Issues:

☞ Do group decision support systems integrate with scheduling systems?

☞ What to do after an electronic meeting? Can you put the resolutions into Notes or other products and track goals and commitments? What is the role of the facilitator? Are facilitators necessary for this technology?

☞ When will desktop video conferencing be affordable? When will multipoint conferencing be available? What are the technologies and standards holding this part of the industry back?

☞ Will corporate cultures use these technologies like email is used today?

☞ How will these technologies change society?

1.2.4 Group Document Handling

Group Editing, Shared Screen Editing Work, Group Document and Image Management, and Document Databases

Sample products:

Face-to-Face—Crosswise	Workflo—FileNet
MarkUp—Mainstay Software	Floware—Recognition Technologies
OnGo Document Management— Uniplex	Documentum—Documentum, Inc.

Issues:

☞ Why is this product category not useful?

☞ What about page mark-up standards such as SGML, HTML, and CALs? Will they support common word processors and page layout programs or do they require a special editor? Do they have version control? How do these standards affect document security? How do they integrate with enterprise document/image databases or repositories?

☞ Where does group document management stop and multimedia begin?

☞ What about obtaining group access, versioning, security, data integrity, compression, integration with other documents, repositories, integration with standard desktop word processing, and group editing?

1.2.5 Workflow

Workflow Process Diagramming and Analysis Tools, Workflow Enactment Engines, Electronic Forms Routing Products

Sample products:

Workflow Analyst—ATI	JetForm—JetForm Corp.
Staffware for Windows—Staffware	Formflow—Delrina Inc.
WorkMan—Reach Technologies	Flowmark—IBM
ObjectWorks—DEC	Workflow•BPR—Holosofx, Inc.

Issues:

☞ Workflow coalition, passing documents and information between products.
☞ Is it worth automating poor processes?
☞ Integration with EDI and other customer services. How is this different than project management?
☞ With 130 workflow products, how do you identify a legitimate workflow product? Where does workflow stop, and group document and image management begin?

1.2.6 Workgroup Utilities and Groupware Development Tools

Sample products:

Microsoft Workgroup for Windows   CoEX—Twin Sun
Lotus Notes—Lotus Development   Replication Reporter—DSSI
Oracle Office—Oracle Systems

Issues:

☞ What should be part of the OS, and what part of the application?
☞ What are the decision-making issues when deciding whether to develop for the OS, GUI, or network?
☞ How to ensure issuer compatibility; standards; object-oriented (reusable) code; licensing (network, multimedia, intellectual property rights).

1.2.7 Groupware Services

Service listing:

Planning and Implementation   Business Re-Engineering
Application Development   Process Re-Engineering
Training and Maintenance   Electronic Meeting Facilitation
Change Management   Consulting

Issues:

☞ Expertise is a most valuable commodity in the groupware market. It is highly unusual to find all the necessary expertise in-house. Additionally, no single vendor offers a complete groupware solution, and re-engineering often requires multiple products and service vendors to collaborate. How do you identify and pull together the resources best suited to your organization?
☞ How are meetings successfully facilitated?
☞ What tools are best suited to your re-engineering needs?
☞ How do you identify the problems with the greatest potential for turn-around from groupware?

☞ How is a consultant best used? What does he/she know that people in your organization don't?

☞ It is imperative that top management and all stakeholders support any process change. How do you enlist and sustain their support?

☞ How do you evaluate the return on investment of using groupware?

☞ How do you find out what other organizations have done in groupware? This kind of "homework" will help direct planning efforts toward projects with the greatest potential for success and away from the disaster-waiting-to-happen.

1.2.8 Groupware Frameworks

These are products that help coordinate other groupware and desktop products.

Sample products:

Cooperation—AT&T GIS   LinkWorks—DEC
TeamOffice—ICL   Uniplex—OnGo Office
GoldMedal WorkGrp—Decathlon   Notes—Lotus Development

Issues:

☞ How can these products integrate the desktop as well as aid in collaborative efforts?

☞ What about security? Does this type of collaboration increase the security hazard?

☞ If framework products help to coordinate the enterprise, can they be used as intra-enterprise products to help collaboration outside of the organization?

☞ If standards emerge in the groupware market, will framework products be necessary?

1.2.9 Groupware Applications

Sample products:
BAI-5000 Distribution Management System—Business Automation Inc.
Patient Tracking System—Management Directions
CustomerFirst—Repository Technologies
ProTEAM—Scopus
HelpDesk—Trellis

Issues:

☞ How can this application be customized for your particular organization?

☞ What are the costs of customization, and will it run on your current collaborative infrastructure?

☞ If this solution is in the marketplace, how do you know your competitor is not using it?

☞ Will this application provide true collaboration and solve the business problem you have?

☞ How will this collaborative application tie into your legacy systems, and access data critical to your business?

1.3 THE GROUPWARE MARKET?

Groupware is not a new idea. Many of the technologies that compose groupware have been around for 20 years. Why is groupware hot right now? Because groupware lies at the convergence of a number of technical, economic, social, and organizational trends that have combined to propel groupware into the minds of managers in both the business and technical communities. Groupware never took off in the '70s and '80s because there wasn't sufficient network infrastructure. However, the infrastructure is now in place, and businesses are using groupware to restructure themselves for global competition.

Is groupware just a buzzword of the '90s or is there an enduring market for these technologies? Many industry analysts who follow collaborative technologies believe that groupware is a legitimate market and that it will endure. However, to call groupware a market is misleading. More accurately, groupware is a collection of technologies that can be applied to specific business problems. One of the problems with "the groupware market" is that no one knows what it is. If there is no common definition for the term "groupware," how can this market be measured and tracked? Nevertheless, several market research firms do track the sales of the technologies that commonly compose groupware (such as workflow, email, electronic conferencing, etc.).

In a recent report on groupware, Bob Flanagan, formerly senior analyst at Workgroup Technologies, Inc. and now an analyst at the Yankee Group, estimated the market for groupware software at $1.7 billion in 1993. He predicts rapid growth, estimating that by 1998 groupware sales will be $5.5 billion worldwide!

This corroborates the figures reported by the British market research firm Ovum, Ltd. In their report, "Groupware: Market Strategies," Ovum states that the groupware market is growing at a robust 15% per year, and they also estimate total groupware sales to be $5.5 billion by 1998. More important, 60% of that $5.5 billion figure will come from training and implementation services rather than software sales. This growth is due to the benefits derived from collaborative efforts and increased communication, both of which are enabled by groupware.

The fastest-growing segments of the groupware market are email and workflow, but even that is changing in this dynamic market. Ovum states that one-third of the 1993 groupware market was workflow, with over 130 vendors. This will still be true in 1995. They also believe that stand-alone email systems, which today make up 19% of the groupware market, will be only 10% of the market by

1998. This means that email functionality will be integrated into other technologies like workflow, calendaring/scheduling, and group decision support systems.

Organizational re-engineering is fueling the groupware market for two reasons: first, because groupware technologies provide many of the tools needed to develop re-engineering strategies and second, because groupware is the primary tool used to implement re-engineering programs. Although some say re-engineering is last year's buzz-word, Ray Manganelli and Mark Klein, authors of *The Re-engineering Handbook* (Amacom Press), claim it's the No. 1 initiative senior executives will use to meet strategic goals. When surveyed, these executives voted the following techniques for meeting strategic goals: re-engineering 88%, process automation 78%, restructuring 77%, downsizing 67%, and outsourcing 40%.

1.3.1 To Re-Engineer or Not to Re-Engineer?

Unfortunately, many who have taken the path to re-engineering have failed. Michael Hammer, the prophet of re-engineering, predicted that American companies will spend $32 billion this year in re-engineering efforts and that two-thirds of those efforts will fail.

When the roadblocks to re-engineering were examined by a 1993 Delloite-Touche survey, it turned out that re-engineering (like the technology it uses—groupware) has two major obstacles: people and technology. By nature, people are resistant to change. This resistance is the largest organizational problem in re-engineering. The second problem is technological and can be defined in terms of the limitations of existing systems. Without solving both problems simultaneously, your enterprise may not be successful in re-engineering or with groupware.

1.3.2 Re-Engineering for the Virtual Organization

Decathlon Systems is a 30-employee, UNIX-based groupware vendor in Colorado. In order to reduce overhead and provide better client service, they re-engineered their own organization with groupware. Decathlon's solution was to use groupware to create a "virtual organization." Decathlon products are run in-house on an SCO UNIX server and consist of email, group calendaring and scheduling, group resource management, cooperative document editing, and personal information management tools.

Initially, all Decathlon employees worked in one 6000-sq.-ft. office. After deploying groupware, the entire Decathlon staff telecommutes. They maintain a 500-sq.-ft. office for staff meetings, get-togethers, and customer demonstrations. The office is now used to house the central groupware servers for the company. For Decathlon, this was an inexpensive and trouble-free process. All the employees were enrolled in the transition process. Everyone provided input during a six-month period prior to the rollout. Because all the employees were already familiar with the software, the rollout went smoothly and quickly.

Decathlon's primary advantage was that personnel was already familiar with the software, so no training was needed except for new people. The only re-organization-related expenses were for upgrading the network and telephone infrastructure, under a few thousand dollars. "The transition cost us less than one month's rent would have been," notes Bob Williams, Decathlon CEO.

"There have been many advantages to distributing our organization: people are more productive, morale is better overall, we have saved not only on overhead but in commute time for employees. Even though we have only been doing this for a short time, my estimate is that we are saving 30% on our overhead. We found this works especially well for our technical people who often work at night. We have assigned people to be available at certain hours so there is always coverage," noted Williams.

Decathlon is still structured with departments, but they are moving to a team structure, coordinating through email or their software's conferencing facility. Each team works with a prime government contractor. However, the requirements are often multidisciplinary. To deal with the issues of cross-platform support, training, and complex customer issues, all account management is done by teams.

All aspects are accomplished electronically. If the prime sales person is not physically available, all account knowledge is in a repository so that other team members can review the account activity and status. Additionally, problems of lost or unacknowledged mail and other client-related information are eliminated because the groupware's forwarding functions resend the mail to another team member if the lead account representative does not respond within an hour.

Williams admits that security could be a problem (although it has not been as yet). For additional security, Decathlon maintains two parallel servers—an internal server and an external server in a firewall configuration. Other groupware vendors, such as DEC, IBM, RSA, and Bull, are keenly aware of the security issues and have implemented additional levels of password protection and centralized security facilities in their products.

What is unusual about Decathlon is that it is a small company. Most studies about companies adopting groupware have shown that groupware is being adopted by larger organizations (usually over 1000 people) and that it has not yet been fully embraced by smaller organizations (under 100 people) unless the smaller organization is required to do so by a large organization partner.

1.3.3 The Mail Must Go Through

Many larger organizations have used various forms of groupware for years. Electronic mail (email) was the first of them. "Electronic mail has become a strategic line of communication and provides some of the infrastructure for other collaborative applications," notes Nina Burns of Creative Networks, Inc. (Palo Alto, California). "A messaging store and forward infrastructure is currently being built in many organizations, for forms routing, and workflow as well as sales force automation. About 78% of employees in Fortune 1000 companies have email today. This number should reach over 90% by 1996."

Again, just using the technology may not solve the business problem. In the case of email, using email technology created some new challenges. Carol Anne

Ogdin, a principal consultant at Deep Woods Technologies, surveyed 250 employees at a large Silicon Valley chip maker regarding their use of email. She found that the average worker spent about one hour per day on email. The survey concluded that better education on the use and abuse of email could save each employee 12–15 minutes per day, which would result in a savings of $40 million per year. This re-education program, which uses groupware as its delivery vehicle, is in progress today. The cost-to-benefit ratio is almost 20:1.

Many organizations that grew up in the '80s implemented mail on their legacy (mainframe) systems. According to International Data Corporation (IDC), a Framingham, Massachusetts-based market research and analysis firm, in 1987 more than 90% of all email users sent messages via a single, mainframe-based system. But as client-server (LAN) architectures became popular in the early '90s, departments were free to implement whatever mail system would meet their needs. This shift to diverse email systems has followed a corresponding shift from legacy to client-server systems.

1.3.4 Tower of Babel

Most companies have found that email is critical to their daily business. Email's popularity is evidenced by the estimated (by IDC) 130 million email users worldwide by 1997. By far, the largest number of mail users are using Novell LANs, although most of today's companies also use UNIX and Apple Macintosh computers and need to be networked to ensure complete enterprise connectivity. But the diversity of computing and email systems presents today's organizations with a challenge characterized as the "Tower of Babel" problem (see Figure 1.4).

Most companies, as they change to a more distributed organizational structure, find that communication becomes critical. Yet those disparate mail systems which were chosen on a department-by-department basis create problems of interoperability (i.e., the ability for software to run on different computers, or the ability for messages/data to be passed from one program to another, transparent to the user). A good example of this is Motorola, a 50,000-person multinational technology company. "Ensuring interoperability between the different mail systems has been a challenge," notes Gene Eggleston, Technical Advisor.

Motorola uses mail systems from Lotus, Microsoft, CE Software, and others. To deal with this problem, a groupware/messaging infrastructure had to be developed. In Motorola's case they decided on the X.400 messaging standard and used WorldTalk 400 to integrate the various messaging systems, allowing every Motorola email user to transparently talk to every other email user no matter what system they were on.

"It's not enough to just translate between different email systems," notes Mike Humphries, Vice President of Sales at WorldTalk. "Now groups want to collaborate on the way they work together." "Rather than just sending and receiving messages, they want to have transparent translation between various groupware products like Lotus Notes and Microsoft Electronic Forms or Novell/WordPerfect's Informs," stated Dave Atlas, VP of Marketing at Worldtalk. "At the applications level, transparent linking of workflow process redefinition, the

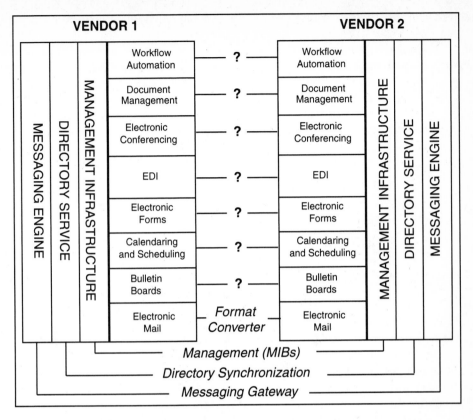

Fig. 1.4 Tower of Babel Problem. Source: David Atlas, Worldtalk Corporation.

routing of intelligent forms, and script translators are the current stumbling blocks for enterprise-wide cooperation on a variety of workflow and groupware products."

1.4 TO MEET OR NOT TO MEET?

But electronic mail is not the only technology to help organizations evolve to higher levels of productivity. Meetings are a prime candidate for efficiency and productivity enhancement. Up to two thirds of a manager's time may be spent in meetings. If those meetings can be streamlined or eliminated, travel time reduced, or the meetings themselves made more efficient and productive, the cost savings and productivity increases could be enormous! Products like TeamTalk from Trax Softworks and Ventana's GroupSystemV have led the way in productivity in this arena.

The second technology under the groupware umbrella is electronic meeting support. Given that managers spend most of their day communicating with others and up to half their time in meetings, anything that will either cut down the number of meetings or make the meetings more efficient will realize enormous productivity gain.

Electronic meeting support is a good example of the way groupware changes organizations by impacting interpersonal interactions. There are four categories of groupware technologies aimed at greater productivity in meetings:

1. Group calendaring and scheduling to automate the process of setting up the meeting
2. Electronic meeting support systems to increase meeting output, productivity, and the quality of decisions
3. Group project management software for meeting follow-up
4. Workflow software to route and track documents and action items generated from the meeting

On Technologies, Microsystems Software Inc., and CE Software all offer cross-platform calendaring and scheduling products which successfully meet the meeting-automation needs of most organizations. These and other companies are working on "knowbots" or "intelligent agents" that act much like your staff to set up a meeting, freeing personnel to handle other tasks. The "agent" or program responds to your instructions. You tell the program who you want to attend the meeting, date and time options, and the proposed agenda. The agent goes out onto the network and checks the schedules of the staff members specified. The agent sends an email message which notifies you and the other attendees of the room, date, time, and topic of the meeting. If there are time or resource conflicts, the agent will also notify you by email and ask you to choose another option for your meeting and begin the process again. By automating this process, untold hours of phone tag, email tag, and logistical time wasters will be saved.

Once the meeting attendees, time, and location have been set, there are groupware technologies to include remote sites and to manage the meeting itself. These electronic meeting systems, or EMS, include products such as C.A. Facilitator from McCall-Szerdy and Associates, Council from CoVision, and GroupSystems for Windows from Ventana. These Windows- or Macintosh-based systems are applications that help facilitate meetings and capture the knowledge and decisions made in those meetings. The use of these systems is covered extensively in the chapters by Dr. Jay Nunamaker, Carl DiPietro, and Frank Lancione.

Once the meeting is over, the EMS captures and exports the decisions and action items to software for administering the project. Tracking the action items for everyone from the meeting as well as developing a coordinated plan for the project can often be a challenge. There are two types of software that can aid with these business challenges. The first is group project management tools such as Microsoft Project, MacProject, or AutoPLAN II from Digital Tools.

Workflow software is also useful. This software helps enact the plan developed in the meeting. Workflow software will not only aid you in developing the optimal business process, but it will route and track the documents involved in the process (see Chapter 3 by Ronni Marshak). This, combined with a group project management software, EMS, and group scheduling system, can make meetings much more productive, support higher-quality decisions, and coordinate and optimize the actions resulting from the meeting.

But what can we expect from these technologies in the future? Dr. Jay Nunamaker, professor at the University of Arizona at Tucson and recipient of the GroupWare '93 Lifetime Achievement Award, sees that meetings of the not-too-distant future will change radically with the addition of groupware technologies. He sees face-to-face meetings via desktop or laptop video gaining in popularity. Traditional meetings will never be eliminated because people have a need to be social, and some issues simply require face-to-face communication. However, when you consider the inefficiencies and disruption that result when people travel to each meeting, it is clear that meetings of the future will be augmented with technology.

In his research at the University of Arizona, Dr. Nunamaker sees the video conference of the future (within 5–10 years) as being so real that people will feel they are in the same room together. However, Dr. Nunamaker rightly notes, "People are still the critical resource in an organization, and groupware and other technologies only augment what people do."

1.4.1 The New Process for Processes

Groupware technologies indirectly support rightsizing, the current trend in business. While many companies shed employees at a rapid rate, those employees left in the organization are often required to produce work previously performed by two or three people. In order to meet this productivity challenge, processes are re-engineered and, when possible, automated. The groupware technology that supports business process re-engineering (BPR) is called workflow.

There are currently 130 workflow vendors who see the potential to evolve organizations to greater productivity through process efficiency. Fortunately, these vendors have realized that the ability to pass information between their products will be critical to the organization. Therefore, they have organized the Workflow Coalition to create a common standard to be used to transport this process information. However, implementing a standard has proven difficult and controversial.

Stowe Boyd of Work Media has been examining workflow product offerings in conjunction with a report on workflow that he is developing for a client. Stowe says, "I don't think the standard coming out of the Workflow Coalition will be useful. All the products I have evaluated so far are so different that I don't see how any standard can address them. Furthermore, if a standard were developed that was able to allow data to move from one workflow vendor's product to another, it would be at such a low level it wouldn't be of great use anyway." The forthcoming report on workflow will be available in March 1995.

Insofar as Stowe's statement is rather controversial, I discussed it with another workflow analyst and the author of the workflow chapter in this book, Ronni Marshak of the Patricia Seybold Group. Ronni agrees with Stowe—to a point. She believes that the coalition has only agreed on terminology. She also agrees that any products which initially meet this Workflow Coalition Standard will do so through APIs and gateways, and that there will be native implementations which will support this standard until 1998. Furthermore, Ronni believes that a big shake-out is due in the workflow arena, most likely in 1996. "When you have over 100 vendors competing for a small market like this, something's got to give."

Whether there is a coming shakeout in the workflow market or not, workflow uses electronic mail, electronic forms routing, and process engineering methodologies to optimize business processes for increased productivity. Workflow grew out of, and is still closely associated with, group document and image management.

In its simplest form, workflow can consist of electronic forms routing. Products like FormFlow from Delrina and Jetforms from Jetform offer this functionality. So do Apple's new PowerTalk/PowerShare products. NASA Ames Research Center used Apple's products to streamline their purchase request form process. Using Apple's PowerTalk/PowerShare, any employee with access to any of NASA's 3500 Macintosh workstations can utilize this form to request a purchase. Simply using the electronic form triggers a complex process that involves form completion, submission, routing, approval, and fulfillment. Routing the forms electronically resulted in drastic improvements in routing time and reduced the labor needed to process them.

Another use of workflow is in time-critical tasks. Medical Test Laboratories (MTL) provides 24-hour turn-around laboratory services for a variety of physicians' offices in southern California. For a business like MTL's, service to the customer is a priority! In the case of MTL, both time and money are critical.

Although MTL has always met its delivery deadlines, as a growing business the demands on its organizational infrastructure and delivery systems were increasing. MTL was looking for a way to meet the increased demands of a growing customer base while downsizing staff. To make matters worse, their budget was frozen by management. A thorough analysis of their business processes highlighted process bottlenecks. This is where they started.

MTL chose Workflow•BPR, a new product from Holosofx, Inc., to identify and graphically display the work units that composed MTL's process. This allowed managers to see the process bottlenecks and explore alternatives that might improve process productivity, reduce cycle times, and increase customer response.

MTL's analysis showed problems in timing, scheduling, and routing of information from their clients, as well as the delivery and pick-up of samples. Once they were able to see the whole business picture graphically, they were able to optimize the scheduling of pick-ups and deliveries. Changing this process alone resulted in a 25% increase in savings in overhead and an estimated 20 to 30% time savings!

In a third example, CACI, a consulting firm with U.S. government and commercial clients, needed to provide high-quality software to their clients quickly. Groupware enabled their competitive advantage by increasing collaboration in the development team, which led to a significant decrease in the time required to deliver projects to clients. However, CACI first used groupware internally to catalyze a reorganization of their company.

CACI currently has 2700 employees. Their organizational challenge was to accommodate a rapidly expanding organization (800 new people over the last nine months) while still meeting the deadlines of deliverables for 200 current projects. Their solution was to employ groupware to leverage corporate knowledge as well as streamline and simplify project management. Groupware was also used to dramatically reduce operational documentation. Mail-enabled workflow management cut the amount of paper needed to document a project and increased its velocity in movement around the organization.

CACI used Quality At Work (QAW) from Quality Decision Management of North Andover, Massachusetts, as their groupware tool. They picked QAW because of its ability to support mail-enabled applications, its integration with Lotus Notes (currently being used at CACI), and its ability to collect and consolidate information from a variety of offices. Lotus Notes had been selected because of its replication capability and security features. "We want to look for the best methods we can find to tie the organization together to make a synergistic organization, instead of all the parts fighting each other or working in a vacuum. This allows us to leverage our success in other areas," notes Steve Hunt, Vice President of Advanced Technologies.

CACI is extending their organization to include their clients. Currently, clients get to participate in selected on-line conferences and structured databases focused on their projects. They also get direct project interaction, like status reports and correspondence, through mail-enabled forms. "The object of this organizational extension is not cost savings but rather to develop a stronger relationship with the client, and it's working," notes Hunt. The program is only being used in a few U.S. sites today, but it will be extended to their European offices later this year.

CACI is one of a new breed of consulting and service firms that are using groupware internally and with their clients. Providing groupware services is probably the fastest-growing segment of the groupware market. But those who provide these services have many challenges.

1.4.2 The Role for Groupware Services

Many consultants become discouraged because even though the technology is adequate for the organization, many organizations do not want to change the way they work. Nevertheless, firms such as Andersen Consulting provide a wide variety of groupware services to their clients. These services include planning, consulting, implementation, custom applications development, organizational consulting, change management, business process redesign, and meeting facilitation.

Attendees at GroupWare '93 were asked what necessary services were not being supplied by software vendors. The most requested service was planning. However, this is not a service that internal consulting groups at Lotus or Microsoft generally provide. Their consulting is usually focused on implementation services or custom applications development, which can be very profitable. Lotus Consulting makes $3 to $5 in consulting for every $1 of Notes sold. However, the need for planning and other consulting services to help integrate groupware into the organization is often filled by consultants of another breed, such as EDS, the "Big Six," or even management consulting firms such as Mackenzie, Inc.

The reason these firms are becoming a major channel for groupware is that groupware requires software products, customization, organizational consulting, and change management consulting. Because every enterprise is different, there is no one firm that can provide a complete groupware solution to a large organization.

Even a worldwide consulting firm the size of Andersen Consulting (25,000 consultants internationally) cannot supply all the pieces. Andersen does not believe they are in the groupware market. "At Andersen, we don't sell groupware," notes Anatole Gershman, an Andersen groupware researcher and consultant. "We provide business solutions for our clients. Increasingly, groupware is a part of those solutions. We will provide whatever groupware products and services our clients need to be successful."

Firms such as Andersen Consulting use groupware (Lotus Notes, GroupSystemsV, and PictureTel system 1000) in-house to leverage their expertise. At their international headquarters in Chicago, Andersen has an emerging technology group that has been examining groupware for the last five years. They pass their findings on to a strategic technologies group that examines technologies such as groupware on a 3- to 5-year time frame. Those findings are passed on to the technology integration services group, which looks at emerging technologies a year away. The integration services group begins to establish expertise in the emerging technology prior to requests by clients. Andersen Consulting has similar "area" groups in Europe and Asia/Pacific. These groups provide an organized pipeline of knowledge about groupware for the Andersen consultants. Recently, one of the partners at Andersen's headquarters in Chicago, Hugh Ryan, started a worldwide program to coordinate groupware activities within Andersen. Hugh has written Chapter 16 in the implementation section of this book, which explains groupware's role in Andersen, and how it is being used with their clients.

Although Andersen uses Notes and other products internally, the major benefit offered by their consulting practice is the ability to integrate a variety of resources, including industry expertise, project management skills, and change management services, to ensure the project is successful.

Andersen has three categories of groupware consulting: infrastructure, knowledge management or information exchange, and process management. For a process management (workflow) engagement, Andersen performs requirements definition, software selection, custom programming, implementation and rollout, and change management as well as maintenance and support services.

For a process management client, Andersen typically develops a workflow application prototype in Lotus Notes. This prototype can be developed in just a few months and can be used to test the redesign of the business process. Generally, Andersen finds that they can cut the cycle for a business process by a factor of 4 to 5, from a six-month cycle to a one-month cycle. The success of this proto-type is usually enough to justify a multi-year business process redesign project.

In the process of rolling out a project of this nature to the enterprise, there may be organizational changes, with personnel and resources being redeployed. Change management services provided by Andersen can help the client to smoothly adapt to significant changes in their organization.

Chapter 16 is a shared chapter, written by groupware practitioners at two different Big Six firms: Andersen Consulting and Coopers & Lybrand. Although both accounts are included in one chapter it is apparent that both organizations use groupware very differently, both internally and for their clients.

1.4.3 Integrators Get Into Groupware

Systems integrators, such as PRC, are also providing groupware services. PRC recently created a re-engineering group populated by former Coopers & Lybrand personnel. The group's charter is to provide clients with turnkey solutions (hardware and software) as well as the services needed for groupware and re-engineering.

1.4.4 Using Groupware to Teach About Groupware

When non-groupware users experience groupware tools first-hand, the impact is startling. Therefore, using groupware as a training tool in a realistic business simulation provides users experience with the human-to-human inter-actions fostered by these tools. Using groupware to teach about groupware has proven highly effective.

This model, using groupware to teach groupware, is being used in a work-shop we (Collaborative Strategies) developed in conjunction with the Workgroup Technologies group at PRC. In general, people resist changes to how they work. To make learning interesting we had to make it fun! We followed the "Murder Mystery" game format, except the only thing murdered is a business process. In the game, each person is assigned a role, usually a business role such as VP of Sales, CEO, CFO, and so on.

Each person has a laptop computer connected to a network. We identify a broken business process to be fixed with groupware. First, everyone reviews the public and private information about his/her role. Then we begin to repair the process without groupware and, as usual, pandemonium ensues. After we discuss the shortcomings of traditional approaches to solving the problem, we move on to a facilitated electronic meeting. The EMS application we are currently using is GroupSystems for Windows (Ventana). In this context, the problem is discussed in a facilitated manner, brainstorming generates viable solutions, and anonymous voting takes place. When a solution is reached we proceed to the next phase.

The next step uses Lotus Notes (Lotus) to create a variety of discussion databases. The participants enter ideas about requests for more information, the impact of the decision, and other issues, essentially creating a virtual forum or discussion around this problem. The discussion is available to all meeting partic-ipants and can be accessed locally or remotely.

Finally, we move into the solution phase where the broken process is fixed using workflow tools from Action Technologies. Participants cooperate in an interactive demonstration, adding information as needed. As you can see, this is a highly streamlined and optimized process. Discussion continues throughout the exercise, until the participants are familiar with what groupware is, how it can be used, what business problems they can apply it to in their organizations, and what an automated vs. re-engineered solution will look like.

Groupware is uniquely suited to use as a teaching tool because of the collaborative and interactive nature of the learning process. When groupware tools are introduced, users are often overwhelmed by the newness of the technology or the plethora of choices. Our workshop format provides everyone, technical and business professionals alike, a chance to focus on the greater challenge of the groupware equation, the business and organizational issues! Also, the hands-on approach helps people understand the requirements and benefits of these tools in a realistic setting. Finally, we encourage group interaction. Unfortunately, traditional training about groupware involves groupware tools displayed on a desktop in a demonstration format; but this is not how groupware is actually used. We believe that groupware tools are best appreciated when they are seen and used in a networked group environment, since it is the interaction groupware facilitates between people that is the source of its power.

Much of the business community's education about groupware has come from vendors like Lotus, Microsoft, and Novell. They believe, and wisely so, that an informed customer is more likely to buy than an uninformed one. However, vendor-developed education is often limited to the vendor's product, and the potential groupware user must look at what product(s) will best solve their business problem(s) in an unbiased manner. Consulting firms and integrators like PRC are providing one-stop-shopping groupware services where a customer can evaluate the offerings of many vendors and determine what will work best in their organization.

We can see that the groupware market, while new, is fraught with activity from vendors, users, and analysts. But what are the forces driving this wave of collaborative technologies, and what are the forces that hinder it?

1.4.5 Forces Driving the Groupware Wave

If, as the industry analysts claim, groupware will be a multi-billion-dollar market in a few years, who will be the customers? Why are businesses the world over so interested in groupware? What is driving the growth of the groupware market? The answers are provided in part by the businesses that have already invested in groupware. The following list represents the primary motivations for making the move to groupware:

☞ Better cost control
☞ Increased productivity
☞ Better customer service
☞ Support for TQM

☞ Fewer meetings
☞ Automating routine processes
☞ Extending the organization to include both the customer and the supplier
☞ Integration of geographically disparate teams
☞ Increased competitiveness through faster time to market
☞ Better coordination globally
☞ Providing a new service that differentiates the organization
☞ Leveraging professional expertise

As you can see, groupware uses technology to provide solutions to business processes. Looking more closely, we see seven major forces that provide the initial propulsion toward groupware:

1. A network infrastructure capable of supporting groupware is now available.
2. Improved price/performance of both groupware hardware and software has made it more available to a larger population.
3. The worldwide recession and downsizing is forcing increased white-collar productivity.
4. Well-known vendors such as Microsoft, WordPerfect, Lotus, IBM, and Digital Equipment Corporation (DEC) are promoting groupware products, thereby increasing awareness in the marketplace.
5. Increased competition imposes change on organizations, making them flatter and more flexible, often requiring groupware for this transformation.
6. Increased complexity in today's products and business procedures is driving the use of ad hoc teams supported by groupware.
7. Articles in the trade and business press have increased awareness of groupware and aroused the curiosity of business leaders.

By observing the groupware market, we see that the laws of physics can also be applied to markets and technologies. The groupware market is driven by three forces: an initial force used to overcome inertia, followed by momentum, and finally a reaction that is equal and opposite to the initial force.

There are also equal and opposing forces that inhibit the growth of groupware, including:

1. There is a low level of education in the business community about groupware.
2. There is confusion in the marketplace as to the nature of groupware. Much of the conflicting/competing information distributed by groupware vendors has increased this confusion.
3. The recession is decreasing budgets, and many firms perceive that they cannot afford the investment in groupware.
4. The distribution channels for groupware are new and not fully implemented.
5. MIS shops worry that they will become dependent on a groupware vendor.

6. Organizations are resistant to change.
7. There are few standards in the groupware market to foster rapid growth.

Additionally, when 500 groupware users were surveyed at the GroupWare '93 conference about their success and/or failure with groupware, those who were not successful noted that the greatest problems with groupware were not technological. Instead, problems stemmed from the lack of support from top management or lack of a well-defined business problem. Users were surveyed again at the 1994 groupware conference with essentially the same results.

1.5 GROUPWARE TRENDS

Just as the groupware market is emerging, so are the classification schemes for groupware. Earlier in this chapter, we looked at three different classification schemes for groupware products. Current groupware product categories are going through a cycle of expansion as many new products become available in the next year. However, consolidation is also occurring. Small, innovative companies with their technology are being snapped up by larger firms at a rapid rate. However, as with most natural and economic systems, expansion today usually leads to contraction tomorrow. At Collaborative Strategies (my San Francisco-based consulting firm), we believe that the product offerings in the groupware category will increase, but the number of categories of products will decrease as users become more sophisticated, standards develop, and the market matures. By 1997 there should only be five categories for groupware products: email/messaging, group document handling, conferencing products, workflow tools, and workgroup utilities and development tools. Of course, there will still be those that offer groupware services, and more and more industry-specific groupware applications will appear.

1.5.1 Groupware Applications

Because the workgroup computing market is still immature, the only items previously classified were those produced by software vendors. However, the market is now five years old, and many of these products have been applied to specific business problems. We are beginning to see a new application-based class of groupware produced by several channels.

Vertical applications using groupware are becoming available from VARs. These applications support sales force automation, human resources, customer service, and product development. Consulting firms provide another example of a developing vertical market. Once a consultant develops a solution for one client, he may be able to apply that solution to another organization with only minor modifications. Finally, companies are developing business-problem-specific solutions themselves.

These trends follow a normal pattern of market development with generalized horizontal software tools entering the market first, followed by more specific tools focused on specific business challenges. 1994 was the first year applications-oriented groupware products were available commercially. Loan applications processing, customer service, sales force automation, credit applications processing...all of these collaborative applications appeared as commercial products in 1994, and we see this trend accelerating in 1995 and beyond.

1.5.2 Will All Software Be Groupware in the Year 2000?

When is groupware groupware, and when is it something else? Applications sold as groupware today may not be sold or even tracked as groupware in the future. Similar to artificial intelligence, as a set of technologies, groupware has the potential to become ubiquitous and hidden.

For example, email support could be pushed down to the operating system level. This would have several advantages such as making messaging available to all applications, providing a common directory structure, and establishing messaging standards. This is also true of database functions. We have already seen this trend in some of the evolving Microsoft operating systems. UNIX has always included calendaring and email as part of the operating environment, so there are precedents for this already!

Some time toward the end of the decade, the term "groupware" may have evolved to encompass all applications. All computer applications may then be group-enabled, workflow-enabled, or support teams on a network. This means that groupware may no longer be useful as a term. So will all software be groupware in the year 2000? The answer is usually yes!

1.5.3 Groupware Worldwide!

So far, our discussion of different groupware technologies and applications has been focused on American companies. However, many of these companies are multinational, and it is important to note that groupware is being adopted at a great rate outside the U.S.

In the U.S. and other western countries, the workplace often already has technology, and people know how to work with it. Adopting a new technology raises people's fears that their skills will become obsolete or that they will be replaced by a computer (automated process). Excuses and rhetoric such as "people are too busy to learn" and "don't fix it if it is not broken" abound, but competing globally means taking the lead, not just keeping up with the Joneses. In other words, this resistance to change does not bode well for the future of western business.

According to Andy Grove, CEO at Intel, "there will be two types of organizations in the future, the quick and the dead." Because groupware increases the velocity of information within and between organizations, those who fail to keep up become extinct faster. But this seems to be a dilemma only for the western world. Many third-world countries see technology as a springboard to economic prominence and fundamental to being a "first-world" country. Therefore, they embrace rather than resist the changes it brings. Introducing groupware technologies does not meet the same resistance it does here in the U.S. because technology is seen as an improvement and a tool to accomplish their economic goals.

In the Middle East, Pacific Rim, and South America, technologies like groupware are embraced with a religious ferocity. "Often the first reason a worker gets a PC on his/her desk is groupware," notes Babur Ozden of Bilpa, the data processing division of Yapi Kredi Bank in Istanbul. Managers are willing to embrace these technologies, effectively changing the way they do business and their organizational structure, because they want to rise to the level of the western world. Groupware enables essential competitive advantages that are necessary to transact business with the western world. Often, these companies do not have to support a base of computer users or proprietary hardware and software. They can engineer, rather than re-engineer, their business right into the information age.

Yapi Kredi Bank, the third largest private bank in Turkey, has invoked YAPI 2000, a company-wide re-engineering effort. The goal is to develop a new kind of automation platform that will give them a competitive edge. They decided on Lotus Notes and Action Technologies Workflow Tools as the tools for re-engineering the bank.

Yapi Kredi's pilot is an application for customer sales representatives in each of their 360 branches. The pilot replaces telephone communications with a Notes application package for loan and credit approvals. They are also using Action Technologies Workflow management software and cc:Mail. Finally, they will integrate all of these groupware products, as well as group document and image management and multimedia products, to bring their bank into the information age!

Budget Rent-A-Car used FileNet's workflow software to streamline their accounts payable operations. Accounts payable is one of the most paper-intensive operations in companies today. The FileNet software was used to match invoices to purchase orders and then process them for payment, with little human intervention, allowing clerks to be free to deal with nonmatching invoices. Budget processes 90% of their invoices with FileNet. Added benefits of automating this process include faster transaction turn-around time, increased productivity, and increased job satisfaction. Budget is also using FileNet to process expense reports four times faster than before. Kraft Food Service uses this system daily to process 2500 invoices from 7000 different suppliers. They have improved productivity by 50% and saved $2–4 million in labor and interest charges.

1.6 JUSTIFYING GROUPWARE TO YOUR ORGANIZATION

One of the biggest challenges is justifying groupware to your organization. You want to reap all the promised rewards of productivity, competitiveness, organizational streamlining, and better customer service promised by groupware, but you are not sure how to justify the expense to your boss.

Imagine this likely scenario. You are positive that your organization can benefit from groupware. However, management is a hard-nosed and tight-fisted bunch. It's not just a case of hard money expenditures vs. soft money savings. Selling groupware to management can be tricky, especially since some of the intangible benefits offered by groupware may be impossible to measure and more important than the measurable benefits.

How should you justify the expenditure of resources for groupware? How should you set your management's expectations? Once you receive approval for groupware, how can you ensure that you will be successful with it?

There are three ways to justify groupware: cost (such as expected return on investment), competition, and increased functionality.

As with many other technologies, relying on cost justification alone can be a dangerous strategy. One of the problems with groupware is the "productivity paradox."

1.6.1 The Productivity Paradox

In a management study performed by MIT, outlined in *The Corporation of the 90's: Informational Technology and Organizational Transformation*, Michael Scott Morton recognizes and explains this concept. "The productivity paradox is the lack of evidence at the aggregate level indicating improvements in productivity or profitability that can be attributed to the increased use of IT within businesses today."

There are several reasons for the productivity paradox. Groupware is often applied to areas of low payoff, such as elaborate financial accounting systems where it is laid on top of existing inefficient practices in such a way that the new technology cannot be used to advantage. Even if the technology is implemented correctly, poor management of the technology will result in lower impact on organizational productivity and may not significantly increase productivity and justify cost.

Besides this paradox, a second and more important reason that the benefits of groupware are not optimal for justification in terms of cost is that the greatest benefits of groupware are often intangible and therefore not measurable in traditional ways.

1.6.2 Intangible Benefits from Groupware

Bullivant, Houser, Bailey, Pendergrass & Hoffman, a Portland law firm, uses groupware not only to save their clients legal fees but to extend their organization to include their clients. "Clients often want reports at periodic intervals. This is an expensive process for the clients and time consuming for our lawyers," noted Don Evans, COO at Bullivant. "Rather than reporting to clients on a regular basis, we can change the process and bring the client into our organization. Using groupware, the client can examine documents in the working file or database, so the reporting time goes away. This can save the client up to 20% of their cost."

Although the major goal of Bullivant's program was not cost savings, it has turned out that they have received some return on their investment. Bullivant invested $250,000 on Lotus Notes software and to build a suite of custom applications to support their lawyers and clients. Training costs were low due to the design of the application, but maintenance and support costs ran up to $100,000 per year. Including these expenditures, actual cost savings include $50,000 in redundant data entry in 1993 alone. Another $75,000 in savings is expected in 1994.

"The biggest benefits we have seen from this system are the intangibles," explains Evans. This application differentiates Bullivant in the mind of the client. "We can now measure how long it takes to resolve a matter, which has raised the level of consciousness on the client side of how much it costs to work with Bullivant. From the client's perspective they want their problem resolved quickly and inexpensively. This system lets them track that and see how well we are doing."

1.6.3 Cost-Justifying Groupware

One caution about cost-justifying groupware is that management, because of their different perspective, may not see the return on investment (ROI) the same way you do. Management is more likely to see groupware as a survival tool or tool for competitive advantage rather than a financial advantage. Competitive advantage is an excellent justification strategy for groupware. Competition forces companies to increase product quality, lower prices, or offer new services just to stay in business. Can you imagine a major financial institution without an ATM service? In this case, although a new technology was used to implement a service, no increase in profits resulted. Yet financial institutions continue to spend millions of dollars on ATM development and installation. ATM technology has become the status quo for the banking business, and these organizations go to great lengths to advertise the convenience and added service ATMs provide to their existing customers.

Another example from the financial sector involves loan applications processing. Using sophisticated workflow software, one bank was able to cut loan processing time from three weeks to three days. This involved using email for messaging and faster routing of documents. Using electronic conferencing software decreased the loan application committee's meeting time and allowed remote members of the committee to attend the meetings. Although process time decreased significantly, and the committee made better decisions, management did not perceive this as a productivity increase because one of the bank's competitors was advertising loan approval within a 24-hour period. In this example, management viewed the use of groupware as an intangible aspect of providing increased service quality and a cost of staying in business.

1.6.4 What Is the Cost of Not Changing with Groupware?

Aside from the competitive and opportunity costs, there are some real costs to keeping your systems and process at the vanguard. David Ferris of Ferris Networks in San Francisco focuses on the financial benefits of groupware. "It is our belief that by judiciously choosing applications, an annual saving of 1–2% of gross revenues can be easily achieved. Our cost/benefit analysis of a variety of forms routing applications has shown this to be true."

"Typically, the major factors for cost savings are the paper handling, data entry, and edit and validation cycles. Additionally, the turn-around time for forms is much faster. A less quantifiable benefit (but still of high value) is the ability of management to respond faster and with more accuracy using more timely information and computer-readable data to examine trends and company directions. We have found that business procedures must be re-engineered, simplified and optimized, and the forms routing exercise acts as a catalyst for this re-engineering," notes Ferris.

1.6.5 Keeping the Corporate Assets

Maintaining confidentiality and ownership of intellectual assets presents a significant challenge to corporations. "It's the assets that walk out the door every evening that we are talking about," notes Jeff Conklin, CEO of Corporate Memory Systems. "Storing corporate knowledge and experience is becoming more critical as more and more companies become distributed across the globe, and both the products and the organizations become more complex."

For example, John worked for a company for 40 years. When he retired, his knowledge left with him. But if John had shared his knowledge over time through an electronic conferencing system, that knowledge would have become part of a collective, corporate memory or learning, which could be leveraged across the organization. In this way, John's knowledge becomes an asset, intellectual property, of the organization as he develops it. Products like Lotus Notes, CM/1 from Corporate Memory Systems, Collabra Share from Collabra, DCA's Open Mind, Team Talk from TRAX, Pacer Forum from Pacer Software, and ICL's TeamWare can all support a corporation's effort to preserve their most valuable asset—people's experience.

As we can see, groupware provides a number of technologies that support collaboration, communication, and coordination in the enterprise, department, or work group. However, Dr. Jay Nunamaker warns us, "Today everyone is the solution provider. It's understanding the business problem that is the hard part!" Many consulting firms, while dealing with their clients' issues around groupware, are becoming aware of their clients' business problems.

The groupware business simulation developed by Collaborative Strategies and PRC goes right to the heart of this challenge. When business professionals actually work with groupware technology and go through the process of solving a particular business problem, they can more readily appreciate how it will help their organization. The next challenge is for these visionaries to secure the support of corporate management.

1.7 MAKING GROUPWARE WORK FOR YOU

At the GroupWare '93 Conference in San Jose, attendees were surveyed to determine their level of success with groupware. The survey showed that 24% felt they were currently successful with groupware. Another 29% felt they were somewhat successful with groupware, and 47% felt they were not yet successful with groupware. When those who were not yet successful were asked why, the two major reasons were lack of support from top management and lack of a specific, well-defined business problem.

1.7.1 20 Rules for Success with GroupWare

The following list of 20 common-sense rules to ensure success in deploying groupware within your organization is based on the author's experience with groupware:

1. Find a groupware champion! The higher up in hierarchy, the better. Get management's hands on the keyboard. By getting top management involved, they see the benefits, and you will get a lot more support!
2. Groupware changes the corporate culture. Plan for it!
3. Pick a pilot project rather than trying to roll groupware out to the whole organization.
4. Pick a bounded project with a group that is supportive of both technology and innovation.
5. Pick a project with visibility and financial impact.
6. Realize that training, maintenance, and support will be the majority of the cost, rather than the initial cost of the software.
7. Measure productivity factors before and after the project has started. This is a good way to cost-justify groupware!
8. Pick groupware software based on a specific business problem that needs to be solved and has not been solved successfully using traditional methods. Corollary: Don't pick the groupware first and then try to find a problem.
9. Make sure you have adequate planning, support, training, and maintenance for your project.
10. No single groupware product can do it all. Don't expect it to!
11. Don't expect software vendors to offer you all the services you need for groupware. You may need to use internal people or consultants to ensure your project's success.
12. Groupware is not a quick fix! As part of a re-engineering effort, it may take 2 to 4 years to see the results.

13. Listen to the people involved in the pilot project. They are experts on what needs to be done and can often suggest ways to better the process.
14. Don't be afraid to make changes! A pilot project is an experiment. Learn as you go.
15. Make sure the software you pick fits with existing systems. Try to amortize your LAN investment by connecting to your mainframe or other legacy systems.
16. You can't change people overnight. Be prepared for resistance!
17. People take time to change. Organizations take even longer!
18. It takes courage to change a corporate culture! Applaud those who are willing to change.
19. Be careful about paving the cow path. There is no point in automating a very inefficient process. There are no big productivity wins here!
20. Groupware can be very political. Make sure it is a big win!

1.8 THE CHALLENGES OF GROUPWARE

The two major challenges to groupware are technical and organizational. Of the two, the organizational challenges are more difficult. For the technical challenges, a technical solution must be found. However, even if the technology solves the problem, works well, and is rolled out efficiently, if the corporate culture does not support it, the groupware implementation may not be successful. Even if the culture supports it, but there is no economic justification for a groupware solution, it will fail. Finally, even if technology, culture, and economics combine to support groupware, the success of a project can be destroyed by politics.

Groupware Success = Technology + Culture + Economics + Politics

The further to the right a factor is in this equation, the greater the potential impact on the success of the project. It is important to take into account all of these factors in any successful groupware implementation.

1.8.1 Technical Challenges of Groupware

One of the most interesting technical challenges facing organizations today is how to integrate groupware systems with their legacy systems. A good example is Intel, which has several IBM 3090s. The mainframes are used for everything from order entry and factory loading to finance. Unfortunately, the Notes applications they currently have for their field sales force does not integrate well with the mainframe applications and does not allow access to legacy data. As a result, field applications specialists can obtain information on bug fixes, new features, or the latest benchmarks for a customer, but they cannot use Notes to find out product availability, shipping times, or prices. To solve this problem, Intel is using the DataLens in Notes Version 3.0, which allows access to data stored in mainframe databases such as DB/2 or ORACLE.

1.8.2 Charging for Groupware

In talking to various MIS groups faced with groupware, one of the issues that always surfaces is how to charge users for groupware services and how to regulate these services. For example, would you charge users a flat fee, or by the word or byte? What if one user wanted to have a desktop video conference from California to an office in London? Video data takes up much of the network's bandwidth. If five or six people did this at the same time, it would dramatically affect network throughput. Supporting groupware technologies like this would mean having a fiber optic network with a bandwidth 100 times greater.

1.9 GROUPWARE: CHANGING THE ORGANIZATION

Management gurus have been writing about technologies that will change organizations for the last 40 years. F. W. Taylor, Peter Drucker, Tom Peters, Michael Porter, Michael Hammer,...the list goes on, have all proposed ways to change and better the organization, such as "scientific management" or "re-inventing (re-engineering) the corporation," "total quality management," "thriving on chaos," and "strategies for competitive advantage." With the words of these management gurus ringing in their ears, managers are constantly looking for the means to accomplish some of the lofty goals set by these giants of management science.

The '90s is a decade of change and paradox. This paradox is no more strongly reflected than in the changing organization. Organizational development consultants speak of "coaches" rather than managers, and "self-directed teams" as well as total, enterprise-wide commitment to the customer. How can today's businesses achieve these goals when many of them still follow the principles of scientific management set out by F. W. Taylor over 80 years ago?

One way to change the organization is through technology. Fortune 500 companies have integrated technology into their organizations over the last 40 years, and yet none has significantly changed the structure or organization of their company. To be sure, many technologies have helped to change business behaviors or small group structures, but very few technologies have changed the structure of the enterprise. Groupware, a set of technologies that aids collaboration, communication, and cooperation via the computer, has the ability to change the way groups, departments, enterprises, and even societies work.

A recent study done on technology in business at MIT noted that often technology does not translate into productivity. Yet today re-engineering experts like Dr. Michael Hammer emphasize the need to remake the organization; but what tools are used to remake these organizations, and are they really effective?

The world is shrinking, and through technology we now have quicker national competitors as well as international competitors. In this competition, the advantage goes to the swift, not always the mighty. The organization that has the most knowledgeable staff will be able to respond more quickly, provide better service, and deliver products to market quicker, thereby giving it an enormous competitive advantage. According to Andrew S. Grove, President and CEO of Intel, "As businesses spread out around the globe, information proliferates and competition grows ever more intense. Computer supported collaboration will become perhaps the most important source of competitive advantage."

However, today's corporate organizations still support a traditional hierarchical chain of command, a structure that cannot respond with the fluidity and quickness needed to be a top competitor in today's marketplace. Changing an organizational structure is about as hard as re-inventing your business, and often they go hand in hand.

How can groupware change the organization? How can it help move the productivity increases seen on the factory floor in the '80s into the executive office in the '90s? How can it improve customer service, and aid in developing more flexible, adaptable, and globally competitive organizations? What effects will this technology have on our and other societies?

The changes brought on by these technologies will be sweeping. Not only will they affect our culture, but they are already affecting almost every culture around the world. But what are these technologies that seem to have the same impact as the internal combustion engine?

Most businesses today still follow a hierarchical command chain organizational structure (see Figure 1.5). However, groupware is changing the nature of organizations themselves. Alvin Toffler (*Future Shock,* 1970) popularized the term "adhocracies" to describe organizations that relied heavily on shifting project teams and lateral communications instead of the rigid vertical communications that many companies use today (see Figure 1.6).

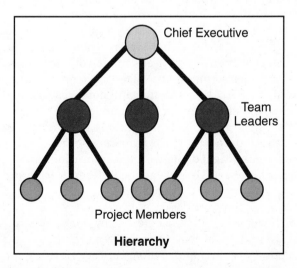

Fig. 1.5 Hierarchical Organizational Structure with Vertical Information Flow. Source: T. W. Malone & J. F. Rockart, Scientific American, September, 1991

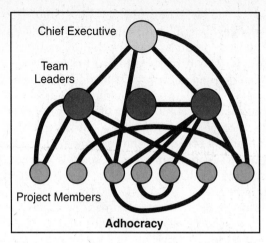

Fig. 1.6 Non-Hierarchical Organizational Structure Using Vertical and Horizongal Information Flow. Source: T. W. Malone & J. F. Rockart, Scientific American, September, 1991

"Some industries are already organized this way," notes Thomas Malone, a professor at the Center for Coordination Science at MIT. "Most consulting firms and law firms today use project-based organizations. An even more extreme example of a networked organization (which I believe will become much more common) is the project team based organization, where the team is assembled from individual contractors or consultants in the marketplace. Two industries that already use this organizational approach are the movie industry and the construction industry."

What is it about groupware that fosters these types of organizations, and how will the integration of these technologies change our future? "Groupware supports geographically distributed teams, and electronic networks can aid in finding and assembling the teams of diverse specialists needed for a specific project," notes Professor Malone. Other technologies that will aid in this process include the information highway and electronic commerce. Early harbingers of electronic commerce in use today are EDI (Electronic Data Interchange) and electronic markets like SABER for airline and hotel reservations."

Anita Roddick, the entrepreneur who founded and continues to manage the Body Shop, also sees the need for organizations to change: "Liberated thinking comes from the team approach, which transcends traditional corporate boundaries. The future for enlightened, pioneering corporations must be based on partnerships between different business leaders, different corporations, and different cultures, in short, the team-net approach."

Another view of tomorrow's organization is seen by Peter and Trudy Johnson-Lenz of Awakening Technologies. They concur with Professor Malone about the structure and evolution of tomorrow's organization. They also believe that the fundamental organizing principles of corporations and institutions are changing. "The old hierarchical patterns no longer work. We used to think of our organizations as independently operating, well-oiled, efficient engines of profit, reflecting the Newtonian mechanical clockworks world view which gave birth to the industrial era. As the new living systems world view develops and matures, we are learning to use its metaphors to understand and create new organizational patterns that reflect our essential interdependence," noted the Lenzs.

In *The TeamNet Factor*, Jessica Lipnack and Jeffrey Stamps describe the teamnet approach: ever-shifting networks of teams that cross traditional, formerly forbidden boundaries, linking once-competing organizations into ecosystems of cooperation. As Lipnack and Stamps explain, "While teamnet means 'network of teams' the two ideas are complementary—each brings a unique element to the other. 'Teams' implies small, in the same place, and tightly coordinated; 'networks' have a sense of large, spread out, and loosely linked. Teamnet brings the best of both together. In an ideal teamnet, people work in high-performing teams at every level, and the network as a whole functions as though it were a highly skilled and motivated team."

Teamnets create bridges within organizations and bridge boundaries outside with customers, suppliers, and competitors. Teams are the foundation unit of these new patterns of interconnection and interdependence. Telecommunications technology is the nervous system that holds these networks together. Groupware is the collaboration support technology that shapes and holds the activity of teams within those networks."

The next case study profiled, Oticon, is a good example of how teamwork and the groupware tools to support it helped a company turn itself around and become very profitable in a short time.

1.9.1 Oticon: Reorganizing for Better Customer Service

Oticon A/S of Copenhagen had a customer service problem. Their customers were elderly and not receiving the kind of service they needed. Oticon was taking too long to get new products to market, morale was low, and profits were down. Oticon wanted to use groupware not only to enhance the quality of their products but to re-organize to better meet the needs of their elderly patients.

This reorganization was focused around greater customer contact and greater contact among employees. Oticon examined a variety of groupware technologies like electronic mail and video conferencing but decided to use a group document and image management system tied to workflow software (from Recognition Technologies) as their solution.

Oticon's goal was to improve responsiveness to customers by decreasing the amount of time it took to process paperwork. They set a goal of 30% productivity increase over three years. This is not the radical re-engineering proposed by Dr. Mike Hammer and Jim Champy, authors of *Re-Engineering the Corporation*, which looks for a 70–100% change after re-engineering a business. Even though Oticon's goals were not as ambitious, they were rewarded with a 500% increase in their bottom line.

To accomplish this rate of return, Oticon re-engineered their IT systems and organization simultaneously. Cultural changes, such as a customer focus, abolishing departments, assigning all employees to multiple projects, and decreasing the layers of management, went a long way in helping turn Oticon around. "This way change is not traumatic or the result of a crisis, and the whole company is more flexible. A departmental structure is only good if the market stays stable, and departmental structures make the organization resistant to change," notes Torben Peterson, Information Technology Coordinator.

To show their commitment to the new technology and organizational structure, dramatic changes were made at the first point of contact: the mail room. All incoming mail except critical documents was scanned and the originals then shredded. Oticon installed a transparent tube in the employee cafeteria where employees could continually see the volume of paper being shredded, which continually showed Oticon's commitment to greater efficiency through less paper.

Oticon estimates that this paperless system and new workflow methods allowed them to bring products to market in half the time over the last two-and-a-half years. Paper storage was decreased by 70%. Oticon easily reached their goal of 30% productivity efficiency. Their reduced expenses attributed to the system and organizational change are 10–15%. They have decreased employee turnover and cut costs by 15%, and sales have increased by 20%. All of these changes have impacted the bottom line positively, with increased earnings of 500% from 1992 to 1993.

1.9.2 Organizational Challenges for Groupware

Over the last few years, SRI International (formerly Stanford Research Institute) has done a multiclient study on groupware. It is interesting to note that the majority of the clients for this study were Japanese, not American, yet most groupware is produced and used in the U.S. Alexia Martin of Co-Development International (who also wrote the final chapter of this book) was the project leader for market research on this SRI multiclient study, which concluded in June 1993. She was able to identify four organizational challenges to groupware:

1. A lack of senior management buy-in and use of groupware. This is particularly a problem with electronic meetings, email, and scheduling.
2. People sometimes resist sharing information and are competitive. There are industries where this is more prevalent such as the military, financial services, and academia.
3. The need for new roles to aid the new organization. Electronic meetings or Lotus Notes discussion databases often need a facilitator. However, in a time of downsizing companies do not want to add new people or a new position which they don't understand. Companies often assign a technical trainer to become a facilitator. This strategy usually fails. The trainers often have the wrong skill set for the facilitator role. This reflects management's lack of understanding of the facilitator's role and the need for good meeting facilitation. Many managers feel they are effective at running meetings, but most are not.

4. Many of the groupware technologies are slipstreamed in with business process re-engineering, TQM, or distributed teams. These organizational
change initiatives are not quick fixes and take a long time to implement.
Business process redesign can take 2–4 years on the average. Management
is often looking for a payback from groupware part way through the process.

A good example of an organization overcoming the organizational challenges of using groupware occurred at General Foods. The reason this project
was a success was that General Foods was able to learn from a prior failure. The
systems manager, Bob Sickles, was successful because he was aware of these
challenges and worked with both the technology and the organization to overcome them.

General Foods has 4000 people at its headquarters in White Plains, New
York. Trying to schedule meetings can be not only frustrating but a waste of
time. It got so bad that Bob Sickles, Systems Manager for Dinners and Enhanc-
ers Division (110 people), created a video called "Nightmare on North Street: The
Scheduling Monster." This 20-minute video detailed the frustration and inefficiency of scheduling a meeting at General Foods in a humorous way. It was just
one of the things Bob Sickles did right in integrating groupware into General
Foods successfully.

Success often grows out of failure. Five years ago General Foods tried to
implement an electronic scheduling program with PC clients and a VAX server.
It failed miserably. "It was too much of a behavioral change," said Sickles. "People
were not used to having their PC on and running the whole day. Now with email
so prevalent, keeping the PC on is standard. If you are not on email, you can't do
your job."

Bob first found a champion in top management: Jim Cook, who is responsible for both TQM and Information Systems at General Foods. Next, Bob went
one step further and got buy-in at both the staff and the secretarial levels, so
that the middle managers who would use the scheduling software heard good
things about it from both above and below. Taking both a top-down and a
bottom-up approach proved to be a successful strategy for General Foods.

After hearing about the initial failure to introduce electronic scheduling
systems, Bob realized he would have to change people's behaviors, overcome
their fears, and competently train them to use the system in order to have a successful rollout. A decree from the division president stating that everyone must
attend the two-hour training session for the scheduler was also helpful.

To tackle the specter of fear, Bob asked the staff about their anxieties. The
most common concerns were loss of control of personal calendars and a fear that
they would be inundated by meetings because they were now easier to schedule.
Bob finessed these fears with a two-pronged strategy. First, he rolled the product
out in a phased manner and only gave it to specific functional groups to start.
These were groups that had considerable contact with everyone else in the division, so the word spread that these fears were unfounded. The second prong of
the attack was to publicize the success of the project. He wrote articles for the

company TQM newsletter about how much time the scheduler saved in the initial pilot tests and how easy it was to use. The word got out, and the fears evaporated.

Finally, Bob made sure it was fun. He used the video to poke fun at the current process and get buy-in from the whole division, so that when rollout occurred he was only fighting technical battles, not organizational ones. Bob realized that he was dealing with not only a technology but behavioral changes on the part of the division. They had successfully rolled out Microsoft Mail a year before, and it had become the predominant way to communicate in the division. Bob was part of the company-wide TQM effort, and in the spirit of TQM he did a survey before and after electronic scheduling. He found that the time needed to schedule a meeting using Network Scheduler 3.0 was reduced by 74% from 5.1 hours to 1.4 hours. Average actual time to schedule a meeting (the actual number of work minutes needed to schedule a meeting) was reduced 71% from 19.5 minutes to 5.6 minutes.

General Foods has had a LAN for two years, and Bob's division is one of the first to be up and running on a LAN. There is a 386 or 486 PC running Microsoft Windows on every desktop of this 110-node LAN Manager/Token Ring network. The current groupware products in use at General Foods are Microsoft Mail and Network Scheduler 3.0. They are evaluating Lotus Notes and other bulletin board systems to access market reports and the on-line clipping service.

When asked about his secret to success, Sickles stated, "The TQM focus on measurement and the customer, as well as thorough planning, helped us in the long run." Sickles was not looking for a quick fix and was willing to invest the time up front to deal with the users of the technology. He had the support of his management and was able to train managers and administrative staff to adapt to their new roles. He used the lines of communication within the organization to allay the fears of the users and publicized the project widely within the company, both to help spread information and to focus the division's and the TQM's program on the project.

In our view, Bob learned from General Foods' prior mistakes and was rewarded with success in the form of a dramatic productivity increase. For those of you considering similar projects, learn from Bob's success. Plan well and reap some groupware successes of your own!

1.10 SUMMARY

This rather lengthy chapter covers a lot of ground. It introduces the book, its goals, and its organization. It covers definitions and a framework for groupware. It looks at the business reasons for groupware, justifications for groupware, and why groupware is the right tool in some circumstances. It includes some short case studies on groupware successes and warns of pitfalls other pioneers have found. Finally, this chapter mirrors the book and ends with a focus on implementation and organizational issues of groupware. This chapter is meant as an introduction to both groupware and the rest of the book. Many of the issues touched on in this chapter are dealt with in depth in later chapters of this volume.

I believe case studies are a great way to learn, especially about how people adapt to and learn to use technologies like groupware. I believe that many organizations learn the same lessons about the use of groupware tools for re-engineering and that if these lessons could be codified, they would save many organizations a great deal of time and effort. To this end, my next book will look at a variety of case studies on groupware and will be organized not by industry or technology, but by "lessons learned." It is my hope this next volume will prove as useful to the reader as this one.

BIBLIOGRAPHY

1. Michael S. Scott Morton, London: Oxford University Press, 1991.

2. Is Information Systems Spending Productive? New Evidence and New Results, Paper #143, MIT Center for Coordination Sciences, June, 1993.

3. Robert Johansen, Page 210, *GroupWare '92 Conference Proceedings*, San Mateo, CA: Morgan Kaufmann.

BIOGRAPHY

David Coleman is the founder and conference chairman for the GroupWare '9X Conferences and expositions which are held on an annual basis in Boston, London, and San Jose. He is also the editor of *GroupTalk*, the newsletter of workgroup computing, and of *The GroupWare Products and Services Catalog* and *The Groupware Buyer's Guide*. He is also co-author of a forthcoming groupware book called *Collaborating for Competitive Advantage*, which will be published in 1996.

Mr. Coleman is a frequent author for technical and trade publications, and in the last year has written a groupware supplement for *NetWork World* magazine, a white paper on groupware for *ComputerWorld*, and a special supplement on groupware for *Fortune* magazine. Mr. Coleman has also done work to advance groupware throughout the world by founding G.U.A.V.A. (Groupware Users and Vendors Association).

Mr. Coleman is a principal at Collaborative Strategies, a San Francisco-based consulting firm focused on technology assessment, marketing, and information in the workgroup computing arena. Collaborative Strategies provides business and technology assessment and marketing and business strategies for workgroup products and services. Collaborative Strategies also provides market research, competitive analysis, collateral development, product positioning, and management for increased competitive advantage on a worldwide basis. Collaborative Strategies works with groupware users as well to define groupware projects, examine business processes with an eye toward redesign, and aid in the selection and implementation of pilot or enterprise-wide groupware projects.

Mr. Coleman has an eclectic educational background that covers a wide range from cybernetics to neurobiology. He has held marketing positions at Natural Language and Oracle, and has consulted for many major hardware and software vendors as well as user organizations.

Mr. Coleman can be reached by electronic mail at david121@aol.com or on the World Wide Web at davidc@collaborative.com. He can be reached by phone at (415) 282-9197.

Introduction to Chapter 2

The first section of this book focuses on computer technologies that help collaboration. Email and messaging technologies are among the most critical pieces of technology on which collaborative applications are built. Almost every collaborative application requires that some information, be it a document, mail note, or routing form, be passed to another person.

Karl Wong used to be a product manager at cc:Mail; from there he moved on to a principal analyst position at Dataquest, where he covers the groupware industry and much more, making him the perfect person to write this chapter and cover the technical and marketing issues for this category of groupware.

Karl begins his chapter with a primer on messaging, explaining terms and functions and bringing the business readers not familiar with this technology up to speed. He moves on to look at the "add-on" components to email, and then classifies the types of email systems. Finally, he moves on to email standards.

Standards and APIs for email have been controversial over the last few years and have been the subject of a major struggle between vendors, specifically between the VIM and MAPI standards. However, it looks as if Microsoft with their MAPI standard are winning this war, as Lotus in Version 4.0 of Notes has agreed to better MAPI support. Although Karl mentions Apple's AOCE standard, Apple is not known as a large player in the collaborative market. It is unfortunate, because Apple computers and their intuitive operating system probably offer one of the best platforms for collaboration. Apple has produced some very interesting collaborative software in PowerTalk, but never marketed it well and never understood that collaboration occurs between people, and people use different types of computers, so the software they use also has to be compatible with different types of computers.

Karl then takes on the sticky issues of privacy and security. With the Internet being the hot topic this year, and reports of security compromises appearing frequently in the papers, this is an issue anyone looking at collaborative technologies will have to deal with immediately.

Karl spends some time looking at the scalability of messaging systems and looks at some of the approaches organizations and vendors are taking to deal with the expansion of these systems.

Since not everyone you collaborate with is sitting at a desk down the hall, collaborative technologies, including email, must deal with mobile or nomadic users. Some of this issue is covered (from a user's perspective) in Hugh Ryan's chapter, and it is touched on in a variety of other chapters in this volume, but nowhere else are the technical issues explored in such a clear and succinct way.

Karl then moves on to cover specific messaging vendors. He examines their products and looks at future enhancements. This section should be especially interesting to those planning messaging infrastructures for the future.

Finally, Karl has a section on groupware products that are commonly built on a messaging infrastructure. Because all groupware products require communication between people for coordination and ultimately collaboration, electronic messaging is an enabling technology for much of groupware except for shared screen applications and electronic meetingware. Karl covers many of the other groupware categories, such as group scheduling, forms and workflow, and even some technologies that are not collaborative, like faxing, paging, and telephony. He ends this chapter with a brief look at the future of messaging.

His conclusion, that the market is dominated by Microsoft, Lotus, and Novell, is one I agree with. However, there is usually only one market leader, and it will be interesting to see which one of these three is the winner. The competition is good for the consumer, but with MAPI as an emerging standard, and Exchange and Windows 95 on the way, the Microsoft marketing engine may prove to be too much even for Novell and Lotus. Whoever wins the messaging wars, it is a sure thing that messaging and the applications that run on top of it are here to stay and will become both more tightly integrated with the operating system over time as well as more sophisticated.

Karl's chapter is a wonderful overview of messaging. It reflects a keen insight into the market, and broad knowledge of the technologies that make up messaging and those that are built on top of a messaging infrastructure. This chapter leads you from the simple to the complex, from messaging components to the complexity of workflow applications!

Electronic Mail and Messaging

Karl Wong
Dataquest Incorporated

2.1 INTRODUCTION AND OVERVIEW

Depending upon your point of view, groupware is at various states of maturity. As the other authors in this book will claim, groupware is what you make of it. It can be simple or complex. Either way, the desired result is the same: to foster a mechanism between two or more people to enhance communication and productivity.

One of the enabling technologies within groupware is email or "electronic messaging." Email at its basic level is a simple yet powerful form of groupware used either by itself or as a foundation for other groupware applications to build a total solution. This chapter will discuss the basics of electronic messaging and current issues as they apply to groupware.

This chapter will cover:

☞ Electronic messaging primer—This section offers a brief overview of the components of electronic messaging.
☞ Types of messaging systems—An overview of the different types of messaging systems in different environments such as host systems, LAN/WANs, and public systems.
☞ Client-server messaging vs. file-based messaging—What the differences are in these two major messaging architectures.
☞ Standards—This section covers the major messaging standards in use today.
☞ Overview of major vendor messaging products—An overview of Microsoft, Lotus, Novell, and other messaging product offerings.

☞ Messaging APIs—An examination of the messaging applications programming interfaces.

☞ Building on the messaging foundation—A look at various enabling technologies and how they interact with messaging.

☞ Mobile and remote messaging—Remote access to messaging systems and wireless technologies is examined.

☞ Future messaging—A look at the messaging market in the months and years to come.

2.2 LAN EMAIL PRIMER

2.2.1 Introduction

Electronic messaging is as important to a local area network (LAN) as its print and file services. Just as with printing and file services, the electronic messaging system is a critical component to any successful groupware implementation, whether starting off small or growing larger to enterprise-wide solutions. Electronic mail can be defined as the transmission of text from one computer to another. The analogy of paper mail applies to electronic mail as well. Just as a paper mail message can be sent via the postal system to other users, an electronic mail message can be sent to one or more users. Once again, as with a paper mail message, the content of the mail message or envelope can contain more than just simple text. While the majority of email messages are text only, electronic messages can also contain graphics, file attachments, faxed images, sound, and video.

2.2.2 Email vs. Messaging

Throughout this chapter and in your conversations with others regarding email, you may have been confused by the terms "email" and "messaging." In the beginning, "email" often referred to the entire system of people exchanging messages on usually monolithic host systems. As email began to evolve to do more and more tasks, the concept of email began to change. An easy way to think of it is this: Email is an application. It performs the task of creating and reading electronic mail messages. Messaging is the electronic infrastructure upon which email and other applications can reside. Email, along with scheduling, workflow, voice, and fax among others, uses the messaging infrastructure for delivery. While the distinction between email and messaging is often gray, many people use the two terms interchangeably. The important thing to remember is in what context the term is being used.

2.3 ELEMENTS OF MESSAGING

Electronic messaging in its basic form is composed of two components: the user agent and the messaging services. As Figure 2.1 illustrates, the basic architecture of a messaging system is divided into these two components.

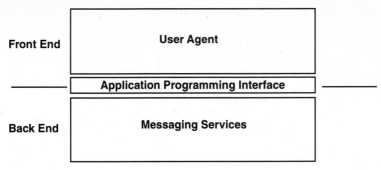

Fig. 2.1 Basic Elements of Messaging

The middle component, the applications programming interface (API), is a very thin but important layer residing between the front end and the back end of a messaging system. Additional information on messaging APIs is provided later in this chapter. Let's break down these two basic components a bit further and explain them and their functions.

2.3.1 The Front End—User Agents (UA)

The user agent (UA), sometimes referred to as the "front end," is the client or the mail agent of an electronic messaging system and is what most people see or think of when the term email is used. The UA is the part of the email package that users see and interact with. Within the UA, users create, edit, send, and read email messages. In addition, the UA may provide some form of notification of incoming mail. While the user interface (UI) may be radically different from one package to the next, all UAs have a common set of basic features for the creation and reading of messages. The UA is probably one of the most significant elements that differentiates one email package from another. Because users will be spending a considerable amount of time within the UA, often the successful implementation of a messaging system is based on how users interact with the UA user interface. If users don't feel comfortable with the UI of the email package, they will be less inclined to use it and see the benefits of email as a tool.

2.3.2 The Back End—The Messaging Services

The messaging services component of an email system, sometimes referred to as the "back end," is the infrastructure responsible for moving electronic messages. The back end of a messaging system is further subdivided into three components:

☞ The message transport agent (MTA)
☞ The message store
☞ The directory store

Figure 2.2 illustrates where these components fit into the overall messaging back end.

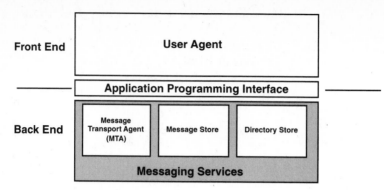

Fig. 2.2 Components of the Back End

2.3.2.1 Message Transport Agents   The message transport agent or message transfer agent (MTA) is the software responsible for collecting, sorting, and delivering the email from one computer, or mailbox, to another. Depending upon the type of electronic messaging system, the MTA will move or copy the mail message from the sender's mailbox to the recipient's mailbox or to a type of database from which it is read by the recipient. The MTA is the portion of the electronic messaging system that the typical user does not see or has little knowledge of. The MTA also defines the overall connectivity possibilities and limitations of an email system. MTAs are broken into two separate camps: open, or standards-based, and proprietary. X.400 and SMTP are open or standards-based examples. The MTAs used today within popular electronic messaging systems such as Microsoft Mail or Lotus' cc:Mail are closed or proprietary. These proprietary MTAs can communicate with any other MTAs of the same type, but they must interact with a gateway (see below) to exchange messages if the MTAs are of different types.

2.3.2.2 Message Store   The message store is where electronic messages are stored. The message store, usually found on the hard drive of a file server or messaging server, is often referred to as the "post office." As with the paper mail analogy, the post office contains the mailbox of each user on the mail system. The sender of a message creates and sends an email message to another user. The MTA will direct the message to the appropriate recipient's mailbox, where it is stored until the recipient picks it up. If a user is not on that particular post office, then the message is forwarded to the post office where that user's mailbox resides. Hence, the mail message is "stored" and "forwarded" to the recipient. The term "store and forward" is often referred to when describing an electronic messaging system.

2.3.2.3 Directory Store   The directory store, sometimes referred to as "directory services," provides the address book from which users can address email messages. The directory store usually provides each user's name and also maps those users' names to specific email addresses. Users access the directory and address messages from within the user agent transparently much like a regular address book. The directory can contain more than just users' names and email addresses. Often the directory store will contain additional information on the users such as their positions or titles, physical locations, or telephone extensions. Often the directory store is a subset or superset of an existing LAN directory. Basically, the directory store of an electronic messaging system is a flat-file database containing records, or users, and the information about them. In fact, many organizations map existing human resource or other personnel databases to their electronic messaging directory to tie this information in with their email.

2.3.3 Accessories—Expanding the Basic System

Although not always an essential part of an electronic messaging system, certain accessories are needed to expand beyond the basic electronic messaging system. Some of these include:

☞ **Gateways**—Gateways act as translators between dissimilar electronic messaging systems. In essence, a gateway will translate an email message from one MTA, such as cc:Mail, to another MTA, such as Microsoft Mail. Unfortunately, because most email UAs provide additional functionality beyond simple text messages, most gateways are forced to the lowest common denominator, usually text. Any added elements of a message a certain UA may add, such as rich text or sound, may be lost during the conversation, depending on the gateway.

☞ **Switches**—There is often confusion between the terms gateway and switch. In short, the difference between a gateway and a switch is that one switch can do the work of many gateways. As an example, Figure 2.3 shows an organization that needs to connect four different messaging systems, which would need six gateways. A messaging switch provides a many-to-many solution. In essence, the switch may include the necessary MTAs of the four messaging systems in order to do the translation between systems. One of the most obvious benefits of a switching system is reduced management. There are also fewer points of failure than a complex gateway solution.

☞ **Message management**—The tracking and routing of messages can be a daunting task. Message management tools help facilitate the management of electronic messaging systems by providing useful tools such as troubleshooting capabilities for bottlenecks in an electronic messaging system, notification of MTA failures, remote management of post offices, disk usage of the message store, and so on.

☞ **Directory management**—Management and synchronization of electronic messaging directories can be one of the biggest nightmares of novice mail administrators and seasoned veterans alike. Directory management applications aid in the management of messaging directories by providing tools and systems to facilitate directory synchronization, duplication of directory

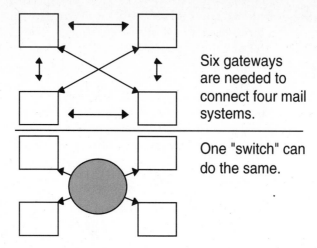

Fig. 2.3 Gateway versus Switch

entries, directory synchronization across disparate electronic messaging systems, and network operating system directory interoperability.

☞ **Agents and filters**—As the popularity of email expands, so does the number of messages. Agent and filtering technologies provide a mechanism for users to cut through the flood of both inbound and outbound messages. One form of messaging agent is "rules," found in many email systems today. An example of a rule would be the classic "I'm on vacation." In this example, a user could implement a rule stating that all inbound messages from a certain date would return or "auto-reply" back to the sender a message stating that he/she is on vacation. Other examples include auto-forwarding, auto-delete, and auto-printing. Agents can reside at the UA and/or the message services level.

2.4 TYPES OF EMAIL SYSTEMS

Email, like everything else, comes in all shapes and sizes. In the past, email was found mainly on large mainframe, or host, systems in which users "logged in" via a terminal or terminal emulation program. Today, email systems can be found in any of three environments:

☞ **Host-based**—Examples included IBM PROFS, OfficeVision/VM, and DEC All-in-1/VMSMail.
☞ **LAN-based**—Examples include Lotus cc:Mail, Microsoft Mail, and Novell GroupWise.
☞ **Public/On-Line Services-based**—Examples include the Internet, MCI-Mail, AT&T Mail, SprintMail, CompuServe, and America Online.

Each of these systems can be used independently or in conjunction with one another; the latter is often the case in large businesses.

2.4.1 Host-Based

The birth of email came on a host system. While many consider the mainframe and mini-computer relics of the past, many corporations still depend on existing infrastructures of PROFs and DEC All-in-1 for their day-to-day email business. While host-based messaging systems are on a definite downturn, a late 1993 Dataquest survey found 39% of all corporations are still host-based-only sites. Another 34% of the surveyed sites used host-based messaging systems in conjunction with newer LAN-based electronic messaging systems.

The important thing to remember with host-based systems is not that mainframes and mini-computer systems are being used, but that the software running on them is important. While these electronic messaging systems are in a state of transition as they move toward LAN-based electronic messaging systems, the hardware itself may find a new life. Many corporations and public messaging services are increasingly finding that well-established host system disk and back-up management services can provide yet another option to growing messaging storage demands.

2.4.2 LAN-Based

The majority of electronic messaging systems installed today are LAN-based. The growth of LAN-based electronic messaging systems has exploded in the last five years. Much of this growth has come from corporate downsizing of both personnel and systems in the late 1980s and early 1990s. This is a trend that is continuing.

Companies leading the charge in the advancement of LAN-based messaging include Lotus Development with its cc:Mail product, and Microsoft and its Microsoft Mail product. Products like cc:Mail and MS Mail, along with Novell's GroupWise, provide a friendly user interface and relatively simple administration when compared to host-based systems. In addition, the LAN-based systems provide a much lower cost of entry solution than do other types of messaging systems.

2.4.3 Public/On-Line Services-Based

Depending on your needs, a public or on-line messaging service provider may be just the right amount of email or groupware necessary. On-line services have been around for several years, but competition has increased considerably in the past few years. The type of on-line service depends on you and your groupware needs. Almost all of these services provide access or gateways to other messaging systems, including the Internet. There are two ways to look at an on-line messaging service provider.

The first way is for your sole message needs. As a user on one of these systems, such as MCIMail or AT&T Mail, you can let the service provider handle all the infrastructure requirements. You and your company would be defined as a user account or accounts. All messages would go through the service provider. This type of arrangement has many benefits. Little or no hardware is required on your site other than a personal computer and a modem. In addition, you can often access your mail account in other cities while traveling on business. The downside is that you have little control over the host system, and all these benefits come at a cost. Most of these services charge by the message or byte count. Depending on your messaging traffic, this cost could be large.

The second way to use these on-line service providers is as messaging hubs or gateways to other messaging systems such as the Internet. CompuServe, for example, provides a hub service for most of the popular messaging MTAs such as cc:Mail and MHS. With this capability, companies would use the service provider in addition to their internal messaging systems. By linking with the service provider in a hub fashion, companies can link disparate sites, or vendors and customers, to the service provider's vast network. Once again, cost may be an issue if your messaging traffic is high. You must weigh the costs of building and maintaining your own enterprise wide-area messaging network against the costs of using a messaging service provider.

The Internet could be a category in itself, but for this chapter on messaging, it is included as a public messaging provider. While the Internet is much more than email, many people have come to think of it as an electronic version of the postal system. The Internet is nothing more than a network, albeit a very large network. Sometimes referred to as the information superhighway or Infobahn, the Internet's large size and popularity offers some exciting messaging opportunities. Much like the options of a regular public messaging service provider such as CompuServe, the Internet can be used as a standalone messaging option or as a backbone or hub.

Many popular Internet service providers such as NETCOM and PSI provide both individual and corporate Internet accounts. Basic Internet email can be had for as little as U.S.$10.00 and is often free in some communities via access to local universities. Whether through an Internet shell account or through one of many graphical Internet readers such as Mosaic, the Internet and its services may provide enough messaging services for your groupware needs. Commonly, though, the Internet is used by small and large corporations alike as a messaging backbone or a common gateway to vendors, customers, and other users. Since many companies have a connection of some type to the Internet, you'll often find that the Internet provides a common transport mechanism for the delivery of email inside and outside the corporation.

2.5 STANDARDS

Someone once said that the nice thing about standards is that there are so many to choose from. Messaging is no different. A standard, or specification, as defined by a standards organization enables programmers, engineers, and information technology professionals to create and work on interoperating products. Some of the standards organizations involved with messaging are the same found in other areas of software and information technologies. They include ANSI (American National Standards Institute), CCITT (International Consultative Committee for Telephony and Telegraphy), IEEE (Institute of Electrical and Electronics Engineers), and ISO (International Standards Organization).

While standards cover a broad area, the focus within messaging revolves around the core messaging services portion or back end. Within the messaging category, the following standards are important to any persons interested in messaging:

☞ **X.400**—A CCITT standard method for the exchange of electronic messages between computer systems. Traditionally thought of as only existing at the MTA level, the X.400 specification includes information at the UA and message store levels. X.400 is most often found exclusively within large, global corporations. As the messaging industry continues to move towards open standards, messaging standards like X.400 are emerging at the top, at least at the corporate level. In many ways, X.400 is competing with SMTP/MIME (see below), especially with the increasing importance of the Internet.

☞ **X.500**—A CCITT standard method for the exchange of messaging directories. The X.500 standard is designed to provide directory information in a global setting; or at least, that is the goal. While this general directory has many advantages, including a hierarchical tree structure, the standard remains in a state of continuing maturity. Unlike the X.400 standards, which were defined as early as 1984, certain X.500 standards were not defined until as recently as 1992. As a result, a variety of "X.500-like" services were developed. In addition, many corporations have been reluctant to exchange sensitive directory information (including personnel information) in any global directory exchange within a public directory.

☞ **SMTP**—Simple Mail Transport Protocol. This messaging protocol is used in TCP/IP networks for exchange of electronic messages between computer systems. Widely used within the government and universities, SMTP is finding large adoption among corporations as the importance of the Internet continues to grow. Many people within the TCP/IP community believe the SMTP and MIME (see below) will win out over X.400 as a corporate message transport standard.

☞ **MIME**—Multipurpose Internet Mail Extensions is a standard used in conjunction with SMTP. MIME is used for the standardization of exchanging electronic objects such as attachments, audio, video, and other large binary files over Internet mail. The inclusion of MIME adds even more fuel to those who believe that the Internet, TCP/IP, and SMTP will become the dominant standards moving into the 1990s.

☞ **MHS**—Message Handling System. MHS is often used generically; most of the time, it refers to Novell's MHS. Novell MHS, through its one-time inclusion within the Netware network operating system, has become a popular MTA on many LANs. While it still maintains a large installed base, MHS as a standard has seen better days. Today, it is found mainly on smaller messaging networks or used as a backbone bridge between messaging systems.

2.6 MESSAGING APIs

Writing applications for electronic messaging systems, whether they be email clients (front ends) or message reliant add-ons, all rely on one thing in order to work with the messaging services back end: application programming interfaces (APIs). An API is a tool used by the programmer to simplify the task of writing software. An API is prewritten code with "hooks" that enable a programmer to integrate one portion of code to another. A person writing an application for a messaging system would need to write new code for each electronic messaging system he or she was developing. With common messaging APIs, the programmer would need to write to one set of APIs instead of to multiple ones. Messaging APIs are much like those found in the database world. What Microsoft's ODBC is to database systems, Microsoft's MAPI is to messaging. While there are other messaging APIs, as we will discuss below, developments toward the end of 1994 have made Microsoft MAPI the clear winner in the heated messaging wars of years past.

Important messaging APIs of interest:

☞ **MAPI**—Messaging Applications Programming Interface. Developed by Microsoft of the Windows operating environment, MAPI comprises two separate versions: Simple and Extended. While not having all the cross-platform advantages of VIM, the MAPI architecture of client and server interface levels is well designed for open messaging. In 1994, Lotus and WordPerfect, both supporters of the competing VIM API standard, announced support for MAPI for inclusion within cc:Mail and Notes, and GroupWise, respectively. With this announced support for MAPI, the messaging industry can move more rapidly towards the goal of ubiquitous mail enabling of applications.

☞ **VIM**—Vendor Independent Messaging API. Originally developed by Lotus Development, the VIM API was adopted by a consortium of companies including Lotus, WordPerfect, IBM, Apple, and Oracle. The additional benefit of VIM over MAPI is its cross-platform support, where MAPI is strictly Windows only. During 1992 and 1993, much debate within the messaging industry occurred over which messaging API should be supported. As Microsoft and the rest of the industry fought this issue out, the customer was caught in the middle. The result was a lack of progress. While the future of VIM remains in doubt (Lotus announced discontinuation of further development), the existing set of tools available make VIM an option for those companies with serious cross-platform messaging needs.

☞ **CMC**—Common Messaging Calls API. As mentioned above, the 1992/1993 messaging API war that erupted between Microsoft and the rest of the industry caused much confusion. For a possible soothing of tensions, the XAPIA (X.400 Application Programming Interface Association) developed the CMC API. With XAPIA members from most of the major messaging companies, including Microsoft and Lotus, the XAPIA was able to establish a set of specifications for basic messaging interface calls.

☞ **AOCE**—Apple Open Collaboration Environment. Apple's AOCE environment includes mail and messaging, catalog services, and various levels of security. The PowerTalk messaging system found within Apple System 7.5 is an example of a messaging application using AOCE. Currently, AOCE is only for the Macintosh operating system. Apple's attempt to establish a messaging foundation built around the Macintosh operating system seems to have failed in the market. If you are in a strictly Macintosh environment and use the core messaging services from Apple, then AOCE may have some interest.

☞ **SMF**—Standard Message Format. The SMF API is supported in Novell MHS systems. SMF-71 is the current version supported. Novell, through its acquisition of WordPerfect and its GroupWise product, is moving away from SMF and towards the MAPI API as it moves to the next generation of messaging products. As part of its migration plan to move existing MHS customers to GroupWise, Novell has announced support for the SMF-71 API in the GroupWise environment. This support allows existing SMF applications written for MHS to move to GroupWise as the preferred Novell messaging platform.

2.7 MESSAGING ISSUES

As messaging continues to gain momentum as a groupware tool, so come the issues or problems that surround any expanding technology. This section examines some of these issues and the trends towards their solutions.

2.7.1 Privacy and Security

As millions of users begin to rely on email for a variety of purposes, including personal letters, business correspondence, information and messages, many of these messages are sensitive, and users want their privacy protected.

Yet, after pressing the "send" button, a message can pass through a handful of mail forwarders and dozens of packet-switching nodes. A system administrator or someone who has gained privileged access to any of these transfer points may also read those messages, depending on the email system used. More users are becoming aware of such risks as email use grows.

The technology for email security breaks down into two approaches:

☞ Message confidentiality—The contents of a message can be encrypted using a conventional encryption scheme such as the Data Encryption Standard (DES). The most difficult technical challenge for such schemes is the secure exchange of encryption keys between pairs of correspondents.

☞ Message authentication—Message authentication is often referred to as "digital signature" security. A digital signature, implemented using public-key encryption, makes use of two keys: a private key, known only to its owner, and a public key that is disseminated so all other users have access to it. If a block of data is encrypted with the sender's private key, any recipient may decrypt that block with the sender's public key. The recipient is assured that the block must have come from the alleged sender, since only the sender knows the private key.

Another development that may help in messaging security is the adoption by email vendors of the PEM (Privacy Enhanced Mail) standard, which describes a common way of encapsulating encrypted messages and defines when software should decrypt a message. The standard, approved recently by the Internet Engineering Task Force, should help them bring standard, secure email to market more quickly.

2.7.2 Scalability and Manageability

As mentioned before in this chapter, LAN-based messaging systems have evolved beyond simple mail for small workgroups. Now they must be able to support so-called information-sharing or messaging-enabled applications, such as group scheduling and workflow.

As the move toward distributed LAN-based messaging systems continues, and organizations continue to turn away from mainframe and minicomputer systems, some of the luxuries these centralized systems provided are missing. Traditional mainframe and minicomputer systems often supported enterprise-wide operation all in one box or machine. Such systems are clearly incapable of handling the kinds of applications needed for doing business in a distributed fashion. On the other hand, LAN-based messaging systems don't have the scalability and manageability of the old host systems, and that's creating major problems for IS managers. LAN-based messaging systems are strong on application functionality, but don't yet include the robust services and management features that customers desperately need.

One approach towards placing some solutions in distributed messaging includes a three-tiered architecture:

☞ User agent level—The email user agents and mail-enabled applications provide the basic layer at which the typical end user sees the messaging system.

☞ Workgroup and departmental server level—At this level, messaging servers are placed to handle the workload where most of the communications happen. It is estimated that 80% of all electronic messages are communicated at this level.

☞ Messaging backbone—The highest level. The backbone is used to connect different systems—both inside and outside the company. The backbone exists solely to enable interoperability between systems, and make that interoperability manageable.

One example of a messaging provider embracing this idea is Lotus Development. Lotus recently acquired SoftSwitch, the leading supplier of messaging backbone switches (Soft*Switch EMX, renamed Lotus Messaging Switch or LMS). This important development signals a maturity of the LAN-based messaging business, and that's good news for system administrators of enterprise messaging systems. LMS products manage directory synchronization between connected systems, and over time that synchronization will include externally connected public and private directories.

Over the next several years, we will begin to see some relief for managers of enterprise messaging systems. As these systems continue to mature, we'll see continued tools and products to enhance LAN-based messaging systems.

With all this information sharing happening, some serious improvements in directory support will be necessary. The manual synchronizing of internal mail directories often done today is difficult at best, but wait until you try to synchronize with the rest of the world when standards like X.500 become more prevalent.

In the end, the most important trend happening today will be management tools. As messaging vendors begin to offer integrated products capable of providing a backbone in a three-tier architecture, such management issues will be easier to answer, and you'll be more capable of managing the messaging network as a whole.

A relatively new messaging standard gaining support is MADMAN, a standard for managing email via SNMP. MADMAN, the Mail and Directory management information base (MIB) is the first step towards alleviating problems associated with email. MADMAN administers an email system by monitoring the flow of messages, a time-consuming task for messaging administrators. The MIB is designed to work with SNMP management platforms.

To date, over 20 vendors in the Technical Subcommittee (TSC) of the Electronic Messaging Association's (EMA) Messaging Management Committee are supporting MADMAN by working to adopt a specific implementation schedule. Lotus, Microsoft, Novell, AT&T, Banyan, and Intel are among some of the companies already in full-fledged implementation development.

2.7.3 Interoperability

The issue of interoperability transcends messaging. The integration and interoperability of different hardware platforms and networking protocols, such as TCP/IP, SNA, NetBIOS, and IPX/SPX, and messaging protocols like X.400 and SMTP is difficult at best. Networking managers and messaging administrators must deal with the issues of interconnecting not only PC LAN-based systems, but messaging between host-based systems, external systems such as the Internet, and emerging messaging-enabling technologies like faxing, paging, and telephony.

2.8 MOBILE MESSAGING

Mobile computers have revolutionized the way we work. Packing the power of desktop systems, mobile computers are small enough and lightweight enough to carry in a briefcase. They've also become portable communications devices. This holds true as we move forward into wireless messaging. What was once a luxury is now often a growing necessity. Wireless communications are becoming an effective mechanism for enhancing the enterprise-wide messaging system.

Mobile computers have already freed users from the restrictions of power cords and the desktop. The next step going forward is to go completely wireless by breaking mobile computers' other tether: the telephone cord. Wireless computing is possible today because of the convergence of several enabling technologies. First, wireless radio modems, like mobile computers, have become relatively small and inexpensive. Also, communications companies are offering services for wireless computer users in urban areas and major transportation corridors. Additionally, the leading software companies are enhancing their applications to take advantage of these wireless networks.

2.8.1 Circuit Switching

Circuit switching is the technology behind all cellular telephone communications—both voice and data. When used in wireless data communications, circuit switching establishes a dedicated, end-to-end connection between two computers. The connection begins with the initiation of the call and ends when the computers disconnect. Users pay for the entire time this circuit is in use.

Because the typical email message is fairly short, operators of the major cellular networks have announced a new technology to make their existing systems more cost effective for wireless email. The proposed new system, called Cellular Digital Packet Data (CDPD), would intersperse packets of data with voice conversations. This technology could, in the future, give users both the cost efficiency of circuit switching for sending long messages and the lower cost of sending short ones as packets.

2.8.2 Packet Switching

Unlike existing cellular networks, wireless packet-switched networks are designed specifically for data communications. Packet switching breaks messages into packets and sends these packets individually over the network. There are two major providers of packet radio networks: RAM Mobile Data Wireless Networks and Ardis.

Packet radio is particularly cost-effective for wireless messaging because most email messages are short enough to fit easily into the packet structure. Users pay only for the data they send, as measured by the number of packets. Packet radio also offers some security advantages over today's cellular technology. Transmissions are digitally encoded, so listening in is not as simple as it is with cellular voice communications.

Packet radio networks provide wireless messaging services in major urban areas, including airports and transportation corridors. The RAM network, for instance, divides metropolitan areas into geographic zones called "cells." Servicing each cell is a base station that sends and receives data packets from your mobile computer. When you send a message, the base station receives it and can either route the message to other mobile users in the same cell, or route it to the local switch for transport to another cell or wired connection such as a LAN.

Other key issues in mobile and wireless messaging to think about include bandwidth, data compression, security, filtering methods, and coverage.

2.9 MESSAGING TODAY AND TOMORROW

While there are several vendors providing electronic messaging products, the email market is dominated by three primary vendors: Lotus Development, Microsoft, and Novell. This section briefly describes their existing products and a glimpse at what the future holds for these respective messaging systems.

2.9.1 Lotus Development

2.9.1.1 cc:Mail   With over 6 million users, cc:Mail is one of the most popular LAN-based email systems on the market today. Based on a shared file architecture, cc:Mail is a cross-platform email system. On the UA or workstation level, cc:Mail is available on Windows, DOS, Macintosh, OS/2, and UNIX operating systems. The Windows user agent provides rules for message management and message searching. You can address messages to recipients on local networks, on distant LANs, and to recipients who receive mail through fax machines all through a simple unified directory. cc:Mail provides a rich and complete set of tools for network and directory synchronization and management. Also provided is the ability for posting of messages and viewing of messages in company-wide bulletin boards. cc:Mail provides message transfer software enabling server-to-server communication and remote user access. cc:Mail also includes single-copy message-store technology, global directory services, and store-and-forward design. The server platform supports a rich set of networking protocols, including TCP/IP, SNA, and X.25.

Future cc:Mail enhancements are planned for 1995. Included are 7-day-by-24-hour on-line back-up and mail database maintenance, an enhanced user agent to take advantage of Windows 95, and hierarchical folders and bulletin boards. MAPI will be supported as well at both the user agent and the service provider levels.

2.9.1.2 Lotus Notes   Lotus Notes is by far the leader in the groupware category. It is best described as a platform. This client-server platform supports multiple network and desktop operating systems in order to connect heterogeneous workgroups, and it includes an integral messaging system, a distributed document database, and a robust development environment. The Notes applications that reside on this groupware platform represent group-enabled software. Far beyond simple support for email, Lotus Notes applications improve the business performance of people working together by enabling them to access, route, track, share, and organize the information they use in their everyday business processes. Developers can build Lotus Notes applications using the platform's tools or by using traditional programming languages such as C or Visual Basic through a set of open interfaces.

In 1995, Lotus Development is expected to release a new version of Lotus Notes, version 4.0. Version 4.0 will contain an enhanced scripting language, LotusScript, for applications development in addition to the existing macro language. Also included are an improved user interface, additional server platforms, and increased scalability. MAPI will be supported as well.

2.9.1.3 CommServer   Lotus recently renamed its future messaging strategy from Lotus Communications Server to CommServer to better reflect its new positioning of Lotus Notes and cc:Mail. CommServer is based on Lotus Notes and provides cc:Mail integration via the "cc:Mail Connector" module, optional X.400 and SMTP/MIME component support, and a high-performance hub routing mechanism.

2.9.2 Microsoft

2.9.2.1 MS Mail   Sold alone and also included as part of Microsoft's Office and Windows of Workgroups products, Microsoft Mail has an installed base of over 6 million users. Available for the Windows, DOS, and Microsoft operating systems, Microsoft Mail's strength is found primarily in the Windows environment. With a rich user interface, and strong editing and OLE support, the Microsoft Mail user agent is very approachable. Also included are nested public folders. The back-end services provide communications and file distribution over the LAN. Message transfer software enables server-to-server communication and remote user access. Microsoft Mail also includes single-copy message-store technology, global directory services, and store-and-forward design; and permits communication with a variety of email systems, including PROFS, X.400, FAX, MHS, SMTP, MCI Mail, and SNADS.

2.9.2.2 Microsoft Exchange   The future of Microsoft's groupware strategy lies solely with the Microsoft Exchange server product. This client-server messaging system provides host-based email, fax, and voice mail integration capabilities. In addition, Exchange integrates group scheduling, electronic forms, and business productivity applications under one unified user interface. Based on the Microsoft NT operating system, Exchange provides centralized system monitoring and administration. It supports Internet SMTP/MIME mail transfer, agents, X.400 protocols, and X.500 directory services. Clients are expected to run on DOS, UNIX, Macintosh, Windows 3.1, and Windows 95. The Exchange client is expected to be included within Windows 95.

2.9.3 Novell

2.9.3.1 GroupWise   Novell GroupWise is more of an integrated groupware application than strictly an email package. Formerly called WordPerfect Office (acquired through Novell's merger with WordPerfect), Novell GroupWise includes email, an integrated personal calendar, an integrated group scheduler, rules-based message management which allows users to assign actions to incoming and outgoing email messages, and task management. Also available is the ability to track the status of a message, which permits users to monitor a message's progress through the system. In December 1994, Novell signed a deal with Collabra to integrate it into collaborative discussion software within the GroupWise product.

2.9.3.2 CCE   With the acquisition of WordPerfect in 1994, the task of development and marketing of Novell's future messaging products fell on the newly formed GroupWare division. Recently, Novell announced a new strategy as it moves forward within the groupware market. Collaborative Computing Environment (CCE) is a modular/component architecture where Novell or third parties can create a variety of groupware solutions. The current product line of the Novell GroupWare Division includes SoftSolutions, a document management product; InForms, an electronic forms application; and two messaging products, GroupWise and MHS.

In the future, CCE will enable network administrators to centralize groupware management and administration under NetWare and will promote the smooth integration of third-party groupware products. The GroupWare Division is projected to have a groupware framework fashioned under the CCE principles by 1995. The first goal of CCE is to be interoperable with a range of operating environments, including UNIX, OS/2, NT, DOS, and Macintosh. Second, CCE will work to enable groupware applications to take advantage of network services within NetWare.

2.10 BUILDING UPON THE MESSAGING INFRASTRUCTURE

Email as a form of communication is equal in function and utility to the telephone, fax, and paper mail, but, as you have read, email is much more than sending memos or attaching files. Messaging is a transport for delivering information, and the next generation of messaging software will provide the underpinnings for applications that will deliver new productivity gains to information workers.

Workgroup software, as this book illustrates, is designed for a group of users, but it is also suitable for core business applications, such as accounting, inventory control, and database management. Group scheduling, forms, and workflow are a few of the applications built on the messaging infrastructure one installs just for simple email.

2.10.1 Group Scheduling

Calendaring and scheduling, often referred to as group scheduling, are typically the first applications to be added to a messaging backbone. Because of the relatively low barriers and required customizations, users can employ electronic calendars within their email to set appointments for themselves and others relatively fast. Group scheduling products are usually provided in one of two ways: as either a standalone scheduling product designed to work with an existing messaging system, or one designed to be integrated within a unified messaging architecture like that of Novell's GroupWise product. The more tightly integrated applications use APIs such as Microsoft's Mail API (MAPI) or Lotus' Vendor Independent Messaging (VIM).

Group scheduling products like CE Software's Network Scheduler or Microsystems' CaLANder work with messaging systems such as Microsoft Mail or Lotus cc:Mail in providing group scheduling capabilities on top of the existing email user agent.

An important recent development by the XAPIA association is the approval of a common group scheduling API. CSA, or calendaring and scheduling API, is designed as a common method or procedure for group scheduling programs and non-group scheduling products to obtain access to the underlying group scheduling system. In theory, with CSA, one group scheduling UA should be able to access the database of another scheduling system. Likewise, a program such as a project management program will be able to poll and post times and tasks through the CSA API. Like CMC, this opens new opportunities for exciting groupware applications using group scheduling.

2.10.2 Forms and Workflow

Electronic forms, or e-forms, can also take advantage of a messaging infrastructure transport system. Typically, a company ventures into workflow with e-forms, because it is looking for ways to reduce the volume of paper, and because the routing paths and interfaces for forms are straightforward. Many companies start with e-forms and workflow routing for expense reports or purchase order requisitions. Companies such as JetForm have led the way, but Lotus, Microsoft, and WordPerfect have entered the market with their Lotus Forms, MS E-Forms, and InForms, respectively.

Implementing an e-forms solution requires that you jump the hurdle of the security and authorization issue. You can't authorize an e-form by typing your name, because anyone could type your name and it would look the same. You must have a secure form of digital signature. Companies such as RSA Data Security are attempting to tackle this issue with some of the encrypting techniques mentioned above. Electronic forms can also handle the results of database queries. With e-forms for data access, you can turn the query results into an email message.

Workflow's future lies not in simple tasks, such as routing expense reports, but in real large-scale corporate applications. Workflow software can automate business processes so the software can routinely decide where to send documents. For workflow to be effective for core business applications, the system must be scalable and robust. It must be usable in a wide-area network as well as by mobile or remote employees. For this to be achieved, messaging and database systems must adopt some of each other's characteristics, such as the standardization of SQL within the email user agent and messaging API support on the database systems.

2.10.3 Faxing

Besides email, probably the most common text-based form of communications is faxing technology. With the boom in faxing technologies in the 1980s and the advent of cheap faxing units, it would seem that the integration of faxing technologies and electronic messaging would be a natural fit. Many vendors have just those solutions in place.

Basically, there are two ways in which to use faxing technology within an email system: outbound and inbound use. Both have benefits and disadvantages over a more transitional faxing machine solution.

Outbound faxing allows a user to fax directly from within the email user agent either through a fax server on the LAN or directly through a local modem. With an email faxing solution, the user need not worry whether the receiving location's fax machine is busy or on. Fax messages are queued till the line is available. Also, outbound faxing eliminates the need to print the message before transmission.

Inbound faxing, either through a fax server connected to the LAN or directly to the desktop using DID or DTMF direct routing, offers users the capability to receive faxes in digital form. Once within this digital format, users are free to import the messages into a word-processing document or spreadsheet. Often an optical character reader (OCR) is used by fax messaging solutions to transform the digital fax into standard ASCII characters.

2.10.4 Paging

Once used only by professionals such as doctors, today paging technology is a ubiquitous tool used by a wide cross-section of people. Some even use it as a social statement, as the ultimate in being "wired." Many people now believe that the lowly pager will lead us into a promised land of carefree wireless communications. But this isn't your ordinary beeper. Instead, a new generation of display pagers and enhanced paging services, coupled with future two-way services and pager-like communicators, are refashioning the beeper business into a far more attractive wireless option.

A wide variety of new paging services have been introduced in the past three years or so. In particular, nationwide networks such as MobileComm, PageNet, and SkyTel have extended their services to include email messages, news briefs, stock quotes, and other information. They can even notify you of faxes and voice-mail messages, and arrange to have them forwarded to you.

SkyTel's pagers, for instance, can receive email from public networks such as AT&T Mail, the Internet, and MCI Mail, as well as private networks like cc:Mail, Microsoft Mail, and WordPerfect GroupWise, or any other mail service, using the X.400 protocol. Lotus and SkyTel recently introduced a Pager Gateway for Lotus Notes workgroup software, and SkyTel says it will connect its network to Microsoft's new Exchange messaging system.

Wireless paging communication has some unique advantages. Rather than depending on users to initiate connections, paging systems simultaneously broadcast, or simulcast, data to all parts of their covered areas as they receive it, using radio towers linked by phone lines and, in some cases, by satellites. Simulcasting ensures that you get messages instantly and automatically wherever you happen to be. A paging system's redundant and overlapping radio coverage also makes it extraordinarily reliable and able to reach spots other wireless systems often can't, such as inside office buildings or tunnels.

However, there are disadvantages too. Primary among them is that phone numbers in numeric paging or messages in alphanumeric paging are sent to you, but you can't respond. Instead, you have to reach for a phone or a portable PC. Moreover, many paging services can transmit only short messages.

This could be changing soon, though. Two-way paging is on the horizon. Already some paging networks are experimenting with what's known as acknowledgment paging—or an automatic response to the sender indicating that the message was received. Future pagers will also be able to send canned responses, such as "Yes" or "No" or "Call me."

However, more robust two-way messaging will require vastly updated paging networks and a new generation of personal communicators. One such effort is already underway. Microsoft and SkyTel's parent company, Mtel, is in the process of building a $150 million system called the Nationwide Wireless Network (NWN) that uses pager-like signals to let you receive and send messages.

2.10.5 Telephony

One of the social stumbling blocks to the use of email comes from the widespread use of telephony and voice mail. Voice mail has gained wide acceptance based on its approachable format, that of the telephone. It often seems that one is either a dedicated voice-mail or email user. The differences in the two technologies transcend the average users. The conflicting use of either of the technologies is the subject of hot debate depending if you are talking with a voice-mail vendor or an email vendor. However, there may be some light at the end of the tunnel. There is a growing trend towards products to merge the worlds of PCs and telephones.

Our workday lives are run by the mundane routing of calls to appropriate people, answering seemingly endless voice-mail messages, and trying to tie all these different points of information (voice, fax, and email) into one cohesive mental and digital database. Electronic messaging and telephone integration offers one way out of telephone turmoil.

The integration of the telephone and the computer is nothing new. Everybody who's ever had their dinner interrupted by computerized telephone-sales systems can attest to this. With this new generation of integration come new standards or APIs competing to become the next standard.

At the center of the telephony battle stand two big camps: the Microsoft/Intel alliance with their TAPI API; and the AT&T/Novell alliance with their TSAPI API. Their respective APIs specify how to integrate computers to control dialing, answering, routing, and conferencing phone calls.

☞ **TAPI**—Microsoft and Intel, as you might expect, have a personal-computer-centric vision of telephone integration. Their viewpoint is that TAPI (Telephony Application Programming Interface) is to telephone-enabling what MAPI (Microsoft's Messaging API) is to message-enabling. With various TAPI-enabled products, you'll be able to do such things as control your phone from your computer, screen your calls (with Caller ID) and have the information about that caller pop up on your computer screen, create your own personal interactive voice-response system, and place calls directly from your word processors or applications. The TAPI specification does not require a network connection. It focuses on what are called first-party features. This means the call that comes in on your personal phone is under your control; once you route or forward the call, that control is gone.

☞ **TSAPI**—AT&T and Novell's TSAPI (Telephony Services API) handles first-party features, but it extends to third-party call features. These make it a better solution for the large-scale office. Architecturally, the fundamental difference between the two is that TAPI specifies a physical link between your PC and the phone, while TSAPI's links can be logical—a map between your server and your phone address. Third-party features include the ability to maintain and track a call as it is routed throughout your system. TSAPI requires that the private branch exchange (PBX) be linked to a server. Because the server is linked to the PBX directly, it has greater and more far-reaching control of the call.

There are pros and cons with each API. TSAPI is available as an add-on module to versions of Novell's NetWare 4.01 and above. TAPI will become an integral part of Windows 95. Only time and the market reception of these competing APIs will decide how and when the convergence of messaging and telephony takes off.

2.10.6 Electronic Data Interchange (EDI)

The merging of EDI and electronic mail promises to produce new opportunities for companies at integrating their messaging systems with existing transaction based systems. EDI involves the exchange of business transactions in a computerized format. EDI's integration with messaging opens up another avenue of this exchange. Many organizations have placed EDI on top of existing email or messaging hierarchies as the X.435 specification for EDI/email merging becomes more prevalent. With prototype X.435 not expended until 1996, IS organizations have time to orient and establish themselves as contenders in this emerging marketplace.

2.11 THE FUTURE AND CONCLUSIONS

Moving forward in 1995 and beyond, the future of the messaging market is at best described as "controlled chaos." The future of the market is pretty much dominated and determined by the three large players: Lotus Development, Microsoft, and Novell. While other players such as On Technology and CE Software will continue to profit in the continuing email expansion, the "big three" software vendors will drive the market. With this control comes chaos, and within these three spheres of influence comes chaos. Each of these three vendors have big challenges ahead of them. Lotus continues to formulate a strategy of integration of its cc:Mail and Notes products. Microsoft needs to complete and ship its Exchange Server and provide the rich set of tools and applications already found within the Lotus Notes environment. Lastly, Novell, with its recent acquisition of WordPerfect, must migrate its remaining MHS installed base while continuing to develop upon and around the GroupWare product line.

For organizations planning or maintaining an electronic messaging system, the future remains bright. Increased competition and continued expansion of email will only enhance the amount of options and tools available for messaging environments and their administrators.

BIOGRAPHY

Mr. Wong is the principal analyst with Dataquest's worldwide software research organization. He is responsible for all research and consulting in the personal computing and workgroup software markets. Prior to joining Dataquest, Mr. Wong was the Senior Product Line Manager for User Agents Technologies at Lotus Development's Electronic Messaging Division, cc:Mail. At cc:Mail, Mr. Wong was responsible for the development, implementation, and marketing of several of cc:Mail's award-winning products. In addition, Mr. Wong has an extensive technical background in the PC desktop and LAN operating systems, gained through his previous positions of Senior Support Engineer and Technology Analyst at Businessland, Inc. Mr. Wong has over 15 years of experience in the PC software industry.

Dataquest Incorporated, headquartered in San Jose, California, is a 23-year-old global market research and consulting company serving the high-technology and financial communities. The company provides worldwide market coverage on the semiconductor, computer systems and peripherals, communications, document management, software, and services sectors of the information technology industry. Dataquest is an international company of The Dun & Bradstreet Corporation.

Introduction to Chapter 3

Workflow is one of the hottest areas in groupware today. At last count there were over 130 different workflow vendors, and it seems like everyone is jumping on the process automation bandwagon. The Workflow Coalition (WARIA) has been formed to define standards and has created a users' group, to help meet the needs of those interested in workflow.

Workflow is often explained with the analogy of the factory floor. In America, manufacturing made great strides in productivity during the late '80s and early '90s, mostly due to automation. Now, visionaries want to take the automated processes of the factory floor and apply them to the office.

Initially, there were some exciting success stories of applying workflow tools and techniques. Automating production-oriented processes like processing claims forms or loan applications has yielded dramatically lower cycle times for processing this paperwork and improved customer service. This has translated into a competitive advantage for organizations using these tools. Additionally, competitors are frantically trying to catch up and surpass early workflow tools users.

Lotus, the biggest name in groupware (right now) has a special group investigating workflow because they believe it is a "strategic" technology and critical to the future of Notes. Unfortunately, Lotus has chosen to not fully implement a workflow strategy for a few years. Notes 4.0 does have some simple workflow features, and Notes can be used as a workflow engine, but in general, workflow functionality is integrated into Notes through the API.

In this chapter, Ronni Marshak, a well-known author and workflow industry analyst, takes a closer look at this popular technology. She defines workflow, gives examples of processes, and discusses products. She looks at the introduction of object-oriented technologies into groupware, and also looks at the role of workflow in the current craze for business process re-engineering or design.

As an entree into a detailed explanation of the components of workflow and workflow architectures, Ronni begins with an examination of the barriers faced by new entrants into the workflow arena. She touches on the same architectural issues that confront all groupware products, such as whether there is a message-based or database-based architecture supporting the product, and whether this is the best architecture for your particular business challenge.

Next, Ronni takes a look at how to choose a process to automate. She wisely dedicates a good section of the chapter to dealing with people as well as the workflow tools. Again, it's the people issues that usually sink a project, not the technical ones!

The final section of this chapter looks at workflow vendors. Who are the key players in the workflow market? Why are they key players? What is the technological advantage of each product? Where is workflow going? Will "workflow" be a useful term in the year 2020?

Additional questions to keep in mind while you read this excellent chapter are: Is it possible to automate the chaos that characterizes the front office? After all, the front office is not a factory floor, and automating can sometimes squeeze the creativity out of a process. How do those workers who are now using these automated workflow processes feel—more or less satisfied and empowered at work? Is automating a process a strategy for downsizing? If it is, how do you re-deploy your personnel? Has anyone in your organization started a workflow pilot project? If so, how was that project selected? What does "workflow" mean in your organization? How can workflow provide an organization with a competitive advantage? Has your management grasped the concepts of workflow? If yes, how are they supporting workflow, and enrolling the organization? Why are there so many workflow vendors, and when will the shake-out happen?

Workflow is a new area in groupware, and it has just become popular in the last few years. Many of the above questions do not have answers...yet. And many have answers that are organizationally specific. But answering these questions will help you get the most out of the cogent summarization of the technologies and issues presented in this chapter.

Workflow: Applying Automation to Group Processes

Ronni T. Marshak
The Patricia Seybold Group

3.1 WHERE WORKFLOW FITS IN GROUPWARE

If you look at technology through sports-colored glasses, then groupware is the basketball team, passing and rebounding to score team points—or it's the crew team, rowing together to speed past the competition—or it's the cheerleading squad, standing on each other's shoulders and jumping into each other's arms to whip the crowd into a frenzy of support—well, you get the picture. In this sporty world of groupware, workflow is the relay race, where only one team member at a time is actually running, but the hand-off of the baton spells the difference between success and failure.

There is a basic difference between other sports and a relay race, and that difference has to do with teamwork—or collaboration. Typically, you think of collaboration as an active explicit joining of minds, working together to achieve a certain goal: brainstorming, co-authoring, and so on. This is the sports team model, where the football team huddles together to plan the next play. But workflow is more focused on process, combining individual achievements into a sequence of actions that achieve a goal.

3.2 WORKFLOW DEFINED

I define *workflow* as the *automation and management of business processes*. A business process is a sequence of actions or tasks which must be done to achieve a business goal. These tasks are performed in a specific order by specific people, or by automated agents taking the role of a person to complete a task. The actual processing of the information within each task, such as performing a credit check or writing a letter, is usually performed in the organization's personal productivity applications and line-of-business applications (such as an accounting system). Typically, the order of tasks changes based on business conditions or rules.

Let me give you an example. In a claims-processing application (the archetypal workflow application), auto theft claims are handled differently than accident claims. When the receptionist at the insurance company takes your claim information, the type of form used depends on the type of claim being made. In an accident claim, claims under $1000 can be approved by a claims adjuster, but claims over $1000 must be approved by a claims supervisor. If the claimant is at fault, the underwriter determines if coverage should be continued or if a surcharge should be applied. The claims workflow application provides the proper form based on the claim type; routes the information to the correct approver depending on amount of claim; and launches the underwriting process based on fault determination.

3.3 USEFUL DEFINITIONS

3.3.1 The Workflow Coalition Is Working to Define the Vocabulary

Over 30 workflow vendors have joined a coalition to work on interoperability standards for workflow products and applications. The first task they have undertaken is to determine a standard vocabulary of workflow-related terms. And, let me tell you, this is no easy job. Everyone has a different shading of meaning for each word. Table 3.1 presents a list of terms pretty much agreed-upon by coalition members. They are presented here to facilitate your understanding of the technology area. Understand that this list is by no means complete; nor are the definitions yet carved in stone.

3.3.2 A Taxonomy of Workflow

Basically, workflow applications consist of the following:

Tasks: An automated workflow application is made up of the different tasks—a collection of activities—that must be completed to achieve a business goal.

People: These tasks are performed in a specific order by specific people—or automated agents taking the role of a person—based on business conditions or rules.

Tools: The actual work—processing of the information within each task, such as performing a credit check or writing a letter—is not really handled by the workflow application. Usually, these tasks are performed in personal productivity applications and line-of-business applications (such as an accounting system).

Table 3.1 Coalition-defined Terms.

Term	Definition
Process	A collection of coordinated parallel and/or serial activities that have explicit and/or implicit relationships among themselves in support of a specific process objective. (Synonym: work process)
Business process	A collection of coordinated parallel and/or serial business activities, in the context of a business organization's structure and policy, for the purpose of achieving clear business objectives.
Process definition	The computerized description of a process. The process definition consists of a network of activities and their relationships and specific criteria to indicate the start and termination of the process.
Process definition instance	Represents an instance of a process definition. It is created and managed by a workflow management system.
Activity	A single logical step within a process definition that contributes to the achievement of the process objective. It represents the smallest grain of abstracted work that can be defined within the workflow management reference model. It is considered complete when it has met the conditions that are defined within the process definition. A work item is considered to be a run-time manifestation of an activity. [Note from author: In this chapter, groups of related activities are considered tasks.]
Data	Information that is provided as a component of a work item. Types of data include application-relevant data and process-relevant data. Examples of data include a word processing document, spreadsheet, image, alphanumeric strings, voice, video, and/or database data. A work item's requested operation(s) may require data in support of accomplishing the objective of an activity within a process instance.
Workflow	The full or partial enaction or facilitation of a process.
Workflow management system	Consists of one or more workflow management engines.
Workflow management engine	A software service, or "engine," that provides the runtime environment for process definition instantiation, the ability to activate one or more process instances, and the ability to manage the operational progress of each process instance as each interacts with human and software application events in the environment.

Data: The documents, files, images, database records, and so on used as information to complete the work—the tools must access multiple shared data sources.

Figure 3.1 depicts a simple workflow application where a single person performs a single task and then forwards the work along a preassigned route. Notice, however, that even in this simple process, the same productivity tool is used for two separate tasks performed by different people. Note also that a variety of data sources are accessed at each task.

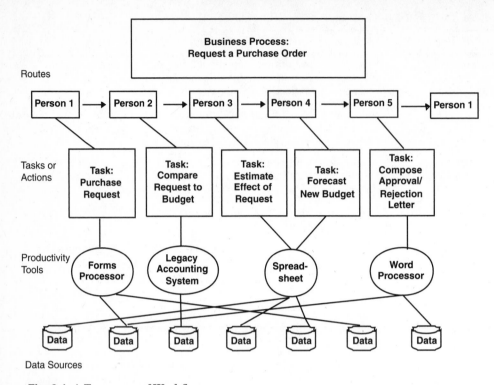

Fig. 3.1 A Taxonomy of Workflow

3.3.3 A Modular Approach

Many of the new generation of workflow products on the market take their lead from object-oriented technology, separating the basic components of the workflow definition into separate objects, which can then be reused and modified. Products such as FlowMark from IBM, InConcert from XSoft, and ViewStar's Workflow Designer separate the information/data/documents being routed from the routing order of the information—or the sequence in which people handle the information. A third component is the tools, or applications for processing the information for each task (see Figure 3.2).

For example, in a workflow application, the information or documents being routed include an imaged application for credit, a form front-ending a customer database, and a credit rating sheet. The route the information takes goes from the application clerk to the supervisor, to the manager, to the approval clerk. The tools for processing the information are an image management system, a forms processor, a database management system, terminal emulation software for accessing credit ratings, and a word processor for sending out the approval or denial letter.

Business rules can become attributes of any of these components, or they can be separate objects themselves.

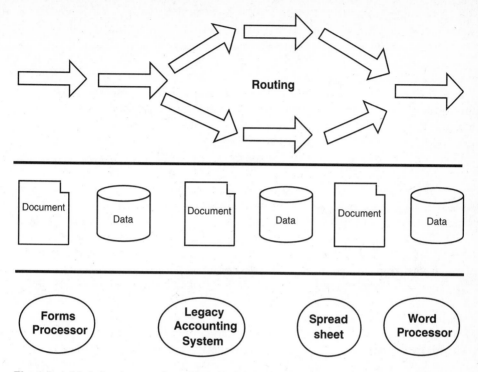

Fig. 3.2 A Modular Approach to Workflow

By keeping these components separate, they become interchangeable. For example, you can easily swap in a new routing using the same information packets and processing tools. Or you could change the productivity tools without affecting the information or the route.

3.4 THE RELATIONSHIP OF WORKFLOW AND BUSINESS PROCESS DESIGN

In most people's minds, workflow is tied to business process design. (I hesitate to call it business process re-engineering because that implies that the processes were "engineered" to begin with. Usually, processes evolve out of common business practice and are formalized after the fact.) And business process design has become a major hot button in today's competitive environment. The increasing pressures of global competitiveness are causing organizations to reexamine the ways in which they do business. All of the processes that make up an organization have fallen under scrutiny. No longer is it enough simply to streamline your manufacturing operation or upgrade your customer service operation. Now the pressure is on to improve the competitiveness of organizations by examining entire business processes from conception to the consumption of the products and services being offered.

Any opportunity to examine your business processes is valuable, but this examination takes time and effort. Organizations don't usually have the time and resources to undergo business process design efforts without the promise of some payback. Automating the processes with workflow tools can be that tangible payback. Once the process is identified, examined, and streamlined, you have a much-improved process to automate. Again, this can be an expensive proposition. Hiring one of the Big 6 consulting firms, such as Coopers & Lybrand or Andersen Consulting, can start at about $250,000. The effort can be well worth the money, but it is a daunting undertaking.

Recently, a new category of tools is emerging on the market: tools that automate the BPD phase but do not generate workflow applications. Products such as Action Technologies Workflow Manager and Virtual Management Inc.'s Workflow-BPR capture the business process design in a graphical map, but never translate that map into an online process. The value of the products is in the methodologies used to generate the information that makes up the map and in the graphical view of the process itself. These maps can be the basis for automation by tools from almost any workflow vendor.

Realize, though, that in some cases it is not necessary to undergo the time-consuming, expensive, resource-intensive BPD sessions. Many times, it is very valuable to "pave the cowpath"—automate the existing process without redesigning or streamlining. The actual act of automating and running the process for a while identifies areas for improvement. Sometimes the best thing to do is to "slap down" the application—rapid prototyping and piloting—continuously improving the process as requirements or new ideas surface.

3.5 WHERE WORKFLOW IS BEING IMPLEMENTED

Today, you find workflow being implemented in four primary types of applications:

- ☞ **Image processing:** Workflow first gained visibility as part of production imaging applications, where images were scanned, collected into folders, and routed in a specific order for approval or comments. When workflow capabilities—primarily routing features—were added to image processors, they were pretty limited, requiring coding at the programmer level to create a workflow application and allowing little, if any, flexibility. The newer generation of tools from vendors such as FileNet, ViewStar, Sigma, and Recognition are much more flexible, supporting graphical development, object-oriented designs, and user-level definition of business rules.
- ☞ **Forms processing:** In the mid-1980s, a British-based company called FCMC (now called Staffware in the United States) introduced forms-based workflow in its Staffware workflow processor. Originally conceived as an enhancement to FCMC's financial software products, Staffware was designed on a proprietary flat-file database which held the data entered

into forms designed in the system. These forms were routed based on rules and conditions of the data. WorkMAN from Reach also uses a forms model for routing work via email. In the past two years, the popular forms designer vendors, such as JetForm and Delrina, have added workflow routing to their traditional form products, which have already been mail-enabled to the most popular LAN-based mail products. As a result, you can specify conditional routing of these forms via your company's email system.

☞ **Mail rules and filtering:** In addition to using email to simply route forms or other information, products such as Lotus cc:Mail, WordPerfect Office, and BeyondMail from Banyan have workflow capabilities built directly in the mail system. BeyondMail also includes a complete Rules Language and Rules Engine for processing mail-based rules. These rules can range from the filtering of incoming mail to launching external applications and macros, thus creating full workflow applications based on the mail rules.

☞ **Shared database applications:** Most commonly seen in UNIX-based (soon to also be found in Windows NT-based versions) client-server workflow products, offerings such as X-Soft's InConcert and AT&T GIS's ProcessIT store information, rules, role tables, and so on in server-based relational databases, executing the workflow on GUI clients—typically MS Windows. Another very visible platform for workflow applications is Lotus Notes, which uses a shared document database model. Notes is becoming an increasingly popular environment for workflow applications, both designed directly in Notes and developed using third-party tools from the many Notes Alliance Partners such as Quality Decision Management, Workflow Inc., Action Technologies, and Reach Software.

3.6 CATEGORIES OF WORKFLOW APPLICATIONS—USEFUL GUIDELINES

Because workflow can be a difficult area to understand, many have attempted to separate types of workflow applications into categories. International Data Corporation (IDC) has proposed three separate categories for types of workflow applications (see Figure 3.3):

☞ Ad hoc
☞ Administration
☞ Production

These are very useful categories, and they have helped customers get their minds around a very complex and diverse set of products and methodologies. However, I believe these categories should be used as guidelines rather than gospel—general category buckets where people can look at the processes used in their businesses and figure out where to start looking at technology solutions to automate them. Some vendors and users have taken these categories too literally, and are therefore ignoring what really needs to happen in the workflow world.

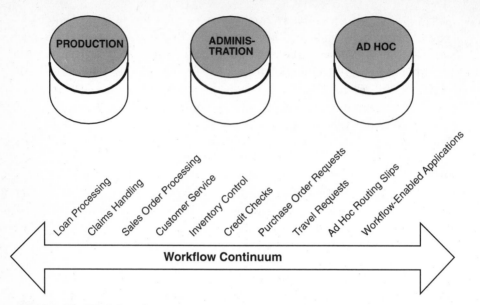

Fig. 3.3 The Workflow Continuum

The ad hoc/administration/production categories are not different countries with impenetrable boundaries. I suggest that you look at workflow applications as a continuum of automated processes, not mutually exclusive arenas. Workflow solutions often start at the ad hoc level, developed by business users without a lot of preliminary planning, and are very flexible within predefined rules and structure. But these same ad hoc workflows quickly grow into more well-defined administrative workflows. And once administrative workflows—such as purchase order requests and expense reporting—are used extensively and have the bugs worked out, they often identify areas that can and should be rigorously structured and automated, thus becoming production workflows.

Determining whether a process is a one-time-only (or few-times-only) ad hoc operation—such as a task force decision-making process for designing a new corporate logo—or a departmental administrative procedure—such as travel requests or expense reimbursement—or a full-time, heads-down, mission-critical production application—such as insurance claims—can be a good starting point. But you need to understand that these applications need to be scalable, both up and down, and that often two or more processes might be combined.

3.7 BARRIERS TO IMPLEMENTING WORKFLOW

3.7.1 Customers Find Workflow Daunting

Even though workflow can be approached from the bottom—small, tactical, departmental automation of standard procedures—as well as the top—enterprise-wide strategic re-engineering of processes—it is the latter view that most customers envision when thinking about implementing workflow in their organizations. And this can be very intimidating from both a cost and time commitment standpoint. Customers working with the major consultancies often spend so much time in the planning stages that, once it comes time to implement, the vendor landscape has changed significantly from when the project began, and new plans need to be made.

3.7.2 Workflow Might Not Work

Even when customers attempt to develop workflow applications, there are a lot of barriers:

☞ **Technologically:** Too often, new systems, especially group or enterprise systems that depend on networked communication, actually bring the network to its knees. Sudden increased traffic, incompatible commands, unexpected glitches—all these happen when new systems are put into place. Heck, they happen when you load a new word processor!

☞ **Design:** Work processes change—sometimes overnight. Workflow applications, especially those with long planning cycles, are often so complex and so difficult to modify that they are out of date before they have a chance. Another classic workflow design problem is that of efficiently automating an inefficient process. Even long and painful business design sessions sometimes yield poorly designed processes.

☞ **Culturally:** If a workgroup isn't properly prepared or motivated to use a new workflow application, the application won't succeed. Too many good applications have failed because they were basically sabotaged by users who liked the way things were done before automation.

3.8 FEATURES OF A WORKFLOW SYSTEM

3.8.1 The Three Rs of Workflow

There are dozens of features that make up a workflow application. And these features change depending on whether the workflow application is implemented in an imaging system, document management system, and so on. But I have narrowed down workflow characteristics to the three Rs and three Ps of workflow.

The Rs. The three Rs of workflow are:

☞ Routes
☞ Rules
☞ Roles

3.8.1.1 Routes   Routing is probably the area of workflow that is the furthest along today. Initially found in the imaging world, workflow routing allowed users of image management systems from such vendors as FileNet and Recognition to send images along a predefined route. As these products became more sophisticated—and broke out of the exclusively image-oriented market—routing became more sophisticated, allowing dynamic changes in routing depending on conditions or rules.

In today's world, you need to be able to specify the flow of any sort of object, not just an image. These objects should be able to be routed sequentially (one after another), in parallel routes with rendezvous points (an object can go off on any number of different sequential routes and then reconcile into a single route at a specified point), and to be sent in a broadcast mode (the email model, where everyone gets the object at once), or in any ad hoc order (as described by the user at the time of processing); see Figure 3.4.

3.8.1.2 Rules   One of the most complex and valuable features of workflow automation is defining your business rules. On a purely practical level, these rules determine what information is to be routed and to whom—for example, if the amount requested is more than $50,000, send it to the supervisor; otherwise, send it to purchasing. This is sometimes called *conditional routing* or *exception handling*. The value of conditional routing is not only that the system handles more of the passing off of objects to the correct recipient automatically. Oh, yes, that is valuable and makes us more productive. But a true advantage of defining

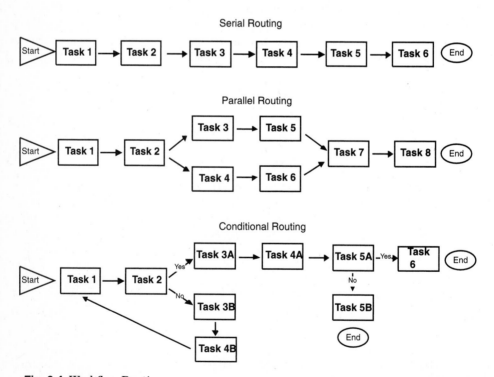

Fig. 3.4 Workflow Routing

workflow rules is the actual act of capturing the assumptions about how your business runs.

3.8.1.3 Roles Then there are roles. In the example above, the request was not routed to Sue or to Max, but to a supervisor or to purchasing. It is important to be able to define roles independent of the specific people who happen to fill those roles. Otherwise, you can get caught in an administrative nightmare. For example, if the system routed the "amount greater than $50,000" to Sue and Sue left the company, the application developer would have to respecify the recipient under the new conditions. If the request was sent to the role, the administrator (not the developer) will simply add the new person's name to the role of supervisor. Now, agreed, it takes the same amount of work to add a name to a role as to change the name in a single workflow step. But consider what happens if Sue is involved in multiple steps in dozens of workflows. The change could be indicated once—in a *role table*, typically a table or database where a person is related to a role—and any workflow that needed to route something to supervisor (Sue) would now route the information to her replacement.

Another area where roles come into play is when a number of different people have the authorization to do the same work. For example, with claims adjusters, it doesn't really matter which one handles the claim as long as someone with that role does.

3.8.1.4 Available Tools The current generation of workflow products on the market provide excellent tools for laying out a graphical map of the routing of a process. Products such as AT&T GIS's ProcessIT, Sigma's OmniDesk, Reach's WorkMAN, and Digital's LinkWorks provide graphical mapping tools that let business users—managers, knowledge workers, etc.—draw the flow of information and steps of the process using drag-and-drop icons and connectors.

Most workflow products have mechanisms for defining rules, but this is the area that is the least advanced in workflow definition tools. In order to define rules, you often have to use scripting or other programmer-like activities. Products in other areas, especially in email, as evidenced by BeyondMail now owned by Banyan, have delivered user-defined rules engines which allow business users without any technical capabilities to write relatively complex rules by selecting options from drop-down lists and from menus.

I acknowledge that defining the rules of workflow can be very difficult; rules can be very complex and convoluted, with multiple options, variations, and exceptions. For sophisticated, multipath, exception-laden processes, you do need trained programmers and application developers, who can be sure to think through the entire set of possibilities that can result from a single rule. However, I am also convinced that business users can think through the more obvious (and more commonly used) rules, such as the example mentioned above, "if amount is greater than $50,000, then send it to the supervisor; otherwise, send it to purchasing." A few of the workflow products on the market, such as WorkMAN from Reach Software Incorporated and OmniDesk from Sigma, allow the end user to define simple rules using Boolean logic operations. This is a very good start.

Many tools also support the concept of roles, providing role tables within the underlying database. The category of workflow products that tends not to support roles is the forms processors, from companies such as JetForm and Delrina. JetForms and Form Flow, respectively, support rules-based routing, but you must send to a named recipient.

3.8.2 The 3 Ps of Workflow

The Ps. But how do you determine the three Rs? I propose examining the three Ps of workflow:

☞ Processes
☞ Policies
☞ Practices

3.8.2.1 Processes   Workflow automates processes—the processes (a.k.a. procedures) that we have established to run our businesses. And these processes are as varied and as personal to our companies as the people who take part in them. Examining your process will help you figure out the steps or tasks that need to be done, the general *route* the steps need to take, and the people or *roles* that need to handle the tasks.

Processes can also span *applications*. By applications, I don't mean word processing and spreadsheets, but customized line-of-business applications such as an insurance underwriting application. For example, a sales process includes an order entry application, a credit check application, and a billing application. These applications can also be considered processes or subprocesses—they require a sequence of steps to be performed based on business conditions. Sometimes an application, such as credit check, can be part of several different processes (loan application, credit card approval, etc.).

3.8.2.2 Policies   Policies are the formal written statements of how certain processes are handled. For example, every company has a vacation policy and a benefits policy, and they should have a policy for how to handle each automated business process. These policies specify the *rules* of the process—for example, orders from preferred customers are filled within 24 hours, while orders from new customers must wait for a credit check. Or, in a help desk process, the next available support person takes the next call.

3.8.2.3 Practices   Policies are wonderful things, but they rarely tell the whole story. To determine how a process really works, you must look at the practices. Practices go beyond the formal written policies of how certain processes are handled; they are the real way the work is done.

Practices identify two things. The first is the historical reasons why a policy was put into place. (Most of this information is anecdotal at best.) "Oh, the reason that everything must go through Charlotte in quality control is that we want to deliver working product. Before Charlotte came on board, Henry in packaging did the final check, and he missed so much!" But, even more, practices are the "breaking of the rules" of the process that make the process really work. For example, "Everything must go through Charlotte, unless it is product type X, in which case, we usually send it right to Henry, because he understands this type of product much better than Charlotte." Or, "Everything goes through Charlotte unless we're running more than two days late, in which case we skip Charlotte altogether and yell at Henry to make sure he does a check at his end." The help desk policy specified above is a real policy of a company I have worked with. Most of the time, the next available support person takes the call, but, when the call was about a specific model of copier, it was always sent to Janice. (She was the only one who seemed to be able to explain how to get the paper to stop catching fire! True story! I was the customer.) Practices use the pragmatic business rules that policies may never surface.

Too often, when designing a workflow application, we identify the routes, rules, and roles by examining the processes and the policies. Then we wonder why they don't really work. I propose that it is because we ignore the real-life practice of how the process has evolved. Only when we capture the practices will we truly automate how we run our businesses.

3.9 COMPONENTS OF WORKFLOW PRODUCTS

3.9.1 Product Modules

Now that we have discussed what makes up a workflow application, we need to look at what makes up the workflow products available today on the market. Workflow offerings really provide any combination of four types of tools:

☞ The workflow definition methodology
☞ The workflow deployment environment
☞ The workflow builder
☞ The workflow management engine

As discussed earlier, you don't have to conduct a workflow design session or use BPD software before you define a workflow process. But the other three components—deployment environment, builder, and engine—are part of all workflow applications. However—and this is important, now—all three components do not have to be provided by the same vendor.

3.9.1.1 Deployment Environment The workflow deployment environment is where users actually work. It is where they view and claim job or task assignments, and access their personal productivity tools and line-of-business applications.

Lotus Notes is the perfect example of a workflow deployment environment that is separate from a workflow builder or engine. Now, Notes does have some workflow capabilities of its own, but many workflow products, such as Reach's WorkMAN for Notes, Action Technologies WorkflowBuilder for Notes, and flow-

Maker from Workflow Inc., provide workflow engines and builders but use Notes as the users' environment.

3.9.1.2 Workflow Builder   Most vendors provide tools with which to define and build the workflow applications. These builders range in complexity from programmer-oriented scripting languages up to very accessible graphical mapping and flow-charting tools. Correspondingly, they are aimed at a variety of developer skill levels ranging from professional programmers to average business users.

A developer uses a workflow builder to define the rules, routes, and roles of the process; to identify the data, information, or objects that are being worked on; and to bind all this to the deployment environment.

3.9.1.3 Workflow Engine   The heart of the workflow system is the management engine, which manages the actual running of each instance of the process. (An instance of a process follows one particular case. For example, the processing of Hortense Lansworthy's loan application is an instance of the loan application workflow process.) I maintain that in order to qualify as workflow, every workflow application must offer an underlying engine which ensures that the data is being flowed to the right person (or process) in the right order depending on the business conditions. The engine also tracks the status of each instance, keeping track of where each instance is in the process. When you evaluate workflow products, you are shown the builder and the deployment environment, but you can't really see the engine. But don't be fooled into minimizing its importance. Without an effective engine, all the beautifully defined workflow applications designed to run in the most advanced environments simply won't work.

3.10 ARCHITECTURAL MODELS FOR WORKFLOW

3.10.1 The Great Debate: Mail (Message)-Based or Database-Based

There has been a lot of discussion—or heated argument—about the relative merits of message-based workflow vs. database-based workflow. Which is better, we all want to know. But that's not necessarily the right question. The real issue is which is more appropriate for your application.

3.10.2 Three Models for Workflow

Workflow applications can be built on one of three alternate client-server architectural models:

☞ Mail-based model—This architecture is most appropriate for document-routing applications such as expenses or purchase-order approval processes.

☞ Shared database model—The documents are stored in a shared database on the network. The document, at least in read-only version, is always available to be looked at.

☞ Client-server database model—The client-server model extends the shared database model by storing and executing workflow rules on the server.

3.10.2.1 Mail-Based Model   The major strengths of the messaging model lie in its ability to support remote users and sites, and to support multiple network operating systems and multiple client platforms. If the mail system supports server-based actions, these can be used to make sure that the workflow application can run even when the client is not active. The mail in-box can be used to quickly get a user's attention when acting on a task quickly is required.

The greatest weakness of the mail-based approach is the complexity of managing the rules of the workflows. Since these rules tend to reside in multiple locations, most often in multiple users' mail applications, any changes in the process may have to be made to perhaps dozens or hundreds of applications which may exist on workstations and laptops all over the world.

In a messaging-based workflow application, it may be difficult to determine exactly the current status of a given workflow. In addition, in a mail-based application that routes documents, the document is not available to anyone other than the current mail recipient. This is a particularly significant limitation in workflow applications where continual availability of documents is important for managing the process.

3.10.2.2 Shared Database Model   The advantages of this model are continual access to the document and the better management capabilities offered. These capabilities include the management of the rules themselves (a single change can be made to affect all participants) and the management of the status of the workflows themselves. The shared database can also be used to store historical information about the workflows so that meta-management capabilities are possible.

The major limitation of the database approach is the need to be connected to the database. This limitation is taken care of by databases that support replication, most notably Lotus Notes. However, replication introduces the question of how current any copy of a database is at any given time.

3.10.2.3 Client-Server Database Model   The client-server model provides all the benefits of the shared database architecture and can easily be integrated with the mail system to provide these benefits as well. Its primary strength is the ability to control the workflow application from the server; this includes the ability to monitor and manage each workflow and meta-manage the whole business process. Storing and executing the workflow rules on the server provides a high level of maintainability for the application.

3.11 SELECTING PROCESSES TO AUTOMATE

When you think of workflow, you think about mission-critical production processes such as loan processing and insurance claims. Automating these processes results in saved money—reduced staffing expenses, reduced paper expenses, and so forth—and increased productivity—process more applications, more claims, etc. Similarly, departmental workflows, where the primary function is getting something approved (purchase order requests, travel reimbursement, etc.) are also a natural target for workflow automation, with the added attraction of being simpler and less expensive to implement. The benefits of automating these processes are improved management and tracking of status.

3.11.1 Determining Return on Investment

The promise of increased productivity as a result of implementing workflow is twofold. First of all, there are innumerable clerical improvements that can be implemented with well-designed workflow systems. More cases can be handled, more loans approved, more purchase orders authorized. And the increased numbers will be measurable.

A study done at Young and Rubicam during the rollout of an automated workflow implementation revealed several interesting productivity issues. The first was that, invariably, productivity went down during the first few weeks of implementation. People were just learning to use the workflow tools and had to really concentrate on tasks that, before they were automated, had become rote. However, after the initial learning curve, productivity—and job satisfaction— went up. The second factor was that the productivity improvements (i.e., tasks took less time) applied to the clerical, tracking, and paper-pushing tasks only. The time it took to complete tasks that involved decision making or creativity did not change. The time spent looking for the materials with which to make these decisions was reduced significantly.

Justifying the pain and expense of implementing workflow applications based on these clerical improvements may not be enough in themselves. So, as you look to putting in a workflow solution in your organization, take a moment to consider the unmeasurable—the increases in qualitative decisions that could result from information being routed to the right person at the right time, making it available when the decision must be made.

3.11.2 Look Beyond the Obvious

Productivity improvements are very attractive. But is this really where the big payoffs are?

In the keynote address at Workflow '94 in Boston, Ellen Knapp of Coopers & Lybrand gave an excellent presentation stressing that the key to workflow is not just getting the process right, but getting the right process right. This means automating those processes that are directly tied into the identity and goals of the organization. For example, payroll is often a process that gets a lot of attention when selecting processes to automate. Yet the payroll process is not high on the list of company goals—except, of course, if your company is ADP, whose main business is handling the payroll process for its many clients. She also pointed to a company that streamlines loan processing from two weeks to four hours, but neglected to develop a strategy for increasing the number of loan applications that came in; the company eventually filed for bankruptcy.

3.11.3 Find the Differentiators

To most effectively take advantage of workflow technologies and methodologies, you should look beyond automating production and administrative process and try to identify differentiating processes; these are processes that are visible to the market—the ones that make our company different, and better.

3.11.4 Support Business Goals

A business process must be tied into a business goal. A business goal is typically quality of products, excellence in customer service, revenue per employee, and so on. One area in which payoffs have typically been fruitful is in redesigning and focusing on customer-related processes. If you are running a process that doesn't meet a business priority, you are wasting valuable time, effort, and money.

3.11.5 Nonfinancial Goals

Of course, business goals do not necessarily need to be financial. A business goal can be to have a great Christmas party or to improve communications between the marketing and development departments. One of the business goals of the Patricia Seybold Group, the company for which I work, is high quality of life for employees. This goal has no bottom-line price tag but is a very valid business goal; ironically, it is also a goal that usually leads to happier and more productive and innovative employees, which, inevitably, results in increases to the bottom line.

3.12 THE PEOPLE ISSUES IN WORKFLOW

3.12.1 Defining the Problem

As I mentioned earlier, processes are usually not explicitly engineered, but rather evolve as we continue to do them and refine them. And a byproduct of this is great loyalty to our familiar ways of doing things. "We've always done it this way" is a common cry when people try to examine and evaluate processes. Examining and redesigning business processes is an area of great potential and great pain. The rewards of streamlining your way of doing business, eliminating the redundancies, identifying the bottlenecks, and understanding why it is you do what you do can be monumental. But be forewarned: the cultural shock that

accompanies change can also bring a process to its knees. Here are several recommendations that will help you ease the pain associated with change.

3.12.2 Involving the Users

Your people are your greatest asset, and, in some ways, your greatest obstacle. Thus, soliciting input from these actual users of the process buys you two
things:

1. These are the people who truly understand what needs to be done in order
   to successfully achieve the business goal. These are the people who can
   identify the practices and can help determine what works and what doesn't.
2. An added benefit of involving users while designing the workflow is that
   you build in user support and ownership of the application from the start.
   This can go a long way towards overcoming the resistance that always
   comes when implementing new systems.

3.12.3 Setting Expectations

Even if users are involved in designing the process, there will still be problems. However, if realistic expectations have been set, workflow implementations
have a better chance of succeeding.

Expectations must be set in two areas:

1. How the workflow applications will be used and what problems they are
   being implemented to solve
2. How productivity will be affected during the initial stages of rollout

One of the reasons that groupware solutions in general, such as Lotus
Notes, are taking so long to catch on in many organizations is that the people
were given the tool without any good reason to use it. They were encouraged to
"play with it...figure out what you can use this for." But people don't have time to
play. It is important that specific applications with specific purposes—and perceived value—be introduced even at the pilot stage. Otherwise, no expectations
at all are set, and people simply will not use the new tools.

Once you have set expectations about how the solution works and what it is
intended to do, you need to set realistic expectations about the potential benefits.
Invariably, the first few weeks of any new implementation will lower productivity as people figure out how to change their work habits to take advantage of the
new solutions. And people resist change; it will take a while before they get used
to the new way of doing things. It is in this period that you get the greatest number of complaints. If people expect an instant panacea, they will jump ship as
soon as the pain of change sets in. If expectations have been set that there will be
problems initially, but that, over the course of a few weeks, it will get easier; and
if the potential benefits are clearly explained, people will still complain, sure, but
they are more likely to stay on track to get over the hurdles.

3.12.4 Training

Training on workflow is not optional! Unlike personal productivity tools, where each user approaches the software with his or her own set of understanding, willingness to learn, and ways of doing things, these are group solutions, which rely heavily on everyone knowing exactly how the application works and what is expected of them. If one person doesn't play by the rules, the application can fail.

An important way of preparing users is by providing training specific to the workflow implementation that is being piloted. Time and time again, we have seen companies offer generic courses on the base technology that makes up the workflow strategy. Users don't take any ownership of generic applications. But with specific courses designed to teach how your organization is going to manage and route your documents for your application requirements, users take a greater interest and have more to which to relate.

One caveat, though. When a specific solution is being developed in an environment such as Lotus Notes, some organizations have found it much easier to train first on the Notes platform and its behavior, and then introduce the business-specific workflow application. Otherwise, users tended to blame the idiosyncracies of the Notes environment on the customized application. One user organization found that if they spent about three hours training on Notes, they could teach a new Notes workflow in under a half-hour. However, even in the case of generic environment training, the success came by following it up with organization-specific training.

3.12.5 The Importance of Piloting

Because of the many human and organizational implications of workflow applications, it is important that you start small, identifying potential usage problems as well as technical glitches. Try to select a representative group as your pilot so that you can surface the issues most likely to affect the organization at large. Solicit feedback and encourage ideas about how to most effectively use the software from all members of the pilot team. And avoid rolling out to others prematurely. Often, others will start to envy the pilot group and will demand that they, too, get to use the new workflow immediately. Problems can arise, because the pilot group has been specifically prepared for the introduction of the new solution, whereas the other users are reacting only to what they perceive to be preferential treatment or imagined benefits for the pilot team. Roll out on a predetermined schedule which takes into account setting expectations and training.

On the other hand, don't view the results of the initial pilot as the final solution. As use of the applications gets past the bounds of the pilot team, the need for additional functionality and new ways of working with the software will occur to other users as they become more proficient. Keep the users focused on identifying those opportunities and communicating them back to the development team for consideration.

3.12.6 Building Buy-In at All Levels

In order for strategic workflow applications to succeed, you need buy-in at the top; you need a high-level champion. This champion will ensure the funding and support to get the project from the planning stage to rollout. Furthermore, buy-in at the executive level will show the participants in the workflow solution that the company is serious about the application. This type of high-level champion may not be required for smaller-scale, less strategic departmental solutions, where the support of the manager is sufficient to see the project through.

Buy-in at the management level is equally important. The manager is the person who will actually be monitoring the workflow and making sure it is being used effectively. If he or she resents the intrusion of software to do what the manager believes he or she has been doing all along, progress will be difficult.

Finally, you absolutely must have buy-in at the user level. This buy-in will probably not be universal from the beginning. Initially, users will take part in the process simply because the high-level champion has made it clear that they are expected to. But once the project is underway, user buy-in can be solicited. This is accomplished by actively involving the users of the workflow in the process of defining the process to be automated, providing input into the piloting process, and encouraging and rewarding constructive feedback on the actual implementation of the workflow application. In fact, soliciting user input during the workflow definition stage is vital. It is the users who truly understand the practices being implemented in the processes to be automated. Not only does involving users during planning help speed up the buy-in process, but it also ensures a more detailed and realistic definition of the workflow application.

3.12.7 Rewarding Usage

Not only must feedback be rewarded, so must usage of the workflow application. Users must perceive an added value to using the new application. Invariably, there is extra effort involved in using a group tool—at least initially. Users must get something out of making that extra effort. A reward can be as simple as praise from the boss for participating. But the best reward is one that the application itself gives. When designing workflow applications, it is important to consider what added benefit the application gives its users. If there is no benefit to the users, only to the "organization," it will be more difficult to enforce usage of the application.

3.12.8 Providing Support—The Guru Factor

It is vital that every workgroup have someone who is responsible for supporting the users of workflow applications. Your company must plan for this from the beginning. If a "workflow guru" is not designated and trained, then whoever happens to learn the application the quickest or understand it the best will be constantly interrupted from his or her own work to help others with theirs. While the *de facto* expert may be very happy to help out, his or her own productivity will plummet as he or she spends time training others on the workflow. By planning for this type of mentorship, the time this guru spends with others becomes part of the job description, rather than time pulled away from the main job. Be aware that supporting workflow, like supporting a network, is an interrupt-driven job. While it may not be a full-time position, it is an "anytime" responsibility.

3.13 KEY PLAYERS IN THE WORKFLOW MARKET

The workflow market is a moving target; over a hundred companies claim to provide some workflow features in their products. It has become politically correct to provide workflow functionality. But certain vendors and products represent the state of the art (if not the state of the market—though workflow products abound, they are not hot sellers...yet) in workflow. Let's touch on some of them here.

3.13.1 Lotus

Many people believe that Notes is, indeed, a workflow product. And the Notes platform does offer quite a few workflow features, such as serial routing, action buttons, and status-tracking. You can also write Notes macros, which, when combined with other Notes features, emulate rule-based workflow routing and management. But the product isn't optimized to create workflow applications; it is optimized for developing document databases and tracking applications.

As mentioned earlier, a workflow builder provides specific tools and interfaces for defining the flow of tasks in the process to be automated, the roles of the people doing those tasks, and the rules by which the flow is determined. And workflow management engines provide specific information on where each instance of a process is at any one point. Although this type of application can be, and often is, developed in the Notes environment, the application developer has to jury-rig the Notes features to come up with the results that a workflow builder (if it is well-designed) will guide you through.

One of the most intriguing elements of the Notes marketplace is the cottage industry it has spawned. Dozens of companies have sprung up to build companion products to Notes, some of which are completely Notes-based and some of which add functionality to the Notes environment. The workflow industry is very visible in this arena.

Companies such as Quality Decision Management Incorporated (North Andover, Massachusetts), with its Quality *At Work* product, and API (Shrewsbury, New Jersey), with its Workflow Engine, have built tools on top of Lotus Notes to automate and manage processes. Other companies, such as Action Technologies Incorporated, with its recently shipping ActionWorkflow Builder for Notes, and Reach Software Corporation, with its newly announced WorkMAN for

Notes, have built versions of their existing workflow products that integrate with Notes as the deployment environment.

Even those workflow vendors that don't have specific Notes versions of their products, such as XSoft Corporation with In Concert and AT&T Global Information Systems with ProcessIT, have all articulated (or are about to reveal) a "Notes strategy," indicating how their products work with Notes. No one, but *no one*, in the workflow marketplace is stressing a purely competitive positioning against Notes.

Lotus Notes has become existing proof of the concept that business users want to develop, and are eminently capable of developing, group applications that reflect how their businesses run. Workflow applications fit neatly into this arena—they are applications that reflect the group processes that run businesses. The visibility that Notes has given to the concept of desktop-based group applications has brought into the sunlight other tools that were too often overshadowed by the entrenched MIS-focused tools, such as 4GLs and relational database application builders.

3.13.2 Action

Action Technologies is one of the most visible workflow vendors for two reasons. One, the ActionWorkflow methodology, a structured method for laying out a process based on the research of Fernando Flores and Terry Winograd, is one of the few clearly articulated models available for defining workflow applications. The second reason is that the ActionWorkflow product line was originally scheduled to become the Notes workflow solution. For a variety of reasons, including Action's organizational restructuring, Lotus's concern about alienating other partners, and failure to meet the anticipated deadline, the exclusive relationship between Action and Lotus was ended. Action now sells its solutions—the ActionWorkflow Analyst (which allows the customer to capture the Action methodology on a PC), and the ActionWorkflow Builder (which comes in two versions—SQL and Lotus Notes). The Builder takes the map captured in the Analyst and generates the base code for the customized application. Because of the change in status with Lotus, Action has been forced to reinvent itself as a sales organization. The company strengths, however, are in consulting and software development. An entirely new executive team has recently been brought in to turn the company around.

Action has recently been awarded two patents: one for its ActionWorkflow Methodology and the other for the automation of this methodology into workflow applications. There is some speculation in the market that this could impinge on other workflow vendors as they continue their development of their products. I speculate that the patents could have an effect in two areas:

☞ There are certain workflow vendors and consultancies that use the ActionWorkflow methodology and engine as the foundation for their work. They already pay Action a royalty for their use, but, by holding a patent, Action may be in a position to change the nature of these relationships.

☞ A Workflow Management Coalition has been formed to try to establish standard APIs and other protocols in the workflow industry. Action is an active member of the Coalition and is, most likely, promoting its patented technology as the *de facto* standard.

3.13.3 Reach

Reach is probably the second most visible player in the non-image-related workflow market. The company first articulated its workflow vision about three years ago, but just succeeded in bringing its product, WorkMAN, to market last spring. Reach recently introduced its WorkMAN for Notes product, which is a complete workflow development environment for applications deployed in Lotus Notes. Reach has won many accolades for its products and workflow philosophy, which is very comprehensive and visionary; but the initial product was buggy, and newer versions have been deemed difficult to use. The company, which is very small, is having a hard time generating sales. Customers are reluctant to pin strategic applications on a company without a track record.

3.13.4 IBM

IBM is another company forced to reinvent itself, and one of the areas where it is claiming expertise is in workflow. IBM is focusing a lot of development and marketing effort on its FlowMark product, an object-oriented workflow builder, manager, and deployment environment running on OS/2. Preliminary assessments of FlowMark are positive, but it is too early to determine if the product will be successfully implemented in customer sites. Since FlowMark runs exclusively in the IBM environment at this point (OS/2 server and client), the product may suffer the reputation of being proprietary even as other platforms become available.

3.13.5 AT&T GIS

AT&T Global Information Systems has recently reorganized, creating a division which markets the company's software products: Cooperation, the new Cooperation Frameworks, the Liberty Forms Processor, and ProcessIT, a server-based suite of workflow components. ProcessIT offers more pieces of the workflow puzzle than any other vendor—the product line includes a workflow mapping tool, an execution environment (where users get their work), an "Exerciser" that allows you to run dummy sessions and gather statistics on performance, a Process Activity Manager based on an Informix database which captures the session and administration information, an Administration front end with a Status Monitor to keep track of what's going on, and an Enterprise-Wide network connection that lets you connect server to server for WAN processes. Unfortunately, each of the components was built by a different organization, and it shows. There are inconsistencies in interface, paradigms, and behavior. And no one of them is stellar—the components range from mediocre to pretty good. AT&T GIS has also had very little success marketing Cooperation, despite early enthusiastic reviews (though the fact that the product was very late in being released contributed heavily to this failure). The new focus on selling software could help AT&T GIS in the workflow market, but the company is definitely trying to swim upstream.

3.13.6 XSoft

The Cambridge, Massachusetts-based Advanced Technologies group of XSoft offers a document-centric server-based workflow system called InConcert. InConcert has received good reviews, and early customers seem pleased. XSoft, in general, is not doing well with its other products, which include the antiquated GlobalView product line as well as desktop software such as Rooms. Xerox, itself, has recently refocused to concentrate even more on documents and printing/publishing. The fact that InConcert is designed to build document-related workflow applications could bring InConcert support from Xerox Corporate.

3.13.7 Digital Equipment Corporation

Digital offers two different workflow systems: the TeamRoute mail-based component of TeamLinks, and LinkWorks workflow development, which is based on database-supported information sharing among workgroups as defined in hierarchical organization charts. The problem with Digital's workflow offerings is that they are not compatible, and most likely, given their different orientations, will never be interoperable. Thus, customers are faced with two different environments and two different paradigms for automating processes. This is very confusing to customers. Digital needs to clearly articulate when each environment is appropriate and how the two product lines—and workflow products—will eventually work together.

3.13.8 Wang

Wang's OPEN/workflow breaks from the image-oriented software orientation for which Wang is becoming known. OPEN/workflow is a much more generic tool, designed for business users, which allows the mapping, management, and deployment of automated processes where image is merely one of the data types that can be supported. The product is nicely designed and straightforward to use, but the new Wang has not yet proven that it can make a profitable business out of software.

3.13.9 The Image Vendors: FileNet, Recognition/Plexus, Sigma, and ViewStar

These leaders in image-based workflow have advantages over the newer entries into the market. Imaging customers are more familiar with workflow and have already been using the first generation of image workflow tools for a few years. While the early tools were pretty limited, the new generation of tools are similar in capabilities, ease of use, and flexibility as the desktop and server-based workflow product now hitting the market. Another advantage that image vendors have is that imaging processes are more focused, so customers know exactly what type of applications to develop with the workflow tools. The challenge to the imaging vendors is to expand their workflow products to include other types of applications. All of these vendors have already begun to do this.

3.14 THE FUTURE OF WORKFLOW

Despite almost universal agreement that the automation of business processes is necessary and valuable, workflow is not selling well. I believe that part of this is because of confusion in the market—ask 20 different vendors for a definition of workflow, and you get 20 different answers. But a greater part is that implementing workflow is unknown territory which often requires large investments of time, money, and change—three areas of great pain.

3.14.1 Umbrella Application

One of the reasons that workflow is such a source of pain is that it is typically seen as the umbrella application under which sit services such as document management, time management, and messaging. Customers use workflow application builders as the development and deployment environments for automated processes. This means that customers have to learn a new development environment, go through a re-engineering exercise (or at least some sort of process definition), train the users on a new system, and so on. Pretty intimidating, no?

3.14.2 Workflow-Enabled Applications

Recently, however, an alternative view of workflow is popping up, modeled on Microsoft Corporation's view of groupware: Group-enable all software by providing group functionality in the operating system rather than in specialized products. We envision workflow-enabled software becoming available. Take, for example, a document management application. Users are familiar with their document manager, using it to save and locate documents, to check in and out of documents, and for version control. By adding workflow capabilities, you will be able to route these documents based on certain rules and/or conditions. Rather than building a workflow application in a new paradigm, you will be able to add these workflow capabilities to the existing document management application.

3.14.3 Workflow Becomes Ubiquitous

Ultimately, I believe that almost every business application written is, in some ways, a workflow application—automating business processes to get work done by a group of people. And, eventually, as a result of this ubiquity, the term "workflow" will disappear. It will simply be synonymous with application development.

BIOGRAPHY

Ronni T. Marshak, vice president of The Patricia Seybold Group, has worked in the computing industry for over 13 years, 12 of which have been with The Patricia Seybold Group. She specializes
in workgroup issues and products, including workflow automation, document management
systems interface design, and product competitive positioning. Marshak has provided consulting for such vendors as IBM, Microsoft, Lotus, Digital, and Hewlett-Packard, as well as for
many users' organizations.

Marshak is the editor-in-chief of the *Workgroup Computing Report: Applying Technology to
Business Processes*, a monthly research newsletter, now in its 16th year, that explores the
issues, technologies, products, and vendors that surround organizational computing, specifically at the departmental level. She also acts as senior editor for *Open Information Systems*
and *Distributed Computing Monitor*. Her articles have appeared in such publications as *ComputerWorld* and *PC Products*. Marshak is author of *Word Processing Packages for the PBM PC*
as well as co-author of *Integrated Desktop Environments* and *Database Software for the IBM
PC: The Desktop Generation*, all of which were published by McGraw-Hill as part of the Seybold Series on Professional Computing.

Marshak has appeared as a speaker at such industry conferences as GroupWare, the Workflow
Conference, Comdex, Windows-OS/2 Conferences, UnixExpo, Unisys Open Forum, and the
Office Automation Conference. She is currently a member of the Advisory Board for Group-
Ware '94 and serves as a founding member of the Groupware Users and Vendors Association
(GUAVA). Marshak also acts as chairperson of the New England office Systems Round Table, a
regional group of high-level corporate technology decision makers founded in 1984, and is
cochair of the Seybold Executive Forum.

Prior to joining The Patricia Seybold Group, Marshak taught word processing and office procedures. She holds a B.A. from the University of Massachusetts and a Master's degree from
Northeastern University.

Introduction to Chapter 4

In some ways, group calendaring and scheduling is a lot like email. Unless everyone is using it on a regular basis, it serves no productive purpose. If everyone is using it, it can be a great time saver and facilitate coordination.

This chapter is by Jack Perry and Jerry Zeephat of CE software. CE develops calendaring and scheduling systems as well as email. The authors' assignment in this chapter was to review the issues and technologies in this segment of the industry without focusing too much on their products. I believe they met this challenge.

Mr. Perry starts the chapter with a scenario of how one might use a group calendaring system. As you can see, the tasks performed without the system are very different than those performed with the system in place. For Jack, this technology is critical to running his day and being productive on a day-to-day business.

Because this chapter is on group calendaring and scheduling, we focus on the resource of time. Group calendaring and scheduling programs have had great success in increasing efficiency while reducing much of the repetitive drudge-work associated with setting up meetings and scheduling tasks. The front office is often characterized as controlled chaos as opposed to the more regimented factory floor. But manufacturing has reaped great productivity gains over the last decade using workflow, group calendaring, and scheduling in production environments. The question is, if these technologies are applied to this controlled chaos, will we still reap the benefits of improved information flow without regimenting out the spontaneity that also adds to the productivity of the office?

Mr. Perry takes us through the evolution of group calendaring and scheduling systems, bringing us to the three types of systems in use today. After describing their architectures, as well as their strengths and weaknesses, he looks at some of the issues in implementing such systems and then moves into various implementation strategies.

He concludes the chapter with a look toward the future. What will we see in the group calendaring and scheduling systems introduced over the next few years? He examines the issues of interoperability, use with PDAs, open APIs, and how the availability of such on-line schedules will affect our daily lives.

One issue that was not completely covered in this chapter is the integration of workflow systems and group project management software with group calendaring and scheduling systems. I see this kind of integration as a future trend. This trend is evidenced by products like CaLANdar, which will have group calendaring and scheduling incorporated in its next release.

A second concern I have about this category of software is its future viability. The function is a necessary one, and the technology to support it will not disappear. The question is, will this technology be incorporated into the operating system, much like messaging technology, which is already moving in that direction? There are ample precedents for this, such as the UNIX operating system which has both email capabilities and calendaring. Also, Windows 95 is rumored to have some of these same capabilities.

I don't doubt that there will always be third-party vendors like CE who will provide software with greater functionality than is offered in the operating system, but the OS software will become a standard. Eventually, this will result in everyone using group calendaring and scheduling to some degree. With groupware functions like this generally available, it will be just as common to schedule a group meeting as it is to receive an email message. I see a future where on-line personal and business calendars will be as critical to our everyday life as our DayTimers are today!

Uncharted waters. That's the first thing that came to mind when writing this section of the book. Groupware applications are a new entity in today's business world. They are not just a better way of working, but an entirely new way of working. When speaking to a prospective customer, it is apparent that the vendor must still sell the concept first and product second. Group calendaring and scheduling is not a better mousetrap. It is not a faster processor or a better word processor. It is a radically new internal system from which business can better optimize its collective efforts. It helps cut the chaos, providing a method of keeping connected users on the same page. It is wonderful technology, and it is still in its relative infancy. The group calendar will soon maintain the same business foothold that electronic messaging enjoys today. This chapter is meant to provide a broad overview of the evolution of this groupware tool, along with current and future issues surrounding its implementation.

When David asked me to write this chapter, he asked me some difficult questions. Most of them concerning technology, but some about myself. Specifically, why was I qualified to write a chapter on this technology in a book like this, where everyone writing a chapter is an expert in their particular area? First, I have an extensive background in the field of time management software, and have worked for firms such as Prisma Software, Campbell Services, Powercore, and CE Software Inc. Also, I believe it is my view of the industry from the perspective of one who has seen it mature (even though it is still in its infancy) that gives me some of the expertise needed to write this chapter. And finally, I speak daily with customers about group calendaring and scheduling issues. That's what I do.

Group Calendaring and Scheduling

Jack Perry
CE Software, Inc.

4.1 A SCHEDULING SCENARIO...

CE Software's marketing department is one of the busiest places in the company. Several marketing managers and their staffs are constantly on the go, spending time at either of our two locations, meeting with members of the R&D department, flying to and from industry affairs, or brainstorming at our advertising agency across town. About the only time they are all at their desks simultaneously is 8:00 a.m., and even then, some have already come and gone! I receive a report from "upstairs" that we'd better cut a couple of expenses before the end of the quarter. It is apparent that I will need to speak with the four managers together, so that we can, as a group, discuss the relative merits of each program and their respective costs. No big deal. The only trouble is getting hold of all of them to let them know that we must discuss these things some time before the end of business Friday.

4.1.1 Without Group Calendaring and Scheduling

I call Jerry. He's away from his desk, so I'm bounced to his assistant's voice mail. I hope she's there to retrieve it later. Left a message. I call Jim O. He's also out of the office. He's at the ad agency designing t-shirts or something to give away at the next trade show. Left a message. Jessica is next. Her assistant notifies me she is in the conference room being courted by an ad rep. One more call:

Jim T. He's at the other building attending a product team meeting. Patience, I remind myself; it's a good thing that they're all so busy. Flustered nonetheless, I dispatch an email to all parties: "We must meet tomorrow afternoon at 4 o'clock to talk budget. By the way, don't spend anything." Noon rolls around, and I've received two confirmations that Friday at 4 is fine. Unfortunately, now it's my turn to leave, as I must meet with the CEO and others to discuss next quarter's projections. When I return wearily to my desk after 6, I've received two emails stating that Friday morning is preferable for both Jim O. and Jim T., since they are flying to a conference at 3:30 that day. I take a stroll through the department, finding that everybody is gone except Jerry. He's rescheduling a conference call to attend the meeting. I make a mental note to give him a raise. Regretfully, though, we're no closer to coordinating a meeting now than we were this morning, and I easily spent a half hour of my day trying to get this thing together. I'm just grateful that I don't have to get ten people together, as four is quite the challenge. I go back to my desk and commence another round of voice mail and email....

4.1.2 With Group Calendaring and Scheduling

I open my group scheduling application in Windows. I select "Marketing Managers," and their schedules are individually overlaid with mine into one view. I click on "free time search" and define the fact that we need to meet for one hour. The scheduler notifies me that everybody is free at 10 a.m. Friday. Would I like to schedule a one-hour meeting for that time? You bet! I then enter a brief message describing the purpose of the meeting. I also attach a spreadsheet so that the invitees will know what numbers we need to discuss. This process took two minutes, start to finish. When I return from my meeting after 6, I see that all parties have confirmed. No problem.

The example above is just one possible scenario. Undoubtedly, all management has encountered a similar problem at one time or another, maybe many times every week. Step back and look at how the process for many routine business tasks has changed over the past five or ten years. Technology has increased the pace of business and, with it, the value of every minute. Each individual is empowered to accomplish more in a shorter span of time. The next logical step, then, would be to allow that same wonderful technology to help manage that increasingly valuable resource, time.

4.1.3 Time, the Scarce Resource!

There are two fundamentally different ways of looking at time as a resource. At once, it is unlimited; constantly replenishing itself. If the job can't be done today, there's always tomorrow, and a day after that, and so on. Conversely, time may be viewed as an all-encompassing, one-dimensional vector. Every second of every day ticks by just once. There's no going back. Fortunately for the group calendaring and scheduling vendors, business favors the latter view.

There can be no arguing that technology has accelerated the pace at which business operates. Information retrieval and communications have become nearly instantaneous, when, in the not-too-distant past, these procedures alone could easily double the time required to accomplish even routine tasks. If Client A wants an amended copy of his current contract along with a billing summary, he can have it on his desktop in an hour, nicely formatted and complete in every respect. From there, the business transaction can proceed. In years past, this request may have taken days or weeks. From this example, it's easy to see how efficient usage of time is becoming an increasingly important concern among management, since an hour of "business time" is constantly rising in value.

4.1.4 Chaos Is the Norm

Consider the value associated with each employee's time line. Throughout each day, these individual time lines must intersect frequently. Every phone call, every chat around the water cooler, and every email represents an intersection. Imagine charting a workgroup's intersections over the course of a week. In all likelihood, it would be a mishmash of lines, increasingly chaotic around points where multiple workers' schedules converge, meetings being a prime example.

In Figure 4.1, manager f decides an afternoon meeting with the members of his workgroup (a–e) is in order. Each line represents communication, diagonals being time-delayed (voice mail, email). Without group scheduling, the individual group members must communicate multiple times to coordinate and rectify their respective schedules. This rough diagram illustrates six busy individuals. Obviously, the chaos level rises substantially in larger groups.

Group calendaring and scheduling serves to lessen the chaos and provide an ongoing organized base from which individuals allocate their efforts. It allows even impromptu meetings to be held without the associated barrage of back-and-forth phone calls, voice mail, and email. Consequently, less time is spent *coordinating* and more time can be spent *doing* (Figure 4.2). In this diagram, manager f can automatically locate a block of free time among group mem-

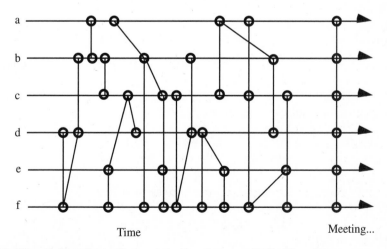

Fig. 4.1 Chaotic Employee Communication Across a Daily Time Line

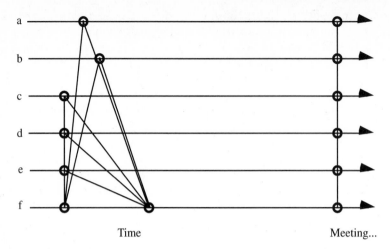

Fig. 4.2 Coordinated Employee Communication Using Group Calendaring and
Scheduling

bers and then create the meeting in his scheduler. He needs only check back once
to see that everybody has confirmed.

4.1.5 Chaos Costs!

Studies have repeatedly shown that offices waste vast sums of money on
schedule coordination activity. When this activity involves scheduling a meeting
between multiple busy schedules, say a managers' meeting, these costs increase
dramatically. Consider these statistics:

☞ Senior managers spend as many as 23 hours per week in meetings.
☞ Middle managers spend 14 hours per week in meetings.
☞ Planning for the average meeting costs $55 per attendee.
☞ 85% of meetings don't start on time.
☞ The average cost of a one-hour meeting of eight attendees is $692.

The adage "Time is Money" never rang so true. This is the problem that
group calendaring and scheduling seeks to address. As a result, today's business
market is rapidly moving this groupware genre into the mainstream.

Buying a group calendaring and scheduling application on a group or enterprise level is similar to buying a personal organizer on an individual level. It is
only as useful as its owner decides to make it. If that personal organizer falls by
the wayside as they sometimes do, the financial loss is minimal. Acceptance of
group calendaring and scheduling brings with it higher stakes. When a groupware application is implemented, its usefulness is limited to the end users' dedi-
cation to the concept. Instead of betting $20 that one person will use it, it's a
wager of thousands of dollars that everybody will use it, or at least everybody
whose job will benefit from its use. Once adopted as a business standard, though,
it becomes an extremely powerful and indispensable tool.

Profs and Office Vision provided the first glance at the practicality of a group calendar tool, but the initial cash outlay required to deploy this technology was out of reach for most businesses. The accessibility of LAN technology made it possible for groupware to reach more of the business world.

4.2 GROUP CALENDARING AND SCHEDULING GROWS UP!

Taking separate roads, three pioneers created applications that would later come to the forefront of productivity-enhancing solutions for business.

In 1989, Don Campbell, president of Campbell Services, was in the early stages of finding a market for a time management application he called OnTime. Back then, the idea that the masses would want to place their calendar on their PC seemed farfetched. Time management via personal computer had been around for quite some time, but widespread use seemed to be nothing more than a pipe dream. As two years passed, Don's concept gained wider acceptance and outright praise from its dedicated users.

At roughly the same time, a true entrepreneur named Guy Chiatello, president of Prisma Software, was developing one of the first GUI time management applications, titled Your Way. Its initial target customer was the salesperson seeking to organize and manage their calendar and contacts. Today this product is known as Borland's Sidekick for Windows. Its original incarnation was one of the first products that fit into the now-crowded software category of PIMs (Personal Information Managers). Its success was not fully realized until it moved away from its vertical sales professional market and into the horizontal applications market. To varying degrees, every business person has a calendar and contacts to maintain. One of its best (and subsequently most emulated) selling points was its incorporation of the Rolodex tab metaphor.

Also at the same time, another pioneer was approaching the time management application from a different perspective. Bill Drummy, who is perhaps the "father of group scheduling," had been working on a product called Medi:For. Its focus was not on providing a means to store a personal cache of information, but enabling networked users to connect to the same calendar database. This application, too, emerged from its vertical market and became Powercore's Network Scheduler. By combining an inviting time management interface with group abilities, Drummy succeeded where others failed. Early adopters were among the first to enjoy the productivity-enhancing abilities of LAN-based group scheduling.

4.2.1 Improvements

Progressively, advancements were made in each product's feature sets and interfaces, while their core concepts remained the same. OnTime added group scheduling capabilities. Bill Drummy and his development team reverse-engineered cc:Mail to provide two main benefits: native usage of directory services for the scheduler, and automatic dispatch of electronic mail in conjunction with the creation of an appointment. Network Scheduler sales increased greatly as a result. Your Way continued to improve its customizability and user-friendliness. As Microsoft Windows mushroomed, these products and their now-sizable group of competitors gained even further acceptance. Windows allowed them to present more information on screen with more intuitive, user-friendly interfaces.

4.2.2 Change as a Constant

Today, the business user is presented with a wide selection of products that offer similar front-end functionality with various back-end methods of providing "groupness." As the market matures, attention is shifting toward how exactly these products work behind the scenes. The big-name vendors each provide their own solutions, but this market has resisted their dominance, in large part due to the methods used to provide group enablement, which will be discussed later. There also appears to be a certain degree of resistance in the IS community to succumb to any one standard for fear of being locked into proprietary infrastructures.

Microsoft's Schedule+, for example, works in conjunction with Microsoft Mail only. From experience, network administrators have learned the hard consequences of "outgrowing" an application. It's difficult enough to switch from one mail system or network operating system to another, but when an application is entirely reliant on either system, it presents an exponentially larger number of headaches for those responsible for the transition, should the need ever arise. Experienced systems professionals have seen the market's landscape change dramatically from year to year, and most have made systems purchases they've later severely regretted. In their profession more than any other, the only constant is change.

The simplest way to avoid these possible future problems is to implement solutions that don't require the presence or operation of any one network component; hence the catchphrase, "Open Systems" computing—a grand, as-yet-unrealized, concept.

4.3 PROVIDING "GROUPNESS"

There are three basic methods of group-enabling a calendar application, each with its own strengths and weaknesses. Not surprisingly, larger vendors have provided solutions that leverage their respective infrastructures and nobody else's. The smaller third parties, on the other hand, have responded by supporting all or several of those same infrastructures. They also use different methods to achieve their groupware functionality.

4.3.1 The Calendar-Enhanced Mail System

This type of group calendar, exemplified by Microsoft's Schedule+, is what its name suggests; groupware functionality is limited to individual point-to-point connectivity. Its robustness is limited by the impracticality that would be involved in the perpetual transport of all calendar data via the messaging system. Figure 4.3 illustrates how it works.

4.3.1.1 Strengths   It does provide several benefits, however, that make its implementation worthwhile for sites where "groupness" is not of the highest import.

☞ Like electronic mail, its adoption can be incremental. It's also pretty handy for the administrator who regularly adds and deletes mail users, since the mail and calendar share a common directory. This can pose a limitation for schedulers that simply reference the mail directory.

☞ A calendar-enhanced electronic mail system offers end-user niceties as well. Since the messaging and scheduling are usually provided by the same vendor, and intrinsically stacked atop one another, their interfaces have a similar look and feel. In order to achieve its full effectiveness, a group calendaring application must be accepted and used by the community it serves. A nonintimidating and familiar interface will be more readily adopted, while reducing training demands. Generally speaking, when any group calendaring and scheduling application is tied in some way to the messaging system, the creation of a meeting between multiple users results not only in an updated calendar for each participant, but also in an automated dispatch of an email message to each invitee.

☞ The calendar-enhanced mail system allows users to RSVP or decline an appointment directly from the email application, a very attractive feature.

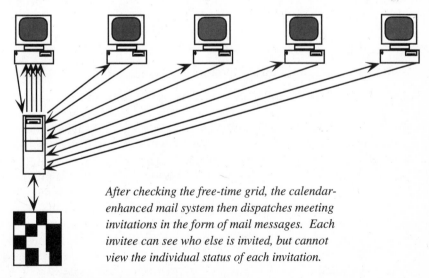

After checking the free-time grid, the calendar-enhanced mail system then dispatches meeting invitations in the form of mail messages. Each invitee can see who else is invited, but cannot view the individual status of each invitation.

Fig. 4.3 The Calendar-Enhanced Mail System.

4.3.1.2 Weaknesses   Available information is limited since there is no central data store.

☞ Other users' free and busy time slots can be viewed (in limited increments—15-minute blocks, for example), but schedule details cannot. A central free/busy time grid is maintained on the mail server. If the granularity were set to one-minute increments, the grid's size would increase by a factor of fifteen multiplied by the number of users. Limiting the granularity to 15-minute blocks keeps performance reasonable.

☞ Each user's schedule is also only as current as the last time they gathered their email, which can become tiresome among workgroups that aren't at their desks constantly.

☞ Additionally, email users aren't the only entities in the building that have schedules. What about the main conference room or the overhead projector? The only way to identify schedulable resources is by giving each resource an email address, meaning that user licenses must be purchased for both mail and scheduling. It also necessitates that users log in as "Main Conference Room" in order to update the currency of its schedule or to view its schedule in detail. Executives wouldn't care to hold a quarterly revenue meeting in the hallway simply because somebody had earlier scheduled the main conference room for a mouse-cleaning clinic. Along the same lines, schedule items and attachments (i.e., agendas) involved with any conference room meeting are public knowledge for anybody with access.

4.3.1.3 A Two-Way Conversation   The bottom line is that electronic mail is essentially a two-way conversation. Calendaring in the two-way mode simply doesn't provide the level of sophistication, or "groupness," that a shared calendar database does, though it does maintain features that make it a viable solution.

4.3.2 Mail-Enhanced Calendar System

The mail-enhanced calendar system employs a centralized calendar database on the file server. This database puts a more extensive amount of information at its users' fingertips. CE Software's TimeVision (formerly Powercore's Network Scheduler) is one such application, as are Campbell Services' OnTime for Networks and Microsystems' CaLANdar, among others. Mail enhancement usually means that the scheduling application addresses the email platform natively through mail APIs, permitting automatic email dispatch and directory referencing. The mail-enhancement aspect of each package is usually an optional feature, and requires that the purchaser buy a scheduler compatible with their mail package. Lotus Organizer will not integrate with Microsoft Mail, nor will Meeting Maker XP integrate with QuickMail, for example. Figure 4.4 shows how this type of system works.

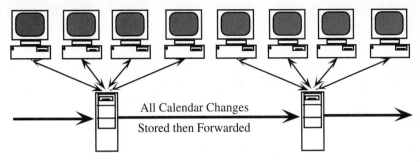

All Calendar Changes
Stored then Forwarded

Fig. 4.4 The mail-enhanced calendar system keeps local calendar databases at each server. Changes are updated between servers in a store-and-forward chain.

4.3.2.1 Strengths   The nature of an extensive shared database offers a more robust level of calendar interaction for its users.

☞ More information is available, and therefore alterable.

☞ To ensure privacy, most schedulers offer numerous security levels assignable to any event or calendar note. This way, personal items can remain just that, while items that may only concern one particular group can be accessed only by that group, and so on.

☞ Also, the database can be easily augmented to include resources or even nonscheduled email users without additional licenses or hassles.

☞ The centralized database provides a much higher level of "groupness" as well, since numerous detailed schedules can be simultaneously loaded onto the user's screen. If a sales manager needs one of his reps to visit a customer in Chicago on Tuesday, he can simply select his staff and overlay their Tuesday schedules into one view. If he sees that Johnson the sales rep will be in nearby Schaumburg that day, he can simply schedule Johnson to visit the Chicago client that same day. If the sales manager could only view free and busy times, he would not have had adequate information to assign the task to Johnson.

☞ The robust feature set possible with this architecture excels when multiple users must coordinate free time to meet. A free-time search is a simple affair in this setup, as is the ability to find only the available people for a specified time slot. Because each user's calendar is always current (or more current, depending on the particular package) on the local server, erroneous double-bookings can be avoided, unlike group schedulers, whose currency relies on frequent email gathering by its users.

☞ Depending on how the particular package works, the scheduler can even work across multiple mail systems, assuming gateways are already in place. TimeVision NS, for example, synchronizes calendar data between servers simply by bundling all recent changes into a piece of mail that is sent to all other schedule databases on the network. Cross-server calendars are only kept as current as the servers communicate their email. Because the contents of the mail message are encapsulated through the email gateway, Office A and Office B can share calendars despite use of disparate email and network operating systems.

4.3.2.2 Weaknesses   There can be several drawbacks to implementing this type of system. Because of its higher core functionality, it is a more complex system overall.

☞ Calendar data is constantly building, and since the application is distinct from the email system, a separate administration module must be employed to keep it under control. Also, because it is separate, users must be added and deleted apart from the mail system. The scheduler will read the new names and delete data related to former employees' calendars, but these functions must be performed at the hands of the systems operator.

☞ Scalability can also prove problematic in this scheme. When an employee leaves the company, his schedule stays behind. If there are 30 servers containing the scheduler database, all of the ex-employee's schedule data must be deleted from each server. This can be a very time-consuming operation, considering that the departed user is named in 100 separate schedule items at each of the 30 servers.

☞ As with any database, corruption can occur as well, which, depending on the particular package, can throw the whole scheduling store-and-forward chain into disarray.

☞ In this model, the end user is also denied the convenience of accepting or declining an appointment from email, which is usually the first place they may notice a new schedule item.

4.3.2.3 The Price of Robustness   In development of future versions, the mail-enhanced side of the scheduling package must remain current with the advancing email APIs to remain cutting-edge. Overall, this solution offers a high level of robustness and interoperability while it suffers at the hands of scalability and administrative burdens.

4.3.3 Host-Based Systems

For years, character-mode Profs and DEC's All-In-One reigned as the only products to perform group calendaring and scheduling. Russell's Calendar Manager and Oracle Office have come along in the meantime to provide Windows and Macintosh users a somewhat friendlier interface with the same enterprise scalability. In the past, users were restricted to dumb terminals and intimidating character-based interfaces, but the functionality was enough to propagate their continued use at organizations that successfully deployed them. Figure 4.5 illustrates a host-based system.

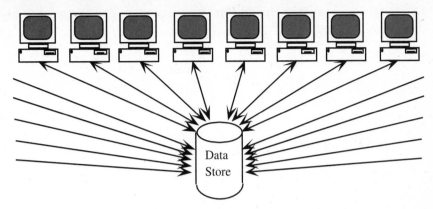

Fig. 4.5 The host-based system is a client-server solution. All data is stored in one centralized data store.

4.3.3.1 Strengths One single database is quite appealing for those who must manage information systems.

☞ Troubleshooting is simplified, as are routine maintenance and administrative operations.
☞ Robust feature sets are also possible in this architecture with the ready availability of a high-end database structure.
☞ Perhaps the biggest selling point of this type of system is its innate scalability. This type of system can support many more users than can a LAN-based server system.
☞ Since this model is a client-server application, it ports more readily between desktop O/S platforms. It would seem, then, that this would be the ideal solution, but it does have its own distinct set of limitations.

4.3.3.2 Weaknesses

☞ These solutions can be very costly, and furthermore, expensive proprietary hardware is often required. Calendar Manager, for example, requires a DEC VAX system and associated communications software to allow Windows and Mac users to tap into the VAX.
☞ Integration with email, if available at all, is usually limited to the mail system proprietary to the hardware on which it runs, though gateways may provide a work-around fix.
☞ For the end user, this type of group calendaring and scheduling package will sometimes fall short of satisfying the current level of customer expectations from a GUI desktop application. Today's users demand colorful, clear icons and interfaces. Of the products above, only Calendar Manager offers a modern-day-style GUI, while the others are limited to character-based graphics, if there are graphics at all.

4.3.3.3 Where Are Host Based Systems Going?   The group calendaring and scheduling packages that run on host-based systems are basically a sidebar to the other functions of the host (i.e., inventory management). As many businesses migrate from host-based systems to desktop PC LANs and WANs, group scheduling's early adopters are often former Profs or DEC's All-In-One users. They have already experienced the sweeping benefits offered by a group calendaring and scheduling solution.

4.3.4 Summary of Group Calendaring and Scheduling Products

Table 4.1 shows what to look for as group scheduling products are considered. Remember that the features found in the various packages vary widely, so by all means investigate all options. Product reviews in periodicals may be a helpful place to start a search, but don't trust the reviewers to approach group scheduling the same way you do, or the way your organization would. Keep in mind that the test lab may have used the products between five or 20 users for a day or maybe a week. Consequently, the analysts may not locate what could be a major problem after a month of heavy use between 100 people. You'll thank yourself later for investigating the long-term ramifications of the "behind-the-scenes" activity generated by candidate packages.

4.4 IMPLEMENTATION ISSUES

Before a purchase decision is made, the evaluating parties and their superiors must be committed to a successful implementation of the product, selecting a package that will make this shift as smooth as possible. Evaluators should scrutinize each package from three different perspectives: the end user, the workgroup, and the enterprise.

4.4.1 The Individual

As technological achievement marches forth, even the casual PC user has become sophisticated, demanding more and more from his or her applications. It's entertaining to note that if a process takes three mouse clicks when it should only take one, it's "cumbersome." If a particular print format isn't available, it may prohibit the calendar's use, despite the other productivity-boosting features. Today's high-performance hardware running fifth-generation mainstream applications, like word processors and spreadsheets, causes the standard for excellence to keep rising.

Software developers are tasked with providing more features while making the software interface as clean and simple as possible. Too many buttons or icons on the screen at once can intimidate users, while wading through several menus to perform a simple task brings resentment. Because of this, interface design has become an art form unto itself, now blending form with its underlying function.

Table 4.1 Group Scheduling Products' Strengths and Weaknesses.

Product Type	Common Strengths	Common Weaknesses
Calendar-Enhanced Mail System	Simplicity	Low "groupness"
	Interface	Not real-time
	Acceptance	Proprietary to email
	Personal features	
Mail-Enhanced Calendar System	High "groupness"	Scalability
	Not email-specific	Administration
	Central database	Performance
	Nearly real-time	
	Robust group features	
Host-Based System	Real-time	Hardware requirements
	High scalability	Interface
	Administration	Cost
	Performance	Configuration
	Email integration	

Customization can solve this problem readily enough, though users may go on for many months before they realize that they even have the option of customizing.

Users don't want to read the user manual anymore. Since the advent of the GUI operating system, the user manual has become a last-ditch read. Users expect to be able to figure it out on their own. It might take a while, maybe years, to discover everything an application does. What aspects of a group scheduling package must meet the needs of the individual?

☞ Informational views
Think of the many types of paper calendars people use. There's a three-year calendar in most checkbooks, a monthly calendar on the wall, and a weekly or daily calendar inside a paper-based organizer. Users expect an interface that allows them to toggle between macro and micro calendar views with information that readily translates between views.

☞ Acceptable printed output
No matter how electronic the workplace becomes, paper is still the medium that never crashes and easily fits into one's wallet if necessary. A selection of handsome and information-rich prints is a feature that many users mandate. It is now common for scheduling applications to print formats specifically for the market's common personal planners.

☞ Performance

Today, a ten-second network lag time can be an eternity, to hear some people describe it. Most products in each of the three types perform similarly to each other since they share similar back-end structures.

☞ Do they like it?

When all is said and done, the individual wants an application that he or she likes to use. When it comes time to schedule a meeting with the manager, will the individual enter his scheduling application and set up an appointment, or will he march down the hall and ask for a meeting? If the user has a doctor's appointment during a workday, will he enter it in his scheduler, or will he only write the message on a sticky note?

4.4.2 The Group

Without group usage, a group calendaring and scheduling application is a squandered investment. If the group allows the application to become "shelfware" (lingo for unused software), then it must not be meeting their needs, assuming that they gave the application a fair chance to work for them. What does the workgroup demand?

☞ Informational views

A group can better coordinate their activities if they can navigate through informational views. Being able to view multiple calendars in a single overlapped view is a desirable feature, especially from macro and micro perspectives.

☞ Enhanced productivity

The group calendar's goal is to increase productivity. The workgroup users will usually accept a product that makes them more effective members of the team. Scheduling a fully attended meeting in about 30 seconds can build a following. A key role in management is to constantly seek methods or resources to improve production, so often they are the ones who drive both the purchase and the implementation of groupware.

4.4.3 The Enterprise

When group calendaring and scheduling is bought into at the enterprise level as opposed to the group's, one simple requirement must be met: adequate return on investment of both money and people. It is pretty difficult to quantify or even guess the extent to which group scheduling will help an entire organization. Trial user groups can be an effective barometer of improvement before deciding on enterprise-wide implementation. A trial group, however, won't reflect the beneficial procedural changes that will occur once *every* department is up and running.

☞ Cost

Let's say that a 250-user site wants to go enterprise-wide with their scheduling application. If the cost is $10,000, that works out to $40 per user. Over the course of one year, it boils down to slightly more than $3 per month for each user. There are other costs involved, though, namely those associated with personnel. The network administrator will have a new set of responsibilities. He'll have to spend a portion of his time adding and deleting users, configuring servers, archiving data, and performing general maintenance. By no means will this be a full-time job, but if the administrator is already having a hard time keeping up with his current batch of network applications, adding scheduling might cause him to start perusing the want ads. Scalability

☞ The methods used by group schedulers to support many users play a key role in their respective administrative requirements. If a store-and-forward data distribution scheme is utilized by the application, it will require more work. Some organizations disable the cross-server calendar connectivity of these applications because of the performance and administrative burden they can cause. The same thing can hold true for the calendar-enhanced mail service type. Heavy usage can generate large volumes of electronic mail. Occasionally, the utilities provided to delete these pieces of mail are inadequate, if they exist at all. This is something to consider when evaluating an enterprise application. The scheduler may operate nicely between ten people as a group, but consider the big picture, since that friendly group calendar may be generating a lot of "junk" behind the scenes.

☞ Deployment

Wide-scale deployment requires training procedure and a certain amount of administrative work. Many customers set up a series of brief in-house training sessions to educate the end users about the practice of group scheduling and particular features of the application purchased. As these group scheduling tools improve, enterprise implementation is becoming increasingly common.

☞ Interenterprise scheduling

As organizations communicate more frequently with customers and suppliers via interenterprise email, the trend would indicate the same increase with calendaring and scheduling as the genre matures. This is a concern for the future as disparate group schedulers do not yet contain a common set of instructions to talk to one another. Recently, the XAPIA created an open API for group calendaring and scheduling applications that will allow two different systems to communicate. This API, which will be discussed at the close of the chapter, is a crucial first step towards future interenterprise utilization of group scheduling.

4.5 IMPLEMENTATION

4.5.1 Start with a Strategy

Introducing groupware applications to a pool of users is an entirely new phenomenon to many organizations. While the mega-corporation customer may employ an entire group dedicated to software training, the fifty-member law firm may hire a lone "computer guy." Many small to mid-size companies simply lack the resources, or just don't allocate enough funding for such a luxury as computer training. The best way to get the ball rolling with a new scheduling application is to start with a strategy.

4.5.1.1 Workgroups
At larger organizations, group scheduling usually infiltrates the network at a workgroup level. The application naturally appeals to the department that needs it the most. As a word processing application is used far more heavily by some departments than others, a group calendar will be utilized at varying degrees throughout an enterprise. When the scheduler is introduced to the group, it is wise to have management commit to its propagation. Every meeting between members of the group must be entered into the scheduler. Assigned tasks can be initiated orally, then reiterated in the calendar. Management must follow up with co-workers who don't use their calendar. Shortly, the group sees the inherent usefulness and needn't be reminded to use it.

If all this talk of strategy sounds difficult, it actually isn't. Implementation is just a matter of building momentum. Once this momentum is reached, group calendaring and scheduling becomes an integral part of the job.

When one workgroup benefits from an application, word spreads. In some instances, the application will proliferate around the company unchecked, while at other locations it will undergo stringent analysis and competitive evaluation before it is even acceptable at a group level. It is a good practice to re-evaluate a groupware application when more than one workgroup requests it, simply because a smart administrator doesn't want an inferior application to become entrenched. Suggesting the removal of a group scheduler once it is entrenched can elicit some very angry responses from those whose lives revolve around their calendar! Unfortunately, most group scheduling applications are unable to import data from other similar products, which places a high level of importance on product selection. It's a lot like choosing a personal paper-based organizer. A fancier one may appear on the shelves next month, but at that point it's impractical to switch because it would take many hours to copy over all of the information stored in the first one.

4.5.1.2 Entserprise
The migration of applications from the workgroup to the enterprise has caused the formation of a new corporate entity: the standards committee. The growing landscape of hardware and software makes the formation of such a group a wise and inevitable step for many companies. Smaller firms often opt for the services of an experienced local integrator for selecting network applications.

As with workgroups, successful implementation usually starts from the top down. Management is mandated to use it; then it can be progressively implemented by each department, with the department's manager driving continued daily use.

Every enterprise works differently, so the appropriate roll-out strategy should be formulated to accommodate the organization as a whole.

4.6 WHAT'S NEXT IN GROUP CALENDARING AND SCHEDULING

Because a calendar is a very personal item, it makes sense that everybody be able to select the calendar that best suits their needs, while providing the same underlying groupware functionality to all users; in other words, interoperability.

Interoperability will allow other time-reliant groupware applications such as workflow or project management to be able to exchange and share data with the enterprise calendar. Interoperability also extends to multiple platforms. If users want to be able to select the calendar of their choice, the calendar vendors are tasked with making all of them "speak the same language." When the pretty interface of Desktop Calendar A can interact with the high-performance back end of Enterprise Calendar B, which links up with PDA Calendar C, group calendaring and scheduling will finally be the solution that will please all users. As the calendar choice should be personal, so should the hardware. Platforms can extend from Windows and Macintosh all the way to PDAs and alphanumeric pagers. The creation of an open API (application program interface) for group calendaring and scheduling would remove a factor that today limits market growth.

It has been suggested that some day, everybody will keep a mega-schedule on-line, accessible from any platform or network. This schedule would connect not only to the doctor's office for appointment-setting, but also to the home to schedule the air conditioning to turn on at 4 p.m. The Internet has allowed for electronic messaging to be accessible from just about anywhere; some day soon, it may be able to update calendars in the same way it does mailboxes.

Real group calendaring and scheduling for interenterprise applications will in all likelihood be limited to a calendar-enhanced mail system at first. Company "A" probably would not benefit from external access to a very proprietary store of information. The largest barrier to interenterprise calendaring and scheduling is security. Until security is absolutely flawless and, more important, trusted by all, acceptance will be limited. Security is also paramount to the individual. The workgroup calendar can never replace a personal paper-based calendar unless privacy can be absolutely ensured.

4.6.1 The XAPIA CSA

In November 1994, the XAPIA (the X.400 Applications Program Interface Association) agreed to its first CSA (Calendaring and Scheduling API). This group, representing every major group calendaring and scheduling vendor and some very large corporate MIS leadership, together defined an open, public-

domain API. The group began as a "birds of a feather" session at a gathering of
the EMA (Electronic Messaging Association). The top group scheduling programmers and industry pioneers gathered to discuss their common future goals, and
what they could do as a group to benefit this entire genre of groupware. Their
decision was to define a set of common instructions that would allow group
scheduling applications to share a core set of instructions. After a lot of brainstorming and back-and-forth work between the developers, they agreed on a set
of 20+ common instruction calls and their definitions.

After the API is incorporated into the next-generation scheduling applications, a wide variety of practical, useful features will be available to the networked user. Any workflow provider who wants to tap into GC&S functionality
may do so by programming to this API, for example.

The possible scenarios for open API usage are seemingly limitless.
High-end calendar functions (i.e., dynamic conflict detection or viewing 50 schedules at once) will still be limited to the actual group scheduling application,
though, since the API only covers a core set of instructions. Still, use of this core
set will provide excellent feature sets for other groupware applications.

☞ If a travelling salesman creates an appointment in the field on his wireless
   PDA, his manager will be able to view it on his Macintosh at the home base.
☞ A deadline in a project manager will appear as a memo in each team mem-
   ber's calendar.
☞ A marketing representative on the road will be updated regarding appoint-
   ments automatically via an alphanumeric pager.
☞ The degree of cross-application calendar usage will be limited only by the
   API and the creativity of the developers who decide to utilize it.

The XAPIA CSA is also a groundbreaking advance towards interenterprise
calendaring and scheduling. If two disparate CSA-enabled scheduling systems
can recognize a piece of inbound email as a schedule item, an appointment can
be created from wherever that email was dispatched. Undoubtedly, even more
powerful applications of this technology have yet to be invented, but an open API
is the first step to realizing all of these possibilities.

4.7 A VIEW FROM THE INSIDE

Beginning with electronic mail, the software industry has seen business become
more and more comfortable with network technology. As the products add features and stability, the networks and machines get faster. Companies are beginning to add components, one by one, to their respective technological arsenals.
Entire file cabinets are being replaced with a single DAT tape, while typewriters
have gone the way of the mechanical adding machine. Paper usage will decline
with the advent of workflow. It may not be too readily apparent, but business is
in the midst of a momentous shift. The graphical networked desktop is becoming
the rule rather than the exception. As long as there are smart developers to see a

better way of doing things, there will be powerful groupware tools to aid business.

Many industry analysts have forecasted tremendous growth in the sales of group calendaring and scheduling software. Why? Because, quite simply, it is a concept that works. It increases productivity. It lessens frustration. People like to use it. Group calendaring and scheduling, in whatever form it may evolve into, is here to stay.

BIOGRAPHY

Jack Perry is the executive director of sales and marketing of CE Software, Inc., an $11.5 million company best known for its TimeVision Network Scheduler 3.5 and its number-one-selling electronic mail software application, QuickMail. Under his direction, CE Software posted its largest quarter sales increase in the company's 13-year history.

During CE Software's acquisition of Powercore, Perry acted as general manager of Powercore and played a pivotal role in the acquisition process. Prior to the acquisition, Perry was the vice president of sales and marketing, where he engineered Powercore's direct selling program which delivered over $2 million in sales within its first 6 months. Perry is credited with the successful launch of Network Scheduler.

Perry has held other senior management positions where he established successful sales models which resulted in dramatic sales increases in very short periods, and he has developed and launched many direct marketing programs.

Perry's technical credits include the development of RunningCounts, a statistical reporting systems calendar for an individual's aerobic activities.

Perry is a graduate of the University of Iowa, where he received a Bachelor of Arts degree in business and communications.

Introduction to Chapter 5

Jim Bair is an analyst for The Gartner Group. He has an impressive academic background and has been in the groupware industry far longer than I. His knowledge of groupware and document management systems (DSM) is both voluminous and incisive.

Jim is a visionary. In this chapter he presents his vision of what a collaborative document management system should be ... not that there is a product, or set of products, that fulfills this definition. Jim effectively uses this opportunity to highlight interesting issues about document management systems.

With the popularity of networking computers, document management systems are becoming more popular. Jim looks at the "hyperdocument model" for document management. First, he defines document management and then examines the products that are purported to support this function. He looks at why current DMS products do not support collaboration well and moves into the requirements for such a collaborative system. Fortunately, Jim not only focuses on the technology and how it links documents, but looks at how it links people, either to documents or into a "community."

Next, Jim moves into the software functions needed in such a collaborative system and emerging standards. He looks at document management as a universal service that should be available to programmers and users alike, spanning applications and even companies.

Part of the technology of collaborative document management is text retrieval. Jim applies this technology to a variety of challenges to six different industry groups and talks about both the implementation and the outcomes. Then he moves into an analysis of text retrieval and the new technologies that are creating the leading-edge products in this field.

Finally, Jim concludes with some words for corporate management about document management and closes the chapter with the idea that DMS will eventually become part of a networked operating system, that documents are containers for idea and information, and that documents should be "tokens" in a business process.

This chapter is more intellectually oriented than some of the other chapters in this volume. Mr. Bair raises critical issues about document management. As illustrated in the introductory chapter (Oticon case study), new technologies for document management, as well as organizational change, were able to turn Oticon around and improve their bottom line by 500%. We all deal with documents every day! Every chapter in this book is a document! I don't see this trend changing, even with the collaborative nature of groupware. Remember, technology is supposed to support the way people work, and not all work is collaborative.

If you have ever worked on a document collaboratively, you know it can be a heady experience. Work which normally took several days or weeks to complete can now be executed in just hours. Jim did not cover collaborative editing, which could rightfully be listed in the category of shared screen interaction or desktop conferencing.

The process goes like this. Let's say you want to produce a corporate brochure. This is a document that everyone will see and must represent the company in the proper light. It must also get the right message across (the same is true of an advertisement). Because of the critical nature of this kind of document, many people have a role in its development: corporate management, advertising or copy writers, production people, editors, and so on. In order to decrease the time to develop such a document, shared screen technologies are often employed.

In this scenario the author contacts the reviewer by phone and establishes an audio link. He then contacts the reviewer by modem (or on a LAN) and makes sure the reviewer has the same document the author has on his/her screen. The author and reviewer can collaborate, redesign, rewrite, and cut and paste the document until both are satisfied with the results. The original document is never changed, and the reworked version is saved by both parties so each has a new original. Rather than sending changes back and forth by email, Federal Express, or snail mail, this process allows the brochure copy to be created in a fraction of the time it would normally take. Products like "Face-to-face" from Crosswise and Mark-up from Mainstay Software support this function.

In the near future, proprietary desktop videoconferencing systems like Intel's Proshare will become more affordable. There are even free systems like "See you See me" that work over the Internet. I believe this type of collaborative document management will become more popular and become an integral part of many document-oriented processes, much like desktop publishing is used in production environments today. In the meantime, Mr. Bair's chapter provides an interesting resource for collaborative document management and points the direction for future products.

CHAPTER 5

The Collaborative Imperative for Document Management Systems

James H. Bair
The Gartner Group

5.1 INTRODUCTION: DOCUMENT MANAGEMENT HAS COME OF AGE

Document management systems (DMSs) are becoming popular as users increase their purchases by 30% to 40% per year. This is not merely because the infrastructure of networks, databases, image processing, and interfaces is maturing. It is driven by the need to deal with the increasing number of digital documents from word processors to email and scanned images. But even though the use of computer-based documents for sharing information goes back to the first use of computers for teamwork in the 1960s, the collaborative capabilities developed in the laboratory have not appeared in contemporary products. The myopic view of documents has largely overlooked the primary purpose: to support human collaboration.

This chapter focuses on the collaborative functionality for DMSs, including "hyperdocuments," managing document "views," document management standards coalitions, and text retrieval technology and management issues. The goal is to help users understand how to obtain greater business value from DMS implementations by expanding their view beyond the paper-based legacy.

DMSs are accelerating in importance because they can help manage the awesome increase in documents. We are producing digital documents at an enormous rate, from word processors to email. To wit, 1680 million pieces of paper were processed by U.S. business in 1986. Since that time, the amount of paper processed has increased by 100% to 3360 billion pieces. In addition, 750 million pages spew out of computer printers every day in the U.S., 958 million photocopies are made daily, and (unfortunately) 356 million are considered unnecessary (source: Xerox Corp.). At the same time, information is streaming in from external news feeds and on-line services, and this is just a dirt road compared to the digital highway off-ramp under construction in our offices. Not only is information increasingly originating in digital form, but paper documents are finding easier paths into the same document bases via image scanning, facsimile, and workflow.

While attention is captured by large numbers, the industry is pregnant with a new emphasis on the fundamental purpose of documents. Documents are the token of collaborative action in commerce. They initiate, trigger, systematize, record, and orchestrate the human collaboration that constitutes organizations. Documents are comparable to the music we play from in business settings—many of us get to be composers as well as musicians. As documents become increasingly digital, their collaborative purpose will enable them to be born again as the grist of business.

5.1.1 What Is Document Management?

Managing documents is something we all do. The average knowledge worker spends 25 to 50% of his/her time processing documents. These include memos, reports, magazines, letters, and the like, which often end up in desktop piles. Most recently, email and word-processed documents have become the majority of information stored in our offices. As with paper documents, most digital documents remain in the author's office and are printed for delivery to others. There are many reasons for this, but it is *sharing* digital documents, as opposed to paper, that is the purpose of DMSs.

DMSs are software systems for storing digital documents in a shared environment. They are implemented on computer servers (mainframes or LANs) and accessed from terminals or networked PCs. They retrieve documents by matching stored attributes to what users specify, such as title, author, date, keywords, and so on. They are distinguished from other shared filing systems such as groupware by the following basic functions:

- ☞ Version management
- ☞ Check-in, check-out control
- ☞ Archival/retention management

These functions are in addition to all the underlying capabilities needed for computer file systems. Versions of documents are maintained so that updates become a new document from the user's perception. Versions are associated with the author who did the editing. If one author makes changes to a multi-author document, then other authors will see those changes in a new version. Versions are retained for a specified period, but the version history is a permanent trail of a document's life.

When documents are stored in a shared system, authorship/editing still must be limited to one user at a time. Thus, documents are checked out by an author for editing, creating a new version, and locking (no one else can edit) the version in the shared library. This avoids a "collision" that would occur if a document were checked out by more than one user, changed, and then checked back in. There is no generally accepted way to resolve conflict over which changes would prevail. DMSs support check-out with different permissions for different users such as "document read only," "read and write," and other privileges.

Documents are a permanent resource for users and organizations, but they cannot be retained on-line indefinitely. Magnetic media is still too expensive, and optical storage varies widely in cost, retrievability, and longevity. DMSs provide retention schedules for different types of documents. When a document ages to its archival date, it is transferred to an off-line medium such as computer tape, optical disks, or micrographic film. The DMS index keeps track of documents indefinitely by providing pointers to off-line locations.

Since most documents are still shared in paper form, DMS can manage indices which provide the physical location of paper documents. This enables users to search the document record (a form with such attributes as author, title, date, and keywords) on-line and then retrieve the physical document from a paper filing system.

Document management is defined by the confluence of user needs and technology development. DMSs were born of the need to support co-authorship and document routing through production systems. Production publishing environments such as aircraft manuals, government policies, or user guides have required computer management of the document life cycle for over 25 years. However, today the area is dominated by products that exploit client-server computing and are not custom-oriented solutions. We will list some of the current products and focus on the evolution of DMSs toward collaborative functionality in the next sections.

5.1.2 Current Products Look Like Repositories

Current DMS products generally fall into two categories: those explicitly positioned for document management, and products that do document management as a secondary function, such as most text retrieval systems. Both types of products serve as repositories, not communication media as does groupware (e.g., Lotus Notes) or email (e.g., Beyond Mail). Current DMS product vendors with significant market share include Novell SoftSolutions, PCDocs, Saros, Interleaf, Keyfile, and Odesta. The relatively new players include Documentum, Global Systems, and Portfolio Technologies. Currently, some of the DMS players are adding workflow, but they are not yet industrial-strength workflow vendors.

Text retrieval products use inquiries to search document indices, rather than focusing on document management per se. The indices are generated from an analysis of the words in the document and/or a document form containing author, title, date, keywords, and so on. In general, building document collections is analogous to publishing documents in final form. The overhead of this analysis and indexing is not appropriate for sharing documents for quick and dirty daily work. The largest market share products, such as BasisPlus from Information Dimensions and BRS/Search from Dataware Technologies, serve the needs of users to search for information when they do not know where it is located. Newer entries are more oriented toward retrieval from servers or PCs, such as products from Verity, Fulcrum, Folio, Conquest, Personal Library Software, and Zylab. However, these products still look like repositories rather than document managers despite claims to the contrary. Services such as Lexis and Nexis from Mead Data Central have not deviated from the original repository orientation of text retrieval systems.

5.1.3 Repositories Do Not Support the Critical Business Need for Collaboration

The problem with DMS products is that documents are "put away" into a centrally controlled and structured repository. These are appropriate for public repositories of literature, not vehicles intended for collaboration among colleagues. Repositories use a predetermined structure for cataloguing and indexing rather than a dynamic scheme generated by users in their daily work. Documents are the active media of ongoing work, ranging from proposals and correspondence to reports and manuals. The DMS products listed here can support these activities, but the repository model does not capture the dynamic interrelationships in and among working documents and their authors.

5.2 COLLABORATIVE DOCUMENT MANAGEMENT REQUIREMENTS

5.2.1 DMSs Need to Capture Community

DMSs tend to ignore the need for quick and facile access to the much larger context of a particular document, which includes cross-references, authors with pertinent expertise, and other people associated with the content area. Providing a repository for sharing documents is a worthy contribution of a DMS, but better ways of representing relationships in information and among people are needed. It is true that "living" documents can reflect the latest information, whether it is a business plan or a technical policy, because they are electronically updated by their co-authors. However, it is important to easily retrieve related documents, current and precedent. Legal research, for example, is largely dependent upon preceding documents.

For example, when a document is authored it is usually related to other documents, either as sources or as a part of an ongoing "collaboration." Documents are also related to people, not just as authors but as part of a community. While reading this chapter, you should be able to quickly retrieve information on the companies and products mentioned. Moreover, you should also be able to learn about the people behind the documents, the company founders, the thought leaders, and the analysts. If seeing this information were easy and fast enough, you would be able to have a more meaningful and informed reading experience. Of course, the author of this chapter and the authors of the related documents, would have to be able to easily connect the related information during the authoring process.

5.2.2 Products Should Link Documents and People

The most important missing functionality in today's DMSs is general-purpose linking, originally called "hypertext," not to be equated with "hypermedia" (see Figure 5.1). Since links can be everything from synchronous network connections to connections between programs provided by Microsoft's DDE and OLE, the best term to describe hypertext links is *hyperlinks*. At the simplest level, users can "jump" on a hyperlink causing the linked-to part of a document to be displayed. Hyperlinks are easily installed when a user points at a graphically displayed document and then points to another document in a different window. A hyperlinking command connects the two locations; this connection remains persistent regardless of the state of the applications or the computer. This enables users who see the first document to point to an icon representing the hyperlink and quickly see the linked-to document. The display of the linked-to document is the same as when the hyperlink was set up. The icons inserted into a document to traverse a hyperlink are "buttons," although any machine-readable address would do. Hyperlinks, as opposed to hypermedia links, are intended to be traversed from one point to another, indefinitely, within or across many documents. Hypermedia is commonly the linking-in of images or video to a multimedia document, a confusing usage of "hyper."

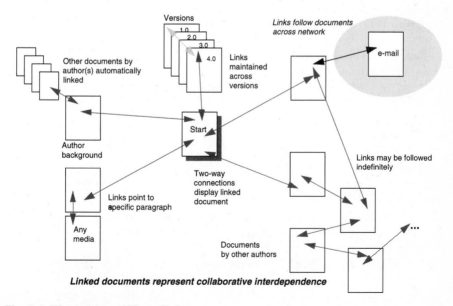

Fig. 5.1 Illustration of Hyperlinks

5.2.2.1 Lost in Hyperspace   Hyperlinks should have additional features as they do in most prototypes. They should be two-way so users can "jump" back from the linked-to document at any time. The simplicity of hyperlinks belies the powerful complexity that arises from extensive hyperlinking. Since users can follow several hyperlinks within or across unlimited numbers of files, navigational assistance should be provided to show the hyperlinkages and a user's location in a linked document collection. This is often done by a graphic overview feature showing the documents as icons and the hyperlinks as lines. The path created when several hyperlinks are followed should be stored for future use.

5.2.2.2 Surviving Editing   Many issues arise when adding hyperlinks to a document management system. Managing revisions is the most onerous because the part of a document that contains the link (the "anchor") may be edited or deleted in succeeding versions. Hyperlinks should survive across revisions as long as enough of the original material remains in the document to make sense. The best implementations should retain the link as long as any of the original paragraph remains. Using the paragraph as the smallest textual object supports features such as co-authoring by keeping a record of authorship per paragraph.

5.2.2.3 Hyperpeople   When hyperlinks are added to current document management systems, paragraphs and other multimedia objects can be linked by authors and readers with permission. However, there is a need to link people and information, and to do so automatically if possible. The first prototypes, such as Augment at the Stanford Research Institute, associated each paragraph with an author and then provided links to other documents by that author. The prototypes maintained a collaborative support system of documents by individuals and teams. When a document was entered into the DMS, it included links to preceding documents as well as all other documents by the author(s). By following links based on author through a DMS, a user could find relevant information without having to rely on text inquiries.

One of the earlier (1985) and better examples of a hyperlink product is Guide from InfoAcess Inc., Bellevue, Washington. But Guide is not positioned as a document management product, nor does it offer sufficient functionality. By offering hypertext, Guide essentially lets users build interactive, electronic documents. In other words, hypertext is a document design and delivery vehicle for InfoAccess. For example, a large bank uses the Windows version to deliver its two-volume, 1500-page Retail Banking Guide. Other applications include an illustrated parts manual where users can link to images, drawings, descriptions of related parts, installation instructions, and so on as needed by simply clicking on the button icon. An impressive implementation of Guide enabled Ford Motor Co. to provide electronic documentation to its factory floors.

5.2.2.4 Back to the Future   Guide and products that include similar capabilities, such as Apple's HyperCard, illustrate the power of hyperlinks, but they do not provide collaborative support. Users should be able to easily generate as many interlinkages across the shared document collection as they would like.

The World Wide Web (WWW) available on the Internet harkens back to Augment. WWW enables authors on the Internet to include hyperlinks in their documents to be traversed to documents on other Internet servers. The attractiveness of hyperlinking in the Internet milieu may encourage its market acceptance.

The dollar savings from publishing electronically and integrating multimedia is enormous, especially when large documents are published frequently. However, the full value from hyperlinks inserted by an author to permanently reference pertinent information is untapped. Future offerings in high-end publishing products such as FrameMaker from Frame, San Jose, California, will allow more flexible hyperlinking, but how well linkages can be built and maintained across a collaborative document collection remains to be seen.

5.2.3 Document View Memory

Documents may be "opened" by finding and pointing to a name or icon in a GUI. But the windows through which users view documents are at best transitory keyholes into the information space. DMSs need features that treat views of documents as valuable presentations to be "remembered" for later use.

5.2.3.1 View Management   DMSs should remember the exact contents of a display window for as long as the user wishes. At first this ability might seem trivial, but the alternative ways of viewing documents are increasing. For example, outliners such as that in Microsoft Word allow the user to see one or more levels in a hierarchical outline, to hide or display the text, or show one line only of text (each paragraph). Spacing and other variables can also be selected. Users typically switch between outline views and formatted views quite easily. But often, they are looking at a two-level outline, then an all-level outline, then a full text display, and so on, with no ability to retrace their steps. In prototypes with this feature, users found it valuable to be able to "jump" through several views, avoiding having to respecify the levels, and so forth, and more important, to review what they had seen. Where the document has more structure than a typical word processor, as with SGML, remembering the view "setup" can be very time-saving.

5.2.3.2 Filtered Views   Filtering is becoming a more acceptable function as products such as BeyondMail from Banyon become accepted. The current function, which actively filters an entire document or email message on the textual content or headers, is just a start. Often, users need to view particular parts of a document and not others. Users should be able to view only those paragraphs or headings that meet their criteria (e.g., "paragraphs which contain mention of legal case xyz"). Prototypes have demonstrated the value of specifying any combination of textual characters or other attributes to determine what part of a document will be displayed. Users should be able to include filters in hyperlinks which would automatically present only parts of documents that passed the filter.

5.2.3.3 Filtered Views of Paragraph Objects   A realization is emerging that documents should contain objects, not merely be flat files conforming to operating system architecture. DMSs should treat an arbitrarily small unit of text as a paragraph (in SGML it would be tagged as a heading, subheading, etc.) and enable it to have attributes as do objects. Attributes used in the first prototype, Augment, include date-of-last-revision and author. With this feature, a user can view only those paragraphs changed by a certain author since a certain date; or a user could request a printout that contained only his contributions. Essentially, documents become multi-author workspaces. A publication becomes a snapshot of co-authored information to be shared with a larger group.

5.2.3.4 Collaboration in Disguise   The ability to view pieces of information based on creation date, date last read, topic, and so on, is essentially what Lotus Notes does to support information sharing. DMSs with the kind of viewing and linking functionality discussed here could support collaborative work as well as Lotus Notes. Future offerings from relational database vendors such as Oracle are likely to provide the capabilities discussed here. It may be technically easier to map the linkages using a general-purpose relational database engine, a technique used in the early prototypes such as Intermedia at Brown University.

5.2.4 Leading-Edge Developments

A number of users have joined forces to learn about the functionality missing from current DMSs. The Open Hyperdoc System Alliance is being facilitated by EPRI (the Electric Power Research Institute), a nationally funded R&D center for the utility industry. The first system to use hyperlinks for collaborative document management, Augment, has been the inspiration and basis of the Open Hyperdoc System (OHS). Several companies have banded together to build an OHS that would test the feasibility of maintaining a hyperlinked document collection for a distributed and diverse community of users.

OHS will enable users to link to public documents that may be revised and transported. Maintaining hyperlinks when documents are moved both physically and logically across a network is the challenge being addressed by promoting standards as well as viable prototypes. Hyperlinked document management will minimize the potential for losing documents, even in worldwide networks, and maximize the ability to find all the related information users need.

When DMSs are available on networked computers across an enterprise and ultimately interenterprise, it is inevitable that systems from different vendors will need to be connected. Currently, if an organization has two or more DMSs they will be accessed completely independently, through different interfaces and different filling schemes. A user will have to search each DMS separately unless he/she knows which DMS contains the desired document. Hyperlinks do not work across different DMSs either, unless custom-programmed or conforming to a standard such as provided by the World Wide Web on the Internet. Thus, standards are being developed in the interest of users that can overcome the multivendor incompatibility, as we will discuss in the next section.

5.3 DOCUMENT MANAGEMENT STANDARDS

5.3.1 Collaboration Transcends Product Differences

The collaborative nature of documents requires equal access from all the appropriate users in an organization. Document access cannot be denied because it is stored in a different product. However, it is likely that management both in and outside of IT will be seeing proposals and requests to implement one of a number of products. The companies mentioned earlier, such as WordPerfect-SoftSolutions, PCDocs, Saros, Interleaf, Documentum, Odesta, and IBM Visual Document Manager, are the better known candidates to manage your document repositories. These companies' products have different architectures, different platforms, and a variety of databases, and thus do not work well together.

The variety of alternatives is ultimately a curse for customers of any size. Given today's software acquisition anarchy, companies will probably have more than one product and might have several in a geographically distributed enterprise. Since document management products have typically focused on one department using one server, scalability to enterprise-wide applications is often overlooked. Typically, applications are monolithic, such as proposal production, product documentation, technical manuals, legal briefs, and personnel records.

There are three alternatives to beat the odds against document management product compatibility:

☞ Wait until the technology matures to provide enterprise-wide solutions.
☞ Purchase a departmental product now and implement a cost-benefit plan that provides payback before enterprise interoperability is required.
☞ Align the solution with a vendor that is working on standards for product interoperability, and evolve the system toward multivendor standards.

Choosing among these alternatives is tricky because basic values come into play. Selecting the first alternative, waiting for the technology, implies that there is low user need and little perceived payoff in the near term. The second alternative, purchasing a product that will become obsolete, places little value on the significant effort to design, re-engineer, implement, train users, and so on required for each new product. This is the least desirable alternative because it is mostly a matter of luck for typical products to stay current for more than three years. Thus, it will be extremely difficult to achieve payback before obsolescence.

The third alternative, vendor standards, has become more appealing in the past year. Standards have evolved in the areas of operating systems, network protocols, graphic user interfaces, database languages (SQL), and even document content architectures (ODA). But in document management, choosing a system has been a one-vendor street. The advent of document standards coalitions is rapidly increasing the desirability of the third alternative.

5.3.2 Collaboration Among Document Managers

Most of the vendors in the DMS arena have formed a coalition to agree upon how their products will "collaborate." The coalition of vendors and users, called "Shamrock" (see "Appendix"), was formed by two major forces in the industry, Saros and IBM (Software Solutions Division). Subsequently, a different standard was launched called ODMA (Open Document Management API [Application Program Interface]), led by the SoftSolutions division of WordPerfect. ODMA was organized to address a different level of standards than Shamrock. Both coalitions have published specifications that are endorsed by their members and available to others who wish to write software to the specifications.

These standards efforts address different parts of the software system. Shamrock defines standards for access to the document library, usually running on a server in a client-server system. ODMA addresses standards on the client. The Shamrock specification is far more complex and lengthy because of the software issues it addresses.

5.3.2.1 Just Wait for Microsoft
A major concern for document management vendors and users over the past few years stems from Microsoft's ability to extend the operating system platform. Microsoft will continue to add capabilities to its client-server operating environment that encroach on application areas such as document management, for example, Microsoft *Exchange*. The first major thrust into applications was the provision of email transports (c.f. MAPI) to complement its LAN offering. Database applications are a similar encroachment (c.f. Access). Microsoft's *de facto* strategy is to dominate the client-server product area in the same way it has dominated the PC desktop with Windows. Any customer contemplating new purchases in these areas is probably in transition to a client-server architecture, using Microsoft Windows, and skittish about committing to other vendors when Microsoft may provide the solution. The problem is compounded by the ease of building new applications by exploiting Microsoft's "user-friendly" application development tools such as Visual Basic.

5.3.2.2 Standards to the Rescue
Microsoft is one of the participants in the Shamrock coalition. Thus, there is hope that the document management services, otherwise known as "enterprise library services," will be standard across both ISV (independent software vendor) products and Microsoft. We hope that Microsoft complies with the Shamrock specification, but in any case, the selection of a Shamrock vendor is recommended.

5.3.3 Standards Should Qualify Products

The Shamrock specification describes an API called Enterprise Library Services (ELS). As members of the coalition release new versions of their products, they will comply with the specification. This process will be accelerated by inclusion of the Shamrock specification as a purchase requirement by customers. ELS enables all users to have access from anywhere and from any platform to shared

documents with uniform security and administration. The key is vendor independence of the services, permitting ELS to be provided by any participating vendor.
Targeting Shamrock-compliant products meets the following customer needs:

☞ The ability to share documents digitally even when stored on different vendors' DMSs
☞ DMS integration with legacy systems, desktop applications, email systems,
  and workflow systems
☞ Access to the enterprise's different DMSs from a single application
☞ The ability to retrieve documents from all the related DMSs in the enterprise (searches across repositories will require specification beyond the current release)
☞ Access control through user login and standardized security techniques

Users of noncompliant DMSs cannot reasonably access other systems.
Since documents are used for interdepartmental collaboration, the digital version of the document is often in a different system in a different LAN. Shamrock-
compliant vendors deliver a significant increase in the usefulness of documents
to users: access to the current version regardless of location in the enterprise.

5.3.4 The Specifications Are for Different Layers

There are two problems in a multivendor environment that occur at different
layers of the software architecture. First, document management requires each
desktop computer to run each document management product separately. For
example, a user has to run Saros to access Saros libraries and PCDocs to access
PCDocs libraries. In addition, accessing the library services for products on different servers and/or different LANs is very difficult. Second, each product on the
desktop client also has to "understand" each word processor, spreadsheet, graphics program, and so on. For example, SoftSolutions must be able to recognize and
act upon WordPerfect, Word, AmiPro, Harvard Graphics, Excel, and so forth.

5.3.4.1 Layers of the Solution The Shamrock ELS and ODMA address
these two problems by focusing on the different layers of the software architecture, as shown in Figure 5.2. Shamrock specifies a standard layer between the
different document management vendors and the document repositories, ELS.
Thus, the user interacts with the desktop document manager (e.g., Saros),
which then interacts with any of the Shamrock vendors' repositories. This
enables the user to retrieve a document from SoftSolutions, Saros, Interleaf,
and others.

ODMA is a local layer that enables the desktop applications to interact
with any document manager transparently to the user. The user will see the document manager functions as part of applications such as WordPerfect or Excel.
In applications built with objects compliant with ODMA, each object has the
same interface to the document manager. ODMA is like a common language for
managing the documents of all applications on the desktop. The ODMA empha-

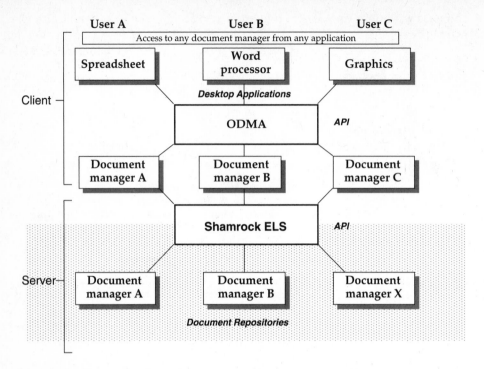

Fig. 5.2 Positions of Standards APIs in a Collaborative Environment

sis on tight integration of document managers into desktop applications makes filing documents in a shared repository much more appealing to users.

5.3.5 Document Management as a Service

Document repository management standards are relatively new, but will have profound effects on the ability to find and retrieve documents within enterprises and ultimately across enterprises. The Shamrock and ODMA specifications, Version 1.0, were published in 1994. The implications for product selection are enormous, and it appears prudent to carefully evaluate the three decisions discussed above.

Document management should be a universally available service that spans across all applications. Having a group of leading companies agree on how to provide services consistently to both programmers and users is of tremendous value. It addresses a fundamental business need—the ability to mesh current solutions with future ones.

5.3.6 Architecture

Layers in an architecture define how different parts of the same or different programs talk to each other. The most familiar example of a "layer" is the graphical user interface (GUI). The GUI is a layer on top of applications that translates between the user and the application, among other things. The current state of document management requires that each desktop application, such as a word processor, interact with each document manager. Typically, the document application hands off the document (which could be a spreadsheet, graphic, etc.) to the document manager. The document manager then uses its desktop (client) program to interact with the server program to move or copy the document to or from the document storage repository. Much of the interaction between the desktop application and the document manager is user-controlled through the GUI (i.e., Windows or Macintosh).

5.3.7 Fishing or Spearing

These standards have focused on the traditional notion of "document management," which implies that retrieval is done by specifying attributes. It is a routine process to retrieve all the documents authored by yourself for a certain month in 1994. However, attributes are insufficient when users do not know exactly which documents they want. They need to search the full text of each document in order to match words that describe their interest with those the various authors have used. It is like fishing with a hook and line compared to the spear fishing of attribute retrieval. The next section will discuss text retrieval and issues in the industry today.

5.4 TEXT RETRIEVAL, CONTENT COLLABORATION

Several years ago, an experiment at Xerox PARC (Palo Alto Research Center) demonstrated a different angle on the retrieval of documents. While working on advanced techniques for preparing and searching the text of documents, the scientists decided to create a database of biographies for scientists at PARC. It included interest areas, past projects, and current research efforts. A potential collaborator could enter his own biography and "ask" the system to find all those people who were similar. Biographies, photos, and organizational location of potential team members were retrieved. In effect, a community was described in an organizational context. The new staff member or the scientist needing collegial support was facilitated through the collaborative use of text retrieval technology in a way more commonly occurring through word of mouth over a long period of time.

5.4.1 Creating Connections Among People Through Knowledge

All users should be able to share documents not only by "sending" them to specific people, or assigning key attributes, but also by searching based on content. Browsing or "fishing" is a powerful way to create connections among people through knowledge, whether it is done automatically as at PARC or by reviewing sets of documents. However, documents have been difficult to find. One reason, based on a Gartner Group survey, is that roughly 80% of that information is on PC hard drives sitting on individuals' desks. This means users cannot typically search for information that is not on their PC.

The second difficulty is well understood in specialized communities such as librarians. Finding a document in a document base of any size depends on how much you know about the document you want, such as author, title, or date. But if you have a more general inquiry, such as "the impact of computer conferencing on the amount of time spent in meetings," then many documents will be recalled that you do not want, and you may miss several you do want. Finding the right documents can become critically important when searching for correspondence that defends a position in legal suit.

5.4.1.1 It's a Matter of History
A special class of product has been applied to the retrieval of documents based on content, not only attributes, for over 30 years. For many of these products the techniques have not changed. They still use the same Boolean search on keyword indices that has been applied since the beginning. In this context, Boolean refers to the combining of search terms or groups of search terms in an inquiry using the connectors "and, or, not." New techniques are embellishing the Boolean tradition, but users, government, and researchers are inventing different ways to represent the meaning of information. Users do not need to know the "new math" of text, but it is vital to have a list of some of the key factors that will enable selection of the right technology.

Digital text has been traditionally stored on large, central machines accessed by terminals, which require significant user effort to find documents. Today, the Library of Congress and Stanford University, to name two, still use character-terminal-based interfaces to their document bases. When text is stored in a large, structured collection, it follows a library model. Libraries are repositories where you store information that has been published for people to share indefinitely. The effort to index, catalogue, and maintain on-line publications implies high-value information. Therefore, high levels of effort to formulate inquires and then reformulate inquiries is warranted to comb the "stacks." A high-value example would be finding recent research relevant to "rhinoviruses and immune system function." Indeed, the whole area of on-line retrieval originated to serve scientific and technical communities.

Documents, the generic units of textual data storage, are retrieved easily if the "fixed field" data is known: author, title, keywords, date, subject category, and so on. Documents can be treated like records in a typical database in this case. The problem is we do not remember this exact information, even for documents we author such as the memo to that key prospect sent last year. In many cases, we do not know anything about the documents but want information relevant to a question. Historically, the Foreign Technology Division of the U.S. Air Force pioneered text retrieval technology to search foreign publications for intelligence. It was very useful to see occurrences of "plutonium" in the nuclear physics literature from the USSR in 1967. Intelligence analysts did not know which documents would reveal threatening developments, but they did know the concepts that would identify the Soviet reports.

Recently, intelligence has become a competitive edge for businesses, especially when financial deals are in the plans. "Free-text searches" can reveal everything from insider trading relevant to certain companies or news of all mergers and acquisitions over $10 million. Intelligence is often about regulatory decisions; for example, U.S. West regularly searches the FCC rulings by Judge Green to see if new product ideas have been ruled legal. Recently, computer companies have been developing new models of business workflow. When a company such as Action Technologies (Alameda, California) receives patents on its models, other companies need to know about the patents and related published discussions to avoid infringement and costly litigation. Intelligence is not always external. For example, a company like Clorox is continually documenting R&D developments that often affect its product formulas and production processes. People in manufacturing need to be able to find research relevant to product problems, which results in comments like "great, they are working on this and we can go with a temporary formula modification." Before research documentation was on-line, manufacturing would have to phone or travel to the R&D facility, leading to mixed results (delays and mistakes).

5.4.1.2 Expanded Definition of Documents   Documents in libraries are an ever smaller proportion of textual information. Now everything, including correspondence, email, trip reports, customer contacts, administrative manuals, contracts, trip reports, plans, and so on, is being produced on-line. Information that was once stored in file cabinets is now on-line in servers and PCs—often duplicated in paper and digital form. The text retrieval solutions now available turn the plethora of digital information into the basis of collaboration and avoid duplication. Text retrieval can enable users to avoid recreating information or making decisions without the relevant information created by unseen collaborators.

5.4.2 Applications for Finding Documents

5.4.2.1 Application Examples   Many users are still not convinced that they need technology to find digital documents. But the rapid growth of industry revenues from text retrieval software (for the major players, over $200 million in combined revenues) indicates that many businesses are making the investment. Here are some examples of applications of products such as Verity's Topic and Fulcrum's TextSearch.

☞ Manufacturing and engineering

  ✘ Technical documentation
  ✘ R&D knowledge base

☞ Legal

  ✘ Litigation support
  ✘ Patent search and submission

☞ Publishing and media

    ✗ News wire alerts

    ✗ News morgue

☞ Government

    ✗ Intelligence gathering

    ✗ On-line policies and procedures

☞ General business

    ✗ Corporate library

    ✗ Human resources

☞ Pharmaceuticals

    ✗ New drug applications

    ✗ Medical documents

5.4.2.2 Pharmaceutical Documents Related to Life The pharmaceutical industry provides important applications because information can be life-saving. Medical documents are used by pharmaceutical companies to protect us from the side effects of drugs—that is, if the documents can be found. Take, for example, a billion-dollar health care manufacturer faced with the challenge of decreasing time to market. It currently has a Medical Information Group that maintains a library of more than 300,000 medical articles, trade publications, and internal research reports and memos. In this mass of text are critical pieces of information about products from the manufacturer itself and competitors. This fits the historical library model of document retrieval, and thus they have depended upon information specialists to mediate between the staff and the document files. For example, the marketing manager may ask for all the internal documents on a drug trial within a segment of the population. In some cases there are a thousand documents relating to a particular product.

Searching this document base manually is almost inconceivable. It would require scanning the tables of contents and indices of publications. In addition, a filing system would have to be maintained with categories (file folders) structured to represent the anticipated needs. In this case, files labeled by drug name, researcher, department, and type of activity (such as clinical trial) filled the file cabinets until just recently. Within these files, correspondence was mixed with reports and other internal documentation, often requiring multiple filings to ensure that something could be found. This is a typical filing situation for a business unit compounded by the inclusion of medical literature.

The computer-based solution had to meet three requirements to increase end-user access. It had to be usable by medical professionals and managers who might not have had computer experience; it had to be compatible with the company's standard word processor; and the system had to run in a distributed computing environment for remote access and future expansion. These requirements portray three important benefits of the solution:

☞ Information can be retrieved by any person who needs it through a friendly interface at any time

☞ Word-processed documents can be added to the document base to become shared knowledge

☞ Documents are accessible from any PC, permitting every user to become his own librarian, retrieving information at his convenience.

The solution was implemented by a major vendor with substantial benefits. Establishing the value of finding the right information when you want it and with reduced labor is beyond the scope of this chapter. It is crucial that management understand the key factors leading to the best solution.

5.4.3 Finding Digital Document Retrieval Solutions

The three benefits of document retrieval solutions belie the limits of current products to find your documents. Assume that the technical problems are solved providing a friendly user interface, conversion of all word-processed documents into a common readable format, and networking the appropriate clients and distributed servers together. Then we have the following three deadly diversions of your resources.

5.4.3.1 Document Management Does Not Mean Text Retrieval   Document management systems may not have adequate text retrieval capabilities. Document management has meant a common repository for sharing documents, often focusing on the co-authoring process by providing editing "check-in, check-out" controls. These systems use a form to represent the searchable part of the document. The fixed-field data is used to retrieve documents (e.g., author, date, title, and keywords). The keywords have to be assigned by either the author or a labor-intensive manual indexing process. These systems are fast because the entire document is not searched (the full text is not part of the index). But unless the keywords are perfect, the likelihood of finding the articles written about "dinosaurs in the Jurassic period but not about movies" will be difficult.

5.4.3.2 Laboring Over Documents   There is a serious labor diversion associated with preparing documents for document management. The form for each document must be prepared, often requiring the author to fill in the specific fields. Some systems can automatically extract title, author, and date from a document. However, authors are left with, and often ignore, the process of assigning keywords, obsolescence date, access privileges, subcollection, project name, and so on, because it is an intrusive nuisance. This labor diversion might not be so egregious except that it often does not describe a document adequately for retrieval. The words in the titles and keyword fields have unique meanings to each person and leave the retriever with a mighty guessing game to decide which words will work. The ambiguity of language becomes a labor-consuming liability with such limited document representations. Using a retrieval word such as "plane" might retrieve documents about airplanes, geometric planes, water planing, wood planes, and even misspellings of plains.

5.4.3.3 Not All Text Retrieval Systems Are Created Equal   Vendors have struggled with the representation of documents for accurate retrieval for several decades. Traditional techniques have become quite sophisticated in products ranging from SoftSolutions to Zylab. However, these systems continue to be limited by the meanings of words—semantics—for retrieval. They typically process every word in a document, deleting common words (stop words), reducing words to the root form (stemming), and creating a rich-text index which also includes the structured data (author, title, etc.). Sophisticated retrieval techniques have been added that measure word occurrence to make the meaning of search terms more specific, for example, "find all documents where *communications* or *networks* appear in the same paragraph or regularly within a certain number of words of *highway* and *data*." The variety of techniques that exploit word occurrence is complemented by synonym dictionaries that provide words with meaning similar to the meaning of your search terms. More advanced approaches use special concepts consisting of a weighted constellation of search terms.

There are three techniques that are offering more effective document representation than the inverted indices of systems from the library tradition. Managers can evaluate products based on the presence of these techniques. They are fuzzy search, dictionary augmentation, and multidimensional spaces. Although they sound far out, these techniques can be thought of in straightforward terms.

Fuzzy searches analyze the document text for patterns in words, characters, and bits. Inquiries can be done by providing a sample of text, a document, or even an image. The documents retrieved will have similar patterns to the inquiry. One leading vendor, Excalibur, uses a fuzzy search technique that can search images by comparing the patterns of the bits.

Dictionary augmentation extends the user's terms to include dictionary definitions such as those in "Webster's." Inquires can be extended to include words and phrases that define the search terms. More important, users can be questioned during inquiry formulation about the meaning of their terms—"there are three definitions of your term, please select the best one." Conquest Software (Baltimore, Maryland) provides almost a million definitions or "concepts," exploiting the valuable work of lexicographers, not just programmers.

Multidimensional spaces show the most promise because they treat similarities in meaning like proximity in distance. The use of distance is easy to imagine in three dimensions, where your inquiry is positioned in the same part of a room as the documents that are similar. The user can vary the distance to include more or fewer things that are near each other, thus controlling the number of documents retrieved. The real power of multidimensional spaces comes from hundreds of dimensions (mathematically possible). HNC (San Diego, California) uses a 300-dimension space, which enables users to find documents with terms that are *similar* (close in the space) without using similar search terms. For example, HNC's MatchPlus can find "car" when "automobile" is used; or it can distinguish between "star in the sky" and "movie star" when the term star is used in an inquiry.

Multidimensional spaces have been under study for at least 25 years, and recently have received funding from the U.S. Defense Department (DARPA) through the Tipster program. The funding was spawned by a recognition that Boolean combinations of search terms were simply the perpetuation of inadequacy. Multidimensional spaces combined with traditional technology hold the most promise for finding digital documents.

5.4.4 Management Pointers

Management can take an informed position regarding finding documents in a variety of applications. There are some clear pointers that have been briefly introduced here:

☞ The growing mass of digital documents is becoming a business resource that is being leveraged by successful companies.

☞ Document retrieval technology is being implemented to exploit the mission-critical, collaborative documents of companies, not just the libraries of technical publications.

☞ Numerous applications have been implemented by companies who are serious about the competitive value of information often unavailable in ponderous paper files.

☞ Managing documents has meant filing them laboriously, while text retrieval ensures finding them if you have the right retrieval solution.

☞ Choosing a system that will find the documents wanted and not those unwanted has been a long-term challenge, finally being met by new document representation techniques.

At long last, finding documents will not be a matter of semantic roulette, but a navigation through a multi-user information space that enables the digital document to create the collaborative linkages vital to organizational effectiveness.

5.5 SUMMARY AND CONCLUSION

This chapter has addressed the collaborative imperative for document management systems. It represents a discussion of DMS as a medium of collaboration that is possible when interlinked systems are available and used on a par with other communication media such as phone, meetings, and email, as illustrated in Figure 5.3. The issues are summarized as recommendations to:

☞ Make document management technology more a part of day-to-day work than a repository/library mind-set permits

Traditional Relationships Among People and Document Bases (DMSs)

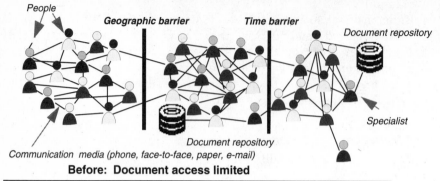

Before: Document access limited

After: Anybody's documents accessible from anywhere

DMSs as an Underlying Collaboration Medium

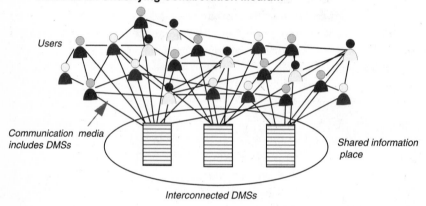

Fig. 5.3 The Collaborative Use of Document Management Systems

☞ Represent relationships among pieces of information and the people who create them

☞ Manage views of information not just the stored form and content

☞ Support the collaborative purpose of documents

☞ Adopt the specifications developed by document standards coalitions

☞ Use text retrieval technology that exploits the latest understanding of the nature of language and of pattern recognition

5.5.1 Related Technologies

Image management and workflow are related areas which will be discussed elsewhere. Images are basically one of several data types that can be part of a compound document. Although extensive software and hardware systems have been developed to manage images, including storage in optical file systems and techniques to transfer them over networks for reasonably fast display, images should not be an end in themselves. Perhaps for high-volume transaction processing (e.g., bank checks), processing images becomes the center of interest. But in the context of documents, images may be incorporated through the use of technology that is rapidly becoming a commodity.

5.5.2 Conclusion

We have discussed document management as if it were an isolated technology—a place to put shared information. DMSs in actuality are an integral part of networked operating systems, different only in the specialized functionality we have discussed. It is probable that DMSs will eventually become extensions to operating systems, building on the distributed file systems already in place.

We have also taken the contemporary perspective of the document as something that is static, to be stored and retrieved. Documents should be part of business processes and flow through organizations, serving as tokens of collaborative action. Documents are also ever-changing containers, not the end result of a publishing effort. The discussion of hyperlinks emphasized this point. However, the workflow and document management vendors are just beginning to come together, each starting to embrace the other's treatment of "documents" or "workflow."

The final word must emphasize that documents as an *end* will disappear and be replaced by documents as a *means* to the communication and collaboration that is the modern organization. Documents will evolve to denote a collection of relevant multimedia objects of information, created on the fly to suit the ever-increasing demand to capture, define, organize, and, above all, share what we know.

5.6 APPENDIX

MEMBERS OF THE SHAMROCK ADVISORY COUNCIL
as of: 11/14/94
Adobe Systems, Incorporated
Aetna Life & Casualty
Andersen Consulting
Arizona Public Service Company
The Coca-Cola Company
Dataware Technologies, Inc.
Documentum, Inc.
EDS Corporation
Frame Technology
Hewlett-Packard Company
IBM Corporation (Co-Chair)

Information Dimensions, Inc.
Interleaf
Merck & Company
Microsoft Corporation
Mobius Management Systems, Inc.
Moore Advanced Services
Open Vision Technologies
PC DOCS, Inc.
Recognition International, Inc.
Saros Corporation (Co-Chair)
Sybase, Inc.
Vantage Technologies, Inc.
Verity, Inc.
ViewStar Corporation
Wang Laboratories
X-Soft Division of Xerox

BIOGRAPHY

James H. Bair is Research Director with The Gartner Group Company and founder of Cooperative Systems Consulting, which designs business processes for workflow and groupware systems. He is a widely recognized contributor to the computing field with over twenty-five years as a consultant, senior manager, and researcher.

Mr. Bair was recognized as an industry pioneer while a senior scientist at Stanford Research Institute (SRI) in the 1970s. He participated on the team that invented the mouse, windows, and groupware. He became the leader of the Office Automation Consulting Program at SRI, consulting to large organizations. He has authored dozens of publications, including the book *The Office of the Future: Computers and Communications*. He was sponsored as an international lecturer for NATO and on a world lecture tour by the United Nations.

In the early 1980s, Bair was manager of Information Systems Research at Bell-Northern Research where he founded a department which combined consulting with research. He chaired the International Conference on Emerging office Systems at Stanford University and cochaired the National Office Automation Conference in San Francisco, which drew over 25,000 attendees. He has been an invited speaker and session chairman at over a hundred industry conferences, ranging from InfoWorld to the National Computer Conference. Additionally, he has chaired and participated in several private conferences, whose sponsors include Hughes, Syntex Corporation, Citicorp, AGIP Oil Company, The Gartner Group, and IDC.

In 1984, Bair became Manager of Advanced Functions for Information Systems at Hewlett-Packard, where he worked with customers to meet their computing needs and provide direction for HP's office products. By bridging the functions of R&D, marketing, sales, and research, he was able to help move HP into new areas such as groupware, image processing, and object-oriented systems. In 1989, Bair was recruited by Xerox as manager of Advanced Solutions for Integrated Systems, to design and launch new information retrieval and document and image management systems.

Bair has also been on the editorial boards for scientific journals, been vice chairman of research conferences, and continues to publish, including two more books. He continues to chair conferences and lectures at the premier universities and companies in the United States and abroad. In 1992 he was the technical lead for the SRI multiclient study *Collaborative Technology Environments* for IBM, DEC, Microsoft, NCR, NTT, Fujitsu, and others, and consulted to the Electric Power Research Institute (EPRI).

Introduction to Chapter 6

This chapter is all about meetings between people. Even though it is a chapter written by an electronic meetings systems (EMS) software vendor, Ventana Systems, the chapter is based on academic research and therefore provides a wide perspective on electronic meetings systems as well as just some rules of thumb on what makes a good meeting. Ventana's chapter encompasses the technology and lessons that Ventana has learned during its more-than-10-year history.

This chapter does a great job of defining EMS, while providing some history of the development of such systems (especially Ventana's). Most EMS meetings have between 10–40 people, but some EMS vendors are starting to use EMS for larger group meetings. Whether this is a new market for EMS systems or an experiment remains to be seen. These systems are being used successfully by groups of any size when the meeting requires consensus or buy-in of a large number of people. It is frequently used for a new initiative like re-engineering, where the feedback and agreement of large numbers of people are fundamental to the success of the process.

Another avenue for electronic meetings is in locations such as Headquarters Company or other executive office suites. Currently, Marriott, other hotel chains, and a variety of consulting firms have EMS facilities for rent. Some of the consulting firms that require you to use their facilitators (which is a good idea anyway) have portable EMS systems. But firms that rent executive office space could provide rooms set up for EMS, with a list of facilitators and technographers who are familiar with the software used in the rooms.

As problems become more complex and meetings more necessary and longer, business will look for ways to get more out of these interactions at a lower cost. As the technologies that support desktop video conferencing drop in price (and they are dropping, very rapidly), more and more people will have this option available to them, and multipoint conferencing should be a reality before the end of the decade.

Although EMS is not a technology covered in great detail in this volume, it will be significant in two or three years as the cost of the software continues to decline (currently at about $200/node, it should be under $100 by 1998). Hardware is around the $1000 range (it should be under $500 by 1998). The current infrastructure bottleneck is ISDN (i.e., the bandwidth of the phone line between computers). As more and more of the U.S. gets wired to ISDN, and the price of ISDN drops, SOHO (Small Office, Home Office) businesses will start to use this technology. Larger businesses already wired for ATM already have video conferencing rooms and will undoubtedly move this function to the desktop as soon as the price drops.

The other significant factor affecting the adoption of meeting technologies is cultural. People are not used to having meetings from their desktop or from a videoconference room, and it is not part of the culture in most organizations to have meetings this way. People still fly to meetings all the time. One reason is that the bandwidth of information is higher than that for just audio (over the telephone); and if you are in negotiations, you want to pick up every cue you can get. Desktop videoconferencing, as in the Jetsons, is a new cultural phenomenon, and one which will have to be worked into those leading-edge corporate cultures that adopt these technologies. Scheduling programs would have to reflect whether the meeting was in person or by video. Some of these videoconferencing issues are covered in the "Futures" section of this chapter, which deals with geographically distributed groups. Videoconferencing is also covered in greater detail in the description of the "Mirror Project" and "The Future of Group-to-Group Interactions."

This is an excellent chapter for someone who wants to read about EMS; EMS is well defined, its pitfalls are examined (lessons learned), and the direction for EMS is thoroughly discussed. What I particularly like about this chapter is that even though Ventana is a vendor, they do not present a hard sell on their product. Instead, they educate the reader about the field of EMS in general and provide some information about GroupSystems in particular. It is this commitment to education that will contribute to moving product but, more important, move groupware forward into the 21st century.

Electronic Meeting Systems: Ten Years of Lessons Learned

Jay F. Nunamaker, Jr.
Chairman, Ventana Corporation
Center for the Management of Information

Robert O. Briggs
Center for the Management of Information

Daniel D. Mittleman
Center for the Management of Information

> A meeting is a gathering where people speak up, say nothing,
> and then all disagree.
> —Kayser, 1990

A great deal of organizational work gets done by individuals who set their jaws, put their shoulders to the wheel, and bear down. The first generation of computer technology focused on improving the productivity of individuals and automating routine tasks. However, many problems organizations face are not routine. They cannot be solved by the rugged individualist because no one person has all the experience, all the insight, all the information, or all the inspiration to accomplish such a task alone. And so teams form. Teams of people have successfully scaled seemingly insurmountable heights. But teamwork brings its own set of problems. All who have suffered the grinding drudgery of meetings-without-end know how unproductive teamwork can be.

There are many reasons why people meet when they are working together: to share information, to make decisions, to avoid decisions, to socialize, and so on. Many things can go wrong with a meeting (Figure 6.1). Participants may lack focus, or may be focused on hidden agendas. Some people may be afraid to speak up, while others may dominate the discussion. Misunderstandings occur as people use the same words for different ideas and different words for the same ideas. The wrong people may be at the meeting, and the right information may be unavailable. Besides being difficult, meetings are expensive. A meeting between

149

Fig. 6.1 Meetings Are Difficult

several managers or executives may cost upwards of $1000 per hour just in salary costs. The 3M Management Institute reports that in the United States alone, there are more than 11 million formal meetings per day, more than three billion meetings per year, consuming between 30 and 80% of a manager's day. These numbers do not include informal discussions between colleagues in hallways and between offices. One Fortune 50 company reports losses in excess of $75 million per year due to poor meetings.

For all their difficulty, meetings are still essential; for all their expense, they are not likely to go away. Meetings will remain absolutely essential and valuable, as they have been for thousands of years. However, they have not changed until now. Electronic meeting systems are a fundamental breakthrough in communication and the results are real. The way we conduct meetings will change, and the work we do in meetings will change. Indeed, the very concept of the meeting is undergoing radical change.

A new breed of computer technology has emerged that targets the trouble spots for team productivity. It is known by many names: groupware, group support systems (GSS), and computer supported cooperative work (CSCW), to name but a few. Groupware is any technology specifically used to make groups more productive. Table 6.1 lists a number of technologies that fall under the groupware umbrella. Sometimes people become familiar with one or two of these technologies, and presume they represent the whole of the field. However, groupware is a very diverse collection of tools. Besides supporting information access, groupware can radically change the dynamics of group interactions by improving communication, by structuring and focusing problem-solving efforts, and by establishing and maintaining an alignment between personal and group goals.

Organizations are now using groupware to leverage their existing information infrastructures in ways that have clearly improved overall productivity. This chapter begins by presenting the Arizona Groupware Grid, a useful model for analyzing and comparing groupware technologies. It then summarizes the lessons learned during a decade of developing, testing, and using electronic meeting

Table 6.1 The Many Definitions of Groupware[a]

Groupware is...	
Computer Supported Cooperative Work (CSCW)	Team Database
Group Decision Support Systems (GDSS)	E-Mail
Group Support Systems (GSS)	Project Management
Coordination Software	Group Conferencing
Group Memory	Video Teleconferencing
Information Filtering	Electronic Brainstorming
Electronic Conferencing	Shared Drawing
Groupware	Electronic Meeting Systems
Group Scheduling	Workflow Automation
Team Calendar	Electronic Voting
Group Development Tools	Shared Editing

[a]Groupware is any technology specifically used to make groups more productive. This table lists many technologies that fall under the groupware umbrella.

systems (EMSs). Before discussing electronic meeting systems in detail, it will be useful to clarify their place within the wider domain of groupware, and to explain the diversity of contributions groupware can make in an organization.

6.1 THE ARIZONA GROUPWARE GRID

Why are teams more productive in one environment than another? How can technology make teams more productive? How can one evaluate the potential contributions of very different groupware packages? In this section we present the Arizona Groupware Grid, a model for addressing these and other questions about groupware. The Groupware Grid has two axes. The vertical axis of the grid represents three different levels of group work. The horizontal axis represents three processes for group productivity. The cells of the grid permit one to classify and evaluate the contributions a given technology may make to group productivity.

6.1.1 Three Levels of Group Work

Group work occurs at three different levels (Figure 6.2), and different technology will support the group at each of these levels. Sometimes, like sprinters on a track team, people exert individual effort towards a group goal, but there is no coordination between individual efforts. Team productivity is simply the sum

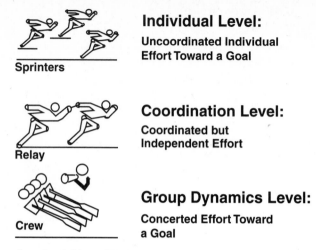

Individual Level:

Uncoordinated Individual Effort Toward a Goal

Coordination Level:

Coordinated but Independent Effort

Group Dynamics Level:

Concerted Effort Toward a Goal

Fig. 6.2 Three Levels of Group Work

appears at the Individual Level, the first, most basic level of the Groupware Grid. Word processing, spreadsheets, file managers, and presentation graphics packages are all examples of technology at the Individual Level. However, making individuals more productive may or may not make the group more productive. If individual efforts are not coordinated, group members may unknowingly be working at cross-purposes.

Like runners in a relay race, some groups coordinate individual efforts, handing off tasks and deliverables to one another and sharing critical resources to accomplish group goals. Technology to improve coordination among individual efforts falls into the Coordination Level, the middle level on the Groupware Grid. At this level, one finds tools like team schedulers, project management, team databases, and workflow automation, to name but a few examples.

Sometimes, like members of a rowing crew, group members make a concerted effort, rather than working as coordinated but independent individuals. As anyone who has been to a meeting can report, such collaborative group work introduces a whole new set of opportunities and challenges that only arise because people are working in concert. Just as a rowing crew has a bos'n, teams working in concert often make use of a facilitator, a specialist who attends to the efficiency and effectiveness of group processes. Technology that makes groups more productive as they work in concert appears at the Group Dynamics level on the Groupware Grid. Electronic meeting tools like shared whiteboards, electronic brainstorming, shared editors, and electronic voting are examples of technology at the group dynamics level.

6.1.2 Three Productivity Processes

The horizontal axis of the Groupware grid derives from the Focus Theory of group productivity [Briggs, 1994], which asserts that regardless of the goal, group members accomplish their tasks by exchanging and thinking about information. There are therefore three processes in which group members must engage to become productive: communication, thought, and information access. However, group members cannot pay attention to everything, and each of these processes demands attention. Any attention devoted to one process is not available for the other two processes. Technology can make groups more productive by reducing the attention costs of engaging in communication, thought, or information access [Briggs, 1994].

The communication process involves choosing a set of words, behaviors, and images and presenting them through a medium to convey information to other team members. The medium could be paper, telephone, video conference, computer, and so on. Sometimes groups are less productive than they might otherwise be because their communication is so constrained, so demanding of attention, that people do not have time to think about what they are hearing. If technology can improve communication, it may make the group more productive.

The thought process involves the forming of intentions toward accomplishing the goal (Figure 6.3). It begins when group members try to make sense of the conditions in which they find themselves. If they decide conditions are unsatisfactory, they form mental models of the problem, trying to identify its causes. They begin to formulate alternative courses of action, and they evaluate their alternatives in light of their desired outcomes. They select a course of action, make a plan, and then act. They then try to make sense of the results of their actions, which may, in turn, lead to the discovery of a new problem, and so the process repeats. Sometimes groups are less productive than they might be otherwise because their thinking processes are unstructured or unfocused. For instance, they may begin to evaluate alternatives before making sense of the problem. They may choose a course of action before considering other alternatives. Or they may act on a solution before planning its implementation. If technology can focus and improve thinking processes, it may make the group more productive.

The information access process involves finding the information the group members need to support their thinking or arguments. Information is knowledge that increases the expected value of choosing one course of action over another. It has value to the extent that it is available when a choice must be made, accurate, and complete. However, the value information derives by being timely, accurate, and complete is offset by the cost of acquiring it, storing it, processing it, and retrieving it. Because people cannot pay attention to everything, the cost of accessing information can become so high that participants are prevented from thinking and communicating. If technology can reduce the attention costs of acquiring, storing, processing, and retrieving information, it may make the group more productive.

The Arizona Groupware Grid crosses the three productivity processes with the three levels of technology support for group work, giving a nine-celled grid (Figure 6.4). One can map the contributions of a single tool or an entire environment into the cells of the grid. A given technology will probably provide support in more than one cell of the Grid.

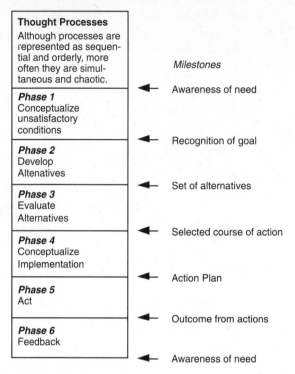

Thought Processes
Although processes are represented as sequential and orderly, more often they are simultaneous and chaotic.

Phase 1
Conceptualize unsatisfactory conditions

Phase 2
Develop Altenatives

Phase 3
Evaluate Alternatives

Phase 4
Conceptualize Implementation

Phase 5
Act

Phase 6
Feedback

Milestones

◄— Awareness of need

◄— Recognition of goal

◄— Set of alternatives

◄— Selected course of action

◄— Action Plan

◄— Outcome from actions

◄— Awareness of need

Fig. 6.3 Structured Thought Processes

Classification of benefits from group support technologies. Each cell contains examples of the kind of support available for a particular process at a particular level of work.

| | Productivity Processes | | |
	Communication	**Thought**	**Info Access**
Group Dynamics Level	Anonymity Parallel Contribution	Structured and Focused Processes	Session Transcripts, Automatic Concept Classification
Coordination Level	Asynchronous Communication	Team Scheduling Automated Workflow Project Management	Shared Data Stores
Individual Level	Preparing Stimuli	Modeling Simulation	Info Filtering Local Data Stores

One can compare the potential for productivity of different environments by comparing their respective grids. For instance, an electronic meeting system offers a great deal of support for communication, thought, and information access at the Group Dynamics level, but little support for the Coordination Level.

A team database like Lotus Notes offers little support at the Group Dynamics level but offers strong support for communication and information access at the Coordination Level. A team database offers little support for thought processes at the Coordination Level, but a workflow automation system offers strong support for thought at that level. An electronically supported work environment that included electronic meeting systems, workflow automation, and a team database would support communication, thought, and information processes at the Group Dynamics and Coordination Levels.

6.2 WHAT IS AN ELECTRONIC MEETING SYSTEM?

Electronic meeting systems (EMSs) sit firmly astride the Group Dynamics level of the Groupware Grid, improving productivity by reducing the attention costs for the communication, thought, and information access processes for groups engaged in concerted work. An electronic meeting system is typically based on a network of personal computers, usually one for each participant. Participants use the technology to support both distributed and face-to-face work. Distributed work occurs when participants are geographically or temporally separated. Face-to-face EMS work often takes place in a specially equipped facility (Figures 6.5 and 6.6). EMS facilities often have one or more large public display screens (systems for geographically distributed participants often have software that substitutes for the public screen) [Nunamaker *et al.*, 1991].

EMS technology had its beginnings in the first computer-aided software engineering (CASE) project in the middle 1960s [Teichroew and Hershey, 1982].

Fig. 6.5 A Portable Electronic Meeting System.

Fig. 6.6 The First EMS Installation at the University of Arizona, c. 1985.

Developers of large information systems found it excruciatingly difficult to capture user requirements for a new computer system. Users found it nearly impossible to express what they needed the system to be until they saw it running. Only then would developers discover that key users had different, often mutually exclusive expectations. In the PSL/PSA project researchers created a structured methodology and an unambiguous structured language for people to use to record their needs. Requirements expressed in this special language could be run through an analyzer program to check for completeness and correctness. Technically, the project was a success. Requirements could indeed be captured and checked. However, the users refused to write their requirements in the structured language. It just appeared to be too complex and too demanding for the inexperienced person to use successfully. Furthermore, it did not incorporate a means to allow users with differing points of view to negotiate their differences.

The Teichroew project, which won the Warnier Prize in Computer Science as the first instance of CASE technology, was the jumping-off point for the early work in EMS by Jay F. Nunamaker, Jr. and his team. They conceived of the first electronic meeting systems in the late 1970s so that analysts could capture natural-language discussions of systems requirements from many users simultaneously, so that all points of view could be considered, and users could negotiate their differences before information systems were built. The first prototype, called Plexsys, came on-line in the early 1980s, and was surprisingly successful (Figure 6.6). Users could say what they needed to say, build on one another's ideas, and quickly identify areas of disagreement that needed discussion, and they could do so with less than half the labor costs. Using Plexsys, the elapsed time needed for the requirements definition process could be reduced by as much as 90%, and the final requirements definitions were more complete and correct than anything that had been possible with traditional methods. Furthermore, it became clear early on that Plexsys was not only useful for requirements definition; it was useful for any group of people expending cognitive effort to achieve a goal. Because of this, Plexsys began to evolve an identity distinct from CASE. Initially, Plexsys researchers at Arizona made a conscious decision to focus on improving the dynamics of face-to-face meetings because the difficulties of that environment were well understood. Once researchers had a grip on the face-to-face environment, they began to explore issues of distributed meetings.

In the mid-1980s, the University of Minnesota also developed an electronic meeting system called SAMM. It was a UNIX-based system on a hardware platform of NCR towers accessed by five dumb terminals. Minnesota researchers used their system in early efforts to develop a theoretical basis for explaining the successful use of electronic meeting systems [DeSanctis and Gallupe, 1987]. The University of Michigan also created several EMS tools on a Macintosh platform, and conducted some of the early research into room and furniture designs for EMS environments.

The late 1980s saw the birth of the commercial EMS market. In 1989, the University of Arizona chartered Ventana Corporation to transfer Plexsys technology to industry and government. Ventana's flagship product, which was derived from Plexsys, is called GroupSystems. University of Arizona researchers in turn used GroupSystems for extensive field and laboratory studies. About this time, the University of Minnesota researchers also turned their SAMM system into a commercial product, but discontinued active GSS development at the university. Also in the late 1980s, the founder of Execucom Corporation created VisionQuest, the first EMS to be developed from the start as a commercial venture. At present, the commercial market includes perhaps half a dozen vendors of electronic meeting systems.

The lessons presented in this paper by and large derive from the experience of taking GroupSystems out of the laboratory and into the field. (It has been installed at over 400 sites to date, including over 120 research university sites. Several dozens of research papers have been published, reporting both experimental and field research.) However, the lessons presented here apply to electronic meeting systems in general. Researchers have learned a great deal about electronic support for team work: what features and functions are important, how to wield the tools effectively, and what kinds of results are possible.

6.2.1 Communication Support in an EMS

To understand the potential communication benefits of an EMS, imagine a meeting where dozens of people came together to work on a pressing and perhaps politically sensitive problem. Imagine that after the meeting leader explained the problem, on a pre-arranged signal, everyone started talking at once. Imagine further that in the cacophony everybody heard, understood, and remembered everything that was said by all the other participants. Imagine that all ideas were considered strictly on their merits, regardless of who offered them, and that as everybody gave honest and open opinions, nobody's feelings got hurt and nobody felt pressured or threatened by either peers or their boss. Clearly, this scenario would be impossible under normal circumstances, but an electronic meeting system can provide the communication support that makes it possible.

As the number of people in a conventional meeting increases, people spend more and more time waiting for a turn to speak. With little or no hope of getting the floor, some people withdraw, letting a few personalities dominate the discussion while good ideas go unspoken [Diehl and Stroebe, 1987]. In an electronic meeting the opportunity to express an idea is never lost; everyone can "talk at once" by typing into his or her computer. The system makes all contributions available to the other participants almost immediately. This means that people do not lose track of their own ideas while listening to someone else, nor of what others are saying while trying to remember what they want to say when they get the floor. All contributions become part of an electronic transcript. Strong (or loud) personalities find it difficult to dominate a meeting or sidetrack it into unproductive or irrelevant issues. All participants have an equal opportunity to contribute. Because their input can be anonymous, people can float unconventional or unpopular ideas without political risk.

Electronic meeting systems can dramatically increase the number of people who can participate in a meeting. A great many studies have shown that when a traditional meeting includes more than five or six people, the productivity drops. Each subsequent addition to the group further reduces productivity. Electronic meeting systems permit dozens of people to work together effectively. Studies of groups using EMS have measured increases in productivity for groups as small as three, with increasing productivity for groups as large as sixty. Although an EMS-supported meeting typically has somewhere between 10 and 40 people, practitioners in the field report having run successful electronically supported meetings for groups of more than 200. For example, former president Jimmy Carter used an EMS to run several meetings of nearly 300 people from all walks

Fig. 6.7 The Multimedia Collaboration Center. An Advanced EMS research laboratory at the University of Arizona, it accommodates 29 users.

of life in Atlanta, Georgia. The group developed a set of ideas for improving economic conditions in Atlanta.

Because an EMS permits large groups to work more effectively than small groups, all the key players can participate in the same discussion instead of developing their understanding of the issues through a fragmented series of small meetings. The large group can quickly evolve a shared vision which accommodates the needs of a broad set of stakeholders. When all interest groups are represented, the group also has access to much more information. A meeting need not be interrupted or postponed until information or approval can be obtained from someone who is not present.

Large electronic groups also experience more instances of idea triggering. One person may say something that sparks an entirely new thought in someone else, a thought that might otherwise never have occurred. Furthermore, studies have shown that the quality of ideas generated is directly related to the number of ideas generated. Large groups supported by electronic meeting systems have been shown to generate more ideas of higher quality than groups of any size that do not use electronic meeting support.

6.2.2 EMS Support for Thought Processes

An EMS is not a single piece of software, but rather a collection of computer-based tools, each of which can structure and focus the thinking of team members in some unique way. For example, an electronic brainstorming tool encourages a group to diverge from standard patterns of thinking to generate as many unique ideas as possible. All users type their ideas into the system simultaneously. The system randomly passes ideas from one person to the next. The participants can argue with or expand on the ideas they see, or can be inspired to a completely different line of thought. An idea organizer, on the other hand, encourages a group to converge quickly on key issues and explore them in depth. Electronic voting tools can uncover patterns of consensus, and focus group discussion on patterns of disagreement.

Every phase of the thinking process requires information gathering, idea generation, idea organization, and idea evaluation. These activities are often accompanied by idea exploration and exposition. The GroupSystems toolkit focuses participant efforts on the activities appropriate to the task at hand (Figure 6.8). Table 6.2 describes some of the most commonly used tools in the toolkit. It is a suite of tools to support the fundamental thinking activities of the problem-solving process.

A group can use any of several tools to support a given activity, depending on how they wish to structure the group dynamics. Moreover, each EMS tool can be used in multiple ways to achieve different group dynamics effects. For example, Idea Organizer can be used to generate a list of ideas that will later be evaluated with the Electronic Voting tool. But Idea Organizer can also be used to cull key concepts from a previous Electronic Brainstorming session and support parallel discussion of those key concepts.

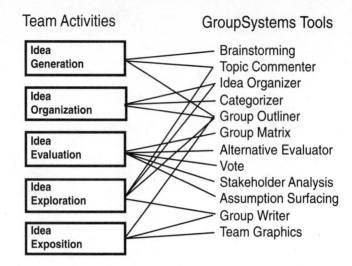

Team Activities   GroupSystems Tools

Fig. 6.8 Group Systems Support for Thought Process

Table **6.2** Summary of the GroupSystems Tool Set

Electronic Brainstorming allows rapid generation of a free flow of ideas.

Topic Commenter permits people to generate ideas and assign them to "file folders" or topics.

Idea Organizer gives structured methods for generating, synthesizing, and categorizing ideas.

Group Outliner allows a group to explore issues and develop action plans using a tree or outline structure.

Group Matrix supports analysis of interrelationships between information sets.

Alternative Evaluation compares a set of alternatives against a set of group-developed criteria.

Vote helps evaluate ideas, measure consensus, and make choices using seven voting methods.

Stakeholder Identification helps the group to analyze the impact of actions or policies on identified stakeholders and on fundamental assumptions.

Group Writer supports collaborative preparation of a single document.

Policy Formation facilitates the process of developing consensus statements and action plans.

Questionnaire allows the group to respond to a questionnaire.

Group Dictionary allows the group to develop common definitions for critical concepts.

Briefcase provides a set of personal productivity tools, including Calendar, File Reader, Notepad, Calculator, Clipboard, and Quick Vote.

An electronic meeting system is more than just software for electronic brainstorming and voting. An EMS includes not only the software, but also the processes and methods, to accompany the use of the tools as well as the environment in which the tools are used. Handled with skill, an EMS can enhance group productivity dramatically. EMS is a new paradigm for collaborative work. The experience of doing business with an EMS is so different from conventional group work that many people have difficulty understanding why they would ever want to use it until they have experienced it personally. Having tried it, many people feel thwarted if they have to return to conventional group work methods.

6.2.3 EMS Support for Information Access

An electronic meeting system can support the information access process in several ways. First, many group support tools include modules that permit users to define key words and phrases, which the system will then use to scan and filter external information sources. Such tools can significantly reduce information overload.

Second, an EMS permits much larger meetings to be conducted productively, which means that a much larger information base is actually present in the minds of the meeting participants. In many cases, this appears to be an important key to increasing productivity.

Third, electronically supported interactions result in electronic transcripts. These transcripts themselves become a valuable information resource for the organization. For example, one aeronautical manufacturer had been using an EMS for nearly two years when a manager faced a particularly intractable problem with a vendor. He asked that the meeting transcripts be searched to find out how many times in the previous two years a particular problem had been mentioned along with the name of that vendor. There had never been a meeting about that particular problem, nor had there been a meeting about the vendor. However, the transcripts showed 19 different instances where the vendor and the problem were linked. Armed with that information, the manager was able to gain major concessions from the vendor and correct a problem that had been plaguing the production line for years.

6.2.4 EMS Support for Alignment of Goals

People always bring personal goals into a team effort. The team can only be productive to the degree that the goals of the team are congruent with the goals of the individuals on the team. Over the long term, people will not work against their perceived self-interest. There are a number of features and functions in an electronic meeting system that encourage the alignment of group and individual goals. Some tools permit anonymous input, which encourages people to speak up immediately if they perceive their ox is about to be gored. Because larger numbers of people can work together effectively, the whole group can learn about individual constraints early in the process, rather than having concerns fester under the surface, only to bring a project down after the investment of much time and expense. Some EMS tools specifically ask team members to identify the stakeholders in a project and to explicitly state their assumptions about each of them. This activity often surfaces misconceptions and unrealistic expectations, permitting a re-alignment of group and individual goals.

6.3 LESSONS FROM THE FIELD

Perhaps the best place to begin a discussion of lessons learned is with the bottom-line results from EMS use, because without the bottom-line benefits the other lessons are of little interest.

6.3.1 The Bottom-Line Benefits of Face-to-Face EMS Meetings

Most of the early EMS work focused on improving the productivity of face-to-face collaboration because the dynamics of traditional group work were already well understood, and the problems were only too clear. The first field trials of EMS took place at the Owego, New York plant of IBM Corporation in 1986 [Vogel *et al.*, 1990]. In a year-long study, 30 groups used GroupSystems to solve problems in production-line quality. Teams using the technology saved an average of 50% in labor costs over conventional methods. They also reduced the elapsed time from the beginning to the end of their projects by an average of 91%. The results were so dramatic that they were suspected of being anomalous, a fluke of the circumstances surrounding the study, so a second year-long study was conducted at six other IBM sites, each with a different set of business problems. In the second study, which tracked more than 50 groups, average labor costs were reduced by 55% and elapsed times for projects of all types were reduced an average of 90% [Grohowski *et al.*, 1990]. IBM now has more than 90 electronic meeting rooms, and the number continues to grow (see Table 6.3).

In 1991, Boeing Corporation ran an independent study to determine whether there was a good business case for the use of electronic meeting systems. Over the course of a year they carefully tracked the results of 64 groups that were using the technology to define requirements for the shop floor for the soon-to-be-built 777 aircraft. The groups used EMS for problem definition, alternative generation and evaluation, implementation planning, and documentation of group outcomes. The result was an average labor saving of 71% and an average reduction of elapsed times for projects of 91%. A conservative evaluation of

Table 6.3 Key Lessons About Bottom Line Benefits

Savings from shorter project elapsed times of 90%.
Savings from reducing labor costs by 50–70%.
Savings from improved decision quality.
Savings from improved buy-in to the decision.

the return on investment for the pilot project was 170% the first year [Post, 1992].

Besides finding quantitative benefits, the IBM and Boeing studies documented improvements in the quality of results and the satisfaction levels of the participants. Since these studies, other organizations have conducted independent evaluations of the benefits of electronic meeting systems. The U.S. Army reported a total savings of $1 million in eight one-week sessions to design a new Army-wide personnel tracking system. Bellcore found a 66% reduction in labor costs for teams using the technology. The Army National Guard saved over 70% in labor costs and 90% in project elapsed time over three information systems documentation writing projects.

While the Boeing case illustrates a financial success using electronic meeting systems, it also illustrates some of the difficulties associated with implementing new technologies in an organization. By the end of the pilot project, Boeing had documented seven-figure bottom-line benefits. Estimates of the ROI for the project rose to more than 600% during the second year. Nobody disputed the results, and yet at the end of the second year the project was terminated, and it was nearly three years before another group at Boeing tried an EMS. Several political problems developed around the use of EMS. First, the people involved decided to use the tools in a way that significantly changed the balance of power within the groups. Throughout the history of the company, the senior engineers had absolute authority and autonomy when designing aircraft facilities. The decision was made to include many other stakeholders in the design process. The new approach brought input from many directions. The senior engineers were not ready to accept the substantial cultural shift represented by the inclusive design approach. Second, the people who introduced EMS to the company were not part of the engineering team; they were a group of internal Boeing business consultants. Some members of the engineering group regarded the consultants as interfering outsiders, even though they were Boeing employees. Finally, Boeing's corporate structure changed near the end of the project. The internal consultants were re-assigned from their centralized group to a number of locations in the field. Thus, no center of competence remained to support the fledgling EMS project, and so it was canceled.

An important lesson learned during the Boeing case is that powerful stakeholders must participate in the planning for early EMS sessions. Busy, powerful people are tempted to delegate EMS planning to others, but choices that appear arbitrary to others may turn out to be critically negative to the stakeholders. An EMS is neutral with respect to power shifts. The tools can be used in ways that reinforce the current structure or in ways that create dramatic power shifts. Sometimes a shift is desirable, but changes in power can cause resistance. These issues must be carefully weighed, or the benefits of the technology to the organization may be lost.

A number of organizations have had difficulties maintaining a center of EMS competence for a very different reason. As people begin to use EMS to make those around them more productive, their value and visibility rise rapidly, and they are often quickly promoted, leaving nobody with the skills to run the electronic meeting system. One solution to the problem is to make sure that there are always several apprentice facilitators in training so that a promotion doesn't strip the company of its EMS expertise. One general in the Marine Corps, however, adopted quite a different strategy. He insisted on being the first person trained with the EMS and ran all the early meetings himself. He reasoned that nobody would be able to claim EMS was too hard to learn. "After all," he quipped, "if the general can do it, anybody can do it." Others in his command soon acquired the skills, and EMS expertise spread throughout his organization. Minor changes in personnel could therefore not disrupt or terminate the use of EMS.

The use of electronic meeting systems may increase the likelihood that participants will buy in to the final results of the group effort. For example, a task force in a large bureaucratic organization tried for over a year to draft a document detailing acceptable field procedures. In that time they were not able to persuade both the field experts and the central administration to accept the same draft of the document, despite a long series of meetings. The team decided to bring the field experts and the administrators to an EMS facility for another try. Using anonymous brainstorming, group writing, and electronic voting tools, the group quickly identified the key issues standing in the way of resolving the disputes. Within three days the group had negotiated their differences and rewritten the bulk of the document. The revised document was accepted and used thereafter by both sides. Because all parties worked simultaneously, a unified shared vision emerged, and key constraints from both sides could be incorporated into the document. Both sides bought into and championed the final draft to the rest of the organization.

The field studies clearly show that substantial benefits, both economic and intangible, accrue from the use of electronic meeting systems. Experience also shows that success depends on both the way the tools are designed and how they are used.

6.3.2 EMS Lessons on Leaders and Leadership Style

Leader characteristics range from democratic to autocratic; situations, from chaotic to static; and organizational cultures, from fragmented to cohesive. The best leaders vary their styles according to situations. An electronic meeting system does not replace leadership, nor enforce a particular leadership style. Rather, it enhances a leader's ability to move a group forward in a given set of circumstances (see Table 6.4).

6.3.2.1 The Democracy Paradox   Organizational problem solving often requires collaboration among cross-functional teams of specialists. These teams, which often comprise experts of equal level, call for democratic leadership to coordinate communication, facilitate the group process, and make sure resources are available. A leader must be sensitive to the subtle cues that indicate whether a team is approaching consensus or spinning its wheels, but it is the team that establishes priorities, sets goals, and decides how best to advance them.

Table 6.4 Key Lessons About Group Leadership

Technology does not replace leadership.

Technology can support any leadership style.

Some people resist EMS: The game has changed; oral/verbal skills and ramming an agenda through a meeting are *not* as important.

Loss of engagement for distributed teams: The lack of visual and nonverbal cues and low accountability appears to reduce the involvement of remote participants.

Change of emotional engagement for face-to-face teams: The technology makes work more exciting for some, more ordinary and mundane for those who feel a loss of power.

There is a need to develop group incentives.

Be willing to accept criticism of you and the organization.

Make sure there is an individual incentive to contribute to the group effort.

As any leader can tell you, however, democratic processes bog down decision making in endless meetings, conflicting proposals, and narrow interests. When crises arise in quick succession, a strong, autocratic leader is often needed to make rapid decisions. A centralized approach is not practical for most ad hoc teams, however, and therein lies the rub.

Electronic meeting systems make it possible to involve more people in arriving at decisions while ensuring that decisions are timely. Larger group size helps to keep the big picture in focus and eliminates a group leader's need to communicate separately with smaller subgroups. Because all subgroups can be represented at an electronic meeting, all perspectives may be heard without jeopardizing the speedy response necessary in a crisis. As the group builds an understanding of problems and tasks, there is less wheel-spinning, more cooperation, less chaos, and more acceptance of decisions.

Traditionally, the larger the team, the slower the democratic decision-making process. More subgoals must be considered, and less time is available for each person to speak. One solution is to break a large group into smaller ones with narrower responsibilities.

Subgroups can operate democratically, but their leaders must still resolve any intergroup problems that arise. It also becomes harder for individuals to see the big picture from the narrow viewpoint of the subgroup. Computerized group support systems increase the practical size of a democratic group from a handful to several dozen. Thirty individuals can share their ideas in the same amount of time that two or three could in a conventional meeting. Furthermore, electronic tools can organize the team's contributions in a form that can be assimilated faster and more easily than can a sequential verbal stream.

It is also possible to use an EMS to permit experts from different geographic locations to participate in a discussion on a few minutes' notice. However, there is still much to be learned about how to manage distributed collaboration successfully. Presently, it is far easier to receive advice from a distance than to complete full projects without ever working face to face.

6.3.2.2 Re-Aligning Leadership with Group Values   EMS technology can help resolve counterproductive conflicts between leadership styles. One man, who considered himself to be very democratic, presided over weekly 2-1/2 hour planning meetings with his staff. For the first hour and a half he would let the staff speak, but then he'd grab a felt marker and move to the whiteboard with the comment, "Let me see if I understand what you're saying." He would then describe his own agenda using words and phrases culled from the group discussion. This vice president's superiors recognized the problem and decided to try using an EMS to alter his autocratic management style. The staff was enthusiastic about the results, but he was not; he could no longer dictate the agenda, and he ultimately decided to stop using the system. The staff, with the support of top management, refused to let him. Group morale rose quickly, and the team prospered under a new, shared vision.

6.3.2.3 Leadership Pitfalls   Failure to make a meeting's objectives explicit can lead to disenchantment, particularly when participants spot phony democracy. If a leader includes a group in the decision-making process after the fact simply to "let them feel ownership," the group process breaks down. Leaders who merely want a team to understand a problem before they propose a solution should say so up front. If the objective is to develop a set of alternatives and recommendations, it should be so defined. Once the team has been commissioned to make a decision, however, a leader can contribute, advise, and argue, but the team will rebel against a leader who overrides its collective judgment.

False promises of anonymity are equally damaging. Any attempt to find out who said what in an anonymous session undermines the leader's credibility and defeats the purpose of anonymous input, which is to solicit risky, unpopular, or opposing viewpoints. It is interesting to note that people often try to guess who said what in an anonymous session. Indeed, they are sometimes quite sure. Experience has shown, however, that such guesses are most often incorrect.

6.3.2.4 Role Clarification   Group support systems can also be used to identify those with a stake in a project and reveal underlying assumptions. When a national library attempted to develop a computer system, it formed a team composed of representatives from different departments such as circulation, cataloging, acquisitions, and computing. For several meetings the groups tried and failed to develop a shared vision of the project. The team leader decided to use an electronic stakeholder and assumption-surfacing tool.

It turned out that the various departments had unrealistic expectations of the computer group, and the computer group had unrealistic expectations about the others. During the next few months, through vigorous and sometimes acrimonious debates, the team arrived at a common understanding and a shared vision. Until the participants engaged in stakeholder analysis, they had not even been aware that fundamental differences existed. The group support system allowed them to share critical information and correct mistaken assumptions, solving an intractable problem and fixing a major oversight in the process.

Any tool is only as good as the artisan who wields it. This is just as true of sophisticated group decision support software as of a screwdriver. To realize these systems' enormous potential to expand the productivity of today's team-oriented organizations, leaders must recognize both tangible and intangible benefits.

The intangibles, which depend heavily on the style and quality of leadership, include greater group cohesiveness, better problem definition, a wider range of higher-quality solutions, and stronger commitment to those solutions. The tangibles, already demonstrated, are dollar savings through greater productivity and reduced staff hours to reach decisions. On the bottom line, more time is free from the demands of frequent—and often frustrating—meetings.

6.3.3 Lessons About EMS Application Software

One of the key constraints on group productivity is that people can only pay attention to a few things at a time, and group work involves many competing demands for attention. Therefore, everything in an EMS must work together to reduce distractions for a group. Over the years, through six generations of GroupSystems development, we have learned a number of lessons about what is important for successful EMS software in terms of structure, use, and interface (Table 6.5).

6.3.3.1 The Values of Modularity
Interface Choices Affect Group Dynamics   It turns out to be very useful to build EMS software into a collection of special-purpose modules rather than use a single module. For example, it is possible to build a single tool that can be used for idea generation, idea organization, idea evaluation (voting), and

Table 6.5 Lessons About EMS Application Software

Interface choices affect group dynamics.

Separate special-purpose modules permit flexible process design.

Templates assist in mapping tools and processes to group tasks.

Group support must integrate with individual desktop application.

Simplify the interface. No more than 30 seconds of instructions. It can never be too easy to use.

The user interface must flow seamlessly from tool to tool.

Data must move from module to module seamlessly.

The system must be robust in terms of stability and data recovery. An obvious point: groupware has many more ways to go wrong, and a higher failure cost, than individual software.

Users must have ready access to external data and past session transcripts.

idea exploration. Subtle differences in user interfaces can make large differences in group dynamics. Therefore, different software tools focus group effort in different ways. For instance, an idea generation tool with a five-line limit per comment submission encourages concise expression of ideas and enables the group to quickly explore a broad range of ideas. On the other hand, an idea generation tool that permits long comments about a few items will encourage in-depth examination of issues. Because interface choices affect group dynamics, and because group dynamics are a critical concern for group productivity, it is useful to build separate interfaces, each to support a particular dynamic.

Simple Interfaces Are Vital   Another reason for building separate modules is that group interfaces must be kept very simple. Group members must talk, listen, think, and remember what has been said. Doing any of these things limits the ability to do the others well. If the computer interface poses an additional distraction, it will hurt rather than help group productivity. By building separate modules for each activity, it is possible to design interfaces that are so obvious the user has no question about what the group is doing and how it is to be done. The screen has no extraneous cues. In the EMS development effort, we attempted to create tools that would permit groups to begin productive work with less than 30 seconds of instructions. Users are often able to begin work with no instructions at all.

6.3.3.2 Process Templates

Because many group problem-solving efforts will involve similarly structured efforts, it is very useful to build an EMS environment that can provide templates for sequences of activities. For example, many groups follow a brainstorm-organize-vote-explore-vote pattern. Another common sequence is generate solutions-generate criterion-evaluate solutions-select a solution. Having a set of standard templates for processes can make it easier for a group to decide what tools to use and what processes to follow. There are two forms a template can take.

First, it can supply a pattern for deciding which tools will be used in what order in conjunction with what group processes. Second, it can design a structure determining which features of a particular tool will be enabled during a given process. Both process-level and tool-level templates permit a leader to quickly adapt the EMS to team goals.

6.3.3.3 Data Portability

When building an EMS in modules, it is also critical that the designer provide a simple and seamless way to move group information from one module to the next. For example, if a group spends time generating a broad set of ideas and then wants to evaluate which ideas are best, it must be easy to move the ideas to the voting module without undue effort. Long or awkward transitions between modules will disrupt the group dynamics and ultimately doom group processes to chaos.

Even when people are working as a group, there are still pieces of the work that will be done by individual members at their own desks. It is therefore desirable to integrate group productivity tools with individual productivity tools wherever possible. It is useful to be able to move information to and from spreadsheets, text editors, databases, and other individual productivity applications.

6.3.3.4 Stability and Robust Recovery   It is an obvious point that all software must be stable and that data must be protected from loss. However, with groupware the attention to robustness must be carried to a near-religious passion. Groupware by its very nature is more prone to failure than standalone software. Hundreds or thousands of events occur simultaneously and randomly in the system, and the system is made up of dozens of computers all acting in concert. Computers fail, networks fail, and people using them fail. An electronic meeting room full of busy and expensive senior executives will not tolerate systems that "hiccup." They will not be understanding when a morning's work disappears in a puff of virtual smoke. In a large group, many person-days can be invested in a few hours of electronic collaboration. When the system goes down, the data must be safe. This means that all contributions should be written to disk almost as soon as they are contributed. Nothing should be maintained solely in volatile memory. Furthermore, data should be stored in more than one location, and the system should back itself up frequently.

6.3.4 Lessons About Group Participation

An electronic meeting system can permit people to make anonymous contributions to group efforts. Putting staff members in a room full of networked workstations where they can express their true feelings may have about as much appeal for a project manager or CEO as joining a weekend encounter group. But the results of adopting the technology turn out to be shorter, more productive meetings and a freer flow of ideas (see Table 6.6).

Table 6.6 Key Lessons for Outstanding Participation

Anonymity will increase the amount of key comments contributed.

The parallel nature of the interaction increases participation. Participants sense they are part of the plan, that they are moving towards consensus and resolution.

Good ideas are a function of the quantity of ideas generated. Adding participants to an EMS meeting almost always improves the outcomes.

When participants anonymously criticize ideas, performance improves. It keeps the group searching for better answers.

Any idea may inspire a completely new idea that would not have otherwise occurred. Develop activities which encourage frequent generation of new ideas.

Provide feedback to groups to let them know how each activity they undertake maps to the entire agenda. Groups stay better focused if they understand how what they are doing ties into the big picture.

In face-to-face groups, peer pressure keeps people moving. Distributed groups tend to lose momentum.

Because ideas enter the system and are circulated without attribution, an EMS frees people to spark ideas off one another or to criticize ideas without fear of rebuke from peers or superiors. It encourages people to participate in meetings without inhibition and reduces the tendency for a few to dominate a meeting. A manager at Hughes Aircraft observed, "People who are usually reluctant to express themselves feel free to take part, and we've been surprised by the number of new ideas generated. We also reach conclusions far more rapidly."

6.3.4.1 Dealing with Criticism When they first hear about anonymous input, some people express concern that the discussion will quickly degenerate into "flaming" sessions where participants launch vitriolic personal invectives laced with four-letter words and slanderous epithets. In tens of thousands of sessions in business and government organizations, however, we have not seen a single such disintegration.

This does not mean, however, that people are not critical in electronic meetings. They are. Participants will often raise issues that would never come out in face-to-face discussions. There is less sting in an anonymous electronic criticism than in a direct rebuke during a face-to-face meeting. The screen buffers the negative emotions that may accompany such criticism. Because nobody knows where a particular idea came from, people criticize the idea rather than the person who presented it. However, we have seen egos get bruised and people having difficulty dealing with honest feedback.

For instance, after the feedback on a reorganization plan in a traditional meeting (without an EMS), the president of one high-tech company was told that there were problems with the plan but that the staff could handle them. In an EMS meeting, however, he found out what his management team really thought. During the discussion, his staff responded both verbally, as in conventional meetings, and anonymously, by entering comments into their workstations. Everyone started typing at once. A list of ideas scrolled down the large overhead screen behind the podium. Rapid-fire key clicks were an indicator of the energy that the meeting generated. People suggested options and argued over alternatives, inspiring one another to think in new and sometimes unexpected ways. But it was through the EMS that negative comments emerged: "The new plan doesn't stand a chance. It addresses the wrong issues entirely." "Once we've spent all the money to do this, the real problems will still exist, only worse." "We're way off-center with this one." After 40 minutes, the president was baffled. "We've been working on this plan for a year. Why didn't you people tell me this before? What do you think we should do now?"

Anonymity may also encourage group members to view their ideas more objectively and to see criticism as a signal to suggest other ideas. "I wasn't as uncomfortable when I saw someone being critical of someone else's idea, because I thought, 'Nobody's being embarrassed here at all,'" says Sam Eichenfield, president and CEO of Greyhound Financial.

"I noticed that if someone criticized an idea of mine, I didn't get emotional about it," says the Hughes Aircraft manager. "I guess when you are face to face and everyone hears the boss say, `You are wrong,' it's a slap to you, not necessarily to the idea."

Despite the safe haven it provides for most participants, EMS isn't always so comfortable for the leader of a project or enterprise. Sometimes it takes courage for a manager to deal with the issues that surface in an anonymous meeting. It's hard to learn to deal with unpleasant input, but if problems lie buried for too long, they may become intractable.

In a rare incident, the founder of a very successful medical technology firm called together key personnel from multiple levels in the organization for an EMS session. Thirty minutes into the meeting he turned red in the face and stood up. Pounding a fist on his PC for emphasis, he shouted, "I want to know who put in the comment on the problem with the interface for the new system. We're not leaving this room until I know who made that statement!" He glared around the room waiting for a response. Everyone greeted his outburst with silence.

After a week's reflection he returned sheepishly to the group and said, "I had no idea there was trouble. I guess I'm more out of touch than I ought to be. Let's try again."

6.3.4.2 Diminishing Dysfunctional Politics Anonymity helps to separate ideas from the politics behind them. Ideas can be weighed on their merits rather than on their sources. Each member of a team tends to view problems from his or her own perspective, often to the detriment of the project or enterprise. For example, in traditional meetings engineers see engineering solutions, salespeople see marketing solutions, and production people see manufacturing solutions. In discussion and exchange of ideas anonymously from many different viewpoints, the big picture is more likely to emerge. EMS groups often achieve a unified, shared vision of problems and solutions—something that's difficult with traditional meeting methods.

Another striking example of the use of EMS to overcome political difficulties occurred in Slovenia, formerly part of Yugoslavia, shortly after the fall of the Iron Curtain. The newly elected president and his cabinet faced the task of redesigning their economy from scratch. By using anonymous electronic brainstorming, they were able to separate ideas from old political rivalries and argue the merits of each suggestion purely on its content (Figure 6.9). Slovenia now has a thriving and growing economy.

Electronic meeting systems can translate negative comments into a positive influence on group productivity. Groups that are only allowed to make positive comments tend to stop looking for solutions when they have identified only a few. After all, everyone seems to like the ideas that have already been generated. On the other hand, when people are allowed to anonymously criticize anonymous ideas, people are not so sure they've found the best answer right off the bat. They continue to search for solutions until they have exhausted the possibilities [Connolly, Jessup, and Valacich, 1990].

Fig. 6.9 The President of Slovenia (third from left) with his cabinet at a facility in Bled, Slovenia, using GroupSystems to make economic policy shortly after independence from Yugoslavia.

6.3.5 Lessons About Electronic Voting

As corporations rely more on teams, with increasing emphasis on participative management, their need to create and measure consensus grows. In most cases, electronic voting tools play a very different role from those of conventional voice or paper-ballot methods of voting. Traditional voting usually happens at the end of a discussion, to close and decide a matter once and for all. Electronic voting, however, tends to inspire a "vote early, vote often" approach. Because it is so fast, teams use electronic voting to measure consensus and focus subsequent discussion, rather than to close debate. In these ways, the technology is more accurately described as polling than as voting. While it can shorten discussions, saving time is not the only reason to use electronic polling tools. Teams find that polling clarifies communication, focuses discussion, reveals patterns of consensus, and stimulates thinking. The following case studies, taken from confidential research of actual events, illustrate the diversity of benefits organizations can derive using electronic voting (Table 6.7).

6.3.5.1 Confidence Voting   A management crisis loomed for a major telecommunications company. For six months, 39 senior managers had wrangled to come up with an ordered ranking of 89 technical researchers on the company's payroll. When they finally completed this arduous task, a new vice president rejected the process by which they had achieved their results.

Table 6.7 Lessons About Electronic Voting

Voting clarifies communication, focuses discussion, reveals patterns of consensus, and stimulates thinking.

Anonymous polling can surface issues that remain buried during direct conversation.

Voting can demonstrate areas of agreement, allowing the group to close off discussion in those areas and focus only on areas of disagreement.

Electronic polling can facilitate decisions that are too painful to face using traditional methods.

Care must be taken to ensure that voting criteria are clearly established and defined.

This vice president didn't believe that the results accurately reflected the technical researchers' qualifications. An outside consultant was hired to engineer a new computer-supported voting process. The new scheme required each participant to submit both a ranking of each researcher and a measure of how strongly they felt about the ranking they were giving. The senior managers then reviewed several different graphical analyses of their votes and found much confidence and consensus on some of the rankings, and a great deal of variation on others.

Subsequent discussion revealed that many managers did not know some of the people they were ranking, relying instead on secondhand information and public opinion. After much discussion and information sharing the group voted again, this time with a much stronger consensus. After the second vote, the group discussed their remaining differences and in short order arrived at an overall ranking of their technical staff that all participants could live with. They agreed that the new computer-supported voting process was much more efficient than traditional voting methods and inspired a more open and focused exchange of ideas. More important, everyone from the vice president down felt that the new rankings were more legitimate than those obtained from the earlier process. The confidence-weighted votes and graphical representations of voting patterns provided managers with a larger picture than they had previously seen.

6.3.5.2 Getting Past Violent Agreement Sometimes members of a team will vigorously debate issues upon which they actually agree. A startling example of this phenomenon of unneeded debate occurred in a health care organization that encompassed a dozen hospitals throughout a major metropolitan area. Three interest groups—doctors, administrators, and directors—set out to define a mission statement and to decide how various special services should be distributed among the hospitals. For reasons that were unclear, the process degenerated into an acrimonious battle—at which point someone noted that it had been three years since the groups had met without their attorneys being present.

The groups decided that electronic polling might be helpful in locating the source of the conflict, and decided to perform an experiment. Approximately 200 people attended a meeting where every participant was given a handheld, radio-linked voting box. Using a large public screen, a facilitator displayed a number of policy statements such as, "When patients need emergency care it shall be given without reservation, regardless of ability to pay." Participants voted by agreeing or disagreeing with each statement as it was displayed.

Prior to the meeting, it was assumed throughout the health care organization that doctors, as a group, were responsible for obstructing agreement and thus progress. The prevailing wisdom was that hospital administrators and directors were the peacemakers in the group, and that a good deal of their energy went into persuading the physicians to be less intractable. This assumption was destroyed by the results. Analysis of the votes by subgroups revealed that, contrary to everyone's expectations, doctors and directors were in nearly perfect agreement on every issue. It was actually the staff administrators who were out of step, although for three years the administrators had been telling the directors that the doctors were causing problems.

6.3.5.3 Voting to Surface Information

Sometimes people do not think to share critical information until they are puzzling over the spread of electronic votes. Traditional methods of measuring consensus that do not reveal group thinking patterns can prove costly. The head of a mining company used a computerized voting system for the highly charged political task of allocating a budget across multiple corporate sites and projects. He asked a number of key executives for their opinions, but the results of the first poll were widely scattered. No one seemed to agree on budget priorities.

The president pressed his executives in order to understand why their voting patterns were so dissimilar, given that they all presumably had the good of the corporation in mind. Finally, one vice president ventured, "None of us really knows what goes on at all these places. We can't really make an informed recommendation."

The president then arranged to have electronic comment cards included on the ballot and advised the group, "If you know about a project, type in what you know. If you don't know, read what the others have typed." Within half an hour, the group had exchanged a great deal of information about the various projects and sites, and the subsequent vote-and-discuss cycle resulted in high consensus on the budget allocation.

As the team left the room, one of the vice presidents pointed at an item on the bottom of the budget priority list, and commented ruefully, "We dumped $5 million into that turkey last year." An eager champion had pushed the project, and when no one had information to dispute his arguments, the management council had simply taken a chance. Traditional consensus building had failed to uncover people's doubts, whereas electronic polling had revealed people's true feelings about the project.

Olympic ice dancers are rated on the brilliance of their performance during a brief moment in time, rather than on their potential for future greatness. So, too, managers often make choices about how to spend money based on the quality of formal presentations rather than the quality of proposed projects. A slick presentation that creates an aura of competence can overwhelm evidence of a poor proposal. An EMS provides a mechanism for organizing and evaluating and analyzing information during and after formal presentations. It also makes this information available during the time voting is taking place so participants can reflect on the facts before them rather than on the impressions received during a presentation.

6.3.5.4 No More Mr. Nice Guy

Electronic polling can sometimes facilitate decisions that are too painful to arrive at using traditional methods. A corporation with a particularly difficult budget crunch chose to use an electronic polling system to help decide how best to downsize. In many previous meetings, the possibility of eliminating a large but ineffective division was raised but was set aside for fear of offending the division's head, who was a very personable and effective lobbyist for his employees. Although the division was generally unproductive, no one wanted to hurt the manager's feelings by pushing to have the division eliminated. Instead, using traditional voting methods, the group consensus indicated that across-the-board cuts should be implemented. Everyone would bleed a little, sacrificing some efficiency in the interests of harmony.

When the electronic votes were tallied, however, it was clear to all involved that the most sensible and most widely supported alternative was to eliminate the ineffective division. In doing so the organization did not have to make potentially crippling cuts to mission-critical functions, and at the same time it distributed responsibility for the decision among the participants.

6.3.5.5 Limits on Electronic Voting

Not all electronic voting sessions are successful. Occasionally, when all the votes are in, all the terms defined, and all the hidden assumptions have surfaced, it turns out there are fundamental and irreconcilable disagreements between parties.

A savings and loan company faced a crisis that threatened its survival. During most of the discussion people were optimistic that they would reach a consensus and proceed accordingly. Rather than converging, however, group members' views diverged as electronic voting proceeded. An analysis revealed that the group was, in fact, made up of several factions with mutually exclusive, deeply held positions. The session came to an end with an agreement to disagree. The only thing the participants knew was that in light of the bitter disagreements they had uncovered, the viability of the current management team, and thus the company, was at stake. On the bright side, the team was now focused on the difficult problem, rather than wasting time squabbling about minor disagreements.

In addition to making face-to-face meetings more productive, electronic voting plays a critical role in supporting geographically dispersed meetings. Remote meeting participants lack such nonverbal cues as shifting gazes, body positions, and gestures that let speakers sense it's time for a discussion to move on.

Although many teams save time and money with electronic voting, it would be a mistake to view that as the technology's main advantage. Some groups spend more time on their deliberations when using electronic voting than with traditional methods. Research has shown that groups using structured voting schemes and response analyses to clarify communication and focus discussion consistently reach higher-quality decisions than groups using traditional voting methods. Electronic tools that permit any participant to change his or her vote at any time, and provide a real-time display of group voting patterns, establish a different dynamic by indicating shifts in consensus. New network-based voting schemes permit a group to begin interacting long before participants arrive in the meeting room, and to extend interaction after the face-to-face meeting is over.

6.3.6 Lessons About the EMS Facilities and Room Design

Electronic meeting systems work well for distributed meetings where participants are geographically separated, and they work well when groups participate face to face. However, the dynamics of face-to-face work are very different than the dynamics of distributed work. When large groups work face to face, the design of the physical space in which they work can contribute substantially to the success of the group. EMS facilities range from the basic to the sublimely sophisticated, from the inexpensive to the massively costly. An electronic meeting room need not be expensive to be successful, but there are some fundamental design considerations that can ensure successful use of the technology (Table 6.8).

6.3.6.1 The Public Screen   Most EMS facilities include one or more public screens. The interactions between participants tend to alternate between on-line engagement via computer and oral engagement with face-to-face discussion. Availability of the public screen or screens is a way to give the group a common focal point for discussion, as well as a way to share public information. One public screen is sufficient for most group activities. When more than one screen is available, facilitators use the second screen to support electronic slide shows,

Table 6.8 Lessons About Electronic Meeting Facilities

Lighting issues are extremely important and a common source of error in room design.

A public screen is important for focusing group attention.

Sufficient desktop space allows for spreading papers about and affords some visual privacy for participant work screens.

Provide space for social interactions like eating and chatting.

Choose a seating configuration that maps to expected group activities.

Minimize background noise.

Provide the facilitator with easy access to all room systems.

Select room appointments to match with the type of group expected to use the room.

Be sure everyone can easily see everyone else in the room. Partially or fully recess monitors into tables if necessary.

Provide back-up systems for servers, user workstations, and so on.

provide a group view of a participant screen, display information from two EMS tools, or present a public view of an external document.

6.3.6.2 Lighting Is Critical   Lighting is an extremely important consideration. Fluorescent lighting, for example, tends to wash out the images on a projected public screen. Incandescent lights can be focused on the areas that need light while not impairing the public screen. It is also important to attend to how lights and windows may cause glare on computer screens (Figure 6.10). Indirect lighting helps to reduce glare. Some installations have had to be completely rewired because participants could not see the screens well enough to do their work.

Lighting is also a useful way to direct and focus participant attention during a session. For example, during on-line interactions, lighting in the room can be reduced to spots on the work surface next to each participant. During general discussion, lighting can be raised in the whole room. During presentations, lighting can focus on the front and center location. If a large room is being used by a small group, the unused parts of the room can be darkened to give a more intimate feel to the area being used. Independent control of a variety of lighting fixtures enhances the ability of the leader to move the group forward toward its goal.

6.3.6.3 Seating Configuration   The first EMS facilities were built with the participant stations arranged in a horseshoe-shaped configuration. This allows for the participants to have reasonably good line of sight to other participants as

Fig. 6.10 A face-to-face EMS facility with monitors buried under glass. Group dynamics improve because people have unobstructed views of one another. However, glare from ceiling lights makes the monitors difficult to read.

well as to the public display screen at the open end of the horseshoe. It also allows the facilitator to step into the middle of the horseshoe to gain the attention of the group. Several other configurations have been tried in other EMS facilities with varying results. Some facilities have been built in a simple conference table arrangement with the public display at one end of the table. This focuses group attention quite well, but does not allow for very large groups. Other facilities have made use of a round table with participants on every side. Again, this focuses group attention well, but requires some participants to sit with their backs to the public screen. Still other facilities have been designed to resemble tiered classrooms. These facilities provide excellent focus on a public screen, but it is sometimes difficult for participants to pick up nonverbal cues from other participants [Fuller and Mittleman, 1994].

All seating configurations will require trade-offs. It is important to consider what the primary purposes of the facility will be to decide the relative importance of group focus, public display screen access, and support for large group size.

6.3.6.4 Lines of Sight and the Work Surface   Some consideration must be given to the configuration of the work surface that will be made available to the participants. First and foremost, the participants must be able to see their screen clearly, but they must also be able to see one another clearly (Figure 6.11). Some electronic meeting rooms have the CPUs sitting on desktops, and the monitors sitting on the CPUs. The result is a "design by Kilroy" effect. People must strain to see over and around the technology. In such a setting, people tend not to engage in the proceedings; they lose interest, and participation drops. Ideally, the monitors can be partially recessed into the desktop so people have clear lines of sight to one another. Some room designers have completely buried the monitors under a glass panel in the desktop, completely uncluttering the surface. As mentioned above, this approach turns out to be a mixed blessing because lights and windows create glare on the glass. It is also difficult to keep the monitor viewing area free of papers and clutter during the meeting. The partially embedded monitor turns out to be a good compromise.

Along with space for the monitor, the work area must provide room for participants to spread out at least two full-sized legal sheets of paper. Participants often need to work from documents while interacting in an electronic meeting room. Providing adequate work surface produces a side benefit. By adequately spacing monitors apart, each participant is afforded a small amount of visual privacy so that participants are less likely to see anonymous contributions typed in by other participants.

6.3.6.5 Social Space   It is important to provide social space along with the work space in an electronic meeting environment. The social space should allow for serving snacks and drinks, and should have ample room for casual conversation. Because the nature of electronic group work is different from traditional group work, breaks tend to be handled differently. For example, at a three-day document writing session the facilitator decided not to have formal breaks. As

Fig. 6.11 A special table to support electronic meetings in Helsinki, Finland. When the computers are not needed they slip into compartments in the table top. The wings of the table articulate to create different seating patterns.

the participants were largely doing individual or dyadic work, the facilitator brought food and beverages into the meeting room and suggested that participants simply get up and stretch whenever they felt the urge to do so.

In other meetings, breaks have been used as a core component of the meeting process itself. A great deal of important activity can happen during breaks. Besides clarifying positions and informally negotiating agreements, people build a rapport with one another that simply cannot be achieved during the computer-supported interactions. Facilitators sometimes schedule breaks to allow for informal conversation and coalition building. One facility at the University of Arizona supports this sort of informal communication by the placement of an outdoor fountain just outside the meeting room. The running water provides a white noise which ensures acoustical privacy for small groups engaging in conversation or negotiation during breaks.

6.3.6.6 Noise   Background noise in an electronic meeting room can be distracting and wearing during a long session. The CPUs for the workstations and the fans on the public screen projectors are prime culprits. Anything that can minimize such noise will improve the usability of the room. Placing CPUs in closed cabinets is one solution, although one must ensure sufficient ventilation to keep the machines from overheating.

One should avoid the temptation to place the CPUs in a separate room. Keyboards, mice, and monitors can all be wired for long-distance connection to the CPU, so all the noise and heat from the CPU is removed from the room. However, as technology evolves it is often desirable to add peripheral devices for each workstation, and some of these devices must reach both the CPU and the user.

Lightpens, digitizers, sound cards, and video cameras, for example, are all available for personal computers, and all can be useful in electronic meeting rooms. However, each requires a special adapter card that must be placed in the computer, and each must be available to the user. These devices cannot be used if the computer is some distance away in another room.

6.3.6.7 Redundancy   It is important to provide redundancy for every key component of the electronic meeting room. Back-up systems such as a second file server, multiple facilitator stations, and replacement components for user stations should be available. When key people are involved in a critical interaction, they will not tolerate "hiccups." This is also an argument in favor of having at least two public screens. Should anything go down, there is something in reserve.

6.3.7 Lessons from the Facilitators and Session Leaders

Table 6.9 lists the key lessons garnered from EMS facilitators. The person who chairs an electronic meeting is the leader or facilitator. This person may be the group leader, another group member, or a separate, neutral individual who is not a group member. Using a non-member enables all group members to participate actively rather than having to lose one member to serve as the chair. A non-member can be a specialist in EMS and group work, but may lack the task and group knowledge of a regular member. The meeting leader/facilitator provides four functions. First, this person provides technical support by initiating and terminating specific software tools and functions, and guiding the group through the technical aspects necessary to work on the task. This reduces the amount of training required of group members by removing one level of system complexity. In some cases, technical support is provided by an additional technical facilitator or technographer.

Table 6.9 Key Lessons from Facilitators and Session Leaders

Preplanning is critical.

Find a fast, clean way to do idea organization—people hate it, and you will lose them if you take too long.

The group must always see where they are headed and how each activity advances them toward the goal.

Be cognizant of nonverbal interactions. Even small nonverbal cues can tell a facilitator a lot.

Expect that ideas generated will change the plan and the agenda.

Group dynamics can be affected by the selection of switches in the EMS tools.

Mix modes between electronic interaction and verbal/oral interaction. Change locations and alternate between large and small groups every few hours to minimize burnout.

Second, the meeting leader/facilitator chairs the meeting, maintains the agenda, and assesses the need for agenda changes. The leader may or may not take an active role in the meeting to improve group interaction by, for example, providing process structure in coordinating verbal discussions. This person also administers the group's knowledge. In an EMS designed without support for meeting leaders/facilitators, any group member may change or delete the group memory. When disagreements occur, members' competition for control can create a dysfunction. While this is manageable for small collaborative groups, it is much less so for larger groups with diverse membership, where competitive political motives and vested interests exist. With EMS, members can view the group memory and add to it at their own workstations, but in general, only the meeting leader/facilitator can modify and delete public information.

Third, the meeting leader/facilitator assists in agenda planning by working with the group and/or group leader to highlight the principal meeting objectives and develop an agenda to accomplish them. Specific EMS tools are then mapped to each activity. Finally, in an ongoing organizational setting where the meeting leaders/facilitators are not group members, the session leader provides organizational continuity by setting standards for use, developing training materials, maintaining the system, and acting as champion/sponsor, which is key to successful technology transfer. The roles of the meeting leader/facilitator may also change over time. For example, after a group has some experience using EMS, the need for technical support and agenda-planning advice may decrease.

6.3.7.1 Preplan the Agenda Carefully   The most basic principle for successful use of electronic meeting systems is that the task must be very obvious to the group, and the activity in which its members are engaging must obviously advance them toward accomplishing that task. Where a conventional meeting may wander for three or four hours before people realize it is off track, a computer-based meeting can resemble a train wreck in about ten minutes if it is not well planned. If the participants feel that the technology is engaging them in irrelevant activities, they will quickly grow hostile and refuse to continue.

The importance of preplanning cannot be overemphasized. Before an electronic session, the session leader must define exactly what concrete deliverables the group will create—be it a problem statement, a list of possible solutions, a documented decision, a plan of action, or whatever. Defining a deliverable can in itself be a difficult task, but without it an electronic meeting is likely to founder. Having defined a deliverable, the meeting leader must then decide on a process for achieving the deliverable. This requires an awareness of the electronic tools and the different dynamics each can produce. Having mapped out a process for achieving the goal, the leader must also be sure that appropriate people are included in the meeting. Any group with a stake in the outcomes can and should be represented. With electronic meetings this is much more feasible than with conventional meetings, because electronic meetings can include many more people without hampering group productivity.

6.3.7.2 Alternate Style of Group Interactions One source of group fatigue is the monotony that comes from repeating the same kind of activity over and over. This work strain can be reduced if the agenda permits alternating among different interaction styles. One dimension to alternate along is electronic and oral interactions. Another dimension to alternate along is to move the participants between full group activities and smaller subgroup activities every so often. Varying the work environment in these ways reduces monotony, which in turn improves productivity.

6.3.7.3 Control of Participant Interactions The facilitator can affect the amount of on-line discussion among participants with subtle verbal cues and with switch selection choices in the EMS software. For example, if the facilitator wants participants to respond to one another, then s/he can select for the EMS discussion tools to number all participant comments and can provide verbal instructions to the group as to how easy it is to respond to a comment simply by referring to its number. On the other hand, if the facilitator wishes participants to focus attention on developing already present ideas and wishes to discourage cross-discussion, s/he can turn comment numbering off.

6.3.7.4 Nonverbal Communication It is important for the facilitator to remember that the use of electronic communication technologies does not eliminate the power of nonverbal communication in the meeting room. The facilitator must remember to be careful about delivering nonverbal cues. Position in the room, posture, eye contact, and gestures are all important parts of the guidance the facilitator provides the group. In return, the facilitator can receive significant nonverbal information from the group if attentive to the cues. For example, facilitators should learn to gauge group energy and interest in an electronic discussion topic simply by listening to keyboard clicks. The noise level in the room will tell an experienced facilitator when the process is producing diminishing returns and it is time to move on to the next item on the agenda.

6.3.7.5 Verbal Communication Even though much of the group discussion takes place on-line during an EMS session, verbal communication can have a huge impact on the results of a session. For example, one cue a facilitator uses to determine whether a group is anxious or bored is the amount of humor present in on-line comments. When a group is focused on the topic at hand, there will be only a moderate amount of humor embedded in the conversation. Once the level of humor noticeably increases, the group is ready to move on.

Facilitator cues can have a large impact on group performance as well. One recent experiment found that the facilitator could boost group performance in an idea generation task an average of 30% simply by changing two phrases in the instructions to the participants. Performance increased if the facilitator adopted a jocular tone and urged the participants to "kick butt" rather than to "try," and suggested the participants would be "brain-dead" instead of "below average" should their performance flag. This small example illustrates a key point: Electronic meeting tools, like the tools of a craftsman, must be used with skill and understanding. The success of the technology depends on the quality of both the system and the processes in which it is used.

6.3.8 Lessons About EMS Implementation

With the productivity gains that have been demonstrated for electronic meeting systems, why hasn't this technology spread rapidly throughout all organizations? Some organizations do adopt, and adapt to, electronic meeting systems so quickly and effectively that the process seems effortless. More often, however, people do not perceive the benefits of the technology until they have used it to solve a real problem. This creates a catch-22 dilemma. The experience of EMS use is so different from traditional experience that often, people cannot visualize its usefulness even after thorough demonstrations. They therefore reject the possibility that the technology can be useful. Once they've used the tools, the benefits become readily apparent, but how does one go about convincing a skeptic to try? Before they've tried the technology, potential users often raise a number of objections. This section addresses some of the most frequently raised concerns.

Only an idiot would put computers in a meeting room! People who express this idea either have not heard or do not believe the data about productivity gains with EMS. Often, the only way to reach them is to include them in an electronic meeting in which they have a substantial stake, but someone else has planned and convened.

Real Executives won't use keyboards! People frequently raise this objection and believe it strongly, but in practice it has not materialized. Executives do type when they have a reason to type. In meetings with tens of thousands of senior executives, we have seen only three cases where executives brought typists to an electronic meeting. These executives took such ribbing and kidding from the other participants that they quickly sent the typists away. In the past there was no reason for an executive to use a keyboard; anything that needed typing could be delegated. In the electronic meeting, typing is the most effective way for executives to communicate, so they type without objections.

People who can type fast have an unfair advantage! Research shows that people with no keyboard experience contribute as many ideas to an electronic meeting as those who type at high speed. The nontypists tend to submit concise, pithy statements, while the fast typists tend to make more lengthy, wordy contributions.

Meetings with more than five or six people are unmanageable and unproductive! Vast research results support this objection. In meetings *without* electronic meeting tools, the productivity of the meeting tends to go down every time another person is included. However, the electronic meeting system changes the dynamics of meetings in a fundamental way. Electronic meeting productivity tends to go up as the group size increases.

We don't need anonymity. We are all open and honest here. Imagine that you were making payments on two cars, two of your children were in college, your mortgage was due, and your boss asked you for an open and honest opinion about a pet project. Self-preservation instincts might preclude direct criticism. In every instance we know of where this objection was raised before an electronic meeting, the participants were surprised at the value of issues and ideas that came out of anonymous EMS sessions. Participants reported feeling liberated by the anonymity. Even small groups that have worked together closely for many years find anonymous input useful at times. In no case that we know of has a business meeting degenerated into vitriolic and personal "flaming" attacks.

We don't vote here; we arrive at a natural consensus. Often, the phrase Natural Consensus is a euphemism for "we do what the boss thinks is best." As noted above, voting does not necessarily imply decision making. It is a good way to stimulate focused discussion on key issues.

The structure imposed by an EMS is unnatural and constraining. The structure and focus provided by an EMS is like the structure and focus provided by traffic signals, signs, road dividers, and the like. When people observe the protocols of the road, the traffic moves efficiently. In places where the protocols of the road are ignored, traffic becomes snarled and dangerous. The structure of EMS keeps participants moving efficiently through their meeting process.

I'm paid to make decisions. Why would I want to involve others in the process? An EMS supports all phases of the goal-attainment process, not just moments of formal, identifiable decision making. As mentioned above, even autocratic, hierarchical organizations use EMS effectively for gathering information, defining problems, developing and evaluating alternatives, and planning implementations.

How can I evaluate my people if their ideas are anonymous? It is an unusual thing for someone to be rewarded for simply mentioning an idea. Rewards are more often based on successful execution of ideas once they have been evaluated and adopted. Performance and productivity count for a great deal. Furthermore,

Table 6.10 Top 10 Worst Excuses for Not Using EMS As Reported by Facilitators from the Field

10. If someone is working at home I can't manage them.

9. I don't have the time and money to write, read, and evaluate all those ideas.

8. I can think faster than I can type.

7. We don't need participation. I already know what my people think.

6. I don't have any time to play with computers.

5. If groupware is so good, why don't I know about it?

4. I can't trust anybody who won't tell it to my face.

3. I didn't get to be an executive by being anonymous.

2. I need to know who said what so I can do annual reviews.

And the Number One Worst Excuse for Not Using EMS:

1. Any damn fool can plan, but it takes a real manager to jump from crisis to crisis!

when people think they have a really good idea, they sign it. Anonymity is voluntary, not mandatory.

This EMS will undermine my power and authority. This is a serious barrier to the adoption of EMS. The technology itself is power-neutral, but it can be used as an instrument to change the existing balance of power. Facilitators should be aware that powerful people tend to resist anything that seriously threatens their power, and they often have the power to make their resistance effective. Due consideration must be given to power issues in order to prevent unintentional confrontations. Powerful people should also be aware that the technology need not threaten them. It can be used effectively and efficiently to support their goals.

There are probably as many objections to EMS as there are skeptics. Table 6.10 presents a compilation of the most humorous excuses heard by many facilitators. In the end, there seems to be no better way to convince people of its usefulness than to have them use the technology to solve one bad problem.

6.4 LESSONS YET TO BE LEARNED

After more than a decade of EMS research, a great deal is known about how and why electronic meeting systems work. However, there are still many lessons to be learned. This section discusses the ongoing research at the University of Arizona, and previews the lessons likely to be learned over the next several years.

6.4.1 Artificial Intelligence to Support Group Work

For instance, to what degree can the role of the facilitator be automated and supported? Research is underway to apply neural network and other AI technologies to the organization of randomly generated ideas [Chen *et al.*, 1994]. Other researchers are looking into the use of expert systems for planning group processes, matching tools to group needs, and monitoring group progress toward a goal. However, real-time use of expert systems for these purposes is still some distance away.

6.4.2 EMS and Business Process Re-Engineering

It is interesting to note that after a decade of development, EMS research is coming full circle. Researchers are beginning to develop specialized EMS tools to support requirements definition and business process re-engineering (BPR). BPR is a process whereby members of an organization create a model of their business activities and information systems, then search for ways to achieve dramatic improvements in productivity, profitability, and customer service. The participants then model new business processes and design new information systems to support them.

An organization need not become very large before there is no single person who knows how and why all parts work. Modeling a large organization is a daunting task. If a model is not sufficiently detailed, it is not useful. If it is sufficiently detailed to be useful, it can be so large that participants suffer information overload. Further, modeling techniques tend to be fairly cumbersome for novice modelers. The models are made up of arcane symbols, and there are strict rules about how the symbols can be placed in a diagram. The people who understand the business tend not to be the same people who understand how to draw useful models, and so large quantities of information tend to get lost in the translation as models are created.

The Enterprise Analyzer project at the University of Arizona is an attempt to use EMS technology to overcome these barriers and make it easy for business experts to create models of their enterprise. Researchers created an electronic meeting system that permits very large groups of participants—often 50 or more people—to work simultaneously to create a model of organizational activities. From the participant point of view, the system is almost magical. Participants need to know little or nothing of the modeling method. They simply type what they know about their piece of the organization in plain language, and the system draws a graphical model from what they typed in (see Figure 6.12).

In the Enterprise Analyzer, as in any magic show, there is more going on up the sleeve and behind the cape than what the audience perceives. Sessions are

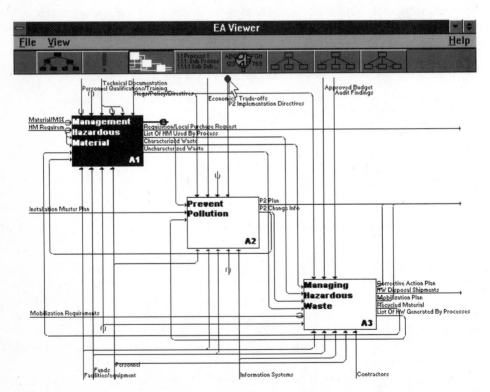

Fig. 6.12 The Enterprise Analyzer Viewer displaying part of an activity diagram created by 54 users working in concert. Users typed what they knew about their system in plain text, and the Enterprise Analyzer drew this picture.

led by a facilitator with expertise in the modeling method. The system provides a number of different input forms. The facilitator controls the participant screens so that the participants are always typing in response to an appropriate prompt. Each prompt is in turn linked to an appropriate data structure in a database. The plain-language descriptions are stored in a database which captures the semantics of the model in its data structures.

Once users have typed what they know, the Enterprise Analyzer evaluates the contents of the data files and constructs a graphical representation. The users periodically review the graphical model as a group to look for inaccuracies and incomplete sections. They are often surprised by the structure of their model, having only known the organization from a narrow point of view before the exercise began.

Early field trials of the Enterprise Analyzer have been fairly successful. Participants complete the modeling in less than 25% of the time required by other modeling procedures, and their models typically contain 10 times the detail of those created by manual modeling groups. Because the system organizes and abstracts the details, however, participants have been able to deal with the more detailed models.

There are some interesting political implications to the use of the Enterprise Analyzer. Because a model can be constructed in a week or ten days instead of six to ten weeks, high-level executives and powerful stakeholders are more willing to participate in the process. Thus, the people who are in a position to negotiate differences and make agreements stick are actually in the room as the model is built. One result is that the models are more acceptable within the organization once they are complete, and so they are more useful as instruments of change. Another ramification is that the sessions tend to be much larger than planned. As the session date draws near, more and more people decide they had better be present to defend their turf and express their points of view. A meeting planned for 20 people can easily grow to 50 or more by the time the session actually begins. This, in turn, leads to more complete models, more acceptable models, and, in the end, better systems.

6.4.3 Encouraging Emotional Engagement in Rational Decision Making

A majority of EMS users walk away from electronic meetings feeling enriched and empowered by the technology and by the collaboration they've had with their colleagues. They often feel somewhat exhilarated by having covered so much work in so little time. Not everyone walks away feeling satisfied, however. A minority feel a loss of power, and find electronic meeting work mundane and ordinary. For instance, in a recent meeting of senior executives at a large high-tech manufacturing firm the participants conducted an annual tactical planning session. For each of the previous five years the session had taken three days. Using EMS the executives achieved their goal in under two hours, and all agreed that the resulting plan was of better quality and had more detail than any plan they had ever generated. Still, when asked how they had liked the session, the executives expressed a general sense of mild discomfort. "It moved pretty slowly," one said.

"It felt kind of routine," another replied.

"I've made my career on being able to drive an agenda through in a tough meeting," another added. "Today there wasn't any need for what I do best." Electronic meeting support is intentionally designed to eliminate many aspects of traditional meetings that tend to get the adrenaline pumping: criticism stings less, you can't be interrupted, you do not pound the table for emphasis. The result appears to be less emotional engagement for some, which may mean less satisfying work. Researchers are only beginning to investigate the importance of this emotional engagement, what the consequences of its loss may be, and what can be done to restore it without reducing the benefits of the EMS.

6.4.4 Support for Geographically Distributed Groups

Although it is technically possible to create group support technology that can be used by participants who are separated in space and time, it turns out to be difficult to engage people in teamwork when they are geographically dispersed (Figure 6.13). Present technology permits full participation by remote users, but experience shows that these users are much more easily distracted from the work than are people who are colocated. Phones ring, people knock on the door with papers to be signed, the user decides to check email. Often, the remote user winds up more an observer of the electronic meeting than a full participant. In the face-to-face meeting room peer pressure helps to keep people active. We often see somebody nudge the person next to him or her in a kidding fashion with an oral comment like, "Say, I don't hear any keystrokes coming from you. Did you go to sleep?"

Fig. 6.13 Technology now supports desktop meetings with participants separated in both space and time. The human challenge is to learn to work productively in the virtual meeting space.

Part of the answer for more complete engagement may come from a set of software features that replace some of the missing nonverbal cues that engage a person in a meeting. Adding video teleconferencing may help. An electronic public screen that is visible on the console of the remote user may also help. If all users were given telecursors that let them electronically point at objects on the public screen, this could substitute for missing hand gestures. Temporary electronic scribbling over the public screen with a pen-based interface may also assist remote participation. There is even the possibility that virtual reality may play a part in creating the illusion of shared presence for remote meeting participants, thereby engaging them more fully in the group activities.

The collision of telecommunication, cable, and computing may have a dramatic effect on electronically supported groups. Currently, the cost of data communication channels is a major constraint on remote collaborative computing. A channel with sufficient bandwidth to support full-motion high-resolution video teleconferencing can cost as much as $10,000 per month. But communication hardware is rapidly decreasing in price, and a nationwide digital fiber network may reduce such a channel cost to less than one percent of that amount. With the ability to pass vast quantities of data to and fro, the meeting environment of the future may look quite different from the meeting environment of today.

6.5 THE MEETING ENVIRONMENT OF THE FUTURE

Technology exists today to permit team members to work any time, any place, and nearly any way they want. Electronically supported groups can work as individuals linked by electronic media in a virtual meeting; they can be located in several meeting rooms that are connected electronically, they can work at the same time, or different members can work at different times. They can work in small groups of four or five, or they can work in very large groups of 50 or more people. However, today many of these technologies are developing independent of one another. To date there is no single environment that combines individual and group support, remote and face-to-face collaboration, text, graphics, video, and voice links, and shared computer applications. Each working mode requires electronic tools specifically tailored to the situation. Each kind of collaboration requires different kinds of information. For example, some information is formal, as with corporate reports. Other information is less formal, as with hallway conversations or notes on the back of a placemat. As we move toward the future, all group support technologies will be integrated into the same working environment.

New experimental environments are now under development at the University of Arizona: The Multimedia Collaboration Center, The TeamRoom 2000, and the Mirror Project. Research in these facilities focuses on the integration of many technologies to support group work, including automating traditional group processes, real-time video and audio through the computer, and intelligent information retrieval and group support.

The Multimedia Collaboration Center (Figure 6.7) opened in November 1993. It combines audio and video teleconferencing technology with GroupSystems and other electronic meeting support. It supports 29 users with workstations and three 10-foot public display screens. It also provides a full arsenal of multimedia display equipment and gives users on-line access to an electronic library and other external databases. Phase Two of this project will include desktop audio and video links at every station. This center will also be fully integrated with the two other environments, the TeamRoom 2000 and the Mirror Project.

TeamRoom 2000 extends the capabilities of existing group support facilities to create an any-time/any-place meeting environment. TeamRoom 2000 combines pen, voice, and wireless network technology so that distributed groups can work in a virtual team space. A dedicated facility with a network of pen- and voice-based notepad computers is the hub of this team environment, but users will move in and out with their portable computers as their needs dictate. TeamRoom 2000 extends the Multimedia Collaboration Center concept beyond the four walls.

The Mirror Project (Figure 6.14) addresses questions relating to group-to-group interactions. Current audio and video teleconferencing technology does not support the rich and subtle communication possible in face-to-face meetings. Where the TeamRoom 2000 project focuses on the interface between the individual and the group, the Mirror facility focuses on creating the illusion of presence that is lost when groups use today's video teleconferencing facilities. The Mirror facility features floor-to-ceiling high-resolution video display walls and addresses optical, mechanical, and human issues to enhance the connection between remotely collaborating groups.

6.6 CONCLUSIONS

We have learned a great deal about how to engage in successful electronically supported collaboration, and we still have a great deal to learn. The field is growing rapidly in many different directions. Looking back ten years from now, today's technology may look horse-and-buggy. Nonetheless, the fundamental principles of collaboration technology will still apply. There will still be problems so intractable that no single person will be able to solve them. Technology will still improve communication, still structure and support thinking processes, and still provide access to information. Yet technology will still be no substitute for leadership.

Fig. 6.14 An Artist's Rendition of the Mirror Project. This project will focus on creating the illusion of presence for geographically distributed teams.

REFERENCES

1. Briggs, R.O. "The Focus Theory of Group Productivity and its Application to the Development and Testing of Electronic Group Support Technology." Unpublished Doctoral Dissertation, MIS Department, University of Arizona, Tucson, 1994.
2. Chen, H., Hsu, P., Orwig, R., Hoopes, L., and Nunamaker, J.F. Jr. "Automatic Concept Classification of Text from Electronic Meetings." *Communications of the ACM*, 37, 9, 1994.
3. Connolly, T., Jessup, L. M., and Valacich, J. S. "Effects of Anonymity and Evaluative Tone on Idea Generation in Computer-Mediated Groups. *Management Science*, 36, 6, 1990, 689–703.
4. Dallvalle, T., Esposito, A., and Lang, S. "Groupware—One Experience." *The Fifty Conference on Corporate Communication: Communication in Uncertain Times*, Fairleigh Dickinson University, May 20, 1992, 2–9.
5. DeSanctis, G., and Gallupe, R. B. A Foundation for the Study of Group Decision Support Systems. *Management Science*, 33(22), 1987, 589–609.
6. Diehl, M. and Stroebe, W. "Productivity Lost in Brainstorming Groups: Toward the Solution of a Riddle." J. *Personality and Social Psychology*, 53, 3, 1987, 497–509.
7. Fuller, M. A. and Mittleman, D. D. "The Collaborative Technology Classroom: On

Active Learning, Group Support Systems, and Physical Environment." Working Paper, Baylor University. Waco, TX.

8. Grohowski, R. B., McGoff, C., Vogel, D. R., Martz, W. B., and Nunamaker, J.F. Jr. "Implementation of Electronic Meeting Systems at IBM." *MIS Quarterly*, 14, 4, 1990, 369–383.

9. Kayser, T. A. *Mining Group Gold*. El Segundo, CA: Serif, 1990.

10. Nunamaker, J.F. Jr, Dennis, A. R., Valacich., J. S., Vogel, D. R., and George, J. F. "Electronic Meetings to Support Group Work." *Communications of the ACM*, 34, 7, 1991, 40–61.

11. Post, B. Q. "Building the Business Case for Group Support Technology." *Proceedings of the 25th Annual Hawaii International Conference on Systems Science*, IEEE, 1992, Vol. IV, 34–45.

12. Teichroew, D. and Hershey, E.A. "PSL/PSA: A Computer-Aided Technique for Structured Documentation and Analysis of Information Processing Systems." In *Advanced Systems Development / Feasibility Techniques*. J.D. Cougar, M.A. Colter, and R.W. Knapp, (Eds.) John Wiley & Sons, New York, 1982.

13. Vogel, D. R., Martz, W. B., Nunamaker, J.F. Jr., Grohowski, R. B., and McGoff, C. "Electronic Meeting System Experience at IBM." *J. of MIS*, 6, 3 (1990).

BIOGRAPHIES

Dr. Jay F. Nunamaker is professor of management information systems (MIS) and computer science at the University of Arizona. In 1974, he established the MIS department and served as department head for 15 years, developing the B.S., M.S., and Ph.D. programs. Among Dr. Nunamaker's many academic accomplishments, he was recognized as the college's Andersen Consulting Professor of the Year for 1992/1993. Dr. Nunamaker is known for innovative research related to group decision support systems, the automation of systems development, databases, expert systems, systems analysis, and design and strategic planning. He has published more than 200 papers and seven books dealing with these subjects and holds editorial positions on major journals. Dr. Nunamaker has received more than $20 million in research grants over the past ten years, and under his direction, the MIS Department has achieved international recognition.

An internationally renowned authority on groupware, his is considered "the father of electronic meeting systems." As a result of his research, the spin-off software, GroupSystems, is now being used at over 500 sites internationally for idea generation, issue identification, issue analysis, communication, and consensus building. Users include Fortune 500 companies, U.S. government agencies, and foreign governments.

Nunamaker's work has appeared in *Fortune, Business Week, The Wall Street Journal, The New York Times,* and *The Los Angeles Times*, and in television coverage by the BBC, CNN, and other networks.

Nunamaker holds a Ph.D. in operations research and systems engineering from Case Institute of Technology, and he was associate professor of computer sciences and industrial administration at Purdue University prior to joining the University of Arizona's College of Business and Public Administration.

Robert O. Briggs is a research fellow in the Center for the Management of Information in the MIS Department at the University of Arizona. He investigates the nature of group productivity and the application of technology to group work. He developed the Focus Theory of Group Productivity to support research on the design and use of group support technologies. His recent work involves the use of electronic meeting systems to alter the dynamics of the classroom to improve writing and thinking skills and to reduce the drop-out rate. He has published and presented his work in various academic and trade forums around the world. Briggs hold a Ph.D. from the University of Arizona. He completed a B.S. in MIS and a B.S. in Art History, along with an M.B.A. at San Diego State University.

Daniel D. Mittleman is a research scientist in the Center for the Management of Information in the MIS Department at the University of Arizona. His research interests include the use of group technology to support architectural planning, the design of group meeting environments, and the use of electronic meeting systems to support group document writing. His recent work was the design and use of group technology to support the programming and planning of three separate architectural building projects. Mittleman holds a Ph.D. from the University of Arizona as well as an A.B. in History and an M.B.A. from Washington University in St. Louis.

Vendor Strategies

Introduction to Chapter 7

This first chapter in the vendors section of this book is presented by Lotus—the undisputed king of groupware...right now. Lotus has done an excellent job capturing "mindshare" in the groupware or collaborative computing arena for two reasons. First, Notes is a good product and development platform; and second, they are the only game in town...right now. Microsoft Exchange is scheduled for release later this year, but I don't think it will compete directly with Notes. Exchange will offer services such as messaging, replication, shared document database, and so on to third-party vendors who will develop functionality similar to Notes. Also, given Microsoft's marketing effectiveness, some of these applications could potentially be real competition for Notes.

Traditional marketing efforts for Notes have been successful in reaching much of the technical community, and Lotus' visionaries and innovators are now pursuing business professionals who have not grasped the benefits of Notes. Recently, Lotus instituted a TV advertising campaign designed to increase their market by familiarizing a broader base of the population with Notes. Only time will tell if this expensive strategy will work.

The assignment I gave to each vendor author was to educate readers rather than sell to them. That's a tough assignment for any vendor, but Jeff Papows and Lotus did an excellent job. I also asked each vendor how they use their own product(s) internally and how their customers use it. Finally, I asked about the product's architecture and direction for the future.

In answer to these and many other questions, Jeff has produced a chapter that looks at the history of Lotus (to show Notes' evolution), initial sales/marketing strategies for Notes, some of Notes' functions, replication technologies, and security issues, and specific examples of how Notes can best be used in an organization.

This chapter gives the reader an inside view of the early days of Notes, before it was popular in corporate America and on TV ads. Lotus is a missionary organization, trying to educate people and potential customers about Notes. Generally, business professionals have not been exposed to groupware strategies and products, so they don't understand groupware in general, let alone any specific product, to appreciate what it can do for their organization. Educating the business community is the biggest challenge facing groupware. That is one of the main reasons for this book!

After a general bringing-the-reader-up-to-speed, Jeff examines Notes as a "change agent" or a tool for re-engineering. Lotus commissioned IDC to perform an analysis of 65 Notes-using organizations worldwide. The results of this ROI study were so startling—most companies showed an ROI of 40 to 100% on an investment of $100,000—they were also hard to believe. So the study was repeated with roughly the same results. It is fair to conclude that Notes did make a big dif-

ference to these organizations, both financially and in other less measurable ways.

Jeff punctuates his chapter with quotes from customers and anecdotes from researchers and MIS people who are using Notes. He also examines how introducing Notes affects the corporate culture. A ready-made case study is Lotus' sales organization, which uses Notes as a tool for sales, coordination, communication, and collaboration. Jeff examines several other case studies, including production environments where groupware applications stand up to the rigors of a production environment. In other words, Notes is being adopted by mainstream businesses for common business challenges, and this bodes well for Notes and all of groupware.

Notes is more than an application, it is a platform on which Notes Partners are building applications. Jeff looks at 11 different, successful products and vendors. Finally, he looks at where Notes is going in the near future. He examines Lotus' partnership with AT&T for network Notes, their relationship with Oracle, and Notes 4.0, which is scheduled for release in mid-1995.

Lotus announced many of the Version 4.0 changes at LotusSphere. Also, it appears their strategy for Lotus Communications Server (LCS) has changed somewhat, so the LCS section in this chapter may already be outdated. Jeff talks about an X.400 messaging backbone for Notes and cc:Mail; however, I don't believe that is the current strategy. To get more up-to-date information contact Lotus directly, or check any number of the Notes-oriented newsletters. My newsletter, GroupTalk (which covers all of workgroup computing), often contains articles on Lotus, its products and strategies, and can be an excellent resource.

This chapter gives the reader insight into the background and motivation for Notes, a summary of some of its functions, the architecture, and third-party programs. It is a great introduction to today's leading groupware product, Lotus Notes.

Lotus Development Corp.'s meteoric rise was fueled by the most popular application in software history, the electronic spreadsheet Lotus 1-2-3. The phenomenal success 1-2-3 has enjoyed virtually from its inception in January 1983 straight through to the present day has become the stuff of legend, and for good reason: it revolutionized the way individuals do business. For the first time, a user could simply and easily model financial and engineering systems, and quickly perform "what-if" analyses. The spreadsheet radically improved the productivity of professionals, and became the essential tool of a burgeoning new class of "knowledge workers."

Meanwhile, the personal computer spent the decade taking corporate America by storm. Neither years of mainframe domination nor the brief ascendancy of the midsized computer could stop the eventual move to the desktop; no timesharing system could match the power of a processor, a graphical display, and a key-

board wholly dedicated to a single end user. Today, the PC is a ubiquitous fixture in the corporate environment, not only in the United States but worldwide. To a great extent 1-2-3, by channelling the power of the computer such that users could focus the processing power directly on everyday tasks, drove the digital revolution of the 1980s.

Even as that occurred, the seeds of the revolution's next stage were beginning to sprout.

While the benefits of PC computing abounded, a few problems were beginning to show as well. For starters, every manager knows that a team working together can achieve things that a group of equally skilled individuals working separately and independently cannot. PCs, however, did nothing to encourage group effort; to the contrary, each existed as a separate island of computing. It was difficult for PC users to exchange data, to coordinate tasks, to incorporate computers into business processes. In fact, in some respects PCs actually diminished communication—people who once spent time in meetings stayed locked in their offices, glued to their keyboards!

The advent and subsequent proliferation of the high-speed digital computer network triggered the next phase of the digital revolution. No longer did each PC function independent of all others—now, they could actually exchange things.

But what? The first—and still most prevalent—use of computer networks involves the file server. Appearing as an extension to the user's hardware configuration, the file server allows programs and data to be stored centrally; thus, the notion of "sharing" began to evolve.

Yet file servers tapped only a minuscule portion of the new environment's potential, the depths of which we are still plumbing today. A slew of vendors attempted to capitalize on the processing power synergy inherent in the PC and the server; for example, they put intense calculations such as database query optimizations on the server, while relying on the PC for graphical presentation services—hence, the birth of "client-server" computing. But even these applications only improved response time for the individual user; they accomplished little for the group.

In the mid-1980s, work began at Lotus on a project that would exploit the network's power and return the investment in the network back to the workgroup. In 1984 Lotus founder Mitch Kapor staked a young programmer named Ray Ozzie to another florally named startup, Iris Associates, to build this product. In 1989 the fruit of this investment emerged as Lotus Notes—and, just as 1-2-3 changed forever the way individuals work, so is Notes revolutionizing the way individuals work together.

If Ozzie is the father of Notes and Mitch was its midwife, however, then surely its godfather is Jim Manzi. An early adherent to the Notes vision himself,

Manzi pitted the combined powers of his persuasive personality and his high corporate offices—in April 1986, he replaced the departing Kapor as CEO; later in the year, he was named chairman as well—squarely behind Notes, which many viewed as a longshot at best. "There were times when things really became shaky," recalls an early Notes division employee, "but whenever we asked for more money, we got it; Jim was pretty unwavering."

From placing significant corporate resources—including perhaps the most prized: autonomy—at the disposal of the Notes organization to going on record time and again to espouse Notes as the key to the competitively urgent emergence of the "electronic keiretsu," he made it clear at home and abroad that he was willing to bet the company on the concept.

Notes for Lotus and the World: Sighting the Goal

Jeffrey P. Papows
Lotus Development Corp.

7.1 WHAT IS NOTES?

Just what is this thing called Notes? Answering that elementary question has proven to be as difficult as it was to explain the electronic spreadsheet in the early 1980s. In fact, coming up with a concise, crisp definition of a product the breadth and power of which defy categorization was one of our earliest hurdles—and I wouldn't say we're entirely over it, even now.

The fundamental concept underlying Notes is the *database*: a repository of information, a collection of documents—"notes"—that can be viewed and organized in a panoply of different ways.

Generally, Notes databases reside on *servers*—usually, high-performance systems with large amounts of disk capacity. Users can keep personal copies (i.e., *replicas*) of databases locally—that is, on their own PCs. Any number of users can access a server-based database simultaneously via a highly intuitive interface that looks like Figure 7.1.

Each database is represented by a separate button. As an individual's databases begin to proliferate, they can be organized logically through use of the tabs at the top of the interface display. It's entirely up to the user which databases he wants to see, and they're laid out on the desktop.

The hard news about using a Notes database is that it requires a vocabulary shift. Most users are accustomed to navigating the repository of choice for *structured data*: the SQL-accessed relational database. But Notes databases

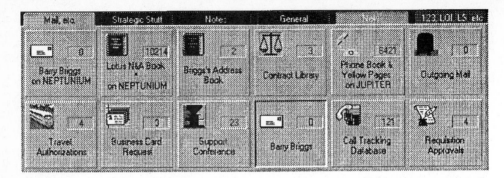

Fig. 7.1 Interactive Interface

aren't relational, because Notes deals with *unstructured information* as opposed to structured data, and new ways require new means. It is this departure from what has long been the norm that both gives Notes its initial critical differentiation—its ultimate potential to actually change the way people do business—and also makes the Notes database difficult for some to conceptualize at first.

The easy news, however, is that "at first" is the operative phrase. Once you learn how to use any one Notes database, you've basically learned how to use them all. This is so because they're all built on the same two concepts: *views* and *forms*.

☞ **Views** are the ways of accessing and eyeballing documents stored in a database.

☞ **Forms** are new combinations of information extracted from the database.

To "open" (i.e., get access to) a Notes database, a user simply double-clicks on its icon. The user then sees a view of the documents in the database; for example, see Figure 7.2.

Views can display any number and variety of documents; the amount of detail shown, and the sorting convention used, are optional with the user. For example, let's say we're looking at a customer records database for XYZ Widget Corp. We could ask for a very expansive view—for instance, "all customers with

Status	Authorization	Traveler	Destinations	Req Date	Age
In Process					
	12124-00003	Bill Brown	New York	01/19/93	0
	22334-00006	Venessa Vincent	Chicago	01/07/93	13
	37378-00002	Carol Clayton	New York	01/19/93	0
	42423-00004	Hattie Henderson	San Francisco;Seattle	01/19/93	0
Approved					
	11333-00005	Kerry Kingston	Dallas	01/19/93	0
Rejected					
	12124-00001	Bill Brown	New York	01/07/93	13

Fig. 7.2 The Database Opened

complaints." On the other hand, we could also ask for a considerably more contracted view: say, "all customers in the Chicago metropolitan area who complained within the most recent calendar quarter that they received ordered widgets more than one week late." Any view can be either expanded or collapsed: pull-down menus, clicks, and keystrokes are all it takes.

Once documents have been sorted according to the user's needs, double-clicking on any one of the documents referenced opens the document itself. Document structure is highly configurable in Notes, thanks to a powerful forms editor that defines fields which can be used to index documents in any number of ways. (The view itself, in fact, is one of the applications of the indices.)

Say you've just double-clicked on one of the documents listed in Figure 7.2; to wit, Hattie Henderson. Figure 7.3 shows what you'll see on your screen.

Each item above—Traveler Name, Employee Number, and so on—is a Notes field. Not only can all such fields be organized in any number of ways, they can also be *encrypted* so that only certain users can see their contents.

There you have a quick tour through the way in which information is organized in a Notes database. But the key thing to always bear in mind is that Notes is much more than a means of managing data: it's an application platform upon which we ourselves at Lotus and our customers can build systems that coordinate and extend the processes by which we run our businesses and activities.

Herein lie two additional concepts: *routing* and *replication*. Routing is the process through which documents can be directed from one individual to another. This is, of course, the foundation for electronic mail. However, routing technology is useful well beyond simple point-to-point mail delivery—for instance, in sophisticated workflow applications.

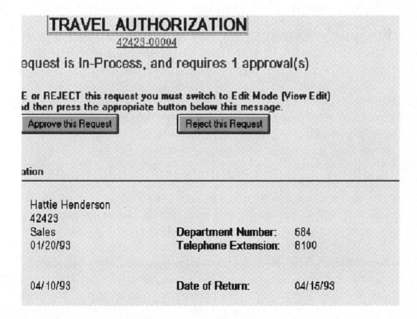

Fig. 7.3 A Single Document from the Database

The essence of workflow is the provision of electronic support for business processes previously accomplished by means of laborious manual procedures: for instance, hand-carrying an approval form from office to office. Notes applications can be built to replace and improve these processes. Take, for example, an applicant-tracking system used by a Human Resources department. As resumes are received, they are electronically scanned into Notes. An HR professional can then read them, identify potential department managers who may wish to interview a particular job candidate—of course, selecting only managers who appear in the database as having openings in their departments—and forward the applicable resumes. The document each interested manager receives contains not only the resume, but two buttons, "interested" and "not interested"; if the former is pushed, an email message automatically goes to HR, apprising the relevant parties of the interest and keying off the formal interview process.

The second linchpin of Notes is a technology pioneered by Lotus: replication, through which copies (or *replicas*) of databases can stay synchronized even though the computers on which they reside may not be connected. Here's how it works:

Imagine one Sales Tracking database in San Francisco and another in Paris. Users in each country are constantly adding and updating documents within each database. At some predetermined time, one server automatically and literally calls the other on the telephone, and they (forgive the pun) compare Notes; that is, they build up lists of documents that have been altered in any way since the last such reconciliation—called a *replication*—and copy these documents over.

In Figure 7.4, replicas of the Sales database in San Francisco and Paris call each other to determine which documents are missing from which replica, and quickly fill in the gaps with copies passed to each other.

What if someone in San Francisco changes the same document that someone in Paris wants to modify? Unlike traditional database systems, Notes allows *both* documents to be changed. When replication occurs, a *replication conflict* is marked; a user can manually update both documents to resolve the conflict.

Replication is a particular boon to laptop users, the burgeoning breed of "road warriors." A salesperson on the road, for instance, can dial into a Notes server and replicate databases to a laptop in just the same manner as can another server. And, in order both to conserve disk space and limit retrieved documents to those of interest, a wide variety of controls and constraints can easily be placed on the replication process.

Finally, recognizing the security issues inherent in a multi-user system, Notes subsumes a pervasive and consistent security-architecture-based public-key cryptography—the technology of which Lotus pioneered in cooperation with RSA Data Security—as well as certificate management based on international standards (X.509) and a thorough implementation of access controls. Via the security engine, a user can encrypt mail or any other document, assign various individuals different forms of access, and build sophisticated workflow applications based on digital signature technology.

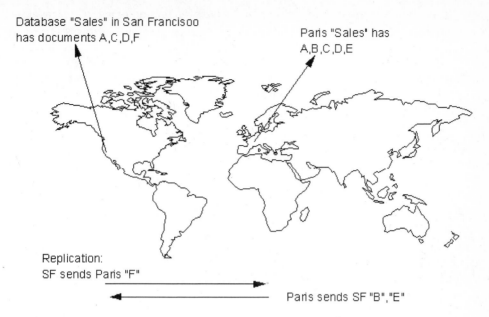

Database "Sales" in San Francisoo
has documents A,C,D,F

Paris "Sales' has
A,B,C,D,E

Replication:
SF sends Paris "F"

Paris sends SF "B","E"

Fig. 7.4 Replication

7.2 ACHIEVING THE GOAL

To accomplish the ambitious goal Lotus set for Notes, the company knew that it had to make Notes a platform standard, much as Microsoft's Windows had become a graphical user interface standard. Also, it had to be platform-total from the word go—a hard-to-implement concept that is just now really taking off. But none of this could even be contemplated until the groupware concept took root, and the groupware market took off.

And therein lies the truly daunting conundrum of the whole Notes venture: in order to be a player in the market, first Lotus had to see to it that the market was created.

How do you do that? Looking back, I think the one-word answer is "iteratively": put the product out there as early as possible, be ready to work closely with any company willing to try it out, and never forget the three most important commitments: Communicate, communicate, and communicate.

With Notes, it was very hard to explain to people what it was and the breadth of what it could do. There was simply no precedent. The impact of that fact can be gauged to some extent in the words of Forrester Research, Inc. analysts Heidi Dix and Stuart Woodring, who wrote the following in a November 1993 Forrester Software Strategy Report:

"Notes defies simple categorization: To different people with different problems, it can appear to be very different things. This is because Notes combines four common, but otherwise separate, technologies: 1) email and messaging services; 2) object store and related services (replication, security, administration); 3) graphical user interface; and 4) a development environment. The result is a technology melting pot that enables a new class of systems focused on...sharing knowledge, not performing repetitive transactions[;] managing qualitative information, not hard data[;] and supporting geographically distributed users, not desk-bound clerks."

If Forrester was still wrestling with these difficulties four years after Notes' debut, imagine what it was like trying to market the concept fresh off the drawing pad!

In retrospect, it looks easy—but an army of M.B.A.s kept extremely busy just trying to figure out how to define the darned thing beyond email.

"Notes was very much of a visionary idea," recalls Eric Sall, a director at the Lexington, Massachusetts-based public relations firm Lois Paul Partners. "To make it happen, lots of technologies had to be investigated—if not invented." Sall got to view this process from a front row seat: when he parlayed his new M.B.A. degree into a position as a strategic marketing analyst at Lotus back in 1986, little did he know that he was about to become the first employee in the Notes organization.

In fact, it was Sall—then a member of a team of internal consultants assigned to evaluate the nascent product line—who ended up writing the first Notes business plan.

"It was the summer of 1986, and we had just brought the thing over from Iris after what was basically a two-year R&D period to install the first application: a sales opportunity tracking application," he recalls. "As soon as it was up, in addition to using it, we started to look at the marketing and technical issues we were going to have to deal with." It wasn't long, says Sall, before his team made a disheartening discovery: "We realized that in both areas—technical and marketing—there were a lot of questions we simply couldn't answer. There had never been anything like this before; we had no precedent, no model, no pioneers to learn from." Left with no alternative, Lotus set out to give Notes, at least in small, the one thing it desperately needed and didn't have: a history.

There was a real Catch-22: in order to actually understand it, you had to go beyond what you could currently do with it. Lotus 1-2-3 was revolutionary in that it automated a series of cumbersome, time-consuming, and often intimidating tasks, but it didn't ask users to completely recast their way of thinking about information. In allowing users to manage unstructured information, such as text, in a flexibly structured fashion, Notes does just that.

"The first thing we did was try to target some likely companies to be the first users—and you've got to understand, I'm talking way pre-beta," says Sall. "We got it down to those that were already networked, and that already had a close relationship with Lotus—both for obvious reasons."

In 1987, this initiative took shape as the Notes Application Partners Program, under which some 25 companies got a free on-site Notes installation and consulting to aim at applicable projects. In return, Lotus got its invaluable first feedback "without which we never could have finished the product, much less marketed it," says Sall.

Even for a team steeled to expect the unexpected, he remembers, the Application Partners Program experience always seemed to pack an extra surprise. "One big revelation was that we had no way of predicting who was going to really *do* something with Notes," he says. "Enthusiasm, which we initially thought was a pretty reliable indicator given the kind of companies we had picked for the program in the first place, turned out not to be any great predictor." Some firms that seemed unable to wait until Notes was installed, says Sall, let the software languish or used it for workaday email-type applications. Others seemed underwhelmed at the prospect of having Notes aboard, "but once it was in, it went like wildfire. And that's another thing we discovered: there was very little middle ground. Users either loved it or couldn't care less." Both of these early observations continue to hold true today.

Difficult as it was and continues to be to fully demonstrate what Notes is, it has proven almost as stiff a challenge to get across what it is not. Never in its most zealous "marketeering" moments has Lotus suggested that Notes is a tool for all occasions or a cure for all corporate ills. Most prominently, Notes was never intended to be, and should not be used as, a transaction-processing front end to an operational database system—that is, traditional order entry, billing, or accounting system that performs, captures, and analyzes business data. Where high-volume, data-intensive, real-time-oriented transaction systems are in question, Notes is not the best answer. Neither is Notes, which was specifically designed to handle unstructured information, a relational database.

When Notes usage extends—as it can and, in many cases, ideally should—beyond the discrete departmental application to enterprise-wide usage, a new set of caveats comes into play:

☞ Lay the foundation for the implementation by carefully creating and *communicating* the business goals and benefits sought, and the specific ways in which Notes might be expected to help attain them.

☞ Make certain that the appropriate technology infrastructure—prominently, the network—is already in place.

☞ Assume that separately allocated training and management will be needed; then, double your assumption. Those who kid themselves that Notes can be learned in employees' spare time or tacked on as the network manager's umpty-umpth task are courting failure.

In addition to an ongoing attempt to ward off misassessments of Notes' technological aspects, Lotus has also been involved ever since the start in a missionary effort with respect to Notes implementation. While there are a slew of consultants addressing the issue these days, the company literally will be the first to remind you that Notes is unlikely to foment change among the change-resistant, or create an information-sharing culture where an information-hoarding, team-averse culture existed before.

"Notes works when watching work in progress is part of the cultural norm, rather than a jarring departure from it," says James V. McGee, a partner in the Chicago-based management/IT consulting firm of Diamond Technology Associates. "A developing idea is a very fragile beast. If you throw it open to discussion [via Notes], the operative question is: will it be nurtured, or will everyone get out their shotguns and try to bring it down—with the biggest reward going to the one who brings it down the fastest?"

In response to the difficulties of marketing Notes, the company made two dramatic moves: Manzi brought a host of non-PC, mission-critical management aboard, and Lotus went into channel-creating with a vengeance, detonating an explosion of allies. The community of Notes third-party products, 170 strong in the fall of 1992, now numbers into the thousands. Envisioning it from the start and kicking it off along simultaneously with the Notes introduction required of Lotus two psychological steps not commonly characteristic of companies that grew up in the 1970s boomtown: admitting what we didn't—and, in many cases, wouldn't—have, and giving other companies a blank check in creating around our core. Both were a reach—but only fitting, since Notes itself was nothing if not a reach.

The management change, on the other hand, was no reach at all; neither was it a "Saturday Night Massacre" that replaced a deposed "old guard." Rather, it was a logical and necessary infusion of large-firm, mainframe-oriented experience into a corporate management that was heavily PC-oriented. I came aboard as part of this initiative, fresh from a three-year stint as president and COO of Cognos Corp. and still very mindful of lessons learned as an executive, first at Software International and then at Cullinet as these originally mainframe-oriented software houses extended their offerings across other platforms. John Landry, now Lotus' Senior Vice President for Software Development and Chief Technology Officer, is a veteran of two decades in the software industry and was a major force behind the development of McCormack & Dodge Corp.'s breakthrough Millennium software operating system. Bob Weiler, who heads up marketing for Lotus, also grew up with and in the software industry at executive posts at McCormack & Dodge, Cullinet, and Interleaf.

7.3 NOTES AS A RE-ENGINEERING AGENT

The need to re-engineer is so critical—and the buzzword so prevalent—that it is hard to find a company today that does *not* claim to have some level of re-engineering initiative afoot or at least on the drawing board. Re-engineering means different things to different companies. Up and down the meaning spectrum, however, the concept of working smarter rather than harder, usually in a highly cooperative format, lies at the heart of the initiative. It is only logical, then, that Notes—conceived and developed with genuine sharing in mind—lends itself to a high percentage of re-engineering projects, at anywhere from a minimal to a sweeping extent.

Just how extensive the role of Notes in re-engineering efforts has become recently took a team of analysts from the Framingham, Massachusetts-based research firm International Data Corp. by surprise. "We started this project with a simple goal: interview Lotus Notes customers and determine their return on investment," IDC senior consultant Ann M. Palermo wrote in the subsequent published report. But what the IDC team found in its visits to 65 worldwide Notes sites went well beyond the original goal. In Lapland, noted Palermo, a Finnish executive described Notes as an agent of change in the way people develop applications, communicate, work together, and view automation. "In effect," he told the IDC analysts, "Notes has the power to transform a company and the people who work for it."

While Lapland might be isolated, the executive's observations were not. "Nearly every [Notes] customer we visited had articulated a similar message," wrote Palermo. Combine the impressive financial returns revealed by the IDC study with "the uniform embrace of change, and the result is much more significant than the simple acquisition of a new type of productivity software," she noted in the report. "Lotus Notes exemplifies a new class of software, allowing companies to automate business processes that have resisted previous automation attempts. Notes may be the elusive Holy Grail of white collar productivity."

For many organizations, the urge to re-engineer a process is sparked by the need to cut costs. Where this is the case, says Santa Clara, California-based technology and management consultant Carol Anne Ogdin, Notes is likely to be a valuable tool, for three reasons:

☞ It's off the shelf: "Nobody has to develop special hardware or software, the software is widely supported by third parties and educators, and it's available on a wide array of popular platforms." Moreover, shifts in Lotus' distribution policy are encouraging more competitive pricing of Notes; for example, the Passport program debuted last spring, a "frequent buyers" initiative that offers decentralized customers the chance to earn volume discounts.

☞ It's scalable: "A small-scale solution is easily expanded into ever-larger scales of implementation without sudden disruptions in methods, technology or service," says Ogdin. "The ability to economically add more clients to a server and more servers to the system is straightforward."

☞ It comes with a slew of available applications—for starters, the so-called "Nifty Fifty," complete, tested, ready to be customized and spread among four categories: tracking, discussion, broadcast, and reference.

How quickly these characteristics can translate into bottom-line savings became clear, for instance, to Mead Paper Co.—a business under the unremitting financial pressure of serving an increasingly demanding customer base while battling ever more stringent environmental and legal constraints.

"The economics of the paper industry require a continuously high level of output with very little quality variation in the final product," noted IDC's Palermo, who featured Mead's experience in the IDC study. "Therefore, the production process is highly automated and monitored by sophisticated equipment. Paper companies require such long production runs and have invested such large quantities of capital in their manufacturing capacity that any quality problem requires immediate diagnosis." Irregularities that might seem minuscule in most contexts—disparate thickness, or an unrecognizable blob—can bring a portion of the manufacturing process to a standstill.

When that happens, samples of the nonconforming compound are dispatched to a central R&D facility for analysis; R&D has to respond to quality queries and production mishaps on a daily basis, in addition to managing long-term projects requested by the company's various divisions.

"How do you prioritize and assign inquiries which may span several scientific disciplines when the response time required is too short to formalize a team and have a structured project methodology in place?" asked Palermo. "How do you provide an acceptable level of service to each division on a daily basis while also ensuring that the longer-term R&D projects remain on schedule?" Faced with these questions, and armed with a mainframe-based project accounting system that was providing less than complete answers, Mead Paper turned to Notes.

The system on which the company had been relying, says Palermo, allowed R&D to track projects, but had no reporting or management capabilities. The Notes system that replaced it also provided project reporting, and added project management and cost accounting budgets—the latter of which was of particular value in light of the fact that Mead R&D charges project costs back to its various intracorporate user divisions. The divisions then use their R&D "bills" as data for coming-year budget projection.

Albeit not in the original Notes game plan, Mead also ended up moving its mainframe-based purchase system onto Notes.

The new groupware system went to work in Mead's research lab as well as in its back room. The paper manufacturer's analytical group, noted Palermo, "is required to identify and explain the behavior of more than 1,000 samples per year with a staff of fewer than 10 people. Each individual is required to document all analysis. Prior to Notes, a Digital [Equipment Corp.] VAX-based Laboratory Information Management System was in place; however, it was expensive to administer and only about 10% of the R&D group were willing to use it. After the analytical group adopted Notes, their service improved to become the best in the facility."

That result alone would go a long way toward justifying Notes to a company so heavily reliant on quality control. However, Mead Paper also realized quantifiable savings in every area in which Notes was implemented:

☞ The functionality differential between the firm's mainframe-based project accounting system and its Notes-based project reporting, management, and accounting package accounted for an annual cost savings of $140,000.

☞ The mainframe-based purchase system cost $245,000 and required the assistance of 1.5 dedicated purchasing agents/application support workers, according to the IDC study; the Notes-based purchase system saves approximately 2/3 of the cost—Mead estimates its annual cost at $80,000—and logs a similar saving in person-hours, requiring only 1/2 a person to manage.

☞ The analytical group's VAX-to-Notes move saved half a person, $50,000 in maintenance, and $17,500 in software support, according to IDC—not to mention increasing the usage rate from 10% to 80%.

Their experience was far from unusual, according to the IDC study. Calling the results "simply staggering," IDC reported finding "return on investment from Notes applications ranged from 16% to an incredible 1,666%, on a median investment of just over $100,000." Some 90% of the 65 companies included in the study and reporting quantifiable benefits showed returns of 40% or more; more than 50% showed returns in excess of 100%, and approximately a quarter of the firms showed returns in the 200% ballpark.

The same attributes that make Notes an effective cost-reduction catalyst also render it a particularly apt tool for quick and easy systems implementation—a need that looms large in re-engineering initiatives. While many management scholars are striving to hammer home the idea that *information* and *information technology* are not synonymous, nevertheless it is also widely accepted that effective information systems can and ought to be a major enabler of the information-enriched organization. The trouble is, "effective" information system all too often means "new" or at least "heavily retooled"—which in turn tends to translate into "expensive" and "time-consuming."

On the other hand, says Ogdin, "Lotus Notes is specifically designed to implement small, quick-response projects...and to foster incremental growth." Built-in design tools, she notes, "mean that each and every copy...has the ability to be used to enrich, enhance and improve the specific application system, on the fly, in immediate response to changing needs and perceptions." Scalability allows for growth from a small base to a large system without disruptive changes in method; meanwhile, Notes' security control features allow the ability to change the system to be restricted to a select few specialists even as the ability to use it expands.

Enticing though it may be, the prospect of creating eventually complex systems with quantum savings in time, effort, and cost is only the second best promise Notes holds out to companies whose re-engineering initiatives involve systems development. More valuable still is the fact that such savings get to the root of one of the key barriers to re-engineering: fear of failure.

True change, says Sheila Smith, a partner at Ernst & Young's Boston-based Center for Business Innovation, is likely to occur only in business contexts in which it is clearly understood that well-intentioned failure will not be penalized. Risk aversity and change, she notes, are counterindicative: a fact of business life that has scuttled many an ostensibly strong re-engineering effort. Notes, says IDC's Palermo, "reduces the barrier to automating business processes by allowing users to simply 'try it' and if it doesn't work, to throw it away with little penalty." In contrast with traditional methods, she points out, Notes development tends to bare potential problems early in the game, allowing the company to fix the error or cut its losses. "Effectively, the investment equation has been changed to the point where there is very little risk of doing something new."

Sometimes what Notes brings to the re-engineering party is as simple—and as critical—as the ability to curtail the paper chase that has traditionally hobbled so many organizations or departments. In New York, for example, The Banker's Trust Co. is two years into a Notes-based project aimed at restoring thousands of man-hours to members of its domestic custody department who were formerly drowning in paperwork and delaying customer service accordingly.

Prior to the advent of BT Edge—the trading house's name for its new system, which lets bank administrators work with Notes-based customer case files across a Novell LAN—each of the 20 to 30 customer queries the bank receives on an average day was apt to trigger a cumbersome research process that often entailed a slew of administrators, thousands of pages of paper, and hundreds of hours. Customers, vice president of global assets Roger Porcella told a *Computerworld* editor last spring, often had to wait a week for answers to even fairly routine questions. [Maglitta, J. (1994), Re-engineering the Workplace, *Computerworld*, May 16, pp. 100, 102.] Now, same-day replies are considered a worst-case scenario; most customers are answered within minutes. According to Porcella, replacing dumb terminals, screen dumps, microfiche, and reams of paper forms and reports with Notes-based "case files" saved "thousands of research hours and eliminated the need to print 50,000 report pages a day" in its first 16 months—freeing 27 researchers to be redeployed upward.

In recent years, the literature of business management has become flooded with testimonials to the urgency of converting sluggish behemoths—hogtied by hierarchical bureaucracies, suffocating under a barrage of useless data, and confounded by mixed signals—into "learning organizations": firms invigorated by easy access to relevant information from a panoply of internal and external sources, poised to embrace and implement change. Only in a learning organization, one author after another posits, can bona fide re-engineering take root.

Creating and sustaining such an organization, however, is proving a great deal more difficult than paying homage to it in print. "In an era of highly mobile workers, grass roots computing, and mercurial environments, the goal...seems more challenging than ever," noted Ernst & Young's Center for Business Innovation in a recent internal publication. "A company may recruit the smartest of workers and invest heavily in their ongoing training, but end up with a knowledge base smaller than the sum of its parts." ["How do we manage the knowledge of the organization?" *E&Y Centerpoint number one*. May 1994]

The problem, according to the seasoned analyst/consultants, comes down to an egregious—and widespread—corporate cultural tendency to make the least of potentially valuable information. "A salesman sees a competitor's new product," the piece continues, "but has no mechanism or incentive to share his impressions with marketing. R&D on the West Coast reinvents the same wheel envisioned the previous year on the East Coast. A planner spends time and money getting information that is already in her office mate's files. The problem is universal, but increasingly hard to live with." If this is the problem—and a host of industry observers are in accord with E&Y—then it is hard to see how Notes, which ideologically encourages true information sharing and technologically enables it for the first time, can *avoid* becoming a key component of the solution in many cases.

Unlimited information flow coupled with multiple ownership of information makes a heady combination, IDC's Palermo noted in the ROI study report. "Notes offers the opportunity to record a corporate memory, whereby everyone in the company can tap into the problem-solving record of the past as well as pose questions in real time. The notion that the entire resources of the corporation can be brought to bear on a single problem is a very powerful concept."

So powerful, in fact, that it spurs idea generation from corporate citizens who formerly feared their input would be neither recognized nor rewarded. In striking contrast with email, "where there is a tendency for users to carbon copy everyone on their list just to prove they are busy," she said, Notes tends to elicit contributions from formerly unheard-from personnel, "while nonproductive members become aware that indeed there is no place to hide."

One of the aspects of traditional organizational culture that is undergoing early and visible change is the whereabouts of the workforce. A confluence of factors, from environmental concerns to workers with increased commitment to family responsibilities to various federal and state employee benefit mandates that drive financially pressed employers into widespread outsourcing wherever possible, is quickly seeding a nation of part- or full-time telecommuters. *BusinessWeek* recently pegged the number of U.S.-based "lone eagles"—professionals who can, and do, work virtually wherever they wish, regardless of their employer's location—at 10 million, noting that the number is likely to mushroom as the Information Highway opens up [*BusinessWeek*, Nov. 15, 1993, p. 58]. Notes is among the technological advances enabling lone eagles to fly, and to do so without endangering their employers' or clients' work product reliability or continuity.

For instance, says Carol Anne Ogdin, "with workflow computing under Notes, where documents prepared for processing are delivered automatically to the employee's desktop computer, the work can be done independent of physical location. An accounts payable clerk can reconcile documents, look up on-line policies and procedures, forward completed work to another station for check issuance (or reject the document to the appropriate party), all the while tending to the infant in the crib next to her." Here's how minimalist "central HQ" can get: Dallas Helps, a Texas-based drug treatment information clearing house, has only two employees. Through Notes, however, the minimally staffed organization serves as the research and analysis 'department' of some 19 Dallas-area drug abuse programs.

Enabling telecommuting, however, is far from the only way in which Notes is helping to redraw corporate boundaries. Ultimately even more revolutionary than such structural changes, for instance, is a subtle shift in the status and relationships of the people within business organizations that is occurring as groupware occupies an increasingly significant place in the business toolkit. At the accounting and consulting firm of Coopers & Lybrand, for instance, outsourcing division manager Dan Hickox waxes enthusiastic about Notes' ability to turn data into information—in this case, information that is directly honing the firm's ability to bring in clients even as it gears up to sharpen the skills of the auditors who will serve the expanded clientele.

"Before, there could be times when some of us didn't have a clue about what engagements others of us were going after," admits Hickox. Inevitably in a huge and dispersed organization, he says, situations arose in which C&L account executives inadvertently bid against each other for one account while other attractive possibilities went unnoticed.

No more. Over the past two years, C&L has phased in a Notes system to help build, and then serve as the anchor of, an all-inclusive electronic auditors' workbench. Potentially, says Hickox, some 25,000 auditors will be communicating nationwide via Notes, leveraging each other's skills and experience while avoiding each other's mistakes. But well before that lofty goal is attained, interorganizational efficiency has skyrocketed, and with clear if not yet quantifiable benefit to the firm.

"Now," says Hickox, "Bob puts into the system an engagement he's trying to sell to XYZ Co., and gets a message from Tom saying 'I'm already working on that one.' Meanwhile, though, five other folks have sent him promising leads." Within minutes, says Hickox, Tom and the firm have avoided wasting anywhere from hours to days, C&L is a contender for engagements on which it might otherwise have failed to bid, and collegial feelings have been enhanced instead of eroded.

Similarly, General American—a St. Louis, Missouri-based life insurance company whose $185 billion in controlled life insurance and 2,000-plus group clients place it among the 50 largest insurance carriers in the U.S.—is relying on Notes not only to drive sizeable near-term cost savings, but to recast the way in which the business of the business is done.

During the past six years, General American has enjoyed significant growth; but to stay on its upward trajectory, it must compete with much larger competitors with higher name recognition and deeper pockets. Like so many other firms, it knows that the route toward meeting so stiff a competitive challenge is paved with superior products, customized insurance programs, and responsive customer service.

Meanwhile, General American must also maintain strict internal efficiencies so as to keep its pricing competitive. Intense competition in the group insurance industry, where cost-conscious corporate customers don't hesitate to shop carefully for the lowest bid, has pared the industry's profit margin to less than 2%—reducing administrative costs and working more efficiently is critical to General American.

In 1992, the company resolved to improve its methods for channeling new account information from the field to the home office. One agenda item was the replacement of an outmoded mainframe-based application, which had grown to include millions of lines of code. More important, however, it hoped to find an effective and attractive tool for the field sales force, most of whom disliked and avoided the unwieldy, often inaccurate mainframe-based system.

General American considered a raft of options, from reverting back to a paper-based system to an approximately $1 million investment in artificial intelligence. What it opted for was Lotus Notes. Now, 250 users within the company rely on a Notes application called Link, whose 40 forms confer a host of benefits on General American:

☞ In the key business area of new account creation, Link strips the limits off the level of detail field personnel can include in their target customer profile submissions to the home office. Once limited to specific types and amounts of information, they can now include all details relating to the large group accounts, which all have different insurance needs. Notes takes specific information input from the forms and channels it automatically to 15 functional departments. When and as conditions change, field personnel simply use an update capacity sadly lacking in their former system to alter the forms in Link, which serves as the repository for all new account information during the initial setup period.

☞ Attracting users to technological aid and training them to leverage it is no longer a problem at General American, either at the training or budgetary level. Link provides a structured walk-through of the entire information-gathering process, speeding up the work while improving its accuracy and thoroughness. The Notes interface is bringing folks aboard without extensive training, and the application even fills in some information automatically. The result? According to General American, input time has been cut in half—down from two days to one—allowing salespeople to focus on sales rather than becoming mired in administration and improving the accuracy of the information in the process.

☞ The company had allocated a year for developing Link, but the intuitive and iterative Notes development environment brought them from first team meeting to final rollout in less than eight months.

☞ The company's $100,000-plus annual maintenance bill on a $250,000 mainframe system has shrunk to $30,000 a year to maintain a $70,000 system.

Perhaps the most telling result, however, is the traffic reduction on the company's internal help routes. The general complexity and myriad details of General American's large accounts used to generate some 40 questions per account—even after the field force submitted information. Because Link both promotes thoroughness and makes it easier for field personnel to submit better information, the home office now logs 15 to 20 questions on each new account: a 50% increase in quality.

And the company sees this as merely the beginning. Now that they've been introduced to Notes via Link, for instance, General American's sales representatives are beginning to use Notes databases to share their expertise.

Moreover, the way in which firms like Portland, Oregon-based law firm Bullivant, Houser, Bailey, Pendergrass & Hoffman [see Chapter 1, "Intangible Benefits of Groupware"] are expanding the meaning of "enterprise" to include customers and suppliers, says IDC's Palermo, "suggests that Notes has the potential to be a tool which will standardize the way in which companies can share electronic information, as opposed to simply data." And while this is still a relatively infrequent use of Notes today, the IDC report concludes, "extending the enterprise will ultimately have the greatest business impact."

7.4 PARTNERS IN NOTES

"The next round of [Notes] customers will not buy Notes because it is 'neat technology,' wrote Forrester analysts Heidi Dix and Stuart Woodring in a recent report [Forrester, cited above]. "They may not see an immediate use for its generic capabilities. Instead, many will want to buy turnkey applications from software vendors and VARs."

Forrester recognizes what Lotus knew from Day One: it is virtually impossible to overstate the integral position of the Notes third-party industry—a community that at recent count stood at approximately 170 companies and is still very much in the growth stage.

Notes may not be all things to all people, but right from the start, it's been a host of things to third-party developers. Notes, points out editor and consultant Sally Blanning DeJean, affords third parties an environment in which to work, an integrator, a container for information, a superstructure framework, or all of the above. Most tantalizing, perhaps, it represents a product with missing pieces.

And the missing pieces are not dispensable. User organizations need third-party products to extend Notes' capabilities; complete or ease existing functions; and tighten or refine integration between Notes and nonrelated software.

Much as Notes itself can't be maximally leveraged without a user base that is primed to share information and ideas, so Lotus has known from the start that this was not a product that could be produced and controlled by any one manufacturer. The cultivation of third-party *partners*, in the deepest sense—a symbiotic relationship that would go beyond the strategic alliance—was a critical part of the original Notes blueprint, starting with the Application Partners Program that made approximately 25 outside companies pre-Alpha users and, essentially, codevelopers.

Just how physically huge a part of Notes the partners would be, however, is something that Lotus underestimated. Like so much else about Notes, we are finding hands-on experience to be our best teacher, and have learned to regard the development of the third-party industry, like the development of a Notes application, as an overwhelmingly iterative process. In several short years, the list of third-party companies offering products and services that expand the breadth and depth of Lotus Notes has grown from some 170 to over 1000. While a

third-party industry of such scope fulfills Lotus' dreams, it makes it hard to fulfill requests for lists of Notes partners and what they bring to the party. Lotus'
most recent attempt is a booklet 238 pages long. To offer a sampling, however:

☞ Waltham, Massachusetts-based Trinzic Corp.'s InfoPump offers users who
   need to import information into Notes from outside sources or export Notes
   information to such sources a "middleware" route. The product moves data
   and metadata between database management systems on an event-driven
   or scheduled basis, transforming the data according to instructions written
   in a high-level scripting language.

☞ Courtesy of Cambridge, Massachusetts-based SandPoint Corp., Hoover—
   working completely within Notes—dispatches electronic agents to retrieve
   information from a wealth of on-line databases, CD-ROMs, newswires,
   broadcast feeds, and corporate computing environments. Once directed,
   Hoover will also update the information as frequently as required.

☞ Electronic Workforce, offered by Santa Clara, California-based Edify Corp.,
   harnesses the well-known communications trio of fax, phone, and email to
   provide remote access to Notes information—messages and data alike—as
   well as to extend Notes' capabilities via integration with other applications
   residing on host computers, LAN servers, and PCs.

☞ ELF, Inc., in Mercer Island, Washington, creates and deploys elfs—members
   of the Electronic Labor Force—within networked environments. Using
   Notes, among other systems, elfs are at work today in the legal profession,
   tracking client matters from initial assignment through conflict of interest
   searches and, once a case is accepted, through all stages until final closure.

☞ VisionQuest, from Austin, Texas-based Collaborative Technologies Corp., is
   a LAN-based electronic meeting support software package that helps teams
   focus on desired outcomes and work toward agreement. A dialogue agenda
   structures and documents the group's collaboration on idea generation,
   evaluation, and prioritization. Among the group-oriented tasks for which
   the system provides tools: brainstorming, commenting, rating, ranking, voting, multicriteria scoring, and resource allocation.

☞ For users looking to analyze and automate business processes, Alameda,
   California-based Action Technologies, Inc. offers Action Workflow: a package tightly integrated with Notes that lets the business process owner
   draw, document, and print a map of a business' processes and its network of
   workflows; enables developers to specify the business rules, forms, participants, and data in the process workflow; creates or edits the definitions
   databases that define the business process; and unifies workflow operations.

☞ From Watermark Software, Inc. in Burlington, Massachusetts comes Watermark Discovery Edition, image-enabling software for Windows applications

that leverages OLE to offer Notes users complete integration of paper documents into their office computing environment.

☞ San Diego, California-based Simpact Associates' Remark! PhoneClient for Lotus Notes invites mobile or remote users into the Notes workgroup by letting them access, create, and manage voice information and data in Notes databases with no computing platform other than a touchtone telephone.

☞ Danvers, Massachusetts-based PictureTel's LIVE-PCS100 integrates live, interactive video conferencing within a Notes document.

☞ New York University now allows students to matriculate in The Virtual College: an on-line teleprogram that trains managers and professionals to both design and work within electronic environments. Participants receive instruction, interview clients, conduct analyses, resolve problems, and build Notes applications—at work, at home, or on the road.

☞ Distributed Systems Solutions International, Inc. in Westlake Village, California, offers DSSI Helpdesk Management, a Notes-based application that lets any department within an organization track customer service/support requests.

And, as mentioned, this is just a small taste of what's already out there—not to mention what's on the drawing board.

7.5 UP AND COMING

Notes—unsurprisingly, considering its start as a product that had to invent and advance its own market before it could take root—is very much a concept and product in evolution. What we've seen so far is only the bare beginning.

Where we're going, at least in the near future, can be glimpsed in developments such as Lotus' partnership with AT&T to produce the NetworkNotes public Notes service, the debut of the NotesView package that lets IS managers centrally administer Notes.

It can be seen in the groundbreaking pact signed with Oracle Corp. in September 1994: an agreement that turns a long-time rival into a creative partner and expands Notes' utility as an enterprise-wide application development platform by integrating Notes with Oracle's emergent Documents multimedia software package. Under the terms of the agreement, Notes users will be able to store data in several Oracle relational databases as well as having full access to Notes' document storage capabilities. Transaction processing capabilities will enter the Notes package for the first time as a result of the pact. In addition, the enhanced Notes interface that will make its debut as part of Version 4.0 will be able to front-end a slew of network resources—including Oracle servers.

And, of course, we are nearing shipment of the most sweeping upgrade in two years: Notes Version 4.0, due for release in the first half of 1995.

The overarching goal of Notes 4.0 is to continue Notes' core strengths: the ability to foster communication, collaboration, and cooperation amongst people—

not just seasoned computer professionals, but users regardless of their level of technological proficiency—by providing a way to rapidly build applications with minimal programming resources and maximal user ease and flexibility. As was the case with earlier versions, this latest iteration addresses the needs of all three sectors of Notes' user community: end users, programmers, and administrators. And where Version 3.0, which emerged as folks were still trying to get a handle on the Notes concept, weighed in a bit more heavily on behalf of end users, 4.0 packs a few extra goodies for programmers and administrators—partly to even up the attention, but also to fuel Notes toward its coming role as creator and enabler of enterprise-wide groupware applications.

Thus, 4.0's five areas of focus:

☞ For nontechnical end users: a substantially more intuitive user interface
☞ For developers: quantum leaps in programmability
☞ For administrators, a triple treat:

✗ Advances in reliability and manageability
✗ Increased scalability and performance
✗ A single mail user interface and infrastructure

Just as it doesn't take a rocket scientist to use Notes, it also doesn't take one to realize that 4.0's attention to reliability, manageability, scalability, and performance and programmability is aimed at users involved in mission-critical systems.

Here's a sampling of the features behind the five-way focus.

7.5.1 Intuitive User Interface

Up until now, most nontechnical end users have availed themselves of comparatively little of Notes' functionality. Version 4.0 invites them to help themselves to more—first, by making the taking considerably easier. A series of functions that existed only in syntactical form in V.3 are now a mere mouse-click away. The list of newly accessible functions includes, for instance:

☞ Enhanced search bar functions such as query builder and query by form
☞ Customized views without any need for design knowledge
☞ Selective replication, available on a point-and-click basis
☞ Editor improvements
☞ Most significant, perhaps: OLE2 support that will let users edit within Notes objects that were created in non-Notes applications

In addition to expanding user access to existing functions, however, Notes 4.0 also adds new user capabilities, including:

☞ Full-text search and indexing of attachments and OLE objects
☞ Attachment viewer
☞ Documentation enhancements such as "Guide Me" help assistance that gives users button-click access to a set of help options, rather than forcing

them to launch a confusing on-line search for aid, and V.3-to-V.4 functionality mapping to guide migrating users

☞ A panoply of interface enhancements such as multipane windows, document
preview, collapsible sections, hierarchical folders, context menus, and a
facility that allows users to "drag and drop" items between receptacles such
as databases

And for the increasingly large group of remote users, Notes 4.0 creates an
unprecedented level of synergy between all stages of mobile use:

☞ Simplified and abbreviated setup procedures that basically render remote
Notes access no more difficult a transaction than direct-dialing a long distance telephone number

☞ Selective replication to allow a user departing from primary access to take
along only that which is needed for the particular trip

☞ Local reduced-size Help functions for the unconnected user

☞ A much-requested server transparency and pass-through dialing capacity
that lets the user reach databases stored on multiple servers with a single
call as opposed to the former necessity of having to dial each server separately

7.5.2 Programmability

Notes 4.0 takes two tacks toward improving life for application programmers: it increases their number by lowering the programming skill level, and then
increases programmability options for end users and seasoned developers alike.

New DAPI access controls, LotusScript language support—a critical step
toward qualifying Notes as a heavy-duty application builder—and the Integrated
Development Environment, a pop-up window in which you can debug and edit
the script you've written, rank high amongst the Notes 4.0 additions aimed at
powering up programmability. Most likely to capture popular attention under
the programmability banner, however, is the introduction into Notes of Agents:
user-created automated processes that can search and retrieve information tailored to an individual user's specifications.

And you don't have to be a programming superstar to have your own Agent:
4.0 features geared toward expanding the class of developers beyond the technologically adept include an Agent-builder for nontechnical users and an Agent
Manager for user-built Agents and Agent templates, as well as routing slips for
workflow control and a nonscrollable region on forms engineered to aid users
who have complained that their forms literally keep getting away from them!

7.5.3 Reliability and Manageability

For administrators, Notes 4.0 ups the integrity of the server and its components—the replicator, indexer, mail router, background exchange, and agent processor—and includes debug code in dynamic load libraries.

To boost manageability as well, Lotus took notice of the tight link between manageability and availability: Version 4.0 brings much-requested early warning and monitoring capabilities to Notes.

When used in conjunction with the new NotesView central administration package, Notes 4.0 supplies administrators with a raft of tools that allow them to view and control a collection of Notes servers as a single entity:

☞ Replication, mail routing, and server task and analysis can be performed from a single central console.

☞ A real-time graphical map of servers aids the administrator in preventing as well as fixing any problems that might spring up anywhere on a Notes network.

☞ An SNMP (Simple Network Management Protocol) management station gives the Notes network administrator access to all SNMP-compliant third-party tools, including, for instance, Hewlett-Packard Co.'s OpenView and IBM's NetView.

☞ The same Agent support available in 4.0 for other purposes gives administrators the ability to automate and schedule management tasks.

What's more, Notes 4.0 packs all existing administrative functions into a graphical user interface client.

And with expanded capacity comes beefed-up security: Notes 4.0 provides local data protection via local encryption and local enforcement of Access Control Language. It also clarifies and strengthens the administrator's control by separating server administrative duties from read, delete, change, and other authority. Thus, for instance, it will be impossible to replicate, say, a name-and-address change throughout the network without explicit authority.

7.5.4 Scalability and Performance

With Lotus' sights fixed firmly on Notes' taking its place as a large enterprise applications player, Version 4.0 also takes aim at increased server scalability and performance for better response time and users-per-server ratio, following the traditional user demand pattern—More, Better, Faster:

☞ **More** transactions per processor: now up 4%, en route to a 50% improvement; improved peak sustained update transaction throughput; bigger name and address book; increased maximum size of Databases and Views; and—a significant move toward enterprise strength—increased numbers of concurrent users per server, databases per server and workstation, servers with which a given server replicates, databases in common when a server replicates, and replicas with which a database replicates.

☞ **Better** replication and indexing—including a unique ID feature whose capacity for shortening the replication process promises substantial efficiency boosts, a multithreaded rather than sequential pull function, field-level replication, and a replication completion indicator.

☞ **Faster** opening of Views and Documents, mail router functions, @ DatabaseLookUp—and the list goes on.

7.6 SINGLE MAIL USER INTERFACE AND INFRASTRUCTURE

When "Unify the Mail!" became a rallying cry among users, it won the same status in the Lotus Notes organization. Version 4.0 harnesses the capacities of a new unified mail interface and the Lotus Communications Server (LCS) X.400 messaging transport backbone to allow Notes and cc:Mail users to mix-and-match mail to suit their individual needs—and to give beleaguered network managers a major break by stepping up the move toward standardized back-end directory administration.

Notes Mail itself gets a sizable shot of flexibility in Version 4.00:

☞ Full client-server mail—a feature likely to get an especially warm welcome from peripatetic users, who will now be able to travel with their mail!
☞ Single message store in Notes, for greater storage efficiency
☞ A new mail template
☞ Quick mail addressing and "type ahead" features

And of course, in keeping with Lotus Notes' underlying philosophy, Version 4.0 will be interoperable across all platforms.

So where do we stand, a decade after a handful of visionaries got their go-ahead from Lotus? The only real answer is: Right here at the beginning. Groupware is still in its infancy. "I don't know if we know 10% of what we're [eventually] going to get from this," says an executive at a company whose Notes application currently ranks among the more sophisticated. Out in the marketplace, the competition is only now beginning to heat up. Given the extent to which Notes is already rewriting the organizational rulebook, the potential for future change in the companies that use it—and the changes in the technology itself that will be driven by such organizational change—is breathtaking. Not only hasn't the whole book been written on Notes—we're still on the preamble.

BIOGRAPHY

Jeffrey Papows is vice president of Lotus' Notes product division. He is responsible for growing the scale of Lotus' Notes business by managing all efforts associated with the product's design, development, distribution, market development, and third-party developer relations. Papows joined Lotus in 1993 from Cognos, where he was president and chief operating officer for more than three years. Previously, he held senior-management-level positions at Cullinet Software, Software International, and Para Research.

Papows, a former flight officer in the U.S. Marine Corps, earned Bachelor's degrees in biology and secondary education from Norwich University, a Master's degree in human resource management from Pepperdine University, and a Ph.D. in business administration.

Introduction to Chapter 8

If Microsoft is not a player in the groupware market, why do they have a chapter in this book? One answer is "because it's Microsoft." But a better answer is that in June 1994, Microsoft announced Exchange, their vision of what workgroup software should look like, and put their stake in the sand, saying, "We are entering the groupware market." For years Microsoft, with their focus on the desktop, has developed products that work across desktops for collaborative functions, like Workgroup for Windows and Schedule+, but never have they really espoused a cohesive workgroup strategy. With this chapter Microsoft comes of age in the workgroup arena.

This chapter looks at the current and future architecture for Microsoft Exchange. As I write this chapter introduction, Microsoft is beta testing Exchange, and those tests should be complete about the time this book is published. However, when Exchange will be available and fully functional is a question that has been hotly debated in the press.

Microsoft has based Exchange on a messaging architecture, like many other groupware vendors. This type of architecture, as well as Microsoft's dominant role in operating systems and desktop applications, brings up a number of technical questions. My observation of many vendors' architectures shows that those with a database architecture (Lotus, IBM, etc.) are currently much more successful with their products than those with a messaging architecture.

Why is this? Is it possible to build a comprehensive groupware product around a messaging architecture? How will Novell, Oracle, Microsoft, and others accomplish this? When will the second version of Exchange that does incorporate full replication be available? How many of the services like email and scheduling will Microsoft start to incorporate into the base operating system (Windows 95 or whatever it will be called), and when will this migration of functions begin to occur? How is Microsoft's marketing tactics of giving away Microsoft Mail affecting the economics of the rest of the mail vendors and what the mail user now expects as "value" software? How will these Exchange products tie into Microsoft's new online network strategy?

In some interesting discussions I have had with Microsoft over the course of the writing of this chapter, it is clear that some "group" functions will start to be incorporated into the operating system. My guess is that before the end of the century we will see functions like email, scheduling, calendaring, intelligent agents, transparent database retrieval, discussion databases, forms routing, and other group functions as part of a Microsoft operating system.

This chapter gives an up-to-date overview of Microsoft Exchange, Schedule+, and other Microsoft group-enabled products. It ties together the latest product thinking at Microsoft with current literature and marketing messages. We are all awaiting Exchange, and Microsoft's entry into the groupware arena.

CHAPTER 8

Microsoft Exchange: Integrating Messaging and Groupware in a Unified Information-Sharing Environment

Greg Lobdell
Microsoft Corporation

8.1 OVERVIEW

Distributing, analyzing, and acting upon strategic information is crucial to the survival of modern corporations. With the growing use of information technology as a strategic planning tool, businesses are demanding improved access to critical information. Given the current global business climate of limited budgets, reduced head counts, and increased worldwide competition, many organizations have been turning to their Information Systems departments for help with improving the bottom line, not only through reduced costs and improved workflow management, but also by developing a whole new breed of information-sharing applications, which open new business opportunities.

Fortunately, as current business strategies increase the demand for these new applications, computer software vendors are delivering advanced products that provide the tools necessary to make these new applications possible. However, in addition to supporting existing systems while trying to keep abreast of the rapid advancements in software technology, the Information Systems department is tasked with learning new tools for deploying advanced information-sharing applications at a faster pace. With new system solutions come new user training requirements. More training, more support. More support, less development. Less development, bigger backlog. Soon, the question arises: "Is there any way to speed up this information railroad without derailing the train?"

Microsoft's answer is to make it easier and more cost-effective to deploy these new information systems by combining them in the single, unified archi-

225

tecture of Microsoft Exchange. Microsoft Exchange lowers training and support requirements by integrating existing systems and platforms, and empowering users to share information through the applications they use every day. Microsoft Exchange also extends information sharing beyond the bounds of the organization by supporting a broad range of industry standards and protocols. With Microsoft Exchange, Microsoft is making it easier to access, organize, and exchange information, and turn it into a competitive advantage.

8.2 INTRODUCING MICROSOFT EXCHANGE

"The goal of Information At Your Fingertips is to improve in fundamental ways how users manipulate, integrate, store, retrieve, and share all kinds of information, both individually and as part of a workgroup." Bill Gates, Chairman and CEO of Microsoft Corporation, first presented this central theme of the Microsoft Windows vision at the Comdex trade show in November 1990. On April 19, 1994, at the annual conference for the Electronic Messaging Association, he introduced Microsoft Exchange, a system for accessing, managing, and exchanging this information.

As Figure 8.1 illustrates, Microsoft Exchange combines electronic mail with groupware and integrates them into the operating system shell to provide a unified information-sharing system.

Microsoft Exchange merges the electronic mail capabilities for sending, reading, and storing messages and file attachments with the groupware functionality provided by electronic forms and public folders for creating and storing workgroup applications, such as discussion databases, sales tracking systems, document libraries, and product information databases.

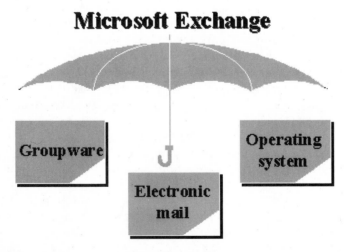

Fig. 8.1 Microsoft Exchange Integrates Messaging and Groupware with the Operating System

Specifically designed to work with existing applications and networks and across desktop platforms, Microsoft Exchange simplifies the process of migrating to a unified information infrastructure. In addition to merging two leading information technology products into a single system, which decreases the training and administrative overhead required to set up and maintain separate systems, Microsoft Exchange makes it easier to access information by providing a universal client that is integrated into the operating system.

8.3 WHAT IS MICROSOFT EXCHANGE?

Microsoft Exchange is a client-server application that combines the power, security, and scalability of a mainframe with the lower cost of a LAN-based system. For larger organizations seeking to downsize from host-based systems and smaller businesses looking for an affordable entry into the information-sharing environment, Microsoft Exchange provides a robust system that is economical to extend and adapt to changing business needs.

As shown in Figure 8.2, Microsoft Exchange consists of the following modules:

☞ A messaging client built into the desktop operating system for sharing not only electronic mail messages, but also files, forms, and other objects

☞ Individual and group scheduling for creating appointments, managing meetings, sharing tasks, and keeping track of contacts

☞ Information sharing beyond electronic mail through replicated public folders that function as repositories for messages, documents, electronic forms,

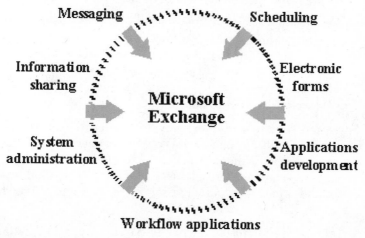

Fig. 8.2 Microsoft Exchange Modules

discussion databases, and workgroup applications, all of which can be distributed throughout the enterprise

☞ A replicated directory that exchanges configuration, routing, and addressing information within the enterprise and with other messaging systems

☞ Electronic forms for viewing, gathering, and exchanging the structured information essential to workgroup applications

☞ An applications development platform for automating business processes that is flexible enough to enable end users to develop their own customized applications without programming, and extensible enough to allow solution providers to build integrated workflow applications with Microsoft Visual Basic and other standard third-party development tools

☞ A system administration program that provides a single view of the entire enterprise, and ensures system reliability through advanced monitoring and management tools

8.4 MICROSOFT EXCHANGE ARCHITECTURE

As mentioned earlier, Microsoft Exchange is based on client-server technology. The Microsoft Exchange client enables users to organize, retrieve, and exchange all types of information. The Microsoft Exchange Server provides the processes that deliver the information to workstations within the enterprise and to other foreign systems. Together, these components provide the following services and functions:

☞ Information services that enable users to exchange a variety of information through their client applications

☞ Directory services that allow users to access and exchange information with other directories

☞ Messaging services that update the directories and transfer, deliver, and route messages and information throughout the enterprise

☞ Connectivity services that transfer and deliver messages to foreign systems

Figure 8.3 shows how the client and server layers are integrated in Microsoft Exchange—a system that combines the services previously available only through a number of separate, proprietary systems.

8.4.1 The Microsoft Exchange Server

The Microsoft Exchange Server provides a distributed communications infrastructure that is built on the multitasking, client-server, and security capabilities inherent in the Windows NT Server architecture. The Microsoft Exchange Server is network-operating-system-independent, and runs well on Novell Netware and other network operating systems. Some of the characteristics of the Microsoft Exchange Server include:

☞ Interoperable—The Microsoft Exchange Server supports existing network transport protocols, such as IPX/SPX for Novell Netware, NetBIOS for

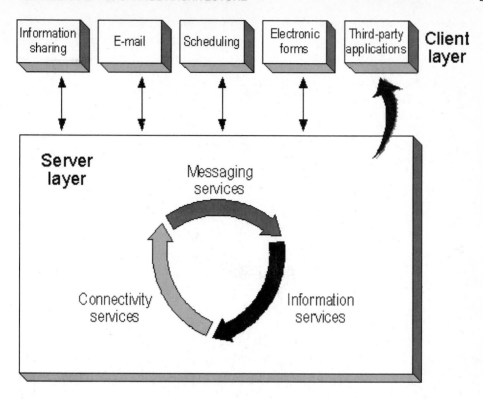

Fig. 8.3 Microsoft Exchange Client-Server Architecture

Microsoft, IBM, and others, AppleTalk, and TCP/IP for UNIX. It also supports industry standards, such as X.400 message transfer compatibility, X.500 directory service compatibility, an SMTP connector for communicating with the Internet and other systems based on an SMTP backbone, Point-to-Point Protocol (PPP) for remote access, MAPI for application integration, and ODBC for access to information stored in diverse database management systems.

☞ Enhanced, centralized administration—The Microsoft Exchange Server provides an easy-to-administer graphical user interface for configuring and maintaining user accounts, directory attributes, servers, and gateways for the entire enterprise from a single workstation. To ensure that the system is functioning at peak performance, the Microsoft Exchange Server provides three types of performance monitoring programs. The Service Monitor displays the status of all services running on all the servers in the system; the Link Monitor displays the status of the links between servers and sites; and the Performance Monitor displays server statistics, which alert administrators to those servers that need adjustments.

☞ Reliable, scalable, secure—The Microsoft Exchange Server takes full advantage of the underlying Windows NT architecture to offer a high level of fault tolerance, scalability, and security through features such as: disk mirroring, which automatically duplicates data among disk drives to prevent the loss of data should drive failure occur; uninterruptable power supply, which provides an alternate backup power source; symmetrical multiprocessing, which enables servers to distribute processing between multiple CPUs; and C-2-level security, which provides access control to system resources.

8.4.1.1 Microsoft Exchange Server Components   The Microsoft Exchange Server consists of the following components:

☞ Message Transfer Agent (MTA)—The Microsoft Exchange Server MTA is a native X.400 message transfer agent that fully conforms to the 1988 CCITT X.400 specification. Along with transferring and delivering messages between other Microsoft Exchange Servers, the MTA communicates with foreign MTAs by sending X.400 messages over standard transports, such as IPX, TP4, Ethernet, RCP, TCP/IP, and X.25.

☞ Information Store—The Microsoft Exchange Server information store is a server-based, structured repository for user mailboxes, messages, and public folders, which provide universal access to groupware applications and shared information of all types.

☞ Directory—The Microsoft Exchange Server directory is a replicated database that contains all the information for users in the Microsoft Exchange enterprise, as well as external recipients, including distribution lists and configuration, routing, and addressing information for users, MTAs, and other parts of the Microsoft Exchange system. The directory is an X.500-type directory service that runs as a Windows NT process on the Microsoft Exchange Server.

☞ Directory Exchange Agent—The directory exchange agent uses the Microsoft Mail 3.x directory synchronization protocol to share directory information with Microsoft Mail 3.x and other systems.

☞ System Attendant—The system attendant is a Windows NT process that builds MTA routing tables and gathers information for tracking messages and monitoring server performance.

☞ Microsoft Mail Connector—The Microsoft Mail Connector provides connectivity to Microsoft Mail for PC networks, Microsoft Mail for AppleTalk networks, and gateways for Microsoft Mail for PC networks.

Figure 8.4 shows how these components interact with each other, and how the client applications, the Microsoft Exchange Administrator program, and the Microsoft Exchange clients interact with the Microsoft Exchange Server to share information with other systems.

8.4.2 Microsoft Exchange Universal Client

Microsoft Exchange makes it easy for users to share information by providing a universal messaging client that is built into the Windows interface and inte-

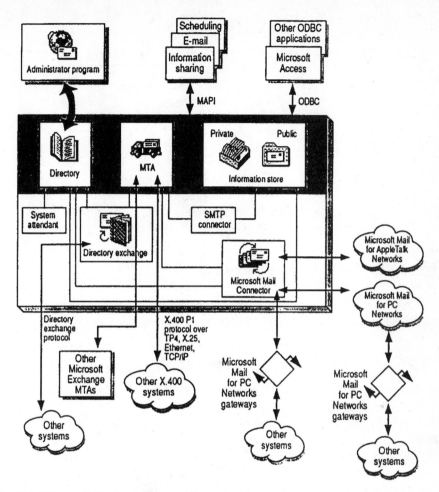

Fig. 8.4 Microsoft Exchange Server Components

grated with the file system. From the user's perspective, the universal client is the tool that accomplishes the unification of the information system because it provides a single interface for managing information of all types. As shown in Figure 8.5, the universal client provides a common entry point for accessing messaging systems, information-sharing applications, on-line services, and the file system.

This means users work with a single Inbox and Address Book for electronic mail messages, faxes, voice mail messages, messages from on-line services such as CompuServe and the Internet, documents from users on other servers, forms for discussion databases and news services, and so on. This radically reduces training costs, because users do not have to learn separate interfaces for disparate systems, and they do not have to understand the complexities of the underlying network to exchange information with users on other servers. This consistency also extends beyond the Microsoft Windows environment, since the Microsoft Exchange client is also available for MS-DOS, Apple Macintosh System 7.x, and UNIX. It can also be used on a variety of networks, such as Win-

Client To A
World Of Information

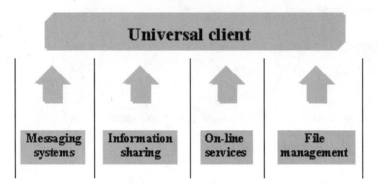

Fig. 8.5 Microsoft Exchange Client Components

dows NT Server, Netware, LAN Manager, Windows for Workgroups, AppleTalk, and others.

8.5 PUTTING MICROSOFT EXCHANGE TO WORK

The first part of this chapter introduced the Microsoft Exchange strategy, architecture, and main components; the next part discusses, in more depth, how the Microsoft Exchange features work together to provide the information-sharing services an organization needs to stay ahead of the rapidly escalating pace of change in business.

8.5.1 A Typical Corporate Profile

To better illustrate the benefits derived when an organization migrates to Microsoft Exchange, the fictitious company Trager International, a composite drawn from the characteristics of a number of our corporate customers, is used as an example.

Trager International markets over 300 products, which are sold through 200 sales representatives throughout the world. Orders are taken in the field and sent to distribution centers in North America, Europe, and Asia, where the products are shipped to customers. In addition, a line of products for the home and office are merchandised through retail stores in the United States and Canada. Trager International also provides a large support organization of over 100 representatives who answer questions concerning the entire product line.

At the headquarters complex in the midwestern United States, Trager International houses the administrative, finance, and marketing departments. The product development and manufacturing divisions are located offshore. The sales and customer support groups are distributed to locations near the world-wide distribution centers.

8.5.1.1 A Heterogeneous Computing Environment   Trager International's Information Systems department works out of the main headquarters and supports a heterogeneous desktop environment of approximately 1,110 Apple Macintosh computers, 4,800 computers running Microsoft Windows applications, and 1,200 computers running MS-DOS.

The Information Systems group supports three separate communication systems: a host-based system for electronic mail and scheduling, another host-based system for manufacturing and inventory management, and their local area networks for storing information created with their personal computer applications. The desktop systems are connected to large AppleTalk and Novell Netware networks, with the mainframes connected through an SNA backbone.

Their goals are to downsize their inventory management system, to place personal computers in their retail sites, and to move their host-based electronic mail and scheduling accounts to a messaging system that will take advantage of their existing LANs. Since they're keeping their manufacturing system on a mainframe, their new messaging system must be able to communicate with the remaining users on the host-based messaging system. Also, they've got to find a better way to share information within the organization, with strategic business partners, and with their customers.

8.5.1.2 Mission-Critical Objectives   To achieve their goals and stay ahead of the competition, Trager International has identified the following objectives:

- Improve communication and distribution of timely information within the organization.
- Manage the unavoidable information overload.
- Make it easier to retrieve stored information from anywhere, at any time.
- Reduce the amount of time spent scheduling appointments and group meetings.
- Automate the delegation of shared tasks and message management.
- Facilitate teamwork, regardless of the location of the team members.
- Make it easier for salespeople and support technicians to find product information.
- Distribute market information throughout the organization.
- Speed up the process of creating new business applications and ensure compatibility with legacy systems.

The following sections explain how Microsoft Exchange provides solutions for these essential concerns.

8.5.2 Improving Communication and Distribution of Information

Information is much more accessible when it's delivered directly to a user's Inbox. With the Microsoft Exchange client, users can ensure deliverability to selected users, distribution lists, and public folders by choosing recipients from a universal Address Book. Similar to a telephone book, the Address Book lists user addresses by real user names—even the addresses for the employees and customers who hold user accounts on different messaging systems. Microsoft Exchange simplifies complicated addresses and makes them transparent to the user.

8.5.2.1 Distributing Monthly Reports   To improve status reporting, department heads at Trager International have been tasked with providing upper management with monthly reports that clearly identify progress. Status reports contain OLE objects, which are portions of a document or spreadsheet or a complete chart that are copied within the message. For example, Figure 8.6 shows a portion of a Microsoft Excel worksheet that has been placed within a message.

Users can also apply rich text formatting, such as bulleted lists, boldface, and underline, to the text in a message to better express themselves. In the previous illustration, the message text shows some of these formatting capabilities. These formats are preserved when the message is transported to clients that support rich text on other platforms or converted to plain text when it's delivered to an application that doesn't support rich text.

Users frequently send messages that include "intelligent" file attachments, such as documents, spreadsheets, schedules, and graphics, which show up as icons in the body of the message. To display the attachments, there is no need to leave the message and launch an application; the attachments can be opened by clicking the icons.

Since the status report is put together by a group of people and needs to be annotated or approved before being passed on to others, it can be routed to each individual in the correct sequence and modified before reaching its final destination.

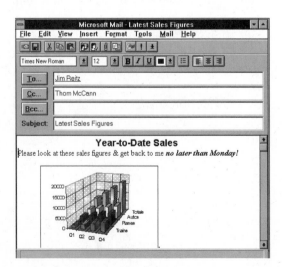

Fig. 8.6 Mail Message Containing a Chart and Rich Text Formatting

With Microsoft Exchange, everyone at Trager International can communicate effectively with the right people at the right time.

8.5.2.2 Managing Information Overload with Rules

Improving electronic communication within an organization has a tendency to "flatten" that structure and encourage open access to all levels of the management hierarchy, which can lead to an increased amount of mail messages for everybody. This can make it time-consuming to find a specific message in a crowded Inbox.

The Microsoft Exchange client helps manage the incoming flow of messages by supporting rules, which are a set of conditions and corresponding actions for automatically processing and organizing messages as they are delivered. For example, Trager International's Vice President of Marketing receives a monthly status report from each of his Marketing Managers. With rules, these status reports are automatically deposited in a designated Marketing Status folder for easy retrieval.

Another example of a frequently used rule is one set up to handle the typical "out-of-office" scenario. For example, it's simple to fill in a form and set up a rule that automatically forwards specified messages to a designated assistant. This automatic message management makes it easier to deal with an overloaded Inbox after returning from an extended business trip or vacation.

Microsoft Exchange rules solve Trager International's concern about information overload by automatically managing messages before they become a burden.

8.5.2.3 Retrieving Stored Information from Public Folders

Prior to the introduction of Microsoft Exchange, electronic information was shared using one of two basic models: the "push" model of electronic mail systems, where messages are delivered to specific users or groups, and the "pull" model of local area networks, where stored information is retrieved from locations on shared network drives. With systems based on these models, users were required to work with two separate applications to access information. With Microsoft Exchange, users can send, retrieve, and organize information from a single application.

As mentioned earlier, the Microsoft Exchange client provides a single interface to the information originating from messaging systems, information-sharing applications, online services, and the file system. This information is stored in folders and is accessible to anyone with the proper permissions. A folder can store information of any type, including documents, forms, graphics, voice messages, and so on. In addition, a folder can be private and available only from a user's computer, or it can be public and stored on a server.

Storing project information in a public folder is especially useful for team members who join a project after the initial phase and have not been included in the original messages and exchange of information about that project. Public folders also eliminate the need to predetermine who might be interested in the information. From public folders, anyone with the proper permissions can easily trace information from a project's inception and gain insight into the many aspects of a project's history.

8.5.3 Creating Workgroup Applications

Trager International needs to do much more than improve access to critical information; they need to find better ways to apply it. To accomplish this, they identified the following mission-critical applications:

☞ Account Tracking System—To improve the timeliness and accuracy of customer activity information, this application must enable account managers to track the frequency and types of customer account contact. Because account managers travel extensively, this status information must be available from company networks in offices throughout the world, and also available through remote access from hotel rooms, airports, and homes.

☞ Sales Tracking System—To clearly identify the products or sales regions that require special attention, this application must include the capability to display current sales volume by region, product, customer, and sales representative.

☞ Product Information Library—To lighten the load while keeping the sales force and customer service representatives up-to-date on the latest product information, Trager has decided to convert its product information library from a binder and paper-based inventory system to an easy-to-reference-and-update online system. Besides text and illustrations (and the appropriate security required to view or update the information), the online library must be able to store a variety of information types, such as word processing documents, spreadsheet workbooks and charts, slide shows with presentation graphics, and multimedia images, voice messages, and videos.

☞ Customer Support System—Currently, Trager International has no formal process for sharing customer support issues with its product engineers. This system must allow the customer support technicians and the engineers to both send and receive pertinent product information and to route requests or complaints to the responsible individual.

☞ Market and Competitor Newswire—Trager International subscribes to several executive newswire services, which they would like to share with a larger audience within the corporation, but they do not want to install another set of specialized applications on desktops throughout the company.

8.5.3.1 Sharing Workgroup Information in Public Folders
Public folders are more than just a shared repository of electronic mail messages and other information items; they are the key groupware element in the Microsoft Exchange architecture. With public folders and electronic forms, Trager International provides controlled access to the information contained in their workgroup applications.

The following list describes the characteristics of public folders that facilitate workgroup communication:

☞ Users can retrieve from and post information to any public folder. These folders can be used as a centralized location for storing related information, reducing the number of locations users need to search to find the information they need. For example, to find all the product, address, and service information related to a specific customer, Trager International's customer service representatives only need look in one location.

☞ Public folders support long names, so users no longer need to remember arcane pathnames and drive designations for storage locations. For example, end users at Trager International can quickly find information stored in a folder named CUSTOMER SERVICE or PAPER PRODUCTS.

☞ Public folders can be replicated so that the information in them can be distributed to designated servers throughout the enterprise, speeding up access time and making it easier to retrieve information. For example, administrators at Trager International can distribute the information in the Sales Tracking application to any site in the enterprise.

☞ Public folders are stored on the Microsoft Exchange Server, allowing an administrator to restrict access to public folders by user, group, or password. When working with outside consultants or partners, Trager International can provide access to specific information while maintaining security for confidential information.

☞ Electronic forms can be associated with public folders, so they can be used to launch workgroup applications that automatically route reports and update all relevant servers when a change is made to the form. By filling in forms, end users at Trager International can find information without learning a new query language.

8.5.3.2 Customizing Folders with Electronic Forms   Microsoft Exchange provides electronic forms for viewing, gathering, and sending structured information so that the structured information can be easily manipulated in a folder view. For example, the Name, Subject, and Date fields of the standard Send and Read forms that are provided with the Microsoft Exchange client are examples of structured information that can be filtered, sorted, and arranged in a customized folder display.

With the Microsoft Exchange custom form tool, users can create their own custom forms to use with the client without programming. For example, one of Trager International's customer support technicians could start with a standard Customer Service form and modify it to add fields for tracking additional information, such as a unique part number or support category, which could be used later for tracking related support calls.

Along with custom forms supplied by third-party vendors, Microsoft Exchange provides sample forms, including a routing form, telephone call report form, group discussion form, and service request form, among others.

When combined with public folders, electronic forms are ideal for setting up public forums or electronic "bulletin boards" and information exchange applications.

8.5.3.3 Easy-to-Modify Views   When users open a folder, they see a collection of columns with headers that indicate the nature of the items in that folder. As the icons in Figure 8.7 show, folders can contain a variety of items, which can be arranged in a variety of ways.

For example, the folders below are arranged according to customer name, but they could very easily be sorted by author or date. To change the sort order to one based on the most current date, the user simply fills in a dialog box. To create their own views, users display another dialog box and choose the properties they want to include in the view.

Working with Microsoft Exchange views, there is no need to run complicated macros or consult expensive experts.

8.5.3.4 Simplified Techniques for Storing Information   To make information available for public consumption, users can mail the information directly to a public folder, using the same methods they use to send an email message. Because Microsoft Exchange folders are tightly integrated into the operating system environment, users can also drag and drop items from the file system directly into a folder.

With Microsoft Exchange public folders and electronic forms, Trager International can create workgroup applications and achieve its objective of making it easier to retrieve stored information.

8.5.4 Scheduling Appointments and Group Meetings

Scheduling meetings and getting busy people together in one room is often the most irritating, time-consuming aspect of solving a problem, especially if key decision makers are off-site. With a new, more advanced version of Schedule+, the Microsoft Exchange combines personal appointments, group scheduling, and

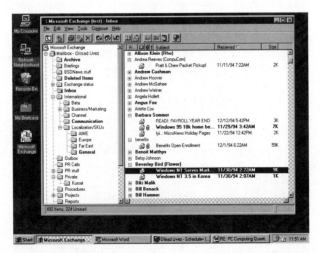

Fig. 8.7 Microsoft Exchange Client Makes it Easy to View Information

task management, and enables users to coordinate critical activities from their desktops or while they're away from the office.

8.5.4.1 A Variety of Appropriate Views To reduce the amount of time spent scheduling and reviewing appointments and meetings, Schedule+ presents views appropriate to the specific activity. For example, Figure 8.8 depicts the Daily Calendar view, into which users can directly enter appointment information and any associated tasks. For different displays of the same information, users can choose from the Weekly or Monthly views.

Appointments and meetings are kept in a personal schedule file that is accessible to other Microsoft Exchange users with the appropriate permissions, enabling them to choose available meeting times at a glance. And for those who authorize assistants to help with their personal scheduling, Schedule+ provides special permissions for providing access to their schedules.

8.5.4.2 Setting Up Group Meetings To save time when scheduling group meetings, users can specify the attendees and any required resources, such as a conference room or audio-visual equipment, by choosing them from the Address Book—the same Address Book they use when sending electronic mail. When it comes to choosing a meeting time, users can let Schedule+ automatically choose the next available time or use the Planner view, as shown in Figure 8.9, to overlay free and busy periods and pick the most convenient time. When there simply isn't a time that works for all the participants, users can choose to remove selected users or groups from the attendee list and view the impact on the available time slots.

When the meeting time has been determined, Schedule+ delivers a meeting notification to each participant. Users can then view their schedules, accept or decline the meeting, and return a reply, all within the Microsoft Exchange client.

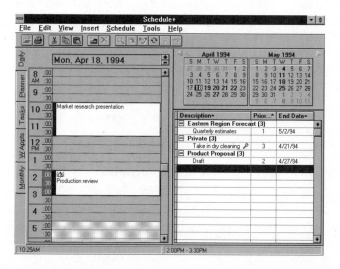

Fig. 8.8 Schedule+ Daily Calendar View Can Be Shared with Others

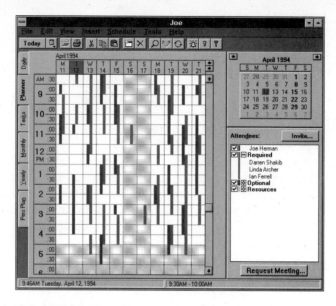

Fig. 8.9 Schedule+ Planner View Displays Free/Busy Times

With Schedule+, Trager International gains a built-in tool for reducing the amount of time users spend scheduling meetings, no matter where the people are located. Think of the time they can save setting up conference calls.

8.5.4.3 Coordinating Tasks with the Task Management View As was shown in Figure 8.8, task lists can be coordinated with specific dates and displayed when the dates are displayed in the Daily Calendar view. Figure 8.10 shows the Schedule+ Task Management view that enables users to organize tasks by projects, and sort them by start date, end date, priority, billing code, and so on. These tasks can also be arranged in an outline format to provide quick overviews, or filtered to display only those tasks that match specific criteria.

The Task Manager view can be also accessed by anybody with the proper permissions, allowing assistants or supervisors to assign tasks, and users to share tasks and status.

With Schedule+, Trager International achieves its objective of automating task management.

8.5.5 Sharing Information Anywhere, Anytime

Trager International is a company on the move. The entire sales force and an increasing number of support personnel are out in the field talking to customers. To stay in contact, this mobile workforce needs to consult their personal computers and receive timely information while they're away from their offices. In addition, these mobile workers need full access to all their information, not just email messages.

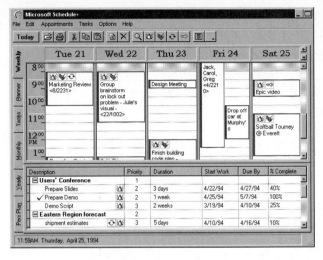

Fig. 8.10 Schedule+ Task Management and Weekly Calendar View

8.5.5.1 Remote Access Microsoft Exchange offers remote access that is integrated into its basic client-server design, providing remote access to all its clients and eliminating the need to support a dedicated, proprietary, remote infrastructure. Because the Microsoft Exchange client is designed to work in a network-independent fashion, it can effectively communicate via many remote access products, such as Microsoft Remote Access Service (RAS) and AppleTalk Remote Access, among others, and a broad range of network protocol standards, such as TCP/IP, Novell IPX/SPX, NetBIOS, and Point-to-Point Protocol (PPP). By supporting these leading technologies, Microsoft Exchange offers a wide range of remote connectivity solutions, from simple 2400-bps modem connections to public X.25 data network communications, including high-speed ISDN digital connections, as well as cellular and wireless capabilities.

With Microsoft Exchange, Trager International's field staff can work with any public folder from different computers in different offices, through a remote connection to the appropriate server. They can also store their Inbox and Outbox on a local machine and work "off-line" with their messages, saving the actual message transfer for the next time they make a network connection, either remotely or by direct connection at the office.

8.5.5.2 Downloading Selected Messages with Message Preview To further maximize the efficiency of mobile connectivity, Microsoft Exchange provides a Message Preview feature for the Windows and Macintosh clients. With Message Preview, users can quickly download message headers before choosing the messages they want to transfer to their remote computers. To help determine the impact of downloading individual messages, Message Preview displays message size and estimated time to download. To help users choose the best time to download messages, Microsoft Exchange also supports scheduled connections, which enables users to preselect the most convenient and cost-effective time to make a remote connection.

8.5.5.3 Wireless Communication

Most market forecasters are predicting rapid growth in the cellular and wireless modem markets in the coming years. Microsoft is working closely with wireless network providers to ensure Microsoft Exchange servers and clients are tightly integrated into their emerging standards.

With its built-in remote connectivity, Microsoft Exchange facilitates teamwork for all of Trager International's mobile workers by helping them keep in contact and share information from anywhere at any time.

8.5.6 Extending Workgroup Applications with Standard Development Tools

The Microsoft Exchange supports the industry-standard data exchange components of the Windows Opens Services Architecture (WOSA), which present programmers with a consistent interface for communicating with back-end services, such as database managers and messaging systems.

8.5.6.1 Workgroup-Enabling Existing Applications with MAPI

The Messaging Application Program Interface (MAPI) provides a layer of functionality between applications and their underlying messaging systems, which enables developers to add messaging features to any Windows-based application. With MAPI, end users can work with applications and share objects without being concerned about messaging service compatibility. In essence, MAPI ensures that the Microsoft Exchange client, or "front end," is independent of the messaging service, or "back end."

The Routing Slip command in Microsoft Word and Microsoft Excel is an excellent example of one of the many ways MAPI can be used to extend existing applications. By choosing the Routing Slip command from the application's File menu, and using the universal Address Book, a user can send the document or worksheet via the underlying messaging system to a series of team members who can add elements to the object and pass it on to others, thus completing a simple workflow assignment.

With MAPI, developers in the Information Systems department at Trager International can access a standard programming interface for integrating messaging into their custom applications.

8.5.6.2 Leveraging Legacy Systems with ODBC

Open Database Connectivity (ODBC) APIs provide "seamless" access across heterogeneous database management systems from within Windows-based applications, making it possible to integrate information stored in Microsoft Exchange applications with existing sources of information on legacy systems. Based on a call-level interface (CLI) developed by an industry consortium, ODBC is an open, vendor-neutral standard that has broad support from both application and database vendors.

ODBC provides application developers with a common API set and uses drivers, in the form of Windows DLL files, written for diverse database systems, such as Microsoft SQL Server, DB2, Oracle, dBASE, and so on.

With Microsoft Exchange, developers in the Information Systems department at Trager International access a standard programming platform for integrating messaging functions into their custom applications and ensuring compatibility with their legacy systems.

8.6 SUMMARY

Microsoft Exchange provides the solutions that Trager International requires to better distribute, analyze, and act upon critical information. With a universal client that is available for all the leading operating systems, Microsoft Exchange makes it easy for users to share information with their coworkers. With cross-network support and built-in remote access, the Microsoft Exchange Server makes it practical to access information from anywhere, at any time. By supporting standard messaging system protocols and connectivity solutions, Microsoft Exchange leverages existing technology investments and makes it possible to communicate with strategic partners on foreign systems.

By integrating messaging and groupware into a single, unified information-sharing environment that is built into the operating system shell, Microsoft Exchange makes it easier to extend the messaging systems that organizations already have in place and delivers powerful new information-sharing capabilities without requiring the deployment of multiple, disparate systems. It's a major step forward in unifying the world of information systems technology.

BIOGRAPHY

Greg Lobdell is a group product manager for Microsoft's Mail and Exchange electronic mail family. He is responsible for product definition, customer and industry relations, and marketing programs.

Mr. Lobdell joined Microsoft in 1983 and most recently managed the Windows NT 3.5 Product Management team. Starting in 1983, his responsibilities have included being program manager for Microsoft BASIC, GW-BASIC, COBOL, Quick BASIC, and BASIC Compiler. In 1988, Mr. Lobdell became Product Manager responsible for Microsoft's line of C and C++ development systems and moved into the Windows NT business in 1993.

Prior to joining Microsoft, Mr. Lobdell was a development engineer with Hewlett-Packard's Personal Office Computer Division.

Mr. Lobdell holds a Bachelor's degree in computer science from Washington State University.

Introduction to Chapter 9

IBM has always been focused on the enterprise. Whether selling mainframes or groupware, IBM takes the "large" perspective. This chapter looks at what IBM has to offer the workgroup environment. Because IBM has been going through so many changes in the last year, their strategy for workgroup computing has changed also. However, IBM has some strong offerings in the workflow arena because their databased architecture is robust enough to stay the course.

IBM's goal is to convey a knit-together, cohesive, all-inclusive groupware scheme made up of its piecemeal groupware strategy. Whether this strategy will be successful, only time will tell. The current market is intensely competitive, and it will take several years for all the pieces of IBM's integrated strategy to be implemented. However, because IBM takes the "big view" they also take the "long perspective." FlowMark and Office Vision are IBM solutions which can be used now, and IBM hopes to knit these together with a database backbone that supports messaging solutions.

Like many other vendors, IBM is putting their money where their mouth is; that is, they are using and testing groupware tools internally. As IBM's focus has broadened to accommodate a dynamic computing market, they have had to re-invent themselves. IBM has been frantically downsizing for years, but downsizing can't go on forever. This situation presents an excellent opportunity for corporate re-engineering. The questions are: Will IBM's current culture allow such sweeping change? How will groupware be implemented and rolled out? Which groupware tools will best serve IBM's new leaner and meaner organization? How will the cultural and technical changes be coordinated? What effects will groupware have on centralization/decentralization issues within the IBM culture? What are the primary and secondary goals for change? Besides Mr. Gerstner, who are the agents of change at IBM?

Let me paint a scenario. I don't know the likelihood of this, but suppose IBM's new management decides that a total re-engineering is the only way to bring it into the 21st century hale and hearty. Furthermore, management decides they want to implement this program exclusively with IBM tools. The program is rolled out internally over the next three years. Much to the surprise of many, one success acts as the foundation for another. Eventually, the company transforms itself. As this happens, all personnel at IBM become familiar with groupware products, enough so that the salespeople who usually sell hardware (already a commodity in most cases) can now act as a reference to sell software: "See, if Big Blue can use groupware internally to improve our company...why can't you?" A very strong reference indeed! In this scenario, it's not the multilayer architecture of IBM's groupware product line that becomes significant, but how IBM uses what they have built.

We are already seeing some of these changes at IBM. On the cultural side, the old IBM dress code is gone. On the technical side, IBM's proposed new corporate headquarters will be wired for collaborative computing and adapted to new collaborative technologies.

Like DEC, IBM has plenty of groupware technology. But unlike Lotus and Microsoft, these groupware technologies are a well-kept industry secret. Part of the problem is that the software is sold by a sales force trained and compensated to sell hardware, not software. The second problem is that either third-party resellers do not understand what they are selling or are not fully behind the products. In the 21st century, groupware is sure to play an even greater role, whether IBM chooses to adopt it on a wholesale level or not.

Historically, IBM had an incredible advantage in groupware; one that eroded rapidly. Profs is IBM's mainframe-based email system with literally millions of users. This population is tailor-made to migrate to client-server architectures. Rather than focus on selling mainframes to these sites, IBM could have developed a migration strategy to focus their customers' attention and dollars on increasingly popular client-server computing and its applications. While this has started, it may be years too late. Just as DEC experienced with its All-in-1 customers, IBM has started to lose its previously dominant customer base to a variety of other vendors' solutions.

What is important in this chapter is not how IBM is trying to tie all the pieces together as a cohesive IBM WorkGroup offering (obviously some of their customers asked for this) but their enterprise focus. Once again, IBM has staked out the high ground, in groupware this time. Let's see if they can hold it! IBM asks and answers several questions about groupware, but the one question they do not ask or answer is "What is IBM's internal commitment to groupware, and how will they be using it within their enterprise?"

IBM and the Role of Groupware in the Enterprise

Richard J. Sullivan
IBM

This chapter is about the IBM WorkGroup strategy and the products that make this strategy a reality. Our goal is to provide the tools for automated collaboration across the physical and cultural boundaries of modern-day computing. We intend to achieve this goal through evolutionary change. In fact, we believe that the surest route to solving business problems is a truly collaborative computing environment which leverages existing industrial-strength technologies and supplements them with tools that fully utilize emerging technologies. In this way, users can move toward enterprise-wide workgroup solutions in an orderly fashion.

This chapter explains how we intend to accomplish this and highlights the benefits of this strategy for users and businesses. As director of IBM's Work-Group Marketing, I am leading this task. We are supported by a worldwide organization that focuses on the way people work, and on providing tools and solutions to improve the way their work is done. It is our mission to provide a business-wide integrated electronic desktop that reflects the work to be done and the various layers of infrastructure and to support this with a highly focused set of tools. We are devoted to the development and marketing of software that fosters collaboration.

In my 28 years of service to IBM, I have personally seen the necessity for computing based on the needs of users rather than the requirements or limitations of the computer system. Not only are our customers asking for this, but so are workers and managers within IBM. So we are busy planting the seeds of groupware in our own backyard. In many ways, IBM is a prime testing ground for the fruits of my division's work.

Automated workflow, collaboration, mail, document management, scheduling, information access, forms—all of these are workgroup applications on which modern corporations must rely to supply business solutions. IBM is implementing consistent enterprise-wide solutions for these pressing requirements. We already have over six million users of our workgroup software, and our in-house workgroup system alone has over 250,000 users (Figure 9.1).

9.1 THE ENVIRONMENT FOR GROUPWARE

It is no longer possible for workers to ply their trade in splendid detachment. For corporations, the combined pressures of global competition and rapid change make today's business environment a perilous place. It takes knowledge, skill, and resourcefulness to deal successfully with these forces.

It's a familiar story. Keeping customers satisfied requires faster development of better products at lower costs. Getting maximum productivity from

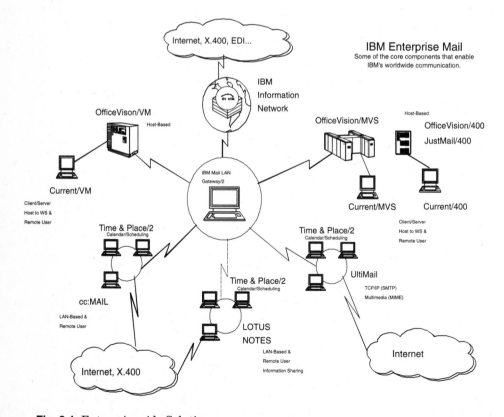

Fig. 9.1 Enterprisewide Solutions

workers requires a re-evaluation of the business processes, which often results in re-engineering and reorganization.

Businesses can no longer rely on their installed information systems to help resolve these issues, because many of these systems were not designed to accommodate the rapid change that characterizes the '90s. Yet these systems contain the information that drives corporations, which must be up to date and readily available to decision makers.

Let's start with an example that's close to home—the typical knowledge worker at a corporation like IBM—and we'll elaborate as the chapter progresses. Our worker is an analyst, advisor, and decision maker. He or she collects information from a number of sources, including coworkers, printed matter, and electronic data, filters and summarizes this collection, and produces a report in some form for distribution to others.

What system exists that can help our worker organize and cope with the vast array of material and media available? How is he or she going to deal with the dual issues of communications and information processing, and how is all of this going to be coordinated with the work of others?

In a sense, computing has tended to isolate workers who sit alone in offices with two main tools for communication: a telephone and a computer. The telephone is familiar; you never have to worry about the packet-switching network or underlying protocols. You just connect and talk. But the telephone system does not in any way integrate the information you've collected.

Computers have been a boon for information processing, and they have the raw power necessary to integrate communication into this function. But the conglomeration of interfaces, gateways, and interchange standards that exists constrains users and keeps them from going very far from their own backyard. They are prevented from getting all the information they need in a timely, coherent manner.

Electronic mail systems have helped make the computer a conversational tool, but automation and collaboration have not yet been well integrated into this basic function. Even with the necessary foundation for communication in place, our worker is distracted by masses of unfiltered data and an electronic desktop covered with a surfeit of tools. Instead of focusing on business goals, users have become desktop traffic controllers, searching for efficient routes to their data sources without getting caught in a gridlock of too much information.

We often think of this as a new problem, but it is not. More than a decade ago, the first groupware products, IBM's Office Vision, DEC's All-In-One, and others, were introduced to help users of host-based systems share access to information, exchange mail, and create office-wide directories.

These systems retained the tight centralized control and strong data security features that are considered essential by IT departments. This has provided a powerful paradigm for collaboration for years and, in the case of IBM, has given rise to a worldwide mail system that, in many ways, is the backbone of the business.

But the emergence of ad hoc collaborative teams to work on specific business tasks has changed the demands on computing systems. For word processing, quick data analysis, and smaller-scale project support—the strengths of personal productivity applications—advanced host-based systems lack the necessary flexibility to be helpful.

Users have wrested a tremendous amount of control over their own computing environments from IT departments, and the compelling need for cooperative computing has resulted in the spread of client-server networks. This has allowed for limited data and file sharing and has given rise to the first groupware applications—basic email. At the same time, the use of disparate LAN-based tools has proliferated.

Our typical worker has realized substantial productivity gains from LAN-based systems. Now that these gains have been achieved, where can further improvements be made? Additional efficiency and better cooperation among systems and tools must be fostered to keep up with business needs. Groupware is the answer.

9.2 IBM's Workgroup Strategy

Our customers tell us that they would like to bring the disparate ends of the computing spectrum together through the new paradigm of workgroup solutions. This means further use of client-server, the adoption of object-oriented technology, and providing groupware applications that allow for evolutionary migration.

As shown in Figure 9.1, IBM's existing products are already providing solutions with both host-based and client-server systems. For instance, the host-based OfficeVision system is supplying fully integrated groupware functionality to its over six million users—mail, address book, calendar, and text processing, at both the personal and workgroup levels. We have turned this into an equally powerful PC-based solution through our family of Current-OfficeVision Workgroup products.

Take our typical knowledge worker again. Originally, OfficeVision gave him or her the capability for endless sharing and collaboration across the host-based network. But once he or she left the centralized network, this ability to use any of the information was lost. (The move towards mobile computing has made this issue even more important.) More important, users were forced to choose between the power of Office Vision and the convenience of client-server networks. Current-Office Vision frees the user from making this difficult choice.

Current gives PC users a consistent graphical front end to all OfficeVision functionality, and host-based users get a more convenient route to begin their migration to client-server LAN-based environments. All users, regardless of location, have equal access to information and each other.

Current-Office Vision embodies the first stages of our strategy toward a complete workgroup environment:

Address the needs of existing customers. Let them continue to use their systems and software while they migrate to a client-server environment. This provides important continuity and protects investments in existing systems.

Introduce products that span diverse operating environments, and at the same time give LAN-based users more consistent user interfaces and more transparent access to data sources. Leverage IBM's core technologies and strengths in database management, message queuing, systems and network management, and application development to bring groupware to a heterogeneous world.

IBM sees these as necessary steps towards the creation of complete workgroup solutions. But we stress the necessity for a rational evolutionary approach to this migration.

All vendors share the desire to build groupware solutions based on their traditional strengths. Building from depth is admirable, but without the breadth of experience, results will be limited in scope and applicability.

Our knowledge worker is faced with conflicting problems. If he or she moves to a client-server architecture from a host-based system, he or she loses access to host-based tools and information. If the move is from a standalone PC, suddenly security becomes a much larger concern.

Our experience has taught us the critical importance of security and reliability. We have also learned that client-server solutions must be capable of enterprise-wide, system-independent, and platform-neutral workgroup solutions. Furthermore, these solutions must provide seamless access from any worker's desktop to information at any location.

With this workgroup strategy, the knowledge worker can access information from existing systems regardless of location and participate in tasks that are structured and driven by new technologies. It's a best-of-both-worlds scenario. Users can access and share data no matter where it resides, and the data can be stored and processed wherever this can be done most efficiently. It's the most effective and successful way to automate business processes.

Most important, this strategy leads to a blurring of the lines between traditional host-based and evolving client-server environments. True cooperation can only be achieved by removing these barriers to the free flow of information. At the same time, the desktop must reflect the tasks to be performed, not just the tools used. IBM sees object-oriented programming and the introduction of componentized software as the key to providing both solutions.

IBM's experience in workgroup computing is well-established. Our host-based offerings, the OfficeVision family, have made us the leading provider of electronic mail and calendar capability in this environment. As a major reseller of Lotus cc:Mail and Notes, we have in-depth knowledge of LAN-based workgroups as well. We started introducing our own family of client-server products in early December 1992:

Scheduling & calendaring	Time and Place	12/92
Workflow management	FlowMark	9/93
Forms	FormTalk	12/93
Multimedia mail	UltiMail	3/94
Data Analysis	Visualizer	5/94
Document management	Visual Document Library	6/94

In November 1994, we introduced IBM WorkGroup, a comprehensive port-folio of integrated functions for workgroup computing spanning communications, information management, and work automation. All of our previous client-server products serve as the base technologies for IBM WorkGroup and form an inte-grated offering that will be extended over time to include additional capabilities, tighter integration, and better workgroup functionality.

The following functions are included in the first IBM WorkGroup offering—multimedia mail (UltiMail), group scheduling and calendaring (Time and Place), and facsimile (FaxRouter), along with new technologies for directory services, agents, and filters. The architecture of IBM WorkGroup allows for tight integra-tion among these functions as well as the inclusion of additional functions. Real-time conferencing, voice dictation, and document management are examples of future areas for expansion (see Figure 9.1).

9.3 WORKGROUP TOPOLOGY

To realize complete workgroup solutions, IBM has defined a three-layered struc-ture that allows for the integration of applications and the introduction of new products as we develop them. This gives us the broad framework necessary to help users take advantage of this emerging groupware technology and, as men-tioned before, differentiates our workgroup strategy from those of other vendors (see Figure 9.2).

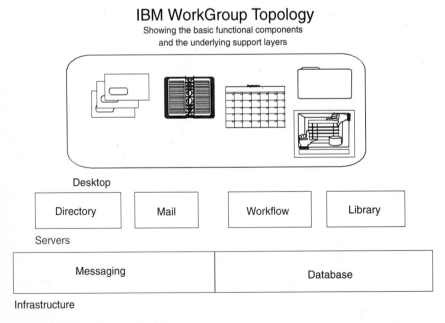

Fig. 9.2 IBM WorkGroup Topology

9.3.1 Layer 1: Foundation

This level of our topology is made up of fundamental services that provide the solid infrastructure necessary to build successful workgroup solutions.

Messaging is one of the key building blocks for a complete business communications strategy. IBM's MQSeries (Message Queuing) distribution backbone, an example of a bulletproof core technology extended for workgroup use, was initially developed for mainframe-based financial applications.

MQSeries provides messaging underpinnings for distributed business applications that are mission-critical. So it has to have industrial-strength characteristics. For example, the finance and banking industries rely on MQSeries for applications like funds transfer, where there is zero tolerance for errors.

Database support is provided by another of IBM's time-tested technologies, the DB2 relational database family of products. DB2 has been thoroughly proven at our customer sites for applications over a wide range of environments and applications.

Our mail and library servers will use DB2's proven design to provide the reliability, security, manageability, and recoverability that are traditional IBM strengths.

Directory services are provided by our WorkGroup Communications technology, discussed in the "Functional Building Blocks" section later in this chapter.

9.3.2 Layer 2: Workgroup Services

We have divided this layer into four functional categories. Each has the ability to scale applications from single-user to enterprise-wide, while maintaining transparent access to basic services.

In each category IBM already has robust applications to provide support, and we are working to extend and open up these applications across the entire workplace.

Workflow, the orderly progression of work from desk to desk and stage to stage, is one of the hallmarks of any workgroup solution. No standalone application can provide this crucial service, which is dependent upon cooperation across desktop LANs and host environments.

FlowMark, the workflow function of IBM WorkGroup, provides work automation tools. These tools allow users to review, design, refine, document, and ultimately optimize business processes. Enabling business process re-engineering through workflow is a key aspect of our workgroup structure.

IBM WorkGroup includes multiplatform mail server software. Essentially a network post office that stores and forwards messages, the mail server is tightly integrated with messaging and network directory services.

Information management is another important function of IBM WorkGroup. It must provide more than simple access to text-based documents. So much business information is in graphic rather than text form that storage of and access to this information must be seamless and transparent.

In today's organizations, the management of electronic information has become as challenging as the management of paper files in the past. The information management function of IBM WorkGroup help customers search for, locate, and process information, images, and documents.

With these programs, line-of-business applications can be linked to electronic folders containing faxes, scanned images, photos, spreadsheets, and other objects. Seamless integration is provided across distributed networks and disparate systems. Multiplatform access is available to all library services and is configurable from the desktop. At the same time, safeguards against illegal access and inadvertent data loss are combined with document logging, locking control, and version control to provide secure storage for mission-critical information.

Data Access—There is always the need to turn data into useful business information. So provisions must be made for explicit data gathering, report generation, and analysis across client-server networks.

Sharing information across workgroups means giving access without writing formal SQL queries or setting up specific lines of communication. It means providing this information in a way that allows users to use their desktop tools to carry out analysis and create reports for further distribution.

The data analysis function of IBM WorkGroup provides this service as a data intermediary. It links data in any form, including multimedia, from underlying DB2 structures, across client-server networks, to desktop icons that can be manipulated in visual form. (The decision support function is also available to perform many desktop-oriented functions, and can access Oracle and Sybase databases.)

9.3.3 Layer 3: Desktop

This is the layer that users see on their desktops, and in many ways its components are the most diverse. Our goal includes integration of IBM applications and services at every level. This includes the products of our business partners and competitors. In our quest for integration and ease of use, we have emphasized the development of common features across these diverse products—common installation procedures, administration, and user interfaces.

Desktop environments thrive on choice. Desktop systems are powerful and popular because users are free to customize their own computing environments.

IBM WorkGroup offers a range of desktop-oriented groupware functions, including chalkboard, mail, address book, calendar, document management, workflow, query, report, and forms. Integrated offerings are available today. For example, the document management function of IBM WorkGroup, Visual Document Library combines document management, search, and relational database technologies.

IBM's mail client software is another example of tightly integrated functionality, combining email, address book, and group scheduling.

Object technology and its resulting componentization will blur distinctions among desktop applications. Object technology already allows us to provide integration across applications. For example, notes can be sent directly from address books, meetings requested via calendar applications and mailed directly to attendees, and tasks forwarded from workflow applications via the mail system.

Our goal is common look and feel, administration, and installation: a task-oriented desktop. Users will customize their own environments by selecting object components. They will be free to pick and choose among the products of many competitors, just as they are with current personal productivity applications. The only difference is that groupware decisions affect a group rather than just a single desktop.

Object encapsulation makes it possible to achieve this level of integration and user customization. Tools are stripped to their essence. Broad functionality is achieved by combining only the tools that are needed. Efficiency is fostered, and the confusion of today's "everything-into-the-pot" applications is avoided.

Object technology, adherence to industry-wide standards, and the three-layer structure described above allow us to offer new products that integrate with existing tools. From the perspective of a groupware user, this is critical. It means that instead of retraining or starting from scratch to use new productivity tools, they can be added in an evolutionary and orderly fashion. The investment in existing systems is protected. The desktop becomes a springboard to increased cooperation with other users and services instead of an impediment to workflow and information exchange.

9.4 FUNCTIONAL BUILDING BLOCKS

A development structure gives integrity and strength to IBM's present and future offerings. But the direction for this development comes from a set of functional building blocks constructed in response to users' needs.

9.4.1 Communication Across Organizations

There is no groupware without the ability to connect to other users—to create, maintain, and expand workgroups.

IBM WorkGroup offers an integrated suite of several functions that make it possible to coordinate group efforts by linking people and resources. It also links the address book/administration function with times and places, and includes group scheduling functionality. An intelligent rules-based filtering tool provides additional productivity.

As shown in Figure 9.3, the mail function of IBM WorkGroup supports all major mail standards, including VIM (Vendor Independent Messaging), MAPI (Mail API), and CMC (Common Mail Call). It also supports native protocols, such as SMTP/MIME today, and X.400 and SNADS in the future. It also includes gateways for OfficeVision, other client-server email systems, and X.400-compliant mail systems (see Figure 9.3).

MQSeries provides the critically important robust messaging transport for these core communication offerings and extends communications beyond mail to embrace business applications—applications which require the security and reliability that MQSeries guarantees.

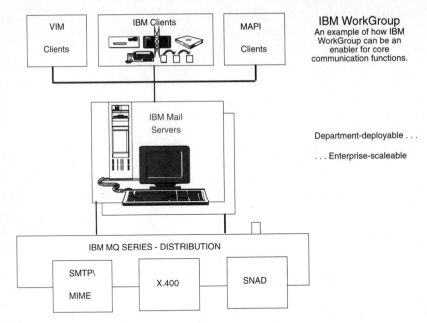

Fig. 9.3 IBM WorkGroup as Enabler

The mail, calendar, directory, fax, and agent functions of IBM WorkGroup are an exciting new product combination for us. Not only will our typical knowledge worker use it, but so will our CEO.

9.4.2 Connection to Data and Documents

Information management refers to the way in which information/data/documents are stored and accessed. For workgroups to succeed, explicit structures for information sharing must exist. This is opposed to the haphazard procedures for setting up servers and directories that exist on most networks today.

IBM's solution is built on a series of library offerings, already partially discussed in this chapter as part of layer 2.

At the desktop level, the information management capabilities provide seamless access so that the right information is available to the right person at the right time. Built on client-server architecture, it provides a coherent way to store, organize, and retrieve vital business information, regardless of location or type of file. The library feature was designed for collaborative use and facilitates easy access to text documents and other forms of information.

The information management functions provide the means to store diverse information across the network on workstation- or mainframe-based servers, at the same time providing tools for administrators and safeguards to protect against data corruption or unauthorized access. It includes the underlying facilities that allow administrators to set up and manage libraries. The result is a collection of secure repositories containing images and other object types that users can access seamlessly from their desktops.

9.4.3 Coordination of Business Processes

Tracking and managing the flow of business processes through the enterprise is critical for success in the '90s. Once again, IBM delivers both middleware and desktop functionality.

FlowMark, the workflow function of IBM WorkGroup, a visually oriented tool for business process modeling and implementation, draws heavily on the underlying database layer to coordinate the steps in a business process, including different desktop and host applications spread across distributed client-server and host environments (see Figure 9.4).

9.5 SOLUTIONS

This wealth of strategy, structure, and products we've been discussing would be meaningless without real-world applicability. How do you use these powerful tools to create orderly solutions to the untidy problems and mixed environments that every business contains? Here is an example of automating complex processes with combinations of workgroup software.

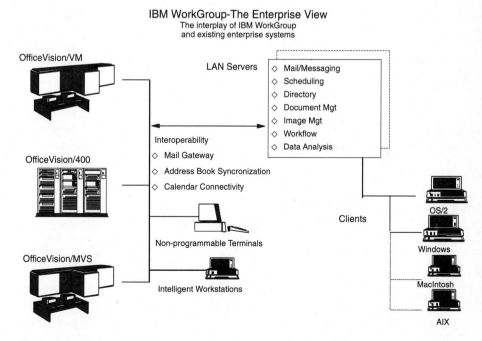

Fig. 9.4 An Enterprise View

9.5.1 Ad Hoc Workflow Example: Travel

Our knowledge worker must take a business trip. This decision triggers a complex workflow which can be streamlined and automated with workgroup tools.

The first step is a travel request. This is the kind of task that our knowledge worker might find particularly irksome—unproductive time spent filling out forms and tracking them through the system. But now he or she is spared this annoyance, and his/her valuable time is saved.

Since our worker travels on business several times a year, he or she has installed the travel initiator application on his or her workstation. This includes a travel icon on his desktop (perhaps the image of an airplane) that he clicks on to start the process. This launches an electronic form so that he can supply pertinent information about his travel plans—purpose, dates, cost estimates, and so on. This is a smart form, and is already partially filled out with our worker's personal information.

When the form is complete and our worker presses the done button, several actions are triggered. The form is filed on a server in the travel archive and, at the same time, is sent by electronic mail to a manager for approval. Information from the form is used to update our worker's calendar with the tentative travel dates.

Before the manager even opens the travel form that has arrived in his electronic mailbox, an intelligent mail processor has scanned the incoming message. From its header, the processor recognizes the form and looks up additional pertinent information in the department's information archives: the travel budget, year-to-date expenditures, a calculated value for the remaining travel budget, and so forth.

The manager has all the information needed to approve or turn down the request. His action, yea or nay, will trigger the appropriate follow-up actions. Rejected proposals are automatically returned to the user; approvals receive the manager's electronic signature and are routed on to the travel agency.

As the form is forwarded, it generates another work task to look up the user's traveling preferences for the agency and to update the budget database with new travel information (most likely host-based data that can be accessed later). Allocation is made for the expenses at this point, but actual expenses aren't deducted until the bills are paid.

The agency doesn't need the entire travel request form. They only need to know the dates, destinations, and the preferences of the person traveling. This information is automatically routed to the appropriate person at the agency. The agent supplies the traveler with tickets, itinerary, and expense report forms that have been automatically customized for the trip. Our worker's calendar is again updated with the specific travel times.

When our worker returns from his trip, he will find expense report forms that have been customized and automatically mailed to his electronic mailbox. Once again, these are intelligent forms. The fields of the expense form are linked to a database which rejects improper data and totals fields as necessary.

There's no need to copy and file receipts, because they can be scanned and stored in the library. If our worker has used a corporate credit card, those charges are automatically added as they are received.

The completed expense reports are forwarded by the intelligent processor to the manager for approval, and then forwarded to the accounting process. Accounting stores the information, updates the appropriate databases, and generates either a printed check or an electronic file transfer to our worker's bank account.

This level of automation allows our worker to concentrate on his job while clerical tasks are handled by this workflow solution. Paperwork and lost time are minimized. Automation can be extended to include forwarding action items when a manager or agent is not in the office.

It takes many well-integrated pieces to attempt a fully automated workflow of this complexity. In this example, integration is possible through the use of several key IBM technologies: MQSeries for messaging and mail, DB2 for the databases, and OpenDoc for the intelligent documents. It is natural to assume that this travel application would be built using object technology to componentize the pieces and allow disparate elements to work together.

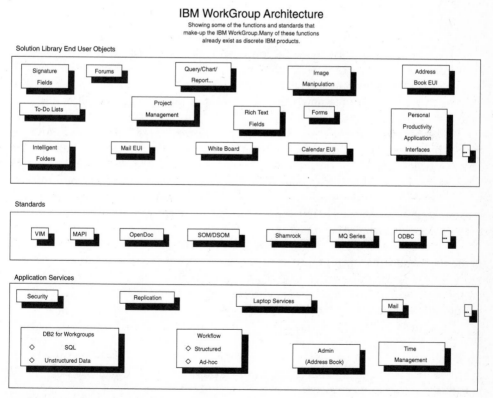

Fig. 9.5 The Interplay of Technologies

9.6 CONTINUED EVOLUTION

Heterogeneity is one of the great strengths of modern computing. Groupware allows users to capitalize on this strength and benefit from increased access to existing environments. At the same time that host-based systems are evolving into more user-controlled environments, PC-based systems are providing more cooperation and better collaboration capabilities through client-server technology. This makes groupware the obvious choice for software solutions, and the forces of modern competition make this choice a necessity.

This migration to groupware has made several things evident. Seldom can a single vendor satisfy all needs. IBM WorkGroup, by necessity, must accommodate the investments already made in multivendor environments.

Groupware is most effective when it is built on existing environments. The fact that groupware can be introduced in an evolutionary, rather than revolutionary, manner is one of its key advantages. Both the corporations that adopt groupware and the vendors, like IBM, who supply groupware are able to build from a powerful base and evolve into stronger, more cooperative environments.

9.7 SUMMARY

The IBM WorkGroup view of groupware cannot help but emphasize the role of existing systems in enterprise-wide computing. We owe it to our existing customers—nearly every Fortune 1000 company and most large corporations worldwide—as well as our potential customers, to build on existing systems as we plan for future systems. This is how we see our role in answering the following questions.

What is the role of groupware in the enterprise?   Groupware helps to make the enterprise more responsive and productive by providing the essential links between people, whether they are connected to host- or LAN-based systems, part of a mobile network, or even temporarily disconnected from any network. Groupware also improves efficiency by creating a more cooperative computing environment so that knowledge workers can get the information they need, where and when they need it.

How can legacy systems be used effectively in a new client-server groupware environment?   At most corporations it is more accurate to speak of line-of-business applications rather than legacy systems. While it is true that many of these systems have a legacy in the past, most of them are existing applications that are crucial to the information-processing role in these corporations.

For these systems to be used more effectively, they must be integrated into the new client-server and groupware environments. This is the evolutionary approach to what would otherwise be radical new technology—build on existing systems, link to existing sources of information, and provide access beyond the scope of existing environments.

What lessons learned from proprietary systems can be applied to today's groupware products? The most basic lessons of computing came out of the development of proprietary systems. These concern reliability, manageability, data integrity, and security, and can be summed up in one word: trust. Users, both individuals and corporations, must be able to trust their systems to be accurate and dependable. Nothing is more fundamental.

What is IBM's groupware strategy, and how does your architecture support the enterprise in its redesign and automation? The three-layered structure discussed earlier in this chapter not only provides the basis for our future product offerings, but also allows corporations to restructure their systems without giving up all of their pre-groupware investment.

This structure is based on the premise that host-based users can choose client-server-based workstations and that standalone personal computers should share in the processing power available over LANs and WANs. The networks act as a computing backbone that can be modified to suit the changing needs of the corporation.

What trends, standards, and issues does IBM see for the future of groupware? It is the nature of computing that change will always be the norm. So groupware, like all other computing strategies, will continue to evolve. The standards that exist today, like those for network protocols and mail systems, will have to deal with faster speeds, larger volumes of information, and tighter security. Many proposed standards, like those for sharing objects across diverse systems, will become integral parts of application software.

The move towards greater standardization goes along with demands for more openness in systems, and this is key to the success of groupware. IBM's strategy endorses many of these standards, both industry and *de facto*. We actively participate in numerous standards organizations, including the Workflow Coalition, the Shamrock Document Management Coalition, and the Object Management Group (OMG).

The adoption of object technology will help facilitate the creation of software components. Components allow users to assemble environments that best suit their requirements, enabling them to create custom-tailored desktops for task-centered computing. Components can also be tailored to group activities, making the coordination of workgroups a more natural process. As groupware evolves, information will exist independent of applications, free to be passed around and accessed as needed.

Shared information repositories and the underlying transport for information will be maintained by what are now IT departments. Decisions about storage, networks, and processing technology will not affect user access to this information.

On the other hand, users will be able to decide what works best on their desktops without losing access to the information and communication services they need for decision making. Such a level of openness and cooperation creates the possibility for enterprise-wide groupware.

When groupware reaches the point of full adoption across the enterprise, it will no longer be correct to identify it merely as a group entity. It will instead become true enterprise-wide cooperative processing.

We are convinced that workgroup solutions, by adapting to the way people work and facilitating intelligent computing functions, improve efficiency, productivity, and the business bottom line. In fact, we see groupware as a strategic necessity.

BIOGRAPHY

As director of WorkGroup Solutions Marketing, Mr. Sullivan has worldwide responsibility for developing and driving IBM's workgroup strategy. This strategy is based on providing integrated, open solutions that streamline the way teams conduct business today and adapt to the new ways teams will work in the future.

Sullivan is building a sound reputation in the industry as an expert in group communications, workflow, and information management, and most recently spoke on IBM's workgroup vision at Fall COMDEX.

During his 28-year career at IBM, Sullivan has been on the vanguard of helping customers apply new technologies to solve their business problems. Through a number of marketing positions in the areas of data communications, telephony, and office technology, Sullivan has been instrumental in driving IBM Token Ring, voice/data integration, and imaging strategies.

Sullivan has also held key IBM assignments in the Far East where he was manager of Industry Marketing for IBM Asian Operations in Tokyo and executive assistant to the chairman of IBM Americas/Far East.

Sullivan holds a Bachelor of Science in mathematics from Boston College and a Masters in business administration from the Amos Tuck School at Dartmouth.

Introduction to Chapter 10

Someone once told me that half of the Fortune 500 companies formed 10 years ago are no longer in existence today. What this shows me is the dynamic nature of our global economy. Nowhere is this dynamism more apparent than in the high-tech industry.

We have all heard the stories of downsizing and rightsizing. Both IBM and Digital have become "leaner and meaner" organizations over the last two years, but how does that tie in with groupware? Digital has always been a technology company—built by engineers and run by engineers. For the past decade they have been hardware-focused. But like IBM, Digital is facing the reality that large proprietary hardware systems are no longer leading the computing market and that software functionality has become the primary criterion which drives hardware purchases. Software to support collaboration is one of the driving forces in this arena.

Although Digital is known for its hardware and has a thriving PC business, Digital has lots of software, and produces software at a prodigious rate. They even have groupware, but it is the best-kept secret in the business. In one of the later chapters in this book, Michael Frow looks at how LinkWorks, one of Digital's groupware offerings, was used to unify information and improve customer service at the Bank of Montreal.

LinkWorks is almost in a category by itself. If you look at the product taxonomy in the introductory chapter, you will see I have LinkWorks categorized as FrameWorks. The other two products in that category have either evolved into something else or are no longer available. LinkWorks is unique in that it provides an overall linking structure for both group and desktop applications. Through object-oriented technology, it transparently connects all the software and application functions together. That is why LinkWorks is one of my only prospects for the currently evolving enterpriseware category.

Digital is credited with having one of the first and most successful office automation products, ALL-IN-1. Today, when automation products support collaboration, they are called groupware. Digital's challenge is to convert those millions of ALL-IN-1 users to their new groupware offerings...like LinkWorks.

But Digital has several other groupware products besides LinkWorks: TeamLinks, MailWorks, MailBus 400, and ObjectBroker round out the Digital family. The first section of this chapter covers a lot of ground and looks at how DEC plans to move deeper into collaborative computing in the future. The second half of the chapter is a description of Digital's product portfolio and describes the product features and functions. Each product has a few customer case studies to round out the chapter. The object-oriented products are developed by other groups at Digital so they are not covered in this chapter, even though object-oriented technology is a big part of Digital's current groupware offering.

This chapter may well reveal the best-kept software secrets in the groupware market. It is well worth reading to see not only what Digital has to offer today, but where they are going in the near future. Clearly, Digital is focused on both the customer and open systems. The real variable, then, about Digital as a vendor is not their software offerings, but their organization and distribution channels.

Digital has always been known for engineering rather than marketing. Digital's current challenge is the same as IBM's: to create a sales force with incentive to sell software (groupware in this case), with knowledge and autonomy to meet rapidly evolving customer needs. They also have to make the software available, make it easy and inexpensive to buy, and try to get some "mindshare" of business buyers looking for tools to re-engineer or more tightly integrate their organization. Digital's organizational structure has been in turmoil for the last two years, while Lotus has grabbed the majority of mindshare with Notes. Lotus is now starting to focus Notes on the enterprise, the territory both Digital and IBM have staked out. Digital's challenge for the future is to keep up the high quality of their collaborative software and to build a third-party community that will resell or develop after-market products. Distribution channels and internal organization will be the cornerstones of Digital's future success.

Digital's Client-Server Solutions for Workgroup Integration

Dilip Phadke and Don Harbison
Digital Equipment Corporation

10.1 BUILDING ON EXPERIENCE; TAKING ON THE FUTURE

In many companies today, the personal productivity revolution ignited by the personal computer has given way to a focus on the productivity of teams or workgroups. These groups are usually interdepartmental, frequently ad hoc, and distributed across the globe.

They tackle bigger problems, often related to significant re-engineering efforts, such as:

- ☞ Business process re-engineering
- ☞ Total quality management
- ☞ Value chain initiatives
- ☞ Electronic commerce
- ☞ Health care administration
- ☞ Just-in-time systems

Like individual users, groups depend on complete, timely, and accurate information—whether in another PC or workstation, a different department's server, or the corporate mainframe. But they need more than just information. They need solutions that help them to collaborate; systems that let them move easily from personal productivity applications to shared applications to corporate databases and production applications. They need unified access and interactivity with their business information.

10.1.1 New Organizational Model

The need for flexible, group-oriented solutions is here to stay. Out of the global recession of the 1990s, a new model of the efficient, competitive organization has emerged. It has a smaller workforce, fewer levels of management, and much closer coordination and interaction between departments. It makes full use of technology—both existing system assets and new acquisitions—to achieve corporate goals, including:

☞ Faster time-to-market for products and services
☞ Greater utilization of assets
☞ Improved quality
☞ Better customer service

The goal is clear, but for many companies it's much less clear how to get there—affordably. Companies have already made substantial investments in technology: mainframes, minis, PCs, personal productivity software, local area networks (LANs), corporate databases, production applications, and, in some cases, early use of shared applications, such as electronic mail, conferencing, workflow, and calendar management.

10.2 DIGITAL'S GROUPWARE STRATEGY

To meet customers' need for integrated systems that empower them to succeed in a fast-paced global marketplace, Digital's mission is to deliver open client-server groupware solutions for the leading desktop and server environments. With workgroup integration products from Digital, companies can become the kind of organizations they strive to be—lean, flexible, and responsive to customer needs and market demands.

Let there be no confusion. Digital is dedicated to helping customers reach this goal. Digital-developed software continues to remain the focus of investments even while the company is restructuring and turning the corner in a remarkable transformation. Many of these products continue to win awards for "best in class" in the software community, including recent COMDEX and CeBIT awards for our LinkWorks software. At Digital, we are intent on making our software as well regarded as the Alpha AXP chip, the world's fastest RISC processor.

Digital's strategy is to build and deliver innovative products and services that add value to customers' current investments in technology and business processes. Far from trying to supplant alternative applications, Digital is fully committed to the concept of open client-server computing. This commitment is nowhere demonstrated more completely than in the range of solutions Digital offers to empower the workgroup.

At Digital, we do not believe a total groupware solution should force users to buy all their products from one vendor. Our experience has taught us that companies are looking at groupware technology to achieve multiple goals. No single vendor or strategy will satisfy all of an organization's needs.

What's needed is an infrastructure that will link together disparate elements from different vendors and make them all work as a single integrated system. To meet the infrastructure needs of customers, Digital has developed what we call a solution integration framework—a framework for integrating desktop, shared, and production applications.

Using a solution framework does not require a massive overhaul of existing technology. In fact, an effective solution enables better use of current systems by integrating them into a client-server framework flexible enough to grow and change with the evolving needs of the business.

10.2.1 Shared Applications and Information Frameworks

The term "groupware" has become an umbrella in the industry for two different types of software:

☞ Applications that promote collaboration (shared groupware)
☞ Solutions that link individuals, groups, and the enterprise to critical business information and processes across the enterprise (frameworks)

One way to understand the difference between groupware applications and a solution framework within an information system is to compare them to a much more familiar system—the transportation system. The highway system, from superhighways down to country roads, can be considered the framework, the vehicles the applications. Roads are designed to accommodate a full range of vehicles, from 18-wheel tractor-trailers to motorcycles, all built by an unlimited number of manufacturers.

In a similar fashion, in a business communication system, a solution framework product such as Digital's LinkWorks accommodates a growing number of client and server platforms, networks, relational databases, and software applications.

10.2.2 Digital's Groupware Portfolio

Digital's groupware portfolio embraces both shared applications and frameworks, as well as messaging agents and backbones, and had its beginnings in the 1980s with the introduction of the world's first integrated time-sharing office system.

Today, Digital's groupware product portfolio consists of:

☞ **ALL-IN-1 Integrated Office System:** Our traditional office solution framework for video terminal OpenVMS customers using VAX and Alpha systems
☞ **MAILbus 400, MailWorks:** Our enterprise mail and messaging solutions for customers using OpenVMS and DEC OSF/1 UNIX on VAX and Alpha system servers
☞ **TeamLinks Office:** Our integrated suite of enterprise client-server groupware applications for customers who need to integrate their personal appli-

cations on PCs and Macintosh desktops with their ALL-IN-1 enterprise applications or MailWorks wide-area messaging systems.

☞ **LinkWorks:** Our open client-server enterprise solution framework offering customers a true object-oriented solution development environment complete with "out-of-the-box" document management, workflow, information access, and security for today's leading desktops and servers.

    10.2.2.1 ALL-IN-1   ALL-IN-1, in its own right, was a revolutionary product, offering terminal users a powerful electronic mail system integrated with a set of office applications essential to any business, including word processing, filing, routing, scheduling, and time management. Introduced in 1982, ALL-IN-1 exploded to become the market leader and has over 5 million active users today.

    ALL-IN-1 was very successful because it gave users (many of whom were new to computers) all the capabilities they needed to perform their jobs efficiently. ALL-IN-1 continues to meet the needs of terminal users, because it:

☞ Provides a high degree of integration with personal as well as shared groupware and business applications
☞ Is customizable to meet the unique needs of each business situation
☞ Offers strong system administration, security, and management capabilities

    Digital is fully committed to maintaining ALL-IN-1 as a viable framework for group computing for both its terminal users, and PC and workstation users as well. It continues to be enhanced. For example, ALL-IN-1 users can now add such new functionality as:

☞ Personal assistant (rule-based mail agent)
☞ TeamRoute (routing and approval)
☞ Distributed sharing

    Digital has evolved ALL-IN-1 to be a TeamLinks server and to support OpenVMS Alpha systems. These features are built into the base ALL-IN-1 product without an increase in cost, which means investment protection for Digital's customers with ALL-IN-1 installations.

    ALL-IN-1 gives customers a very cost-effective path from time-sharing to client-server computing with TeamLinks. Moreover, ALL-IN-1 can also be an object within a LinkWorks environment; that is, LinkWorks currently integrates the ALL-IN-1 file cabinet and mail.

    As illustrated in Figure 10.1, an evolving ALL-IN-1 installation can benefit from the addition of ever-new technology, without the need to jettison existing investments in hardware, software, applications, and training.

    10.2.2.2 Worldwide Enterprise Electronic Mail and Messaging   As a full-service vendor, Digital offers the industry's most complete portfolio of messaging products—from user agents to a powerful electronic mail backbone—and backs everything with comprehensive consulting services to assist customers throughout all aspects of distributed, integrated messaging, including planning, design, implementation, and management.

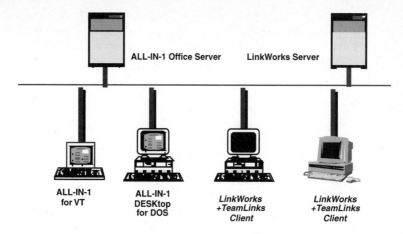

Fig. 10.1 The Path to the Future

Products include MailWorks, which provides a rich set of mail services to a choice of multivendor desktops, mail clients, and mail-enabled applications; the MAILbus 400 distributed messaging backbone, which provides reliable, high-volume, store-and-forward services for guaranteed message delivery across the enterprise with gateways to SMTP, fax, telex, and numerous third-party PC LAN mail systems, as well as the DEC X.500 Directory Service, which organizes people and system resource information in a format that can be accessed by any authorized user or application in the enterprise network.

No other vendor can match Digital's experience in providing electronic messaging solutions. We have the largest installed base of any vendor—more than 7 million electronic mailboxes and more than 2000 X.400 installations. Digital's own mail and messaging system is one of the world's largest electronic mail networks—encompassing our worldwide workforce, consultants, business partners,vendors, and more. This system has more than 100,000 mailboxes and directory subscribers, and delivers more than 50 million messages per year.

10.2.2.3 TeamLinks Office: Enterprise Groupware Applications TeamLinks Office helps users on the industry's most popular desktops—Microsoft Windows and Macintosh—communicate, coordinate, access, and share information across LAN and platform boundaries. TeamLinks Office works with Windows and Macintosh spreadsheets, graphics, and word-processing applications to enhance existing productivity capabilities and simplify business procedures. Servers currently offered with TeamLinks are DEC OSF/1 UNIX and OpenVMS.

The TeamLinks Office low-cost client-server suite of groupware applications is available as a complete set of shared applications. This suite of products offers capabilities comparable to other well-advertised products at a competitive price—mail, administrative workflow, scheduling, conferencing, and library services. What the others can't offer, however, is the seamless working environment of TeamLinks.

At the heart of the TeamLinks Office product family is TeamLinks Mail, an easy-to-use electronic mail service based on the international X.400 mail standard. TeamLinks Mail uses MailWorks or ALL-IN-1 servers, together with Digital's messaging backbone capabilities, to integrate diverse messaging systems and provide a seamless, secure, reliable delivery system across workgroups and across the enterprise.

TeamLinks leverages mail and messaging technology to address customers' needs for flexibility, choice, and investment protection. TeamLinks is an ideal client-server groupware application solution for PC and Macintosh workgroups. In addition, use of TeamLinks with ALL-IN-1 provides an office system that integrates low-cost VTs and distributed PCs into a common set of workgroup services. This use of TeamLinks further enables ALL-IN-1 users to evolve toward open client-server computing. And finally, TeamLinks is also a path to Digital's next-generation framework environment, LinkWorks.

10.2.2.4 The Newest Technology: LinkWorks
LinkWorks is the next-generation enterprise solution framework that carries on the ground-breaking tradition of ALL-IN-1. A product for the 1990s and beyond, LinkWorks allows customers to fully embrace and benefit from the dual use of open client-server computing and object-oriented system design.

Customers deploying LinkWorks solutions are never tied to a "one-size-fits-all" type of system. They have the freedom to develop and evolve their business solutions using a flexible, vendor-neutral component approach.

Focus on Customers' Key Issues   LinkWorks is designed for line-of-business managers who want to build a custom business solution using business process re-engineering concepts and object technology to achieve improved business operations. It provides the opportunity to streamline existing business processes or define new ones.

LinkWorks can tightly integrate personal, workgroup, and business applications. Workflow and team information sharing can be designed from the bottom up (by power users or integrators) in LinkWorks; rapid prototyping, customization, and solution evolution is the name of the game. LinkWorks is purposely designed to address the ever-changing requirements of teams working in a distributed environment.

Organizations today want technology that supports flexible, efficient processes for developing and deploying solutions that can be easily distributed and reused in other parts of the enterprise. The LinkWorks development process supports software reuse and evolution.

Organizational Impact   LinkWorks is to today's groupware products what word processing was to the typewriter—a revolutionary new way of doing business by enhancing and reusing information.

This new model does not rely on email or related bulletin board technologies that store information in shared file structures. Rather than having information routed from user to user, the object routes only the message notifications to those individuals who need to know, at the right time in the process. This is particularly important when people need to share large amounts of information, such as complete file cabinets, digital videos, or graphic presentations.

However, one cannot immediately throw away traditional mail-based communications in favor of object technology. Customers using LinkWorks solutions have discovered that email is best suited for simple interpersonal messaging. So just as word processors coexist with typewriters in a traditional office, LinkWorks provides coexistence with email. LinkWorks offers a basic email application, yet has the ability to fully integrate TeamLinks Mail, MS-Mail, or cc:Mail clients.

LinkWorks: The Future of Integrated Applications—Today! LinkWorks defines a new category of software in the breadth of its capabilities and its truly open, object-oriented environment. It supports, in encapsulated form, the most popular personal productivity applications. It integrates most popular desktops as clients, and offers a broad choice of servers. LinkWorks delivers an unprecedented ease of integration across all the levels in an organization—desktops, workgroups, corporate systems, and production systems.

LinkWorks becomes the organizing and enabling focus for the re-engineered enterprise by allowing companies to harness the assets they already have—expertise, equipment, and processes. The applications users know and prefer—personal productivity applications like word processing and spreadsheets; shared applications such as mail, scheduling, or workflow processes; business applications such as general ledger or manufacturing resource management—can be woven into an enterprise-wide information system. Thus, LinkWorks enhances the applications an organization already has by providing an underlying framework for sharing with others regardless of location or desktop environment.

LinkWorks allows people to continue using the applications they're comfortable with and makes it simple for them to do tasks and solve problems by providing unified access to information regardless of where it is. In other words, the learning curve with LinkWorks is so minimal that increases in productivity result almost immediately. Users appreciate the fact that LinkWorks supports their preferred desktop environment. IS management appreciates its lower support costs, security controls, and more "manageable" management features.

The greatest value can be achieved by tailoring LinkWorks to identified needs and well-defined business processes. This can be done sequentially—starting with individual departments or business processes. Digital works in close partnership with its customers and business partners to design and implement customized solutions built upon LinkWorks. Alternatively, LinkWorks can be installed and tailored by customers themselves. With LinkWorks, solutions are never static. LinkWorks powerful solution development environment, based on object technology, ensures that organizations can modify solutions rapidly to successfully adapt to changes in business demands.

10.3 DIGITAL'S GROUPWARE FUTURE

Digital's fundamental core competency in complex systems architecture and distributed networking, combined with our global multivendor support capabilities and commitment to standards, allows customers to deploy the appropriate workgroup solution with confidence that all parts will work together reliably and securely.

Organizations that have adopted LinkWorks and TeamLinks have discovered that these products positively impact their business. They tell us that Digital's workgroup solutions are fundamentally changing the way they work, and for the better.

TeamLinks, MailWorks, and LinkWorks clearly show Digital's excellence in technology. TeamLinks allows ALL-IN-1 customers to move to a more open, client-server-centered environment. MailWorks provides a reliable, scalable, departmental mail server for popular mail clients. For new customers, LinkWorks provides organizations with an exciting and powerful new business solution framework.

But advanced technology and broad-based strategic plans are not enough to ensure a leadership position in today's fast-paced worldwide groupware market. Customers need a company that understands what it takes to integrate applications which can solve business problems not only today, but for the future. Digital is such a company.

TeamLinks and LinkWorks are not designed merely as standalone groupware products; rather, they are components of a much larger plan. They are designed to easily link with other important technologies to solve ever greater problems. For example, TeamLinks and LinkWorks work with products like ObjectBroker in Digital's enterprise software portfolio, where ObjectBroker manages the messaging of objects. Similarly, LinkWorks and TeamLinks will also connect with innovative new products now being developed to leverage the Internet and multimedia for workgroups.

Systems integration services from Digital and its business partners complement product offerings and further serve to connect various elements for comprehensive solutions.

The breadth and availability of such comprehensive solutions enables Digital to solve the complex business process requirements of organizations, while providing tangible improvements for individuals in the workgroup. If you are exploring groupware or have begun to implement groupware technology in your company, perhaps it's time for you to talk with Digital or our business partners.

10.4 DIGITAL'S GROUPWARE PRODUCT PORTFOLIO

The remainder of this chapter provides more specific information on Digital's groupware product portfolio. Case studies are also included to illustrate the variety of solutions our customers have realized using these products. Product information is presented from the customer's perspective, and each section can be read independent of the others.

Information is provided for:

☞ LinkWorks (pages 275-85)
☞ TeamLinks (pages 285-91)

☞ MailWorks (pages 291-3)

☞ MAILbus 400 (pages 293-8)

10.4.1 LinkWorks

Digital's award-winning LinkWorks business solution software provides a development environment in which you can integrate personal productivity, groupware, and business applications for departmental and line-of-business success.

LinkWorks weaves various applications together into a whole solution, like weaving many colorful and vibrant threads into a distinctive tapestry—a tapestry that is all the more valuable for the diversity of its threads and the uniqueness of its pattern.

LinkWorks can create solutions on many levels. It's highly scalable, from simple integration of personal productivity applications and groupware to a sophisticated industry- and customer-specific solution. From use in a single department to enterprise-wide solutions, LinkWorks provides a uniform environment for both ad hoc and formal work teams. It "group-enables" existing applications by providing facilities for document sharing, versioning, access control, electronic mail, and automation of workflow processes throughout the LinkWorks environment.

Its innovative use of open, client-server, object-oriented technology makes it a superior framework within which to customize business solutions, and allows Digital and its Business Partners to offer a range of industry solutions based on LinkWorks. As a development environment for customized business solutions, it is second to none.

10.4.1.1 Revolutionary Solutions Development Environment
LinkWorks provides a revolutionary environment for designing, distributing, and deploying software components. Combining groupware functionality with object-oriented technology, LinkWorks lets software professionals create solutions unmatched in flexibility and cost efficiency. With LinkWorks, developers can:

☞ Add value to personal productivity applications

☞ Create dedicated industry-specific solutions

☞ Create customer-specific solutions and enhancements

The foundation for this unique value is the uncompromised use of key object-oriented techniques like inheritance, dynamic binding, and reuse. Compliance with emerging object-oriented middleware technologies such as Digital and Microsoft's Common Object Management (COM) and the Object Management Group's Common Object Request Broker Architecture (CORBA) ensures both unique integration capabilities and investment protection.

Easily Create LinkWorks-Enabled Software Components LinkWorks allows software professionals to both extend LinkWorks functionality to existing applications and extend the LinkWorks framework itself. In a significant step forward for reusable software development, any set of modifications or extensions can be grouped together and extracted for distribution, reuse, and evolution as LinkWorks software components (see Figure 10.2).

Extend LinkWorks Functionality Itself   In another significant step forward for reusable software development, LinkWorks lets developers extend the framework itself with external functionality. This capability enables the functionality and data of legacy applications to be presented in an object-oriented way, making them candidates for further modification, extension, and reuse.

The LinkWorks development process is evolutionary—you never start from scratch. You use what is already there, improve and extend it step by step, and reuse it.

LinkWorks extensions are created on the LinkWorks Workbench, a graphical tool that lets developers navigate and browse through the object-oriented structure of LinkWorks and modify and extend the behavior of the system. External functionality is included within LinkWorks software components via industry-standard calling conventions (see Figure 10.3).

The results of a set of modifications and extensions—new functionality—can be grouped together as a LinkWorks Software Component and extracted for distribution with a unique worldwide identification. This component is then available within the LinkWorks hierarchical structure for further evolution.

LinkWorks is already at work in solutions that address commonly experienced problems in several industries. More are under development by Digital and its Business Partners.

Totally Customizable   LinkWorks readily lends itself to customization in order to devise a solution tailored to the unique needs of different types of users,

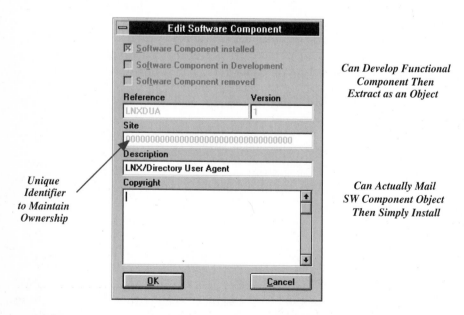

Fig. 10.2 LinkWorks Software Components May Be Extracted and Commercialized

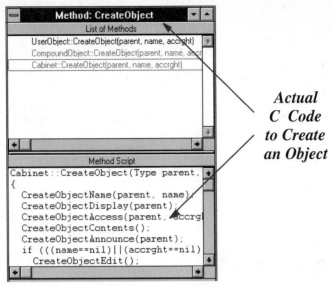

Fig. 10.3 Editing Methods in LinkWorks Class Programming

groups, or enterprises. Customization can occur immediately after installation, or at a later stage if desired.

Maximize Investments LinkWorks ensures the preservation of legacy systems and applications, while at the same time providing the opportunity to re-engineer business processes for greater efficiency, customer satisfaction, and profit. LinkWorks protects existing investments in installed hardware and software. It supports a wide range of server platforms, desktop clients, installed databases, and popular personal and groupware applications. LinkWorks also protects investments in training by building on existing user expertise and established user comfort levels. Users continue to work on the desktops they prefer with the applications of their choice. And new industry-standard applications and tools can be seamlessly added as desired or needed.

Easy to Learn and Use LinkWorks presents users with a graphical environment, based on Windows 95, which closely resembles the physical desk. Documents, filing containers, and tools exist as objects, represented as icons, on each user's electronic desk.

Users work efficiently and intuitively by moving icons with the mouse. For example, if a user has created a document with his favorite word-processing application and wants to make it available to all members of the team, he simply selects the document with the mouse and drops it on a shared cabinet.

The document is now available to all team members who have access rights to this cabinet. All authorized users can retrieve data stored in it and work with it. Access rights to a cabinet (read only, read and write, etc.) can be flexibly assigned even to the level of an individual object. Because LinkWorks can integrate the applications users are already comfortable with, and makes it simple for them to attack new tasks and solve problems, users quickly adapt to it. User acceptance and empowerment—combined with the ability of LinkWorks to disseminate information and automate processes—yield productivity gains for the individual and the organization.

Unified Access to Information   LinkWorks provides unified access to information. Information can be generated by any personal productivity, groupware, or business application integrated into the LinkWorks environment. LinkWorks users can share information by dragging and dropping documents and other information objects into a shared filing container, by emailing them, or by utilizing a share option on the menu.

A directory service locates individual users or groups of users. So it's a simple matter to create distribution lists for information sharing within LinkWorks or for standard fax or electronic mail to a person or an organization outside LinkWorks. LinkWorks also provides automatic version control—for an individual's own objects, such as a document, and for shared documents. When a user opens a shared document for editing, a new version is created, and other users can still read the previous version. And users can register their interest in particular documents, so that they will be notified immediately when changes are made.

10.4.1.2 The LinkWorks Desktop   The LinkWorks desktop (see Figure 10.4) is unique in that it retains the personal user's environment no matter what hardware or operating system is underneath it. The desktop can be moved from one client to another unchanged, since the user and their related desktop environment are maintained as an object. An individual sees four kinds of objects on the desktop: tools, applications, documents, and containers. Tool icon examples include a calculator, a clock, a wastebasket, and a shredder tool that writes erasure patterns over an object's reclaimed disk space to provide an added level of security. In addition, LinkWorks provides a search utility tool that can find any object attributes in the entire system.

The LinkWorks desktop may be presented in the user's local language. In fact, languages can be mixed within a single LinkWorks cell cluster. For example, a French desk and a German desk in the same organization. LinkWorks is a globally engineered product, available in over 24 languages (see Figure 10.5).

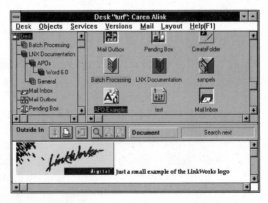

Fig. 10.4 The LinkWorks Desktop

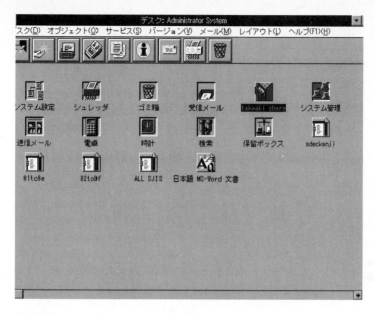

Fig. 10.5 LinkWorks Is Internationalized in Over 24 Languages

Application icons represent PC or workstation applications programs. Document icons identify their associated memos, video or clips, drawings or graphics, and spreadsheets. An application program can be executed by opening either the application icon or an associated document icon. Both the application or document object may be stored on either the local workstation's hard disk or the server disk.

The fourth kind of object, the container, is an intelligent directory that can hold other container objects and act on them in certain ways. Anyone who uses file cabinets can relate to this container object. For example, a container icon for a LinkWorks file cabinet represents a shared file area. File cabinets allow people to exchange documents with one another. More complex containers, such as LinkWorks' main In Box and Out Box containers, allow users to distribute or print files by simply dragging and dropping the file's icons into them. Since a spreadsheet is considered an object, you can pick it up and drop it on a file cabinet or email it or the entire file cabinet.

10.4.1.3 Sharing and Communication with Objects An object, such as a document, created in one of the applications programs on your desktop can be shared in several ways. You can place the object in a local desktop container and designate a list of other people who have access to it. Alternatively, you can place it in a shared container on the LinkWorks server or route it to other users as a special object that can be shared. Recipients can read, modify, file, search, or digitally sign objects, depending on their access rights. It is even possible to pick up a whole file cabinet as an object and place it in a different location.

One of the biggest differences a user experiences when working in the Link-Works desktop, versus other non-object-oriented integrated workgroup products, is the way information flows within the workgroup. It does not flow via email. Instead, it flows through an object-based sharing mechanism. An individual can create an object, such as a document, in his or her own private workspace and define it with no sharing or viewing rights. To open up the document for review, discussion, or editing, the user simply modifies the object's attributes. The object is not moved along, as in an email system; instead, it announces to the system who will be notified next.

LinkWorks has not ignored the need for the interpersonal communications that email provides. A very basic email application is included on the desktop. In addition, LinkWorks provides gateways to a number of industry email systems (X.400 backbone, HP OpenMail, MS Mail, etc.) to help the user who must send information beyond the LinkWorks confines.

Workflow and Process Automation   In every company, information circulates among various departments and offices in the form of documents, notes, forms, presentations, images, and more. Recipients then read, modify, file, search, or sign off on the information. The functionality of LinkWorks makes it possible to automate these standard workflow processes to promote efficiency within and across groups and ensure procedural control.

LinkWorks presents the company's organizational structure in an easily manipulated chart. User profiles maintain information regarding preferred applications, desktop clients, and security parameters. This allows for a flexible and secure work environment.

Workflow is an object class, and can be modified and reused like any other object within LinkWorks. The workflow elements in LinkWorks are stored on a database, and any activity is tracked. Workflow is not confined to members of the LinkWorks workgroup. By use of Protected External Methods, the routing mechanisms to other workflow systems or applications outside the LinkWorks domain can occur.

Workflow is designated through a workflow "map" that can conditionally route a document, such as an expense report, through the organization based on conditions the organization sets up. For example, a value in a given spreadsheet cell can alert individuals who may not normally be part of the process. The workflow map handles the job of routing each discrete task to the correct addressee. The sender can track the location of the document along the path defined by the map.

Business processes requiring an audited tracking trail can make use of the LinkWorks electronic signature feature which records formal document review and/or approval. In addition to documents in the workgroup, the desktop elements, such as icons and folders, can be routed, along with the data in each document.Distributing icons and folders as objects can be used to replicate a mini-environment for participating workgroup members. For example, such a mini-environment could be created on a project basis, including definition of individual tools, templates, access rights, and so forth.

10.4.1.4 Administering a LinkWorks System
LinkWorks has a server-centric architecture that provides major subsystems for object storage, administration, and object management. The three server components of the architecture include a management component, a data cell (or cells) component, and a personal desk manager component. This architecture makes it possible for Link-Works to provide an open environment that integrates all the existing components of a system: multiple repositories, multiple servers, multiple networks, multiple clients, and multiple databases.

The management component provides a graphical user interface (GUI) specifically designed for server administration. Client-server connections can be established by the administrator via the DECnet or TCP/IP networking protocol. Data cells contain information regarding each LinkWorks user's environment and the attributes of LinkWorks objects. The final component, the personal desk manager, includes the user's initial desk and the tools available to the user.

Since all system and user configuration data is stored independent of the workstations, users can easily switch between various desktop devices and locations whenever required, and still work with their personal "desk."

Storing object metadata in industry-standard relational database systems (including Ingres, Informix, Oracle, Rdb, and Sybase) is key to the LinkWorks architecture. Information created by LinkWorks users is automatically stored as metadata in a relational database. LinkWorks uses relational database technology to ensure the integrity of information created, the total availability of sharable information, and protection of the data against unauthorized access or virus infection. Improved security and manageability of departmental systems relieve IS burdens and worries, without adding to their work load. Indeed, use of Link-Works benefits both business departments and IS. Functional business units are able to more directly control their own processes and priorities. IS realizes improved system management, data protection, data security, and information sharing in departmental computing. Because it's easy to manage, almost all system administrative functions in LinkWorks can be performed by a nontechnical person.

LinkWorks administration can be centralized or distributed to individuals throughout the organization. For some organizations, centralized administration is a real strength, enabling the administrator to define an environment that allows individuals to work together more effectively while ensuring that the organization can keep track of its software assets. For example, the administrator can ensure that only two or three approved word processors are available to members of the workgroup on a given project. Limiting the number of potential document development tools makes it easier to implement group document templates. However, some organizations prefer distributed workgroups with their own autonomy in administering the system, and LinkWorks is designed to allow this.

10.4.1.5 Customizing the LinkWorks Environment
LinkWorks is customizable and extensible (see Figure 10.6). There is no modification required to integrate "off-the-shelf, shrink-wrap" software. Icons, menus, and even the

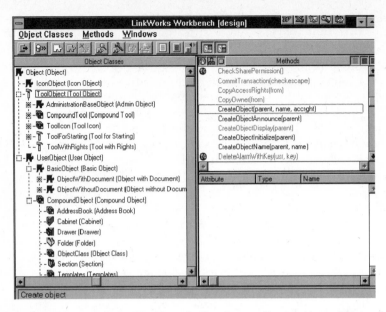

Fig. 10.6 With the LinkWorks Workbench, Developers Customize and Extend Link-Works Objects

underlying C++ programming code can be tailored for a particular user, group, or organization. In addition, desktop applications can be "encapsulated" within the LinkWorks environment. Encapsulation is a relatively simple process. First register the application in the LinkWorks framework, and then assign the new object's defining attributes, including type of application, location, icon, and object class.

Going beyond simple encapsulation of applications is a little more complex. Digital has added out-of-the-box capability in the form of programmable objects, called Application Programming Objects (APOs), that will act as a developer's workbench. APOs will include LinkWorks service definitions, linkable services, and utilities available as objects for easier programming and reuse. For example, one APO will allow the programmer to create, modify, and maintain hyper applications. Hyper applications allow the target user to click on a word or figure in a document and jump to another window or related information. This new location can contain, among other things, another document. This is sometimes called "live link" or "hot link" capability.

The APO toolkit also allows programmers to integrate sections of code, written in any language they choose (from pervasive languages like Visual Basic for Applications or C++ to application-specific macro languages), into the environment. There is a wide choice of development tools, ranging from formal languages to application-specific macros. LinkWorks also includes a collection of callable routines whose main function is to enable applications to participate in the LinkWorks environment. In addition, generic user interface and object manipulation capabilities will reside here.

Another interesting object will provide the capability to automatically record events or classes of events. The resulting record will be editable. Of course, the toolkit also provides the necessary testing and debugging tools to support the programmer's task.

In addition, there are two scripting language mechanisms for power users. One of these supports Microsoft's Object Linking and Embedding (OLE) paradigm, including OLE 2 automation. The other is Digital-specific and meant to enable development for multiple platforms. These scripting languages will provide linking and navigation capabilities.

10.4.1.6 Examples of LinkWorks Business Solutions at Work   The following examples demonstrate innovative ways in which Digital customers are achieving their business goals of time to market, quality, and customer satisfaction.

VW-GEDAS   VW-GEDAS is an information technology consulting firm and value-added reseller (VAR) of high-performance information systems. As one of Digital's Business Partners, VW-GEDAS has worked closely during the past two years with Digital.

In addition to developing information-based solutions for its parent company, the well-known auto manufacturer, VW-GEDAS meets the information technology needs of government agencies and diverse commercial clients worldwide. Under an agreement with Digital, the firm is currently marketing Link-Works-based solutions under the name "Synergy for Windows."

Among the most successful projects that VW-GEDAS has implemented thus far with LinkWorks is an 80-user integrated sales and logistics solution for a special equipment dealer that supplies Volkswagen customers with custom accessories.

To classify LinkWorks software as either "groupware" or "middleware" would be too limiting—it actually represents a new class of group productivity software. Before choosing LinkWorks software, VW-GEDAS evaluated numerous alternatives, including Rhapsody from AT&T and Lotus Notes. "We chose Link-Works because it's much more 'in the future'; it's completely object-oriented, it's secure, and the workflow component is unmatched," said Wiesner.

"LinkWorks is really unbelievable," said Wiesner. "At one site we have users sitting at Macintosh computers, and they can share the same 'objects' with users on the PC, OS/2 workstations, and UNIX workstations. They have a mail gateway to IBM MEMO too, as well as a mail gateway to Digital's ALL-IN-1. To have this running without many 'tricks' is a big step for information technology."

Wiesner emphasized the importance of workflow. The workflow component of LinkWorks takes advantage of the product's object-oriented attributes. "The idea behind LinkWorks is this: I take a box, and in that box there is a WinWord file, an Excel spreadsheet, and perhaps some drawings coming from a designer. All these things together are available for a special group of users—everyone has access," explained Wiesner.

He added, "Where there's a process involved, such as filling an order, approving a request, or collaborating on a project, the box can be routed from one person to another. The process can be tracked from beginning to end, and members of project teams can be alerted when new information becomes available."

Another feature of LinkWorks that Wiesner praised was the ability to control access to information—protecting security, yet freeing the flow of information to those who need it to make decisions and perform their jobs. The system permits restricted access to specific documents, protecting sensitive materials from unauthorized use.

VW-GEDAS is using LinkWorks to gain control of unwieldy networks of PC users as well. "One of the biggest problems for large organizations is having a network with 300 or 400 or more PCs," said Wiesner.

VW has now chosen LinkWorks for company-wide implementation for all its divisions. The implementations have already begun at Audi.

Siemens Integra Switzerland's leading supplier of railroad switching technology, Siemens Integra, was looking for a way to bring the administration of its business up to the standards of quality and efficiency embodied in its products. The company found the answer in LinkWorks.

With the LinkWorks solution, managers, administrators, and secretaries at five sites in Wallisellen, Switzerland, and one in Bern, 100 km away, can share information and work cooperatively as never before. Best of all, the transformation of its approach to information technology didn't require a wholesale replacement of the computers and software it had before. Siemens Integra employees use the same PCs. They use the same applications software, too. All that has changed is that they have a new integrated client-server environment in which to work—one that offers a common, easy-to-use graphical user interface to all of the tools and information they need to do their jobs as efficiently as possible.

But Markus Elsener, Information Systems Director for Siemens Integra, likes to point out how it happened with LinkWorks at his company.

"The decision to buy LinkWorks was not made by the top management or the EDP department; it came from the users—with management approval, of course," said Elsener. "I think this is very important, because they are the ones who will be using it. It is good because they say it is good."

The reason their users like LinkWorks so much is that it not only makes them more productive as a team, it makes the computer-based environment itself friendlier. "The user interface appealed to us right away, within the first five minutes of seeing it," added Elsener. "The look and feel is really excellent, and it makes sharing data very easy."

Projects at Siemens Integra generate a lot of data. Work in process represents about 30,000 files that need to be managed, coordinated, and shared.

"We looked at Lotus Notes but it was not the right product for our application. With LinkWorks we can use our existing applications, linking them to big data archives. With Lotus Notes we would have to write our own applications."

With PC clients networked with a UNIX server, LinkWorks gives Elsener's organization the flexibility to build on the company's established technology base. They can include widely used off-the-shelf products in their integrated client-server environment. The same will hold true when they migrate their database server to an OpenVMS system, which they plan to do.

"Scalability is also very important," added Elsener. "We will integrate all of our PC users, including the 60 or so we have at our Bern site. LinkWorks makes that possible."

For Mr. Elsener and Siemens Integra, LinkWorks has turned out to be more than a quick solution to a pressing problem. It has spurred thoughts about fresh ways to approach their business processes, for the simple reason that LinkWorks opens the door to new possibilities.

"For some departments, we are analyzing how we can solve problems differently with LinkWorks than we are now," said Elsener. "This is particularly true in the finance area. We want to see if we can speed up the process for bids. And we haven't even started to use the workflow management features of the system.

"The longer you work with LinkWorks, the more ideas you get for how you can improve your company. It took us just a few months to see all of the possibilities. Then we began to realize them and use LinkWorks to organize our office."

As Mr. Elsener said, "If you were to take LinkWorks out of our department, we could not imagine how to work." And that says it all.

10.4.2 The TeamLinks Workgroup Solution

TeamLinks Office makes organizing, accessing, and sharing information easy, no matter how large or small the number of users, or how many miles separate them.

TeamLinks Office works with the applications you use every day—Microsoft Windows and Macintosh spreadsheets, graphics, and word processors—enhancing your capabilities and simplifying the most tedious business procedures. What's more, you can start with TeamLinks Mail and add any of the other options as you go along.

TeamLinks is a family of "enterprise" client-server groupware applications—scalable from small LANs to large implementations of tens of thousands of users. TeamLinks is built on Digital's proven and reliable servers and is easy to use. And your TeamLinks applications are fully interoperable with users on DOS PCs and video terminals. If your organization needs to communicate through diverse systems and messaging services, TeamLinks is your solution. TeamLinks Mail uses MailWorks or ALL-IN-1 to provide seamless electronic mail service, no matter how many networks and applications your organization uses. Based on the popular international standard X.400 mail, TeamLinks Mail breaks through technological barriers to integrate diverse messaging systems. It provides the most reliable delivery system available today.

TeamLinks Mail (see Figure 10.7) lets you create messages within your favorite Windows or Macintosh application and mail them without leaving the application. For example, mail-enabling macros let users mail documents directly from WordPerfect. The whole process is seamless.

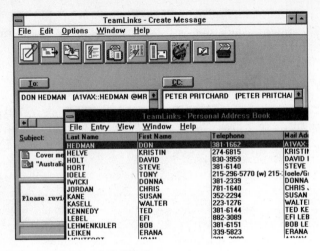

Fig. 10.7 TeamLinks Mail for MS-Windows

TeamLinks Mail offers a rich selection of functions and capabilities. In addition to commonly found features such as create, reply, or file, TeamLinks offers the following messaging functions:

☞ Create and edit distribution lists
☞ Carbon-copy and print mail
☞ Search incoming/outgoing mail
☞ Prioritize delivery
☞ Flag unread mail
☞ Broadcast mail receipt
☞ Collate delivery and read receipt (not available with ALL-IN-1)

TeamLinks also offers the following directory functions:

☞ Sort by first name, last name, and mail address
☞ Look up local and remote users
☞ Support for nicknames
☞ Transparent access to global directory

It also provides gateways to public mail carriers:

☞ AT&T Mail
☞ CompuServe
☞ MCI Mail
☞ USEnet
☞ Bitnet
☞ Internet
☞ SprintMail

You can alter the look and feel of TeamLinks for Windows to suit the way you work by customizing the button bar. More sophisticated customization of TeamLinks is possible with the TeamLinks Software Development Kit.

While more vendors are beginning to incorporate the X.400 standard into their messaging services, TeamLinks Mail users are in the forefront, already working with the most widely accepted mail standard in the world. Using X.400 today translates into investment protection for tomorrow.

10.4.2.1 TeamLinks Routing   Processing review and authorization documents manually can be time-consuming and difficult to track. TeamLinks Routing automates your workflow process for procedures such as purchase orders and expense vouchers (see Figure 10.8).

Simply route the form, document, drawing, or graphic that you want reviewed and approved; or route the application you want distributed. These items are then automatically sent from one user to another once action has been taken. TeamLinks Routing lets you track an item's progress and ascertain its status throughout the entire review cycle. At the conclusion of the cycle, TeamLinks Routing delivers a history of the process to keep for future reference.

10.4.2.2 Electronic Filing—Maximum Organization and Efficiency   With the TeamLinks Shared Filing features, stacks of paperwork and cumbersome file cabinets are things of the past. Not only are your PC and Macintosh files easy to organize, but you can share and organize electronic files, data, and documents with other TeamLinks users, eliminating tedious disk swapping and manual file transfers.

Here's how it works: You create electronic file cabinets containing drawers and folders to hold documents in the format of your choice. Name the documents, file cabinets, folders, and drawers whatever you want—you're not required to follow conventional DOS file naming. And Macintosh users can continue to use their familiar Macintosh file navigation tools.

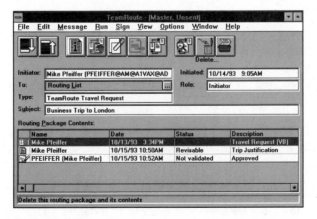

Fig. 10.8 TeamLinks Routing

You have consistent access to all your documents, anywhere in the network. Call up documents, mail messages, images, and spreadsheets from the same file menu simply by clicking on the name.

10.4.2.3 TeamLinks Conferencing—Around-the-Clock Networking   With TeamLinks Conferencing for Windows and Macintosh, users can collaborate and share information any time, anywhere. TeamLinks Conferencing can accommodate a small group within the same building, or thousands of people on a worldwide network.

TeamLinks Conferencing is easy to use through its simple topic-and-reply format. You can request a directory listing of notes (topics and replies) written by one person, notes with a particular word or phrase in their titles, or notes written before or after a specific date.

Conferences are arranged as a chronological, titled series of topics and replies.

10.4.2.4 TeamLinks Library Services—Information at Your Fingertips
TeamLinks users have access to the latest information when they need it and where they need it with the DEC VTX electronic reference library.

Information is offered in a variety of formats, including images, graphics, and text. And with content-based retrieval, finding information is fast and easy.

Selecting from menu and keyword searches, users can view, print, or mail themselves reference materials from the on-line library. And DEC VTX is a less expensive alternative to hard-copy distribution methods, since it eliminates the costs of printing, warehousing, and shipping information.

10.4.2.5 Group Scheduling   Each TeamLinks user has an individual calendar (see Figure 10.9). To correlate work and schedules, the day-planning system links all individual calendars, including those of remote users who are not continuously connected to a LAN. When individual and group calendars are called up, they show what meetings are already scheduled and what times are available. Simply select the time desired, and all calendars are updated. RSVP/Confirm/Decline messages will then inform each participant of the meeting's status. You can also add information such as the meeting location, the purpose of the meeting, and any special notes you feel are important. You can even schedule items needed to conduct the meeting, including conference rooms, slide projectors, and phone equipment; all the scheduling details are handled for you.

Calendar Manager makes organizing projects and plans easy and efficient. Users can make notes and action lists for themselves and for others showing appointments, priority levels, and target dates. These lists can be managed separately or merged with daily appointments.

10.4.2.6 TeamLinks Office—The Easy Way to Start   The TeamLinks Office suite includes all five TeamLinks applications—Mail, Routing, Conferencing, VTX, and Calendar Manager—in one easy-to-order package.

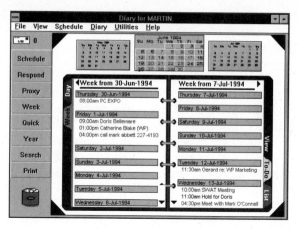

Fig. 10.9 TeamLinks Scheduling

10.4.2.7 How TeamLinks Is Helping Digital's Customers The following examples demonstrate how some of Digital's customers are utilizing TeamLinks to improve communications.

Hydro-Electric Commission in Tasmania "We use TeamLinks from the CEO on down, and it has dramatically changed the way we do business," says Mike Williams, Manager of Information Services for the Hydro-Electric Commission (HEC) of the state of Tasmania, Australia.

The emphasis at the HEC is on business. The Hydro-Electric Commission is the largest state-owned enterprise in Tasmania and supplies power to all of Tasmania.

However, too much time and money was being spent in a traditional, paper-based approach to communicating throughout the company. To increase productivity and reduce overhead, the HEC moved to streamline their internal communications with TeamLinks.

Williams initiated a pilot program of approximately 150 people from various levels in the organization and made sure to include all the senior executives and their secretaries. "We wanted to get the top people involved and have them push for universal use," related Williams. "We got a lot of support from our chief executive; he was very enthusiastic."

HEC is largely a PC organization, whose users run TeamLinks Mail for Windows. However, a few critical users are on Macintosh systems, including the corporate general manager. HEC users are now able to share Word documents and Excel spreadsheets not only between PCs, but also between PC and Macintosh systems.

Now at approximately 840 users, the implementation continues to roll out. The two most widely used applications across the enterprise are TeamLinks Mail and DEC VTX.

TeamLinks Mail, at the heart of the TeamLinks Office suite, provides seamless electronic mail capability across diverse platforms and personal productivity applications. It is the most important component of TeamLinks for HEC. "I expect it will form part of many things we'll be doing in the future," said Williams, "and it's easy to use. Anyone who can move their way around a Windows screen can use TeamLinks Mail."

HEC's main purpose in installing electronic mail capabilities is to improve internal communications.

DEC VTX is the Hydro-Electric Commission's other most widely used TeamLinks family application. VTX helps the HEC update, distribute, file, and retrieve information on-line. The Commission's telephone directory, company policies and procedures, chart of accounts, and human resource information now reside on VTX, and are updated and accessed there. Employees receive up-to-date information faster, and at a lower cost to the company. A personnel directory for VTX, including photographs of employees, has recently been custom-developed for HEC by Digital.

HEC has reaped several benefits from its implementation of the TeamLinks solution. Overhead reduction has been impressive—$A1.2 million (U.S. $900,000) per year, according to HEC's calculations. That includes twice the savings in reduced post-initiation paperwork handling that the Commission had expected. Payback was achieved in 12 months.

"Many more people know many more things about many more subjects now," observed Williams. "And our ability to communicate better with each other improves our ability to communicate with customers. We can respond better and more quickly externally now that our internal turnaround time has improved. Our TeamLinks solution is helping us achieve our number one business goal— customer satisfaction."

State of Ohio's Rehabilitation Services Commission   "Counselors in the field were authorizing services before they knew they were out of money," advises Karen DeLong, MIS Manager for the State of Ohio's Rehabilitation Services Commission (RSC). "There was no real-time budget information. Counselors had to wait weeks for paperwork to be processed before they could activate a service plan. This was time that could have been put to better use making Ohioans with disabilities employable."

Putting consumers on the road to employment is one of the most important goals of the Rehabilitation Services Commission, a state agency charged with assisting individuals with physical or mental disabilities. The RSC's most often requested services are job training and placement.

The antiquated paper system that RSC used slowed down both training and placement services. Using the old system for developing a rehabilitation plan that, by Federal regulation, must be signed by the client before service can begin, counselors had to visit the client, write up a plan, return the document to the field office for typing and processing, mail the typed document to the client for signature, and wait for the document to be mailed back. All of this had to take place before services could be authorized. Other procedures were similar throughout the formal counseling process. With over 30,000 active consumers requiring service, DeLong knew she had to find a better way to get things done.

To improve timeliness of service and reduce operating costs, RSC chose TeamLinks. Their solution includes mobile computing, which is vital for RSC.

TeamLinks allows counselors to create reports and other documents anywhere in the field. Then these documents can be electronically mailed and routed anywhere on the Commission's wide area network (WAN).

The enterprise WAN capabilities of the TeamLinks workgroup solution sold DeLong. "We needed a system that can integrate wide and local area networks into a seamless enterprise-wide network. We also needed good security to protect consumer confidentiality." TeamLinks—with Digital's network software and robust messaging backbone—allows RSC to do just that. Ease of use was another key reason the Commission chose TeamLinks software. "A lot of the people who will be using this system have never used a computer before. We needed a solution that is intuitive, easy to learn, and easy to use wherever one may be," continued Ms. DeLong. "Counselors need to be able to access the system as easily on the road as they can in the office."

Not only will service quality be vastly enhanced through the new solution, but operating expenses will be reduced at the same time. "We've calculated that we will save the taxpayers approximately $2 million per year with the full implementation of this system," estimates DeLong. "We will be able to speed up the rehabilitation process, generate taxpaying workers sooner, and redeploy clerical staff to other assignments. Everybody wins."

10.4.3 MailWorks for UNIX

When different workgroups in the department use competing LAN mail systems, it is hard to share information quickly and easily. MailWorks for UNIX® maximizes your productivity by smoothly linking separate and diverse workgroup mail systems within the department and beyond.

Digital's MailWorks for UNIX provides a reliable, flexible, cost-effective way to tie diverse desktop mail systems together. Its client-server technology allows Macintosh, Microsoft Windows, DOS, and UNIX Motif workstations to participate as peers in an integrated workgroup that may be distributed across wide geographic areas. Its support for a wide range of platforms is matched by support for an ever-growing list of mail clients—including TeamLinks, Microsoft Mail, Lotus cc:Mail, MailWorks Motif, and others. MailWorks lets you easily communicate within the department, with other departments in the enterprise, with business partners, and with public and private service providers, including the Internet, all without expensive gateways. MailWorks supports simultaneous connections to both SMTP and X.400 mail systems, so that the same message can be sent concurrently in both environments.

The MailWorks client-server user agent can also be used with the Digital MAILbus 400 distributed messaging backbone and Digital X.500 Directory Services to build a complete, reliable, standards-based enterprise messaging solution with long-term investment protection.

10.4.3.1 Within the Department and Beyond   For starters, MailWorks for UNIX supports messaging needs within the department. It lets users of diverse workgroup mail systems exchange the kinds of information they work with every day, including faxes, spreadsheets, documents, and scanned images.

Beyond that, MailWorks enables workgroup users to communicate freely across the heterogeneous enterprise and with suppliers, customers, and other partners. Simultaneous support for SMTP and X.400 messaging protocols makes it easy.

MailWorks users can exchange messages with users of UNIX SendMail products—including the Internet via the SMTP messaging protocol. At the same time, MailWorks connects seamlessly to MAILbus 400, Digital's best-in-class, 1992-conformant MTA, for communication with X.400 environments. With Mail-Works a single message can be addressed to any number of Internet and/or X.400 recipients. MailWorks provides easy integration with the SendMail community, the Internet, Digital's VAXmail, and X.400 Services. The MailWorks server can distinguish the type of address and send the message to the appropriate trans-port(s) automatically (see Figure 10.10).

10.4.3.2 Time-Saving Group Message Stores Groups of users, such as project teams or special interest groups, can set up group message stores. These group message stores can be accessed by more than one user at a time, and can serve as a bulletin board or forum for discussion.

10.4.3.3 Easy Message Management With MailWorks it's easy to keep track of all the messages that flow throughout the organization. MailWorks pro-vides such features as hierarchical folders for filing mail, cross-indexing of fold-ers, and a query facility to retrieve messages.

10.4.3.4 Flexible Configuration MailWorks can be tailored to support any site's configuration because of its client-server design and its ability to use

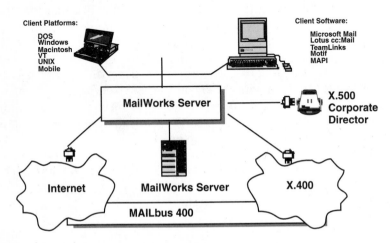

Fig. 10.10 Digital's Messaging Framework

remotely mounted message stores, remote X.400 MTAs, and remote X.500 directories.

10.4.3.5 Familiarity and Ease of Use   With the choice of clients offered by MailWorks, users of Microsoft Mail and Lotus cc:Mail clients can continue to work as before, using the mail applications with which they are familiar. Within this familiar environment, they enjoy the added benefits that the MailWorks server provides.

In addition to the flexibility and ease of communicating outside of one's own workgroup, MailWorks offers users a Personal Address Book to make it easy to reference frequent mail addressees. Access to corporate directory services simplifies the task of locating and sending mail to others in the organization.

10.4.3.6 Secure and Reliable   MailWorks provides superior security and reliability—a significant improvement over LAN file-sharing techniques. Unlike PC LAN mail systems, all messages are uniquely identified in the MailWorks X.400 mail system. Messages are easy to trace. With MailWorks, there are no lost messages.

10.4.3.7 Cost-Effective Distributed Management   PC LAN mail systems do not support distributed management. As a result, the cost of management is quite high because each LAN server (dedicated PC) and LAN router (another dedicated PC) must be managed individually, at the physical location of the PC. When you add up all the PCs required to set up a backbone, including high-availability requirements—CPU backup, disk shadowing, alternate network paths, and nondistributed management time—the cost of management is significant.

With the ability to configure MailWorks to meet your expanding needs, you can eliminate the need for large numbers of post offices and gateways. With MailWorks it is easy to add users. You don't need multiple directories and excessive system management.

10.4.3.8 Investment Protection through Choice   MailWorks provides freedom of choice in desktop client, server platform/operating system, and network protocol. This freedom allows MailWorks to coexist with existing PC LANs and preserves your investments in existing equipment and training. It allows you to implement your messaging environment in the most cost-effective manner.

10.4.4 MAILbus 400

MAILbus 400, Digital's native X.400/X.500 messaging environment, offers unparalleled performance to meet needs for increased throughput required to support the growing use of your messaging system and mail-enabled applications. Built on the 1992 CCITT X.400 electronic messaging standard, MAILbus 400 is a set of products that offer extended management, high performance, standards support, and low cost of ownership.

Digital designed MAILbus 400 to deliver high availability and reliability. This is accomplished by having MAILbus 400 work in sets rather than be colocated. As a result, MAILbus 400 provides failover capabilities. This means, for example, that if a system failure occurred in a facility in New York, another MAILbus 400 Message Transfer Agent (MTA) could pick up the mail traffic. The result? No disruption of mail service and no lost messages!

10.4.4.1 Messaging Without Boundaries   MAILbus 400 makes "messaging without boundaries" a reality. It offers interconnections to other systems and services, integrating the messaging environment and extending it beyond the boundaries of your enterprise. Offering high performance and unmatched reliability, MAILbus 400 supports the X.400 and X.500 standards.

The MAILbus 400 product family includes the MAILbus 400 MTA, an Application Programming Interface (API), X.400 user agents, and various gateways from Digital and Digital's business partners. With this extensive set of products, you can extend MAILbus 400 services to other user agents and messaging systems—both inside and outside your organization.

10.4.4.2 MAILbus 400 Message Transfer Agent   Digital's MAILbus 400 MTA is designed to meet the performance requirements of large-scale, global messaging networks, and is capable of transferring more than 15,000 messages per hour.

The MAILbus 400 MTA delivers a reliable message transport service to applications such as user agents and mail gateways. Incorporating the 1992 X.400 MTA, it includes Digital's leading-edge DEC X.500 Directory Services, which enable MTAs to share routing information.

One of the advantages of a native X.400 environment is that any vendor's X.400 gateway or MTA can connect directly to the MAILbus 400 MTA. Connection to the Internet and other UNIX messaging systems is provided by the MAILbus 400 SMTP Gateway. Digital also offers the DEC MailWorks user agent, which connects the most popular UNIX desktops to MAILbus 400. For multivendor interoperability, Digital provides gateways to popular PC LAN mail systems through third-party relationships with Retix and Innosoft. In addition, access to fax services is available from Softline and Innosoft.

The MAILbus 400 MTA can exchange messages with other vendors' MTAs that conform to either the 1984 or 1988/1992 X.400 recommendations. It can perform conversions on the content of a message, based on which data types each message recipient can process.

MTA Management   Conforming to the Enterprise Management Architecture (EMA), MAILbus 400 can be managed from any DECnet OSI node with an appropriate EMA director such as POLYCENTER Network Manager 200. Since MAILbus 400 is supplied with default settings, installations are easy—reducing setup time and costs.

The MAILbus 400 MTA Management provides continuous operation, 7 days a week, 24 hours a day, 365 days a year. Best of all, you don't have to bring down the system for housekeeping. And to make management even easier, the MAILbus 400 MTA is designed to be managed remotely, eliminating the need to have management experts at remote sites.

10.4.4.3 Global X.500 Directory Services

MAILbus 400 incorporates the DEC X.500 Directory Services, Digital's comprehensive, global directory for multivendor, enterprise-wide networks. This service lets all MTAs in a network share the same routing information, thus reducing the cost of management. MAILbus 400 also provides full accounting, so you can keep track of exactly how your system is being utilized.

Not only does this powerful directory encompass every user in your extended enterprise, but it also provides information about all services—computers, printers, files, servers—regardless of where they are in the network. Today, such information is usually stored on a per-network or per-application basis, which limits access to the information. And while you might have some level of connectivity, networked information and services are useful only if they can be found and located. An up-to-date, synchronized directory is essential for distributing the necessary information throughout a multivendor environment.

When teamed with Digital's X.500 Directory Synchronizer, X.500 Directory Services can synchronize virtually all directories in your extended enterprise. Supporting an unlimited number of users, DEC X.500 Directory Services provide a high-performance, consistent set of directory services that tie together your heterogeneous mail systems—no matter which or how many mail systems your users are using.

Unlike other directory services that claim to be "X.500-like" or "X.500-compatible," X.500 is built on the 1993 recommendations of the X.500 1988 standard specification—which gives you a major technical advantage over products that are not built on these recommendations. Since X.500 is the undisputed future in directory services, Digital's X.500 Directory Service will allow you to be part of that future.

10.4.4.4 MAILbus 400 Application Programming Interface (API)

MAILbus 400 API is an X/Open® standards implementation that opens the MAILbus 400 environment to any application written to this specification. The API can operate colocated with the MAILbus 400 MTA or remotely.

10.4.4.5 MAILbus 400 Simple Mail Transfer Protocol (SMTP) Gateway

This gateway provides a bridge that allows mail to be exchanged between the traditional UNIX system mail community and the X.400 mail community. The gateway is able to use the backbone management facilities and handle address translations through the DEC X.500 Directory Services.

10.4.4.6 X.400/X.500: The Future of Messaging and Directory Technologies

Committed to providing growth paths into evolving standards-based environments, Digital offers easy migration to the native X.400/X.500 environment. MAILbus 400 lets you extend your MAILbus messaging networks to this new generation of products—without disrupting your current environments.

10.4.4.7 A Commitment to the Future Through International Standards Digital is active in the formation and use of international and *de facto* standards—which provide a common denominator for integrating diverse systems. This commitment to standards lets you preserve your investment in systems and information, while providing a cost-effective path to future technologies.

10.4.4.8 How Messaging Products Are Helping Digital Customers The following examples demonstrate Digital's industry leadership in client-server messaging integration.

United Kingdom's National Health Service (NHS) Syntegra, the systems integration arm of British Telecom (BT), is leading the winning team, and Digital is providing the core messaging technology for a pilot system for the United Kingdoms National Health Service (NHS).

Part of a seven-year investment program by the NHS, Syntegra's proposed message-handling service will link thousands of medical and dental practices, and hundreds of hospitals and Health Authorities across the United Kingdom into one nationwide network. According to Tom Sackville, Parliamentary Under Secretary of State in the United Kingdom, "The system will make substantial savings for patient care and speed up the secure transfer of all sorts of data around the NHS." The message-handling service is a critical part of the NHS-wide networking infrastructure which will support electronic communications throughout the NHS, including the instant distribution of emergency medical messages. Dennis Shaughnessy, Syntegra's account manager for the NHS, states, "Syntegra has recognized the increasing need for partnership and risk-sharing with its customers. We have the technical and business expertise, and the financial resources, to take on this type of project." Syntegra claims the service could eventually handle more than one million messages a day and will use the most up-to-date messaging technology—Digital's MAILbus 400—which is soon to be used for BT's own public messaging service.

CITGO Petroleum Corporation CITGO Petroleum Corporation recognized the importance of enterprise-wide electronic communication and, to realize its vision, sought help from Digital.

Headquartered in Tulsa, Oklahoma, CITGO is a refiner, transporter, and marketer of transportation fuels, refined waxes, petrochemicals, and other industrial products. Each company location, and even organizations within the locations, have different computing needs. Naturally, each evolved its own unique array of computers, applications software, and electronic mail systems. That was the problem. The systems couldn't "talk" to each other. This meant that most communications relied on paper memos and the telephone—not the most efficient way to get the word around for today's fast-paced global business markets.

CITGO wanted to retain computing autonomy for its various operations, but at the same time achieve the enterprise-level electronic communication so important to its business. Digital was able to meet the need with a standards-based communications solution that brought the disparate computing and electronic mail systems of CITGO's domestic operations into one common messaging environment.

CITGO wasn't entirely without electronic mail before it approached Digital. It had pockets of electronic communication, with the most widespread use by Macintosh users who exchanged messages using QuickMail. But they represented only a small fraction of the company—about 300 of CITGO's nearly 2500 computer users.

"It got to the point where CITGO employees would request a Macintosh just so they could access email," said Dan Grady, "We had invested heavily in a corporate network, but that was greeted with a big 'So what?' because we didn't have the applications to take advantage of it."

Without an enterprise messaging system, the word often just wouldn't get out. "If copying everyone on a memo or a voice mail message took too much time and effort, then that information wouldn't get disseminated." And that was all too often the case.

When CITGO first explored enterprise-wide email, it considered starting from scratch with one universal system, but quickly rejected that option. "We had invested too much money in the technology we already had," said Grady. "Besides, we wanted to continue to be able to offer our users a choice of mail clients, which would require a messaging system that could support multiple types of desktop mail applications. We decided that a standardized backbone would work well for us and settled on X.400 for that purpose."

Although a number of vendors offered X.400, CITGO had other significant requirements as well.

"We required the automated directory synchronization, because our parent company runs a PROFS system with 20,000 to 30,000 names," added Grady. "I didn't want to manually keep all of those directory entries current. We also planned to manage our mail network, so we needed some kind of monitoring tool. The only company that could offer all of that, along with the X.400 backbone, was Digital."

Today, with Digital's help, CITGO has all of its locations connected in one electronic messaging network. It includes QuickMail, Microsoft Mail, PROFS, VMS Mail, DEC MailWorks, and UNIX SMTP mail systems along with X.400 connections to outside mail systems. The X.400 backbone comprises Digital's MAILbus with a Distributed Directory Service (DDS) containing about 30,000 entries.

The MAILbus nodes include gateways to PROFS and X.400. CITGO also has an MS Mail gateway to X.400 and gateways to QuickMail and SMTP.

"The number of hard-copy interoffice memos has decreased dramatically," noted Grady. "I hardly ever see one anymore. Our field locations have really begun to rely on email for their day-to-day communication, and everyone is just now beginning to discover the value of our electronic commerce connections through AT&T and the Internet.

Two years ago, before CITGO had installed its electronic mail network, communication in this large company was by paper, telephone, and pockets of email. Slow, but adequate. As Dan Grady recalled, "We knew there were sound technical and business reasons for having an electronic mail network, but CITGO did not know how important it would turn out to be." Now they know.

"If the email were to be down for too long," said Grady, "I would need to escape to a distant land." Fortunately, Digital's messaging products allow him to stay comfortably at home.

The following are trademarks of Digital Equipment Corporation: ALL-IN-1, Alpha AXP, AXP, the AlphaGeneration logo, DEC, DECnet, Digital, the DIGITAL logo, LinkWorks, MAILbus, MailWorks, OpenVMS, PATHWORKS, POLY-CENTER, TeamLinks, and ULTRIX.

Third-party trademarks: Macintosh and Mac are registered trademarks of Apple Computer, Inc. AT&T is a registered trademark of American Telephone and Telegraph Company. Calendar Manager is a trademark of Russell Information Sciences. MacWrite is a registered trademark of Claris Corporation. CompuServe is a registered trademark of CompuServe, Inc. cc:Mail is a registered trademark of cc:Mail, Inc. HP-UX is a registered trademark of Hewlett-Packard Company. Freelance, Lotus, and 1-2-3 are registered trademarks of Lotus Development Corporation. MCI Mail is a registered trademark of MCI Communications Corporation. Excel, Microsoft, MS, PowerPoint, and Windows NT are registered trademarks and Windows is a trademark of Microsoft Corporation. AIX, IBM, and OS/2 are registered trademarks of International Business Machines Corporation. Motif and OSF/1 are registered trademarks of Open Software Foundation, Inc. INFORMIX is a registered trademark of Informix Software, Inc. INGRES is a registered trademark of Ingres Corporation. ORACLE is a registered trademark of Oracle Corporation. SCO is a registered trademark of the Santa Cruz Operation, Inc. UNIX is a registered trademark licensed exclusively by X/Open Company Ltd. WordPerfect is a trademark of WordPerfect Corporation.

BIOGRAPHIES

Dilip Phadke is currently the group marketing manager for Work Group Systems, including leading products such as LinkWorks and Teamlinks, with worldwide responsibilities for product management and product marketing. He has held this position since July 1993. Prior to that, he was the corporate marketing manager for Document Management Systems. His previous Digital assignments were in manufacturing engineering and software engineering.

Phadke has over 20 years of experience in building and marketing software systems. Prior to joining Digital, Phadke was employed at Data General Corporation.

Phadke is an engineering graduate from Karnatak University in India and has an M.B.A. from the University of Massachusetts. He is the author of several papers and has been a presenter at numerous conferences and symposia.

Don Harbison is currently a marketing consultant with Digital's Software Business Group. His responsibilities include design and implementation of marketing programs for the LinkWorks product worldwide. He has held this position since April 1993.

Harbison has over 15 years of experience in communications and software product management and marketing. Prior to joining the LinkWorks corporate product marketing team, Harbison managed and marketed software products for business and technical users in middleware (ObjectBroker, document management, and electronic publishing software product groups).

Harbison received his Bachelor of Arts degree from the Colorado College and a Master of Fine Arts degree in communications design from the Rochester Institute of Technology.

Introduction to Chapter 11

Of late, Novell has seen that groupware and other collaborative applications will be the next battleground for territory in the computing arena. Although Microsoft has won the battle for the desktop, they do not have network dominance; Novell does. However, Novell does not dominate in collaborative applications (right now Lotus has the lead in that arena with Notes). So Novell entered the groupware market through the back door: they bought WordPerfect, thereby placing themselves squarely in the fray for the hearts and minds of groupware users.

Novell is plagued by the lack of a cohesive, understandable workgroup strategy. This chapter attempts to delineate their current groupware strategy, new organizational structure, where the current products fit, and which groupware products will be available in the future.

Novell also discusses their current partnership with Collabra, explains how Collabra Share fills a hold in their groupware product offering, and presents case studies to detail their Collaborative Computing Environment (CCE). It is important to see that Novell has a gap in their workflow offering. While InForms offers forms routing through electronic mail, it is not a full-fledged workflow product. My educated guess is that Novell will acquire workflow technology from Reach (they are currently investors) or some other workflow vendor whose architecture closely matches Novell's. In either case, Novell should make that decision soon after this book is published.

Like IBM, Novell is trying to piece a patchwork of groupware products into a cohesive whole, with an offering for the enterprise. Unlike IBM, however, Novell's groupware is message-based rather than database-based, and it is unclear whether a message-based architecture is the right way to go. So far Lotus' database-based architecture has been most successful. For Novell, the messaging architecture makes sense, since they are a network operating system vendor.

Novell looks to the future with TNG, Sniper, and other code-named products that will fit into their CCE framework. This is a fairly technical, product-oriented chapter, and works well for those with a technical background.

Finally, Novell ends the chapter by comparing their products to Microsoft and Lotus, which everyone will do anyway. This strategy gives Novell a chance to position their products in the market. Since Oracle has the products most similar to Novell (Oracle Office), it would have made interesting reading to hear their take on Oracle. In any case, this is a meaty chapter and one that clears up a lot of the mystery regarding Novell's products and directions.

In this chapter, Bob explains how Novell, Inc., got into the groupware market and why it is so committed to providing groupware solutions. He also describes the products Novell currently offers in the groupware arena and how these products are being used today to gain increased return on investment from their networks. Finally, he presents Novell's groupware vision for the future and compare that vision to our competitors' groupware strategies. The information contained in this paper represents a "snapshot" of Novell's products and strategies as of December 1994.

CHAPTER **11**

Novell's Groupware Strategy

Bob Young
Novell GroupWare

11.1 WHY NOVELL IS IN THE GROUPWARE MARKET

Novell, the world leader in network operating systems, recently entered the applications market by acquiring WordPerfect Corporation. The objective of this acquisition is for Novell to lead in providing true networked applications. Through these applications, Novell will expose the full benefits of the network to end users, thus increasing returns on network investments.

Not coincidentally, Novell inherited several well-respected and established groupware products through its acquisition of WordPerfect Corporation. These products include the email, group scheduling, and task management software, GroupWise; the document management system, SoftSolutions; and the electronic forms software, InForms. These groupware applications take advantage of the network infrastructure to enhance communication, coordination, and information sharing among workgroups. (See "Novell's Current GroupWare Products" later in this chapter for a more detailed description of these products.)

In the reorganization that followed the Novell/WordPerfect merger, four business units were formed: the NetWare Systems Group, the UnixWare Systems Group, the Information Access and Management Group, and WordPerfect, the Novell Applications Group. Within WordPerfect, the Novell Applications Group, are three major product divisions: the GroupWare Division, the Business Applications Division, and the Consumer Products Division.

The mission of the newly formed GroupWare Division is to help people work together by providing software solutions that enable them to efficiently gather, share, access, and manage information.

The GroupWare Division draws on the strengths of three companies for its leadership. Heading the Division as Vice President and General Manager is Ken Duncan, former President of SoftSolutions Technology Corporation. Stewart Nelson, formerly Vice President of Development for WordPerfect Workgroup Products, is now the GroupWare Division's Vice President of Development. And finally, I am the Division's Vice President of Marketing.

Before taking this position in the GroupWare Division, I held several management jobs at Novell in both marketing and development. Most recently, I was Vice President of Product Management for the NetWare Products Division and Vice President of Marketing of that division for the two years prior to that. After selling infrastructure (the network operating system) for two years, I am excited to have the opportunity to provide a face to the user for the network services. Networked applications such as groupware are the vehicle to deliver the benefits of the network services to users. I bring to the Novell GroupWare Division both an understanding of the networking technologies that form the base for groupware solutions and experience delivering network solutions to users through multiple distribution channels. Groupware solutions are inherently a combination of network services and application software. Novell is uniquely qualified to deliver groupware solutions because we are the only company in the industry who has successfully delivered both PC-based network infrastructure (NetWare) and applications (WordPerfect products). That combination of experience will help Novell become one of the leading providers of groupware solutions in the industry.

11.2 NOVELL'S CURRENT GROUPWARE PRODUCTS

In its GroupWare product line, Novell currently has four major products: Group-Wise, Collabra Share for GroupWise, SoftSolutions, and InForms. These products arguably represent the broadest range of groupware products offered by a single vendor in the industry today.

11.2.1 GroupWise

GroupWise messaging software provides electronic mail, group scheduling, personal calendaring, and task management for the workgroup and entire enterprise from a single application. GroupWise provides collaborative solutions today by helping people to:

- ☞ Communicate and share information via email and attachments
- ☞ Keep track of personal and group appointments
- ☞ Check free and busy times and schedule group meetings for people and resources
- ☞ Assign personal and group tasks and track them through completion
- ☞ Route documents and messages for approval or review from one person to the next in a distribution list
- ☞ Configure rules to act on messages automatically on the user's behalf

☞ Connect to PROFS, cc:Mail, SMTP, and X.400-based systems
☞ Be accessible from anywhere by using remote (mobile) technology, whether by fax, pager, or wireless modem

GroupWise provides one of the most powerful and comprehensive email, group scheduling, and task management solutions available on the market today, as well as a solid messaging foundation for enabling other GroupWare applications and functions.

11.2.2 Collabra Share for GroupWise

Novell offers Collabra Share for GroupWise through a joint development effort with Collabra Software, Inc. Collabra Share provides message-based electronic information sharing and conferencing, allowing workgroups to collaborate on many types of information both within the local network and across the external messaging infrastructure. Collabra Share benefits and features include the following:

☞ Virtual discussions or forums, eliminating unnecessary meetings
☞ Access and navigation of multiple information sources, including news wires, company files, email messages, graphic images, and voice files
☞ OLE 2.0 compliance
☞ Discussion database replication
☞ Intelligent tools, including relevance ranking, threading, intelligent navigation, and full-text searching
☞ Policy-based administration
☞ Full integration with GroupWise messaging system
☞ Remote access through GroupWise Remote
☞ Support for multiple desktop and network operating systems
☞ Support for multiple email systems

Collabra Share for GroupWise provides a simple, flexible, and inexpensive way for organizations to utilize their existing GroupWise and network infrastructure to put people together with information.

11.2.3 SoftSolutions

A sophisticated document management system, SoftSolutions enables tracking of information and documents on all networks throughout the enterprise. Advanced capabilities like automated document archiving and deletion, version control, activity tracking, and fax integration make SoftSolutions an outstanding information management tool.

Other specific document management solutions that SoftSolutions provides include:

☞ Fast and easy location of information in any document using a powerful full-text search engine

☞ Powerful document security to control access of shared documents
☞ Dynamic document maintenance
☞ Enterprise-wide management
☞ Tight integration with many popular applications

11.2.4 InForms

InForms works as a front end for databases. InForms lets customers design, create, and use electronic forms to automate the gathering and storing of information in any of more than 20 different database formats.

InForms provides the following forms solutions:

☞ Easy and professional design of both electronic and printed forms
☞ Elimination of entry errors through automatic calculations
☞ Query capabilities for fast analysis on any linked data
☞ Advanced database field and form linking, including cross-database joins
☞ Intelligent workflow routing
☞ Ability to use most major email systems as workflow transport vehicles
☞ Digital signatures with high-level security

InForms can almost put an end to paperwork. Invoices, employment applications, employee records, requisition forms, purchase orders, or expense reports can be filled in quickly and accurately. In addition, the information can be immediately routed to databases that will automatically create data records to help gather, analyze, and share information quickly, efficiently, and immediately.

InForms is another powerful GroupWare tool to automate and re-engineer the way business processes and uses information.

11.2.5 Novell Uses What It Sells

The high quality of Novell's GroupWare products is due in large part to the fact that the GroupWare products are used extensively in-house. As a case in point, one of Bob Frankenberg's first objectives after Novell acquired WordPerfect was to have the new Novell completely connected through GroupWise as quickly as possible. Within a few months, any Novell employee at any site worldwide could send messages and files, as well as schedule meetings, directly with any other Novell employee using the GroupWise client. And because Novell is committed to multiple-platform product development, the change to a new messaging system did not require additional hardware at the desktop. Novell employees run GroupWise on whatever platform they normally use to do their work.

The idea of extensively using our own products is not a new phenomenon. Prior to the Novell/WordPerfect merger, WordPerfect Corporation used GroupWise (formerly WordPerfect Office) extensively from its inception. In fact, the WordPerfect Office email product was originally created to solve a business problem at WordPerfect—namely, inefficient communication and information sharing among employees.

The limitations we have found over the years of using our own products are the same limitations that our customers have found. Our own organization provides a very appropriate laboratory to determine how well we resolve these limitations. If a product is not designed optimally or does not work the way people want it to work, we hear about it immediately. The company's insistence that our products be used extensively internally before they are released to the general public has resulted in products that both work and meet customer needs well.

11.2.6 St. Mary's Hospital for Children—A Case Study

Of course, Novell is not the only organization benefitting from GroupWare technology. One example is St. Mary's Hospital for Children in the New York City metropolitan area.

With the recent emphasis on health care reform in the United States, Novell recently investigated, through focus group studies, what would be the ideal health care information system. The requirements yielded from these studies included many of the features already provided by Novell GroupWare products. To demonstrate the potential of groupware computing in health care, Novell initiated a pilot project that would showcase the benefits of GroupWise and InForms in the health care environment. The main objective of the pilot was to incorporate these products into a controlled health care environment using the products' features to improve the flow of clinical information among a multitude of professionals and points of services.

WordPerfect selected St. Mary's Hospital for Children, located in the New York City metropolitan area, as its partner in this pilot project. Nationally recognized as a leader in rehabilitation services for children, St. Mary's is a full-service pediatric specialty nursing facility that provides subacute rehabilitation services to children with special health care needs, such as premature infants with congenital birth defects, children with AIDS, adolescents who have suffered spinal and brain trauma, and burn victims. Each year, more than 60 hospitals throughout New York and the United States refer more than 1000 children to this 95-bed facility, which provides not only in-patient treatment, but also extensive outpatient and home care.

Well known for its innovative home care program, this non-profit hospital provides services to more than 600 children daily and completes in excess of 120,000 home visits annually. Because of the extensive nature of its home care program, St. Mary's was the ideal facility for a groupware computing pilot project. A myriad of professionals visit each child daily, providing services that range from general nursing care and physical, occupational, and speech therapy, to more complex services, such as specialized programs for traumatic brain injury and coma recovery. Prior to this project, St. Mary's home care professionals had been unable to communicate their clinical findings and treatment recommendations with one another. The hospital has long been aware that the quality of patient care could be greatly enhanced with the immediate exchange of information among its professionals, and was an eager candidate for this project.

Uniquely, St. Mary's does not have a problem with reimbursement because of a New York State law citing that any minor who is hospitalized for more than 30 days is emancipated and thus becomes immediately eligible for state Medicaid coverage. The state's Medicaid program provided the control factor in this pilot project because information flow simply needed to occur. Reimbursement would not impact the measurable results of this project. The hospital's reimbursement situation was, in fact, impacted only by the geographic territory covered by the professionals; therefore, clinical information was not always submitted in a timely manner.

Before implementing this pilot project, Novell visited the hospital and identified several objectives. The first objective was to reduce the number of forms by 75% using InForms Designer and Filler. It was determined that the hospital's professionals, for the most part, were sharing patient information via phone conversations, yet were duplicating a tremendous amount of paperwork each time information was charted. The second objective was to facilitate the collection, storage, and retrieval of important patient information upon the completion of each visit using InForms.

St. Mary's professionals were frequently unable to share their clinical notes with the hospital or other professionals because of the distance traveled daily and/or the traffic congestion well known in the New York City area. The final objective was to increase the quality of patient care by linking together all members of the treatment team electronically through GroupWise, which alleviated the professionals from having to travel back to hospital or satellite facilities, except for staff meetings.

Because of the scope of the project, a three-phase implementation plan was adopted. Phase I—the nursing component—would focus on the streamlining and development of forms necessary to document the delivery of multidisciplinary services to each child. With the installation of a network and the aid of notebook computers, the nurses would be able to transmit relevant patient information to other members of the home care team via the redesigned forms. The flow of information would allow the hospital to bill immediately for services rendered. Phase II would link together the remaining members of the home care team. A systems integrator would be identified to design the forms required to provide connectivity between the home care program's social work professionals, the home care team, and state agencies. Finally, Phase III would target the utilization of wireless networks and cellular phone technology to permit greater flexibility and speed of information transfer.

During home visits, the visiting nurse or other professional fills in a variety of forms to record the patient's progress from one visit to the next and to keep a history of the patient's medical needs. When using paper forms prior to the InForms Pilot Project, the visiting nurse had to fill out all medical information pertinent to the visit, regardless of whether the information had changed or not.

The InForms pilot application uses electronic forms and Paradox databases to enter and store the medical information. This solution provides methods to retrieve and reuse the information from the patient's last visit to update the information for the current visit.

Once the medical information is saved to the Paradox databases on the nurse's laptop computer, the records are then collected and sent through GroupWise Remote to the local area network at Bayside Hospital. These medical records are then available to other staff at the hospital where the patient information is available for billing and other administrative needs. If paper copies of the forms are necessary, the forms can be printed as blank forms, or they can be printed with the medical information as part of the form.

St. Mary's chose InForms for the home care pilot program because it was important that the medical information gathered by the nurses at each home visit be recorded accurately and quickly, and then be made available for others to use where needed. If the forms could be filled in more efficiently, more time would be available for the nurses to make more visits, thereby increasing the number of patients who could receive care through the St. Mary's home care program.

Many of the forms contain information that can be shared between other forms—information such as the patient's name, age, address, and family structure. Since many forms can be filled in for the same patient, each form has a link to the Patient Information form and the Patient Information database. A unique number is assigned to each patient, and that number is then used to look up the patient's personal data as each form is filled in.

Each electronic form is also linked to a printed form. Once the patient's medical information is entered into the screen-oriented electronic form, the data can then be passed to the print-oriented electronic form to be printed.

The electronic forms also have links to multiple Paradox databases. When the form has been filled in, the form data can then be saved to the set of databases linked to the form. The medical records can then be queried and used for reports, used to update current visit information, sent via email to another user on the network, or printed.

Each form is accessed through a menu form, which was developed to allow the user to easily select other forms or to look up or modify patient information. After each home care visit and at other times during the patient's stay in the program, the nurse uses InForms on a laptop computer. The nurse simply selects the appropriate option from the form menu and fills in the form information. The record is then saved to the databases linked to the form.

Because the medical records saved from the form only reside on each nurse's laptop computer, the records are sent on a regular basis to the local area network at Bayside Hospital using GroupWise Remote. To send the records, the nurse first queries the records which need to be sent, and then creates a form transport file, a file which contains all the queried records that need to be sent to the LAN. Once the records are queried, selecting the Mail option from within InForms invokes GroupWise Remote and automatically attaches the transport file containing the records to the mail message. The message is then addressed to a recipient on the LAN and uploaded to Bayside Hospital.

The success of this ongoing pilot project will be measured by St. Mary's project objective, which is to increase nursing productivity by the simplification of charting and reduction of paperwork, resulting in an 80% increase in visits by nursing professionals. Early research already indicates a potential 75% reduction in paperwork.

11.3 NOVELL'S COLLABORATIVE COMPUTING ENVIRONMENT (CCE)

While Novell offers a strong family of groupware products that are delivering solid solutions today, the GroupWare Division is committed to delivering, in the near future, a framework to integrate current and future groupware technologies. This groupware framework—Novell's groupware vision for the next several years—is called the Collaborative Computing Environment, or CCE.

11.3.1 Merging Product Strategies

The challenge for the new GroupWare Division was to take three formerly separate product strategies and merge them into a single, cohesive strategy. Luckily, all three products were already headed in very much the same direction. Similarities among the separate strategies included openness, scalability, and cross-platform support. So merging the three product strategies into one was not nearly the chore it could have been.

Shortly after the Novell/WordPerfect merger, the new Novell presented a messaging convergence strategy that outlines the plans for combining the MHS and GroupWise messaging strategies. Meanwhile, SoftSolutions was working from a strategy code-named TNG (for The Next Generation), and InForms was working from a strategy code-named Sniper.

11.3.1.1 Messaging Convergence Strategy   Novell's current messaging products include GroupWise, MHS 1.5, and Global MHS 2.0d. The Messaging Convergence Strategy outlines how Novell will combine these three different products, along with their previously separate product strategies, into a single, comprehensive, backward-compatible messaging product and strategy.

OME   Prior to the Messaging Convergence Strategy, Novell announced a GroupWise messaging strategy called Open Messaging Environment, or OME. As shown in Figure 11.1, the basic objective of OME is to eliminate direct dependencies of client applications on specific underlying services. Two API layers—one above the base services and another below the client applications—provide this independence. OME provides a true plug-and-play environment for both client applications and services via support for industry-standard APIs as well as published extensions to those APIs.

The grand vision of OME is that it provides not only a complete messaging solution, but also the flexibility to use another vendor's messaging client on the GroupWise back-end messaging services. An organization could also choose to use the GroupWise messaging client on back-end services provided by any number of vendors. For example, an organization might choose to use NDS (NetWare Directory Services) for their directory service, the GroupWise message store, and a standard message transport, such as X.400.

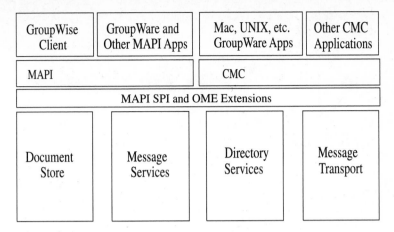

Fig. 11.1 Open Messaging Environment

MHS and Global MHS　MHS has been the native messaging system for NetWare for some time. In NetWare 4.1, Global MHS is specifically designed to take advantage of NetWare Directory Services (NDS) and the product's central administration features. NetWare's X.500-based NDS, coupled with the powerful Global MHS messaging engine, makes NetWare 4.1 a comprehensive platform for workgroup and enterprise-wide messaging applications and services.

To establish the NetWare 4.1 Messaging Services as an open platform, Novell introduces the widest support of desktop APIs in the industry, which include Simple MAPI, VIM, CMC, SMF71, and MAPI 1.0. With more than 900 SMF-based developers and hundreds of MAPI-based applications, NetWare 4.1 will quickly become the industry's largest, most open messaging platform. The goal is to enable any "off-the-shelf" application across the network to become "message-enabled" and use the native services of NetWare's messaging and directory services.

Collaborative Message Server　The Collaborative Message Server is the product that represents the convergence, or combination, of the best of the OME and MHS strategies. The Collaborative Message Server is the key to the third of the three phases in the Messaging Convergence Strategy, as outlined below and shown in Figure 11.2.

The first phase—interoperability—was realized in September 1994, with the release of a set of NLM processes that provide directory synchronization, full message translation, tunneling services, and gateway connectivity between Global MHS/MHS and GroupWise. The primary benefit of the first-phase product is that it allows existing Global MHS and GroupWise systems to coexist and share information.

The second phase—integration—focuses on easier-to-use tools and enhanced services to better integrate both Global MHS and GroupWise with NetWare 4.1 administration utilities and directory services. Delivered at the end of 1994, the second-phase product, also a set of NLM processes, provides common administration for the messaging and network services through NetWare 4.1

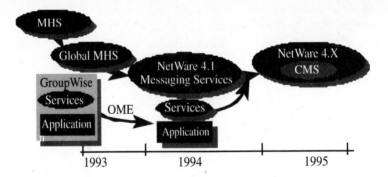

Fig. 11.2 Messaging Roadmap: Converging Technologies

administration tools (e.g., NWADMIN and RCONSOLE) and tighter directory synchronization with NDS, which serves as the master directory service.

The third and final phase—convergence—introduces the Collaborative Message Server, or CMS. CMS will enhance NetWare 4.1 Messaging Services to include support for new collaborative services, such as information sharing (conferencing), group scheduling, workflow, task management, enhanced messaging, forms processing, and replication services. CMS will combine the best attributes of OME into NetWare 4.1 Messaging Services to provide a collaborative computing foundation that supports both MHS and GroupWise systems. This new generation of messaging services will be based on an open messaging environment that supports a wide range of client-server APIs, common directory services, common message transfer agent, common message store (Universal In Box and folders), and a common administration infrastructure. Integrated within the advanced services of NetWare, CMS will take advantage of NDS and NetWare Security (such as authentication, access control, and encryption), as well as NetWare's licensing, file, and print services.

11.3.1.2 TNG   The TNG strategy for SoftSolutions is similar to the GroupWise OME strategy in that it also separates the client applications from the services by means of APIs, with the same resultant benefits as OME. In this case, TNG employs DEN as the service API and ODMA as the client API. Base services include a document store, an image store, and database access. These services can be accessed from clients on the Windows, Macintosh, UNIX, and DOS platforms. TNG is illustrated in Figure 11.3.

11.3.1.3 Sniper   Finally, Sniper is built on the same philosophy of connecting applications with services through an API. Sniper employs a single API (INDBLIB), which is used by both the services and applications. INDBLIB provides access to numerous databases, including FLAIM (the proprietary database on which GroupWise is built), SQL databases, desktop databases (such as Paradox, dBASE, and FoxPro), ODBC-compliant databases, IDAPI/

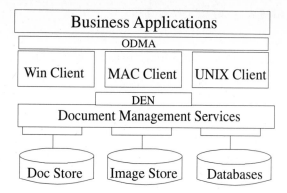

Fig. 11.3 Code Name "TNG"

BDE-compliant databases, and NDS (NetWare Directory Services). Client applications include a security module as well as the Designer and Filler. Sniper includes plans to provide the Filler on Windows, Macintosh, and DOS. Sniper is shown in Figure 11.4.

Clearly, the separate messaging (MHS and GroupWise), SoftSolutions, and InForms strategies are remarkably similar in scope and vision. CCE is simply the natural evolution of bringing together these three product strategies, which were already heading in the same direction.

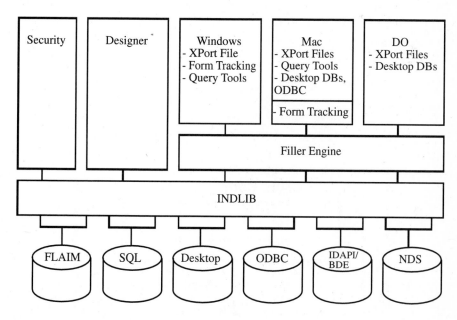

Fig. 11.4 Code Name "Sniper"

11.4 CCE FRAMEWORK ELEMENTS

As shown in Figure 11.5, the CCE framework consists of five basic elements: network services, administration and management, service components, client components, and solutions.

11.4.1 Network Services

Network services surround and support the service and client components, which expose and use the network services as needed. Examples of network services that pervade GroupWare components include, but are not limited to, the following:

☞ NetWare Directory Services (NDS)
☞ Data migration
☞ Telephony services
☞ Security
☞ Print services
☞ File services

11.4.2 Administration and Management

Like network services, administration and management services also surround and support the service and client components. The administration and management services eliminate the need for separate administration utilities for the network, servers, and applications by providing a unified and centralized administration model. GroupWare components will integrate administration and management services such as the following:

☞ Directory and address book
☞ Configuration (installation)

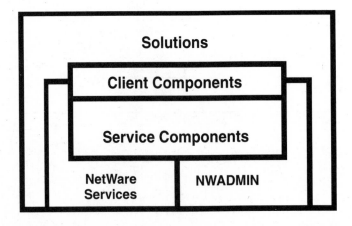

Fig. 11.5 Collaborative Computing Environment

☞ Event notification
☞ Monitoring and statistics
☞ History analysis and modeling
☞ Storage management
☞ Systems management (FSD/ESL)

In NetWare environments, CCE will use NWADMIN as the native adminis-tration platform. A GroupWare-provided administration tool will be used for other network environments.

11.4.3 Service Components

Service components offer a wide variety of base services upon which a wide range of client components and solutions can be built. Service components that CCE provides include, but are not limited to, the following:

☞ Message store
☞ Message transfer agent (MTA)
☞ Connectivity and interoperability
☞ Workflow
☞ Document and image store
☞ Database access

The CCE framework also supports and encourages the development of third-party service components. These service components, whether supplied by Novell or third parties, provide a wide foundation for client components.

To provide easy access to service components, the CCE framework includes an open service provider interface (SPI). The CCE SPI contains MAPI, plus Novell-created extensions to support the services (such as scheduling and task management) not included in MAPI. The SPI allows any customer or vendor to create client applications that take advantage of any or all CCE services.

11.4.4 Client Components

The client components in the CCE framework provide the base groupware functions that can be used individually or in combination to create collaborative computing solutions. Client components provide the following functions:

☞ Email, calendar, scheduler, and task manager
☞ Workflow, forms, and query
☞ Document management and imaging components
☞ Address book
☞ Conferencing
☞ In box, out box, and status tracking

As with service components, CCE supports the addition of third-party client components as well as an open API. The open API is standards-based and allows the client components to run on any standards-based back-end services.

11.4.5 Solutions

Solutions are end-user applications and interfaces that take advantage of all the service and client components to solve collaborative computing problems and create new collaborative processes. Under CCE, Novell provides several powerful "out-of-the-box" solutions for common collaborative computing needs. These solutions include, among others, an electronic messaging application, a calendaring and group scheduling application, a document sharing and control application, and intelligent agents that can perform many collaborative computing tasks on behalf of users.

CCE is, however, much more than the ready-to-use solutions Novell provides. System integrators, third-party vendors, and organizations' in-house developers can use development tools to combine service components and client components in new ways to create solutions to collaborative computing problems unique to an organization or vertical channel. CCE will support Novell application development tools, such as InForms and Visual AppBuilder, as well as industry-standard application development languages, such as Visual Basic and C++.

Still more solutions will emerge in the form of GroupWare-enabled applications. These could include all of the applications in desktop application suites, such as Novell PerfectOffice, Microsoft Office, and Lotus SmartSuite. In this case, the desktop application is the interface to GroupWare component functionalities and services.

11.5 CCE Design Philosophies

Two basic design philosophies also pervade the CCE framework. The first is openness, and the second is cross-platform support.

11.5.1 Openness

CCE's open design consists of support for industry standards, APIs, protocols, and other open interfaces for the functionality that Novell provides beyond basic services. At the desktop application level, CCE includes support for the following APIs:

☞ Simple MAPI
☞ CMC
☞ ODMA
☞ AOCE
☞ OpenDoc
☞ OLE
☞ ALM

Among the client-server protocols CCE supports are the following:

- ☞ TCP/IP
- ☞ IPX
- ☞ Named pipes
- ☞ File (store and forward)
- ☞ LU6.2
- ☞ Async

CCE will also support the following service APIs and protocols:

- ☞ Extended MAPI
- ☞ DEN
- ☞ GroupWare Extensions
- ☞ ODBC
- ☞ IDAPI
- ☞ SNMP
- ☞ DMI
- ☞ MIME
- ☞ X.400
- ☞ TSAPI

Any functional extensions that Novell provides to our services or components will have a defined interface that will be available to all developers.

11.5.2 Cross-Platform Support

CCE includes cross-platform support at the client, application server, and network levels where it makes sense. GroupWare clients support the Windows, Macintosh, UNIX, and DOS operating system platforms. GroupWare application servers include support for the UNIX and OS/2 platforms, with Windows NT support in process. And GroupWare solutions run on the NetWare, Banyan, LAN Server, and LAN Manager network operating system platforms.

11.6 CCE FRAMEWORK SUMMARY

Figure 11.6 presents a detailed, layered diagram of the CCE framework. The diagram shows examples of the types of service and client components, as well as solutions, that can be built upon the CCE framework.

One benefit of CCE's modular or "componentized" framework is the flexibility to bundle components in any number of ways to provide diverse solutions. The component framework also offers higher quality and consistency of products. CCE provides both best-of-class products built on its components as well as the ability to create custom solutions built on the same components. Finally, all solutions work across multiple operating system, server, and network platforms.

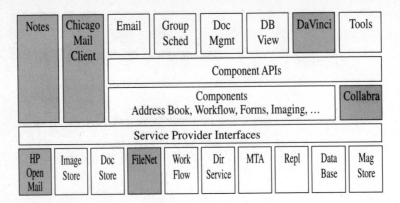

Fig. 11.6 Collaborative Computing Environment

The CCE framework is open to third-party products and can be extended and customized by third parties as well. CCE also enables the adoption of new technologies more quickly because components can be modified and upgraded individually. Finally, CCE is easy to manage because of its integration with network services and its centralized administration model.

11.7 DIVISION REORGANIZATION FOR CCE

In order to deliver on the CCE promise, we recently reorganized the GroupWare Division at Novell. Instead of being split into product teams, the development and marketing departments are now organized into component teams. Our goal is to erase product boundaries and intermix personnel from the previous product groups. We believe the new organization will allow for "cross-pollination" of ideas and technologies, creating new product synergies and ensuring that all components within the CCE framework fit together seamlessly.

11.8 GROUPWARE STRATEGY COMPARISON

There are several essential differences between the Novell CCE strategy and our competitors' strategies. The differences fall mainly in the areas of foundation and design philosophy. Because we consider Lotus and Microsoft our main competition in the groupware arena, I'll give a brief comparison of our groupware strategy and theirs.

11.8.1 Novell Compared to Lotus

Lotus' groupware foundation is Notes—a single product that is supposed to solve many collaborative needs. We see a couple of problems with this strategy.

First, while Notes provides good solutions in such areas as conferencing, discussion databases, and other database-centric needs, such as client tracking, it is not an optimum solution for all groupware problems. Lotus represents Notes as a "one size fits all" product, and yet considerable development and customization are required to build solutions that, in the end, are not always optimal. Second, Notes forces significant change on an organization. All information must be stored in the proprietary Notes database and accessed through the Notes client. Finally, Notes requires a redundant infrastructure as it is not integrated with the network operating system. This redundancy means a high cost of ownership.

Novell, on the other hand, offers a variety of components at all groupware computing levels so customers can pick and choose only those components that provide the specific solution they're looking for. One of these Novell components, for example, is a solid, integrated messaging solution—something Lotus has been promising for quite a while and hopes to deliver in its LCS architecture. In addition to a complete family of groupware products, Novell also offers a way to preserve network and application investments through its open CCE architecture.

11.8.2 Novell Compared to Microsoft

Microsoft centers its groupware architecture around its operating systems. Their strategy is to embed groupware features, such as an email client, in the operating system. Microsoft is also moving to a client-server technology exclusively, with Windows 95 as the primary client and Windows NT as the server. We feel that one of the reasons that NT has not been well accepted is that it requires an organization to install a completely new infrastructure.

While Microsoft does offer a groupware solution, it is one without much variety or flexibility. Microsoft offers a messaging solution, but does not offer a document management, conferencing, or imaging solution.

Novell's strategy is to provide a multiplatform solution at both the client and server levels, as well as at the network operating system level. Novell does not expect its customers to throw away their current investment and go with an all-Novell solution (although we obviously won't mind if our customers decide on an all-Novell solution). Today, Novell provides the widest range of groupware products in the industry, with offerings in every major groupware category. Novell's CCE also supports both client-server and file-sharing groupware services, giving its customers even more flexibility and choice.

11.9 SUMMARY

Novell provides a wide range of groupware products today in the form of the GroupWise, SoftSolutions, and InForms products. These products are providing solid business solutions today—helping to connect people to people and people to information. Building on this foundation, Novell is looking to the future with its

CCE groupware strategy. CCE represents a component architecture at all levels of the groupware computing model. CCE's component architecture, along with the design philosophies of openness and cross-platform support, will provide the most flexible and useful groupware solutions in the industry.

BIOGRAPHY

As vice president of marketing for Novell's GroupWare division, Bob oversees product definition and strategy development for Novell GroupWare products (GroupWise, InForms, SoftSolutions). Prior to this current position, Bob held several management positions at Novell in both marketing and development. Most recently, he was vice president of NetWare Product Management. Bob's background prior to Novell includes experience in the personal computer division of IBM, Hewlett Packard, and Wyse Technology. Bob has an M.B.A. from Brigham Young University and a B.S. with a computer science emphasis from California State University, Chico, in business administration.

Implementation & Management Strategies and Case Studies

Introduction to Chapter 12

In many ways this was the most difficult chapter for me to write an introduction for. Marvin Manheim has not only presented often at groupware conferences, but he was the conference chairman for several years for the GroupWare Strategic Executive Conference, and he and I are also authoring another book focused on case studies and lessons learned from groupware. So with this kind of relationship, it's hard to be objective about a chapter.

Nevertheless, Marvin's chapter is in the implementation section of this book because it focuses on how groupware can support teams to meet specific business objectives. Marvin focuses on order cycle integration and the use of groupware tools to enhance this process. He focuses on something he calls TSS (team support systems). He broaches the idea that no one vendor may have all the functionality in their product to support a TSS, and that different teams within an organization will need different TSS.

He also covers the business reasons for groupware and then moves on to using groupware to re-engineer the order cycle or supply chain integration. Marvin examines the whole supply chain and looks at both suppliers and their trading partners for EDI and coordinated information systems (i.e., extending the organization through groupware).

Dr. Manheim looks at the design and implementation of a TSS. Marvin's example uses Notes for the TSS design team, which is not surprising as Marvin's group at Northwestern University are all Notes users. He also uses Ventana as an EMS and looks at a number of case studies that his group has done with various vendor and user organizations. He even talks about how he is teaching a class using Lotus Notes and its discussion capabilities.

Marvin, like many of the authors in this volume, and especially those in the implementation and organizational change section, notes that "it is critical that the emphasis shift from GW as a technology to a TSS as a set of business-focused applications."

Marvin and I agree so strongly on this point that the book we are doing together focuses on case studies of how groupware was implemented in a wide variety of organizations and what lessons were learned in that implementation. We believe that this first volume, in covering the technologies, market, and implementation issues, will pave the road for our next volume, where our readers can benefit from the experience of others in successfully using groupware for team support, process re-engineering, or collaborative working.

Designing Team Support Applications to Meet Business Objectives

Marvin L. Manheim
J. L. Kellogg Graduate School of Management, McCormick School of Engineering and Applied Sciences, the Transportation Center, and the General Motors Strategy Research Center, Northwestern University

Nicholas J. Vlahos
Cambridge Systematics, Inc.

Yinyi Xie
McCormick School of Engineering and Applied Sciences and the Transportation Center, Northwestern University

Groupware is an important class of information technologies which opens up significant new opportunities for managers to improve substantially the ways in which organizations operate. In order to assist managers in deploying groupware effectively, this paper explores a number of issues in the design of team support systems to meet business objectives.

We view groupware as a set of technologies which enable the development of applications to meet business needs. We call these applications task-focused team support systems, or TSS.

We begin with a lengthy presentation of a number of observations about groupware and groupware implementation.

We first present a number of observations on the nature and role of groupware, emphasizing the role of groupware products as providing a toolkit with which to construct specific business applications. Next, we discuss some of the ways in which groupware can be used to achieve business objectives, focusing on "Order Cycle Integration" as an example. We then look at the role of technology in supporting the interpersonal processes in teams, including the user role in

TSS development. Next, we look at a number of critical implementation issues. Then, we examine several alternative approaches to TSS implementation strategies, including a technology focus approach, an application focus approach, a business process approach, a business strategy approach, and composite approaches. Next, we examine groupware's relationships to other processing modes, especially the structured transaction processes which are the traditional concerns of many information systems professionals. We explore particularly closely the relationship between personal work and group work, a link which is supported by Personal Information Managers (PIMs). We also focus on the role of TSS in an enterprise-wide information architecture.

In the next major part of the chapter, we present an approach to effective TSS design and implementation. Particularly important in our approach is the use of a TSS to support the team doing the TSS design and implementation; we discuss our present version of this, as implemented in Lotus Notes.

In the last section of the chapter, we present several case studies: a workshop for initiating strategic change processes; a business process re-engineering activity in a major global airline; development of a TSS for public-sector urban transportation planning; and the use of TSS to support student interactions in a graduate educational offering.

12.1 OBJECTIVES

Groupware (GW) provides an opportunity for managers to substantially improve the ways in which their organizations compete. In order for managers to be able to exploit this opportunity effectively, managers must choose an effective approach to implementing GW. Our objective in this chapter is to assist managers in thinking through their strategy for planning, designing, implementing, and adapting GW in their organization.

We will discuss:

☞ Lessons learned from GW implementation efforts to date.
☞ What issues should managers consider in choosing an implementation strategy for GW?
☞ What process should managers follow to exploit the potential of GW in responding to these challenges?
☞ How can GW itself be useful as part of the GW planning and implementation?

The work reported here is part of a long-term research program, the Strategic Informatics Research Program, a multicompany program at Northwestern University. In this program, we have been studying, since 1983, the role of information technology as a part of the overall strategy of a business. Particular emphasis in this research has been on the role of IT in enhancing people's working processes, and the role of IT as a competitive weapon in globally competing organizations [Manheim, 1990, 1992, 1993, 1994]. As part of this research, we concluded that technology to support collaborative work was a potential source of competitive advantage to an organization [Manheim, 1990]. As GW products came to market, we began to work with selected products in both research and professional practice. We have been involved in GW planning and implementation activities since 1991. In that process, we have worked with a number of organizations in the planning, design, and implementation of GW for support of critical business processes.

Based on these experiences, we have developed a number of observations about the effective implementation of GW, and we have drawn on these conclusions in developing a methodology for GW implementation. This methodology is supported by the use of GW; that is, we envision the planning and implementation of GW as a team activity which is itself supported by GW applications.

In this chapter, we first present a number of observations about groupware and GW implementation. We summarize these **observations** by statements set off in ***bold italic type*** and indented (see Table 12.1). We then present an overall model for implementing GW, including the use of GW to support the GW implementation process. Finally, we present several case studies that illustrate particular aspects of GW planning and implementation and particular aspects of this model.

12.2 OBSERVATIONS ON THE NATURE AND ROLE OF GROUPWARE

We have found a number of areas of confusion in what groupware is and how it should be viewed, conceptually.

12.2.1 Groupware as a Technology

First, GW can be viewed as a set of technologies. In this sense, groupware is an information technology.

Groupware technology is a class of software and related hardware that can be used to enhance people's interactions.

Groupware technology includes capabilities such as electronic mail and voice mail; audio and videoconferencing; discussion functions such as an electronic bulletin board provides; workflow management; electronic support for meetings; capabilities for working on a shared object, such as electronic whiteboards or shared-screen systems; group calendaring and scheduling; and others.

12.2.2 Groupware as a Toolkit Component for Building Applications

However, we need to recognize that groupware is a component that provides a capability. We need to distinguish the technology from the systems that are actually deployed to meet a business need. In our view, we use groupware components to build task/team support systems.

A task/team support system (TSS) is a system that provides full information systems support to the members of a team who participate in one or more spe-

Table 12.1 Summary of Key Observations on Groupware Implementation

Groupware technology is a class of software and related hardware that can be used to enhance people's interactions.

A *task/team support system (TSS)* is a system which provides full information systems support to the members of a team who participate in one or more specific processes or tasks. A TSS supports the individual work of each team member, as well as their collaborative work in various modes of interaction, and supports their collaboration whether they are working at the same location or at different locations, and whether they are working at the same time (synchronously) or at different times (asynchronously).

Groupware by itself is not a solution to a business problem. To provide a solution, an application must be developed—a full TSS must be implemented.

Groupware applications use information technology to support collaborative work among individuals performing a business process.

The objective of TSS is to enhance the ways that people work—their "Ways of Working" (WoW).

To be most effective, groupware must be delivered in applications—team support systems—which support individual work as well as shared work.

Typically, TSS will include groupware components, standard office automation components, and task-specific components.

Often, in support of individual work management, some type of Personal Information Manager (PIM) capability will also be provided.

Groupware can be a major element of an organization's business strategy, especially for business process integration.

Groupware plays an important role in supporting the people-to-people collaboration that traditional transaction processing, MIS, and DSS systems do not support. Groupware supports unstructured and semi-structured processes in parallel to the support to structured processes provided by traditional systems.

TSS design should reflect the role of a team support system as a component of the social organization of work.

TSS design should consider explicitly the social (interpersonal) dimensions of team participants as individuals and as roles.

TSS design should consider the "Team of Teams" structure.

All forms of team participants interactions are important parts of the team processes, not just the same-time-same-place meetings.

TSS design should explicitly support the evolution of team activities over time.

TSS design should recognize that the team social system may evolve over time, and should accommodate this proactively.

TSS design should expand the ability of team members to enhance the interpersonal interactions of team participants.

Table 12.1   (Cont.)

Users should have a clear role in TSS design, implementation, and evolution in use.

A TSS should be designed so that it can be evolved easily as team needs and desires change.

A TSS requires appropriate technology infrastructure.

Depending on business needs, different TSS strategies, with different systems and related infrastructure, may be targeted to different segments of the planned user community. It is essential that the strategies be complementary and the systems be interoperable.

A TSS can be implemented as a standalone and/or portable system.

Reaching and maintaining critical mass of users is a key implementation challenge. In designing a TSS implementation strategy, a plan for achieving critical mass is essential.

Implementation of TSS should be planned and managed as a process of organization change.

The user role in TSS implementation and adaptation should be carefully considered. In general, a major role for users is desirable.

Visioning the future is a valuable activity in TSS implementation planning.

TSS can be implemented as a part of a business process redesign approach. Business redesign can be radical, incremental, or strategically incremental in philosophy.

TSS can be planned and implemented as part of an overall business strategy process.

Groupware augments, doesn't replace, other processing modes. TSS design should plan explicitly for appropriate roles of other processing modes, especially face-to-face and traditional communication media.

Groupware can be part of an overall information systems strategy.

The major technology components of a TSS consist of applications, platforms, and building-block functions. TSS design requires decisions on these components.

To design an effective TSS, one must build one or more applications based on one (or several) platforms, and one (or more) building-block functions.

It is often useful to design one or more plans of use as part of overall TSS design.

To support individual work in the context of group work, consider integrating a PIM-like personal construct-based action support system in the TSS.

A TSS should be designed as a component of an enterprise information architecture.

Explicit relationships among unstructured, semi-structured, and structured processes should be developed to create an integrated enterprise information system.

Consideration should be given to providing a triage process to route work among business processes, including structured, semi-structured, and unstructured processes.

cific processes or tasks. A TSS supports the individual work of each team member, as well as their collaborative work in various modes of interaction, and supports their collaboration whether they are working at the same location or at different locations, and whether they are working at the same time (synchronously) or at different times (asynchronously).

Consistent with this definition, typically an organization will have a number of different TSS. Each TSS is developed to assist a specific business team in accomplishing one or more specific business tasks. Thus, a TSS consists of one or more "applications."

Such a TSS involves the use of groupware, together with other software (and possibly hardware) components. For example, a TSS to support a sales team might have groupware functions together with customer databases and sales forecasting models, and other tools. A TSS to support a product planning and design team might have CAD, costing, simulation, and other tools in addition to the groupware components.

In today's vendor marketplace, there are perhaps 350–400 groupware products, from perhaps 250 vendors. Each vendor's product provides a platform and a number of specific functionalities. A particular TSS might be built out of one or more vendor-supplied platforms, plus a mix of functionalities provided by one or more vendors.

Task/team support systems support both individual and shared work, with team members both in the same organization and in different organizations. TSS support sharing data, brainstorming and other forms of idea generation, discussing, voting, storing and retrieving data of various forms, monitoring data about the changing conditions in the firm or its environment, working on shared objects such as a proposal, a report, a budget, a design, and so on. TSS also support building and maintaining relationships among individuals and groups to achieve mutually beneficial objectives, both short-term and long-term.

The key point about TSS is that today's groupware product offerings provide a rich range of tools with which to develop task-focused team-specific business applications to meet specific business objectives. The choice of a product is only the beginning; how it is designed and implemented as an integral part of a business strategy is the key issue, as we discuss below.

> Groupware by itself is not a solution to a business problem. To provide a solution, an application must be developed—a full Task/Team Support System (TSS) must be implemented.

12.2.3 Groupware: A Business Process Definition

One of the reasons that GW is important is that GW implementation can be a major part of the technology support for redesigned business processes. GW is important because of its role in supporting the ways in which people interact in accomplishing business tasks. From a *functional* or *business process* perspective, GW is a key technology.

Groupware applications use information technology to support collaborative work among individuals performing a business process.

12.2.4 Objectives of TSS: Individual Enhancement

The objective of TSS is to enhance the ways that people work—their "ways of working" (WoW). In some cases, this is reflected in a narrow definition of productivity: the goal is to increase transactions per person per time period, or some other productivity measure. More generally, however, the goals may be significantly broader: to enhance customer service, increase quality, increase customer satisfaction, increase long-term revenue and profitability, and so on. While the technology by itself is not sufficient to achieve such objectives, a TSS can be a major component of efforts to enhance people's WoW.

The objective of TSS is to enhance the ways that people work—their "ways of working" (WoW).

12.2.5 Individual Work Support in the Context of Groupware

While the primary emphasis in groupware applications is supporting teams, there is also a very important link between individual work and the shared work environment. This was alluded to in the discussion previously of the role of TSS in supporting both individual and shared work.

Quite simply, the issue is this: if GW tools are separate from the basic working environment of the individual, the GW will be far less likely to be used than if the individual-work applications are integrated with the collaborative tools. For example, ideally a TSS should incorporate both GW components and standard office automation components, such as word processing, spreadsheets, address books, calendars, presentation graphics programs; and task-specific components, such as an order entry system or a sales support system. If the collaboration tools are in a different environment, then crossing the boundary may cause resistance to their use.

To be most effective, groupware must be delivered in applications—team support systems—which support individual work as well as shared work.

Often, too, there will be task-specific components of the TSS, integrated with others. For example, in a TSS to support a marketing team, there may be marketing databases, contact management tools, consumer response prediction tools, and newsfeeds from sources of competitive intelligence. In a TSS to support product planning and design, task-specific tools may include a CAD package, cost estimating tools, a project management system, and others specific to product design.

Typically, TSS will include groupware components, standard office automation components, and task-specific components.

Often, in support of individual work management, some type of Personal Information Manager (PIM) capability will also be provided.

12.3 OBSERVATIONS ON USING GROUPWARE TO ACHIEVE BUSINESS OBJECTIVES

12.3.1 The Challenges Facing Business Today

Businesses today face many intense competitive forces: pressures on productivity, costs, profits, quality, and customer service. In addition, many companies face the additional challenges of becoming more international, or, if already multinational, of becoming more effective in their global business strategies (see also the introductory chapter by David Coleman).

To compete successfully in today's dynamically changing environment, firms need to be able to effectively address several key strategic issues:

☞ Cost-quality improvement through coordinated manufacturing, including such coordination strategies as "just-in-time" and overall quality improvement programs

☞ Cost-quality improvement through simultaneous engineering, using integrated design teams, combining representations from product design, engineering, and manufacturing, and, increasingly, marketing and other functions

☞ Integration of the order cycle, or the time between when the customer places the order and the time the customer receives delivery, in order to shorten the cycle time and therefore reduce inventories

☞ Provision of quality after-sale customer support, to provide customers with a high level of service for maintenance, including spare parts availability and technical skills in service staff, and rapid and convenient access to add-on products and services, such as training, documentation, and product upgrades

☞ Improving the product design process and shortening design cycle time, the time it takes from conception of a new product to delivery of that product into the market with full consumer support

☞ Coordinated, flexible manufacturing, to coordinate effectively sourcing of components and subassemblies, distribution into multiple markets, and efficient use of a network of manufacturing and assembly plants

☞ Effectively coordinated R&D, driven by the need for product development for national, regional, and global markets, and by the recognition that unique research competencies exist in many different countries and cultures

These issues are very important for firms of all sizes, whether they are competing in national, regional, or global markets. These issues are especially critical for firms competing globally; and today, almost every company is competing globally, or faces competitive threats from actual or potential global competitors.

12.3.2 The Need for Changed Structures and Processes

These forces demand significant changes. Critical business processes must be integrated and redesigned to operate in substantially more effective ways. The pressures of competition and especially globalization of company operations call for new forms of organization structure and new forms of organizations. Increasingly, companies are discovering that rigid, hierarchical, formal structures do not work well in today's competitive business environment; the rigid "stovepipe" organizations of the past are not capable of responding to today's pressures. Instead, companies are using teams which cut across departments, functions, and geographical responsibilities. Especially important, many companies are moving toward network structures, in which business units operate largely independently and are coordinated more effectively through interpersonal relationships than through hierarchical control.

While these competitive challenges are threatening to many managers, they also provide an opportunity. In this new era, there is an opportunity to gain significant competitive advantage through integration of people skills and appropriate technology support. The companies which can coordinate business processes effectively in this new, more complex business environment can gain a competitive edge. Information technology, particularly groupware used to build task/team support systems, gives companies an opportunity to do this.

For example, some companies are critically examining their basic business processes. This has come to be termed "business process redesign (BPR)" [Hammer, 1990; Davenport, 1993]. In this examination, managers consider what their core business is, and what the critical business processes in this business are. In one model, three critical business processes are proposed (once the choice of product or service strategy is determined) [Manheim, 1990]. These processes integrate a number of functions and cut across departmental and other organizational boundaries. These integrating processes are:

- ☞ Customer relationship management: The *customer relationship management cycle* involves all interactions with prospective customers prior to a sale, the sales process itself, and serving the customer after the sale, with maintenance, upgrades, training, and other services.
- ☞ Order cycle management: The *order cycle* begins when the customer places the order, and ends with delivery of the final product to the customer. It includes production planning and scheduling, logistics for inbound and finished products, production coordination between schedulers and suppliers, and other types of integration and coordination.
- ☞ Product cycle management: The *product development cycle* involves all aspects of designing a new product and getting it to market. It includes research and development, product planning and design, and the related market research and design for manufacturing.

Several key functions support these three integration foci:

☞ The "people management" process—human resources management, in its broadest definition
☞ Information systems and telecommunications
☞ Technology and finance
☞ Finance
☞ Logistics and transportation

In order to accomplish this integration of business processes, communication and collaboration across multiple organizational units is required. Groupware is especially valuable for this role.

> Groupware can be a major element of an organization's business strategy, especially for business process integration.

12.3.3 Business Process Improvement Through Information Technology: The Example of Order Cycle Integration

Consider, for example, the business process of order cycle management, or as it is often called in the logistics field, "supply chain integration." In production and logistics, many parties are involved in coordinating all the processes that are involved in fulfilling a customer's order: manufacturer, suppliers of parts and subassemblies, material managers, logistics managers, transportation carriers, customer service representatives, quality assurance staff, and others. Integrating all of these functions is a business imperative today in many sectors: the goals are to reduce the cycle time to fill a customer's order, reduce the inventory of parts, work in process, and finished goods in the pipeline, increase the accuracy and completeness of filling a customer's order and of billing him for it, and accelerating the payment for the delivered items to put cash in the bank as soon as possible.

To achieve this degree of order cycle integration, manufacturers, merchandisers, and their trading partners are using EDI and other technologies to create coordinated information systems to manage this "pipeline" of materials flow. As materials flow from component and subassembly producers to final assembly, distribution channels, and retail channels, and to the eventual consumer, so also does information flow among these trading partners in the "supply chain." Information includes purchase orders, movement requests, proposals, bids, shipment status messages, inventory status messages, electronic funds transfer messages, and many others. We call these coordinated systems "pipeline management systems (PLMS)" [Manheim, 1992, 1994].

These pipeline management systems deal with **structured** data and structured processes: purchase order initiation, purchase transmission via EDI, purchase order receipt and entry into an order-entry system, production scheduling, and so on. PLMS provide the capabilities for managing high volumes of data for highly structured transactions. To accomplish integration in the order cycle, tightly linked "pipelines" of information flows are being developed, paralleling the pipelines of goods flows. Thus, the pipeline for managing the materials flows is supported by an information systems "pipeline," or pipeline management system. The PLMS consists of transaction processing, management information system, executive information system, and decision support system components.

Many firms in manufacturing, merchandising, logistics, and transportation are already well-embarked on this strategy. Some of the major functions performed within a PLMS include:

☞ Shipment status tracking—location of a shipment at each major transition point as it moves through the transportation segments of the supply chain
☞ Inventory status tracking—current inventories by item while in production, warehousing, or movement through transportation carriers
☞ Movements of ancillary information in document or electronic form

In a typical situation, the PLMS to serve a particular customer is operated by a number of partners, interacting in various ways. Consider the coordination of the overall order cycle in a typical national or global company, as shown in Figure 12.1. Different functions are dispersed in different locations across the region or across the world, and must be linked together to function properly. These teams are located organizationally in different functions—for example, marketing, production planning, logistics coordination—and in different geographic locations.

Teams within this structure must manage quite complex processes, often under difficult time constraints.

For managing the overall process, teamwork involving the representatives of the various business units involved in the order cycle is necessary. For exam-

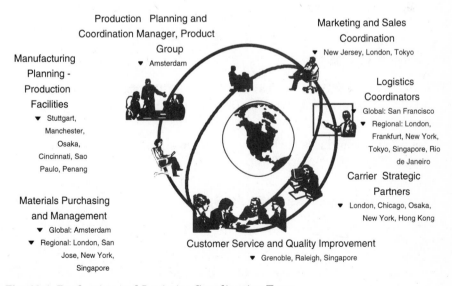

Fig. 12.1 Production and Logistics Coordination Team

ple, if a problem arises, such as weather causing a disruption in transportation in one region, or a machine breakdown causing a temporary shortage of a needed part, or other problems, people must step in and manage the process of searching for a problem solution, gaining consensus among the concerned parties, and implementing the solution and monitoring its effectiveness.

Consider what happens when one of the widget production line sites in Figure 12.1 goes down. Assembly sites in the company are affected, and must scramble to fill assembly time using production from other sites, including possibly production from other vendors. This team must manage a series of complex questions: Where are widgets in transport anywhere in the world? What plants are they being shipped to? What are the relative priorities of these shipments for different assembly plants? Are there inventories for diversion of shipments in transit, and what happens if we do divert?

Structured systems such as PLMS are not capable of handling crises or other complex exceptions, but teamwork **can** handle complex issues.

Thus, the example of order cycle management illustrates the need for *two kinds of fundamentally different processes:* the *highly-structured* processes using transaction processing, MIS, and DSS, represented in this case by the pipeline management system; and the *unstructured* or *partially structured* processes which support people-based problem solving. This is where groupware is needed: to provide information technology support to people-based problem-solving.

> Groupware plays an important role in supporting the people-to-people collaboration that traditional transaction processing, MIS, and DSS systems do not support. Groupware supports unstructured and semi-structured processes in parallel to the support to structured processes provided by traditional systems.

We will return to this point in a later section.

12.4 OBSERVATIONS ON TECHNOLOGY'S ROLE IN SUPPORTING TEAMS

It is very important to have a clear conception of the social processes in teamwork in order to have a perspective on the role of TSS in supporting collaboration in business teams.

> TSS design should reflect the role of a team support system as a component of the social organization of work.

12.4.1 A TSS Is Support to a Social System

The team to be supported consists of a number of individuals. Each individual has different needs, concerns, goals, and desires. Various individuals have pre-existing relationships with one another, and these relationships are multivalent and dynamic. The team as a whole has a dynamic in its relationships, and these relationships evolve over time [Gabarro, 1990].

TSS design should consider explicitly the social (interpersonal) dimensions of team participants as individuals and as roles.

12.4.2 Often, the Team to Be Supported Is a Team of Teams

One way to visualize this structure is shown in Figure 12.2, Team of Teams. Each circle represents a team, either formal or ad hoc, that works together to accomplish one or more functions within the organization. As a manager takes on different tasks during the work week, the manager may interact with other managers from within the company, from customers, from suppliers, and from other organizations such as government agencies. We illustrated one such Team of Teams, for managing a production planning and logistics process, earlier; in a later section, we will discuss a Team of Teams in an airline organization.

TSS design should consider the "Team of Teams" structure.

12.4.3 Team Processes Are Longitudinal: Time Duration Matters

The interactions of a business team take place over time. Early business successes of groupware were achieved through the use of electronic meeting support systems [Post, 1992]. These systems were shown to be useful in supporting many different types of business meetings. As a result, the goal of providing meeting support is often confused with the goal of providing team support.

To design effective TSS, one must consider the interactions of team members outside the same-time-same-place meeting room. For example, consider the typical application of meeting support systems, to support some type of business planning process. This meeting may take place over a period of one-half to four or five days. The actual team process includes many activities in

Fig. 12.2 Team of Teams

addition to the scheduled formal meeting, such as formal or informal meetings or discussions, and conversations, face-to-face or by telephone or email; to set the agenda of the formal meeting, and to decide on the participants, key roles of various actors, and so on; to follow up on the results of the meeting and manage or monitor implementation of the action steps resulting from the meeting; and others.

> All forms of team participant interactions are important parts of the team processes, not just the same-time-same-place meetings.

The processes of interaction of a business team take place over periods of time ranging from days to years. Same-time-same-place meetings may have an important role in these processes, but can never be the totality of the process. Designing a TSS application can include design of meeting system usage, but should, in most cases, include design of TSS components to support other elements of the team processes.

> TSS design should explicitly support the evolution of team activities over time.

12.4.4 The Team Social System Evolves Over Time

John Gabarro [1990] summarized the literature on the evolution of interpersonal relationships over time. Being a careful researcher, the model he developed is described as a model of two-person interactions. While it does not apply directly to all of the complex interactions that take place in a multiperson team environment, Gabarro's model is very valuable because it highlights the ways in which the social relationships in the team evolve over time.

The design of a TSS must, as a minimum, accept the fact that the relationships among the team members will evolve over time. Therefore, the ways in which people use the system may vary over time, and people may want to emphasize different functionalities in different ways as their interpersonal relationships in the team evolve.

> TSS design should recognize that the team social system may evolve over time, and should accommodate this proactively.

12.4.5 A TSS Can Be a Management Tool for Enhancing the Team Social System

For some managers, it may be desirable to have an explicit strategy and plan for how the team should evolve its social structure and processes over time. For example, management of a product planning team may have a specific goal of encouraging communications among marketing, engineering, and manufacturing people, to break down the disciplinary and departmental barriers among these critical functions. This may be an important objective, critical to the success of the product design activity.

TSS design and implementation may be intended to specifically support this strategy for enhancing the team's social interactions.

TSS design should expand the ability of team members to enhance the interpersonal interactions of team participants.

12.4.6 The User Role in TSS Development Is Critical

TSS in many cases use elements of very complex technology, such as databases, security and access control functions, messaging and data transport mechanisms, and so forth. As a result, there is often a tendency to see TSS design and implementation as wholly or largely the role of the information systems specialists and MIS departments.

This is a dangerous view. For TSS to be successful, users must find the system providing highly attractive and useful service. The greater the role that users play in determining the TSS capabilities and controlling their evolution, the greater will be the likelihood of significant acceptance and use of the TSS. As discussed above, a TSS and the social organization of work are closely interrelated.

For these reasons, the relative roles of the users and the technical specialists should be carefully considered and balanced. Ideally, the IS staff ensures the basic installation and functioning of the TSS platforms, and the availability of a library of building block functions (BBFs) which can be used by users or by trained application developers. Then, users take the lead role in identifying priorities and establishing the major functions of applications. In many cases, users may design and implement applications themselves: designing and modifying workflow patterns in a workflow management system; designing and modifying discussion databases for specific focused discussions; designing and modifying forms in forms-based processes; selecting the modules to be used in a specific meeting process, preformal as well as formal; and so on.

> Users should have a clear role in TSS design, implementation, and evolution in use.

12.4.7 A TSS Should Be Designed to Evolve Over Time

A TSS may have many different functions and be composed of a number of applications. It will generally take time for users to master specific capabilities and integrate them into their working patterns. As users use specific capabilities, they will see additional or modified capabilities which they believe would be useful. Furthermore, as the team evolves its social system and the work it is doing, team members' views on what is important and useful to complement their business processes will change.

For these reasons, it is essential that a TSS be designed so that its functions and capabilities can be evolved over time in response to users' needs and desires.

> A TSS should be designed so that it can be evolved easily as team needs and desires change.

12.5 OBSERVATIONS ON IMPORTANT IMPLEMENTATION ISSUES

There are several major factors which have significant influence on the design and implementation of TSS.

12.5.1 Technology Infrastructure for TSS

In general, support to the desktop requires networking and PCs which are adequate to the task. For example, some of the more powerful groupware products may require Windows and significant computer memory and hard disk capacity, and moderately powerful modems. This may require upgrading computer hardware on a number of desktops. In some companies, this has resulted in a strategy of choosing two different TSS strategies, one for desktops and users with high-end computers, and one for users who do not otherwise require powerful computers. Thus, compatibility of TSS platforms is critical.

However, increasingly, vendors are offering strategies which require little or no infrastructure investment. For example, on-line services such as Compuserve, America OnLine, or others can be used to provide some functionalities. A standalone system such as a bulletin board can be set up using one of many packages. Increasingly, vendors are offering support services. For example, both Compuserve and AT&T have announced public-access server approaches in which they will provide the server support for Lotus Notes use, and all that the user needs is a copy of the Client software to get started; the user does not have to support an infrastructure of servers.

> A TSS requires appropriate technology infrastructure.

> Depending on business needs, different TSS strategies, with different systems and related infrastructure, may be targeted to different segments of the planned user community. It is essential that the strategies be complementary and the systems be interoperable.

It is also true that serviceable TSS can be implemented in a flexible, mobile way. A Bulletin Board system requires only a single computer. An electronic meeting system can be assembled in a portable configuration with a number of laptops and a portable LAN using parallel-port network connectors and lightweight portable cabling; projection is provided by an LCD panel display and overhead projector.

> A TSS can be implemented as a standalone system and/or as a portable system.

12.5.2 "Critical Mass" in TSS Implementation

Gaining user acceptance is important. Groupware, to be effective, must be used by all the members of the workgroup and must be used regularly and consistently. If you can't count on someone accessing the system and looking for communications relevant to them, then you will not use it for important communications.

Thus, it is critical to have an implementation strategy, and TSS design, which attracts people to use the system and use it frequently. If only a part of the team exchanges messages via the TSS, then the traditional methods (telephone, fax, paper memo, and so on) remain dominant, and people tend to slip out of use of the groupware methods.

If, however, a strong catalyst is found to make it attractive or necessary for people to use the TSS, then after a certain stage it becomes the "only way to go" (provided it is well-designed, useful, useable, and well-maintained!). Such a catalyst can come from one or several means:

☞ The TSS increases personal productivity and effectiveness so significantly that people can't accept going back to the old way.

☞ Enough people, critical to the team, make extensive use of the TSS, such that if others do not regularly check the email, the discussions, and so on, they find themselves left out of important discussions and even important decisions, or missing information critical to do their jobs.

☞ A senior executive announces that he/she will only act on messages which come from the TSS and will cease to use paper memos, and he/she follows through on this.

Critical mass is not necessarily everyone; what is important is that the people engaged in the critical business processes which are the focus of the strategy should be active and engaged users of the TSS.

> Reaching and maintaining critical mass of users is a key implementation challenge. In designing a TSS implementation strategy, a plan for achieving critical mass is essential.

12.5.3 TSS Implementation as Change Management

It is important to recognize that TSS implementation is a process of organization change. As such, it is a threat to many people. People fear the loss of the known and true ways of doing things—what they are familiar with; and they fear the uncertain future—new ways of doing things. These fears are natural [Manheim, 1988].

These fears lead to resistance in many forms.

Organizational resistance can be anticipated and can be dealt with in a positive, proactive way. Using appropriate diagnostic approaches, the various forms of resistance that might be encountered can be identified. Then a change management strategy can be designed, to be implemented as part of the TSS implementation strategy.

> Implementation of TSS should be planned and managed as a process of organization change.

12.5.4 The User Role in TSS Implementation and Adaptation

It is important that users be involved throughout the process. TSS should support users in their work in ways they find useful and satisfying. TSS should increase the pleasure of work, not degrade it.

For this reason, it is especially important that the very design of the TSS, as well as the implementation strategy, be carefully considered from the users' perspectives. As discussed earlier, the users should be given the opportunity to shape and lead the TSS implementation process, not only initially, but also in the continued evolution of the TSS.

This view is in contrast to the philosophy, implicit or explicit, in some organizations' implementation of TSS, especially workflow management systems (WFMS). In some approaches, there is an initial premise that the objective of WFMS implementation is to cut costs by increasing productivity and reducing head count. In this approach, the WFMS is seen as a way of structuring work so that people work harder, faster, and more accurately; and the design of the WFMS implementation includes performance monitoring and other elements to reinforce this goal. This conceivably is an appropriate approach in some companies in some circumstances; but it should be examined carefully before being adopted. Perhaps an alternative strategy, in which people are given more control over their work, and more opportunity to vary the work and their roles in the processes, may lead to a more substantial and longer-lasting increase in productivity.

> The user role in TSS implementation and adaptation should be carefully considered. In general, a major role for users is desirable.

12.6 OBSERVATIONS ON ALTERNATIVE APPROACHES TO TSS IMPLEMENTATION STRATEGIES

There are a number of fundamental choices for implementation strategy in TSS.

12.6.1 Technology Focus Approach

In a **technology focus** approach, the emphasis is on the groupware technology. A decision is made to purchase product X, it is installed, and then applications are sought for it. In some major companies, this strategy has been adopted successfully. However, there is a risk that the user community may not readily accept the technology. The best way to minimize this risk is to be sure that a portfolio of pilot applications are identified, both for use in determining the most appropriate technology to be selected, and for initial application developments of early pilots.

12.6.2 Application Focus Approach

In an **application focus** approach, a specific application is identified for which groupware seems promising. Based on the needs of that application, a product is selected and the TSS developed for that application. This is often effective in creating an initial beachhead in the organization for groupware, but it is possible to make a choice of a product which is not especially appropriate for other applications in other parts of the organization.

12.6.3 Business Process Approach

In this approach, TSS are implemented as part of the process of redesigning business processes (business process redesign).

12.6.3.1 Approaches to Process Redesign   The redesign of business processes can be done in several ways. The **incremental** approach begins with an analysis of the existing process. Then, the information systems support is designed for the process as it exists or as it may be improved. This is the way many information systems have been designed over the years.

In the **radical change** approach (reflected in Michael Hammer's [1990] oft-quoted approach of "Don't automate, obliterate!", the change strategy emphasizes the development of a radically new vision of the future form of the process. Systems are then designed and implemented to support this radically changed process.

We have found that most senior managers do not trust a radical change approach, because they are fearful of the consequences of major change in systems and procedures simultaneously, and because they do not believe that the systems can be designed and delivered as promised.

12.6.3.2 Strategic Incrementalism: A Practical Approach to BPR   A third approach to changing business processes is that which we call **strategic incrementalism** (adapted from Isenberg's [1986] "strategic opportunism"). In this approach, a vision of a radically changed and improved process is developed. This is then used as a basis for developing a multistage program for implementing the vision in phases. Each phase is designed to have tangible, meaningful benefits. Because of the phased nature, the downside risk is minimized; each stage can be evaluated before a decision is made on whether to proceed to the next.

Visioning the future is a valuable activity in TSS implementation planning.

TSS can be implemented as a part of a business process redesign approach. Business redesign can be radical, incremental, or strategically incremental in philosophy.

12.6.4 Business Strategy Approach—The Vision-Strategy-Processes-Tasks Model

In some situations, the objective of implementing TSS is part of a broader set of objectives involving the business strategy of the organization. In such a case, it may be appropriate to develop the TSS strategy as a part of an overall business strategy process.

This will involve formulating a **vision** of the business. Based on this vision (and perhaps associated mission statements and identification of core competencies), alternative strategies are formulated and evaluated. Then a specific business **strategy** is selected. Based on this selected strategy, the business **processes** which are critical to successful execution of this strategy are identified. If the processes already exist, then the existing processes are assessed and necessary changes to those processes identified. If not existing, then the required processes are defined. For each critical business process, the **tasks** which must be accomplished to execute those processes well are identified. Then, the **information systems** support required for these tasks and processes is identified. As part of this information systems support, appropriate **task/team support systems** are identified.

Thus, the **VSPT** (Vision-Strategy-Processes-Tasks) approach leads to identification of the needs for TSS which are consistent with the selected vision and strategy.

> TSS can be planned and implemented as part of an overall business strategy process.

12.6.5 The WoW Approach

Earlier, we introduced the notion that the fundamental objective of TSS is to change the ways people work, which we called the "Ways of Working" or "**WoW**" (SM) approach.

This leads to a variant on the VSPT approach, the **WoW** approach. In this approach, the visioning process includes conceptualizing the desired ways of working to be built into the organization's processes. Then, this is translated into functional requirements for processes, tasks, and TSS (and related personal construct-based action-support systems—see below). The result is a TSS with explicit support for individual work as well as shared work. (The products described briefly in the PCAS discussion below exemplify some of the possibilities.)

A particularly promising direction for application of the WoW approach is to design new forms of executive information systems for senior management teams. For example, one senior executive of a major software company demonstrated recently how receipt of particular types of messages in his TSS would trigger (via agents) paging messages to his pocket pager: for example, receipt of a press report on a competitor's new product would trigger a message, as would major movement up or down of his company's own stock.

12.6.6 Composite Approaches

Sometimes it may be appropriate to utilize a composite approach, combining several of these approaches. For example, a VSPT process might be undertaken as part of a broad-based strategic management process, concerned with the need to reposition a business. While this process is underway, one or two products might be selected in a small-scale technology approach to TSS implementation and used on an experimental basis for one to three applications as pilots. One of the applications might be the VSPT process itself—team support for the business strategy process. Then, as the strategy process proceeds, experience is gained with specific groupware products and TSS application development. When the VSPT process leads to the identification of a number of critical TSS applications, there is an experience base on which to select a product, including a platform and set of BBFs.

12.6.7 Portfolio Approach for Continuing Implementation

Often, once the initial pilot applications have been developed, it will be desirable to implement a number of TSS applications concurrently. Thus, the TSS implementation team may shift to becoming a TSS coordination team, coordinating a number of TSS implementation teams, each implementing one or more TSS in specific business areas.

12.7 OBSERVATIONS ABOUT GROUPWARE'S RELATIONSHIP TO OTHER PROCESSING MODES

It is important to examine critically how groupware relates to other modes of processing, whether person-based or computer-based.

12.7.1 Groupware as a Complement to Existing Interaction Modes

Groupware is a *complement to existing ways* in which people work together:

☞ Face-to-face meetings and informal conversations
☞ Basic electronic communications, such as telephone, telex, fax, and nonelectronic forms such as paper mail
☞ Computer processes, such as transaction processing systems, management information systems, and decision-support systems

Groupware provides the capability to add additional functionality to these existing capabilities, which enhances significantly the power of the full set of capabilities.

These capabilities will likely continue to be required for the foreseeable future. Under many circumstances, it may be practicable to reduce the amount of face-to-face meetings and replace them with electronically facilitated interactions via groupware. In some special situations, the need for face-to-face may be avoided altogether. For example, in today's business world, numerous business tasks are accomplished by a series of telephone messages, without people ever meeting each other face to face. In general, however, it is important to plan the role of TSS in coordination with and as a complement to other processes.

In addition, there will still be many functions performed in database and transaction-processing environments. Groupware will not replace these, but may provide an additional dimension of functionality to deal with issues that these systems cannot deal with.

For example, in the order cycle management example given earlier, people do coordinate today through face-to-face interactions, telephone, fax, and so on, and do use pipeline management systems as described. What groupware provides is the opportunity to strengthen these collaborative interactions significantly through the use of information technology to support additional modes of interactions.

> Groupware augments, it doesn't replace, other processing modes. TSS design should plan explicitly for appropriate roles of other processing modes, especially face-to-face and traditional communication media.

12.7.2 Groupware as an Information Technology Can Play a Major Role in an Overall Architecture

Groupware applications are often developed and implemented in isolation from other information technology applications in the organization. When this occurs, it is a missed opportunity: groupware is a part of the set of information systems capabilities of an enterprise, and its role and power can be magnified by implementation as part of an overall enterprise information systems strategy.

> Groupware can be part of an overall information systems strategy.

12.7.3 The Components of Groupware Applications: Use of Building-Block Functions in TSS

As indicated previously, a TSS is implemented as one or more software applications. Sometimes, such an application can be implemented directly by simply obtaining a vendor's product, installing it, and running it. This is true of the simplest email and bulletin board systems. However, in almost every case, there is much more required; the software must be tailored to the specific situation. In some cases, this tailoring may simply involve setting up a topic for a specific discussion forum, or an agenda for an electronically facilitated meeting. In other cases, a more substantial application development process may be appropriate.

12.7.3.1 Building-Block Functions When one examines the groupware product offerings available today, one sees that in fact each vendor's **product offering** consists of at least two types of components. The **platform** is the overall software environment (perhaps with some hardware, as in the case of video conferencing systems) which packages a number of functionalities. The **building block functions (BBFs)** are specific functionalities which are provided as separate modules or command choices (Table 12.2).

For example, an electronic meeting system (e.g., Ventana's GroupSystems, Collaboration Technologies' VisionQuest) will typically have BBFs such as idea generation via brainstorming, voting (with different modules for different voting schemes), discussion, agenda-setting, and others. In each application—each

Table 12.2 Building Block Functions (BBFs)—Illustrative List

Information Sharing

  Threaded Discussions

  Brainstorming

  Collaborative Writing

  Group Diary

  Group Dictionary

Group Evaluation

  Classification/Categorization

  Questionnaires

  Ranking/Voting/Scoring

Communication

  Call the Author

  Fax Gateway

  Chatting

  Remote User Access

Links to Personal Work

  Links to a Personal Information Manager

  Reference Databases

  Rule-Based Routing of Information

  Automatic Mail Processing (e.g., Beyond Mail)

Meeting Management

  Access Control

  Team Definition/Assignment

  Group Scheduling

  Agenda Coordination

  Task Assignment

  Deadline Management

meeting to be supported—the meeting facilitator sets up an agenda which utilizes the various BBFs in particular ways for particular areas of discussion at different points in the time plan of the meeting.

As another example, a multipurpose groupware product such as Lotus Notes comes with a large library (50 at present) of BBFs in the form of database templates, for mail, discussions, document libraries, presentation libraries, simple workflow management, and others (Notes' database templates, or *.NTF files). To actually apply Notes, the application developer (who may be the user) selects a template and creates an instance of a database from that template. The same discussion template may be used to create a discussion database about users' needs, another one about customer service issues, a third about product offering ideas, and so forth.

As a third example, in implementing a workflow management system, the various functionalities of the software must be applied to support one or many specific workflows. Each workflow process involves specific individuals in specific roles at specified points in the process. Each workflow is a separate application, in our terms. The various functionalities of the workflow software are the BBFs. In addition, some vendors may provide templates of standard or "useful" workflow processes; these provide patterns which can be applied as starting points in developing applications for a specific TSS.

> The major technology components of a TSS consist of applications, platforms, and building-block functions. TSS design requires decisions on these components.

12.7.3.2 Applications   From this discussion, it should be clear that to build a TSS, one or more application(s) is developed. Each application consists of one (or more) platform(s), together with the use of one or more BBFs. An application may be built up from one or more product offerings.

For example, in a product-planning TSS, one could have several major products from different vendors: Lotus Notes, GroupSystems V, Corporate Memory Systems' CM/1, and a CAD package, together with a suite of standard office applications. CM/1 provides a group brainstorming and idea generation BBF and platform. GroupSystems V provides same-time-same-place meeting support, including other forms of idea generation, voting, and discussion. The office suite provides basic applications such as word processing, presentation graphics, database, spreadsheet, and personal-information manager (PIM) functions. The CAD package provides computer-aided design support for developing and managing the visual representation of a product, which is also described in memos and reports, presentations, and other forms of documents and images supported by other components of the system. Notes provides basic email as NotesMail, a number of specific discussion databases around various topics (marketing, product design issues, manufacturing and design issues, supplier relations, etc.), various information repositories, and so on.

Recently, several vendors have announced versions of their groupware products which come packaged as applications, based on BBFs. For example, QDM, the vendor of Quality at Work (QAW), a set of Notes applications, has launched a QAW Business Solutions Suite, with four initial applications for customer service and customer relationship management; project management; and a PIM-like "QAW Initiative" capability (see discussion below).

To design an effective TSS, one must build one or more applications based on one (or several) platforms, and one (or more) building-block functions.

12.7.4 Plan of Use

Each application is composed of one or more vendors' products, with one or more platforms, and one or several BBFs. We need to also distinguish the application itself from the **plan of use** of the application in a particular setting. As mentioned previously, a meeting facilitator will have a plan of use for using specific applications during a meeting. A team facilitator for a product-planning team will have a plan of use for introducing and making available various of the specific functionalities outlined in the previous paragraph.

In general, a plan of use will be designed to balance the need to support the business team with desired functionalities, with the need to not overwhelm the team members with too much too soon. Therefore, a plan of use will often be tailored to build up team members' capabilities with the use of the TSS in a series of stages, giving them additional capabilities as the need comes to be perceived. In the educational case study described below, the plan of use had the students first learn how to fill out a biography form in the biography database; then move to mail and discussions. Later, they could become familiar with the other applications.

It is often useful to design one or more plans of use as part of overall TSS design.

12.8 OBSERVATIONS ON THE LINK BETWEEN PERSONAL WORK AND GROUP WORK

While the primary emphasis in groupware applications is supporting teams, there is also a very important link between individual work and the shared work environment, as introduced previously. We now examine the implications of this observation in greater detail.

12.8.1 Personal Construct-Based Action-Support Systems

There is an important link between TSS and the personal actions, or "to-do" lists, of each individual in a workgroup.

The discussion of the issues facing businesses today emphasized the variety and complexity of the challenges. Managers are concerned with building the capacity in their organizations to compete effectively in this complex environment. The fundamental objective is to change the ways people work: the ways in which they think, and the ways in which they act. As introduced earlier, we call this the "Ways of Working," or "**WoW**," approach. Whether we talk about TSS or about business strategy, this is our goal. TSS emphasizes the ways people work in workgroups. We must recognize that this is a process which also involves the individual, cognitive level: what people think about, how they think about it, what they do to get something done.

There is a class of software emerging which provides tools for individuals to enhance the ways in which they think and act. We call this class "personal construct-based action-support systems (PCAS)."

12.8.2 Classic Personal Information Managers

These PCAS systems come out of a heritage of personal information managers (PIMs). Originally, PIMs were combinations of basic tools to support personal work: an address book for names, addresses, and telephone numbers; a calendar to track appointments and other scheduled events; and a notebook for miscellaneous short notes. This type of software is almost as old as the use of personal computers; Sidekick, for example, was an early Borland product of this type.

12.8.3 Construct-Based PIMs

Around 1987, a new type of PIM emerged, in the form of Lotus Development Corporation's Agenda. Agenda had a general structure intended to be used by a user to create her own PIM capabilities. Instead of a fixed structure, Agenda allowed the user to create and manage a highly personalized database of connected information about people, including names and addresses, appointments, projects, tasks, issues, concerns; whatever the user wanted. All of this data could be input in a loose freeform way, and then would be organized in a variety of user-defined views, according to a variety of user-defined categories of information. The whole structure was very flexible and allowed the user to construct her own personalized software tool to support her own highly individualized ways of working.

Although designed to be a PIM, Lotus Agenda was a market failure as a PIM. Its very power and flexibility made it difficult for many users to work with. However, for a small number of users who overcame the learning barriers, it was a very powerful tool [Fallows, 1992; Geis, 1991].

Lotus Agenda was the first of a new class of software. Manheim [1989] showed how this type of tool could be used to support the processes of strategic management by allowing the user to manage personal work priorities together with the evolution of insights and information. For example, interview notes could be organized by concepts such as "SWOT" analysis—"strengths," "weaknesses," "opportunities," "threats"—one standard approach used in strategic management. Then, notes from interviews, database scans, brainstorming sessions, and other sources could all be viewed as "opportunities," to serve as a basis for formulating candidate strategies. In this way, Agenda's capabilities to create and manage a library of concepts as a way of managing a loose set of text information provided a very powerful tool to support a strategic management process.

Thus, Agenda was an early example of PCAS.

12.8.4 Emergence of PCAS

PCAS are emerging now into the mainstream through three separate thrusts.

First, a new generation of PIMs in the Windows environment have this same capability (approximately; not all of Agenda's capabilities are available in a Windows tool). ECCO (Arabesque) is a leading example. ECCO provides Agenda-like flexibility, allowing the user to define concepts as "folders" into which items of information are placed. The user can then define "views" using these folders (and filters and other devices), such that a view shows those items in the corresponding folders. In addition, ECCO also provides standard telephone book views, for a name and address directory, and calendar views, for appointments and scheduled events, with items of information appearing in those views also being manipulated by folders as well.

Second, there is a class of "performance support" systems which have also emerged into the marketplace. These systems are designed to provide software support to a user engaged in performing a particular type of activity. ManagePro (Avantos) is a leading example of this class. ManagePro is designed to support managers who are concerned with managing people in a thoughtful and effective manner. The basic conceptual schema of ManagePro is that managers manage People, Goals, and Actions. The user constructs a list of goals, in a tree-like hierarchy, including goals and their subgoals; identifies tasks needed to accomplish those goals; and identifies people as individuals, teams, and roles if desired. By assigning people to tasks and goals, and establishing milestones of various types, the manager can focus on the key issues in her daily management environment. In addition, ManagePro places high priority on coaching and mentoring people, so there are specific concepts about how to do these things well which are reflected in software. Similar systems have come to market for personnel review and for other management tasks.

These performance support systems are like PCAS, except that their designs incorporate specific concepts, and they do not have the flexibility of true PCAS, allowing user entry of individual concepts.

12.8.5 PCAS in the Groupware Environment

The third direction of PCAS evolution is seen in the emergence of groupware products which are linked to personal information management. Several examples have emerged recently.

First, of course, email of any flavor can be sorted and filed by the user's and/or the sender's categories, reflecting their concepts for organizing their work. This sorting and filing can be either explicit, done manually by the user, or implicit, done by intelligent agents [Malone et al., 1989]. BeyondMail was the first commercially successful product to provide this capability; now it is moving into many different email products, and Beyond itself has been acquired by a networking software company, Banyan.

Second, some groupware products have had links to some type of PIM capability. For example, Lotus Notes since its early days has had the ability to import Agenda files (but only import, no other functionality).

Third, some PIMs have developed multi-user capabilities, in which several individuals can share portions of their personal information base, and keep other portions private, with some degree of synchronization. ECCO 2.0 and ManagePro 2.0 have this basic groupware-like file-sharing capability.

Fourth, and most important, vendors of two major groupware products have just launched versions with explicit PIM-like links, each reflecting a particular philosophical approach in their implementation.

QDM is a vendor of Notes add-on products and recently announced a Quality-at-Work (QAW) Business Applications Suite of products. All of the applications focus around mail-based forms (as does all of Notes), with the addition of categories reflecting various concepts of a personal to-do list. For example, the "Pending Work" view for an individual shows items that other people are expecting the person to do, including "action items," approval requests, opinion polls, and brainstorming session participation; items that the individual is expecting of others (the same types of actions); and other messages.

Particularly interesting is the design of "QAW Initiative" which supports concepts about a hierarchy of goals and their interrelationships: Harry can formulate an initiative by expressing a goal or objective. Harry then develops several strategies for accomplishing this initiative. He then issues several directives to specific individuals with particular tastes to be accomplished by particular target dates. Pat does similarly. Each team member can then see, in his own database views, the pending Initiatives, Strategies, and Directives which require action on his part—part of his own to-do list—and the pending items for others which they have initiated.

In a similar way, Action Technologies in its Action Manager for Lotus Notes product provides each user a personal to-do list categorized by the phases of its particular workflow model: preparation, negotiation, performance, and acceptance.

12.8.6 Implications: Personal Work Integrated with Team Work

As this discussion illustrates, individual work is now beginning to be explicitly linked to the groupware support of team work. In our view, it is very important that TSS be designed to enhance individual work in the context of group work.

To support individual work in the context of group work, consider integrating a PIM-like PCAS in the TSS.

In developing a TSS for TSS design, we have followed a somewhat similar philosophy, as described below. The "Notetaker" application is designed roughly along an Agenda/ECCO model.

12.9 OBSERVATIONS ON THE ROLE OF TSS IN AN ENTERPRISE INFORMATION ARCHITECTURE

We have emphasized several times that the role of groupware is as a complement to both face-to-face interactions and traditional information systems. It is valuable to look at groupware as a part of a multilevel architecture of an enterprise.

12.9.1 Multiple Levels of Processes

12.9.1.1 The Structured Processes Level As illustrated earlier in the discussion of order cycle management, the highly structured processes of an enterprise are supported by transaction-processing systems with their related management information systems, executive information systems, and related operational decision support systems. These systems represent a "level" of processing capability where the structure of the information and the processes that operate on them is highly specified, and can be executed with minimal human intervention in the *structure* of the processes.

12.9.1.2 The Face-to-Face Level These are the traditional modes of face-to-face interactions, in meetings both formal and informal, planned and unplanned.

12.9.1.3 The Groupware Level This is the level of electronically facilitated interactions among individuals, including all of the groupware technologies as well as traditional forms of electronic interaction such as voice telephone, fax, and related technologies.

12.9.1.4 Workflow Management Systems One type of groupware is sufficiently different in its functionality that it is useful for some purposes to distinguish it from the others: workflow. There are often aspects of a business process that are neither so highly structured that they can be performed completely by transaction type systems, nor so unstructured that they can only be performed by people using groupware to facilitate their interactions. These process elements are capable of being structured, but they also require human intervention at one or more critical points in the process, for checking, exercising judgments, or doing other things that require judgment and insight beyond what can be coded for computers. For these situations, a workflow management system is appropriate. Such a system routes information from one individual to the next, and varies the routings according to the actions that specific individuals take.

12.9.1.5 The Multilevel Architecture The preceding discussion illustrates the role that structure plays in the productive use of information systems support in the enterprise. Consider structured, semi-structured, and unstructured situations. When situations are novel or "unstructured," and require substantial human judgment, interactions among multiple individuals, and possibly bargaining and negotiation, then the process requires face-to-face communication augmented by those forms of groupware that can provide electronic support for these interactions. When the situation requires some human judgment and processing, but can be structured in a pattern, then workflow management systems are appropriate. When the situation is highly structured, and all the data and rules and conditions for processing the work are known, the processing can be done without human intervention, in transaction-processing systems.

Consider the order cycle management team described above. The TSS that supports this team might have such groupware functions as email, discussions, and other functions to support the work of a team in resolving such situations. Thus, the groupware application is a task/team support system that supports the work of the production and logistics teams, and complements the work performed by the PLMS.

> A TSS should be designed as a component of an enterprise information architecture.

> Explicit relationships among unstructured, semi-structured, and structured processes should be developed, to create an integrated enterprise information system.

12.9.2 The Triage Function in the Multilevel Architecture

In designing the information systems for an organization, in general all three types of processes will be appropriate: unstructured, semi-structured, and structured. What does this mean, operationally? Consider what should happen when a request for information or another type of transaction message arrives from outside the organization for processing. Upon receipt, the message is first passed through a **triage function**, which determines the appropriate routing of the message through the organization.

Such a triage function in a multilevel architecture has been implemented at the Wuerttembergische Insurance Company (WIC) in Stuttgart, Germany. In the WIC approach, a message or query is received from company or independent sales agents or directly from customers. A clerk enters the description of the query or request into the computer, and a "triage" process operates on the data contained in the message, and by reference to any previously stored data about the customer and his insurance coverage. If the case requires only routine processing, like a routine request for a policy renewal, then the request is processed by the highly structured transaction-processing system. If the case requires some human judgment but fits into one of a number of standard patterns, then it is processed as a workflow by the workflow management system— for example, in the case of a request for additional insurance coverage from an existing client. If, however, the request requires substantial human judgment and decision making, or is novel or unusual in some critical respects, then the request flows through the email and related systems to be operated on by managers in face-to-face or electronically mediated discussions—this may be true in the case of a request for a major new form of coverage, or for approval of a major claim.

> Consideration should be given to providing a triage process to route work among business processes, including structured, semi-structured, and unstructured processes.

12.10 AN APPROACH TO EFFECTIVE TSS DESIGN AND IMPLEMENTATION

In parallel with our research on TSS design and implementation issues, we have also been developing and experimenting with various TSS design approaches. In this section, we will outline the general approach we have been using, and then we will discuss a TSS for TSS design and implementation which we have been developing.

12.10.1 A TSS Design Approach

We visualize the design and implementation of TSS as an ongoing, evolutionary process. While there are major decision points, such as the choice of an initial platform(s) and the choice of initial pilots, in general we expect the deployment of TSS in an organization to be a process of incremental implementation of specific applications and evolution of applications in use.

Nevertheless, there is a certain logic to how the process should be managed. Fundamentally, there are several major activities:

1. Diagnosis and Assessment
   In this activity, information is collected about the existing situation, analyzed, and critical issues are identified, together with priorities for further work (the work plan) (the following details are illustrative and are not meant to be complete):

   a. Collect information on the existing situation—identify the strengths and weaknesses in the business, in the strategy of the firm, in technology; in teamwork and social structure; in organizational environment dynamics, morale, and attitudes; and especially in critical business processes; and other potentially useful information.

   b. Identify the key business issues—what are the critical business processes; what are some opportunities; what are the most important threats at the levels of business strategy, goals, and processes?

   c. Establish the initial frame of reference and domain for strategic intervention with TSS.

2. Strategy Formulation and Evaluation

a. If appropriate and if following the VSPT approach, conduct a visioning activity and develop a strategic vision.

b. Formulate goals for strategic and operational changes in the business: long-term strategic goals, mid-range goals, and short-range, implementation-focused goals; for the business as a whole, and for critical business processes.

c. Develop alternative strategies for achieving those goals

d. Evaluate the strategies relative to the goals—preliminary. If necessary, repeat the goal formulation and/or strategy development activities.

e. For the strategy selected (preliminary), formulate an implementation plan.

f. If issues surface in developing the implementation plan that cause questioning earlier choices of goals and strategies, repeat the goal formulation and/or strategy development activities; revise and reevaluate strategies if necessary, and revise the implementation plan to reflect new considerations.

3. Strategy Choice

Based on the preceding steps, select a strategy and associated plan for implementation. If issues surface in the strategy choice process, be prepared to go back to earlier steps and revise them.

4. Implementation, Monitoring, Evaluation, and Plan Revision:

a. Begin implementation in stages.

b. Monitor progress, results, and issues or problems that surface.

c. Evaluate the lessons learned as implementation proceeds.

d. As necessary and appropriate, revise the strategy and the implementation plan.

12.10.2 The TSS Design Team

The team designing and implementing TSS in an organization is itself a task-focused team. In general, this team will consist of some people from units responsible for information systems and possibly for end-user support, together with representatives from user organization units.

One of the best places to begin with TSS implementation is for the TSS implementation team to design and use a TSS itself. This has a number of benefits:

☞ Using the technology themselves, the team members can be sure that it is shaken down and operational, and can evaluate the level of quality of the implementation, and the issues and problems in user understanding (e.g., user interface, commands, etc.).

☞ The TSS design and implementation process is itself a complex process, and the effectiveness of the process can be substantially improved by the use of an appropriate TSS.

☞ The fact that the TSS design team is itself using this type of system helps to convince users that there is a value in this approach.

12.10.3 A TSS for TSS Implementation: An Example

We have built a TSS for use by a TSS design team. This "TSS for Designing a TSS," or "TDT," has been implemented in Lotus Notes and has been used in various ways during its development to support TSS design activities (see case studies following).

The TDT consists of several Notes databases, integrated into a single application system:

Notes Mail: This database provides a standard electronic mail capability for confidential mail among team members.

Biographies: This database has forms for each team member to fill out his/her own biographical data, with whatever degree of humor, exaggeration, and so forth the individuals want to engage in. The purpose is to serve as an initial introduction of members to each other, as well as a repository for telephone numbers, mail addresses, appropriate formal salutations, organization location, and so on.

Design Discussion: The team members use this discussion database to engage in freeform discussion of whatever issues and topics any team member wants to put forward.

NoteTaker and Design Concept Manager: This application has two major functions. First, it serves each individual as a personal note-taker. In this function, notes are taken and entered as desired, in loose form. Notes can be entered contemporaneously, as in a meeting or in a discussion, or afterwards. Once entered, the notes are then analyzed by the user, and can be categorized and classified and sorted in various ways to be useful in the design process. In the role of Design Concept Manager, the NoteTaker also serves as a database for recording the ongoing evolution of the design: for example, alternative strategies can be laid out; alternative sets of information on the strengths and weaknesses of the existing process and proposed alternative process designs, strategies, and so forth, can be viewed and parsed. In both the NoteTaker and Design Concept Manager modes, this application supports the rapid evolution of ideas, in the processes of taking notes and analyzing them, identifying critical issues, and generating and evaluating alternative strategies. This application also supports the development, analysis, evaluation, and selection of various broad elements of the strategic planning process: vision, strategy, process, tasks, organization environment, and others.

Strategy Library: Contains a library of potentially useful strategies, including the ones under present consideration.

Application Requirements and Definition Library: This database contains the evolving statements of requirements (goals) for which applications are desired or proposed. It also contains the preliminary design requirements for those applications which are selected to be implemented.

Implemented Applications Library: This is a catalog of all the presently implemented applications. Closely associated with this are:

> *Design Elements Library:* This database also serves as a repository of application design objects, such as forms, views, macros, buttons and their scripts, and so on.

> *Group Dictionary:* This serves as a repository for definitions (and debates) of special terms peculiar to the team, the task, the organization, and so forth. A subset of this list is the specific terms used for fields in the application system.

Product Selection Toolkit: This application provides forms and procedures to be used in selecting a platform(s) and BBF(s) for a particular application. While this is still under testing and refinement, the present design includes forms for describing processes to be supported and tasks to be accomplished, proposed application system functionalities to support this process, goals and requirements, and so on. Associated databases include:

> *Building-Block Functions (BBFs):* This is a catalog of the various basic building blocks available for use in building TSS applications. The building blocks are described in generic form whenever possible across products, but are product-specific where this appears to be necessary.

> *Product Library:* Contains information on each product (software and, where appropriate, hardware) available from applicable vendors. In addition to general description, price, and so forth, each product is described in terms of the BBFs it provides, and other BBFs which are useful and are available from other sources as add-ons or complements to the primary product.

People-Goals-Actions (PGA) Database: This application is the key management focus for the design team activities. This is a tool for supporting the management of assignments of responsibility to design team members: goals of the process are formulated, people on the TSS design team and other resources are identified, and specific actions necessary in achieving the goals are formulated and assigned to specified individuals. This is a form of project management database. It is used to support management of tasks and assignments of responsibility in the design and planning activities. Specific aids are given for assessing organizational barriers to change.

Other Databases: Also available are standard types of groupware databases, such as document information, mail, and others.

12.11 APPLICATION CASE STUDIES

The concepts and techniques described in previous sections have been tested in several case studies.

12.11.1 A Workshop for Initiating Strategic Change

In one application, we were asked by a major computer firm to develop a process to be used to initiate a strategic change process in a client organization. After discussions with the sponsor, we developed this vision and strategy.

Vision: Our goal as a vendor is to enter into a strategic role with the senior management team of a client organization. We want to catalyze in their organization a dialogue and debate that assists them in formulating a strategic initiative and implementing a strategic change plan. We do not care whether at this stage they identify any specific needs for our particular products.

Strategy: We will focus on an issue which we believe is critical and strategic in many client organizations: "How can we drive a customer-service attitude throughout our organization?" To engage the senior management team of a client organization in this issue, we will conduct an intensive two- or three-day workshop with senior management participants.

Process: This workshop will explore the issues in delivering customer service in a quality way, and will examine experiences of other firms. Our goal is to end up with the team formulating a set of management tasks which they can carry back to their organization and begin implementing immediately.

Process and TSS Design for the Workshop: The content of the workshop will cover a range of topics, such as:

☞ What industry and business forces are driving us to significantly increase the importance of being a "quality service provider"?

☞ What does customer service mean? How can it be measured?

☞ What are other companies doing to achieve improved customer service?

☞ What are the possible actions we can consider implementing in order to achieve substantially improved customer service?

☞ How can the use of information technology assist us in improving customer service quality? in measuring and managing our efforts to improve service? in delivering service?

☞ What are the barriers to change in our organization? How can we overcome them?

☞ What are the important actions or steps for us to begin with? The highest-priority steps to undertake first?

To create the appropriate dynamics, the workshop will consist of a set of sessions in different formats:

☞ Presentations will present basic information, introduce concepts, and frame issues (on an initial, broad basis, to be revised subsequently in the activities following).

☞ Face-to-face discussions in "break-out" groups will stimulate surfacing of issues and wrestling with alternative perspectives, alternative priorities, and problem-solving.

☞ Electronically mediated sessions using a TSS will support specific styles of interaction around specific tasks in the overall process.

To support this process, a particular TSS platform was selected: an electronic meeting system (EMS), using Groupsystems (a Ventana product, in a version repackaged by an OEM partner). The physical support was provided through a number of laptops, connected in a portable network to a laptop serving as a server, which supported the facilitator and also the projection of current results through an LCD panel and overhead transparency projector (OHP).

Supporting this overall design, the workshop was constructed as a series of modules. The modules using the TSS were designed to complement the other modules in very specific ways. For example:

☞ Following a presentation on "Customer Service and Its Importance," the EMS was used for a brainstorming session (anonymous, synchronous idea generation). The session participants were asked to identify reasons why customer service was important to their customers, and to identify specific aspects of service which were important (e.g., accuracy in billing, timeliness of acknowledging receipt of an order, etc.). The results of the brainstorming session were then used in a facilitated discussion, with the aid of the EMS, in which the group discussed which aspects of service were roughly similar and therefore could be combined.

☞ The next presentation was on "Ways of Measuring Customer Service." Following this presentation, the EMS was used to support a second brainstorming session, about ways of measuring the key customer service aspects previously identified. Again, the results were combined. The results were a list of key service variables and ways of measuring them. These were discussed in a face-to-face discussion session. The question was then raised, "Which of these are most important?" After some discussion of relative importances, and of the feasibility of measurements of various kinds, the EMS was used with a voting module to support anonymous voting, and the group prioritized the various service variables.

☞ Later in the workshop, the group was asked to begin addressing the question of "What to do first?" in implementing improved service. Another discussion session focused on discussing alternative management actions which might be considered, and on identifying barriers to change. Then, in an intensive sequence of EMS sessions, a specific action program was developed: first, brainstorming was used to identify issues and action program elements; then, the facilitator grouped action program elements to get major actions listed; then, voting was used to prioritize the action items. This was followed by a group discussion around such questions as, "Did we capture the important elements? Are there key questions or uncertainties still in our minds? What kind of time frame is desired to get these actions accomplished? What kind of time frame is achievable?" and so forth.

This workshop design was tested in an Alpha test as a structured walkthrough, in which the overall design was talked through in a team setting and discussed.

After some revision, the design was then tested in a full-scale Beta test. Participants included senior executive representatives from the information systems vendor and senior executives from customer organizations, prospective clients for the workshop product offering. The workshop was conducted over two-and-a-half days, from about 8:00 a.m. through after-dinner sessions into the evening, at an off-site location away from any offices.

The workshop Beta test was successful beyond all expectations. The content was appropriate and effective, and the dynamic interplay of multiple styles of interaction—presentations, discussions, EMS sessions—was especially effective. Both groups of participants raved about the value to them, and the potential value to their organizations, of this type of TSS-supported senior management workshop.

Unfortunately, the vendor sponsor was shortly thereafter confronted with major downsizing, and the specific business unit that funded the development was abolished within eight months of the Beta. There was no opportunity to carry the success into the marketplace.

This example illustrates:

☞ The use of the VSPT approach

☞ The role of TSS support in an overall process, with social dynamics

☞ The design of a specific TSS application, through the use of a platform (a specific vendor's EMS product) together with specific building blocks—brainstorming, commenting, voting, and other modules—with a specific plan of use.

12.11.2 Business Process Re-engineering in an Airline

In another case, we were asked to participate in a business process redesign (BPR) process in a leading global airline. This particular process focused on the process of scheduling the airline. In parallel, other groups were focusing on five other critical processes.

Prior to beginning this participation, we reviewed the relevant research literature on airline scheduling. In the published literature, the dominant themes are the use of operations research (OR) models such as mathematical programming for performing particular scheduling tasks, such as assigning aircraft to routes, constructing a time-based schedule of flights, assigning crew to aircraft flights and segments, assigning time slots at airport boarding gates, and so on.

The BPR process was designed around four phases. An initial planning meeting of senior executives framed the initial set of questions. Then, a set of three three-day sessions were held, away from the airline's offices, to accomplish the actual process redesign activities. Finally, a brief meeting was held at the conclusion to review the draft of the report, giving the results of the BPR process and providing key action recommendations to senior management.

As the actual BPR process began to unfold at the intensive three-day sessions, it quickly emerged that the dominant issues were those of "trust" and "reliability" among the key participants in the scheduling process. The technical details, such as the need for more accurate data and better analytical tools, while somewhat important, were very much secondary to these people issues.

While the process was not designed around an explicit "diagnosis and assessment phase," in actual fact, the first three-day meeting and a substantial part of the second were devoted to raising issues, discussing them, and eventually getting around to prioritizing them. All agreed that the issue of "trust" was the dominant issue in the process.

To explain further, we will go into some detail (the titles, responsibilities, and other details are modified slightly in order to disguise the identity of the specific airline).

In this case, the relevant team is a "Team of Teams," as introduced earlier. The key actors participate as individuals in the overall scheduling process; but as a practical matter, each key actor is supported by numerous staff members who actually do the detailed work and meet with others in similar positions in the other functional areas to work on the problem. Thus, the team is a team of teams, each constituent team being a group of individuals supporting the key manager in the process from their unit. These key managers are:

☞ The General Manager for crew is responsible for all aspects of personnel in flight, including Cockpit Crew (pilots, navigators/flight engineers) and Cabin Crew (stewards and flight attendants), and including recruiting, training, scheduling, working conditions, and so on.

☞ The General Manager of Hub Operations is responsible for all aspects of on-the-ground support at airports, including aircraft boarding gates, their availability and scheduling, support equipment and operations concerned with fuel, supplying meals and other consumables, baggage handling, and so forth.

☞ The senior manager responsible for marketing strategy is concerned with what services should be offered on what routes, at what times of day and days of the week, at what prices, for what classes of services, with what marketing and promotional campaigns, to serve what target groups, and so on.

☞ The General Manager of Maintenance is responsible for ensuring that aircraft, their electronic systems, their engines and other major components are maintained satisfactorily, including both scheduled maintenance and responding to needs for unscheduled maintenance.

☞ The Director of Operations Management is the single individual responsible for ensuring that an overall airline schedule is developed, is feasible, and is concurred with by all of the responsible managers (such as those described previously) and satisfies the goals, policies, and concerns articulated by the top executive management of the airline who do not participate actively themselves in the scheduling process.

A key characteristic of this process is that the majority of the key managers are roughly equal in position and title, in stature, and in having significant management responsibilities. Although the Director of Operations Management (DOM) is the key individual responsible for the effectiveness and success of the overall process, he does not have line authority over the other participants, each of whom is a key holder of major resources and has independent authorities and responsibilities.

In other words, this is a true "team," in which there is no single manager with authority over the others; collaboration is essential for the team to get their work done.

This is also a "Team of Teams," in that each of the senior managers participates as an equal in the overall scheduling process when it is necessary to coordinate at this most senior level. However, a great deal of the actual coordination—and dialogue, debate, issue surfacing, and conflict resolution—takes place at levels below these senior managers. For example, a particular task—developing a better marketing and service strategy for Latin America—will actually be worked on by a team designated for that task, formed of individuals from each of the major groups. This working team will review their work with the senior managers but will, in general, not call on them for conflict resolution except when the issues are very significant and the conflicts major. Thus, the actual work of the team gets accomplished by many smaller, lower-level, task-specific teams (task forces, committees, or informal groups).

The issue of "trust" was reflected in this way. In order to produce an agreed-on schedule, all of the stakeholders must agree that the schedule meets the concerns which it is their responsibility to enforce.

These concerns have several dimensions. For example, the GM Maintenance is responsible for safety; therefore, he is concerned that all aircraft will be operated within their allowable operating conditions and will be scheduled for overhaul or other maintenance of various component systems at the required times. At the same time, the GM Maintenance is responsible for the workloads, working conditions, training, and job satisfaction of thousands of maintenance workers around the world who fulfill the airline's needs in this function. He is concerned that his people and other resources are not so overtaxed that their ability to perform their key jobs is affected. While he is concerned with fulfilling his own responsibilities, he is also concerned that he not be seen by others as inflexible and unwilling to consider the overall good of the airline, including its ability to try to be profitable.

Each stakeholder is operating under conditions of very tight resources, very little time for analysis and decision, and very difficult operating conditions in the market environment and in terms of resources available to the airline.

Thus, issues of "trust" come up in ways such as this:

☞ The marketing people propose a service change (e.g., adding an additional daily flight on a particular route). The other stakeholders need to comment on this and determine whether it is acceptable to each one of them. It takes weeks or at least several days for each to check out his concerns and be assured that they can, or cannot, accommodate the proposed schedule modification. Several major stakeholders may spend several person-weeks or

person-months of effort in analyzing the proposed change, and may conclude they can meet it only by seriously stressing their operating people
(e.g., working extra hours of overtime or split shifts).

☞ Doing a major analysis only to discover that the original proposer has with-
drawn the proposal for various reasons, or that it is opposed by some other
major stakeholder and therefore is unlikely to be adopted.

☞ Spending substantial effort just to get a meeting of the relevant stakeholders scheduled and held, only to discover that several have met informally
and resolved the outstanding issues; or reached a conclusion that the issues
are not resolvable and the proposal should be dropped.

☞ Finally getting a meeting held only to discover that some party has a major
concern which will block the proposal; and that party has been called out of
the meeting to deal with an even higher priority issue, so the meeting cannot resolve the question.

☞ Discovering that a sequence of specific change proposals can be accommo-
dated individually, but that cumulatively they represent a major drain on
available resources and significant overtaxing of operations people in the
relevant area (e.g., ground operations).

In the BPR process, the present processes were critically examined. Out of
this, a list was developed of some 35 ways in which the process generated mis-
trust, conflicts, failures to communicate, excessive stress on particular stakeholder departments, and other sources of wasted energy.

After this diagnosis was presented to the group as a whole, it was realized
that the central issue was how to improve the communications among the critical stakeholders so that more timely and effective communication could take
place to reduce misunderstandings, delays, unneeded analysis work, unneeded
or unproductive meetings, and other underlying elements that caused lack of
trust.

We presented the role of TSS as a support tool and discussed some specific
applications. A vendor was immediately requested to make a demonstration, and
Lotus Notes was demonstrated to a number of senior managers. They immediately saw applications of this TSS platform, and the process of developing and
implementing a pilot application for operations management was initiated. The
need to implement a TSS to support operations management was included in the
BPR group's final recommendations.

The actual development of a pilot focused around one specific planning
problem, the planned airline schedule (or proposal) for three years out from the
current date. The pilot was set up with one specific application, focused around
discussion of possible changes to the draft schedule under development. By careful design of the forms for posting an issue, the social dynamics of the process
were changed in significant ways. For example, the initial response to a proposal
included allowable responses roughly as follows: "I concur"; "I oppose for these
specified reasons ——"; or "I need to analyze this and I will respond by (a specified date)." Thus, a stakeholder could see very quickly if other stakeholders con-

curred with the proposal, objected, or were planning on taking several weeks to develop a response. If many people objected immediately, then no further work was likely to be required, and it was likely that the proposer would quickly withdraw the proposal. If many people were going to be delayed in their response, then each would see that and could pace their work accordingly.

This early pilot was successful, and is leading to development and implementation of a number of additional TSS for operations management and related processes.

This case demonstrates:

☞ The importance of a diagnosis and assessment stage; in this situation, the original premises of the BPR process and numerous participants turned out to be wrong, and the really critical issues resolved around trust and related interpersonal and intraorganizational issues.

☞ The importance of designing a TSS to reinforce the desired social process of interactions among the team members, in that the design of the pilot reflected specific actions to create an atmosphere of more realistic expectations and responses.

12.11.3 Public-Sector Transportation Planning

In another case study, the objective was to produce a preliminary design of a TSS for the State of California to use in urban transportation decision making, especially about new high-technology systems (such as IVHS, Intelligent Vehicle Highway Systems) [Khannafani *et al.*, 1994; Khattak *et al.*, in press].

The objective of the first phase of the project was to do a diagnosis and assessment, in order to identify the key issues and priorities and to specify the design of a prototype. This included preliminary design of the TSS, including selection of the appropriate platform and building-block functions to be provided for TSS development. In addition, a simple prepilot prototype was developed to illustrate how the proposed TSS would perform.

In the diagnosis and assessment phase, interviews were conducted together with a literature review to identify the key issues to be addressed in designing a TSS. Based on this information, a set of goals for the TSS were developed. Then, the methodology outlined in Table 12.3 was applied. The result was a preliminary design, in the selection of a number of BBFs. These were grouped into six categories of work tasks.

12.11.3.1 Example: Method for Selecting BBFs The methodology for selecting BBFs can itself be supported by a TSS [Xie, in process; Khattak *et al.*, in press]. The development team can use some of the same building-block functions which they are discussing and evaluating to assist in the evaluation process. For example, Step 1 can be supported by the building blocks ***Brainstorming***, ***Threaded Discussion***, and ***Scoring***. We will discuss the BBFs further in Step 3. Table 12.4 shows a software package BBF matrix.

Table 12.3 Methodology for Identifying Building-Block Functions

Step	Participants	Process
1.00	End Users	Determine the goals to be supported
2.00	End Users	Determine the key tasks needed to address each goal
3.00	Developers	Propose building-block functions for each task
4.00	Both	Evaluate each BBF for each task
5.00	End Users	Determine the set of BBFs to be developed for each task
6.00	Both	Evaluate software packages/platforms for each BBF
7.00	Judgment or Scoring Function	Evaluate each software package for each goal
8.00	End Users	Agree upon an implementation plan for team support

Table 12.4 Example of a Software Package BBF Matrix

Software Package BBF	Real-Time Conference	Brainstorming	Rules-Based Routing
Lotus Notes		yes	partial
Group Systems V	yes	yes	
BeyondMail			yes

Step 1—Determine Goals The first step in the process is for the developers to meet with the eventual end users who will be supported and discuss the goals that the end users have for the system. It is quite likely that not all end users will have similar goals that they would like to have supported. It is important, however, for the developer to understand the different points of view. Clashing goals from end users may create a substantial barrier to acceptance of the team support system.

It is desirable for the end users to agree upon a (sub)set of their overall goals to be addressed by the team support system. In many cases, however, the developer will have to facilitate a decision or present an opinion of what goals can be best supported in order for the end users to reach consensus.

The result of this step is a set of goals for the developer to consider. These goals drive the rest of the development process: for example, one important goal of this TSS was to enable people to "give opinions without fear of reprisal."

Step 2—Determine Key Tasks Once the goals to be supported are established, the next step in the process is to determine the key tasks needed to support each goal. Some tasks will be specific to particular goals; others will be supportive of achieving a number of goals. Again, the TSS design team interacts with end users to develop this list of tasks, and to complete a task/goal matrix.

Table 12.5 Example of a Task/Goal Matrix

Task / Goal	Build better proposals	Build proposal faster
Delegate writing tasks	important	important
Hold "meetings" without travelling to central site		important
Build outlines of each writing task for approval	important	
Coordinate with writers of adjacent sections of the proposal	minor	minor

This matrix contains the key tasks for each goal as well as support tasks found in a number of goals. An example of this matrix is shown in Table 12.5.

This task/goal matrix provides a framework for the end users to discuss and develop agreement on what the team support system should achieve, and allows the developers to begin suggesting approaches to provide the needed support.

Step 3—Propose Building-Block Functions In Step 3, the developers introduce the concept of the BBF. Some 80 BBFs have been identified, most but not all using some component of groupware software or hardware. Some of these BBFs are not "computer-system-oriented," such as the BBF "Phone Call." As we will see in the demonstration application, however, even some of these "non-computer" BBFs have potential implementations in a team support environment.

The majority of this step is education and discussion. The developers should discuss each BBF with the end users and obtain initial comments. The session should be designed as an "awakening" for the end user, where questions and ideas are strongly encouraged.

Step 4—Evaluate BBFs by Task Once the BBFs are identified, each BBF should be evaluated based on its ability to support the different tasks identified in Step 2. Both the developers and the end users should be involved in the evaluation process because each group brings a different perspective to the process. The end user has an intuitive understanding of the task but not necessarily of the BBF. The developer has worked with the BBFs before and understands their strengths and limitations, but is not as familiar with the tasks.

Since the set of BBFs can be quite large, we would propose a two-tiered process. In the first step, each BBF is evaluated on a "yes/no/maybe" basis for each task. This can be done quickly and efficiently with either paper and pencil, a spreadsheet, or a group facilitation package.

After an initial pruning of the BBF set in Step 5, the developers would return to Step 4 and conduct a more complex evaluation of each remaining BBF for each task which was evaluated as "yes" or "maybe." This detailed evaluation would identify the following items for each BBF\Task pair:

☞ How the BBF would be used to support the task
☞ The strengths of the BBF with respect to the task
☞ The weaknesses of the BBF with respect to the task

☞ Potential changes to the task definition which would improve the "fit" between BBF and task

Step 5—Determine the Set of BBFs to Be Implemented   As mentioned above, Steps 4 and 5 might be executed iteratively. Each time Step 5 is addressed, the end users should be able to use the information from the preceding step to prune the set of BBFs being considered.

This step is critical because it provides the general functional requirements of the team support system. If the end users are not able to resolve which BBFs should be included, more evaluation in Step 4 is needed. Similarly, if the BBF set identified would require resources beyond those available, the BBF set must be further analyzed and pruned again.

Step 6—Evaluate Software Packages for Each BBF   Completion of Step 5 provides the development team with the list of desired BBFs needed to be implemented to provide satisfactory team support for the end users. Different groupware products provide different mixes of BBFs with different characteristics and modes of use. The next step is to evaluate alternative groupware products in terms of the BBFs that they offer. The outcome of this step should be a matrix linking packages available with the BBFs they provide, such as that shown in Table 12.4.

Of course, the development team might decide to handcraft some BBFs from scratch in order to build a tightly integrated system or because the products available do not provide the desired capabilities.

Step 7—Evaluate Software Packages for Each Goal   The next step is to evaluate the available groupware products in terms of the goals of the end users. In this step, the ability of each product to support the users' goals is evaluated by considering which software packages provide the BBFs that support the tasks required to achieve the desired goals. These results should be reviewed with the users. Often, there is not one software package that will fully support all the goals of the end users. Sometimes, it may be possible to provide the desired functionality with several packages, but the interconnection of the packages may require significant resources. Therefore, the end users may need to revisit the goals developed in Step 1 and resolve which goals (and therefore which software implementations) should be given priority.

Step 8—Agree Upon a Team Support Implementation Plan   The developers should work with the end users to build a implementation plan which satisfies as many of the goals as possible while using software components that can be integrated as much as possible.

12.11.3.2 Application   This methodology was applied to the issue identified previously: The objective was to develop a preliminary design for a TSS for planning of IVHS transportation projects in the San Francisco bay area. As a pilot, a specific limited prototype was developed for planning HOV (High-Occupancy Vehicle) lanes (for buses and carpools) on freeways.

This case study illustrates:

☞ The design of a TSS based on selecting from available BBFs and products

☞ The potential application of TSS to extended enterprises, in this case the collection of organizations and interest groups involved in public-sector decision-making

12.11.4 TSS Support for a Graduate Management Degree Program

In this case, a TSS was designed and implemented to support graduate MBA courses at the J. L. Kellogg Graduate School of Management, Northwestern University. The initial TSS was implemented in spring 1993, and has been used for three courses since then. Each time the TSS design has evolved, and new and/or refined applications have been implemented [Manheim *et al.*, 1994; Xie, in process].

The approach used in designing the TSS was similar to the WoW approach described above. An initial vision of the educational processes desired around the course was developed, and a TSS consisting of several applications was developed, using a library of BBFs. Over the series of courses, the vision of the educational process and the role of groupware in that process evolved, and the TSS design was modified as well. Critical also were the ways the educational processes themselves were evolved to exploit the use of the TSS; this is especially true of the student assignments, as discussed below.

The platform decision was made prior to the design of the courses. Lotus Notes was selected because of its functionality and the prior familiarity of the Northwestern team with the product. Therefore, the TSS design activities focused on what applications to build in the Notes environment to achieve the educational process objectives.

12.11.4.1 Visioning: Educational Objectives
The use of TSS was visualized as a central element of the educational objectives of these courses. These objectives pertain both to the educational *process* itself, and in this respect are relevant to many different types of courses; and to the *content* of the courses, which is relevant to certain types of courses.

Process Objectives With respect to the educational process, the objective was to provide the student with a richer and more valuable *educational experience* than might otherwise be obtained This was based on the belief that education should be a multidimensional, multi-"channel" experience. In contrast, in one classic model of teaching, the student is viewed as "an empty container," and the role of the instructor is viewed as "pouring knowledge" into this container (a caricature!). Instead, the goal at Kellogg was to follow a very different model, with multiple channels of interaction:

☞ Face-to-face in-class discussions
☞ Face-to-face out-of-class discussions, in the traditional faculty-student and student-student interactions
☞ Electronically mediated out-of-class discussions, in which the groupware provides a medium for *student-student*, *student-faculty*, and *student-resource person* interactions.

Particularly important was the goal of enhancing the student-student inter-actions, as this is well known to reinforce learning; and is also consistent with and reinforces Kellogg's commitment to group work. Since these classes typically included students from the Kellogg day and evening programs, and from other university schools (e.g., engineering), a major goal was to stimulate student-stu-dent interactions outside the formal classroom among students of different back-grounds and professional perspectives.

Another goal which became important in the third iteration of the TSS use (spring 1994) was to expand the resources on which a student can draw, to include not only the faculty teaching the course, but also:

- ☞ "Alumni" of the course, students who took the course in previous years and are interested in and willing to engage in continued interaction with the subject matter and the current students; in Kellogg, this promotes interac-tions between second-year and first-year students
- ☞ Other Northwestern faculty and research staff who have an interest in the topics covered in the course
- ☞ Academics, researchers, and executives outside Northwestern who are also interested in interacting with the students

Thus, a part of the vision was that use of TSS could expand the learning community from the traditional model of a teacher and a group of students inter-acting in the physical classroom to an open model of the teacher, students, resource persons, and alumni interacting in the virtual classroom.

Another goal was to motivate more intense learning by providing a variety of stimuli to students' thinking more deeply and more broadly; it was felt that electronically mediated discussions could improve this substantially.

Content Objectives   In addition, for certain courses, the use of groupware was also relevant to the *content* of the course. For example, one of the courses covered globalization, the changing forms of organizations and the emergence of "virtual" and "network" organizations, and the role of information technology in facilitating and supporting this evolution of organizations and of new ways of working. In this context, groupware is a key technology influencing this evolu-tion, and is a potential source of competitive advantage for companies which learn how to use it effectively. Therefore, the groupware experience component of the course was intended to provide a "hands-on" or "laboratory" experience in which the student could learn first-hand about the realities of electronically sup-ported interactions, and their strengths and weaknesses.

In another course, the content covered how managers can be effective in for-mulating and implementing strategic change. In this context, tools which sup-port teamwork among the members of the strategic management team and their "clients" in the organization are particularly useful in bringing out these dimen-sions of the process.

12.11.4.2 The Groupware Experience   Each student had an individual copy of Lotus Notes client software and access to the server.

Notes is a groupware product which can support a variety of different modes of interaction within a group such as a class and its associated teaching staff. Notes provides a basic *electronic mail* capability. In addition, Notes provides a *platform* for developing a rich variety of specific applications, each of which can support group interactions in different ways.

These applications are developed by creating specific Notes Databases (generally, but not always, by using or modifying templates provided by Lotus). Each database is composed of forms and ways of viewing the forms in the database, called views. There may be many different types of forms in a single database, and many different views, all with specific purposes. For example, a discussion database may consist of a Main Topic form and Response forms. Anyone can initiate a discussion by filling out a Main Topic form. Anyone can participate in a discussion by filling out a Response form, in response to either a Main Topic or another Response. The forms and databases are "mail-enabled," in that students and faculty can fill out forms and they are automatically mailed to all other participants who have copies of the same databases on their computers.[*]

The team support system (TSS) for these courses consisted of a number of Notes Applications, using several Notes databases and/or mail interaction modes:

1. *Biographies:* A biography database is provided. Each student is expected to fill out a biographical form. This can be as little or as much information as the individual wishes. It is a mechanism through which each student can introduce himself or herself to his or her colleagues, and get to know something about them in return.

2. *Course News:* A database for providing current information. This will allow rapid dissemination of operational information, such as planned shutdowns of the Notes system if any, solutions to any operational problems that are encountered, policy statements if needed, and other information. For example, we use the News database to announce local tradeshows or exhibits which are relevant to the course, to invite students to late-breaking events, and so on.

---

[*] A student can access Notes either with a copy on their own machine or through a machine in one of the school computer labs.

Each user has personal copies of each database on their machines, and exchanges information with other users by logging onto a Notes Server, through either direct linkage over a network or dial-in access using a modem. Once logged on, the user engages in a process called replication, in which the user's copy and the server's copy are updated and made mutually consistent; in this process, any contributions that the user has made, such as mail or an addition to a discussion, are added to the generally available copies of the databases on the server.

A key feature of Notes is its sophisticated security and access control. Every database has its own restrictions on access. All class databases are open to all course participants as the instructor decides. When several students decide to establish a private database for their own use, they can restrict access to all other participants if they so wish. In addition, Mail is private and cannot be accessed by others. Thus, Notes provides a very dynamic and secure way of managing a variety of databases for different subgroups in the class and for different purposes.

3. *Bibliography:* A database with forms for various types of bibliographic items. This can be used for sharing information about specific references that students come across in their research.

4. *General Discussion:* This discussion database is the primary focus of student activities. Anyone can initiate a discussion by composing a new Main Topic. Anyone can participate in a discussion by composing a Response, either to a Main Topic or to another Response. The sequence of Main Topics and Responses creates a "threaded" discussion.

   The Discussion database also allows the individual to assign his/her comment to one or more categories:

   a. A "theme" category is required: To reinforce the discussion of the key themes of the course, each student entering a new Main Topic is required to identify at least one of the themes to which this topic pertains.

   b. A "class date" category is optional. This is used if the student's topic refers to something that occurred, or was discussed, in a particular class.

   c. A "readings" category is also optional. This is used if the student's topic refers to one or more specific readings on the required reading list; if so, the reading reference is entered as a keyword in the form.

   d. A general category field is also available, to allow a student to assign a topic to any categories he or she wishes, including ones that the student makes up.

   Various views in this database display topics and/or responses by the various category types, as well as by date, author, and other variables.

5. *Notes Mail—Basic:* Notes provides basic electronic mail capabilities. While the information in all the other databases is public and available to everyone who has access to a specific database, Mail is private, and can only be viewed by those individuals (or groups) specifically named as addressees (or recipients of copies or blind copies). Therefore, Mail is especially useful for interaction on a one-to-one basis, as for student-faculty and student-student communications.

   Mail is used for discussions of possible term paper topics, personal problems such as reasons for missing a class, and so on. Students are advised to use the Discussion databases, not mail, for topics that can usefully be discussed by larger groups such as the class as a whole.

   Students can also use Mail for sending items, such as term paper proposals, as electronic attachments or enclosures to mail messages. Students are warned to do this only with a document composed in a widely used word processor or spreadsheet, as the recipient must be able to read the attachment by reading it into his/her word processor or spreadsheet program.

6. *Notes Mail—Grading Application:* We also use Notes Mail for providing grade feedback to students. A Grading Database for each course has specific forms for grading specific assignments and for the overall course grade at the end of the quarter. Thus, the professor in charge, when grading each assignment, fills out a form for each student; this is made available electronically to the student whenever the professor is ready to release the forms and mail them electronically. The grade forms are also printed out as traditional paper copies for distribution in class. The grade forms are confidential, of course. From a faculty viewpoint, we have also incorporated a nice ease-of-use feature which makes final grading easier: the Course Final Grade Form for each student "inherits" and incorporates the grades and other information for each of the student's prior assignments. Thus, the teacher has in front of him an electronic form with all of the component assignment grades and text comments for review when deciding on the final course grade for the student.

7. *Course Evaluation Database:* Kellogg uses several standard evaluation mechanisms. In the middle of a quarter, a form is passed out to the students to provide comments on the course to that point. These are filled out anonymously and returned to the instructor for guidance in adjusting the course during that same quarter. In addition, a more formal evaluation form is distributed at the end of the quarter, which includes numerically scored questions, some of which enter into personnel decisions in the school. As an experiment, we are providing an evaluation database containing electronic versions of these forms. Students can fill out the forms electronically, and their identity is hidden, so these are indeed anonymous evaluations. In addition, we may provide general evaluation forms which a student can fill out at any time to provide direct feedback to the instructor.

8. *Document Repository:* We have also experimented with a document repository. This stores selected documents on-line for student access. For example, a discussion in the Discussion database began exploring patents and other forms of intellectual property protection. One student mentioned that the Secretary of Commerce had recently chaired a committee which had studied intellectual property protection. The student went into Internet resources, found a copy of the cited report, downloaded it, and put it in the document repository for class use.

9. *Student Databases:* If a group of students wishes to have their own Discussion (or other database), we can make that available. In 1993, students working on a group project set up a Discussion database for developing and exchanging ideas and drafts. Any group of two or more students can have their own database; and they can control access, deciding whether to keep it private for their own use or open to some broader grouping.

10. *Other Applications:* Are developed as the course evolves.

12.11.4.3 Creating Readiness to Use the TSS   The Assignments and grading approach for these courses reflect this use of Notes. However, it was recognized that requiring the use of Notes may be a barrier for some students, and the teaching staff were prepared to make individual adjustments in special situations. In addition, an alternative grading option was provided for students who did not want to make use of Notes in a heavy way.

Typical Assignments   Notes could be used to submit term project proposals, term papers, and other assignments to the instructor.

12.11.4.4 Creating "Critical Mass"   As discussed earlier in this chapter, creating a critical mass of users in a TSS application is critical to its success. To strongly encourage students to participate early in the discussions, and to interact frequently, a specific assignment was given in which each student had to lead an electronic discussion among her peers in the class. Each student was responsible for "chairing" at least one major discussion on Notes with classmates. To quote from the assignment:

> You do this by initiating a topic, and by intervening in the discussion from time to time to stimulate, shape and evolve the discussion. Your role is as a catalyst, facilitator, debate leader, ... ???. You will be GRADED on your performance in leading a productive, intellectually stimulating, relevant discussion; we will discuss the criteria during the class.

> To hedge your bets, you may want to initiate and "chair" more than one major discussion, to see which one turns out most interesting.

> We will discuss in class the mechanics of fulfilling this requirement. Tentatively, I will ask you to send me a Notes Mail message before the due date, referencing the discussion you are submitting for grading, and summarizing briefly for me the major ideas which emerged during that discussion.

The TSS is now being redesigned for the fourth iteration of use (fall 1994), in a different course. On this cycle, the TSS design methodology outlined above is being used and refined.

In conclusion, this case illustrates:

☞ The application of the VSPT approach, involving vision, strategy, processes, and tasks
☞ The use of a TSS with a number of specific applications, each implemented by building off of or adapting a specific BBF
☞ The use of a specific application to assist in developing social relationships, through the use of the Biography database
☞ The adaptive evolution of the TSS over time, as lessons are learned in use of the TSS

12.12. CONCLUSIONS: IMPLEMENTING TEAM SUPPORT SYSTEMS

Groupware is a powerful class of information technologies. Effective deployment of GW in an organization offers significant opportunities for achieving important business objectives. To achieve these objectives, GW must be deployed with a thoughtful, careful implementation strategy; otherwise, its promise will remain largely unfulfilled.

We have discussed many aspects of GW deployment.

First and foremost, it is essential that the emphasis shift from GW as a technology to team support systems (TSS) as a set of business-focused applications.

We have also discussed the role of groupware in achieving business objectives, technology's role in supporting teams, implementation issues and alternative implementation strategies, and GW's relationship to other processing modes and other forms of information systems support.

We then discussed an approach to effective TSS design and implementation, and presented a TSS for support of the team doing TSS design and implementation. In our case studies of particular applications, we illustrated various aspects of the methodology we have been describing.

The implementation of team support systems can be a major element of an organization's competitive strategy. Ideally, TSS implementation should be planned and managed as a priority task for senior management. Information systems staff should support that effort. The planning and design of a TSS should reflect the vision, strategy, and goals of the organization.

However, in some companies this will not be accepted or feasible. In these situations, the manager leading TSS implementation should view the activity as an explicit effort for planned organizational change and capacity-building. The technology of groupware is a means, not an end.

ACKNOWLEDGMENTS

Research support from the following is gratefully acknowledged: the Strategic Informatics Research Program and the companies supporting it—British Airways, Avantos Performance Systems, Intertrans, Inc.; Conrail Corporation; IBM; and the William A. Patterson chair at the Transportation Center, Northwestern University.

This paper benefited from numerous conversations and joint activities with David Coleman, Collaborative Strategies, Inc., and the Groupware Conferences; Shinroku Tsuji, Kobe City University of Commerce; Frank LeClerq,, Amsterdam City Planning Department and TNO; Kyoji Kunitomo and Yasumasa Shinohara, Ricoh Company Ltd.; and Tatsuro Ichihara, Omron Corporation.

The authors gratefully acknowledge the benefits of the research support of the sponsors and the collaborations of colleagues, but we alone are responsible for any errors or biases presented here.

REFERENCES

1. Bahrami, Homa, [1992], "The Emerging Flexible Organization: Perspectives from Silicon Valley," *Cal. Mgmt. Review*, Summer. pp. 33–52.
2. Bartlett, Christopher A., and Sumantra Ghoshal, [1989], *Managing Across Borders: The Transnational Solution*, Boston: Harvard Business School Press.
3. Busch, E., Hamalainen, M., Suh, Y, Whinston, A., and Holsapple, C. W., [1991], "Issues and Obstacles in the Development of Team Support Systems," *Journal of Organizational Computing*, Vol. 2, No.1, pp. 161–186.
4. Clemons, Eric K., and Michael Row, "A Strategic Information System: McKesson Drug Company's Economost," *Planning Review* 16:5, Sept./Oct.
5. Cooper, James, Michael Browne, and Melvyn Peters, [1991], *European Logistics: Markets, Management and Strategy*, Oxford, U.K.; and Cambridge, MA.: Blackwell.
6. Davenport, Thomas H., [1993], *Process Innovation and the Management of Organizational Change*.
7. DeJean, David, and Sally Blanning DeJean, [1991], *Lotus Notes at Work*, New York:
8. Ellis, C. A., Gibbs, S. J., Rein, G. L., [1991], "Groupware: some issues and experiences," *Communications of ACM*, Vol. 3, No.1, pp. 39–58.
9. Fallows, James, [1992], "Hidden Powers, Agenda 2.0 Evaluation," *Atlantic Monthly*, 269:5, p. 114.
10. Fast, Robert and Lauren, [1991], *Business Applications with Agenda*, New York: Brady Publishing.
11. *Fortune*, [1994], "Mr. Cozzett Orders a Computer," June.
12. Gabarro, John J., [1990], "The Development of Working Relationships," pp. 79–110, in Galegher, Jolene, Robert E. Kraut, and Carmen Egido, *Intellectual Teamwork*, Hillsdale, N.J.: Lawrence Erlbaum Associates.
13. Geis, George, [1991], *Business Management with Lotus Agenda*, Cambridge, MA: Southwest Publishing.
14. Gray, Paul, [1989], "Managing the emerging information systems technologies: the case of group technologies," in Gray, Paul, William R. King, Ephraim R. McLean, and Hugh J. Watson, editors, *The Management of Information Systems*, Chicago: Dryden Press, pp. 123–156.
15. Grohowski, R., McGoff, C., Vogel, D., Martz, B., Nunamaker, J., [1990], "Implementing Electronic Meeting Systems at IBM: Lessons Learned and Success Factors," *MIS Quarterly*, Dec., pp. 369–383.
16. Grudin, Jonathan, [1989], "Why groupware applications fail: problems in design and evaluation," *Office: Technology and People*, Vol. 4, No. 3, pp. 245–264.
17. Hammer, Michael, [1990], "Re-engineering Work: Don't Automate, Obliterate," *Harvard Business Review*, April.
18. Hiltz, S. R., Dufner, D., Holmes, M., Poole, S., [1991], "Distributed Group Support Systems: Social Dynamics and Design Dilemmas," *Journal of Organizational Computing*, (2)1, pp. 135–159.
19. Hedlund, Gunnar, and Dag Rolander, [1990], "Action in Hetarchies—New Approaches to Managing the MNC," in Bartlett, C. A., Y. Doz, and G. Hedlund, editors, *Managing the Global Firm*, London: Routledge, pp. 15–46.
20. Isenberg, Daniel J., [1984], "How senior managers think," *Harvard Business Review*. November-December, pp. 81–90.
21. Isenberg, Daniel J., [1986], "Strategic opportunism," *Harvard Business Review*.
22. Johansen, Robert, [1988], *Groupware: Computer Support for Business Teams*, New

York: Free Press/MacMillan.

23. Khanafani, Adib, Marvin L. Manhei, Assad Khattak, and Nicholas J. Vlahos, [1994], *The Role of Teamwork in a Planning Methodology for Intelligent Transportation Systems*, Volume 1, California PATH Working Paper WPUCB-ITS-PWP-94-08, Berkeley: Institute of Transportation Studies, University of California.

24. Khattak, Assad, Nicholas Vlahos, Adib Khanafani, and Marvin L. Manheim, in press, "The Role of Teamwork in a Planning Methodology for Intelligent Transportation Systems," *Transportation Research*.

25. Kirkpatrick, David, [1993], "Groupware Goes Boom," *Fortune*, Dec. 27.

26. Malone, Thomas W., Kenneth R. Grant, Kum-Yew Lai, Ramana Rao, and David A. Rosenblitt, [1989], "The Information Lens: An Intelligent System for Information Sharing and Coordination," in M. H. Olson, ed., *Technological Support for Work Group Collaboration*. Hillsdale, N.J.: Lawrence Erlbaum Associates, pp. 65–88.

27. Manheim, Marvin L., [1994], "Beyond the Logistics Pipeline: Opportunities for Competitive Advantage," in James Cooper, ed., *Logistics and Distribution Planning*, Second Edition, London: Kogan Page Ltd.

28. Manheim, Marvin L., [1993], "Integrating Global Organizations through Task/Team Support Systems," in Linda M. Harasim, editor, *Global Networks: Computers and International Communication*, Cambridge, MA.: MIT Press.

29. Manheim, Marvin L., [1992], "Global Information Technology: Issues and Strategic Opportunities," *International Information Systems* 1:1, 38–67 (January).

30. Manheim, Marvin L., [1990], "Global Information Technology: Globalization and Opportunities for Competitive Advantage through Information Technology," *Tijdschrift Voor Ver Voerswetenschap* (Journal for Transport Science), Rijswijk, the Netherlands: Kwartaalschrift van de Stichting NEA, 1990:2, pp. 138–159.

31. Manheim, Marvin L., [1989], *Strategy as Process: Cognitive Concepts and Information Systems Support*. Paper prepared for the International Meeting of the Strategic Management Society, October, 1989. Working Paper. Policy Department, J. L. Kellogg Graduate School of Management, Northwestern University, Evanston, IL.

32. Manheim, Marvin L., [1988], "Information Technology and Organizational Change—Strategies for Managers," in Klaus M. Blache, editor, *Success Factors for Implementing Change: A Manufacturing Viewpoint*, Detroit: Society of Manufacturing Engineers, pp. 123–149.

33. Manheim, Marvin L., and Daniel Isenberg, [1987], "A theoretical model of human problem-solving and its use for designing decision support systems," in Stohr, Edward A., Lee Hoevel, Leonard Haynes, and Arthur Speckhard, eds., *Architecture, Decision Support Systems, and Knowledge-Based Systems, Vol. I, Proceedings of the Twentieth Hawaii International Conference on System Sciences*, sponsored by University of Hawaii, Association for Computing Machinery, and IEEE Computer Society, North Hollywood, CA.: Western Periodicals Co., pp. 614–627.

34. Manheim, Marvin L., Nicholas Vlahos, [1993], *Implementing Customer-Driven Quality*, Final Research Report, Transportation Center, Northwestern University.

35. Manheim, Marvin L., Nicholas J. Vlahos, and Yin-yie Xie, [1994], unpublished working paper, *Enhancing the Educational Process Through Lotus Notes*, Management and Strategy Department, J. L. Kellogg Graduate School of Management, Northwestern University.

36. Nohria, Nitin, and Robert Eccles, [1992], "Face-to-Face: Making Network Organizations Work," Chapter 11, *Networks and Organizations: Structure, Form and Action*, Edited by Nitin Nohria and Robert G. Eccles, Boston, MA: Harvard Business School Press, pp. 288–308.

37. Orlikowski, Wanda J., [1993], "Learning From Notes: Organizational Issues in Groupware Implementation," *Groupware '93 Proceedings.*

38. Post, B. Q., [1992], "Building the Business Case for Group Support Technology,"*Proceedings of the Twenty-Fifth Annual Hawaii International Conference on Systems Sciences*, Vol. IV.

39. "Singapore Tradenet: A Tale of One City," [1990], Case HBS 9-191-009, rev. 9/20/90, Boston: Harvard Business School.

40. Xie, Yinyi, in process, unpublished Ph. D. dissertation, "Designing Task-Team Support Systems for Business Applications: A Methodological Approach," title tentative, to be submitted to Department of Industrial Engineering, McCormick School of Engineering and Applied Sciences, Northwestern University, Evanston, IL.

41. Zmud, R. W., Lind, M. R., Young, F. W., [1990], "An Attribute Space for Organizational Communication Channels," *Information Systems Research*, December, Vol. 1, No. 4.

BIOGRAPHY

Dr. Marvin Manheim is the William A. Patterson Distinguished Professor at the J. L. Kellogg Graduate School of Management, Northwestern University, with additional appointments in the McCormick School of Engineering and the Transportation Center. He teaches and does research in three areas: strategic management, especially the use of information technology as a competitive weapon; computer support for human problem solving (including Groupware, Team Support Systems, and Symbiotic DSS using Intelligent Agents); and the evolving structure and processes of globally competing organizations. He has been doing research on groupware and its strategy implications since 1988. Dr. Manheim is also chairman and founding principal of Cambridge Systematics, a consulting firm with 110 professionals in four offices. He is cochair of the Black Forest Group, a group of user companies active in groupware, workflow, and other emerging information technologies. Dr. Manheim has written and/or edited several books. He received his B.S. and Ph.D. degrees from MIT.

Dr. Nicholas Viahos received his Ph.D. from Northwestern University and was a research assistant professor there while this search was being conducted. Now at Cambridge Systematics, his practice focuses on the design and implementation of team support systems.

Yinyi Xie is a Ph.D. candidate in industrial engineering at Northwestern University. His dissertation topic is the design of team support systems.

Introduction to Chapter 13

In this chapter, Lesley Shneier discusses some of the critical factors in moving groupware technologies into the World Bank, a highly complex organization: overcoming fear of technology, motivation, incentives for change, overcoming hoarding knowledge and expertise, support and training, and communication with the users. As you can see, few, if any, of the factors discussed are technical.

Lesley's chapter reports on a study which evaluated how technology was brought into the World Bank. Insofar as Lesley is a social scientist who focuses on people, rather than a part of World Bank's MIS department focusing on technical issues, her report evaluates the organizational issues confronted by this highly complex organization. The authors of this study concluded that involvement and commitment to the technology on the part of senior management made it possible to realize much greater progress than expected. This underscores the strategic nature of groupware and the commitment necessary from top management.

The World Bank is an international organization facing some unique challenges that a commercial bank (such as Bank of Montreal) would not confront. For example, diversity in staffing reflects their international focus. Furthermore, although they are not a government institution, they have an organizational hierarchy one would expect in a government organization. Actually, they are somewhere between a government organization (with a specific charter) and a commercial organization (that has countries as clients). Personnel come from diverse backgrounds and cultures. Additionally, the studied population contained staff with different levels of technical knowledge. Generally, finance staff was more technically adept than operations staff. The experiences people had with technology also affected how easily the technology was accepted and used. As was to be expected, the more technically adept finance personnel took to groupware more easily than the operations staff. Even where staff was familiar with email technology, the transition to groupware was not always smooth.

It is no mistake that two of the case studies in the implementation section of this book are about banks. Banks have taken to groupware in a big way. As a matter of fact, so has the entire financial industry. Many of the business processes in the financial industry are very old, inefficient, and production-oriented. This marks the industry as an excellent candidate for process redesign. Additionally, banks are sensitive to increased competitive pressures. In the case of World Bank, competition is not the motivator; often, the ability to communicate with others in the organization, or to use a new technology to make better loans, is the motivation.

This chapter should be read in conjunction with Michael Frow's chapter on groupware at the Bank of Montreal (and vice versa). It is interesting to see how two organizations with many of the same organizational challenges apply the same technology as a solution, but in very different ways.

CHAPTER 13

The Implementation of Enterprise-Ware at the World Bank: A Case Study

Lesley-Ann Schneier
The World Bank

13.1 INTRODUCTION

The introduction of new technology into an organization brings with it the need to manage the change that results from the new technology as well as occasioned the need for that new technology. The effectiveness of such new technology introduction into the organization is highly dependent upon the management of the technology, the process, and the people. Management must ensure that the technological product functions well in support of the business processes. This is more of a logistical issue to identify the business needs and then to develop appropriate technology tools. Managing the people is the more difficult issue. People will respond differently to technology depending on their knowledge, experience, attitudes, and culture. Management, therefore, needs to direct the responses of users through leadership, communications, training, and support.

Significant research elsewhere has been conducted to explore the factors contributing to the success or failure of a technology introduction. This report attempts to bring together some of the more salient findings from this research in order to assist organizations in a smooth transition to new technology. This chapter describes the introduction of an enterprise-wide network in the World Bank from the perspective of the end users. The study was conducted both as part of the evaluation of a network pilot and to determine the ways in which new technology influences user behavior, so as to provide guidelines for maximizing the potential of future technology changes. Like many organizations, the Bank invests a great deal of time, effort, and money in hardware and software; it has not really focused on ensuring that this investment is used effectively. The aims of this study were to determine the kinds of behavioral changes that are necessitated by, and/or occur as a result of, moving from a standalone technology working environment to a collaborative technology working environment; and to understand the criteria/conditions that are required or motivate staff to change their behavior.

This particular study also represents a watershed for the authors, since it became a tool for disseminating our thoughts and views about the human side of technology. As social scientists working in an IS department, it has taken a great deal of time and effort to get the technology experts to focus on the human aspects, particularly on the implications the human issues have for the success or failure of the technology being introduced. Here, for the first time, was the opportunity to do so. That it derived from the move to a collaborative electronic environment, with the rudimentary recognition of the potential to form an electronic community, seemed appropriate, given that the emphasis is now to be placed on the community, which is, of course, the people. And that is what groupware is all about—enabling people to work together more effectively.

13.2 THE WORLD BANK GROUP

The World Bank Group (the Bank) is an international organization, affiliated with, but independent of, the United Nations. The Bank's major goal is to help developing countries achieve sustainable economic development through the provision of loans for projects and technical assistance. In doing so, it performs the dual roles of financial institution and development agency. The Bank is both owned and governed by its member governments, representing about 177 countries worldwide which pledge funds to the Bank. While the Bank's explicit business is lending money for development, its implicit business is gathering and applying knowledge about the development process. The Bank's role as provider of information and knowledge is becoming increasingly critical to its success. However, a 1991 study showed that the Bank's knowledge became scattered and inaccessible after its 1987 reorganization. Therefore, capturing and disseminating this knowledge and enabling cross-fertilization has become a priority. Bank staff, who are recruited typically in mid-career from economics, education, nutrition, agriculture, sociology, law, or any of dozens of other fields, come from many countries. Most of the about 7000 staff are based at headquarters in Washington, DC. The Bank also has about 70 field offices around the world, and headquarters staff typically spend up to 120 days per year traveling to countries with which they are working.

Organizationally, the Bank may be thought of loosely as being divided into a Finance arm, an Operational arm, a Research arm, and Support arms. Finance provides the trading and borrowing functions which leverage the funds that the Bank has to lend to developing countries, as well as the controller functions for the Bank itself. Operations is the heart of the organization and is divided geographically into regions that provide lending, supervision, and technical assistance to developing countries. The Research arm provides central information and expertise on a wide range of topics such as agriculture, health, education, energy, infrastructure, environmental concerns, and women in development. The support functions include personnel, information technology, general services, and legal and secretarial services.

The Bank, like all organizations, has an informal organization—or rather, organizations—that cluster around several variables; for example, professional discipline subspecialties, nationality, and influential people. One of the major reasons for building an enterprise-wide network was, in fact, to develop an electronic network of experts in a major field of development work. The electronic mail system currently functions in a limited way as the *de facto* network of the organization.

In Operations[1] the majority of staff are assigned to a division which may have either a country focus or a sector focus (such as agriculture, infrastructure, education). Staff work on projects as Task Managers or members of task teams, often from different work units in different parts of the Bank, and may include short-term consultants and/or field office staff in the applicable country. These teams come together and disband several times over the course of the project life cycle. Almost everything they do is written up in the form of a report, such as a back-to-office report after a mission to a developing country, a loan appraisal report, a loan supervision report, and so on. Most task managers assume the burden of coordinating and integrating the various chapters that are written by their team colleagues. Some rewrite what their colleagues give them; others simply cut and paste from diskettes. Reports are long (over 100 pages), complex documents containing text, economic and financial analyses in the form of tables, charts, and graphics. They are multi-authored, and go through a multilayered review and revision process[2] until the loan is finally approved by the Board and becomes the legally binding document between the Bank and the country concerned.

The Bank is intensively document-based. Estimates show that the organization deals with some 20 million pages per annum, including what is generated internally and what is received form borrowing clients. There is a heavy exchange of documents between the Bank and the clients and also internally, across organizational boundaries. The majority of professional staff—so-called knowledge workers—draft their own reports using WordPerfect 5.1. Some are now using Word or WordPerfect for Windows, and some still write in longhand and have their secretaries do the word processing for them. Those who draft their own reports usually have secretarial staff do final formatting, spell-checking, proofreading, and sometimes even make the changes to the text, charts, or

---

[1] Finance staff are typically more technologically advanced than Operations staff, and their work processes and ways of working are quite different from those of operations staff.

[2] One internal study showed that reports typically go through over 100 reviews and rewrites before they are presented to the Board as final, legally binding documents.

tables. When task teams work together, they typically produce paper copies of drafts, and hand these to the Task Manager with a diskette. However, when staff are physically separated by more than a few offices—and particularly when they are on different floors or even different buildings—then they typically use fax, and sometimes electronic mail, to share their documents. It is this document sharing, and the corresponding compilation of information and directories of experts in electronically accessible forms, that the enterprise-wide network is designed to facilitate and improve.

13.3 THE PROJECT

Industry analysts, academics, and actual experience in the Bank show that information technology transforms the way people work. Rather than "just letting this happen," we decided to try to understand how behavior changes, what the transition phases would be, and whether these are idiosyncratic or can be generalized. If we could then assist managers and staff to plan accordingly, we would maximize the chances of success and better manage our ability to take advantage of the productivity enhancement potential offered by current developments in technology. The study would identify the current styles of work in both a non-networked and a networked environment, then compare and contrast these work styles to derive the behaviors that are different. An attempt would also be made to identify nonelectronic informal networks of people, and to see if there are any changes in the behavior of people on electronic and nonelectronic networks. However, since most of the electronic networks that currently exist in the Bank are limited to local work units, it may be too soon to see any viable behavioral changes across work groups such as might be predicted to appear with the enterprise-wide network.

13.4 METHODOLOGY

The study group identified divisions with similar work programs in networked and non-networked environments. To identify the styles of work in these various working environments, a series of interviews and focus group meetings were held with staff from each division. Other work that had already been undertaken to document the work processes was invaluable as a source of additional information about the way people work. The results of the series of interviews and focus group meetings and the content analysis of the various documents and other studies were analyzed to identify the work styles, and so derive changes in work styles and/or behavior. The study also focused on the training and support requirements and incentives/motivators in the work ethos that have been found to be essential in bringing about and maintaining networked behaviors.

Seventy staff members and managers in four regions were interviewed during the course of the network evaluation and this study. The Information Technology (IT) staff in each region and in the central Information Systems (IS) department were also interviewed. In particular, information was sought about the way staff used technology in general, their needs for support and training, and perceptions of how the network has changed and/or could change the way they work. In addition, focus groups and individual interviews were held at different stages of the network pilot, and the lessons learned from all these evaluative stages are included here.

13.5 SOCIOTECHNICAL APPROACH

For the past four or five years, the IS department has employed staff with expertise and experience in understanding the impact of technology on the organization and its people. These staff members have conducted research into electronic mail usage, voice mail, issues and concerns of staff with technology, how the roles of professional and support staff change with technology, and how electronic networks change the way staff work. The information so gathered is fed back to the technical staff, to Bank management in general, and to the IT training and support functions so that the lessons learned at each stage can be applied to the implementation of future technology changes. IS Management now recognizes that while the hardware and software issues can be solved relatively easily, it is the people issues that are the hardest and most intractable to resolve. Nonetheless, the support and training functions remain underfunded; the Controller still demands increased productivity before more funds may be spent on technology; and managers in general do not believe that they need to spend more time and money on these crucial people areas in order to gain the full effectiveness and potential of the technology that they have deployed.

In a technocentric approach, managers typically assume that the structural changes required to implement the new technology will naturally follow from attempts to use it. It may, but it need not, and workers have been known to find ways to bypass the new system instead of incorporating it into their normal way of working. A sociotechnical approach, in contrast, involves planning for both technological *and* structural modifications. In particular, the sociotechnical approach stresses user participation in all aspects from planning and design through implementation, testing, and evaluation; resources (including time) for training; and norms supportive of learning and experimentation (for example, placing the emphasis on efforts instead of on immediate results). As Ed Schein [1988] says, "the Socio-technical model argues that one must integrate the human considerations with the technical ones in the initial design process—rather than, as is traditionally thought, the human elements are something that follows and must be adapted to the mission and the technical/structural elements." He also stresses that if the people who will use the system are not involved in the initial design phases, then unanticipated problems may arise that interfere with the effectiveness of the system. "We see this especially in the realm of IT where the difficulties of implementation far outstrip the difficulties of invention [1988, p. 8]." Similarly, Peter Keen [1991] observed that "the technical risks are relatively small and manageable, and that the non-technical risks are very high and center around implementation." Consequently, sociotechnical design considerations become primary to integrate the technical and human capabilities. As will be shown, despite the presence of sociotechnical staff in the IS organization, these points are particularly apposite for the project under discussion.

13.6 THE IS ORGANIZATION

There is a tremendous need for the various sections of any IS department to work together; yet it seems that little historically has prepared them for this way of working. Typically, most information technology and data processing (IT/DP) departments have operated in the past in discrete units or divisions that seemed to have little need to work together. Technological developments have made it almost essential that information technology and data processing departments work together. Communications, mainframes, technical support, messaging, wiring, and building design all need to be integrated and to cooperate in the design and delivery of services: as machines are being linked together, and systems are being integrated, so their staff need to work together and be integrated. Yet these services tend to be organizationally discrete fiefdoms that may or may not work in tandem, and usually little organizational effort is made to enable such a change in both attitude and style of work. Nonetheless, if the IS organization is to be successful in the new networked environment, it has little choice but to deliver integrated services to its clients, if not as a single client service work group, then as a conglomerate of cooperating service delivery units.

A further change—and challenge—that IS departments face is the need to become ever more client sensitive and client oriented. This, too, represents a change from the historical perspective of the DP department being the "gurus" of computer programming who descended on the client and then vanished for extended periods to produce what they thought the client wanted. Now that computer power is readily and cheaply available to the actual end user, and those end users no longer need much programming knowledge to use and apply computer power to their day-to-day business needs, they have become far more knowledgeable about what computers can do for them and more demanding in what they require from the IS department. This means that IS staff need to know far more about the actual business requirements in order to supply the appropriate technology.

As organizations mutate from a series of unconnected standalone PCs to an integrated web of connected PCs, the use and function of the IS department must change. The arguments here surround the pros and cons of centralization versus decentralization. Yet, a strong case can and should be made for a combination of both. There is need for greater standardization to ensure that services across the networks will operate interchangeably; and, at the same time, to allow services to be developed when and where required. As Schein [1988] says, "it is this diversity within unity theme that accounts for so many current management statements that the effective organization is one that can both centralize and decentralize, that can be loose and tight at the same time."

The need to integrate, rather than control, has become the key role for the IS department in the Bank. This is not the same as centralization versus decentralization, but is rather about creating some structure within which the users have the freedom to develop their own applications. It also means that the IS department must develop communication channels to ensure that it knows about and can broker information about these applications, as well as ensuring that the common areas, systems, wiring, and so on both support and enable these various applications, and that these applications can operate together in a fairly seamless fashion. In the Bank, this has meant that the various divisions within the IS department need greater communication and integration, and can no longer operate independently. The need for more institutionally oriented technology solutions, such as networking, directories, and electronic document management, also means that the IS department must become far more proactive and reach out to end users.

IS is organized in the Bank as a combination of centralized and decentralized work groups. The central IS department provides institutional solutions such as global communications, operates the various mainframes, provides telephone directory services, electronic mail, voice mail, and fax, and supports hardware that is installed, but does not develop end-user applications. The decentralized IS groups develop local applications, and provide the support and training for their clients. Various governance bodies and advisory groups provide information and feedback to the central IS group on a regular basis. The net effect of this type of IS organization is a reactive and passive central IS group that does not initiate technological change and, in many cases, a user community that wishes the central group would be more proactive and propose changes; in between them reside the local IS groups that serve their end users and wish the central group would go away!

13.7 NETWORKS IN THE BANK

The concept of networks is not new in the Bank; the first LAN was installed in the Bank around 1984 and there are some 4000 Banyan and other connections in various parts of the Bank as well as one Region (of about 1100 users) that is networked via a Banyan LAN. Electronic mail (ALL-IN-1) was installed in 1984 in Finance. After a drastic reorganization of the Bank in 1987, all staff were given a workstation, and soon thereafter, virtually everyone was hooked up to ALL-IN-1. The ratio of staff to workstations is roughly 1:2, since most traveling staff now have laptops as well as their desktop workstations.[3] The majority of workstations are Intel machines, with about 1000 Mac users, mainly in Finance. In late 1990 there was a proliferation in requests for LANs, ostensibly for printer sharing, but deeper probing revealed a need to foster cross-fertilization of ideas and

---

[3] There is also an experiment underway whereby staff only have a laptop, which they use in the office with a docking station and large monitor.

expertise that had been destroyed after the reorganization. During the next 18 months, a great deal of engineering was done to test and develop the "middleware" that would be necessary to integrate the desktop to deliver enterprise-wide networking services. The network was designed to provide the kind of information sharing and information access which would meet the needs that staff had expressed through a series of surveys and interviews. During this time, too, there was a sense of convergence both within the Bank community and in the technology market. For example, we agreed on the need for a GUI, and a communal and common platform on which information could be accessed, stored, and shared. This agreement was certainly not there at the start of the project, and a great deal of time was spent trying to bring the various IS groups together and get buy-in from them.

Staff at the Bank now have at least minimum skill and familiarity with PCs and are no longer dealing with the fear of computing (except for a small residual percentage). However, the Bank is now dealing with the need to apply computing power and skills to improving the business production and staff productivity. There is a demand to tap into the knowledge base—the documents and knowledge of experts. Like many other organizations, the IS department is busy re-engineering its processes to align them with the needs of the key business units.

With the pilot of the enterprise-wide network, various key managers in the Bank became aware that the Bank's individualist style of work, as exemplified by the standalone personal computer, would change to a collaborative mode of work, as exemplified—and enabled—by networks (see Figure 13.1). The idea of everyone being able to share files and access information across the whole institution, and potentially worldwide, led to great interest being expressed by both technology and user managers in knowing how behavior changes when one makes this move.

13.8 RESULTS AND DISCUSSION

There is a fairly good body of research literature on how information technology (IT) changes the way work is done. Very little of this research, however, focuses on how to *manage* the changes that information technology introduces. Those few researchers who do, however, demonstrate that top management commitment and involvement are essential. These research studies demonstrate that successful implementation of information technology projects all have a high-status business manager as the key actor. The key actor, through active participation,

Fig. 13.1 Progression from Standalone to Collaborative Computing

provides support to the business changes that are driven by—and sometimes impel—the IT changes. Much of the body of IT literature that describes what has happened with the introduction of IT demonstrates how hard it is to implement any new technology without such top management support. Other studies (e.g., [Orlikowski, 1992]) and prior Bank experience have shown that collaboration does not occur unless the work ethos requires it and rewards it, and that simply providing technology does not guarantee behavioral changes. We are dealing with human nature, and unless people use the technology given to them, the investment in technology may never reach its potential. This means that people must be helped to use the tools given them, which is the underlying theme of all the work of the authors. To us, this is far more exciting and challenging than making the technology work in and of itself. That's the easy part! Helping people to feel comfortable, to confront and overcome their fears, and encouraging and enabling management to provide the leadership their staff require in order to reach a stage of sufficient comfort with the tools, is very rewarding—and time consuming. We hope that the results presented here will enable others to help their users to a greater extent than they have done before.

13.8.1 The Network Pilot: From Techno-centric to Socio-technical Approach

From its earliest inception, the network project was masterminded by the IS department with an approach that was almost exclusively technical. While there was some limited participation on the part of the pilot organization, there was the *belief* within the central IS group that the end users were fully involved in the development of the pilot product. This belief persisted despite frequent protests from the pilot department that they were excluded from the design process. From the central IS group's perspective, the user was closely involved in the design and testing of the product; after all, joint meetings were held weekly, and their desire not to have their work disrupted by incomplete products was being respected. From the user's group perspective, they were being held at arm's length, as they had not seen anything usable and had not participated in decision-making meetings or the design of an implementation plan. The net result of this disparity in perceptions was a steadily eroding relationship between the parties involved in the pilot project, to the extent that the user group was considering either purchasing a local area network externally, or taking over the project management themselves.

These different perceptions of the various players took on a life of their own that critically affected the progress and outlook of the network. Where the central IS people conceived of the network as a series of technological systems that would link individual workstations together, the user community conceived of the network as a series of integrated applications that would be delivered to their workstations, thereby enabling them to share work and information easily throughout the organization. The central IS pilot group therefore concentrated on what those technological systems would be, while the end-user community concentrated on what applications they required, such as filing and retrieval of documents—and assumed that the technology would provide them the required stability and surety of both connectivity and accessibility to individuals and information. The central IS group could not understand the frustration of the user pilot group at being given what the latter considered a "raw prototype of the pilot product." Much time elapsed before both sides came to understand just what the other meant by the use of the word "pilot." For example, to the IS engineers, "pilot" meant "try this technology to see if you like it or if it works for you"; but to the end users, it meant "fully developed product that we will test to see if it fits with our business processes." Similarly, "document sharing" or "file sharing" (usually used synonymously) meant "computer files with servers to do backup and so on" to the engineers, but "document sharing with issues of version control, archiving, and so on" to document management staff, and "working on the same document" to the end users.

Thus, different sets of people with different concepts of what was being piloted, and, more important, understanding certain words from different perspectives or contexts, led to increasingly confused and hostile meetings. This led to confusion in defining needs and building systems, and made it far harder to understand what was really meant and for these different units to work together and collaborate and integrate their work toward the goal of a single project like the enterprise network.

Similar "language problems" emerged during the evaluation of the pilot project. The problems that the technologists considered to be minor hiccups and were known to exist well before the pilot was introduced appeared to the users to be much more severe. These were actually perceived as major obstacles by users and created negative perceptions of the whole project. Simply put, if a user cannot print or cannot use a particular software package, the user will blame the network for these problems. In addition, the inconvenience experienced by the users can lead to their rejection or, or resistance to, any new capabilities being supplied. They may become alienated and come to question the viability of all the technology and the credibility of the IS staff.

Communication and coordination emerged as key factors in facilitating—in fact, ensuring—that shared understanding and integration took place. During this study, the researchers discovered that those staff who attended multiple meetings knew far more about what was going on (not surprisingly) than those who only attended one meeting a week. More important, we found that those who attended multiple meetings did not realize that others did not know what was being discussed, that they felt isolated, "stupid" for not understanding what was happening, or "talked down to" when the project leader was giving information. Steps to rectify this situation and provide ways and means to keep everyone informed included more formalized meetings with agendas, minutes that were circulated regularly, a newsgroup on the Internet, and better use of the electronic mail distribution list: in other words, the use of groupware tools to support these different groups.

A new series of groups was convened, with greater involvement of the end users. This was a revolutionary change given the culture in the Bank of group decision making and consensus-seeking prior to any decision being implemented.

Without such accountability, however, the project could not move forward. With the aid of a process facilitator, these various groups of people were helped to understand each other, clarify their terms, and also define appropriate roles and responsibilities. Participants began to function as a team and to work more seriously. As the level of trust increased, the central IS installers began to team up and train the local IS staff and to install the network jointly. The result was greater understanding of the issues and problems that each group faced, as well as better trained local staff who would be in position to support the end users. At the same time, the senior managers of the central IS group and the pilot department got far more involved, held joint meetings, and really demonstrated the importance of high-level management playing the leading roles in the project.

The Bank's experiences thus confirmed the findings from other research: when senior management on both sides became involved, the project made far more progress. With the help of a change agent and process facilitator, the technical experts on both "sides" became a team who appreciated the problems that each side was facing. Table 13.1 depicts a model of successful technology adoption [Rousseau, 1989].

13.8.2 The Users: Their Knowledge, Experience, Attitudes, and Cultures

As with any management initiative, employee buy-in to the technology change effort has a dramatic effect on success. They must want to change because they perceive the change to be in their individual best interests. Otherwise, they will passively or actively resist the change, in either case impeding progress. In the Bank, staff commented that they are not often included in the decision process or even the implementation process. Similarly, staff noted that they are asked to pay the price of an installation of new and often "buggy" software without really knowing what the benefits are. Bank staff have neither the time nor the inclination to tinker with technological tools in order to make them function. Nor will they use the tool if they cannot figure out how, if it is unpleas-

Table 13.1 A Model of Successful Technology Adoption

Vision Practical	Key Actor Support	Belief that change is possible	Identify first steps
SPECIFY ⟶	INVOLVE ⟶	COUNTER ⟶	INSTITUTE
System Configuration	Technical Experts	Resistance to change	Pilot projects
Goals and effectiveness	Implementers/ change managers/ users	Negative norms	
Incremental adoption criteria	High-status members	Individual fears and anxieties	
Impact on positions, work groups, and departments			

ant to do so, or if they are afraid. Staff could not articulate real fears, but suggested what one person actually called "irrational concerns," such as fear of losing information, uncertainty or dread over having to learn a new application or new ways of doing things, interference or downtime at the time of a critical deadline, and so on. These fears are real enough to the users, and ought to be dealt with up front, and often, with leadership, communication, training, and support.

13.8.3 User Experiences

The users themselves have significant influence over the success or failure of a new technology. Bank staff typically fall into four groups: haters/resisters, simple users, proficient users, and power users. "Haters/resisters" tend to be staff who are less familiar with technology. They may be older or from cultures where using such tools is not commonplace—or is even beneath their dignity—and they tend to perceive the technology as an infringement, a nuisance, or even a threat. "Simple users" are staff who have learned to use a few applications, but who are not truly comfortable with the technology. These users had such difficulty learning how to get to their current point of technology utilization that they fear learning more. "Proficient users" tend to be higher-level staff with solid experience working in a computing environment in either the private sector or academia. "Power users" also tend to be higher-level staff who have had some specialized experience in a technical field such as engineering. Midway between the "simple users" and "proficient users" is a group of staff who are typically support staff. They are generally fairly accepting of changing technology, interested in going to training classes to learn new applications, and several of them expressed interest in the office technology support function as a potential career move. To use the terminology of other studies, our "power/proficient" users are the early adopters, "simple users" are follower or basic users, and "haters/resisters" are reluctant users. Not surprisingly, user views were mixed, depending on the category of user. Both the proficient and power users tended to play the role of lead user and to champion (or beg for) more advanced uses of technology for their work processes. The majority of staff, however, fell into the basic user/follower category. For these staff, the typical response was, "oh, no, not another technology change! I've only just gotten comfortable with the previous one." As Andy Burnett [1994] says, "as organizations move toward networking as their main communication medium, parts of the workforce could find themselves excluded from the thinking processes, because they are uncomfortable with networking." What we will need to guard against is islands of staff who become isolated from the mainstream simply by their reluctance to use the technology that is rapidly becoming pervasive throughout the organization.

13.8.4 Culture and Age

Culture and personal characteristics, too, have significant bearing on the acceptance of information technology. For example, older staff are typically not comfortable working with a keyboard and are habituated to writing longhand. Many have great difficulty changing their work patterns and are frustrated when they are forced to type because they find it slower. Also, some cultures associate a negative status with working on a keyboard and no longer having a personal secretary. To minimize these feelings, staff should be provided with information very early in the development process to allow them enough time to get accustomed to the idea and eliminate any unrealistic fears. Such advance efforts could also serve to identify and resolve any special needs of staff in advance of the technology introduction.

A study on older staff noted that this group, more than others, needs to have training closely aligned with their work experience [Staufer, 1992]. "The form of presentation should be as realistic and stimulating as possible: it might be quite favorable to visit a similar place of work where the same computer system has already been installed. Seeing the system actually work and talking to some users can dispel psychological reservations for anxious potential users." Within the context of the Bank, this could be accomplished by visiting other units that are using the network and learning from those actual end users as peers: "...(I)t is best to train older staff members at their familiar place of work. Given the opportunity to learn in the environment they are accustomed to, feelings of anxiety will be less likely to arise. Also enhanced knowledge transfer is obtained when the learning context and the working context resemble each other." It is especially important to explain possible changes in work organization, status, and relationships with coworkers. Training programs should endeavor to relieve anxiety and create a positive attitude toward work with a new technology. Training methods should be tailored to the different learning behaviors of older people and of people of different cultures and backgrounds.

13.8.5 Change in Traditional Roles

It is not only in terms of cultural expectations that the technology is changing the roles of staff. In this study, as well as previous studies at the Bank (e.g., [Bikson and Law, 1993]), staff noted that technology has irrevocably altered the roles and relationships of professional and secretarial staff. Over time, as most of the professional staff have produced their reports using word processors, there has been a corresponding decrease in the actual secretarial content of the support staff jobs. Many support staff are anxiously clinging to the vestiges of their old roles, while others are trying to climb the career ladder using office technology and information technology support as the vehicle. Most professional staff, while reluctant to give up having a personal secretary (and the associated status), are increasingly finding that instead of traditional secretarial support, they now need clerical help to copy and distribute final reports at one end of the support continuum, and information search capabilities and sophisticated document editing and formatting at the other. The Bank apparently needs a hybrid layer of staff that falls between the higher level and support levels, who would be able to understand both the business needs and the technology applications, and so assist all staff in using the technology to accomplish their work. Unless the Bank acknowledges this problem, it will not be able to meet the needs of professional staff once the network providing more sophisticated services, such as access to a variety of internal and external sources of information and electronic document management.

13.8.6 Level of Comfort With Technology

The level of comfort felt by staff toward a technology tool also determines how well that tool will be employed. Staff currently do not feel comfortable sharing files over the network because they are afraid of losing data or overwriting an important file. They perceive the network as something of a "black box," and they are not sure that if they put something into it they will be able to get it back out again. Staff are also unfamiliar with methods for joint document creation and with tracking the location and versions of documents. While staff say it is easy to ship documents from one directory to another, it is very difficult to keep track of where the documents end up and which versions are pertinent. The result is a rising volume of clutter on the network drives and less than optimal use of information resources. This lack of comfort with the tools offered by the network will need to be overcome in order to yield effective utilization.

13.8.7 Human Aspects of Technology Acceptance

Some staff members react negatively to technology because they believe that technology is abused by some of their colleagues. They cite electronic mail and voice mail as examples of technology dehumanizing their working environment. While staff receive hundreds of electronic mail messages per month, some say that there has been an increase in the number of messages of limited value, largely due to increasingly large distribution lists. They are disappointed that this form of networking reduces face-to-face interaction because they feel that electronic messaging is a more formal communication which results in diminishing personal rapport and dwindling teamwork. They argue that this is making the Bank a cold environment and placing increasing stress on those who must use the technology even if they do not have a real interest in it. In a similar fashion, technology can enable poor etiquette to become more prominent. For example, voice mail can be used to screen calls, staff use speaker phones to avoid the extra effort required to pick up the receiver, and electronic mail is used instead of handwritten personal notes or telephone calls. The result is that selfish motivations that really are discourteous degrade the value and the level of personal interaction. These actions themselves may turn staff away from technology, but they also may result in degrading the work environment. While there was evidence of some staff using voice mail and electronic mail technologies to avoid personal contact, this was, in fact, very rare. Nonetheless, the concern of technology dehumanizing the workplace is valid, and requires attention from management and technology staff, through training and constant communication, if staff are to truly embrace the concept of the electronically networked organization.

A study on alienation [Minch and Ray, 1986] provides some useful insights: for example, the study found that "computer alienation, powerlessness and meaninglessness...will lessen after students receive education concerning computers." This demonstrates that education can manage attitudes, and therefore needs to be effectively employed in technology introductions. The study also found that people who feel alienated from computers tend to ignore news about them. Along these lines, we have found time and again that notices about technology tend to be ignored, only those who are interested in technology tend to respond to surveys about technology, and many staff and managers resisted being interviewed about their technology experiences, asking us to talk to the technology expert in their division instead.

13.8.8 Electronic Mail as the Archetype of Networking Change Agent

Shortly after electronic mail was introduced, it became the *de facto* network of the Bank, so much so that many of the staff who were reluctant to embrace new technology, believed that, since they already had a network, the "new network" was being foisted on them by the technology experts. Prior studies (e.g., [Bikson and Law, 1993]) showed how critical electronic mail had become for communication among virtually all staff at the Bank. Nonetheless, Bikson also showed that "although use of the communication network is commonplace, *full and effective use* (italics added) is not. That is, electronic mail is now an indispensable medium for brief internal messages and on-line news, but it has yet to become a generic infrastructure that supports the diverse needs of knowledge workers." Bikson found that electronic mail was rarely used to share anything that exceeded two pages, as either part of the message body or an attachment. More important, it was only rarely used as a basis for collaborative work.

What electronic mail at the Bank actually achieved was the flattening of the organizational hierarchy. Prior to electronic mail, staff sent mail through or via their own managers across the organizational unit and down the receiving unit's organizational chain. With electronic mail, however, staff simply sent their mail directly from their own workstation to the next, regardless of the status or position of the recipient. While at first some senior managers were outraged that "anyone" could send them a message, this anger dissipated over time, and now virtually no one sends any mail "through" any manager. This does not mean that formal and official communications, such as lending documents, do not go through the organizational hierarchy; they do, through a process of review of reports which are ultimately presented to the Board. The main message here is that electronic mail has served to lessen the high degree of formality that governed even simple communications—and no other formal system was put in place to negate the effects of electronic mail.

This finding corroborates Harrington [1991], who argues that "the implementation of information technology through the information network changes the nature of information access by individuals and hence ultimately changes who can make the decisions." Harrington goes further to postulate that the shift in power on the information network may create a new elite membership. While we have not investigated the power relationships over the network to be able to comment sensibly on this point, there are definite signs that the electronic mail network has achieved cultural changes. More important, there is a growing acceptance of the need to change the business processes by involving staff to a far greater extent than ever before. Examples of this trend are the formation of a committee that will not only facilitate but actually fund experiments to improve the way staff work. In a highly unusual move, an electronic mail message was sent to ALL staff in the Bank, explaining this committee, and inviting staff to submit proposals for changes directly to the committee. Aside from working on the many task forces that the Bank sets up to examine various aspects of the organization (typically composed of managers rather than staff), this is the first time that staff have been encouraged—what's more, electronically—to think about changing the organization culture.

13.8.9 User Responses to the Network

Given the relative novelty of the network in the Bank, and the fact that there was no concerted effort to alter work behavior, it was probably unrealistic to expect spontaneous dramatic behavior changes. The changes that were observed were therefore incremental rather than major. For example, staff were using the network to share files rather than passing around hard copies and diskettes. The patterns of network file sharing followed the traditional work flow, with the greatest level of activity at the smallest work group level. As the work moved up the chain of command to cross divisions, departments, and eventually regions, the volume of files transferred dropped dramatically; but, arguably, the importance of file sharing is enhanced, since the network reduces the relevance of physical proximity. Access to the network also tended to elevate the level of expectations of staff. They became aware of what tools are available in the marketplace, and wanted to have them *now*. They wanted to be able to share files with colleagues all over the Bank, without the clumsiness of ALL-IN-1. And they expected the network to function perfectly all the time, including evenings and weekends.

At present, there is a general feeling among staff that the real advantages and disadvantages of networking are not yet clear. Partially this is caused by the fact that networks are not yet omnipresent in the Bank. But also, staff are dubious about the benefits of file sharing and joint document creation. Many staff members feel that their work is highly fragmented, that there is not much of a need to share files or other information, and that any need which does exist is already being met by exchanging diskettes and/or by the rather clumsy method of attaching documents to electronic mail. Staff do recognize that one of the main benefits of the network is the greater ease of file sharing, joint document creation, and data collection. Shared files also makes various macros, databases, information resources, and training resources available on demand, to all staff members. These factors offer improved access and management of information, along with some time savings. Staff also recognize that the network provides the necessary infrastructure to deliver the much-needed greater value-added services, such as desktop messaging, directory services (including a "yellow pages" of Bank experts), and electronic document management systems when these become available.

There were quite a few staff members, too, who were not enamored of the new technology, including those who had been networked for some time and those awaiting installation. All these staff members expressed their concerns in human terms: they were afraid that the network would reduce their contact with their colleagues. Instead of going to a colleague's office with hard copy and a diskette, and perhaps talking to other colleagues en route, they believed—and feared—that they would be expected to "dump their document somewhere in space." As Eagle [1994] points out, transmission media impose greater distance and tend to constrain natural communications. "E-mail has allowed the flow of information, but its protocol requirements add a secondary level of language which limits the freedom of communication. It has allowed us to 'talk' to each other but not in fact (as in face-to-face) or in metaphor (as in letter or phone) to create a full human communications event." Although staff who were not yet connected to the network expressed such fears of lessening the social contacts, in actual practice, those staff who had been networked the longest still discussed their documents with each other and tended to use the network only as a transport medium—they simply did not hand-carry or mail the paper copy or the diskette. Thus, the social contacts remained in place and unchanged. The network also reduced the need to rely on the mail service and/or fax when the colleague was on another floor or in another building. In fact, staff on the network began to be frustrated when they had to work with someone more than a few doors away who was not on the network, and even more resistant to the clumsy file transfer mechanism offered by the electronic mail system.

13.9 THE MOTIVATORS AND INCENTIVES FOR CHANGE

Management has a significant role to play in determining the success or failure of a new technology because management controls the resources of the organization. With a new technology introduction, as with any change effort, management plays a critical role in defining the strategy, providing leadership, and then in implementation through training, support, and communication.

13.9.1 The Manager

Our studies show that staff gradually become more comfortable with the functions of the network, beginning naturally with the functions required most frequently, like printing and file sharing. But the transition has been slow and uneven. Placing a "technological box" on the desk does not appear to be sufficient to get staff interested in using it. Staff must have some incentive to shift their behavior. They must have the benefits of any changes clearly demonstrated to them. If those benefits are not immediately apparent, then they must be forced into making changes either by direct authority or by limitation of alternatives. For instance, the manager who placed on the network the various thoughts and ideas resulting from a divisional retreat and then told staff to enter their ideas and comments and to sign up for participation in some of the action plans, created a reason for his staff to try the network. As a result, this division is far more advanced in their usage of the network to work collaboratively.

As we looked at the differences within and between the various divisions that we studied, we realized that the biggest changes in work styles and use of the technology occurred in those divisions where the division chief took an interest in the use of technology, and actively encouraged staff to use the network. The second influence came from the "lead users," who could demonstrate the business benefits of technology in a context that colleagues could relate to and emulate. In fact, this influence was even greater when the division chief was the lead user. Those divisions where there was no lead user, or where the lead user was not influential on the division chief, showed very minimal use of technology, not through any demonstrable fear or inability, but simply because they did not know what to use it for; they were willing to try something if someone showed them what to do, but they could not even begin to imagine creative uses of technology. These findings confirm the critical success factors cited above, particularly the essential role played by management; the importance of the organization as a whole viewing the IT changes as innovations; and peer learning as a major source of training.

13.9.2 Communication

Communication is essential. Staff noted that, generally, they are not given much information in advance of technological change. Consequently, they do not have an intellectual framework for accepting the changes. Presentations, demonstrations (preferably by peers talking of their own uses and successes), and frequent discussions of the new technology in the context of work all played important roles in fostering an environment that was not only accepting of the changes, but actually encouraged the adoption of new technology and the new ways of working.

With the exception of the initial pilot division, staff did not appear to have received sufficient encouragement on how to develop a network culture. To the majority of the staff, the basic physical functions of the network were described, but very little was done to build a sense of enthusiasm. As a result, many users had not "bought into" the network concept and did not dare to explore anything on their machines. Time constraints also prevented staff from attempting anything new unless they could see a clear current business need. The pilot division, which had a formal "kick-off" meeting with senior management in attendance, followed by classroom and one-on-one training, showed a much higher rate of interest, enthusiasm, and use of the network from the very beginning. These differences were also obvious in the actual training sessions, where those from the pilot division attended more regularly and showed interest in the tools; in contrast, the other staff showed a high degree of resistance to training, including avoiding training altogether.

13.9.3 Support and Training

There is a definite positive correlation between the use of the network and the amount and nature of support and training provided. The first division in the pilot received intensive support and training from both the central and regional IS groups; however, the level of support tapered off as more divisions were installed on the network. Also, as the local divisions took over the support function, the support providers tended to be less knowledgeable and therefore of less help than those providing support for the first division, who were actually on the design team. It became clear as this study progressed that the dividing line between support and training had become blurred. In fact, it seemed that if the support personnel responded to each call for support as an opportunity for training, and took the time to teach staff at their desks in the context of the actual task during which they had required help, then the learning was greatly increased, and the staff member would become an avid user of the network. One-on-one training in the context of work, rather than showing staff how to use the software, though seeming expensive at first, actually turned out to be of greater benefit and potentially lower cost[4] in helping staff use the technology in a more productive manner than the typical training class currently offered in the Bank.

Training is an essential element to the effective application of technological tools. The value of training extends beyond the simple "how to" aspect to breaking down cognitive barriers that keep people from trying something new. Most Bank staff do not know what they can do or conceive of what is possible with the given technology, or even what questions to ask. Training should provide the context they require by explaining the benefits of technology and enhancing the ability of staff to effectively use the equipment dropped on their desktops. There is strong evidence to suggest that the process of learning technology occurs in a step-wise fashion, following the classic learning curve. More significantly, the pattern by which new software is introduced can impact that learning curve. We found that management needed to push their staff to progress up the learning curve by providing more directed learning related to their work that builds on itself step by step. Staff needed to be challenged to perform functions in the network to encourage them to learn how to use it.

The technology itself offers novel ways to deliver training to end users. One of the key senior managers is very keen on the concept of "just-in-time" training, to be delivered at one's desk when one needs it. Experiments are underway to produce computer-based multimedia training, and a prototype is currently being offered over the network. There is also talk of embedding much of the training into the applications in the form of on-line help.

---

[4] Based on the costs of the time of eight participants to attend a half or full day of training with one trainer, compared to the costs of the trainer's time to spend one hour with each of eight participants--for us, the costs of the participants' time are more important than the costs of the trainer's time.

Time and again, it becomes apparent that the technology itself is not as significant as the people using it. "Previous research supports the tight coupling of effective computer use and 'humanware', or the knowledge, skills, abilities and other resources needed to take advantage of available system functions" [Bikson and Law, 1993]. Training is not, however, the only avenue to improved humanware. One option is to provide higher-quality technical assistance/support personnel who could come to a user's workstation and, in the course of providing help, teach the user a difficult function (e.g., to install a macro). Another option is to improve the interface, making access to needed functionality more transparent. Practically speaking, an innovative combination of approaches is needed: what cannot be remedied in the system interface can be made more accessible by advanced training, but for rarely used functions, the provision of special technical assistants is probably more efficient.

In sum, the most important motivator is active management to get staff to utilize the technology they are given, to understand the business benefits, and to encourage and foster the lead users' interests in applying technology to the work processes. Similar conclusions were reached in a prior study of electronic mail use quoted earlier, in which Tora Bikson noted that although email is used by virtually everyone, *full and effective* use is not made of the system. For "electronic mail" we could substitute virtually any piece of technology in the Bank, and this observation would still be true.

13.10 HOW NETWORKING DIFFERS FROM OTHER TECHNOLOGY IN TERMS OF ACCEPTANCE

Technology causes shifts in the typical office power arrangement. Higher-level, professional staff with multiple degrees and strong intellectual capabilities are confronted by machines they are forced to use by the organizational imperatives of getting the work done. Since for the most part they cannot master the machine themselves, they must seek help from others, who are typically further down on the status ladder. Many of them resent being dependent on people who are typically younger, have more technical than business experience, and do not have the equivalent intellectual capacity. For some staff, their feelings of frustration and dependence may cause them to choose not to use the technology, to criticize it openly, to retard growth or change, and even to impede others from using it effectively.

All this takes place simply as a result of working with isolated personal computers. A network, however (at least in its current state), presents an additional layer of dependence. The PC is no longer a personal tool to use or not use as one pleases. In fact, if one chooses not to use the network, one may find oneself cut off from the organization, excluded from the exchange of both formal and informal knowledge, to the extent of not knowing much about what is going on in the organization. There is thus a greater level of coercion and a lowering of freedom of choice to use or not use technology. Guidelines and standards are required by the network, and permission and/or assistance from the network administrator (a new role) is required to add anything new or change anything. The network administrator is therefore thrust into a power position—one of controlling or denying access—and the objectives and concerns of keeping the network running may not be harmonious with the needs of their clientele.

In a sense, the conditions operating within a network community are analogous to a social contract model. The individual with a standalone PC is like a person living in the state of nature. Each individual must give up some independence, some freedom, in order to derive the benefits of belonging to a larger community. But in order to willingly enter into such a contract, the individual must perceive the benefits of belonging to be greater than the sacrifice of freedom. Thus far, in the Bank, the benefits of network computing have not been clearly stated to most users.

Additionally, in the Bank, the person with "institutional memory" is a highly valued member of staff. Consequently, the whole idea of sharing information, of placing it in a central repository where others could access it electronically, is anathema to many Bank staff. Information is thus viewed as both a symbol of power and a source of job security. However, "unlike previous sources of power, such as land and money, information has to be made into something else, something usable, to pay off in power. That fact is not yet widely recognized. Indeed, most efforts to capitalize on the power potential of information seem to come from a miserly perspective" [Brown and Wiener, 1984]. Getting this message across to managers who must send the appropriate signals to staff, and to knowledge workers themselves, will be crucial if we are to realize the potential of the new technology that we are rapidly deploying across the institution. Likewise, we anticipate that the real power will come from those who know how to access the information, as well as the people who are the experts on the subject, rather than from those who, through longevity, maintain the "institutional memory." In fact, we will need to demonstrate and teach that "information, unlike other forms of wealth, can be shared and still wholly retained. Indeed, astute sharing can increase the value of information" [Brown and Wiener, 1994].

13.11 GROUPWARE AS A DATA-GATHERING TOOL

Throughout the project, information was gathered from the various groups involved in the pilot stages. Several focus group meetings were held, at first non-electronically; then, once the electronic meeting room was installed, it was used extensively, with the IS staff and end users. This use of groupware tools added significantly to the amount and quality of information collected during the crucial phases of the project. In the early phases, as may be extrapolated from the description earlier of a "we-they" attitude between the central and local IS groups, there was a great deal of resistance to any negative feedback from the local to the central group. The resistance was, however, hidden, until the central group was presented with the printout from the electronic meeting session. This experience, which necessitated a detailed debriefing by the facilitator, led to a better understanding of the differences between the two groups, and was the catalyst for the subsequent team-building work that took place.

The meeting room was again used to elicit feedback from the ultimate end users, although we were unable to conduct as many sessions as we planned due to the difficulty of scheduling lengthy sessions with busy traveling staff. The sessions that we did run, however, yielded rich information that was then substantiated in individual interviews with those staff who had been unable—or unwilling—to attend the group sessions. An additional benefit from the group sessions was the synergy that emerged as the group not only evaluated the network products, but also shared their problems and solutions. In fact, the greatest benefits that we saw came from staff who typed in problems to which another participant responded with solutions. Staff who did not work together made plans to meet afterwards to learn from one another.

An interesting observation concerning group versus individual interviews concerns the nature of staff that favored either form of data collection. At the Bank, the professional staff typically preferred individual interviews, which are usually shorter than group interviews. Support staff, on the other hand, favor group interviews. Those who did not attend the groupware sessions tended to call on colleagues to join them during what had been scheduled to be individual interviews. A similar observation was made relating to preferred modes of training: support staff typically like going to classes and learning together, while professional staff prefer to learn one-on-one at their desks.

13.12 IMPLEMENTATION

As we have demonstrated, an essential ingredient for successfully managing and implementing any change action is the presence of a high-level, well-respected organizational actor to lead the planning effort and to champion the project on a full-time basis. The implementation team must consist of employees with substantial business experience and a strong sense of organizational strategy. Communication across a wide platform of interested and knowledgeable people is essential, both to keep people informed of progress and to gain feedback as to expectations, requirements, modifications desired, and so on. We have also confirmed the need for a sociotechnical approach to implementation. The need to involve staff with a sociotechnical perspective directly in the project and as facilitators during meetings became obvious—particularly once staff perceived the dramatic changes in relationships and progress on the project once the facilitator joined the project staff. From our experience, implementation must be incremental and dynamic, and not expected to produce immediate results, thereby allowing time for users to experiment and gain confidence with the new systems. The implementation team, and indeed the whole organization, must view the new system as an innovation explicitly involving experimentation and risk.

13.13 WHAT GROUPWARE TECHNOLOGY ENABLES YOU TO DO

Network technology and recognition of the value of information access, together with technology that will automate the routine and mundane work, promises a change in the focus of work for knowledge workers. Once knowledge workers no longer have to deal with the routine work, they will have the time and scope to focus on the parts that cannot be automated and to use their brains to be creative and innovative. Of particular relevance in this regard is the ability to quickly locate relevant documents, whether they were created by someone down the hall or across the world. Instead of reconstructing information that exists, or used to exist, on a computer or piece of paper somewhere in your organization, but which cannot be shared or found when needed, knowledge workers will be able to use this time on more creative and productive pursuits.

13.13.1 The Virtual Team or Organization

While the network environment has clearly not yet revolutionized the end users' situation, it has provided the necessary first steps of getting users to start thinking of themselves as part of an electronic group or community, and to think about new ways of using that network power. Sharing common information, such as spreadsheets, budgets, and business plans; developing a common divisional rolodex of clients and other contacts; developing a common telephone directory with flexible searches and automatic dialing features; and electronic bulletin boards are some of the uses to which staff are putting the network. Other areas they are exploring are the provision of calendaring and scheduling systems, shared project management tools to provide all members of a project team with pertinent project information and the capability to update this information continuously. What staff are most interested in is having access to some regular mechanism that would disseminate best practices or good ideas for using the network.

All this points to the emergence of a fledgling electronic community, the faint glimmerings of a virtual organization. Groupware tools such as the Bank is using enable organizations to link electronically dispersed employees to create a virtual organization, which could cross organizational and international boundaries. What the Bank is ultimately aiming for is a global network that will enable staff to tap into information resources and communicate with anyone else regardless of where they are (Figure 13.2). The current limitations include the state of technology, the level of computer sophistication (beyond basic literacy) of the staff, and, for our organization, the limitations of telecommunications capacity of many of our borrowing client countries. "The power of the virtual team is that it overcomes the tyranny of distance...(But), the rise of groupware means that people will work with a wider range of other people in their firms and other organizations" [Watson *et al.*, 1994]. At the Bank, we already have people working on ad hoc teams composed of staff from inside and outside the Bank. Electronic mail made communications between these team members far easier and

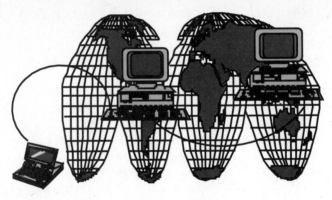

Fig. 13.2 Network Collaboration, the Global Aim

quicker, and for those staff in other countries, has reduced the tyranny of working not only in different countries but also in different time zones. Staff using the network are now asking for electronic contacts with non-Bank team members and clients in other countries.

13.14 HUMAN ISSUES

What has been postulated is that, with electronic networks, individuals will be more frequently involved in ad hoc teams, but paradoxically will be less tightly bonded to colleagues, "because electronic teams tend to have a lower level of social bonding than physical teams" [Watson *et al.*, 1994]. The concerns voiced by Bank staff, of reduced social contacts because of the electronic emotionless network, are thus echoed elsewhere. Without the human touch—or with potentially reduced human contact—managers will need to work far harder on developing team spirit, on ensuring occasions where team members can meet face-to-face, and also exploring the use of other tools in the groupware arsenal such as video-conferencing so team members at least know what their colleagues look like! It is likely that in electronic communities of knowledge workers such as the Bank, the pattern of greater direct horizontal communication will apply equally between the internal organizations, their internal and external clients, and their subcontractors. In so doing, there are very significant cultural and language differences to be taken into account when considering collaborative working between organizations on an international basis.

The most significant and intractable obstacles to the implementation of groupware are not technical, but come from a source much deeper and longer-established than computer science—human nature. Time and again, it becomes apparent that the technology itself is not as significant as the people using it. We have shown repeatedly in this chapter the importance of paying attention to what Bikson called "humanware," the skills, attitudes, and apprehensions of the people who will use the tools. In addition to enhancing training programs, management also needs to track the progress of staff and the relative impact of various programs. "Follow-up measurement is essential if managers are to ensure that lessons stick and stay stuck" [Dale, 1992]. Some suggested methods for gathering such information include random telephone calls, enlisting managers to monitor skill levels and then polling managers, and using help-desk data or on-line polling.

On another, deeper level is the issue of "how, in the individualistic cultures of the West, can collaboration be fostered" [Dale, 1994]. It is very difficult for people to give up their tendency to keep what they know to themselves if they believe this is a source of power to them, and to realize that if they do, then the organization will benefit from having it shared. The sophisticated use of information technology tools, particularly groupware tools, is in fact leading to a situation where the routine and repetitive aspects of knowledge work will be automated, thus freeing up the knowledge worker to deal with the unstructured, nonroutine, ad hoc aspects—potentially the more creative and innovative aspects of their work. The various attempts at business process innovation or re-engineering are also steps in this direction, aiming to reduce the repetitive nature of work, and simplifying work by creating automated versions of the process, which may include expert systems. Combined, these forces will point to a time when the whole nature of office work changes such that knowledge workers spend more time applying their knowledge and less time searching for information that exists, repeating routine tasks, and so on. Robert Heller [1990] postulates that "as information systems take over more and more of the structured activities (which are) tasks that can be shaped in advance, and taught by rote, and which never vary significantly," so the number of people employed to execute these tasks will decline. "At the same time, the number of management staff and professionals working on the 'unstructured' needs will continue to swell. Unstructured tasks cannot be taught by rote, vary continually, and shape themselves as they progress. They fall to executives, professional staff, and knowledge workers." Helping these types of staff use the technology appropriately and effectively will become the major challenge for the immediate future.

Computer networks can be a powerful agent for social change, provided they are tailored to the needs of the function or organization they serve. The IS relationship with the organization is changing to a "computing universe" with the user at the center, instead of the organization [DeLisi, 1990]. A genuine fear of people is that electronic communication will dehumanize their daily working lives. Unless and until this fear is demonstrated to be unrational, and/or alternative ways of socializing are instituted deliberately by managers to ensure face-to-face interaction, people will be reluctant to embrace any concept of electronic community or virtual organization. In this context, DeLisi believes that team building and electronic communication can conflict with each other, and, if this is so, that conflict must be managed. "We do know (three) things: (1) we need to continue face-to-face dialogue even though participants are far away from each other and even though we communicate increasingly through electronic means; (2) many-to-many forms of communication seem to foster team building despite the lack of face-to-face communication...and (3) to develop a shared set of values."

13.15 CONCLUSIONS

Despite having had electronic mail throughout the organization for at least seven years (even ten years in some parts), the Bank is a long way from being an electronic community of electronically collaborating staff, let alone a virtual organization. The human issues involved in implementing new technology, particularly dealing with the rational and emotional fears of people, the need to ensure social contacts with colleagues, and the leadership role of the manager, all require great attention if we are to succeed in becoming a virtual organization.

We found that the effectiveness of a new technology introduced into an organization is highly dependent upon the management of both the process and the people. Technology really is no different from any other organizational initiative. Technology change must be managed in order to be effective. From this study and others we conclude that the following are critical for the successful introduction of technology which will change the way the organization works:

- ☞ Commitment at the highest levels of management to a clearly defined vision of where the organization is headed in terms of technology. Such high-status managers or "product champions" must identify and communicate specific, attainable objectives with clearly defined roles and responsibilities for all staff. Both the implementation team and the wider organization must view the IT changes as innovations that explicitly involve experimentation and risk.

- ☞ Consistent and effective communication of the organizational vision to all staff. Communication should be thought out well in advance and carefully coordinated. Some communication should follow the hierarchical chain of command and take advantage of authority roles, for such things as nomenclature or policy. Others are better delivered on a peer-to-peer level, for pointers on how to do various functions better. Whenever possible, communication should also be used as a means of training, for example, when installing a network, use the network to communicate with staff.

- ☞ Implementation of appropriate training and support programs. Similar to communications, training should be delivered through any and all available means, and those means should be carefully selected by management according to the desired effect. For example, large group training sessions may be the best forum for general introductory information, but one-on-one sessions generally are perceived to be better for getting an individual up to speed. Peer learning should be recognized as a major source of training, particularly because it may take as long as six months to master the new environment. Support needs to be coordinated and managed flexibly because some structures are better than others, depending on the circumstances. Central units, multidisciplinary help desks, and local consultants all have their roles, but each is not useful all the time. Effective support depends on the effective management and allocation of these resources to the appropriate situations.

☞ The focus of all efforts must be on the sociotechnical changes which involve planning for both the technological and organizational structure changes that technology will introduce. The sociotechnical approach includes user participation, interactive systems and program design, resources specifically allocated for training, and norms of supportive learning and experimentation (rather than immediate results).

ACKNOWLEDGEMENT

The author wishes to acknowledge her research associate, Christopher P. Melly, for his contributions to this chapter.

REFERENCES

1. Bikson, T.K., and Law, S.A. [1993], "Electronic Mail Use at the World Bank: Messages from Users," *The Information Society*, vol. 9.
2. Brown, A., and Wiener, E. [1984] *Supermanaging: How to Harness Change for Personal and Organizational Success*, McGraw Hill, p. 243.
3. Burnett, A. [1994], "Computer Assisted Creativity," in *Groupware in the 21st Century: Computer Supported Co-operative Working Toward the Millennium*, ed. P. Lloyd, Adamantine, p. 203.
4. Dale, T. [1992], "Strategic Outlook, End-User Training, Knowledge Experts," *CIO*, September 15, 1992, pp. 35-50, p. 45.
5. Dale, T. [1994], "The Evolution of Interpersonal Computing," in *Groupware in the 21st Century: Computer Supported Co-operative Working Toward the Millennium*, ed. Peter Lloyd, Adamantine, p. 186.
6. DeLisi, Peter S. [1990], "Lessons from the Steel Axe: Culture, Technology, and Organizational Change," *Sloan Management Review*, Fall 1990, p. 90.
7. Eagle, Ron [1994], "Aquarius Dawning: Human Communications in the Twenty-first Century," p. 224, in *Groupware in the 21st Century: Computer Supported Co-operative Working Toward the Millennium*, ed. Peter Lloyd, Adamantine.
8. Harrington, Jon [1991], *Organizational Structure and Information Technology*, Prentice Hall, p.158.
9. Heller, R. [1990], *Culture Shock: The Office Revolution*, London: Hodder & Stoughton, p. 30.
10. Keen, Peter W. G. [1991], Note to the World Bank, *Review of the ITF paper on the Bank's Enterprise Network for the 1990s*, July 25, 1991.
11. Minch, Robert O., and Ray, Nina M., "Alienation and Computer User Attitudes," *College of Business, Boise State University, 7th International Conference on Information Systems*, December 15-17, 1986, ACM.
12. Orlikowski, Wanda J. [1992], "Learning from Notes: Organizational Issues in Groupware Implementation," *CSCW'92 Proceedings*, also *Groupware '93 Proceedings*.
13. Rousseau, Denise M., "Managing the Change to an Automated Office: lessons from five case studies," *Office: Technology and People*, 4, 1989, pp. 31–52.
14. Schein, Edgar H. [1988], "Innovative Cultures and Organizations," *Management in the 1990s Sloan School of Management,* MIT 90s:88–064, p. 8.
15. Staufer, Michael [1992], "Technological change and the older employee: Implications for introduction and training," *Behavior & Information Technology*, vol. 11, no. 1, pp. 46–52.
16. Watson, R. T., Bostrom, R. P., and Dennis, A. R. [1994], "Fragmentation to Integration," in *Groupware in the 21st Century: Computer Supported Co-operative Working Toward the Millennium*, ed. Peter Lloyd, Adamantine, pp. 38–39.

BIOGRAPHY

Lesley-Ann Shneier is a social scientist in the Organization and Business Practices Department of the World Bank. During her ten years with the World Bank, she has applied her knowledge of people and her skills in organizational change and resistance to change, to the process of introducing new information technologies to staff. She has designed and conducted executive development programs to introduce managers to the concepts and benefits of information technology, particularly groupware technologies. She has also conducted action research into how the organization and structure of work and staffing requirements change as a result of introducing information technology, including the impact on staffing structures, and the competencies and skills required. She is particularly interested in enabling staff to absorb and use new groupware technologies, building on their current level of computer literacy, to become more effective and efficient in their work. As an experienced facilitator in electronic and traditional meeting tools, she utilizes electronic meeting room tools in the course of her research projects. She is currently working on implementing the results of this research to enable the World Bank to create a culture of an electronically collaborative community regardless of place or time.

Prior to joining the World Bank, Ms. Shneier worked as general manager, Human Resources for Dun & Bradstreet in Australia and South Africa. Both companies were engaged in a major computerization project in collaboration. Ms. Shneier was responsible for the design and development of training programs, skills assessment programs, and the retraining and re-allocation of staff to different functions.

She has degrees in social work and a graduate degree in personnel management and organization behavior from the University of Witwatersrand Graduate School of Business Administration in Johannesburg, South Africa.

Introduction to Chapter 14

This chapter is in the implementation section of this text because it deals with the use of groupware at a commercial bank and is particularly interesting when compared with Lesley Schnier's chapter about groupware at the World Bank. Both organizations employed groupware as a technology for a solution to a business problem. In the case of the Bank of Montreal, the ability to deliver better customer service was the prime motivator for installing groupware.

Furthermore, this chapter was written by a banker, not a consultant, vendor, or technologist, as were the other chapters. A business person, helping his organization grapple with the technical and cultural changes brought about by groupware, works from a different perspective.

Michael Frow does a great job of characterizing the "CenterPoint" system, the Bank of Montreal's groupware system, and he examines many of the issues that other large commercial organizations are dealing with: moving from the mainframe to the LAN, retooling IS for the 20th century, a focus on clients rather than information systems, empowering the employee, ubiquitous access to information, and redeployment of personnel.

Michael takes us through the reasons the bank decided to embark on this project; he examines the Bank's goals, how they chose the vendor and groupware products to meet their needs, implemented the prototype, and reviewed it and set standards for the whole organization. He then moves into the pilot program and its project management aspects.

Finally, Michael discusses the organizational challenges which confronted his pilot. These challenges were met through the use of multidisciplinary teams.

He then examines the cultural changes this project caused and some of the issues around redeployment of personnel (a touchy issue at best). Specifically, the numbers of support staff and middle managers were reduced because the new system allowed bank officers and managers to assume many of the functions these personnel had previously performed. However, keyboard and other hardware-related skills are necessary to assume these responsibilities, so additional training was necessary before managers and bank officers could use the information systems and groupware that were available to them.

Although not a technologist, Mr. Frow had to become familiar with the technology as well as the business and organizational issues. The primary lesson we learn from this chapter is that to succeed with groupware you really need a strong personality, a champion. This champion should be part of upper-level business management, but with some knowledge of technology and a commitment (and the power) to change.

Finally, Mr. Frow brings us up to the present, or at least where CenterPoint was in November 1994 when this chapter was written. He examines current project status, its success, and where they are planning to take the project over the next year. He looks at the critical factors for their success and gives some advice to others who will follow on this path. All in all, the insight Mr. Frow brings to this chapter makes it a worthwhile read for anyone interested in any aspect of groupware!

Groupware at the Bank of Montreal

Michael Frow
Bank of Montreal

14.1 INTRODUCTION

The Bank of Montreal is one of the largest banks in North America, employing approximately 35,000 people worldwide and providing a full range of personal and corporate financial services in both Canada and the U.S. The Corporate and Institutional Financial Services group (the "Corporate Bank") provides financial services to large corporate clients, financial institutions, and governments worldwide, employing approximately 1200 people, primarily in North America. This abstract reviews the experience of the Corporate Bank in deploying the Center-Point Relationship Management System, a major group-wide, object-oriented, client-server groupware application.

In conjunction with its wholly owned Chicago-based subsidiary, Harris Bank, the Bank of Montreal is unique in North America in the breadth of services that can be provided on both sides of the U.S. and Canadian border. The Corporate Bank's clients typically require individually crafted solutions to meet their financial objectives, which in turn demands the active cooperation of skilled professionals within the Corporate Bank, often in a variety of locations. The market is highly competitive, requiring superior levels of client service and originality, frequently within tight time and price constraints. High standards of internal controls are also important as the failure of a bank to maintain a high-quality loan portfolio will invariably result in either the failure of the bank itself, or at least the loss of its independence.

My own background is very much within the business rather than the technology community of the Bank, having worked in Canada and the United States

in both the Bank's Personal and Commercial Financial Services Group and the
Corporate Bank. At the inception of the project I was based in Toronto, with primary responsibility for the Corporate Bank's credit function, supporting the provision of financial services to other financial institutions worldwide. For the past
year I have been based in Chicago, with primary responsibility for administering
the credit function supporting the provision of financial services to large U.S.-
based corporate clients. My involvement with CenterPoint arose as a result of my
membership in a small steering committee guiding the use of technology within
the Corporate Bank and a long-standing interest in the use of technology to
improve business effectiveness. For the past two and a half years, I have
reported to the Vice Chairman with respect to the implementation of Center-
Point in addition to my credit responsibilities.

14.2 ORIGINS

The origins of CenterPoint™ were somewhat unusual. The Corporate Bank has
relied on mainframe systems to manage and deliver its products for many years,
and with the advent of the PC, rudimentary local and wide area networks were
developed throughout the Corporate Bank. Individuals and individual groups
varied widely in their use of technology with some pockets of innovation in various locations, particularly in the U.S. By 1991 electronic mail was widely available and used, but apart from this, PCs were used primarily as personal, rather
than enterprise, productivity tools. In late 1991 the technology community that
supported the Corporate Bank advised the business community that a backlog of
projects requested by them had developed and that business community cooperation was requested in reviewing the project list to assist with determining project
priorities. A small group of business representatives was established to review
the outstanding project list from a business priority perspective. It rapidly
became apparent that a considerable amount of effort was being expended to further develop existing applications that had limited life expectancy, and that
many requests from individual areas within the Corporate Bank contained significant similarities but were treated as multiple separate projects. Perhaps
more important, however, was that the utilization of technology was not clearly
focused around key business strategies and priorities.

Very few projects survived—most were suspended (and eventually canceled), while a more comprehensive and fundamental review took place centered
around determining what Corporate Bankers needed on their desk to provide the
quality of service demanded by the Corporate Banking clients. The review took
place with the benefit of three key research sources, namely staff interviews, a
client survey, and a continuous improvement study of the lending process within
the Corporate Bank. Approximately 50 staff interviews were conducted with a
representative cross-section of individuals drawn from all areas and functions of
the Corporate Bank. A survey of the Corporate Bank's clients, conducted by an
independent third party, was also extensively used to assist in determining clients' perceptions of strengths and weaknesses of the Corporate Bank's client ser-

vice and ongoing expectations of their bankers. Lastly, a dedicated team of business individuals had been working for some months, undertaking a continuous improvement review of the credit process within the Corporate Bank, identifying areas that could benefit from re-engineering, business process change, or technological innovation.

One key theme that emerged strongly from each of the areas was the need to organize all information and processes around clients rather than around internal functions, departments, or products. Another theme that became evident was the need to leverage the intellectual capital of employees to promote greater levels of creativity in crafting solutions to meet client needs. It was clear that we needed to become better at sharing both information and expertise, and that groupware would represent a key component of the business re-engineering.

14.2.1 Organizing Information Around Clients

The Corporate Bank, like many other large organizations, has evolved over many years around specialty departments or functions such as relationship management, credit, individual product delivery, product development, quality control, and numerous other functions. In organizational terms, these separate areas can be thought of as silos or stovepipes that allow the organization to realize economies of scale and specialization. Each of these areas maintained their own paper-based files and had invested in technology over many years to automate processes or transactions within their specialized area or to provide management information. For example, computer-based systems were developed to manage loans, treasury products, documentary credits, cash management, statutory reporting, and so on. In the Corporate Bank, over 40 computer systems/databases are utilized to manage client relationships. In addition, each department maintains its own paper-based files. This plethora of paper and computer files, together with separate organizational departments, leads to fragmentation in the management of relationships which can be visible to clients, and also a source of frustration and inefficiency for Bank staff when they try to gather a comprehensive view of a client's relationship with the Bank. As noted above, the silo structure of an organization is largely driven by organizational efficiency considerations. While they can and do produce significant efficiencies, they can also promote the growth of solitude with differing sets of values in the various silos. In turn, the maintenance of silo values can compete with organizational values of satisfying client needs. In many instances, silos have little to do with optimizing client service. Indeed, as delivery of products and services to clients frequently requires cooperation between silos, it may become somewhat of a challenge to provide seamless service to clients. Seamless service to clients requires that information within the silos be shared and that high-quality systems are in place to facilitate individuals in different silos working together effectively in multifunctional teams.

In large part, the design of CenterPoint is centered around the importance of drawing information residing in the various silos, whether in the form of paper or computer files, into one shared, comprehensive, client-focused source and providing tools that enable staff to work together effectively in virtual teams—in short, to refocus information and processes around clients and not around internal silos or products.

14.2.2 Creativity

Just as the research indicated a strong convergence of both clients and staff on the need to focus information and processes around clients, so too was the need to be able to demonstrate reliably and consistently creativity in meeting clients' needs reinforced by both constituencies. Financial products are highly flexible and subject to customization, and clients strongly expressed their desire for creative solutions and products to meet their needs. Staff expressed complementary needs for reducing drudgery and process and being provided with improved manipulative tools and access to information from both internal and external sources to enable them to respond quickly and creatively to client needs.

14.2.3 Remote Access

Review of the research material also clearly indicated the need to be able to function effectively anywhere at any time. Many of the Corporate Bank's clients are located geographically distant from the Bank's offices. Professionals working on a particular client's needs may also be located in different geographical areas, and the marketplace is demanding the ability to respond to client needs whenever and wherever the individuals associated with fulfilling that need happen to be.

14.3 THE PROTOTYPE

Armed with the above research and conclusions, work commenced on building a solution. It was apparent that technology, and groupware in particular, would represent a key enabler. As a solution clearly required a high degree of integration of existing automated and nonautomated systems at the enterprise, rather than silo, level, it was also apparent that the solution represented a considerable technological challenge. What was not clear was that a full set of satisfactory solutions existed to meet all the established needs in an adequate manner. To assist with managing the risks associated with such a broad project, it was decided to adopt a prototyping methodology with clearly defined time frames and reviews. An initial goal of demonstrating proof of concept within a three-month time period was established.

It was apparent that the Corporate Bank did not possess all the skills necessary to build a solution within the short time frame established. The search for an external technology partner was more difficult than anticipated, as many vendors were primarily interested in selling their own products and services rather than helping the Corporate Bank integrate pre-existing systems with new products from a variety of different vendors. Additionally, the paradigm of many vendors was still very much based on the use of technology within a silo rather than enterprise-wide across silos. Digital Equipment of Canada was one of a few who truly listened to the Bank's need, and they were selected as the primary external technology partner. The project was seen by a number of companies within the technology community as a valuable laboratory for developing experience in an emerging technology, and many vendors provided product, or knowledge during the prototype period at nominal cost.

The project team itself was drawn from the technology and business communities within the Bank and the external technology partner. The prototype was run as a business project rather than a technology project with three project managers, two drawn from the Bank with both business and technology backgrounds and one from the external partner. Developers were given a month to establish high-level specifications for the products in their assigned areas with business representatives and to pick their development tools. They were then given a month to deliver their applications with constant business user feedback as products were developed. The final month of the prototype was set aside to validate the integrated solution within a real business unit of approximately 25 users.

The prototype (see Figure 14.1) was focused upon:

1. Building an electronic file that could be shared with all individuals throughout the Corporate Bank who needed access to that information; in other words, establishing one shared client file that could replace the existing separate paper-based files maintained by different departments on the same client. A rudimentary imaging facility was incorporated.
2. Providing for electronic signatures and routing of correspondence.
3. Delivery of a real-time news feed to users' desks that could be tailored to their own client base or area of interest.
4. Establishing a library for internal Bank information, which was previously distributed in manual format, that could be electronically searched and accessed.
5. Delivery of an electronic conferencing facility.
6. Establishing the viability of utilizing a customer information file (CIF) that provided for the integration of existing, predominantly mainframe computer systems. The design called for the CIF not to duplicate the information from existing systems, but rather to contain information as to the location of data on other systems. A call for information on the CIF would in turn generate a call to the system containing the required information, returning it to the application that was seeking it. In this way the user does not have to access separate systems to get information and does not need to know where information is actually located or how to retrieve it.
7. Implementing an automated credit application form that would use the CIF above to obtain information from a variety of systems and record it on the document, permit cutting and pasting from other sources, and be capable of electronic routing.

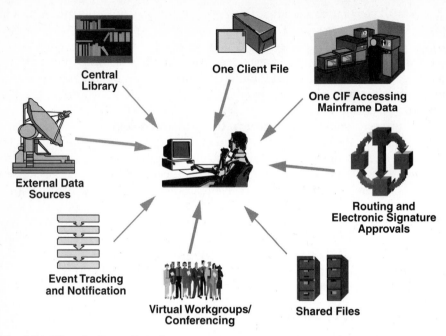

Fig. 14.1 What Is CenterPoint?

A group of users with limited exposure to PCs were chosen as the prototype site to more conclusively demonstrate usability. The prototype was built within the three-month time frame and clearly demonstrated proof of concept. The system was extensively demonstrated throughout the Corporate Banking business community and was embraced as the way the Corporate Bank wanted to conduct its business. The magnitude of the cultural change and potential for business process change also became apparent and will be discussed more fully later.

14.4 ARCHITECTURAL REVIEW AND STANDARDS SETTING

Development of the prototype necessitated implementing technology solutions in areas where standards had not been established within the Bank. The prototype was built to demonstrate proof of concept rather than development of a production-quality solution that could be implemented on an enterprise-wide basis. Accordingly, it was necessary to undertake an architectural and standards review to assist in establishing a blueprint for a production-quality system. This review took three months and represented a considerable challenge to complete, given the number of areas within the technology arena that were impacted and the imposition of generally tighter time frames than were historically the case with tasks of this magnitude. A clear commitment to open systems emerged, with endorsement of an object-oriented, client-server environment as the only framework within which required functionality could be delivered with the necessary performance and security. Additionally, the Bank wished to maintain as much vendor and platform independence as possible and ensure that applications developed were portable between different platforms. From the business community the imperative of remote access was reinforced, which made the technology deliberations that much more complex. The review was completed in January 1993, following which a pilot program was established to build a production-quality system while continuing to build on the functionality established in the prototype phase.

Figure 14.2 illustrates the evolution of the technology implementation.

14.5 THE PILOT

Following the success of the prototype, a pilot program was established, again based on the active testing and involvement of an expanded group of business users located in both Toronto and Chicago. The multifunctional project management structure of business, internal, and external technology resources was maintained. Initially, the focus was on designing and building the production version, which was accomplished within approximately six months, followed by extensive testing and refining based on user feedback. At the completion of the pilot, approximately 170 users in both cities had been brought up on Center-Point. The total pilot period lasted a little more than a year and included a comprehensive analysis of the impact of the technology on the business activities and financial performance of the Corporate Bank.

I have been asked in the past to detail how we structured our teams and established charters, reporting relationships, and the like, and it is probably appropriate to review this aspect in a little more depth. As was previously indicated, three senior project managers were appointed. One of these project managers, who has remained with the project since inception, had experience in the relationship management function prior to her transfer to the technology function a few years before the CenterPoint project commenced. The rationale behind this original transfer was to provide the technology community with a better idea as to the needs of the business community, and when the CenterPoint project commenced she was a natural candidate to be a senior project leader, given her firm grasp of business needs and understanding of and experience working with technology resources. The other Bank-appointed project manager had a strong analytical background, having worked in a number of business and technology areas. As the project matured and the focus shifted away from development to implementation, this individual was succeeded by an individual with more experience in implementing large-scale projects. Throughout the project we have worked with two senior project managers from Digital, both of whom have exhibited not only strong technical and project management skills, but also a well-developed business sense. The remainder of the core team, generally somewhere between six to ten people, has been made up of individuals with primary responsibility for application development, integration, network setup and configuration, training, and project reporting and control.

a. An evolving architecture - before

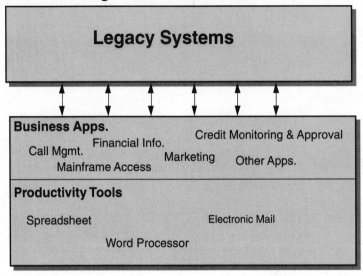

b. An evolving architecture - Phase 1

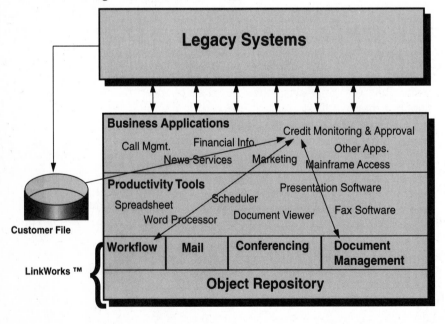

Fig. 14.2 The Evolution of the Architecture

c. An evolving architecture - Phase 2

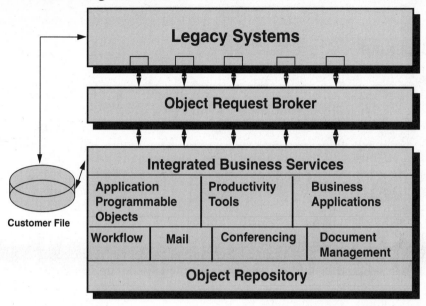

Fig. 14.2 Continued

At the beginning of the project, formal individual mandates were not provided to the project management team—collective responsibility was emphasized. Indeed, prior to any work taking place the whole project team was taken off-site to participate in team-building exercises because it was recognized that the team would have to work together somewhat differently from previous projects where individual roles were more clearly defined, with more formal reporting structures. As many parts of the technology community were impacted by a project of this scope, but often not to the extent that it made sense for a dedicated resource to be assigned to the project team, much of the work was accomplished by ad hoc teams assembled at the time a need was identified and dissolved when the objective was accomplished. Weekly meetings of the project team and key individuals within the technology community management structure were held, and these formed a critical part of the strong discipline that is needed around a project of this magnitude. They provided a senior forum to make decisions quickly as circumstances changed, acted as an important communication vehicle, enabled issues to be tracked and resolved, and ensured resources were made available as needed and bottlenecks minimized. Minutes were also circulated from this meeting to the business and technology communities to ensure that appropriate individuals were kept fully advised of progress and outstanding issues. Above all, teams and individual team members were expected to be proactive—for example, they should not wait for a user to develop a list of specifications but were expected and accountable for developing such specifications with users—they were expected to be as involved with the order as with the delivery of the product.

14.6 CENTERPOINT'S STRUCTURE

CenterPoint is built around Digital's Linkworks framework, which provides a powerful, object-oriented integration environment. It has good administrative tools with users and workstations set up independently, providing the ability to tailor access to the system by geography and time. The Bank's clients are sensitive to the extent information on them is made available throughout the Bank, and the maintenance of access rights at the document or object level is very important, particularly in a shared file environment. While Linkworks has the ability to operate across a variety of server and client platforms, we have chosen to implement it within a Windows environment at the client level, running on predominately 486-based PCs with 12M of RAM. While we have successfully tested using both Macintosh and UNIX-based workstations alongside PCs, the wider availability of Windows software, coupled with cost and support considerations, has resulted in only Windows-based clients being implemented.

The structure at the server level is more complex, with a TCP/IP communication standard being used to tie the various environments together. Linkworks™ is run from an OSF1 server with Oracle as the main database for information objects. One Linkworks server has been established in each site. The Customer Information File, which provides real-time access to a number of mainframe databases, is maintained on a VAX using a Sybase database. A variety of other servers also provide special services; for example, an OS/2 server provides the WAN with real-time news feeds. The Novell LAN has been maintained and provides for delivery of a number of applications and some maintenance and security functions.

14.7 FINDINGS

At the inception of the project it was clearly understood that the business process and cultural implications of CenterPoint were significant. Historically, the deployment of technology was undertaken very much on a departmental or functional basis. By its very nature a departmental or functional type of deployment places bounds within the organization around which the impact of a particular project will be felt. CenterPoint's implementation was different in that being groupware in nature and being deployed throughout an enterprise, it would impact the way everyone did their job and materially impact the content of many of those jobs. It was also understood as an agent of change—a tool to help the Corporate Bank refocus attention and activity externally around clients. The following discussion will highlight some of the principal findings of CenterPoint implementation to date with respect to both the business and technology communities within the Corporate Bank.

14.7.1 Project Management

A prototyping methodology with cross-functional teams is probably essential for applications of the scope of CenterPoint if they are to be implemented in short time frames and yield the functionality required by the end user. In many organizations, the business and technology communities are two solitary areas that do not communicate and work together optimally. Typically, technology orders are "handed off" by the business to technology, who then work on building products to be "handed off" back to the business. They frequently take so long to develop and implement that they no longer meet all the requirements of the business when they are completed, and both parties remain dissatisfied. The response is often to add new processes and checks to ensure that specifications are more clearly documented and adhered to which will, in all probability, add to the delivery time and cost without necessarily increasing the quality of the product. There is also the very real problem of specifying what is required, particularly with complex systems like CenterPoint where a user will probably not be able to fully specify their requirements until they have some elementary experience using it. There can also be problems with accountability. The business takes no responsibility or ownership of the product during the development stage, and it is perhaps not surprising that what is delivered does not fully meet business needs or expectations. The technology community believes it delivered what was asked for and that the business community must take responsibility for inadequate specification of their requirements. The technology community is frequently seen by the business as one community, whereas it has been structured with its own silos that do not necessarily talk or work well with one another. They are also further removed from the Bank's real clients, with the consequence that the sense of urgency attached to addressing business community needs and competition can be severely diluted. The paradigm of "hand-off" referred to above needs to be replaced with one of "hand-shake," where both business and technology remain engaged, committed, and accountable for product quality (see Figure 14.3).

The organizational challenges that are faced when trying to implement major change are severe. The Corporate Bank's approach has been to establish multidisciplinary teams as much as possible—users sitting down with developers, communications experts, data security and mainframe access specialists, and so on. Major components are prototyped since not all problems or requirements can be foreseen on a drawing board, and frequently user requirements evolve as the product itself is developed. Additionally, dispute resolution mechanisms must be clearly and credibly established—where consensus cannot be reached, the issue must be rapidly raised for resolution. Our experience initially was that it was not always easy (even for technologists among themselves) to reach consensus, particularly among individuals who were not used to working in a prototyping environment. After some early testing of the dispute resolution mechanism—final decision by a panel of two technology representatives and one business representative—the mechanism was used less and less, to the point where most individuals working on the project have probably forgotten about its existence today.

Fig. 14.3 The Paradigm Shift

Equally important as prototyping is the need to continually focus on the business drivers of the project rather than the technology itself. With a project of this magnitude, it is all too easy to focus on the tool rather than the reasons for building the tool. It is also easy to become sidetracked into providing interesting technology rather than targeting implementation to strategic business objectives and realization of investment returns. The cultural and business process changes are also of such a magnitude, as we will more fully discuss later, that unless the clear focus is on the business, the chances of successful implementation are significantly reduced. Accordingly, major groupware implementations such as CenterPoint must be run as business projects by the business in close partnership with technology. Business must be the driver with technology being the enabler. This can be as difficult for the business as technology. Business simply has not had to roll up its sleeves and take accountability along with technologists for the technology agenda; it has not been part of the job description.

Prototyping works. The combination of a team-based prototyping methodology and active business involvement and leadership is powerful and capable of producing quality products in short time frames. However, close management is essential, and check points must be built into the system to ensure that results justify continuing development. A prototype approach can result in improved risk management and mitigation as incremental investment is only made when the technology is shown to work and deliver the results that warrant the expenditure. It should also be noted that as the product evolves, particularly when it comes to implementation activities, more traditional technology project management methods become appropriate—the trick really is to adjust management methodologies to suit the circumstances. As the focus of the project has changed from development to implementation, and now to ensuring that appropriate changes take place in business processes to maximize the value of the technology, different skills and tools are needed which must be reflected in the composition and management of the project.

14.7.2 Cultural Change

The cultural and business process changes brought about by large-scale groupware implementations such as CenterPoint are profound. These changes must be understood, embraced, and supported at very senior levels within the organization if major enterprise-wide groupware projects are to be successful. Every individual's job is, to some extent, impacted by such applications, which inevitably results in some pain. Given that in any major change there are short-term winners and losers, one should also expect ready adoption by some and either passive or active resistance by others.

It is important to note, however, that the traditional modus operandi within the office environment was changing anyway—what was really lacking was a technology that truly supported that change. Global competition, the demand for high quality and low price, reducing product life cycles, and the increasing trend of corporate restructuring require individuals in organizations to work together more efficiently, respond more adroitly to dynamic change, and continually streamline business processes. The traditional office can be thought of as comprising, for want of better words, managers, middle-level officers, and support staff. Managers reviewed information, made decisions, had face-to-face contact with clients, and frequently asked their middle-level officers to complete paperwork, perform analysis, and the like. In turn, these officers then turned to support staff to type documents, update computer systems, and the like. In the emerging office, technology enables managers to perform much of this background work themselves. The consequences are multifaceted but will invariably include improved turnaround time for client requests, reduced overhead, improved productivity, and, if properly implemented, improved client service. Let us examine the impact on various individuals within the traditional office.

The need for support staff reduces, with obvious issues raised with respect to how these individuals are redeployed. Organizations solve such problems in different ways; but the more areas going through the same change at the same time, the more complex the redeployment process becomes because it is no longer as simple as moving people to similar jobs in other areas—they are disappearing at the same time. In general, the Bank expends considerable effort retraining staff whose positions have been eliminated, with a very high success rate. With respect to CenterPoint it has always been stressed that the project is not primarily focused on expense reduction but rather on revenue growth—freeing people from routine, helping them be more productive and creative and spend more time in revenue-generating activities. Generally, staff reductions that have occurred have been through attrition. For the support staff that remain after implementation, there are also changes in the composition of their responsibilities which may be difficult to embrace. Individuals may have taken great pride in the way they maintained their paper files, jealously guarding their own files. The sense of pride may have been important to their sense of contribution, role, and self, and suddenly it is a behavior which is no longer valued or appropriate—documents are filed electronically by the creator in shared files. As humans, it can often be difficult to make this adjustment quickly.

The impact on middle-level officers is also significant. As managers are increasingly required and able to do things for themselves, officers are left with less to do. Additionally, more information is purchased from external vendors and delivered directly to people who need it. In the case of the Corporate Bank, middle-level officers frequently took a client's financial statements, transferred the information to a standard spreadsheet, and performed some analysis. Now, 20 years of financial data on public companies is available on-line, purchased from an external vendor, and delivered directly to those who need the information. There are really two important ingredients here: first, work previously completed internally is being out-sourced with corresponding benefits in terms of cost, turnaround, and information availability, and second, the cultural impact that results from reducing barriers to information flow. A component of the self-image of individuals at all levels within the organization relates to the information they control—increasingly with applications such as CenterPoint, information becomes a corporate resource, and barriers to information flow are significantly reduced. The impact on middle-level officers is far-reaching because in many organizations these individuals were responsible for collecting, manipulating, and presenting information from varied sources. Generally, the number of such positions will likely be reduced, but there is the potential for some of these individuals to become junior management.

The impact on management is no less significant. In the past, many of the tasks undertaken by support and middle-level officers are now performed, in a modified form, by them. Previously, they may not have needed keyboard skills—now, they are absolutely mandatory. Particular care must be taken with this group; they are usually the primary contact point with the client. One of the complaints of clients in many industries is that they do not see enough of their company contact. Significant staff reductions are often possible at the support and middle officer levels which may result in additional burdens being placed on management, offsetting positive impacts on this group in terms of information availability, communications, and so on, and hence not result in a net increase in additional "street time." As was noted earlier, clients are also demanding improved creativity, and one of the impacts of technology such as CenterPoint is to make much better tools and sources of information available to management. The ability to deliver creative solutions to clients is closely related to the quality and availability of tools and information, but in many cases requires management to become much more comfortable using the technology.

A practical, but somewhat simplified and idealized, example may help to illustrate the changes in the business environment. Previously, when completing a credit application, the relationship manager would probably have requested an assistant to commence the process following a conversation with the client. This individual may then have requisitioned relationship management's paper copy of the file. A check would be made to see if the financial statements of the client were on file; and, presuming they were, the assistant would have either sent them off to a central department to have them analyzed or undertaken the analysis himself or herself. This generally involves taking the information in the financial statements and inputting information into a spreadsheet program.

A copy of a previous application would also probably be made and requests submitted for up-to-date information from a variety of mainframe databases containing product information. The results of these requests and selected information would then be handwritten on the copy of the previous application. An analysis of the financial information and rationale for the recommended facilities advised by the relationship manager would then be drafted. This draft would then be forwarded to a typist, who would type the application using word-processing software. The typed version would be checked by the assistant, corrected as required, and then forwarded to the relationship manager, who in turn would then probably make her or his own changes, to go through the typing/checking process again. The application would then be signed and routed with supporting material for additional approvals as required.

This may have involved moving the paper request between a number of physical locations. By contrast, in the new electronic environment, the relationship manager can review the electronic file from the desktop, initiate a new credit transaction by selecting the client name, which automatically reads information into the application in real time from a number of mainframe sources. If the company is a public company, 20 years of financial information is available on-line from an externally purchased CD ROM database. Standardized or custom spreadsheets can be prepared using this information database and highlights transferred to the credit application. An on-line news database can be checked for recent news that may be of interest. Information can be put in an electronic credit application folder, and when the relationship manager is satisfied with the transaction it can be signed and routed electronically. At all times the transaction can be tracked electronically. When the last signatory signs, the transaction is "sealed" so that it cannot be changed or deleted from the system.

This example is greatly simplified but helps to explore the change in the business environment, including reduced handling, improved access to information, and shortened cycle times. In practice, many transactions are sufficiently complex or urgent that a variety of people are working on meeting a particular client's need—but increasingly, they produce the final product within their particular sphere of expertise to form part of the final solution. While some information repositories are common to all (e.g., the Linkworks object database and certain client information on mainframes), other information sources accessed by different users may be quite different—just as previously they subscribed to different information sources based on their business area. Increasingly, external information is being purchased electronically either through direct feeds or via CD ROM.

The impact on executives is also worth noting. Historically, this group was often the group least impacted by technology in their day-to-day responsibilities. In extreme cases their secretaries retrieved their electronic mail, printed it out on paper, maybe typed dictated replies, and sent them out under the executive's ID. It can be a daunting prospect for these individuals to become as proficient at using the technology as any other individual in the organization, but when trying to implement change within an organization, it is imperative that this group embrace that change. Another dimension of the impact on this group is the need to avoid the temptation to overmanage. With fewer barriers to the flow of information, it is easier to overmanage and become involved in areas or levels of the business that were just not feasible before and that should more appropriately be left to others.

The above discussion is very brief and has indicated only a fraction of the organizational impacts that have to be addressed when implementing a major project such as CenterPoint. Nevertheless, it serves as an indication of the magnitude of change involved and to underline the importance, as discussed earlier, of viewing such projects not as technology projects but rather as business projects with a technology component. They also raise the interesting question of when one should implement such changes—when the organization is financially sound or in response to a business crisis. There is a very strong sense in the Corporate Bank that the type of change embodied within CenterPoint is absolutely necessary, and that regardless of whether one likes the change or the way it is being done, it is simply a matter of time before competition will force the change if one is to survive. An organization's history of change and culture will determine when it is appropriate to undertake such changes, but timing is an important issue, and the speed of change may be more amenable to control if one is making the change from a position of financial strength rather than necessity.

14.7.3 Cultural Change—Technology Community

Just as the cultural change within the business community is profound, so too is the impact within the technology community. There is a strong tradition within the financial community of professionally managed mainframe environments—high standards of availability and reliability are essential to the functioning of the business. Outside this environment, local area networks were being set up by a more entrepreneurial, experimental, skunk-work type of individual. LANs were used for electronic mail and some personal productivity tools but generally were not vital to the business—indeed, if individuals did not like using a PC, there were often many ways to minimize their use.

With enterprise-scale groupware applications such as CenterPoint, new standards of performance and support are required—if the system is not up, then neither is the business. There is also a quantum leap in technology as the LAN/WAN becomes a highly complex and integrated client-server environment. Not only are skill levels challenged in the process, but the type of individual that prospered in the former LAN environment may not be the asset they once were—one no longer rewards to the same extent the entrepreneurial spirit that takes an old PC and uses it as a key router within the system, even if it does save money.

The primary contact between the business and technology communities was frequently an individual within the LAN area. They were very much the respected experts who got things done, generally within a much shorter period of time than was possible within the mainframe environment. With the change in technology an outside technologist now enters the picture, and some of the qualities of reliability and availability of the mainframe world are more important to the business than before. New levels of support are also required, and the business community takes far more interest in and leadership of the technology agenda as they begin to see technology more clearly as a business tool. As they become more involved and exert leadership, they are no longer content to live with historical time frames, service levels, or approaches. The LAN constituency of the technology community begins to feel threatened from both sides—the business becoming more active and demanding, and the mainframe community who see a future in extending some of the characteristics of their technology platform out to the LAN.

The above challenges have been among the most demanding the CenterPoint project team has had to face. They persist, but are becoming less severe and time-consuming. The crux of the problem can probably be summarized as managing the change from a very loosely knit group of able technologists, enjoying their jobs but focusing more on the technology, to a service-oriented group, focusing less exclusively on technology and more on servicing their client, the Corporate Bank. Such a change can only be accomplished with the highest-quality leadership in the technology community with a clear commitment to client service and willingness to effect organizational and personnel change. The change only reflects what is going on within the business communities of many organizations—reorganization to more clearly address the needs and expectations of clients. The change is more difficult in some ways for the technical community— they were more isolated from the realities of a competitive world, with one comparatively undemanding client who had limited ability to buy elsewhere and with a reward system that was biased towards technical skills. Now that client has raised significantly increased demands that require satisfaction.

14.7.4 Technology Challenges

As if the above human issues were not enough, there are also technology challenges. It was apparent at the time the prototype was established that the former technology infrastructure within the Corporate Bank was incapable of supporting an application like CenterPoint. Hardware at the user level required upgrading, as did LAN and WAN communication performance. Major components of the LAN and WAN infrastructure, including servers, routers, and operating systems, all needed upgrading. With the substantial investment made in mainframe processing and information systems, a way had to be found of integrating these systems, built over many years using a variety of platforms and tools, into the CenterPoint environment. The Bank was also reviewing standards to which new technology implementation should adhere, standards of openness, portability of applications, reusable object orientation, and the like. Most technical problems have technological solutions and, in that sense, are potentially more manageable than human issues surrounding major change, but applications such as CenterPoint represent a major technological challenge to many organizations at the current time. Mechanisms must be in place to ensure that issues are identified promptly and actually resolved and not left unsolved, thereby potentially jeopardizing key project components and milestones.

14.8 THE BUSINESS CASE

We have dwelt heavily on potential obstacles and challenges to be addressed. Is there an upside? The answer is unquestionably yes, although given the discussion so far it is apparent that it is not automatic, and the critical success factors, to be discussed shortly, must be present. Tools like CenterPoint are themselves very powerful agents of change; they facilitate organizational and process changes that would simply not be possible otherwise. Impacts take many forms, some of which we have touched on already: improvements in the quality of client service along both quality and time dimensions, relationship management's ability to spend increased time with clients and in revenue-generating activities, information accuracy and availability, and employee morale and productivity. Ultimately, however, major initiatives like CenterPoint must be justified from an economic standpoint. In this regard benefits come in two flavors, enhanced revenue and improved productivity (or sales and cost of sales). Quantification of the business impact of implementation has proceeded incrementally with technology development. At the prototype stage, the business case was rudimentary but supported the limited investment dollars associated with the prototype phase. Part of the prototype phase was to build a more robust business case, which supported the decision to proceed to pilot, during which phase a more detailed evaluation again was prepared to support the decision to implement CenterPoint throughout the Corporate Bank. Such an approach is consistent with experience that not all impacts, both positive and negative, can be foreseen until experience is gained in one's own environment and organization.

Within the Corporate Bank, the business case has never revolved primarily around head count reduction and productivity improvement. Indeed, the fear of sizable staff reductions can be very damaging and jeopardize the likelihood of success. Rather, the business case has primarily been based upon business process improvement and redeployment of individuals to facilitate improved client focus and increased street time with clients, leading to consequent revenue enhancement. The most valuable resource the Corporate Bank possesses is the intellectual capital of its employees, and the goal of the CenterPoint project has been very much focused on reducing the drudgery and non-value-added component of jobs, and providing tools to leverage creativity and teamwork into enhanced financial performance.

With respect to financial impact quantification, two major initiatives have taken place with the assistance of external consultants; namely, a bottom-up analysis and a top-down analysis. The former analysis was completed by analyzing the activities of individuals from a representative sample of business units throughout the Corporate Bank and building an enterprise model that could be used to model the impact of the business re-engineering and technology introduction. The second analysis focused more specifically on the impact of re-engineering and technology on revenue-generating activities. The Corporate

Bank's consultants with respect to client coverage strategy assessed the impact of such changes from both an external client perspective and internal delivery perspective, and quantified the impact on financial performance. Both studies yielded very similar results and substantiated the material positive financial impact of CenterPoint deployment.

Maximum benefits take time to realize. By its very nature as an enterprise tool, benefits increase more than linearly as more individuals are connected. It takes time for individuals to become fully competent with the technology, and it also takes time and effort to change business processes to take advantage of the technology. The business case supporting CenterPoint has been prepared on the basis of it taking approximately two years after a site has the technology in place to realize all projected benefits because processes are migrated on a phased basis. With fairly conservative phasing of benefits, the return on investment significantly exceeds the Corporate Bank's hurdle for new investments.

Obtaining the payback from a technology investment is not automatic. The benefits of new groupware tools will likely only be maximized if new ways of doing business are adopted; there is a tendency to see many new tools as ways of automating existing practices. CenterPoint has always been viewed as a tool to realign business practices—but in turn, tools are needed to guide this effort as it is not automatic. The discussion below with respect to the use of a "configuration laboratory" indicates how the Bank is ensuring that processes are effectively reviewed and revised, and benefits from groupware deployment realized.

14.9 CURRENT STATUS

As of November 1994, approximately 350 business users are actively using CenterPoint in Toronto, Chicago, and Houston. Approximately 150 people in New York and Chicago are in various stages of training and conversion. By early 1995 all Corporate Banking personnel in the U.S. will have been converted to CenterPoint, with implementation in Canada scheduled for completion by early 1996. By then approximately 850 to 900 individuals will be utilizing CenterPoint.

While implementation represents a significant workload, the focus of activity has very much changed from development and implementation to ensuring that the benefits of the technology are realized by the business. In this regard, the object orientation has very important business consequences. From a business perspective, objects can be broken down into two components: the information object itself, for example, a document, spreadsheet, file, and so on; and attributes of the object. Some attributes will be assigned by the system, author, date and time of creation, and the like, but attributes can also be user- or organization-defined. A credit application, for example, is an object; and the question that then arises is, what are the important attributes of credit applications? They may include amount, whether it has been authorized or not, and whether the client has accepted the facility or not. The environment is capable of recognizing when the transaction changes from "not authorized" to "authorized" and can then trigger other applications automatically. When the client accepts the facility and the attribute changes from "not accepted" to "accepted," a different set of applications may be invoked; for example, update the business plan, start billing, and so on. In this way, by carefully thinking about the classes of objects that one establishes and their attributes, it becomes possible to embed a considerable amount of process within the technology. To further this process, a configuration laboratory is an integral part of the implementation phase—essentially, a room containing eight workstations and tools to assist with capturing and analyzing the process and procedures that are used to control and monitor work practices throughout the Corporate Bank. Users from various areas can use the laboratory to assist in capturing the process involved in their interactions with a view to improving the functionality of objects themselves and the processes associated with them. Analysts and developers can then work with those user groups to design applications that can be developed and tested in an interactive manner, thereby promoting and permitting process change to take place to gain maximum advantage of the technology.

Of course, time saved can be reinvested in the business, realized as expense reduction, or simply squandered. Historically, in too many instances where process improvement has taken place the results have been disappointing, largely because the importance of involving senior management in ensuring that time saved is optimally used has not received the appropriate focus. Technology cannot ensure that time is optimally used; only business managers can. This requires that the technology be "owned" by the business and that senior management is accountable for redeploying resources and for delivering expected results. In conjunction with the activities in the Configuration Laboratory, considerable attention is being given to assisting the business to actually realize anticipated results.

Along with the above, further improvements in network infrastructure are being undertaken. A version of CenterPoint that can be used while traveling is a high priority of the business and has been developed except for final resolution of the cost effectiveness of various security devices. With the richness of the CenterPoint environment, particularly its object orientation, it is also logical to extend a subset of the desktop to clients' offices, and some preliminary work is currently being undertaken in this regard.

14.10 CRITICAL SUCCESS FACTORS

I have been asked many times by people from other organizations to identify critical success factors based on our experience to date. I have been struck by the similarities between the problems that organizations face in a very wide variety of industries, particularly larger established companies. Discussions of silos within organizational structures, the need to share information, and the need to organize more effectively around clients seem to ring true in many organizations. Similarly, the need to accommodate legacy systems and renew the relationship between business and technology communities within companies appears broadly applicable. Against this background there are critical success factors that can be identified, where by critical we mean that without such factors being present the success of the project would be significantly impaired.

14.10.1 Visible Senior Executive Sponsorship

The most important part of the critical success is the need for visible, strong senior executive sponsorship. As we have discussed, applications of this magnitude have a profound cultural impact within the organization that require behavioral change on the part of all employees. Within the Corporate Bank the Vice Chairman has fulfilled this role. In addition to being a Vice Chairman of the Bank, he is also the chief executive officer of the Corporate Bank. He has a strong outward-looking market perspective, is keenly aware of the importance of leveraging intellectual capital, and appreciates the value of technology. In both his internal and external communications he has consistently communicated his vision of how the Corporate Bank will undertake its business. He has communicated that the changes this represents are not options, and that those organizations or individuals that do not continually adapt and evolve to meet changes in the environment will likely suffer the same fate as dinosaurs. There is a natural reaction to change, similar in many ways to the invasion of a biological organism by a foreign body. Corporate organizations are no different in that they are highly complex self-regulating bodies that bring their own immune systems into play when challenged by change. Culture is an important element of the immune system that tends to dictate the way problems are seen and evaluated (or not seen at all!). Organizational structure is another defense mechanism—this is the way that things have to be done, with the number of levels that a change must be reviewed at acting as a natural brake. Immune systems also have a critical survival value, however, and the trick is to ensure that change does not overcome the system but enables it to prosper in a changing environment. Executive sponsorship is absolutely critical to assist in ensuring that the immune system does not maintain the organism in perfect shape for an environment that no longer exists, but rather that it evolves to flourish with environmental change. Executive sponsorship comes in two flavors, visionary leadership and the exercise of position power. Both are necessary to overcome resistance to change—vision to help establish goals, and summon energy and enthusiasm for a common purpose, and position power to occasionally ensure that resistance to change or process delays do not become undue problems.

14.10.2 Business Must Be the Technology Driver

Technology should not be developed for technology's sake but to enable the business. Technology is also changing—at one time its impact was largely confined to individual areas or processes within an institution. With groupware and the growth of networks, it is increasingly becoming a tool with enterprise-wide implications. Business in many organizations would appear not to be exercising true leadership of the technology agenda in conjunction with the technology community. While coming from the business community, I have had the opportunity to meet with many technologists from other companies as a result of my involvement with CenterPoint, and the question I am asked most often is, "How do we get the level of business involvement that you have achieved at the Bank of Montreal?" It is not an easy question to answer. Other commitments and priorities

frequently interfere, as do traditional perceptions of respective roles and responsibilities. However, with the pace of change in the world and forces of competition, globalization, and growing importance of knowledge-based industries, it is
imperative that business strategy, human resources, processes, and technology
are fundamentally integrated. Ultimately, it comes down to the quality of senior
executives within both the business and technology communities to ensure that
technology is appropriately focused on meeting business priorities.

14.10.3 Business and Technology Must Forge a Close Working Relationship

Within the Corporate Bank the ability of the business and technology communities to forge a close working relationship was critical to the success of the
project. It involved a new way of working for both communities, based on a prototyping methodology and multifunctional teams. It involved making real progress
on changing the paradigm from "hand-off" to "hand-shake." It takes constant vig-
ilance still to maintain this relationship—it is not easy for either community to
change deeply entrenched habits established over many years, but it is becoming
easier with time as the benefits become more apparent to both communities.

14.10.4 Careful Identification of External Technology Partners

There are a plethora of vendors trying to sell their products and services.
Because of the multifunctional, team-based prototyping methodology that was
adopted to develop CenterPoint, it was very important to identify a partner that
understood clearly what the Corporate Bank was trying to achieve and would
work as an integral part of a multifunctional team. The Corporate Bank was
looking for both products and expertise with the paradigm required being one of
"partner" rather than "vendor." Few vendors understood this at the time, focusing too narrowly on trying to sell their products, regardless of their true fit with
the Corporate Bank's requirements. When one looks at projects like CenterPoint,
the funds expended on licenses and hardware, which will likely be distributed
among many vendors, represent less than half the expenditures and are frequently commodity decisions with limited added value in their own right. The
added value comes from crafting and integrating those products to meet a particular need, which in turn requires a thorough understanding of the client's objectives. It is the intellectual capital of the vendor that increasingly is the major
contributor to the value creation of the client and what they are prepared to pay
for—not unlike the corporate banking market.

14.11 SUMMARY

Enterprise groupware applications such as CenterPoint have profound impacts
on organizations and are powerful agents of change in their own right. Because
of the wide scope of business process and cultural impacts, the more traditional

approaches to technology development are not always as effective as one would like. Such undertakings must be regarded first and foremost as business projects, enabled by technology. In knowledge-based industries, technology is becoming an increasingly important business tool. The development of the right tools at the right time is critical to the success or otherwise of business strategies, and new forms of partnership must be developed between the business and technical communities within organizations. Because of the degree of business process and cultural change involved, implementation is a very difficult process requiring a high level of executive support, first-class management, and active business involvement.

Within the Corporate Bank of the Bank of Montreal, we now have over two years of experience with developing and implementing CenterPoint. It has been a difficult and challenging process, but the benefits continue to significantly outweigh the costs. It has been embraced as the way the Corporate Bank will conduct its business and is transforming that business. The focus for the next twelve months is very much on ensuring that the maximum return on our investment is obtained. The Configuration Laboratory will be extensively used, and the impact on the jobs of individuals in the Corporate Bank will be significant—indeed, as more information objects are deployed and process embedded in the technology, I suspect that the changes to the way we perform our daily tasks will be greater over the next twelve months than over the past two years. We are also beginning to turn our attention to extending the CenterPoint platform to our client's offices. The ability to work in teams across the silos of an organization, clearly focused on client needs, is significantly improved; and what is gained by the internal team is ultimately also gained by the client and the shareholder.

BIOGRAPHY

Mr. Frow is responsible for the management of the Bank's Credit function in the United States. Prior to assuming these responsibilities in August 1993, Mr. Frow worked in the Bank's Canadian operations in both senior line and credit positions. He is currently vice president, credit, managing the credit functions supporting the Bank's international financial institutions portfolio and treasury function.

Throughout his career, Mr. Frow has maintained an interest in the utilization of technology to attain a competitive advantage through improvement in client service levels and business productivity. In addition to his credit responsibilities, he sits on a steering committee with business and technology representatives, which establishes the merit and priority of technology initiatives within Corporate Banking. This past year, Mr. Frow has been closely involved with a strategic project to re-engineer business practices which incorporates the implementation of an object-oriented, client-server workstation throughout Corporate Banking.

Prior to joining the Bank in 1991, he worked for a major British bank in New York as the manager of the large U.S. corporate market. Mr. Frow holds an M.A. degree in mathematics and philosophy from Oxford University, England.

Introduction to Chapter 15

This chapter is for all of you who have been in unproductive, unnecessary, or poorly run meetings (that should include everyone). Find out how one person used a new groupware technology to make meetings more effective for an $8 billion corporation.

I first met Carl Di Pietro when he gave a presentation at one of my Group-Ware Conferences. His presentation was about "Skunkworks" for Marriott—the development of an electronic meeting room. I found his story so fascinating, I asked him to write it up as a chapter. This chapter tells of Carl's work in HR at Marriott, and looks at what he has done in management consulting and meeting facilitation since leaving Marriott.

Since Jay Nunamaker is in the same industry and focuses on the same technologies in Chapter 6, I recommend you read these chapters consecutively to get two perspectives on a very small but well-leveraged area of groupware.

Looking at some of the comments, it is obvious that Carl brings a strong sense of humor to this chapter and provides an opportunity for those who create and use this technology to laugh at themselves. Humor, we find, is one of the best tools for introducing a new technology. It helps remove some of the fears associated with a new technology and increases acceptance of the technology. Carl also punctuates his chapter with quotes from famous people to highlight the point in a section of text. It makes great reading.

Carl takes a case study approach to "meetingware." He does a great job of analyzing the factors involved in getting the Marriott group started, and looks at what worked and what didn't. Carl has since moved on to join Collaborative Decisions, Inc., a consulting firm. He has worked with many other clients, and he carefully takes us through the meeting room itself, the equipment involved, and finally the results. He concludes with an evaluation of the literature and other research findings on meetingware to compare to his own firsthand knowledge.

Carl never loses sight of the fact that meetingware, or group decision support systems, involve people. He capitalizes on the teachings of Osborne and DeBono for brainstorming and creative thinking for problem solving. He then moves on to an analysis of what goes wrong in meetings, behaviorally and technologically.

I can tell you from personal experience as an electronic meeting facilitator, and one who has sat through innumerable meetings, that the most significant factor in a meeting is the facilitator. His or her impact is magnified by the technology, but not compensated for by the technology. Most managers are poor meeting facilitators. (Why should they be good ones? It's generally not part of their jobs.) These skills can easily be learned, but there are significant advantages to having an outside facilitator run the meeting.

Brainstorming can be done with pencil and paper, but it is much more effective when done electronically. Also, anonymous voting is difficult with pencil and paper, but it can be done easily electronically.

To date, I am aware of only four or five groupware products (computer-based) that support electronic meetings: on the PC are Group Systems V (also sold by IBM as Office Vision), Vision Quest, and CM / 1 (Ventana, Intellect, and Corporate Memory Systems are the respective vendors); and on the Macintosh, Council and CA Facilitator (CoVision and McCall Szerdy, respectively). All of these products have much the same functionality. CM / 1 shines in mining and capturing corporate expertise and experience. Both Group Systems V and Vision Quest offer Windows-based products, but Vision Quest is the only product integrated with Lotus Notes at the time of the writing of this chapter. The Macintosh products, although easier to use and more intuitive, have a smaller market base because of the platform.

In most cases, the platform and software do not make a huge difference. The facilitator's training will determine both. Most of the work in a facilitated meeting occurs prior to the meeting in defining goals and an agenda for the meeting. This is where the facilitator really earns his / her pay!

Because the productivity potential for meetingware is enormous, it is interesting to ask why the market for these tools is so small today. Why are most of the companies selling this software making more from training, facilitation services, and management consulting than they are from the software? What is holding this area of groupware back? Is it technology? Is this the "killer application" that will drive desktop videoconferencing? Is it behavior? Are people just unwilling to use a computer to complement a "face-to-face" interaction?

The real benefit of this chapter is found in the lessons Carl learned in the meetings he facilitated. He details a wide variety of experiences not only about the technology but about the human interactions as well. These "lessons" are distilled from many years of experience and provide some of the same value found in Jay Nunamaker's chapter.

Carl also looks at obstacles and concerns about meetingware and comes to the conclusion that meetingware represents a risk-free meeting environment. What this means is higher-quality input, better answers, and ultimately better decisions. He looks at "moments of truth" in his facilitation of over 6000 people, and provides not only the anecdote, but the lesson learned from it. This chapter is useful for novice meeting facilitators, experienced facilitators, and those looking at electronic meetings as a way to improve productivity in their organizations as well as their own careers.

Meetingware and Organizational Effectiveness

Carl Di Pietro

15.1 FOREWORD

As a Vice President of Human Resources I introduced meetingware technology at Marriott Corporation's International Headquarters in 1991. The technology, which was used by thousands of employees from Marriott and other organizations, was installed in a meeting room called the Marriott Group Decision Center (MGDC). Marriott, at the time the MGDC was opened, was an $8 billion service organization with 200,000 employees worldwide. 3000 employees worked in the vicinity of the MGDC in Bethesda, Maryland.

The MGDC was a traditional meeting room in every respect except that it was equipped with computer workstations which were linked together for communications via a local area network (LAN). When appropriate during the meeting, the leader would instruct participants to use computers to "anonymously" type in their ideas; then prioritize them in the order of importance, profitability, or any other criteria selected. Among the benefits, participants reported that using the computers for meetings provided more truthful responses to issues, a higher quality and quantity of useful ideas, creative synergism, and immediate printed feedback for the participants and the leader.

As a management consultant I now specialize in the use of technology in group facilitation and consensus building. I am a partner of Collaborative Decisions (CD), a consulting firm with offices in Bethesda and Potomac, Maryland.

Using various techniques to include computers, Collaborative Decisions works with clients in such areas as planning, focus groups, quality improvement, process redesign, communications, needs assessment, and human resources. Computer systems used by CD are a type of groupware known by many names including Meetingware, Electronic Meeting Systems, and Group Decision Support Systems.

The use of technology to enhance meetings and group productivity is in its infancy. Meetingware is a "tool" in the facilitation process rather than *the* solution. Group results from computer exercises must undergo the rigors of discussion and human thought before conclusions are reached.

This chapter reflects the diversity of my experiences working with thousands of employees who work in public and private sector organizations.

15.2 THE EMPEROR'S CLOTHES—A CASE STUDY

Over 150 years ago, Hans Christian Andersen wrote his beloved tale *The Emperor's New Clothes*. The Emperor, being a somewhat gullible, egocentric sort, believed the tale of two swindlers, that they could weave him a set of clothes so fine in quality that only the wisest of men could see them. The Emperor assembled his staff and subjects to view his fine new clothes, so regal and elegant. As he paraded through the streets, the crowds cheered their approval. All, that is, except for one child, candid and fearless, who shouted out the "naked truth"—the Emperor has no clothes!

Why didn't the Emperor's closest advisors, his staff, or his subjects expose the hoax? According to Andersen, to challenge the emperor's perception was to be seen as "stupid" or "not suited for their jobs."

Nearly two centuries have passed since Andersen wrote his story. And in terms of human candor, "group think," political correctness, and risk taking, perhaps not much has changed.

15.3 THE VISION

The search for the key that could unlock the power of people, their diversity, their knowledge, their creativity, their candor, and their ability to problem-solve was first inspired in a college classroom in the early '60s. Two concepts, although elementary to the experienced manager, were profound revelations to the young business student.

First, when faced with a problem, for insight, go to the people impacted by or involved with the problem. They can offer perspectives not otherwise available. The leader can then choose to act on, modify, or ignore the suggestions.

> *"The best way to have a good idea is to have lots of ideas."*
> Dr. Linus Pauling

Second, embrace techniques that go beyond superficial "behavior" to unlock the "true" attitudes and beliefs of people. Find ways to encourage people, the problem solvers, to freely and spontaneously share their ideas and feelings.

Along these lines, I was introduced to the teachings of Alex Osborne, considered by many to be the "Father of Modern Brainstorming Techniques." Osborne believed that if you gathered people on most any issue and questioned them in a risk-free small-group environment, they would be eager to offer a plethora of ideas, comments, and solutions. He was correct. The class explored this concept. As students responded to a question, ideas would flow, ranging from the intelligent to the idiotic. Commenting on ideas as they were presented was not allowed. Synergism would eventually begin. Participants would piggy-back on the ideas of each other, creating new ideas that were not owned by any one person but rather by the group. The parts were in fact greater than the whole. Diverse thinking, even absurd ideas, were seen as adding value since they often triggered creative thinking not otherwise achievable.

15.4 SHORTCOMINGS IN MEETING EFFECTIVENESS

In the classroom and later in real business settings, brainstorming became a popular way of effectively collecting ideas from groups. A few shortcomings, however, frequently occurred which minimized the effectiveness of brainstorming.

First, even though not allowed, it was difficult for participants to refrain from commenting on or critiquing ideas as they were offered. The tendency to criticize often led to defensiveness, competition, and discussions that moved in directions which were neither productive nor in line with the group's mission. Comments were sometimes counterproductive and inflammatory. There seemed to be little that could be done to curb this practice without a strong leader or facilitator present. A critique of ideas as they were offered often diminished participants' creativity and willingness to participate. It placed participants at risk when offering an idea that might be met with the disapproval of the group or leader.

While Osborne believed that a group discussion of idea pros and cons was critical, he felt these discussions should take place separately from the brainstorming exercise. There needed to be a time for the collection of ideas, a time for evaluation, and a time for conclusion/resolution.

Osborne's rules for brainstorming specifically prohibited the interruption of idea flow and judgmental or critical comments. Yet groups instinctively engaged in such disruptive behavior. How could this behavior be discouraged or eliminated altogether?

Second, groups often failed to record *all* the ideas that were offered. It was difficult to determine why some ideas were seen as appealing enough to be captured on a blackboard or flip chart while others were not accorded the same respect. It was clear that the formal and informal leader(s) of a group consistently dictated the acceptability of an idea with a spoken word, a nod of the head, or a mere eye movement. Verbal and nonverbal cues from the most influential members of the group determined the life cycle of an idea, observation, or suggestion. The complexity of the group, the "games people play," political issues, hidden or dueling agendas, group think, hierarchical dominance, political correctness, gender, rank, ethnic considerations, and organizational culture are among the factors that impact the processing of ideas in a group meeting.

Third, *production block* is another reason for ideas not to be recognized and recorded. As one person speaks, others listen. Many times those listening do not get an opportunity to advance their own ideas, and drift into their own thought processes, or simply forget an idea they had.

How do you deal with these complexities so the best thinking can be captured and the best decisions made? How do you motivate the group and leadership to focus on the quality of ideas rather than the personalities and roles of the presenters? Or is it even desirable to manage these complexities? Do groups and leaders *really* want to make the changes necessary to surface the best ideas and solutions, or do they embrace the status quo, favoring ideas for other reasons?

Fourth, groups and leaders did not have a simple, "quantitative" way to prioritize the ideas gathered or did not have an inclination to do so. Conclusions were often reached by the leader or group that had little to do with which ideas were most strongly supported by participants, quietly or verbally. How does one motivate leaders and groups to involve themselves in the tedium of a structured discussion, evaluation, and quantification of alternatives in order to select the most desirable? Some business decisions were driven by what I call the "football syndrome." All heck would break loose during the last two minutes of a meeting. With precious little time left and pressure to reach closure, quick conclusions would be made that in no way reflected the lengthy discussions that had previously occurred during the meeting.

Fifth, another meeting phenomenon that occurred whenever groups failed to properly reach closure involved "meeting and organizational memory"; the recording of ideas and conclusions. Usually, minutes of a meeting, if taken at all, were not published until days or even weeks after the meeting occurred. Sometimes they weren't published at all. The production of the minutes often required off-line interpretation of what had been said and agreed upon during the meeting. Conclusions were often drawn from a few poorly written notes, flip charts, or memory. Thus, the resulting minutes often did not accurately reflect the conclusions, decisions, or best thinking of the group.

Sixth, meetings can become not much more than an expensive *tribal ritual*. Taking on a life of their own, with confusion about such things as purpose and mission, meetings often result in little or no productive outcome. Whatever the reasons for holding meetings—informational, problem solving, planning, social, CYA meetings, or whatever—there needed to be significant improvements in the quality of meeting outcomes, reduction of the frequency of meetings, and increased support of meeting decisions by organizations. That is, if the organization really wanted to change!

Table 15.1 Cost of Meetings[a]

Attendees	$40,000 Salary	$60,000 Salary	$80,000 Salary	$100,000 Salary
2	80	120	160	200
4	160	240	320	400
6	240	360	480	600
8	320	480	640	800
10	400	600	800	1000
15	600	900	1200	1500
20	800	1200	1600	2000

[a]Includes cost of payroll while in a meeting as well as cost of lost productivity.

These six shortcomings were frustrating and perplexing. According to a survey of 1000 managers and professionals [Mosvick and Nelson, 1987], management spends 25–80% of their working time in meetings. 53% of this time is considered unproductive. The higher in management one goes, the more time is spent meeting and the more costly such meetings are to the organization. Why have organizations allowed the meeting place to become a safe haven for underproductive group gatherings? Why haven't organizations been more proactive in improving the efficiency and productivity of group gatherings? Why haven't incentives and rewards been implemented to promote more effective use of employee time and organizational resources during meetings?

15.5 IMPROVING GROUP PRODUCTIVITY IN MEETINGS

It isn't that the issue of improving group productivity in meetings has not been addressed by organizations. In fact, hundreds of techniques have been developed to enhance group productivity and effectiveness. Training programs are designed and delivered by most large organizations to help meeting leaders and participants be more productive. Thousands of books and articles have been written suggesting ways to improve meeting effectiveness and communications. Facilitation techniques have been introduced which are simple and effective in improving the productivity of groups. Nominal group and Delphi techniques are among the more popular. Why hasn't it been enough—or has it? What incentives exist for organizations and members to improve the efficiency of meetings? Are the opinions of those supposedly empowered and responsible for implementation of a process or program really valued, or are they sometimes pawns in a decision process that is really driven by top-down preferences? What are the honest attitudes and beliefs of meeting participants, and how do you separate "behaviors" (political correctness) from the "truth" (attitudes and beliefs)? Do meeting leaders and groups really want to know the "truth"? Why are there so many meetings, and why is meeting attendance often seen as unproductive and boring but somehow still "en vogue"? Why is it necessary for meeting participants to leave their "knit-ting" and spend valuable time traveling to a single location to meet? How can timely business decisions be made when meetings are often delayed because the "right" people can't be scheduled? Is there a way to make it better?

> *"Truth is the cry of all, but the game of a few."*
> Bishop Berkeley, 1744

15.6 TECHNOLOGY—A HELPFUL TOOL

The notion that technology might offer dramatic assistance in improving meet-ing productivity began to gain momentum in the '70s. Work at Xerox's COLAB and IBM's introduction of meeting software were encouraging signs that com-puter technology might provide assistance. These and other companies experi-mented with computers placed at each seat in the meeting room. The computers were "linked" together in a local area network (LAN) so that when an entry was made in one computer, it would be seen by every other meeting participant in the room. Participants usually entered their ideas anonymously but had the option of indicating which ideas were theirs. These early computer systems were too expensive and complicated to succeed in most organizational environments. Soft-ware systems available in the '80s required a facilitator as well as a technician to be present while a meeting was conducted. Adding staff overhead to conduct meetings was often unacceptable, especially in a profit-driven organization.

In 1991, Dr. Maryam Alavi, Professor at the University of Maryland (Col-lege Park), demonstrated how a new and unusually friendly software called VisionQuest could be used to facilitate a work group. The software could be oper-ated by a meeting facilitator or owner. Special personnel were not needed to con-duct an electronic meeting. Furthermore, the software could be used in the distributed mode—meeting participants could be connected from their offices or other remote locations in the same way employees are connected via email. Meetings could be held with participants in the same place or different places, at the same time or different times. Although not a replacement for a face-to-face meeting, this powerful feature could dramatically reduce travel expenses, speed the decision process, and result in greater meeting efficiency and productivity. No longer would of a "key" contributor be excluded from the decision process because of unavailability.

15.6.1 Why Better Meetings

Having groups share information over a network was already being done with electronic mail and similar technologies. What was new and exciting about meetingware was that groups could share information interactively and anony-mously. Furthermore, meetingware computer tools were available that would allow groups to analyze information and prioritize it in innumerable ways. This greatly facilitated group focus and consensus. The electronic tools available included brainstorming (collecting ideas), placing ideas in categories, and prioritizing ideas through rating, ranking, voting, allocation of points/dollars/manpower full-time equivalents, and multiple weighted criterion evaluations.

The productivity potential for meetingware seemed enormous, especially considering that the software was so user-friendly and could make meeting at different times in different places a reality. This ability to conduct remote meetings, without necessarily adding expensive staff and hardware/software, could result in reduced travel expenses, fewer meetings, improved attendance at critical meetings, assurance of key personnel involvement, and less time spent away from primary job responsibilities.

> *"The only limit to our realization of tomorrow will be our doubts of today. Let us move forward with strong and active faith."*
> Franklin D. Roosevelt

15.7 THE CHALLENGE

Introducing this technology at Marriott was a challenge. Funding for the project was not initially available since budgets for the year were already in place, and "venture" money was unlikely considering the difficult times that were being faced by Marriott and the service industry at large.

After the software was acquired, $10,000 was earmarked from the Division of Human Resources budget for the experiment. In a "skunkworks" environment, a task force was assembled to study and make recommendations regarding the introduction of meetingware to the corporation. The task force was made up of information systems, human resources, and operations personnel from different divisions of the company. Objectives were established, available competitive software tested, the organizational culture evaluated, facilities and hardware acquired, marketing and training plans developed, and performance measurements established. The evaluation and installation was completed in six weeks.

Practically speaking, there were just three software products available for consideration: Team Focus (IBM), Group Systems (Ventana Corp.), and Vision-Quest (Collaborative Technologies Corp.). Team Focus and Group Systems were virtually the same product. As part of the evaluation, companies that were already using meetingware (Boeing, IBM, Proctor and Gamble, Westinghouse) were benchmarked.

In October 1991, the Marriott Group Decision Center opened. Compared to previous years, it appeared that the time was "right" for such cultural change to be successful because:

1. *Ease of use*—With adaptations, the software selected, VisionQuest, was so user-friendly that no training was required for almost 100% of meeting participants.
2. *Computer acceptance*—The workforce in general, including many senior management personnel, were considerably more at ease using keyboards

and computers than they were just five years before. Email, simplified word processing, ATMs, TV remote controls, and many other keyboard technologies were becoming commonplace.

3. *Rightsizing*—Marriott, and American business in general, was beginning the push to do more with less while doing it better. Leaner organizations and shrinking margins were prevalent. Business process re-engineering and a growing reliance on technology were emerging.

4. *Quality priorities*—The Total Quality Management (TQM) movement at Marriott had been endorsed by senior management in most business units. TQM principles of empowerment, participative management, performance measurement, valuing diversity, self-directed work groups, and quality improvement teams were initiatives that could make use of meetingware.

Barriers to success included the possibility that:

1. There was an innate fear of the unknown which might doom the concept regardless of how productive it was.
2. The organization might reject this method of exchanging information as inappropriate or impersonal—the meeting paradigm.
3. The candor that might surface during meetings could threaten or disrupt the power/authority balance.
4. Keyboard phobia or incompetence might discourage attendance at and support for these types of meetings. This was of particular concern with some of the senior management groups since computer use was not widespread at the highest levels. Also, typing was probably viewed as inappropriate "executive" behavior by many.

15.8 THE STRATEGY

A plan was developed that would hopefully ensure the acceptance, success, and institutionalization of the MGDC.

1. A Champion—The Vice President of Human Resources would volunteer as the Champion of the meetingware project. The Champion's role was to advance the merits of meetingware with select key personnel in the operating and staff organizations, encourage support for the concept, locate future funding, and protect the concept from severe critics during the early period of the life cycle.
2. Staffing—A headquarters Human Resource Department would be fully accountable for the promotion and management of the MGDC. Technical support would be provided by the Corporate Information Systems group.
3. Marketing Scope—The MGDC was to be marketed and promoted across division lines, to all hierarchical levels in the organization and to all job

functions. Marketing plans would include such things as free demonstrations, continuously run videos in heavily traveled areas of the building, biweekly releases in the headquarters administrative bulletin, table tents in the cafeteria, and status charts (showing number of meetings, meeting results quantified, man-hours and dollars saved, and testimonials). After each group met in the MGDC, an anonymous evaluation was completed using the computers. The results, which were consistently complimentary, were reported back to those who participated in the meeting and to prospective users of the MGDC.

4. Meeting Selection—Initial meetings held in the MGDC were evaluated for appropriateness and likelihood of success. The MGDC started with small successes and grew in time so that complex meetings were held routinely with success. This approach also allowed the MGDC support staff to mature in their understanding of the software, the culture, and which techniques worked best.

5. Meeting Templates—Standard meeting computer templates were designed that would allow users of the room to schedule and hold a meeting without involving the services of a professional facilitator or technician. After 18 months of operation about 40% of all meetings were conducted by the owner of the meeting without staff assistance.

6. Staff Support—Free consulting, meeting design, and facilitator services to users of the MGDC would be provided for at least one year.

7. Solicitation—Possible users of the room were directly solicited, demonstrating application of the technology that would help them solve their unique business problems. Every function in the organization was a potential client. Operations, Finance, Treasury, Public Relations, Marketing, Information Systems, Training, Relocation, Planning, Engineering, Procurement, Legal, and so on were solicited—and they came.

8. Training—A two-hour training program was made available to those users who wanted to learn more about conducting a meeting using the software. The training session focused on how to move from one computer tool to another. Standard meeting agenda templates were prepared so that no customization was required. About 70% of the meetings held in the room used the standard agenda templates developed by the part-time meeting room staff. These templates (problem solving, planning, etc.) made the software easy for clients to use without assistance.

9. Targeted Clients—Those most likely to have difficulty accepting the MGDC concept would not be recruited to use the MGDC. Those who did not have keyboard skills and those who would see keyboard communication as an "unnatural" act were identified. For the most part, these included:

   a. *Senior-level executives* who were seen as less accustomed, on a daily basis, to compromising and sharing power in the decision process. Furthermore, these executives would probably see keyboard communications as stilted and unnecessary. Exposing computer incompetence in the presence of peers and/or subordinates could also be seen as a threat and embarrassment to the senior executive. It was hoped that senior-level executives would embrace meetingware, on a highly individual basis, after their staff reported success stories.

    b. *Operative employees* not accustomed to using computers or keyboards as part of their job. Language was also a concern, but numerous meetings were later held in Spanish and German with impressive results.

10. Identity—To gain a corporate identity and ownership for the room, framed pictures of each operating division of Marriott were placed around the room, and the meetingware Champions in each division were identified. The name of the room, MGDC, reflected an organizational client rather than a single group or division.

11. Outside Organizations—To test how outside cultures reacted to meetingware, scores of organizations—industry, government, military, educational institutions, associations—were invited to use the MGDC for business meetings, and their reactions were anonymously measured. It was expected that revenues collected from outside organizations would help fund the MGDC. Also, installing the MGDC concept in selected Marriott Hotels might provide a value-added service for business clients and result in a new revenue-generating opportunity. A business plan was developed.

15.9 THE ROOM

The room selected for the MGDC was approximately 25' x 30'. It looked like a traditional conference room in every respect except that 12 computers were placed on folding tables configured in a U shape. The tables were skirted to hide wiring and system units. 286 and 386 computers were used, and from time to time different types of computers and monitors were tested for acceptance by participants. Participants clearly preferred monitors that did not block the view of other participants but otherwise displayed no strong equipment preferences once they focused on the meeting content. Eventually a table was tested, with success, that positioned the monitor under a glass top. This left the participant with no obstacles, but rather a flat working surface that more resembled a traditional conference room. Having the computers and monitors out of sight was also seen as more desirable by those with computer phobia who entered the room for the first time.

15.9.1 Common Screen

Some electronic meeting rooms have a viewing screen at the front of the meeting room which will serve as a focus for illustrations and discussions. This screen will allow projection of images from one of the computers in the network. Usually, the leader's computer will be used for projection. LCD panels, rear projection devices, and large TV monitors are among the options. Many times the information on the front screen will be a duplication of what participants are seeing on their individual computer screens, but sometimes the meeting leader/facilitator will opt to project other information.

The only drawback to central projection is cost and possible distraction of meeting participants. Front projection is costly: $5000 or more for a quality image in a light-filled room.

15.9.2 Overhead Projector

For many reasons, an overhead projector was seen as an inexpensive necessity in the electronic meeting room. It can be used as it would in any conventional meeting for projecting information. In the electronic meeting, it has the added advantage of using transparencies projecting group results following a computer prioritization or at any time the group leader prefers. A transparency can be run through the printer located in the room and then be laid on the overhead projector for magnification and focus. The printer and overhead projector can be an inexpensive alternative to a central video screen system (LCD panels, etc.).

15.9.3 Printer

It is helpful, but not mandatory, that a printer be located in the electronic meeting room. Results may be printed by any participant or the meeting leader on demand. This provides hard-copy feedback for the group, and the information can be used for small group breakouts or as final reports. The printer should be located in close proximity to the meeting leader. The printer selected should provide an adequate number of pages per minute plus be very quiet in operation. There are many printers which satisfy these requirements.

15.9.4 Computer Processing Units (CPUs)

It is, of course, desirable to have CPUs located outside of the meeting room to reduce heat and noise and for esthetics. The costs of cabling and otherwise remoting the equipment may not meet cost/value tests. Each CPU and monitor was identified. Generic workstation identification allowed for the easy, quick login of participants when security and password entries were not required. In the MGDC, a theme was developed for naming the computers. Each computer was identified as a symphonic musical instrument; some were named after bold musical instruments like the trumpet and kettle drum. Others were named after delicate instruments like the cymbal or harp. These musical instrument workstation names were popular among participants. The names created an ambiance and spirit that suggested to participants that they would be respected for their diverse views and styles. When blended together, as with a symphonic orchestra, participants could make beautiful music. Normally, no passwords were used to log in participants; however, when sensitive meeting issues were to be discussed, unique, personal identifications with passwords were provided to ensure 100% confidentiality.

15.9.5 Electrical Power and Heat, Ventilation, and Air Conditioning (HVAC)

Because of the number of workstations, printers, overhead projectors, and other pieces of electrical equipment in the MGDC, upgrading the electrical and HVAC systems was required. This has not normally been a requirement in subsequent meeting room installations. A backup power system was in place so that power losses or surges did not damage the data, server, or other electronic equipment in the room. The use of notebook computers, which do not require special electrical or HVAC accommodations, can be a simple, cost-effective alternative to full-size computers. Notebook computers allow for a "mobile meeting room" which can be moved from site to site with relative ease. Because of their low profile, notebooks do not block the view of participants. Notebooks provide flexible use of the equipment, and reduce overhead expenses for a dedicated room that may have special HVAC requirements.

15.9.6 Keyboards

Full-size keyboards were preferred simply because they were more comfortable to work with. In addition, they provided excellent numeric pad functionality which made idea prioritization easy. Major keys were color-coded so participants could quickly identify which keys to press for specific functions. Color coding also resulted in more intuitive training of participants. Keys selected for color coding were those used for viewing screens, moving forward or backward, entering ideas, and so on. For instance, the "RETURN/ENTER" key was used by each participant to release an idea to the other meeting participants' computer screens. Therefore, "green" was an appropriate color choice indicating "go" or "yes." The ESCAPE key was "red" to indicate a "stop" or no" response. Color coding should be intuitive to the extent possible.

15.10 THE RESULTS

The performance of the MGDC and its effectiveness were measured from the opening day:

1. Using the computers, standardized closed-ended questionnaires were anonymously completed by MGDC users.
2. MGDC users were asked to make anonymous narrative "comments" about their experience using the computers. These comments were then "rated" by the users to identify how strongly the group felt about meetingware.

3. Focus groups of users and managers were formed to evaluate the effectiveness of the MGDC.

4. MGDC staff, meeting owners, reporters, academicians, and researchers observed and reported on MGDC activities and group dynamics. Articles about the MGDC experience appeared in *Fortune*, *Wall Street Journal*, *Wirtschaft* (Germany), *Human Resource Executive*, and *Forbes*, to mention a few. The MGDC received the Yoder-Henneman Award in 1991 for creative application that would improve organizational communications and group productivity (Society for Human Resource Management).

"Build it and they will come."
Field of Dreams, 1990

Some of the external researchers observing and evaluating MGDC interactions included Dr. Maryam Alavi, Professor, College of Business and Management, University of Maryland; and Dr. Irene Liou, Assistant Professor, Merrick School of Business, University of Baltimore. Dr. Deborah Tannen, Georgetown University, linguistics expert and best-selling author of books on communications and gender issues, also observed a working meeting in process. After nine months of operation, over 3000 participants from Marriott and other companies had used the MGDC. Approximately 60% of the meetings were facilitated by a person trained in the use of the software. Using standardized meeting templates, 40% of the meetings were managed by the meeting owner without outside technical or facilitation assistance. These types of meetings continued to grow in popularity.

The MGDC was booked over 85% of the time, and users generated over 30,000 ideas. Over 90% of the ideas generated were judged by users to be valuable and useful. 10% of the ideas collected were duplicate or unusable ideas. In surveys, users estimated that it would probably take about 10 times longer to accomplish similar results using traditional meeting techniques. Participants often indicated that some outcomes might not be accomplished at all using traditional meeting techniques. Annualized, it was estimated that 35,000 man-hours would be saved by using the MGDC ($1,000,000 per year).

15.11 RESEARCHERS' FINDINGS

During the first four months the MGDC was opened, post-meeting anonymous questionnaires were evaluated by researchers (Alavi and Liou) from 23 randomly selected meetings with 167 persons attending. Participants represented a variety of functional jobs from different areas of Marriott (e.g., Information Systems and Technology, Human Resources, Legal, Marketing). Some job titles represented in the meetings included Vice President, Manager, Attorney, Secretary, and System Specialist. Meeting topics included such things as planning strategic objectives, determining characteristics of a world-class organization, employee recognition award selections, and a survey of operational services.

Each meeting participant completed the questionnaire; none abstained. The results were typical of findings that would continue to be observed on an ongoing basis (over 2000 users would eventually be surveyed).

Using a 1 to 5 Likert rating scale [strong agreement (5) to no agreement(1)], each survey question was answered with solid agreement. The mean scores ranged from 4.06 to 4.87.

Questionnaire Items	*Mean*
1. I would like to use the MGDC again.	4.87
2. Compared to a "traditional" meeting it took LESS TIME to GENERATE ideas today.	4.76
3. Compared to a "traditional" meeting, MORE IDEAS were generated today.	4.69
4. Compared to a "traditional" meeting, it took LESS TIME to PRIORITIZE ideas today.	4.65
5. Using the computer was easy.	4.55
6. Compared to a "traditional" meeting, I was MORE COMFORTABLE in offering my ideas today.	4.35
7. Compared to a "traditional" meeting, today's meeting was LESS STRESSFUL.	4.34
8. The group members worked well together.	4.24
9. In today's meeting, I felt I was a part of the group.	4.20
10. Compared to a "traditional" meeting, the QUALITY of the ideas was better today.	4.06

Anonymous comments that were "strongly" supported (4.0+ score) by the 167 users included:

☞ "It (MGDC) was quick and very effective in accomplishing our goals."
☞ "A large number of ideas in a short time."
☞ "Using the computer made the meeting fun even though we were discussing major topics and how we felt about people."
☞ "This method (MGDC) is great in expanding the thinking of individuals...."
☞ "I think this is a great system; a quick and easy way to gather data and make decisions."
☞ "It maximizes the group's mental resources."
☞ "The whole concept of computerizing the (meeting) process is excellent. Typing from flip charts is ancient, a total waste of time. We are lucky to be able to have access to a room like this. Like a symphony, everyone plays an important role and needs to be heard. This will help motivate associates to use their true opinions. This is QUALITY."

Observations by the researchers included:

☞ There was a high degree of task productivity; the meeting process seemed to be highly improved relative to a "traditional" meeting.
☞ Participants felt more comfortable in offering their ideas, and perceived less stress during the MGDC meetings.
☞ A high degree of group cohesiveness was experienced in the MGDC meetings.

"We make more enemies by what we say than friends by what we do."
Churchill Collins, 1914

☞ No conflict was observed among the group members, and a high degree of group cooperation existed.
☞ A high level of participant engagement in the meeting task and high motivation were noticed during the MGDC meetings.

The researchers conducted post-meeting interviews with participants. Here are highlights of commonly held views:

☞ There was a high degree of participant engagement and involvement in the MGDC meetings. (A meeting leader noted that one often uncooperative and negative staff member had acted enthusiastically cooperative during the MGDC meeting.)
☞ The MGDC environment was compatible with the established group norms and organizational culture.

There were no negative comments or observations cited by the researchers.

15.12 OTHER RESEARCH FINDINGS

The following represents strongly held beliefs of meetingware users that were collected in subsequent anonymous surveys, interviews, and observations made by meetingware staff, participants, and clients.

15.12.1 Positive and Supportive

1. Groups have far more in common than their perceived differences (shared values).
2. Although empowerment and participative management are embraced publicly, in reality, employee ideas are often perceived by some to be of questionable value; meetingware has helped change this perception in most cases.
3. Compared to traditional meetings, ideas in MGDC meetings are more likely to be implemented (76% yes; 22% no difference; 2% no).

4. When in debate, participants often listen more to form their next response than they do to understand the point of view itself. This did not happen using meetingware.
5. Meetingware meetings are likely to have a positive effect on "how" meetings are conducted in subsequent meeting scenarios using traditional techniques.
6. Meetingware empowers participants and managers.
7. Introverts and mavericks are both more productive.
8. Printed feedback on the screen and via printer:
   a. Builds trust, credibility, and motivation
   b. Legitimizes responses as "valued" and increases likelihood of implementation following the meeting
9. Meeting participants process information in different ways and at different speeds. The meetingware scenario respects and cultivates these differences.
10. Meetingware allows bosses to gain power and control rather than lose it.

The truth will set you free."
Anonymous

11. Meetingware is more participant-focused and less facilitator/group-leader focused.
12. 100% participation in meetingware meetings is routine.
13. Meetingware provides clearer objectives and focus with prioritization tools.
14. Participants routinely buy in to group consensus and let go of personal preferences/agendas.

"Talk as if you were making a will, the fewer words, the less litigation."
Gracian, 1640

15. Fewer words are needed to explain ideas when typing than when talking.
16. Those who already have power and influence in the traditional "talking heads" environment will often find meetingware uncomfortable or threatening.
17. Flatten organizations. Self-directed work teams aggressively used meetingware in the absence of the formal leader.
18. Owners of the highest-rated ideas rarely identify themselves; nor do owners of the lowest-rated ideas.

"The best ideas are common property."
Seneca, First Century

19. Participant attitudes move from "me" to "we" thinking.
20. Because all entries are documented in the computer, those who arrive late for a meeting, or leave the room, will be able to "catch up" with the group and remain involved in the decision process.
21. Participants work in a "risk-free cone of silence" which affords them unprec-

edented time and space to think through responses in depth before sharing them with the group.

22. Computers allow for distributed meetings—meetings held at different places and at the same time or different times.

23. Meetingware allows for multiple simultaneous meetings, which explodes productivity. As many as 14 meeting topics have been processed at the same time. Self-directed meetings and teams are commonplace.

"Never argue. In society nothing must be discussed; give only results."
Benjamin Disraeli, 1832

24. Groups Form, Storm, create a Norm group behavior, and only then Perform. Meetingware often minimizes or eliminates the Storm and Norm activities in the cycle.

25. Meetingware is a tool that, if used properly, should enhance the business solution process.

"The great consolation in life is to say what one thinks."
Voltaire, 1765

26. Anonymity:

   a. Results in little chance that bias/prejudice will influence the decision process.

   b. Some of the most powerful ideas often come from participants not normally seen as "productive" contributors.

   c. Consistently, participants found it difficult, if not impossible, to "guess" who submitted which ideas.

   d. Creates an environment that encourages directness and candor.

"All truths that are kept silent, become poisonous."
Nietzche, 1883–1885

   e. Encourages participants to think creatively "outside the box" since there is no fear of rejection or ridicule.

   f. Idea owners have nothing to defend or prove and therefore are rarely defensive or argumentative.

   g. The quality of ideas becomes the group focus rather than the rank, gender, ethnic background, and so forth.

   h. Diverse views add value to the decision/buy-in process.

   i. Surprisingly, rarely are there rude/crude comments.

   j. Having participants view and type in reactions to a situation from different perspectives (wearing "different hats") can greatly enhance understanding, tolerance, and creativity.

   k. Allows participants to "let go" of a personal position that they might otherwise feel obligated, in the presence of peers and supervisors, to defend exhaustively in the conventional meeting.

27. "Teams flourish when objectives are clear, opinions are valued, and communications honest and timely."

28. Those closest to a problem are very likely to have excellent ideas on how to solve it; particularly if they are expected to implement solutions.

29. Organizations, particularly larger ones, have fallen short in "tapping" the creative, problem-solving power of their human resources.

30. Meetingware allows for all meeting participants to "talk" at *the same time*, without interruption, rather than the conventional linear processing of information (one person talks, everyone else listens).

   "As long as a word remains unspoken, you are its master; once you utter it you are its slave."
   Solomon Ibn Gabiroc, c. 1050

31. The "games people play" and the complex interpersonal skills needed to weigh remarks, rebut, critique, and defend are for the most part eliminated. Games played by participants when typing in ideas are usually quietly processed by the group during the prioritization exercise and put "in their place" by the group—without confrontation or risk.

32. It allows for complete documentation of the information collected, which can be printed in hard copy for distribution to participants, printed on overhead projector transparencies, copied to the computer hard drive or floppy disk, and/or converted to an ASCII file for input into other software programs. Likewise, information can be brought into the meetingware from word processing, spreadsheets, and so forth using an ASCII format.

33. Using meeting templates (generic agendas) allows for effective impromptu meetings—even without a trained facilitator/technician.

34. No training is required for participants.

35. Large groups may be divided into smaller groups to expand productivity (division of labor). Then, to reconnect the team, smaller groups can be brought back together as a large group to view all comments.

36. Draft documents, policies, and so on can be reviewed and commented on by key personnel, on-line, to speed and improve the quality of an otherwise protracted task. Participants being asked to review and comment can be in the same room or in other locations at different times. Participants can identify themselves or remain anonymous. Meetingware eliminates the tedious task of distributing hard copy of a document, awaiting "redline" responses, rewriting the document for a second, third, fourth review by participants. It becomes an authorship tool.

37. Through the prioritization tools available in meetingware, groups quickly and consistently focus on those issues/solutions on which they agree rather than on those that divide them.

38. Participants overwhelmingly feel that they are better able to share their "true" feelings on issues/solutions regardless of political correctness. The best business decisions are based on collecting accurate information, valuing diverse perspectives, and respecting the range of human thought and emotion.

39. Participants rarely display a reaction to information appearing on the meetingware monitor that may be critical of their ideas or personal beliefs. Why? Users report that since no one knows who owns the idea, there is nothing to defend. Also, for this reason, verbal and written criticisms provide them with "space" to think over their point of view and quietly alter their position without embarrassment. If, after the prioritization of comments, a participant's idea is not supported, it is often found to be easier to let go of an idea and focus on ideas supported by the group. The computer monitor, as an impersonal vehicle through which information passes, is the messenger that facilitates tolerance and acceptance.

40. Distributed meetings are a reality—same place, same time or different place, different time.

15.12.2 Concerns and Obstacles

Here are some concerns that users have raised about meetingware. Each remains a challenge for the meetingware practitioners. Some possible remedies and suggestions for dealing with the obstacles are shown in brackets [ ].

1. Computers can become the focus of the meeting or the computer results seen as the solution.

[The experienced facilitator can easily manage the software, agenda, and client to provide balance and neutralize this obstacle. "The greatest overall meeting results are produced where computers and facilitator support are used together" (Mosvick and Nelson, 1987)]

2. Meetingware may not be taken seriously. Four different participants at the Senior Vice President level in one organization called meetingware an "odd ball," "microwave cooking," "a video game," "a glorified flip chart."

[The facilitator must know the client and participants to skillfully select the proper use of meetingware applications where success is assured. Although humor is important to a meeting's success, it could be dangerous to use the computer for "game-like" exercises. Criticism will more often come from senior executives who see this process of exchanging information as awkward. They are more inclined to want to "talk it over" or "hammer it out." Those who are persuasive, dominant talkers may be critical of meetingware if their power and influence is compromised. Meetingware is not for all audiences or for all types of meetings.]

3. Extensive preplanning of meeting strategies, keyboard competencies, agenda, and meetingware tool selection are often required. Although careful planning usually results in a more powerful meeting, meetingware can be seen as over-engineering the meeting.

   [A responsibility of the facilitator is to balance the needs of the group, which often include use of technology, conventional facilitation techniques, discussions, physical movement around the room, and so forth. Care must be taken not to overuse the computer tool, particularly with first-time users. The few minutes required to "orient" users to the keyboard will be repaid many times over. Using generic meetingware templates, meetings can be held impromptu with less planning than normally done by a group leader. Use of meetingware need not require additional planning time, if one accepts the premise that all effective meetings require at least some planning.]

4. Facilitation skills are required for complex meetings.

   [This is true and further complicated since conventional facilitators have sometimes resisted using technology to process groups. The selection of facilitators who are open to the possibility of meetingware is critical.]

5. Meetingware advocates "democratic" decisions.

   [Meetingware promotes candid input and involvement of participants to the extent the meeting leader desires. Decisions could be made on the "majority rules" basis, but this is rarely the case, nor is it recommended. Normally, participants are aware that the meeting leader has responsibility for decisions but seeks the group's input to influence those decisions. It is the leader's responsibility to establish the ground rules for decision making and accountability.]

6. A false sense exists that the meeting must be all or nothing; all electronic or all conventional.

   [This, of course, is not true, but it does require an experienced facilitator who will arrange the proper mix of activities and manage the group's expectations. Most groups want to "overuse" meetingware, and this will be a challenge for the facilitator to manage.]

7. There is a natural tendency for "information overload"—more information than the group or leader wants. Redundant information can lead to fatigue if not chaos.

   [This can easily occur when meetingware is used by the inexperienced. The author developed a Meeting Management Formula for managing information overload: $R = Q + P + T$. A simplified explanation of the formula follows:

   R = The number of **R**esponses expected.

   Q = The **Q**uestion asked; the broader, less complex the question, the more responses expected.

P = The *P*articipants; their knowledge, interest level, and number.

T = The *T*ime; the amount of time participants are allowed to respond.

Applying the formula in meeting planning and using numerous facilitation techniques, such as multiple simultaneous group assignments, should control information overload and increase the quality of group input.]

8. Meetingware is "hard work." Participants become enthusiastic about inputting their ideas, prioritizing results, and otherwise being active members of the meeting group. Compared to conventional meetings, meetingware is a vigorous experience that can mentally and physically "drain" participants.

   [The client's drive to overwork the group and the participants' eagerness to participate must be managed by the facilitator to maximize performance and minimize fatigue. Working full-time on the computers must be avoided, however productive it may be in terms of deliverables.]

9. It's not *always* desirable to have anonymous input .

   [Agreed, there are many techniques to satisfy this concern. When appropriate, to identify idea owners, participants can place their initials or some other identifying mark in front of each idea typed. Depending on the situation, giving participants codes to place next to their ideas will provide anonymity among a group of participants.]

10. Fast typists are at an advantage.

    [This may be true in some meeting scenarios. However, when a group prioritizes ideas it is on the basis of idea quality; therefore, users report that typing speed is not a major concern in most situations. The best ideas will be identified by the group when prioritization takes place. Quantity will not override quality.]

11. All voters are not created equal. Some participants' votes should count more than the votes of others. For instance, for certain meetings, line employee votes may be more critical than staff employee votes.

    [Numerous techniques are available to separate voting value issues. For instance, staff votes could be rated separately from line personnel votes. Then a comparison can be made to understand the differing opinions, if any.]

12. Only weak participants want anonymity.

    [Studies do not support this concern. In fact, the most powerful ideas often come from less dominant participants. Differing personalities and styles have little if anything to do with intelligence, creativity, problem-solving skills, or willingness to put oneself at risk voicing an unpopular view.]

13. Those who seek recognition for their work will be unfulfilled in the anonymous environment.

    [This does occur, but the person "needing" such recognition usually finds a way to let the group and/or group leader know of their contribution—publicly or privately. Routinely, participants choose not to identify themselves even when asked by the group or group leader to do so. In fact, contributors often forget which ideas they submitted since they focus more on the group's progress than their own.]

14. Meetingware is impersonal, and the "texture" of feelings and emotions is lost.

[This may be true when compared to the brisk discussion, fluid exchange of ideas, and emotions of conventional discussions. Meetingware will recognize that, dependent on the existing culture, conventional discussion and debate usually need to remain an important part of the meeting. Using computers to move participants into a "risk-free cone of silence" is a valuable tool that needs to be supplemented with discussions for texture and understanding. The balance of discussion, debate, illustration, computer tools, and reaching closure is a manageable responsibility of the facilitator or meeting owner.]

15. People prefer to send and receive information in different ways. Some prefer writing, some talking, some listening, some reading, some illustrating, and so on. Meetingware is not for everyone.

[This is true. At the same time, conventional meetings ("talking heads") are very appealing to some and very frustrating to others. The facilitator needs to recognize the different style preferences within the group (sending and receiving information). The structure of the meeting should recognize the differences that exist in most every group but still maintain high productivity.]

16. Anonymity can result in crude remarks and character assassination.

[This is true. However, this has not been a problem to date. In the 100,000 ideas/comments made by users to date, less than 1/10th of 1% have been considered inappropriate by the client. The facilitator must set the guidelines for "gentle candor" and responsible input, particularly in sensitive meetings where harsh comments are more likely. Furthermore, if inappropriate comments appear on the screen, the facilitator or meeting leader can halt the meeting for further instruction to the group and/or quietly remove the inappropriate comment from the screen. Interestingly, groups usually monitor themselves and will rebut harsh comments made on the screen.]

15.13 Truth and the Emperor's Clothes Revisited

Perhaps the most refreshing and powerful aspect of meetingware is its ability to place participants in a "risk-free" environment; an environment where issues can be explored without outside interruptions (chatter and critique) and in complete anonymity; an environment where truth is tolerated, in fact encouraged, without reprisal or criticism; an environment where people are not seen as "stupid" or in jeopardy of "losing their job" for speaking their mind.

For leaders, the power of truth (knowing where people stand on issues) can be so valuable in social and business settings that a brief discussion on "truth" has been included in this section. There have been extensive research and writing on truth and its power.

"A man's most open actions have a secret side to them."
Joseph Conrad, 1911

For many reasons, getting to the truth in meetings, or any time people gather, for that matter, is difficult. There are scores of reasons that the truth is withheld; cultural, political, ego, job security, self-promotion, courtesy, and economics, to mention a few. The national best-selling book *That's Not What I Meant*, by Deborah Tannen, PhD., is an excellent reference document that will help readers understand why people, even in non-threatening situations, may choose to be "indirect" or not truthful. Dr. Tannen's latest best sellers, *You Just Don't Understand: Conversations Between Men and Women* and *Working 9 to 5*, explore the differing conversational styles that exist between men and women (i.e., games played, indirectness, candor, etc.). Dr. Tannen observed a group meeting in the MGDC largely to study the interaction between men and women using the computers. She was particularly interested in the decision process and gender power issues. Because of the anonymity, there was no way she, or others, could identify which ideas were male or female. The group, as with most groups meeting in the MGDC and elsewhere, displayed little if any interest in identifying the owners of ideas. Following Dr. Tannen's visit, as continuing research, many groups were surveyed to determine if they could identify which ideas were authored by males, females, minorities, high-ranking officials, and so on. The findings revealed that individuals and groups were routinely unable to correctly identify idea owners—much to their pleasant surprise!

"Truth is such a rare thing, it is a delight to tell it."
Emily Dickinson, 1870

The Day America Told the Truth is another best-selling book that deals with truth and its power. Researchers for the book had 2000 Americans in 50 locations across the United States spend a full day anonymously answering 1800 questions on values and beliefs. The findings were startling. In the context of meetingware, there were many results that drastically contradicted publicly accepted beliefs and "politically correct" positions. There were 24 revelations that came from the study. One conclusion of particular interest was:

"Lying has become an integral part of the American culture, a trait of the American character. We lie and don't even think about it. We lie for no reason... And the people we lie to most are those closest to us" (i.e., Family, Friends, and Bosses).

"The world wants to be deceived."
Sebastian Brant, 1494

Lying is a harsh word. Still, the study found that 91% of the 2000 people surveyed admitted lying regularly. In most cultures, offering candid opinions may place one at risk and/or be seen as rude. Participants, consciously or unconsciously, spend time and energy "feeling out" the boss and others, watching for body language cues, and weighing comments before speaking out. Groups often "agree" on solutions that may be compromised or not supported by all participants, even though the "behavior of the group" suggests unanimous agreement (i.e., "group think," Abilene Paradox). Business meeting scenarios, considering the risks and rewards, greatly magnify this kind of dynamic. Messengers with bad news or unpopular views are often killed. Those who are compliant are often rewarded and seen as "team players." Those who are not compliant are sometimes seen as dissenters, or not "in tune." Management must learn how to recognize the difference between "behaviors" (the way people act) and "beliefs" (what people really believe), and value that difference. Unless the beliefs and attitudes of those responsible for implementing a plan or program are identified and processed, the plan is likely to fail. Today's problems often come from yesterday's solutions. Today's solutions are sometimes a product of "making it work for the boss" and do not reflect the true beliefs of those participating in the solution. Scores of examples are readily available in business, politics, and elsewhere.

15.14 REVELATIONS AND VIGNETTES

After facilitating meetings for over 6000 people, many "moments of truth" have been experienced by the author and his staff of facilitators. In fact, in just about every meeting, something powerful has been learned regarding human relations. A brief review of a few of the meetings is presented here as a study in human dynamics and to elaborate and support research data collected to date. The vignettes do not represent atypical experiences. The lessons learned were played out innumerable times, just with different players. On occasion, the descriptions of the clients represented below were slightly changed to maintain confidentiality.

> "Appearances are not held to be a clue to the truth, but we seem to have no other."
> Ivy Compton-Burnett, 1947

1. ORGANIZATION: Fortune 20 corporation
   PARTICIPANTS: 16 executives at Manager, Director, VP Level
   DESCRIPTION: Strategic planning meeting (1-1/2 days)
   The first day was very productive, as anonymously rated by participants and openly by the boss. Except for two participants, the group was enthusiastic about their work. Overnight, two participants lobbied the boss to increase verbal discussion and reduce the use of the computers. The second day, unlike the first day where all participants were prolific, consisted of almost four hours of discussion which was dominated by three participants. 80% of the discussion was managed by 20% of the participants. The

boss spoke less than ten minutes during the entire meeting, and some participants didn't speak at all. The dominant participants engaged in personal agenda discussions and otherwise undid what had been decided the first day.

At the close of the meeting, several participants lingered to quietly voice anger and frustration with the facilitator about how the second day was handled. In fact, one executive wrote a memo on his concerns about the second day and subsequently met with the boss to discuss his displeasure. An unsolicited note written to the facilitator started, "You couldn't have had a better testimonial to the value of the software after today's meeting (second day). The dominant personalities managed the day and did what they were apparently not able to do the day before."

Lessons Learned: Anticipate the political issues and power focus as part of the meeting planning process. Sharing power with others is not always welcomed by those who already have the power and/or feel they have the "right" answers. Although the boss displayed excitement and support for the first day findings, facilitator discussions with the boss at the end of the first day might have produced a different outcome the second day.

2. ORGANIZATION: Fortune 100 corporation
   PARTICIPANTS: Middle managers
   DESCRIPTION: Employee focus group

The focus groups were assembled to offer opinions on the effectiveness of communications within the organization.

This was one of over 30 group meetings being held across the U.S. involving over 300 employees up and down the hierarchy. The primary language for one particular group was Spanish, and the entire meeting was to be held in Spanish. However, during refreshments prior to the meeting, only flawless English was spoken by the group.

"If you shut your door to all errors, truth will be shut out."
Rabindranath Tagore, 1916

At the start of the meeting the facilitator, who conceded fluency difficulty with Spanish, suggested to the group that they might prefer doing the entire two-hour meeting in English instead of Spanish. The group spontaneously and enthusiastically agreed. The interpreter hired for the meeting was excused.

Only moments later, just as the first question was about to be asked of the group, the facilitator had second thoughts and requested that the group begin the meeting by anonymously indicating on the computer whether the next two-hour meeting should be all-English or all-Spanish. To the shock of everyone, seven participants wanted the session in Spanish and two wanted English. No one abstained. The group offered no explanation for the huge shift in sentiment. The interpreter was hurriedly recalled and the meeting begun. Interestingly, only Spanish was spoken and typed during the entire meeting.

Lessons Learned: Don't judge what people really believe by observing "behaviors" (their "game face"), regardless of how enthusiastically and unanimously the behavior supports an idea or course of action. Why did the group verbally indicate that English was their preference? There appeared to be several possible reasons. First, the facilitator, as the leader, suggested "preferred" (English) behavior, which may have biased the group. Second, participants apparently felt more comfortable expressing themselves— thinking, reading, and/or typing—in Spanish. Third, future promotions may have been seen to be "at risk" based on a perceived lack of English fluency. Fourth, there may have been a competitive rivalry among participants on the English fluency issue.

3. ORGANIZATION: Rehabilitation consortium (not for profit)
   PARTICIPANTS: Three groups meeting at different times to determine how each perceived barriers to employment for the disabled.
   DESCRIPTION: Group 1—Rehabilitation counselors
                             Group 2—Employers of the disabled
                             Group 3—Severely disabled persons

Serious concerns were raised during the planning portion of these meetings. The most significant was whether the disabled group could use the computers and what value meetingware would add. In short, the meetings were extremely successful as reported anonymously by each group and the meeting owners. The severely disabled (paraplegic, blind, deaf, amputees) were more highly productive and excited about their contributions than in conventional meetings held previously. The computers allowed each of the groups to work separately and privately. The benefits of anonymity allowed for true attitudes/beliefs to be presented by each group on "tender issues." The computers also allowed for a quantification of results and the comparison of one group's perceptions/beliefs with each of the others. The gaps became the springboard for non-confrontational discussion to follow. The disabled participants reported a "freedom" to express themselves within the confines of their own capabilities. They were not rushed or pressured to perform as was sometimes the case in meeting with those who were not disabled. They were not embarrassed by their inability to communicate at a level beyond their capacity. The technology respected limitations and empowered them.

Lessons Learned: All groups reacted very favorably to the technology and to the quality of information exchanged. Physical and mental disabilities were not a barrier to collaboration; in fact, the technology and techniques used eliminated barriers like never before. The starting point for understanding, communication, and trust may be the acknowledgment that diverse groups may be more effective if separated initially, so that they may come in touch with their own identity/issues, and then brought together for understanding, assimilation, and compromise. The results, which were revealing in many respects beyond the scope of this writing, have been published in the *Journal of Rehabilitation*.

4. ORGANIZATION: Environmental engineering corporation (1000 employees)

PARTICIPANTS: President and Executive Committee

DESCRIPTION: Two major topics were discussed: first, the selection of those who might be promoted to Vice President, if any; and second, strategic planning. The computers were to be used only for the strategic planning portion of the meeting, but the plan was amended.

Without meetingware, a roundtable verbal discussion of possible promotable executives was held. The President summarized the group's lively comments, which seemed very open and candid. He concurred with the group's decision to promote two Vice Presidents. To "validate" the discussions, the facilitator suggested using the computers. Doing so, the group quickly learned that they had overlooked a leading candidate who was a finalist the prior year and remained a viable candidate for consideration. In addition, the group learned that individually, and as a group, they felt strongly about one executive selected during the discussion. The candidate had not spent enough time in grade to be promoted to VP, and his promotion would cause serious morale problems in the organization. The President, with some amazement and embarrassment, changed his decision on who was to be promoted and admonished the group for not being more candid during the open discussion session.

Lessons Learned: The President, in the opinion of the facilitator, had an excellent relationship with his executive group, so fear of reprisal did not seem to be an issue. What occurred, however, was that individually, participants had concerns about the promotion "timing." They confided that they did not bring it up as an issue, feeling they might be alone in that opinion; which was clearly not the case.

5. ORGANIZATION: Association executive staff quarterly meeting

PARTICIPANTS: Executive staff and clients

DESCRIPTION: Clients were asked to meet with association staff to finalize association objectives and project priorities.

Using the computers and working together, a list of project priorities were brainstormed by the staff and clients. However, when prioritizing in order of importance, the staff was asked to rate objectives separately from the clients to see if there was alignment. The staff, having met with the clients on a prior occasion, was stunned to see that there was a serious discrepancy between the order of priorities perceived by the staff and those required by the clients. The clients were amused with the staff reaction since they felt they had clearly articulated their needs on numerous prior occasions.

"Those who never retract their opinions love themselves more than they love the truth."
Joubert, 1842

Lessons Learned: In conventional discussions, we often hear what we want to hear. The staff had been going down the wrong path in what appeared to be a sincere attempt to satisfy the client's needs. The association head was an authoritarian leader who saw himself as participative. The use of meetingware clarified and amplified client priorities that may not have otherwise been identified. The association head and staff committed to the clients' needs.

6. ORGANIZATION: Large division of a conglomerate
PARTICIPANTS: Operations managers, supervisors, and human resource specialists
DESCRIPTION: The group was charged with rewriting job descriptions and identifying, according to the requirements of the Americans With Disabilities Act (ADA), "essential job functions" and "reasonable accommodations."

Participants traveled from many different locations to attend the first of four planned meetings. Each meeting was expected to last two days. Using meetingware, and having 10 to 14 different meetings going on simultaneously in the same room, the group was able to complete their work in one-and-a-half days.

Lessons Learned: Dividing a large group into small teams allowed each group to focus on a piece of the project. The participants were able to work where they added the most value. Using the computers also allowed each participant to view and type comments on work done by other groups. Productivity exploded, duplication of effort was minimized, and the total group was involved in every issue to the extent they wished to be. Division of labor can be a very powerful technique when using meetingware.

7. ORGANIZATION: Telecommunication corporation
PARTICIPANTS: Operations, administrative staff, executives
DESCRIPTION: The group was convened to solve productivity problems in the work group.

In a three-hour meeting using meetingware, the group identified issues and prioritized their impact on productivity. Meetingware was also used to do a cause-and-effect analysis of issues and to identify alternative solutions. The top-rated solutions were innovative, easy to implement, and would have dramatic impact on productivity. The meeting owner, a Vice President, was so pleased with the work done by the group he began to ask who offered the top-rated idea. Finally, the owner of the top-rated idea spoke up. The Vice President, as well as others in the room, were surprised that the owner of the idea was on the administrative staff and not a member of the management team. One participant inappropriately commented about the owner of the best idea, "and she's just a secretary."

"Men are judged more by their appearance than reality."
Machiavelli

Lessons Learned: Rank, gender, knowledge, and so on have little to do with the actual contributions a participant can make to the decision process; particularly in the collection of ideas. For this reason, inviting those with a different perspective and placing them in a "risk-free" environment can produce quality results. This phenomenon is a common occurrence when using meetingware. Excellent ideas and solutions often came from participants not normally valued by the group. Most of the time, owners of highly rated ideas do not identify themselves. It's also rare that a meeting leader will persist in knowing who owns which ideas. Some meeting participants have preferred to identify themselves after an idea had been implemented and was working well.

8. ORGANIZATION: Fortune 25 company
   PARTICIPANTS: National travel group
   DESCRIPTION: This group was responsible for increasing employee use of airline, car rental, hotels where the company had national contracts which offered significantly reduced rates.

Approximately $20 million annually was being lost because employees were not using the national contract companies. The group, which was geographically and organizationally dispersed, was not able to get its arms around the issues in previous meetings and was far from having an action plan. Less than 30 minutes into the meeting, it was clear to the users that productivity would go well beyond their expectations. The group, by their anonymous evaluation, had accomplished breakthrough results. Major issues were identified and prioritized with confirmation. Cause-and-effect analysis was completed and suggested solutions presented. The meeting took about two hours of intense work.

Lessons Learned: The less groups work together, the more difficulty they may have establishing rapport and understanding (norm and storm). This large group was able to sort through a lengthy list of issues, reaching consensus quickly and easily. Having a printed copy of meeting decisions was seen as another major advantage of the meetingware and improved chances of the implementation of results after the meeting.

9. ORGANIZATION: Benefits group from different divisions of a multinational conglomerate
   PARTICIPANTS: Directors and Vice Presidents
   DESCRIPTION: This complex group, representing significantly differ-

ent business lines, had been meeting over a twelve-month period attempting to make recommendations on a benefit program.

On the first occasion of using meetingware, this group realized that there was serious confusion about their mission. They had met monthly for over a year, and many of the participants quietly questioned their direction and purpose. The group spent the balance of their first meeting redefining mission, purpose, objectives, and so on.

Lessons Learned: Many individuals had serious concern about the viability of the group. For political reasons, they continued to attend meetings, dutifully making contributions, but did not talk to each other about their concerns. The anonymity of meetingware helped this group open up, share frustrations and concerns, and complete their mission in subsequent meetings.

10. ORGANIZATION: Fortune 100 company
    PARTICIPANTS: Spanish-speaking hourly employees
    DESCRIPTION: Several separate meetings were scheduled for focus groups to exchange ideas on how to improve the workplace and to receive feedback on the effectiveness of the company's communication and quality improvement initiatives.

These employees spoke very little if any English, and most had never used a computer keyboard. With hunt-and-peck typing skills, each group considered themselves productive. All were able to rate the comments since it only required reading the comment on the screen and typing in a number (rating). The participants, anonymously and vocally, were thrilled with meetingware results and reported feeling empowered in new ways—especially when they rated ideas.

Lessons Learned:

"The greatest hunger of the soul is to be heard and understood."
Anonymous

11. ORGANIZATION: Large national retail corporation
    PARTICIPANTS: District Manager and staff of 12
    DESCRIPTION: The District Manager had been told by her boss that there were serious concerns about her leadership effectiveness as reported by her staff and others. Correction was required or she would be removed from the job.

At the request of the Manager in jeopardy, a staff meeting strategy was developed using meetingware. There were many topics covered during the four-hour meeting, including a "free-for-all" to identify issues that concerned the staff. The staff was asked to anonymously comment on performance styles of key management personnel in the organization. The results, as rated by the group, identified the strengths and weaknesses of the Manager in jeopardy. Although there were improvements proposed for the Manager, the group strongly supported and respected her performance. The District Manager was thrilled with the results, and so was her boss.

"Be not deceived with the first appearance of things, for show is not substance."
English Proverb

Lessons Learned: What was discovered some time after the meeting concluded was that only two employees were dissatisfied with the Manager. The dissatisfied employees were undermining the Manager, who was a stern, no-nonsense leader who could be curt at times. The Manager's boss made it a practice to collect information from employees on the "state of affairs" and entertained feedback from employees without validating its accuracy. The Manager, who was exonerated, was a victim of the grapevine and destructive, inaccurate information passed to senior management by a few.

"The truth is too simple; one must always get there by a complicated route."
George Sand, 1867

12. ORGANIZATION: Service company field operation
   PARTICIPANTS: 13 participants, including two Vice Presidents
   DESCRIPTION: This was an organization in leadership transition. The new VP for the region was interested in finding ways field operations could increase sales.

The group that was assembled would not talk openly. In fact, the group was so suspicious of the new leadership that they were reluctant to use the computers with the leadership in the room. This was the first and only time to date this phenomenon has occurred. The befuddled leadership offered to leave the room, and only then did the group begin to enter information in the computers. They were asked to identify some ideas on sales opportunities and promotions. What they were preoccupied with, however, were the interpersonal and leadership issues that concerned them. Why was there a management change? How was the promotion decided? Who was considered for promotion? What was going to happen to those replaced? Were more changes planned? And so on.

When the VPs returned to the room, it was obvious that interpersonal and policy issues needed to be understood and processed before the group would be able to deal with the other business at hand. This was done. Misunderstandings were identified and explanations offered. By the later part of the meeting, which was extended an additional hour, the group opened up with the new leadership, and guarded verbal discussion began.

Lessons Learned: True progress on business issues may not be processed successfully until underlying issues of greater importance to the work group are explored and resolved. The internal tension and suspicion in this group was very unusual. Routinely, groups with sensitive issues have no problem discussing them using the anonymity of the computers. This group was so paranoid they needed unusual inducements to participate. The new VP held subsequent meetings where the focus moved from trust issues to business issues.

"When everyone is against you it means you are absolutely wrong—or absolutely right."
A. Guinon, c. 1900

13. ORGANIZATION: Government agency
    PARTICIPANTS: Headquarters Executive Director and executive staff
    of 12
    DESCRIPTION: This meeting dealt with operation issues and planned projects.

    The meeting was seemingly uneventful. At the conclusion of the meeting, the executives did the usual anonymous computer critique of the day's meeting. One item that was rated very high by the group was "when using the software, participants could be candid without fear of offending others or being at risk." One executive, joining the organization just two weeks before, was amazed that the group would rate such an item so high. In his opinion, the boss was very open to comments and critiques. Although the new executive insisted on answers to his question, no other member of the group or the boss commented.

    Lessons Learned: The facilitator did not know until after the meeting that the boss was viewed by the group as intolerant of opinions not aligned with his own thinking. In fact, he could be openly harsh with his staff and carry a grudge. After the meeting, one executive mentioned in confidence that "the new guy will learn soon enough about the boss."

14. ORGANIZATION: Multibillion-dollar financial institution
    PARTICIPANTS: Random selection of employees and managers
    DESCRIPTION: A new Division CEO was interested in knowing what issues faced him in the leadership transition.

    Division-wide surveys might unnecessarily disrupt the organization, and time was short. Focus groups of employees were formed representing different parts of the company. By collecting employee issues and concerns in a "risk-free" environment and rating them, the CEO was privy to those issues most important to employees. 20% of the employees in the Division were invited to participate in focus groups. Reports were available immediately following each focus group. The priorities cited in the focus group were responded to by the CEO in a division-wide employee meeting. The priorities that he covered were so on target that employees applauded his insight, concern, and compassion. The focus group was acknowledged by the CEO publicly at the employee meeting, and the meetingware focus group concept was subsequently used before each Division meeting to anticipate issues.

Lessons Learned: Go to the people if you want to know what is happening. Place them in a "risk-free" environment for candid feedback. Interviews, even if conducted by outside consultants, are not usually seen as "risk-free." Paper-and-pencil surveys take a long time to complete, don't allow for adequate evaluation of open-ended responses, and can disrupt the organization. Using focus groups can be very effective, but care must be taken when evaluating results in relation to sample size.

15.15 MEETINGWARE APPLICATIONS

Anytime a group gathers, and their mission can be put in the form of a question(s), there may be an opportunity to use meetingware to facilitate the gathering. Here are some successful applications of meetingware.

1. Planning—strategic and tactical (as is-to be activities)
2. Business process redesign (as is-to be activities and process identification)
3. Focus groups with employees, clients, suppliers, and experts
4. TQM-cause and effect/fishboning/affinity diagramming/quality improvement teams
5. Joint application development (JAD)—needs and requirements
6. Conflict resolution/impasse/team building
7. Selection committee awards—grants, recognition, performance
8. Training—diversity, change management, and so on
9. Resource allocation/budgeting/distribution of dollars, FTE, points
10. Process flow and sequencing
11. Needs analysis/job training, and so on
12. On-line document and policy edit/review/develop
13. Questionnaires/surveys/suggestion systems
14. Americans with Disabilities Compliance (essential functions/accommodations)
15. Marketing research
16. Organizational effectiveness and development

15.15.1 The Breakthrough

There is little doubt that meetingware will be widely used in time and become as ubiquitous as the computer. Friendlier software, voice recognition, artificial intelligence, and integration with other communication technologies are just a few of the innovations that will enhance meetingware's growth. Some breakthrough issues that may need to occur for meetingware to be institutionalized include:

1. **Meeting paradigm**—Not having to meet in the "same place" or at the "same time" is the paradigm shift required to accomplish "critical mass." When this is accomplished, face-to-face meetings, although irreplaceable, will diminish in frequency and importance. Meetingware faces many of the same cultural and technical challenges that have slowed the use of email in some organizations. As acceptance of email grows, more employees will have access to computers and will be more comfortable communicating and exchanging information using keyboards. As more communication networks are installed in organizations, meetingware will become easier to cost-justify. Improvements in the meetingware software and networking will also add to the acceptance of meetingware.

2. **Who's in charge?**—There is no one in most organizations responsible for meeting effectiveness. With the move to re-engineer processes, improve customer quality, reduce operating costs, and do more with less, the meeting has remained relatively unscathed compared to other business icons. Employees are usually not rewarded for the effective use of meeting time and resources; nor are they penalized. Face-to-face meetings are a safe haven, whether they be meetings of standing committees or junkets for conferences. Meetings are of course critical, but until organizations demand meeting time accountability, there will be little incentive to minimize the frequency or improve how meetings are conducted. Too often, managers have a perception that their meetings are very productive and there is little room for improvement. Rarely do managers (in a "risk-free" environment) ask for attendee feedback on their meeting "effectiveness."

3. **Double standard**—Meetingware, as currently formatted, offers users the tempting opportunity to "tell the truth" from their perspective. The truth is what leadership says it wants; but do they really? Until leadership becomes more accepting of the truth and diverse views, the anonymous features of meetingware may make its acceptance difficult.

4. **Loss of power**—Knowledge is power! Sharing knowledge is sometimes seen as a sure way to lose power. Meetingware is still seen by some as a threat to power. Losing control and having contradictory views expressed are seen as risky. With the sharing of knowledge and possible loss of power can come loss of job security. The concept of self-directed teams and flatter organization are already contemporary threats to leaders sensitive to the knowledge and power issue. When meetingware is widely seen by all as a tool to gain power and knowledge, not lose it, meetingware will flourish.

5. **Information management**—Technology has provided an avalanche of information at work and at home—database management, computer on-line services, 500 channels of TV, telecommunication innovation, and so on. There is more information "readily" available now than most people want or can handle. How to manage and use information effectively is the challenge. When groups gather to use meetingware, sorting through the amount of

information that can be generated is a detractor to its use. As mentioned, facilitation techniques can help manage this concern, but meetingware technology may have to build in software solutions for information overload.

ACKNOWLEDGMENTS

Thanks to the professional practitioners who have shared their meetingware experiences with me in preparation of this chapter. Especially Frances Lowe, Potomac, MD.; Robert Zadek, Half Moon Bay, CA; Paul Collins, Lincolnwood, IL; Susanna Opper, Alford, MA; Bernie DeKoven, Palo Alto, CA; Bonnie Kramer, World Bank; Clem McGowan, PhD., Mitre; Joel Reasor, PhD., AARP; and Richard Yellen, University of North Texas. My deepest appreciation to the visionary members at Marriott who supported the meetingware concept and helped make it a success: Chris Bubser, Mark Cross, Gary Grossman, David Kennedy, Charlie L'Esperance, Barbara O'Neil, Jim Moyer, Tony Neal, Mike Wakefield.

REFERENCES

1. Anson, R. [1990] "Improving Meetings Using Computers and Facilitators," College of Business, Boise State University, Boise, Idaho. (Research support by 3M Meeting Management Institute.)
2. Berne M. D., E. [1964] *Games People Play.* New York: Grove Press.
3. Buckley, W. M. [1992] "Computerizing Dull Meetings Is Touted as an Antidote to the Mouth that Bored." *Wall Street Journal*, January 28, 1992 (B1).
4. Carlson, P. [1992] "The Awful Truth About Meetings," *Washington Post*, December 20, 1992.
5. Connelly, T., Jessup, L. M., and Valacich, J. S. [1990] "Effects of Anonymity and Evaluative Tone and Idea Generation in Computer-Medicated Groups." *Management Science*, 36 (6), pp. 689–703.
6. Clark, C. [1958] *Brain-storming; The Dynamic New Way to Create Successful Ideas.* North Hollywood: Wilshire Book Company.
7. Crosby, P. B. *Quality Is Free.* New York: McGraw-Hill.
8. Davis, S., and Davidson, B. [1991] *2020 Vision—Transform your Business Today to Succeed in Tomorrow's Economy.* New York: Simon and Schuster.
9. DeKoven, B. [1990] *Connected Executives—A Strategic Communication Plan.* Palo Alto: Institute for Better Meetings Press.
10. Doyle, M., and Straus, D. [1982]. *How to Make Meetings Work.* New York: Jove.
11. Drake, S. [1992] "Electronic Meeting Rooms...." *Human Resource Executive*, July 1992.
12. Gallupe, R. B., Dennis, A. R., Cooper, W. H., Valacich, J. S., Nunamaker, F. F., Jr., and Bastianutte, L. [1992] "Electronic Brainstorming and Group Size." *Academy of Management Journal*, Volume 35, pp. 350–369.
13. Harvey, J. B. [1974] "The Abilene Paradox: The Management of Agreement." *Organizational Dynamics*, Volume 3, Number 1, Summer; AMACOM, a division of American Management Association.

14. Howard, V. A., and Barton, J. H. [1992] *Thinking Together—Making Meetings Work.* New York: Morrow.
15. Kirkpatrick, D. [1992] "Here Comes the Payoff from PCs," *Fortune*, March 23, 1992.
16. LaPlante, A. [1994] "Brainstorming 90's Style." *Forbes ASAP.*
17. Mosvick, R., and Nelson, R. [1987] "We've Got to Start Meeting Like This! A Guide to Successful Business Meeting Management." Glenview, IL: Scott, Foresman and Co.
18. Myers, D. G. [1978] "Polarizing Effects of Social Comparison." *Journal of Experimental Social Psychology*, Volume 14, pp. 554–563.
19. Myers, I. Briggs, and McCaulley, M. H. [1995] *Manual: A Guide to the Development and the Use of the Myers-Brigs Type Indicator.* Palo Alto: Consulting Psychologist Press.
20. Opper, S., and Fersko-Weiss, H. [1992] *Technology for Teams—Enhancing Productivity in Networked Organizations.* New York: Van Nostrand Reinhold.
21. Patterson, J., and Kim, P. [1992] *The Day America Told the Truth.* New York: Plume.
22. Post, B. Q. [1992], Boeing Corporation. "Building the Business Case for Group Support Technology," Los Alamitos, CA: IEEE Computer Technology Press.
23. Schrage, M. [1990] *Shared Minds—The New Technology of Collaboration.* New York: Random House.
24. Senge, P. [1990] *Fifth Discipline.* New York: Doubleday.
25. Stalk Jr., G., and Hout, T. M. [1990] *Competing Against Time—How Time-Based Competition Is Reshaping Global Markets.* New York: The Free Press.
26. Tannen, D. [1986] *That's Not What I Meant! How Conversational Style Makes or Breaks Relationships.* New York: Morrow.
27. Tannen, D. [1990] *You Just Don't Understand—Women and Men in Conversation.* New York: Morrow.
28. Thompson, C. [1992] *What a Great Idea!—Key Steps Creative People Take.* New York: Harper Perennial.
29. Trocha, H. J. [1992] "120 Problem Solutions in Twenty Minutes," *Wirtschaft, Welt am Sonntag*, June 7, 1992.
30. Von Oech, R. [1990]. *A Whack on the Side of the Head.* New York: Warner Books.

BIOGRAPHY

Carl Di Pietro is a nationally recognized process consultant specializing in the use of decision support systems to facilitate "rapid group consensus." He specializes in the use of networked computers to move groups from divergent to creative convergent thinking in quality improvement, process re-engineering, problem solving, planning, and other business processes. His techniques and methods have been written about in *Fortune, Forbes, Wall Street Journal*, and other publications.

Di Pietro has over 20 years of experience in a wide range of human resource functions in manufacturing and service industries, most recently as a vice president, human resources, Marriott International Headquarters. Thousands of employees from over 200 organizations have participated in business meetings using his methods, which increase the quality of decisions. He is the creator of a computer-assisted meeting facility, the Marriott Group Decision Center, at the Corporation's International Headquarters. He was awarded the 1992 International Yoder-Henneman Award (SHRM) for innovations in communications and human productivity. Mr. Di Pietro, a frequent speaker, has taught in the undergraduate business school at Georgetown University and the University of Maryland. Mr. Di Pietro is a business graduate of the University of Maryland and holds an M.A. in human resources from George Washington University. He is an arbitrator with the American Arbitration Association and a member of several professional organizations which include the American Society of Quality Control, Human Resource Planning Society, Planning Forum, Human Resources Technical Society, and the Society of Human Resource Management (SHRM).

Introduction to Chapter 16

This is a shared chapter and is an interesting study of Big Six experience with groupware and how two different consulting firms used groupware both internally and with clients.

Hugh Ryan is a focal point for groupware at Andersen Consulting, one of the largest and earliest users of Lotus Notes. In this chapter, he discusses how Andersen uses groupware, internally and with their clients around the world. Groupware has become a significant percentage of Andersen's revenue and supports their idea of "team metaphor."

Hugh uses anecdotes and case studies to explain the aspects of implementation in his examples. He looks at how groupware has impacted his practice, and then looks at why groupware is happening today (i.e., the factors contributing to its spread within Andersen and its clients). Some of the same factors I mentioned in the introduction (downsizing, increased competitiveness, etc.) are echoed by Hugh. He introduces the ideas of Knowledge Managers and Knowledge Xchange which comprise the intellectual capital of Andersen. The idea of having this expertise and experience available to company employees is not a new one, but the technology to make it a reality is new. This type of Knowledge Xchange provides a significant competitive advantage.

But the technology has to be tied into the culture. Price Waterhouse found that out the hard way. After a successful roll-out of the technology, Notes was not being fully utilized by PW consultants to leverage expertise. In a consulting organization, an employee's value is determined by the number of billable hours. Therefore, time to learn complex new technologies is at a premium. Furthermore, if it is not clear that the new technology will directly improve personal business productivity or increase personal revenues, there is no incentive to participate in collaborative processes. Once PW realized this, they tied promotions and raises to use of the collaborative databases. This resulted in generating more active Notes users and many more contributions to Notes databases, and PW's intellectual capital soared. The point is, it's the conjunction of technology with culture that is successful, not just technology alone!

At this point in time, Andersen has 10,000 Notes users connected all over the world. Maintaining the directory, replication storms, and other hazards has taught Andersen what works in large organizations and what doesn't. Andersen looks at all aspects of groupware—workflow, electronic meetings, and other collaborative technologies. But Hugh also talks about change management and its importance to the success of these re-engineered processes. Finally, Hugh moves on to cover conditions for the "team metaphor."

Both parts of this chapter are very personal views of large organizations. Frank Lancione was at Coopers & Lybrand when I asked him to write his chapter, but has since moved to a systems integrator, PRC. His writing reflects his perspective and experience with groupware from the perspective of an integrator rather than that of a Big Six executive. Because I have worked closely with Frank, I have had the opportunity to see firsthand the difference in corporate culture and how these differences impact the way groupware is used internally and for customers.

Frank's style is much less formal than Hugh's, but just as effective. Frank talks about his experiences facilitating electronic meetings for many government groups and presents an interesting example of group decision making in electronic meetings against the backdrop of our participation in the war with Iraq. He looks at how these technologies are used on a daily basis and their emerging role at PRC. It is interesting to note that PRC deals with both hardware and software issues. In addition to its commercial IS systems consulting, PRC is often a prime government contractor. PRC takes a view of groupware that is very different from Coopers & Lybrand or Andersen.

Most of the consulting firms must "walk their talk," use the technologies to re-engineer themselves, before their customers will go for it. This has led PRC to a focus on process redesign and an internal restructuring.

I know you will find both parts of this chapter entertaining and informative. They are very different. Keep in mind that both companies are using some of the same groupware technologies, but in very different ways!

CHAPTER **16A**

Building Computing Solutions
with the Team Metaphor

Hugh W. Ryan
Andersen Consulting

16A.1 PART I: GROUPS THAT GROPE AND TEAMS THAT DELIVER

In recent years the business world has moved very quickly toward groupware
solutions. At Andersen Consulting, groupware has grown in just two years from
a small part of our business at a few key sites to a business that accounts for over
3% of our systems integration work. We are convinced that this growth will follow at a rate similar to that we have seen with client-server computing. There,
after just seven years of tracking this technology, client-server solutions now
make up over 50% of our business.

Our work with groupware has convinced us that the core of this practice is
about allowing teams of people to work more effectively on a backbone of computing. The key to a successful team is to have clear goals and a commitment to
achieving those goals. With a commitment to goals, the computing backbone cannot fail; without that commitment, the backbone cannot succeed. Because of this
focus on the *team* we have moved away from referring to the work as groupware.
In our experience, these new computing solutions are being built around the
metaphor of a *team*. Groups grope; teams deliver. So we speak most often in
terms of "teamware." Related concepts can be found in the industry today. These
include Forrester's [1993] social computing and Gartner's New Synthesis.

With the team metaphor, business computing solutions are based on a business team completing a business process. The support includes all things that
teams need—communications, coordination, and sharing—as well as the applications individuals need to perform their work.

477

As an example, consider an insurance office performing the business process of settling a claim. In one common model for this process, it will consist of the subprocesses of collecting the claim information, gathering evidence, adjudicating the claim, and settling the claim. The team for this process would consist of the claimant, receptionist, claim taker, claim agent, and claim settlement specialist. Time and budget constraints are often set by the company based on the desire to deliver a speedy and fair settlement. All of these components become wrapped together in the team metaphor.

Hearing the word "teamware" for the first time, the reader's reaction might well be, "Another consultant making up names to confuse things." However, in our experience, if you are trying to sell these kinds of ideas to management, especially senior management, you will often find that they have a pretty negative view of information technology investment. I have literally had a senior executive tell me, "I have enough groups groping around here trying to figure what they are doing; I want some results."

In addition to the selling aspect, the concept of the team brings to the entire development and delivery process a much sharper focus on what one is trying to do in delivering a solution. With the concept of the team, one leaves the development starting gate asking things like, "Who is the team? What do they need to work together? How will the team succeed?" These are the right questions to ask, because they get you started off in the right direction.

These questions also point you toward a larger problem associated with the delivery of the team metaphor. The "user" of the system is the entire team, and if you thought doing a system for an individual user was hard, watch what happens when the user is a team. The problem is much like the multibodied problem in physics. As the number of interactions and needs increase, coming up with a solution gets harder and harder. A team of several hundred people spread across three continents and multiple cultures and on which the sun never sets is going to face some tough challenges.

In a sense, we have been providing aspects of such solutions for many years. I once worked on a health insurance application which required the claim to be moved around to appropriate claims personnel based on health risk. However, there are differentiating aspects of the definition which make the team metaphor a step forward over prior solutions. These factors include the following:

☞ The focus of computing shifts from the individual to the team. The answer to how the solution works is about how the team interacts to get the job done.

☞ The result of the team's work is a *case*. The case has all the information relevant to the team's work. This may include structured data, text, and media such as image, voice, and video. Individuals access and use the case, but the team's deliverable is the case as a whole.

☞ Many aspects of the building solution focus on how the team works. Questions here include, who on the team has the case? What are they doing as a part of the team? What do they need to complete their work? What parts of the case can be worked on while it is in use by the current team member?

Further questions include, who can and should work on the case as it completes the next stage of work? Where is that person, and how can the case be delivered to them? What are the criteria by which one can move the case to the next person? What do we need to know to evaluate progress and effectiveness of the team?

If one considers these qualities of team work, there are new sets of questions and concerns in the delivery of solutions based on the team metaphor. These new questions suggest that while we have been doing some of these solutions the team metaphor is taking us in new directions and in these new directions lies the opportunity of the team metaphor.

16A.1.1 Impact on Our Practice and Overview of the Material

The following material is largely structured based on how the team metaphor has impacted and is impacting the Andersen Consulting practice. We are helping our clients every day with this form of solution, and we find that their questions and concerns usually come in the following sequence:

☞ What is the team metaphor, and what is its relationship to the terms such as groupware and workflow? This was discussed above and will be discussed below in "Forms of the Team Metaphor."

☞ Why is the team metaphor happening now? Often, this question comes from a feeling that "We've had enough change, why can't we have a little peace now?" This is discussed more fully in the section "Why is the Team Metaphor Happening Now?"

☞ Then the questions shift to the different forms of the team metaphor. In our practice we find that this shift to forms of the team metaphor is essential. It clarifies where the client's problems and opportunities are and can provide a migration path to move into the team metaphor. This is discussed more fully in "Forms of the Team Metaphor."

☞ As the opportunities and problems of the team metaphor become clearer, the focus shifts to the process of building the solution. The underlying technology for these solutions is inherently client-server, and the technical steps and decisions are very dependent on the organization's current commitment to client-server technology. The second, and arguably greater, issue is how to get the group to work as a team. In our experience, the greatest challenge in these systems is not the technology; it's getting people to work as a team. While we may not like to admit it, many enterprises today are really recursive functional fiefdoms; the concept of a team crossing boundaries of the fiefdoms is viewed with about the same anticipation, excitement, and interest as an anthrax epidemic. In this context success requires a focus on getting people to *want* to be part of the team, and this challenge is not about neat-looking graphical user interfaces. Finally, one moves into delivery and once again the focus shifts to installation and operations of the system and evolving it to meet new needs. This is discussed more fully in the section "Issues In Developing Team Metaphor Solutions."

The following sections will take the reader through the typical thoughts, ideas, and approaches that we use in our practice in implementing team metaphor solutions.

16A.2 WHY IS THE TEAM METAPHOR HAPPENING NOW?

The question "Why now?" is a key question, because the answer helps to build the case for solutions based on the team metaphor.

I've already discussed one of the key factors. Until now most of our solutions have addressed the individual, collecting the results of the work that they do. Increasingly, however, strong businesses are being built on teams of people working together to get the job done [Katzenbach and Smith]. The team metaphor provides the basis for thinking about these solutions. It is needed now as businesses ask how can we work as a team? There is the opportunity to do previously unrecognized work which can matter to the business.

Although the team metaphor shifts the focus of the design to the team, these solutions can be built on the work we have done for the individual over the last 25 years of business computing. Thus, for example, a claims agent may still enter claims into the initial entry screen in a legacy system. Given that the information technology industry is facing the reality of 20 or more years of legacy systems, solutions that can build on the legacy are those that will thrive.

The team metaphor is able to take unique advantage of the recent computing technology we have been installing. Specifically, teamware can take unique advantage of the capabilities we find in client-server-based solutions. More organizations are realizing that client-server represents the convergence of computing and communications. With the team metaphor, additional processing (rules) occurs to alert others (roles) in the team of the entry and sets in motion the flow of work (routes), which ensures that the team pulls together to meet the demands of the new claim. This doing and moving of the work intrinsically needs the convergence of computing offered by client-server computing. This convergence makes the most sense in the context of a team, simply because to be a real team, the members of the team must be able to communicate. That is what client-server allows them to do.

In addition, team communications will need to take many different forms—not only traditional data, but also voice, image, handwritten annotation, and possibly phone. These are all components of what I have previously described as the human metaphor [Ryan 1992], which is built on the back of client-server and which we can employ to make the team metaphor more effective.

We are working in a time of downsizing of the corporation. In reality, what this often means is that middle layers of management are removed from the corporate structure. These layers often served the roles of administering the business process and communicating what was happening among the various roles. This was, in a sense, a soft role; it is difficult to show the return on investment for such an individual. As these roles are cut out through downsizing, it is becoming apparent that there was value in such work. Its value must be maintained, and the team metaphor concept provides at least part of the solution.

At the same time, we are delivering solutions focused on reinventing the business process. Reinventing the business process is often understood as going from a traditional functional focus to a process orientation. The process orientation naturally arises when one implements the team metaphor, since it is the process of the team working together that one is capturing in the implementation.

As one reinvents the corporation, one opportunity which arises is that often the business process extends over the traditional corporate boundaries. Upstream, one can look at suppliers as a part of the solutions. Downstream, one can see distributors and even customers as a part of the solution. In this view of things, the corporation becomes a manager of the value chain that delivers the product or service to the customer and is referred to as the virtual corporation. Such a virtual corporation focuses on ensuring that each component of the value chain has what it needs when it needs it, not on doing the work in the component. Given the difficulty of managing such a company internally, managing this extended value chain can be an appallingly difficult effort. To succeed, the team metaphor can and should extend beyond the traditional corporate boundaries to meet this evolving vision of the corporation. Here are some examples of what I mean:

☞ At Andersen Consulting, we have implemented a large knowledge exchange application, which I discuss in more detail later. In essence, this application allows us to move our firms' growing knowledge capital to people who need it, whenever they need it. Because a consultancy is, to a large degree, in the business of applying knowledge to client problems and opportunities, this system has become a major intellectual artery for our firm.

☞ As this is written, one of my clients, a large insurance broker, is beginning to reinvent its processes. Traditionally, brokers divided the risk into pieces and then found insurers to assume different components of the overall risk. With the new process, the broker will manage the process of brokering, which occurs between client and insurer. In this role the broker becomes a negotiation manager. The broking company views the impact on the business as immense.

☞ At a window manufacturer, the customer in the hardware store uses an application developed by the manufacturer to design their windows. The design validates that what the client wants can be built; then, when the order is complete, it submits the order to the shop floor where it is scheduled and built. It is then delivered to the customer's house or to the hardware store. Consideration is being given to providing a list of approved installers to the customer and offering to contact them to supply bids for the installation.

☞ A similar design-to-specification is done now by several auto manufacturers so that the customers select what they want for the auto, and are then given a delivery date and price.

☞ A pharmaceutical company provides workstations to its mobile sales people. As they travel to their customers and take orders, the focus is on finding the drugs the customer wants or needs. There is little focus on who makes the drugs. In effect, the drug company has become a distribution channel for drugs; the source of the drug is not a major issue.

The point is that these types of applications are becoming pervasive, and the key is to focus on the concept of the virtual enterprise that includes the customer and distributor as a part of the solution. Doing so results in more involved customers who feel they are getting what they want, while squeezing costs and delays out of the distribution channel.

It appears that these considerations make the team metaphor a truly different solution. We have been doing solutions for the individual for a quarter of a century; through repetition and improvement, we have gotten very good at them. But the day of the solution for the individual is over. The potential for new solutions and innovation lies in the team. And the convergence of computing and communications means that the technology is now there to deliver solutions based on the team metaphor. Thus, to a remarkable degree, the team metaphor is the right image for our computing solutions at the right time. It builds on where we are and where we want to go for the future.

The question of metrics often comes up during discussions of the team metaphor. This is a difficult question to answer, for two reasons. First, the team metaphor represents a new way to do business. For example, consider Andersen Consulting's knowledge management system I mentioned above. It's a new phenomenon; it didn't replace an existing system, so a cost/benefit analysis is difficult to do. We made a judgment call that because of the explosion of knowledge in our business, we need to make sure our people can get at that knowledge any time they want it. We didn't do a cost/benefit analysis because we knew in our guts that it was the right thing to do. In the case of the pharmaceutical business, the company was implementing a green field application. Nothing existed before, and no company has been run to this point in a similar manner. The cost/benefit is simply hard to determine.

The second reason why metrics is so complex is because the measures that one can find are usually not objective financial metrics, but somewhat more abstract measures of service or quality. In the case of the broker mentioned before, they have been quoted at public forums as saying that their team-oriented system reduced the brokering times by up to 90% in the prototypes. But people involved with the application say that the process has been so changed by the application that one is really comparing two totally different businesses. In the case of the manufacturer, they were looking for 6 sigma quality. Thanks to the team of sales, engineering, manufacturing, and installation personnel, they achieved that goal. The ability of the system to support the team made a direct contribution to the quality of the delivered product.

My point is not that one has to avoid metrics. Rather, the nature of the change rendered by the team metaphor is so profound that doing a traditional ROI may be impossible. The good news in all this is that the team metaphor may well offer the potential to do the business so differently that you will not know it when it happens. The bad news is that there will always be some people who will demand a clear ROI before moving on a solution. With the team metaphor, that may be difficult.

16A.3 FORMS OF THE TEAM METAPHOR

In our practice, when we work with clients on this type of solution we move past the team metaphor pretty quickly to discuss the different forms of the team metaphor. There are several reasons for this. First, the team metaphor is a wide concept covering many things. We find it essential to begin to frame the client's interest by going through the forms to decide which are of interest. Furthermore, the concerns and issues of successful development and delivery of the team metaphor are very dependent on the form of the team metaphor being adopted. Finally, experience suggests that analytical people spend a good deal of time trying to define what a thing is before doing it, so having the forms identified already can save time.

A team's approach to work depends on the nature of its tasks, team size, and work processes and the roles of the team members. A means to differentiate among the various forms of the team metaphor is in terms of defined process, time and budget constraints, and quality goals. Some forms of the team metaphor place great emphasis on meeting time and budget constraints; others put greater focus on the objective of meeting quality goals. The following differentiates the various forms of the team metaphor based on these considerations:

☞ Communication and routing
☞ Information exchange
☞ Process management
☞ Collaboration
☞ Meetings

16A.3.1 Communication and Routing

Effective communications between members of a group or organization depends on choosing an appropriate channel. That choice is based on several factors: the nature of the information to be communicated; the group to be addressed; the level of interaction required within that group; and keeping the communication timely. Electronic mail (email) is a common choice for informal, ad hoc, non-urgent communication. Email is an effective way to request information, track pending issues, update colleagues on project status, or request a meeting. Some examples of email products are cc: Mail, Microsoft Mail, and Word Perfect Office.

In the context of the team metaphor, communications and routing is, essentially, a utility. As such, it is not about defined processes, or budget constraints or quality goals. It is about communications, and this is a necessary backbone on which to base the team metaphor.

Andersen Consulting has received a good deal of attention in the press for our widespread use of Lotus Notes. As this is written, it is deployed to over 10,000 people on a worldwide basis. Our use of it to date has focused on these first two forms of the team metaphor—that is, communications and information exchange (described below). We use it widely as a communications forum to ship and share information and request things of others. It fits well with our highly mobile work force, who tend to spend most of their careers on the road working with clients. This means we must be able to connect into and use the communications where and when we can.

In my own experience on the road, where a particular hotel chain has become a second home, my experience with communications often means arriving at the room at 10 or 11 at night, diving under the bed, and pushing the dust bunnies out of the way to plug into the telephone jack to do an exchange. If I choose to do this night after night, even with allergies to that dust, it must mean that the communications exchange is vital to my work. Today, as I write, I received a resume for a consultant coming from Europe, a request for client-server credentials for a proposal in the People's Republic of China, another round of memos on what is a technical versus enterprise architect that is being argued over three continents in cyberspace, and 400 memos from administrative functions. Only one of these is a slight exaggeration. This is typical, and with the exception of the administrative memos I have no idea how I did the same work for 20 years without the tool. (My treatment of the administrative memos has not changed significantly with the advent of Notes.)

16A.3.2 Information Exchange Applications

Much of the information required by today's business worker is unstructured in nature and does not conform to fixed columns or rows. This information often originates outside of the enterprise—news feeds or company profiles, for example—and must be easily shared to be of real value. Information exchange applications provide business workers with capabilities to easily manage and share vast amounts of both structured and unstructured information from both internal and external sources. The objective of information exchange applications is to make this information available to the business worker when and where they need it. Developing effective information exchange applications requires very different rules, tools, and associated training as compared to even "traditional" client-server applications such as GUI builders and relational DBMSs. Lotus Notes is a common tool to deliver information exchange.

With regard to information exchange at Andersen Consulting, we are making some large investments in what we call our Knowledge Xchange knowledge management system. This is a cybrary (a library in cyberspace [*Wired*, 1994]) containing much of what we know—what we call "knowledge capital." As examples, one can find in the Knowledge Xchange approaches for connecting Windows clients to UNIX servers, architectures for building Visual Basic solutions, or conjectures on the futures of DBMS vendors. In effect, anything that a consultant feels could be of value to others can be placed in the Knowledge Xchange. Being able to capture and make this information available is becoming a major competitive advantage for our firm [*Fortune*].

We are in our second generation of the Knowledge Xchange. One might say that the first generation suffered from success. In effect, it became a bag—and anyone could put things in the bag. The good news was that the bag had a great deal of stuff. The bad news was that the bag had a great deal of stuff that was hard to find when it was needed. The input and the number of people desperately seeking things in the bag convinced us that there was a great deal of value in the concept of the Knowledge Xchange. However, it was obvious that we had to provide structure and a framework for adding things to it.

What we have done is go to a library concept to manage our knowledge in the cybrary. What any library does when it adopts the Dewey Decimal system is defines the dimension of knowledge it will keep. We are doing the same in defining dimensions of knowledge we will keep. So, for example, we have a technology dimension that includes such things as client-server, database, and multimedia. We have a second dimension that includes industries such as insurance and products. There are additional dimensions such as geography and so forth.

In addition, in keeping with the library concept, we have librarians, who we call "knowledge managers." These people ensure the quality of the content in the Knowledge Xchange. As such, they review all submissions to the Knowledge Xchange for quality and content. They may add dimensions to the submission, such as the client-server knowledge manager determining that a submission had content valuable to the data management dimension. They may determine that a submission is redundant and advise the submitter to review what exists already and determine what is unique in their submission. They provide assistance for personnel looking for things in the cybrary, and they may hear of opportunities where the content would help and proactively contact personnel to explain what is available. This happens often when we are developing a proposal. We widely view the knowledge exchange as one of our keys to success in this highly competitive world.

At the same time it must be said that operating such an exchange is a difficult and complex undertaking. The need to classify knowledge was widely debated within the firm. One group (which I refer to as the "fabulists") felt that modern search engines made such preclassifications unnecessary and would be restrictive. The second group (which I refer to as "correct") felt that without classification we would move toward chaos again. In the end, the classification approach seems to be moving in the right direction.

There are other concerns. The telecommunications expense is immense. Obviously, personnel must be as dedicated to the effort as the cybrarians. Furthermore, there are significant numbers of personnel involved in simply running the systems on a day-to-day basis. Simply having 10,000 people turn up willy nilly all over the world wanting to connect in and replicate is a challenge. The implications of a single worldwide directory of 10,000 people is something we are still thinking through. We have had what are referred to as "replication storms" where changes from a set of servers in one site cause a cascade of changes around the world, and the servers get so tied up replicating changes they do not have resources to connect to users. Regaining control of these situations is difficult. As it turns out, taking a server off-line results in all the changes being queued for the server; when it is reconnected, the storm can be restarted by the server. To some degree we are on the leading edge in these efforts, and the leading edge is where you get the cuts. But at the end of the day, no one ever says that we should or even can go back. Our business is based on knowledgeable people, and they find and place much of that knowledge in the Knowledge Xchange.

16A.3.3 Process Management Applications

The essence of process management is the completion of cross-function business activities which meet quality goals within constraints of time and budget [Seybold, 1993]. Routes, rules, and roles of the new business process are defined as key steps in building these applications. The new rules, roles, and routes determine the flow of work within the business team and documents used by the business team. To reap the full benefits of process management, an organization must typically change how it functions. New paradigms and methodologies are required for process management, including the compound document metaphor, workflow, commitment tracking, time and budget management, queue management. Ironically, many popular "groupware" products which claim to support workflow capabilities are inadequate for "industrial-strength" process management, though they may be fine for other types of team applications.

Process management applications focus on situations where there is a defined process. For example, the claims settlement business process in a well-run insurance company will be well defined. The goal of the claims process management application is to see that the process is done with the full participation of the team. Thus, all the roles of claimant, receptionist, witness, and claims agents must be recognized. The application must consider where time is being spent and try to make sure that when work can be done, it is assigned to the right person with all the information they need to get it done. Thus, in the claims example, the claims agent might get a flash to re-open the claims case when a doctor's report comes in. The claims process must have quality constraints which can be measured and tracked.

16A.3.4 Collaborative Applications

Collaboration is the act of working jointly to produce a single product or service. Individual contributions are, of course, a key component of collaborative work, since teams typically divide a project into subtasks, assign them to individual members, and then merge the results to produce the final product. Object management, version control, compare, delegation, merge, and annotation are key technologies.

These efforts differ from process management primarily in the fact that the processes for collaborative efforts may not be well defined. Further, it is in the nature of collaborative efforts that they may not have well-defined time frames and budget constraints. Typically, there is a strong focus on quality, producing one's best from the collaborative effort.

16A.3.5 Meetings

Meetings are a setting for team work suited for "face-to-face" interactions in order to make decisions, solve problems, and craft solutions that are not routine. Applications based on decision support system (DSS) technology can aid in this process, help to structure the discussion of a problem, provide the framework for brainstorming, establish criteria for evaluating proposals, and provide the tools for analyzing the constraints on a business model. Such applications do not lend themselves easily to traditional development tools and techniques.

In these applications the process is not any better defined than is the meeting agenda. Budget constraints tend not to receive much focus, given the meeting has been agreed to. Time constraints are often a dominant concern.

Taken together, these are some of the components of what we mean by the team metaphor. The key point is that the metaphor is a rich way to capture the way we interact with others.

16A.4 PART II: THE ISSUES IN DEVELOPING TEAM METAPHOR SOLUTIONS

Given this framework for the team metaphor, I turn now to the issues of implementing a system based on the team metaphor. One of the values of the team metaphor framework is that, while a set of issues can be identified that are of concern for any team metaphor implementation, the significance and impact of the issue varies, based on the form of the team metaphor being implemented.

With regard to the issues, the following are major concerns when considering an implementation based on the team metaphor:

☞ The reality of the team
☞ Defining the technical architecture for the team metaphor
☞ The systems management of a team metaphor
☞ The network as the team
☞ Implementing the teamware solution

16A.4.1 The Reality of the Team

Probably the single biggest impediment to implementing a solution based on the metaphor of a team is the fact that in many organizations very often few people work effectively as a team. As an example, I did a good deal of consulting with a banking institution. The organization has been widely recognized in the press as a highly effective organization with an ability to destroy the opposition. In essence, the organization viewed itself as a set of very aggressive competitors. I found that this reputation extended into the internal organization as well. If there was no competitor to go after, the organization would go after itself. This made meetings interesting affairs. Some of them bordered on verbal karate with an undertone that they could become physical. This internal competitiveness became an increasing concern in the context of implementing the team metaphor. The client and I finally concluded that a team metaphor implementation in the form of process management or collaboration would be, at best, difficult.

On the more positive side, a pharmaceutical company I noted earlier has used the team metaphor to move toward the virtual enterprise. One of the key concerns in a pharmaceutical company is the question of unanticipated drug side effects. The company uses a combination of tools to monitor automated news feeds for reports on drug problems or side effects. When a problem is detected, the system automatically issues requests for information to the manufacturer to clarify the situation. This information in turn is then available to the salespeople on the same work day. Given the considerations of time zones, the salespeople may be equipped with the facts prior to start of the business day because they are part of the team.

The point is that if an organization does not work well as a team, there is little reason to believe that a systems implementation based on the team metaphor will lead the organization to different ways of behaving and working. The options then are to select a form of the team metaphor which makes sense for the organization, or to exert a change-management effort to bring about the needed change in the organization to work as a team.

What do I mean by change management? The change management process is a formal, well-defined process to move the users of the system to acceptance of the system. The process is typically based on what is called the change curve (see Figure 16A.1). This curve starts by giving the business user awareness of what the change is and why it needs to happen. Then one moves to giving them knowledge of how the change will work and how they will work with the changed approach. There then follows a period of trial and evaluation where the business user works with the system or a prototype of the system, allowing them to provide feedback and see changes from the feedback. Finally, one moves to conversion to the change and acceptance. Depending on the nature of the change, the change management process often includes changes to the measurement and reward system so that the value of the change is made explicit.

The need for a change management process must be evaluated in each case, as a full change management process may not always be necessary. For example, one form of the team metaphor—communications—has worked in a wide variety of organizations, whether they have an orientation to teamwork or not. When one considers experience with this form of the metaphor, this is not too surprising. Whether one likes working with other individuals or not, the fact is that we still need to communicate. With a global mobile work force, such communication becomes desperately difficult, but also essential. To this end, the communications form of the team metaphor facilitates this need and seems to grow natu-

Fig. 16A.1 Managing Change

rally as a part of the organization. Thus, in a number of cases, I have seen email become a part of an organization with little or no encouragement, simply because people need to communicate.

Beyond communications, many of us, as knowledge workers, need constantly to know more than we do and to learn from what others are doing. As a result, the knowledge management form of the team metaphor can be a natural solution in many cases. I have already discussed how Andersen Consulting has rolled out its Knowledge Xchange to over 10,000 consultants, most of whom consult it on a daily basis to find out who else has dealt with the same or a related problem in the global organization. In this case, the rollout of the Knowledge Xchange has happened with essentially no training or incentives. As an organization, competition and the explosion of technology and solutions have resulted in a desperate need to know the best practices available, and the Knowledge Xchange provides at least part of the answer.

When one comes to process management, teamwork becomes more of a challenge. The process management form of the team metaphor means one must work with and be dependent on others. One must trust that others will do the job that needs to be done, so that one may do one's own job. Furthermore, the result of the work is not the individual's results but the team's. For many people in many organizations, this can be a disturbing perspective. For the financial institution discussed earlier, it was an overwhelming concern.

Then the change-management process of addressing awareness, knowledge, trial, evaluations, and measures and rewards becomes more critical. Such an effort must focus on overcoming old views of one's role and defining and building confidence in a new role as a part of the team. It is easy to write this, but far harder to achieve.

As an example, I once worked with a government agency client where the system being delivered had an associated three-year change-management process. It began with explanations of the need for change in business practice and reduction in head counts due to citizen perceptions of service by the agency, and the reality of an aging and declining tax base. From this the effort moved to explain how processes would change based on moving to the single-customer view and sharing of work across the agency. There then ensued an extended trial period with prototypes of the systems in a model office followed by conversion to the live systems with over 25,000 users in 500 local offices. Given that this was a system justified in part by large head count reductions in the face of an active union, the system went live with minimal action. The reasons are almost entirely due to the effectiveness of the change process.

The importance of a change-management process in the team metaphor cannot be overemphasized. As this is written, several articles have appeared in the last year on the sudden surge in productivity of U.S. workers [Magnet, 1994]. The bottom line seems to be that the change has come about due to the impact of downsizing on business users. As a result of being downsized, business users are being forced to use systems they have had for years, as the systems were intended to be used, because the downsizing left no option. The implication is, for many of the systems we have delivered over the years, the user did not make the business changes to use them. Given the number of systems built and installed over the last 20 years, this is a stunning indictment of the effectiveness of change management for the systems to date. Given the prior point that people are often not used to working in a team, it makes it critical that a highly effective change-management effort be mounted for any process management form of the team metaphor.

When one considers collaboration, change management is once again going to be a requirement. Several reasons contribute to this conclusion. First, by definition, collaboration is used when the process is not well defined. This means the users are not accustomed to prescribed styles of work. Even the minimal amount of systemization of process found in collaboration will mean a change in work style for a business user who is often used to working in an unrestricted fashion. Second, in implementing a collaborative form of the team metaphor, often some form of consistent deliverable will need to be imposed [Katzenbach and Smith]. In opposition to this, limited systemization and standardization of the forms are often found in users who have a tradition of doing as they please. In addition, business users brought into a collaborative solution, many times, are professionals who have the option to simply say no to a system. All of this means that change management for the collaborative style of the team metaphor must be approached with a great deal of thought, care, and consideration for the business user to be impacted by the system.

16A.4.2 Defining the Technical Architecture for the Team Metaphor

This issue addresses making all the decisions that one needs to make with regard to the technology to be used in implementing the team metaphor. Experience with the team metaphor suggests the problem can be broken into two situations. One case is found when the enterprise has already moved to client-server technology. The other case is when an enterprise has not yet begun to implement client-server technology.

With regard to client-server and the team metaphor, it seems that client-server is the natural technical base on which to deliver the team metaphor. The client workstation provides both local processing capability and the event-driven architecture. The local processing capability provides a natural fit to the needs of the business user doing a wide range of work, from entering client orders to creating memos to running models.

Also, by providing local processing, the workstation provides a means to ensure that the team metaphor is available wherever the mobile user goes. The event-driven architecture provides for a very responsive nature, which means that the work to be done can be driven by the business users' needs as the work they are doing unfolds around them. It also means that as the team needs to reach out and touch the specific business user, the workstation can respond to these events and alert the business user as the need arises.

The server provides the means for the collective work of the team to be gathered and processed as a whole. It also provides a place where all members of the team, many of whom may be mobile, can meet in an electronic sense and share the results of their work and assess the questions the team is facing in trying to do its work. As such, the server is a critical part of successful delivery of the team metaphor.

The above suggests that client-server is an inherent part of the team metaphor. If an enterprise has not yet adopted a technical architecture for client-server, then the implication is that a great many decisions must be made with regard to the basics of client-server. I have addressed elsewhere the process of doing this [Ryan, 1994]. However, it is worthwhile to note that this can be a time-consuming process, with many decisions to be made on processors, operating systems, DBMS, tools, and so forth. In a calculation I once did for one client in an open systems environment, there were over 6000 possible combinations. While no one goes through all of these combinations, the fact is, these decisions can and often do consume several months before being resolved.

In a sense, the team metaphor represents a significant point in the evolution of business computing solutions. It is a solution for a wide set of business problems built on what has been termed the "client-server revolution." Because the team metaphor assumes the use of client-server, this suggests that what once was a revolution has now become the status quo. It further suggests that those who have not moved to client-server are risking becoming stuck in the business computing past. Given the potential benefits of the team metaphor, becoming stuck is not the way to end up.

If the enterprise has already moved to client-server, then a significant set of decisions have already been made. In my experience, it has not been necessary to reverse the client-server decisions, particularly in the last few years, because *de facto* standards have emerged and we have begun to move toward technological lock-in for client-server. Assuming, then, a base of client-server, the decisions are about what is needed to support the team metaphor.

The team metaphor framework can be a useful guide in such decisions. In a sense, as one goes from implementing communications to meetings, the right technical decisions vary. For example, if one is intent on primarily implementing a communications team metaphor, a wide set of email-based tools will suffice. However, if one's intent is to implement communications and one inadvertently moves to implementing something like our Knowledge Xchange, then the tools selected for communications may provide inadequate.

Similarly, the tools that work for information exchange may not suffice for process management. In the latter, there is often a need to reflect the progress of the team in real time in traditional databases, and some of the prominent tools do not do this. Also, as one moves to process management, one is often building complex business logic, for both the individual and the team as a whole. Finally, the process management activity means that one must deal with rules and roles of personnel in doing the work. Often, this information needs to be recorded in databases for rapid and consistent access. Many of the information exchange tools do not have this built in, and it must be added. The combination of limited real-time access to relational databases, and the need for complex logic and flexible descriptions of rules and routes means many of the team metaphor tools today do not stand up well to such demands.

As an example, I have worked at several clients where the initial prototypes of the systems were developed using tools well suited to information exchange. Prototypes were well received and contributed to building awareness and knowledge of the change. However, as we moved from prototypes to the live system with the need to update databases on a global basis, the need for very complex logic, and the need to change personnel and their roles on a worldwide basis, it became apparent that the tools for prototyping would not withstand the demands of the live system, and implementation proceeded with more traditional tools.

I have had the opportunity to review several cases where initial prototypes were done using information exchange tools and the long-term pervasive impact of the lack of database capability, complex logic, and flexible roles and routes was missed. In each case the system had to be retracted or had an ongoing reputation as being a problem.

The key point of all this is that when making decisions on technical architecture, one must consider carefully the *form* of the team metaphor one is planning to implement. The technical components that work well for communications may be disappointing when pushed beyond this need. Similarly, tools that succeed well at knowledge exchange may disappoint when pushed to critical business needs inherent in process management. At the same time, the more common technical tools used to build custom applications may require far more custom building for pieces that one finds inherent in knowledge exchange or communications. The key is to know where one is going when one implements the team metaphor. Given that one understands where one is going, one selects an architecture based on that goal and ties it to an appropriate change management effort; in this way, the potential to succeed is greatly enhanced.

16A.4.3 Systems Management for the Team Metaphor

In the last few years, more organizations have recognized that systems management is one of the greatest challenges in successful implementation of client-server. Given my earlier comments on client-server being the basic technology for the team metaphor, the same comments apply for the team metaphor. One point worth some emphasis is that the communications and knowledge exchange forms of the team metaphor experience have shown that these forms can spread throughout the enterprise very quickly—often, far faster than is expected by, and with little direct knowledge of, systems personnel. In contrast, typically, systems management is assembled slowly as known applications are moved to the client-server environment. As a result, the rapid spread of these forms of the team metaphor may outstrip the capabilities of the systems management due to the sheet volume of users coming into the team metaphor.

In the case of process management, the business nature of these applications makes the normal issues and concerns of systems management apply. However, my experience has been that these systems are moving into business solutions of business users who may be mobile and apt to connect into the system at any time of the day. Furthermore, the demand of the team often means that the individual must get to the team metaphor applications right now, even if it is eleven o'clock at night. As I have said, if I have wrestled the dust bunnies to get into my system, it is somewhat frustrating to be told that the "server is not responding." In this case, it is essential to have a highly effective help desk facility that can get on top of the problem *now*. Failure to do so can threaten the effectiveness of the team as a whole.

At Andersen Consulting, we run a help desk during normal business hours to help our consultants navigate the Knowledge Xchange. This can be an invaluable service. In essence, I view this as an application support help desk. The personnel on the help desk know the application and understand the questions being asked. In addition, their role is not just to record the problem, but to solve it while the caller is on the phone. The value of this help desk becomes clearer after hours, when we can't get it—when we're up late or calling from Europe or Australia or Tokyo. Indeed, as this is written, our firm is considering outsourcing the help desk support on a 24-hour basis. That obviously represents an additional expense, but it may be unavoidable, given our patterns of usage. Each business needs to evaluate its own specifics; but if the business is done on a global basis or if the usage is such that people are accessing information at all hours of the day and night, such a help desk would make a major contribution toward the success of the team metaphor application.

16A.4.4 The Network as the Team

The title of this section suggests that the successful delivery of the team metaphor is critically dependent on the underlying network. The essence of creating a team on the backbone of computing is to connect the individuals of the team into a cohesive effective whole. The key to do this is the network. It must be available, reliable, and of sufficient capacity that the team never finds their ability to share negatively affected by the network. While this may seem obvious, once again, these systems often happen outside the normal development channels. As a result, the need for ongoing coordination with the network group will require focus. In achieving the focus, it is essential that the network personnel understand what may be exceptional demands of the team metaphor.

My discussion of motel beds and dust bunnies implies another requirement for the network when delivering the team metaphor. The network should be invisible. Too often, networks today imply a tethered network and the associated difficulties of connecting and the mystery of what to do when the network connection does not work. The implication of this is that the team metaphor may be a major driver in the enterprise coming to grips with the mobile business user who must have near-full-time connectivity. The result will be that when the individual can be connected to the network, he or she will be connected, and the connection will happen with no skill or involvement by the individual. This is something for which I devoutly hope, in the interest of my allergies.

16A.4.5 Implementing the Team Metaphor

Change management, technical architecture, system management, network; all of these make a daunting list of concerns when moving to the team metaphor. It would be nice to deal with them in a calm, rational, sequential fashion. The fact is that the demands of business often do not allow such an approach. In all the cases I have seen, the reality has been that these problems must be addressed as a whole in parallel, and yet in a logical and coherent fashion. The key to managing this complexity is a program management approach to the problems. In this form, each of the efforts are addressed in parallel efforts. The essence of program management is to ensure that these parallel efforts are proceeding on schedule with well-defined deliverables of adequate quality to meet the needs of various efforts. Failure to do this inevitably leads to a set of sequential crises and rework. An effective program management effort will avoid this situation and, in turn, build confidence in the team one is trying to support.

16A.5 CONCLUSION

The team metaphor is one of the most far-reaching developments we can see in addressing business needs through computing. It could well represent the next stage in our business solutions and may well suggest where we need to go in providing solutions over the next decade. At the same time, the issues associated with the team metaphor clearly suggest this is a development approach which presents significant ongoing challenges. Some, such as change management or systems management, may present surprises just when it seems the hard systems work is done.

Given what it is, why it matters, and the issues, the team metaphor represents one of those rare intersections of business needs and technology. It is one of those cases where business need and technology capability lift us to a new plane in business computing solutions.

REFERENCES

1. Part 1 appeared as Hugh W. Ryan, "The Team Metaphor," *Journal of Information System Management*, New York: Auerbach Publications, Summer 1994, pp. 83–85.
2. Forrester Research, Inc. "Defining Social Computing," *Computing Strategy Service*, 10, 9 July 1993.
3. Gartner Group, Inc. *SMS Research Note*, "SMS8: Moving IT Into a 'New Synthesis'," March 8, 1993.
4. "Patricia Seybold's Notes on Information Technology," *Action Technologies' Workflow Products* by Ronni Marshak, May 1993.
5. Jon R. Katzenbach and Douglas K. Smith, *The Wisdom of Teams: Creating the High-Performance Organization*, Harvard Business School Press.
6. Hugh W. Ryan [1992], "The Human Metaphor," *Journal of Information Systems Management*, New York: Auerbach Publications, Winter 1992, pp. 72–75.
7. Myron Magnet, "The Productivity Payoff Arrives," *Fortune Magazine*, June 27, 1994, pp. 79–84.
8. Hugh W. Ryan [1994] "Preparing to Implement Client-Server Solutions," *Journal of Information Systems Management*, Auerbach Publications.

The Use of GroupWare in the Big "6"—Coopers & Lybrand

Frank Lancione
PRC, Inc.

Coopers & Lybrand (C&L) is one of the largest auditing and consulting firms in the world. We provide services ranging from classic financial and accounting reviews to process improvement consulting and large-scale information systems implementation. Our clients range from multinational firms and national governments to small businesses and cities. We also deal directly with individual investors who come to us for tax assistance and financial advice.

The past decade has seen both our global and our local markets becoming increasingly competitive. Workgroup computing and global connectivity are key elements of our strategic response. The sections that follow present examples from our client work and our own internal implementation that illustrate how C&L is using groupware tools ranging from electronic meetingware and hypertext-based process automation software, to email, and Lotus Notes. We have chosen examples that showcase the applications where we see groupware providing the most leverage: promoting closure in decision making, linking power centers to build consensus, promoting unity of action among members of decentralized work teams, and providing access to the best of human knowledge in an organization wherever it resides.

16B.1 GETTING CLOSURE: USING GROUPSYSTEMS MEETINGWARE TO FACILITATE TOP MANAGEMENT DECISION MAKING

Vice Admiral Michael P. Kalleres is not a patient man when it comes to the pursuit of excellence. During Desert Shield and Desert Storm he commanded the U.S. Second Fleet. Five of the seven carrier battle groups that were engaged during the war to restore the sovereignty to Kuwait worked for him. As the Commander of the Second Fleet, he was responsible for the training and effective use of the U.S. Naval battle forces from the Atlantic. He was also a customer receiving strategic and tactical logistics services from the Military Sealift Command.

The Admiral transitioned from being a prime "user" to being a prime provider by assuming command of the United States Military Sealift Command (MSC). From August 1992 to July 1994, as Commander of MSC, he managed over $4 billion annually in commercial shipping, and led the nation's Ready Reserve Forces. The Command of MSC spans the globe with over 150 ships, and a partnership with the U.S. shipping industry by use of short- and long-term U.S.-flag charter vessels. The Command employs 8000 military and civilian personnel, 80% of whom are at sea. Leadership and command of the organization mandates centralized policy, but decentralized execution and feedback. Maximizing the use of people, infrastructure, and technology are a must because crises tend to occur at the remotest spots of the world which have the least infrastructure for support. Success in demanding jobs requires high standards. Admiral Kalleres demands results. He wants action quickly. In the spring of 1993, he was not getting what he wanted.

In the spring of 1993, C&L got a call from the Captain who headed the information systems directorate at MSC. MSC has an interesting and important mission. With U.S. military forces withdrawing from overseas bases, our national defense increasingly depends on our ability to quickly get our troops to crisis points in other parts of the world. Once they are there, the Defense transportation infrastructure must provide the bullets, bedrolls, and other equipment they need to fight. MSC is the agency within the Department of Defense (DoD) that is responsible for providing ocean transportation to haul the vast amount of goods needed to sustain U.S. forces overseas. The media likes to show pictures of big C-5 cargo airplanes landing on remote airstrips at the start of a crisis. However, in reality, 95% of everything it takes to support a fighting force anywhere outside the U.S. moves by ship—military and commercial charter ships under the control of MSC.

The Captain's call to C&L late on a Thursday night presented us with both an opportunity and a challenge. He wanted us to submit a cost proposal for conducting several strategic planning sessions for the top leadership of the Command. In the first meeting we were to design a program plan and exercises using electronic meetingware that would guide the headquarters executive group through the steps needed to develop proposed goals and objectives for the Command. The results from this session were to be presented at a worldwide Commander's conference a week later. At this session, too, we were to design a series of exercises using electronic meetingware that would help the overall group reach closure on worldwide goals and objectives for the Command.

Strategic planning sessions using meetingware are great consulting assignments. They are rewarding for clients because tool sets such as GroupSystems dramatically increase a group's productivity. They are fun for the consulting staff because of the high-level client exposure and the great visibility within the organization that the products receive. This particular project had some very tangible risks, though.

Timing was an issue. The executive team could not meet with us until the following Monday to agree on session design, yet the first of the two sessions was already scheduled for the following Wednesday. Equipment was an issue. MSC had no electronic meetingware facility of its own. C&L's facilities were booked. This meant a joint scramble by MSC and us to find an alternative site. The greatest risks for the session, however, turned out to be organizational.

Typically, when a client decides to bring in outside facilitators and technology support for something as important as the development of their strategic goals at a once-a-year conference, they don't wait until three workdays before the session to begin the contracting process. When we asked the Captain to shed light on the extremely short notice, he gave the explanation that every individual who has ever worked in a military organization understands immediately: the Admiral is unhappy.

As we launched into the assignment we found a familiar pattern of behavior. Internal teams had been meeting for several weeks to develop drafts of goals and objectives for approval by the agency leadership. A variety of meetings had been held among the headquarters executives to consider the staff proposals. MSC in-house facilitators had been trying to record and manage the flow of ideas during the headquarters staff meetings with post-it notes, flip charts, and markers. They were not successful in capturing all that was going on—a source of irritation for the Admiral. They also had to rely on the "show of hands" method to try to gauge group support for issues being debated.

The in-house sessions were not resulting in decisions. Time was running out, and so was the Admiral's patience. As Admiral Kalleres described it: "What I needed was closure on ideas. Anyone can talk about a subject, but if you don't have closure there is no 'sale'." From a leadership standpoint, Admiral Kalleres was concerned about the quality of the decisions being reached:

> When you try to collect ideas using post-it notes and paper, 70–80% of the ideas are lost. No one ever collates the paper. Ideas which might not apply to the immediate topic might apply somewhere else. Even if an idea doesn't have immediate support, it may still be worth exploring. The groupware allowed me to collect a vast amount of input from my people, get it collated under a series of topics, and then step aside later and review the results. At the end of each session day, the C&L folks provided me with a complete electronic report of the products. I was able to go through it that evening.

The electronic meetings C&L conducted for MSC's top executive teams were very different from the in-house sessions. In our electronic meetings, each participant is seated before a computer. Input from each individual machine is collected through a local area network which runs GroupSystems software. GroupSystems for Windows is a specialized group decision support software application. It was developed by Dr. Jay Nunamaker of the University of Arizona, and is marketed commercially by the Ventana Corporation. GroupSystems software provides a series of tools for manipulating and analyzing participant input. The tools are used to lead participants through brainstorming, convergence on key strategies, voting, evaluation of items, and group writing to document the results. Data collected through the network are projected on a large screen display at the front of the room so they can be viewed by all participants. C&L meeting facilitators lead the group through structured exercises to build the information required to reach closure on the planned deliverables for the session.

An important feature of an electronic meeting is anonymity. Ideas entered into the system are displayed on public screens without attribution. This requires the group to react to ideas based on their merit—rather than based on the status of the originator. C&L has found that executives at the top of organizations thrive on the candor that results. Admiral Kalleres observed:

> I am concerned when I find that I am the only guy talking at a meeting. No organization can survive if it is limited to the ideas and energy of a single person no matter how active that person is. Because of the cloak of quasi-anonymity you get with groupware, people tend to express ideas they would not normally record. I thought this was useful not only because of the ideas captured, but because it told me about the mood of acceptance. Ideas with only 60%–70% acceptance are still worth exploring. They can be refined.

In an electronic meeting, there is a mix of media. Participants are seeing their own and others' ideas summarized in public screens. Bar charts, graphs, and thermometer-shaped "mood meters" project voting results. Ideas can be captured in narrative paragraphs, in "file folders," or in hierarchical decision trees. Each round of input through the system is followed by extensive group discussion to analyze the information and reach consensus on what is important to take to the next step in the decision process. This variety of displays and methodologies fits a broad range of thinking styles and can be useful in trying to promote a common understanding of the issues. Adm. Kalleres commented:

> Often in a meeting I will be watching more than listening, particularly if I'm already familiar with the subject matter. When the flow of ideas is great enough, the general professional atmosphere of the organization will show. People can be elastic in some ways and inelastic in others. Do they do their homework before they come to the meeting or just show up? Do they understand best through reading the comments on the screen, or in an auditory mode—reacting off-the-cuff to the discussion? When we got to sticking points the facilitator and the mood meter voting really helped the group reach closure.

Participant reaction among MSC executive staff and among MSC field commanders was overwhelmingly positive at all sessions. Admiral Kalleres said, "We accomplished in the first afternoon more than we had in the preceding four weeks. Our field commanders loved the groupware. They said that was the best Commander's conference they had ever attended." Admiral Mathis, who had just reported to MSC as the Deputy Commander, said, "We just did in a day what it took us five months to complete in the Command I just came from."

16B.2 CONNECTING THE POWER CENTERS: AUTOMATING POLICY-MAKING WORKFLOWS WITH LOTUS NOTES

Perhaps you have seen the circus act where a juggler gets a stage full of plates spinning on the ends of sticks. The juggler starts by holding a six-foot wooden pole vertically. He balances a china plate on top of the stick. Then, he spins the plate as though it were an old 33-1/3 record on a turntable. As long as the plate is spinning, its centrifugal force keeps the pole upright. If the plate slows too much or stops, the stick falls and the plate breaks. As the juggler gets more and more plates spinning on one side of the stage, the plates he originally started on the other side begin to lose velocity. As they slow, they threaten to fall to the stage and shatter. By the end of the act the juggler is frantically dashing about the stage trying to ensure that each plate gets whatever reinforcing spin it needs to keep it from crashing to the ground.

C&L is the prime contractor working in partnership with the Synetics Corporation, the Volpe National Transportation Systems Center (Volpe Center), and the U.S. Marine Corps (USMC) to establish a comprehensive document-routing system for the U.S. Marines headquarters organization. Few private sector organizations are as large in scale as Federal organizations. Within Federal organizations the Department of Defense (DOD) is the granddaddy organization of them all. Getting organization-wide agreement to change policy within DOD as a whole, or within an individual service like the Marine Corps, poses problems similar to those faced by the juggler described above. The larger the change, the more constituencies you must consult and try to win support from. Like the juggler, you face the problem of having support from parties whose needs you meet early in the process lose force as you modify your proposal to address the demands of other groups in the clearance network. Finally, as with the juggler, success comes only if you can get a critical mass of stakeholders to concur with your proposal all at the same time, as well as efficiently respond to the subject at hand.

The applications C&L is developing for the Marine Corps deal directly with the challenges of efficient response in the policy coordination and consensus-building process. Once the system is implemented, it will allow USMC personnel to electronically route documents for policy coordination and clearance. Phase I of the project is scheduled for completion in early 1995. It will link 2400 individuals through an integrated PC DOCS OPEN and Lotus Notes architecture. PC DOCS OPEN is a document management software that is being used to index and provide pointers to the vast number of documents that need to be referenced in the current environment. In the future, it will be used, along with Lotus Notes, to provide indexing and document access to much of the business correspondence being created through the network. Lotus Notes is being used to provide the communications links and database applications development platform.

Bob Stouffer, the Volpe Center program manager for the project, explains its goal as providing "increased accountability, control, and visibility—and from this hopefully better efficiency in the document clearance process." Stouffer characterizes the current process as "circulating paper copies of documents through multiple offices for review with little control over the clearing offices other than noting the date that a package was forwarded to them, and proposing a deadline for the completion of their action."

Under the new system, the originator will be able to use an electronic buck slip form to identify who will be included in the document clearance process. He or she will also be able to search for and attach electronic copies of any critical prior correspondence or background documentation that would be relevant to reviewers and include this in the electronic packages they receive for review. Once a review process is underway, all clearing offices can have visibility of comments being made by other offices. The action officer—the individual assigned to broker the package through the clearance process—will have full visibility of concerns being raised as comments are added to the Notes database for that package. The action officer, and all clearing parties, will be able to pose clarifying questions, exchange views, and furnish information through discussion documents that will be associated with the package being cleared. All transactions will be documented, date-stamped, and a part of the record.

The Phase I project will cover staff at the Marine Corps headquarters at the Navy Annex in Arlington, Virginia and at the Marine Corps base at Quantico, Virginia. Stouffer sees the system eventually reaching out to "5500–6000 individuals worldwide." Once the system is up and running, Stouffer explains: "Even if you are located halfway around the world, you will be able to participate in the clearance process as though you were in the next office."

Perhaps the greatest impact of the new process will be qualitative. Stouffer observes: "As the process is envisioned now, there should be no screening out of comments in the data base. Decision makers at the final approval point will be able to peruse the comments in the file and get unfiltered viewpoints from people at lower levels in the organization who contributed to the dialogue during the clearance process. The decision maker can choose to ignore these comments or design around them—but their very presence in the file has the potential to change the way decisions are reached."

16B.3 PROMOTING UNITY OF PURPOSE: USING PROCESS AUTOMATION SOFTWARE TO MANAGE INFORMATION SYSTEMS DESIGN AND DEVELOPMENT

You're on the conductor's podium in front of the symphony orchestra at Carnegie Hall. Before you are 100 concert musicians and their instruments. Behind you are several thousand paying customers filled with anticipation and awaiting your performance. You raise your baton. You signal the orchestra. You begin. But wait! The violin section is playing an old version of the music. You changed that arrangement two weeks ago. And the horns. This is supposed to be classical. They are interpreting the score as jazz. And where are the percussionists? You look down and see a phone message. They missed the bus and will not be able to deliver their part of the symphony on time. They apologize for any inconvenience!

If you have ever managed a large systems development project you may find the preceding scenario all too familiar. Whether your team works in a single building or on several continents, achieving unity of purpose is a continuing struggle. You battle to ensure that everyone is working to the same standards, using compatible methods, and aiming for the same milestones. You hope the individual code modules will work together even though they were developed by different teams. Sometimes it's a losing battle.

As a designer and developer of large commercial and governmental information systems, in the early 1990s C&L was looking for a way to help ourselves and our clients win this war of maintaining control on large systems projects. At that time, C&L had a very comprehensive systems development methodology called Summit. This methodology provided a detailed conceptual framework that spanned the entire systems development life cycle. We implemented this methodology with a wide range of project management and software development tools. However, it was clear that the level of performance we were aiming for would require a much more seamless approach.

Achieving unity of purpose would mean creating a way for every participant on the project, from the overall manager to the lowest-level programmer, to have visibility of all critical data on requirements, progress, standards, and work products. The entire team had to be able to adjust quickly to changes occurring in any part of the project. All project staff, including individuals new to the project or to C&L, would need to have a common understanding of our methods and the desired deliverables at every step along the way. Our solution was to develop a proprietary groupware-based toolset—The Summit Process Management System (Summit Process).

To build Summit Process, C&L encapsulated its systems development methodology into what can be thought of as a process automation tool. The engine which underlies Summit Process is a software package called MATE. We have a proprietary version that has been specially tailored for Summit Process by the program's developers, Advanced Development Methods, in Burlington, Massachusetts. The MATE version we use provides a shell with graphical user interfaces; hypertext; the ability to start up other software tools, complete a task, and then import the data without exiting the program shell; and full network-based communications between all parties.

Summit Process brings to the system developer's job the same types of work process support that have proved so successful in boosting worker productivity in blue-collar industries. For example, if you walk the floor of an aircraft repair depot that maintains and overhauls airplanes, you quickly encounter the concept of "kitting." In order to execute his or her job, the aircraft mechanic requires: 1) the item to be overhauled (e.g., landing strut, fuel gauge, canopy, etc.); 2) instructions or guidelines on what repairs are to be made; 3) engineering drawing and specifications information; 4) the tools required to execute the repair; 5) the materials required to execute the repair; 6) routing information on where to forward the part after he or she is finished. Unless all of these elements are present, the job cannot be done. Instead of making the worker try to collect all of these elements, in industrial settings, they come to the worker. Hence, the idea of "kitting."

In materials staging areas, all the parts, all the instructions, in some cases even special-purpose fixtures, are combined in "kits" that can be delivered by forklifts or in-shop trolleys to the workers areas on the shop floor. Tags attached to the pieces to be worked on tell the mechanic what shop gets the item after he or she has completed his operation. Once the worker signs off, the in-shop trolleys transport the work to the next work center. As a shopfloor supervisor once told us: "When you're paying a mechanic $18 an hour to fix airplanes you don't want them running around chasing down blueprints or parts." The managers in these facilities are able to keep track of the flow of parts, timetables, materials requirements, and process through comprehensive work tracking and scheduling software.

Summit Process emulates these workflow processes by providing a series of work management modules. The Planner Workbench contains a series of "route maps" and a database of project management estimating information. This module walks a project manager through a dialogue in which he or she answers questions about the project's goals and scope, the technical environment, and the technical characteristics of the proposed system. It even addresses risk related to factors such as the skill levels of available resources in the development team and in the client's organization. Summit Process uses the results to generate a tailored technical strategy, a work breakdown structure, a project plan, and even a range of cost estimates. Once a project plan is built, the manager can load it into any of a wide range of commercial project-planning software that can work as an integrated part of the package under the MATE shell. The project manager can assign individual tasks within the plan to members of the development team and communicate these assignments to them through the network.

The assignments from the project manager are accessed by project staff through a Developer's Workbench. When an individual signs on to his or her Developer's Workbench they see all of the WorkSets that have been assigned to them for completion. This can include taskings that have been sent to them by different project managers if they are working on multiple projects. The hypertext capabilities of Summit Process allow the developer on-line access to information on project standards, project schedules, detailed instructions on how to perform the assigned tasks, even examples of completed deliverables. In executing a task, the developer can access whatever modeling or software development tools the task requires through the workbench environment. At the end of a task, the developer can communicate back to the program manager through the built-in messaging facilities that a milestone has been completed.

The final module of Summit Process is the Process Engineer Workbench. This module allows the modifications to the basic Summit methodology database. This allows C&L or a client organization that has adopted our methodology for in-house use to tailor the work breakdown structures, the activity components, and all of the methodology extensions (i.e., the on-line training and documentation materials). Because Summit Process is network-based, developers in the field always have access to the current versions of information, standards, directions—everything that is contained in the central database file.

C&L has been very successful with Summit Process. It is currently being used by clients such as GTE, Bellcore, Smith-Barney, and Anheuser-Busch. Future development includes using Lotus Notes as the communications infrastructure so that all work products will be available in a shared database as well.

16B.4 POWERING UP: TAPPING THE BEST OF HUMAN KNOWLEDGE WHEREVER IT RESIDES IN THE ORGANIZATION OR THE WORLD

7:30 AM. My 12-year-old powers up my PC and dials into the server while I'm shaving. She gets a kick out of checking my email for me. A couple of messages. Mostly routine stuff through our in-house system. Two from clients through our Internet gateway. Only one is urgent. I get breakfast.

8:15 AM. I get the client who's in a hurry on the phone. We need to work out a revised cost proposal. I call up the spreadsheet with the cost data I sent him last week and I work on it while we are talking. I run a couple of "what if" drills by changing key variables in the spreadsheet to reflect the new information. We talk through the implications. When he's satisfied with the numbers, I save the file and fax it to him from my PC. He calls back in five minutes to say he's got the proposal and it's just what he needed. Done deal.

9:10 AM. Next Item. Uh oh. Three reports have been forwarded to me for review through Notes overnight. The first two are good. I forward concurrence memos for the files on those. The third is pretty deadly stuff. I summarize my reservations, and attach a couple of articles I've downloaded from the Gartner Group's on-line service that describe trends the writer needs to address.

10:00 AM. Conference call with the team working in St. Louis. We discuss options for completing the work within schedule despite reassignment of one of the critical team members. While we are talking, one of the managers on that end uses Notes to check the latest staff availability roster for our overall division. We discuss the pros and cons of each of the staff who are available in terms of the skills needed on this job. We both cut over to the resume database in Notes to do a more detailed check on the qualifications of the finalists. Then we decide on a candidate. The St. Louis group calls him up and adds him to our conference call. He confirms he's interested and available. He agrees to report next Monday.

11:00 AM. Finish returning all of my morning voice mails. Update my schedule in Lotus Organizer and add a revised copy in calendar form to the office's staff locator file database.

11:30 AM. Call up the file for one of our standard presentations and make some very minor changes. Use Notes to send the revised slides to the reproduction shop at the office so they can copy and bind the handouts for my afternoon briefing to a client.

11:45 AM. Grab a sandwich, while I call up and review a report on the status of billings and collections for our group. Send out voice mails to several staff asking them to follow up to ensure all documentation required for payment has been submitted on key accounts.

12:15 PM. Traffic has died down, should be able to get to the office in less than 30 minutes. (It would have been an hour at 8:00 AM.) I check voice mail a second time and return messages from my car phone as I'm driving to the office for my afternoon client meeting.

In business process redesign workshops with clients, we stimulate creative thinking about "To Be" process options by having participants write scenarios. We ask them to describe how their workday might look if they had carte blanche to take total advantage of the technologies we demonstrate for them and if they had no organizational limits placed on their redesign options. The stories they write are a walk-through of their day from breakfast to bedtime, which describes: 1) what they are doing in their redesigned world, 2) what others are doing, and 3) how their redesigned ways of operating are better than the "As Is" processes they are forced to use today to perform their jobs.

What we are seeing more and more of are "possible dreams"—reborn concepts of operations that are achievable using the technologies that are already available to us. The recurring themes from the individual's standpoint are:

☞ Easy access to data through networks on the schedule, and in the form in which the employee wants it

☞ Easy access to other people without necessarily having to be physically present for face-to-face meetings

☞ More options for workers of when, where, and how they carry out their work

While employees are seeking options, organizations are looking to groupware technology to create advantages. Recurring organizational goals cited in our redesign workshops are:

☞ Leverage: Being able to tap into the right information and the right people wherever they are in the organization so that you can:

     ✗ Stop "reinventing the wheel"

     ✗ Take advantage of the full resources of the organization

☞ Alacrity: Being able to infuse innovations, critical information, and changes in strategy quickly throughout the organization in order to:

     ✗ Satisfy customers

     ✗ Outflank competitors

     ✗ Exploit shifts in the business environment

What's interesting is that connectivity through groupware can potentially satisfy both sets of objectives with technologies that are far from exotic. For example, in the scenario described above, the technologies needed are already widely in use in most large firms: email, access to the Internet, a spreadsheet program, a fax/modem card, telephone conference calls, file sharing through Lotus Notes, access to on-line data services through a network, access to corporate financial reporting systems through a network, voice mail, and cellular phone.

The employee in the scenario is able to satisfy the organization's goals by using Notes, conference calling, and facsimile to respond quickly to his customer's request for a revised cost estimate. These technologies also allow him to work with his colleagues to identify and access the best staff resource to permit a project to come in on time. The scenario satisfies the employee's objectives as well. He is able to access data when he needs it, and to interact with his colleagues and his client without having to travel to be face to face with them for this particular set of decisions.

Looking at the scenario, the big areas for problems are potentially social, not technical. Will the organization be comfortable allowing the employee to work out of his home at his discretion? If working at home is an option, are there any limits on when he is "open for business"? Can his boss call him at 7:30 AM (while he's in the middle of shaving) to check on the status of the proposal that is in discussions with the client?

Every redesign workshop we conduct has at least one participant who asks: "If this stuff is so good, are you guys using it?" Fortunately for us, C&L staff can say: "Yes." Two years ago C&L's leadership completed a top-to-bottom strategic realignment of the Firm. Out of that process came a Firm-wide commitment to make technology a central part of our competitive strategy. The major elements of C&L's technology strategy derive from our vision of the PC as a communications platform rather than as a computation device. Our goal is to achieve universal access—literally, to give every employee the power to tap into the resources of the global Firm at any time, from any place.

A wide range of technologies and initiatives are building C&L's infrastructure for global connectivity. A major effort is underway to establish standard workstation platforms for our tax practitioners, our audit personnel, and our information systems personnel that specifically support the audit process. Underlying C&L's standard workstation platforms will be a global applications warehouse. The warehouse will be a repository of Notes applications developed within the Firm. For example, there may be several approaches to sales tracking among the different lines of business, and in different parts of the world. Variations in business practices will lead to variations in the requirements for each user's sales tracking system. Under the warehouse concept, a line of business or geographic group will be able to view all of the existing sales lead applications that have been developed within the Firm. They can copy any one they like, and customize it to suit their needs. They contribute their final product to the repository where it widens the options available for practitioners in the rest of the Firm.

A great deal of attention is being given to the use of technology in support of C&L's Client Service Approach initiative (CSA). CSA was developed as a framework to help the Firm's multinational engagement teams deliver world-class service to our largest clients. C&L is developing tailored business applications to make it easy for the teams to integrate collaborative computing into their business processes. An example is a suite of Notes databases that help the Partner-In-Charge of an international engagement keep track of key client personnel at every client site around the world and the C&L staff who are responsible for serving them. The same system provides a network of pipelines that allows the Partner-In-Charge to get visibility of important information from staff at all levels. Video conferencing and electronic meetingware are examples of other technologies that are being introduced to CSA teams. Future initiatives will explore the use of tools such as workflow and electronic whiteboards.

16B.5 CONCLUDING OBSERVATIONS

Much of what groupware brings to business processes is simple in execution, yet profound in its implications. Is it really all that significant that two workgroup members at geographically separate sites are able to see the same version of documents? Considering that this single capability implodes coordination cycle times, reduces by order of magnitude data reentry and rework, and makes it possible to redirect staff resources from paper shuffling to thought work, the answer is most decidedly: "Yes." But these are only the mechanical benefits.

The full promise of groupware is reflected in the concept of what C&L refers to as a "Knowledge Network." Groupware in all of its forms is directed at making accessible the collective knowledge and experience of the "tribe." In business this means using groupware to force your competitors to face off against the total information and expertise of your Firm, not just the expertise of the staff resident in a single project team or office.

For society as a whole, groupware becomes a powerful lever for speeding up the maturation of the knowledge base of our species. The renowned physicist, Stephen Hawking, cites the development of external knowledge transfer mechanisms as having had a watershed impact on the evolution of the human race:

> At first, evolution proceeded by natural selection from random mutations. This Darwinian phase lasted about three and a half billion years and produced us, beings who developed language to exchange information. But, in the last 10,000 years or so, we have been in what might be called an external transmission phase. In this, the internal record of information, handed down to succeeding generations in DNA, has not changed significantly. But the external record, in books and other long lasting forms of storage has grown enormously. Some people would use the term evolution only for the internally transmitted material and would object to it being handed down externally. But I think that is too narrow a view. We are more than just our genes. We may be no stronger or inherently more intelligent than our caveman ancestors. But, what distinguishes us from them is the knowledge that we have accumulated over the last 10,000 years and particularly over the last 300. (Stephen Hawking speaking at the Macworld Expo in Boston, Massachusetts, in August 1994.)

If, indeed, "knowledge is power," groupware, by providing access to knowledge, amplifies our individual and collective strength. From work groups using Lotus Notes in large organizations, to high school study groups sharing lecture notes over America Online, groupware invests the effort of the individual with the wisdom of the whole. In the not too distant future, we are almost certain to view business processes that are not groupware-enabled as relics or, more likely, as harbingers of extinction for the organizations that failed to adapt to the new ground rules for survival.

BIOGRAPHIES

Hugh W. Ryan joined Andersen Consulting in 1971 after receiving a Masters degree in mechanical engineering. He was admitted to the partnership in 1982. He has worked on a variety of engagements with emphasis on on-line and distributed applications. In the last five years, Mr. Ryan has worked extensively in the developing fields of professional workstations, cooperative processing, and client-server systems. Mr. Ryan also writes a column for systems development in the *Journal of Information Systems Management*. He has spoken at numerous conferences and seminars across the United States and in Europe.

Frank Lancione is the Director of Workgroup Technologies for PRC's Business Process Re-engineering Center of Excellence. He and his team are helping PRC and its clients to achieve improved business results using Group Systems for decision support, Novell and Lotus Communications products for interenterprise communications, and a wide range of other network-enabled solutions.

Frank's experience prior to joining PRC is a unique combination of over 11 years of "Big 6" consulting at Coopers & Lybrand, and a variety of positions within the government. While at Coopers & Lybrand, Frank managed C&L's Federal Consulting Group in Cambridge, Massachusetts. He also established C&L's Federal Practice's Electronic Meetingware capability by developing the methodology, training staff, and establishing a groupware center in Washington, D.C. He managed the group that won C&L's first major contract to bring large-scale implementations of Lotus Notes to Federal agencies. In addition, he also provided strategic support to the Defense Transportation System, Military Sealift Command, U.S. Postal Service, and United States Air Force.

From 1971 to 1984, Frank had the unusual opportunity to deal with agency-wide and government-wide human resource and compensation policies. During this period, he worked at the Internal Revenue Service, the Office of Management and Budget, the former Civil Service Commission, the Office of Personnel Management, and the Merit Systems Protection Board. In 1978, he served on the Personnel Task Force that developed the recommendations which led to the passage of the Civil Service Reform Act.

Introduction to Chapter 17

This chapter is probably the most valuable chapter to read in the implementation section of this book. Peter Huckle is the conference cochairman of the GroupWare Conferences in Europe and was also responsible for the marketing of ALL-IN-1 for DEC in Europe. Peter is very knowledgeable on both groupware products and how companies implement them. His wife Tracey Shearmon is an industrial psychologist, and together they have helped many British firms take the first steps on the successful path to groupware.

They focus on some guiding principles for implementation and espouse much of the same change management philosophy and experience that Dr. Manheim does in his earlier chapter. Although groupware is about software and people, the way it is implemented both technically and within the organization is critical to its success.

This chapter has some overlap with the next chapter from Alexia Martin, as both do consulting on how technology is transferred successfully into organizations. Because Peter has a technical background and Tracey has a psychological background, they offer strategies for both implementation and technology transfer. They offer a blueprint for groupware implementation that is actually a cyclic process. They include many of the critical questions that technologists (who are usually focused on the technology and solving technical problems) do not think to ask. They look at how to reward people for collaborating and how to measure the success of collaboration.

They then lead you through an assessment of your current situation and environment, how to select a pilot project, defining success, planning for change, developing a project plan, how to deal with user behavior, how to implement the changes, and finally, how to measure the effects of those changes.

The strength of this chapter lies in the detailed discussion of groupware implementation. It is clear to see that the Huckles have helped many organizations find a successful path to implementing groupware successfully in a variety of different organizations. The Huckles have taken these experiences for us and distilled them down to some heuristics or rules of thumb that can be applied to any organization, making this chapter an excellent complement to the more academic chapter by Marvin Manheim and the greater organizational focus of Alexia Martin's chapter.

In groupware, because the technology has such powerful leverage on the corporate culture, implementation is a pitfall. Reading this chapter is one way to make yourself aware of this pitfall and possibly how to avoid it. The other way is to use an experienced consulting firm that has steered many of their clients through these perilous waters. Either way, it is useful to have some guidance to avoid the myriad of pitfalls like lack of user support, replication storms, lack of management support, focus on the incorrect type of problem for this technology, *lack of clear vision for the project or the business, and choosing software that will not support the functionality you need in your new re-engineered business or requires radical customization to get it to do what you want it to do.*

I can't guarantee this chapter will give you the answers to all these questions, but it will give you a general idea of how to do a successful groupware implementation and how to avoid some of the pitfalls the groupware pioneers found.

CHAPTER 17

Groupware Implementation Strategies

Dr. Peter R. Huckle
The Kingsgate Group
Tracey Shearmon
The Kingsgate Group

This chapter looks at how a successful groupware implementation can be achieved through a balanced implementation strategy and offers some guiding principles to apply together with practical suggestions for planning and managing the organization changes that are needed. It draws on the experience of office system implementations by organization development and IT specialists and looks at how to develop a strategy for success. The implementation approach recommended is to follow well-proven change-management processes.

17.1 CONTEXT BEFORE STRATEGY

Office systems have been deployed for many years now, and there are many millions of users around the world. Although much of the technology of office systems can be labelled as groupware, there is, despite this investment and commitment to success on the part of many companies, an unease that somehow the investment was not fully justified by the returns in hard business terms.

The potential business benefits of groupware are only realized if the impact on the organization structure, and on the roles and behaviors within the organization, are fully considered. Therefore, the management of cultural and behavioral factors is a key factor in the successful implementation of groupware.

More effective groupware implementations are now becoming possible due to the interaction of many complex factors that include both technological and cultural dimensions. It is an understanding of these dimensions and their combination that gives us insight as to how to design successful groupware implementation strategies and the type of skills that are needed to facilitate implementation.

In the world of information technology, we are seeing all of the technological elements that make the successful use of Groupware possible come together today. These elements include networking infrastructures, the widespread use of interconnected personal computers, and personal and group productivity software.

The personal computer has become an indispensable business tool and is becoming an increasingly *personal* tool. The owner of a personal computer sees it as their window on the world of information. It is inevitable that people will want to use their PC as their primary interface to the company—its people and data.

In our personal and business lives we are experiencing cultural changes towards the acceptance of information technology as a facet of our everyday living. The fax machine, banking terminals, the pocket telephone, and notebook computers all play a part in causing this cultural shift—changing people's expectations towards a greater freedom, away from the constraints of a fixed working day and office location towards greater quality of life, flexible work patterns, and working from home.

It is these changes that allow companies to think about employing people and structuring the organization in different ways, hence providing the opportunity for significant improvements in many key business parameters, including customer satisfaction, cost reduction, time to market, and overall organization effectiveness.

17.2 IMPACT OF GROUPWARE ON THE ORGANIZATION

The introduction of groupware into an organization may be contemplated as a means of solving a specific business problem or, more broadly, as a vehicle to help in introducing and sustaining an evolution of the organization's culture.

The possible range of effects of the introduction of computer technology into an organization were described by Malone and Rockart [1991] as consisting of three orders of change:

☞ First-order effect: substitution
☞ Second-order effect: increased demand
☞ Third-order effect: new structures

The prize we are seeking to win by a third-order change is not only one of increased efficiency in the organization but also the building of an organization that is more agile in response to a changing competitive, economic, and legislative environment.

The third-order change can be described as a *transformational change.*

The transformational change that can be achieved with groupware is that many more people will directly add value to the organization. By directly adding value we mean doing jobs where the key responsibilities include, for example:

☞ Dealing with customers
☞ Explicitly supporting people who are dealing with customers
☞ Developing products and services

This is in contrast to the roles many people play in the traditional hierarchical organization, especially in large companies where much of the energy of the organization is focused inward. People spend too much time and effort on company politics, internal reports, and meetings.

The transformed organization will have many characteristics that differ from those in the traditional organization, including:

☞ A flatter structure with significantly fewer layers of management
☞ Blurred functional barriers
☞ People working in dynamic teams which are focused on clearly defined end goals
☞ Changed roles—especially those of middle management
☞ New ways by which people value themselves and each other—the focus being on the contribution made rather than on the position in the hierarchy
☞ Communication flows which are more horizontal than vertical
☞ Decisions being made and implemented nearer the customer
☞ Leadership which is focused on the business rather than the organization

17.3 THE EFFECT OF GROUPWARE ON PEOPLE

For creative and entrepreneurial people at all levels, a large company can be a frustrating and disabling environment. The effect of the traditional organization on people with these qualities is that they will either:

☞ Rise up the management ladder (and spend less and less time adding direct value)
☞ Remain at the "coal face" spending high levels of energy "beating the system"
☞ Opt out of trying to make a difference and play the "game"
☞ Leave to work for a competitor

However, entrepreneurial people have exactly the qualities that are increasingly required to maximize an organization's chances of success in today's competitive marketplace. Groupware provides the means to enable the potential contribution of such people to be harnessed by the organization to maximum effect.

Once installed and implemented, groupware helps people to do their jobs more effectively by enabling them to communicate across the organization as well as up and down the management chain. It therefore allows people to "get on with the job" rather than spending their time circumventing organizational barriers to progress.

Working in an environment where people can access information, are able to make decisions and satisfy customers, and feel part of a winning team all contributes to increased job satisfaction, motivation, and productivity. The entrepreneurial, creative "subversives" will be more likely to stay and to succeed in making a difference.

As well as impacting workers, groupware has a major impact on the role of management. Management has a vital but changed role to play, providing leadership and coaching, and enabling and mentoring the parts of the organization for which they are responsible.

Through groupware, managers will find it easier to canvass opinions from all over the company and from all job functions before making strategic decisions and providing direction. Decisions throughout the organization can be made and communicated more quickly and effectively.

Much of the change required is related to the way that people behave towards each other, the goals of the organization, and the information that they need to do their work.

We have concluded that all of the factors outlined above must be included in a successful implementation strategy for groupware.

We believe that third-order transformational change results from implementing groupware in a receptive environment.

A fully successful implementation strategy is therefore one that creates a receptive environment by taking into account and carefully balancing the following three elements:

An enabling culture—which responds dynamically to the free availability of information and generates and supports behaviors such as information sharing, empowerment, risk taking, responsibility, and initiative

Aligned goals and metrics—where individual, group, organizational, and customer goals and the metrics and rewards that drive them are all congruent

Groupware products—which are functionally adequate and integrate into the "natural" work processes

The rest of this chapter offers a step-by-step implementation strategy structured on these three elements.

17.4 IMPLEMENTATION STRATEGIES

The approach we recommend when developing your groupware implementation strategy is to follow well-proven change-management processes that include:

☞ A vision of the ideal end state
☞ The selection of a realistic intermediate goal that moves the organization towards the vision
☞ An analysis of the current situation

☞ An evaluation of the differences between the current situation and the intermediate goal

☞ The development of a project plan which implements the changes necessary to reconcile these differences

We offer a blueprint implementation strategy for you to adapt to your own needs (shown in Figure 17.1) and describe it step by step. We have added to the change-management process in the context of implementing groupware the need to consider and balance all of the three dimensions of change described above (enabling culture, goals, and metrics, and IT infrastructure) throughout the process.

Before describing each of the steps in the diagram, it should be noted that in practice, much of this work is iterative and there will not be clear boundaries between the steps. Like any journey, however, it is useful to have a map even if you have to make detours on the way to reach the intended destination.

17.4.1 Developing a Vision

The importance of the vision is that it will give you a context for the changes you are planning to implement. Although the initial project you have in mind may impact only a part of the organization, the changes it will make should take you at least some way towards the ideal overall end state.

Once you have developed the vision, try testing it on people throughout the organization—do not forget to ask people in jobs such as telephone sales, shop floor work, the janitor. Take notice of what they say.

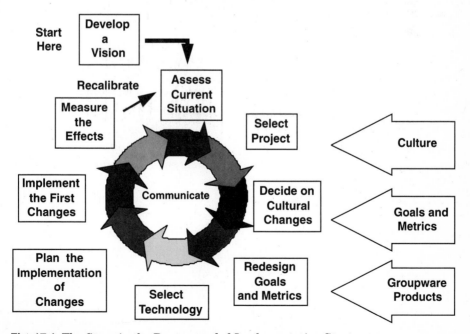

Fig. 17.1 The Steps in the Recommended Implementation Strategy

A helpful way to develop the vision is to ask yourself and those who do the work involved some questions, such as:

☞ How will it feel day to day to work in the organization?
☞ What will be different?
☞ What will they and I be doing differently?
☞ What will be the same?

Express your vision in terms of:

☞ The kind of organization you want to work in
☞ The parameters of the business
☞ How people are measured and rewarded

Culture: Make sure that your vision includes the amount of autonomy you are willing to allow people in the front line to have to make real business decisions. Recognizing that decisions can only be made with the necessary data at hand, think about how much information you are willing to let people have through the system. Consider "formal" data such as product defects, industry surveys, financial results, and product successes and failures as well as "informal" data such as grapevine information, opinion, and rumor.

Goals and Metrics: Think about both the behaviors that you want and the behaviors that you do not want in the transformed organization. This will help you to decide which behaviors to drive with the measures and rewards system. Equally important, it will tell you which things you have to stop measuring and rewarding. You will also need to think about new ways to reward people, and you may need to be radical about who does the measuring and rewarding.

Information Technology: Your vision should include the type of IT infrastructure you want in terms of:

☞ The degree of openness (freedom to source hardware and software) you want to achieve to maximize the competitiveness between suppliers
☞ How much freedom you are willing to allow end users to source their own applications and desktop devices
☞ The degree to which you want to utilize your existing infrastructure
☞ How much effort you are willing to spend in system management
☞ What interfaces you need between your company and its customers and suppliers
☞ The extent to which you are prepared to compromise functionality today for an ability to evolve over time

17.4.2 Assessing the Current Situation

Include all of the three dimensions of change in your assessment and ask questions.

Culture: Do people work in teams today (are any of these teams cross-functional teams)? Are people measured by their performance in these teams? How much "real" information is shared across the organization? Who supports people when they need help? What do people really get rewarded for? Who makes the decisions? Is working with customers seen as a high-status occupation? Who is seen as the competition?

Goals and Metrics: Do you have a corporate and departmental vision? Who knows what it is? Who is rewarded when the organization succeeds? If you work in teams, who gets rewarded if the team succeeds? Is it easier to ask forgiveness than to seek permission or vice versa? Is risk-taking rewarded? Are people rewarded more for "fire fighting" than taking a longer-term view?

Information Technology: How well is the IT infrastructure integrated into the daily working lives of people (in all jobs)? Are users happy with the current infrastructure and their interface to it? Is top management happy with it? Do top management use it? Where is the "real" information kept?

17.4.3 Selecting the Project

The project you decide to implement first will depend largely upon where you are starting from, both culturally and in terms of your IT installation.

- ☞ You may have the technology and need to pay attention to cultural aspects to get people to use it as groupware.
- ☞ You may have the culture and need to select the appropriate technology to sustain the culture and to gain the additional advantage that groupware can give you.
- ☞ You may have neither the technology nor the culture so you will need an implementation strategy that develops both together.
- ☞ You may have both the technology and the culture required, in which case you are ideally placed to gain a rapid benefit from groupware and can contemplate a much more ambitious application.

One of the decisions that has to be made as the implementation strategy is developed is how much change should be contemplated, and how soon. The strategy could range from a transformation of the whole organization to a more gradual evolution, perhaps by starting implementations at isolated points within the organization and then allowing the natural processes of reinforcement to bring about the change over a period of time. This decision will need to be based on external factors such as competitive pressures or changes in the cost and availability of skills or raw materials. Internal factors, such as the current culture of the organization, the budget available, or the degree of willingness of senior management to support a given level of change, also need to be taken into account.

To choose a project for success, we suggest that you consider the following criteria:

1. Choose a project that is as close to the customer as possible. Increased customer satisfaction will result at the earliest possible opportunity in addition to other organization benefits you will experience.
2. Choose a project that involves cross-functional business processes. By doing this the barriers between departments that maintain the current order will be critically examined, and you will begin to sow the seeds of a change that can spread throughout the whole organization.
3. Choose a project which is important to your business so that senior management is both aware of and committed to the change.
4. Select a project that takes you towards your vision.

In addition to these criteria for project selection, make sure that you have taken into account any other initiatives you have underway such as TQM, ISO 9000, Customer Satisfaction, and JIT. Look for opportunities to integrate these efforts with the proposed groupware implementation project. If integration cannot be achieved, work with the owners of these projects to ensure that they fit together and that their respective contributions to the overall corporate goals are understood and valued.

If the initiative to implement groupware is not owned by the most senior person in the organization, you must have visible commitment by a senior person to its success. You will need this because there inevitably will be resistance to change, and especially resistance to changes in the culture of the organization. There is always much vested interest in the status quo, and people feel threatened by change. This commitment at a senior level has another key role to play in terms of exhibiting behaviors that reinforce the values that you want the new structure to embrace. As with any change implementation, if senior management says one thing and does another, people will believe the actions, not the words.

Implementing groupware will cost you a lot of effort. To make a successful and permanent change, the gain you anticipate achieving must be worth (and believed to be worth) the pain of making the change.

Investing time in choosing the best first project will pay great dividends when further projects are contemplated at a later date, as you will be able to build on your success.

17.4.4 Defining Success

Define success using the terms in which your vision was expressed. Imagine that you have implemented the change successfully, and describe in detail what it is like.

Culture: How do people relate to each other? How they go about their work? What roles do managers and supervisors have? What does the organization chart look like? How does information flow? Ask practical questions such as what happens when a customer telephones with a problem, what happens if a customer changes a deadline, or who decides whether to stop the production line if a machine keeps breaking down.

Goals and Metrics: Consider both the business metrics and also the way in which you measure and reward people. Express business metrics in concrete terms such as time to process an order, cost of sales, reject rates, or awareness of your products in the marketplace. The way people are measured and rewarded should be linked explicitly to the business metrics.

Keep in mind that you get the behavior you measure, so it is important to change the goals and metrics to support the new ways of working. Consider informal as well as formal rewards. Think about how people are going to be measured and rewarded once the changes are made. Consider not only the new metrics and rewards that you will introduce to reinforce the changes, but also, and very importantly, which of the current metrics and rewards you are going to abandon. For example, if you currently reward a sales team for beating the others and you do not change this metric, is it reasonable to expect the sharing of customer and competitive data in the field?

If you want people to work in cross-functional dynamic teams, contributing to these teams should be part of their goal set. If you want collaborative behavior you must measure collective as well as individual success.

Information Technology: How are people going to use the technology you have introduced—is it going to be an essential part of getting the job done? Think about this in terms of the informal information channels that you have in place at the moment, such as the coffee machine.

Before answering detailed technical questions, define success in terms of issues that affect the degree to which the technology can be integrated into the working life of everyone in the company. For example:

☞ How well does the proposed system integrate with the user's personal computing environment?
☞ How is the corporate computing infrastructure integrated?
☞ How well does it support remote sites?
☞ How well are occasionally connected users supported?
☞ How well does it enable connections to be made with customers and suppliers?

17.4.5 Planning the Implementation of Changes

The difference between the "current situation" and "success" as you have defined it in previous steps will indicate *what* you need to do (i.e., the work that needs to be done). The next step is to decide *how* to make the changes.

In practice, you will probably have started to formulate an implementation plan in your mind as you went through the previous analysis. The process is an iterative one.

Managing the implementation of groupware is like any other project—you need to define actions, each with an owner and due date. Some other practical points to consider when planning the implementation are discussed here.

Project Team: Nominate a senior person with authority to own the implementation, and work to help this person understand what they need to do in practical day-to-day terms. Recruit project team members from the key people in the organization. These should be the kind of people who "cannot be spared." By doing so you will add greatly to the unspoken importance of the project. Include on the team some of the more subversive members of the organization. You will need their ideas and creativity.

Be prepared to visibly and tangibly reward success. At the end of it all, identify some heroes and celebrate.

Project Plan: Use your organization's processes for managing change. Involve key stakeholders in planning activities to ensure their ownership and commitment to the actions. Decide on realistic timescales and maintain momentum with energy, enthusiasm, and good old-fashioned management control. Plan for ongoing review and further developments—the project will not end with the first implementation.

Communication: Communicate and seek opinions from those impacted, and listen to and take note of their inputs. Make sure that the plan includes managing the expectations of all of those involved—be they stakeholders, implementors, or those affected by the changes (including customers and suppliers from both inside and outside the organization). Let it be known that this is the first of many such implementations and that at least some of the participants in this implementation will play a role in the future expansion of Groupware in the organization.

User Behavior: A critical success factor with groupware implementation projects is that your project plan should include ways to help people change the way they work. The end result you are trying to achieve is an integration of the technology into the daily routine. One of the keys to the successful implementation of groupware is achieving the behavioral changes in the use of technology. Perhaps you can use your implementation to satisfy some of the expectations that people increasingly have in terms of the relationship between work and home. Consider offering personal benefits to users of the system to help draw them into using it. Some examples of what you might consider:

☞ If you are installing a product that provides information sharing between individuals, allow topics of a personal interest nature to be shared.
☞ If you are installing email, make sure that adequate facilities are installed to permit access at all levels in the organization and that sending a reasonable number of personal messages is not frowned upon.
☞ Find ways to reward the use of the system—for example, give prizes on a random basis to those accessing a new information source.
☞ Allow people to advertise their own goods for sale in a bulletin board.
☞ Advertise special offers (company products at special discounts, for example).
☞ Provide personalized newspapers.
☞ Publish your company stock price on a daily basis.

Try and have fun along the way—what you are trying to do is to make everyone's job more interesting and exciting and to enable everyone to feel part of a winning team.

17.4.6 Implement the Changes

In our experience, planning is a "comfortable" activity and can become an end in itself. Many management teams spend more time planning, and planning to plan, than they spend on implementing their plans. So our message is—having considered all of the above, *just get on and do it*.

It is important to be continually sensing the opinions of customers, users, impacted departments, stakeholders, and others. Listen to what they say, not what you want to hear. Make it OK for people to tell the King that he has no clothes and do not shoot messengers. If things are going awry you need to know about it quickly, to learn from it and take visible actions to get back on track. Since you will probably want these behaviors to become the norm once the implementation is complete, it is good to get in some practice during the implementation phase.

Be aware of the impacts of the changes on other parts of the organization's system. Don't go for point fixes of symptoms; take a deeper look at causes. Don't underestimate the amount of energy you will need, or the amount of momentum you will have to create to cause a change that is to be carried into the organization. It will be all too easy for old habits to reappear, reinforced by the parts of the organization that are not directly involved in the change.

As things go well, reward success and take the lessons forward to the next step towards your vision.

17.4.7 Measure the Effects

After the implementation is completed, it is important to check that all is going to plan and, if not, to make modifications. You defined success in terms of three dimensions of culture, goals and metrics, and IT. It is now time to review how you are doing in terms of these criteria.

Be realistic and flexible. There will have been changes in the environment (both internal and external) during the implementation phase that you could not have foreseen when you planned the implementation. Be sure that any deviations from the goals you set are acceptable; but if they are not, you will need to recalibrate.

At this point it is time to begin to think about the next step towards achieving the bigger vision and to start the implementation cycle again.

It will be easier the next time around!

17.5 CONCLUSIONS

The potential gains from Groupware are enormous. Implementation of groupware is about managing change. Your implementation strategy needs to include the three dimensions of change—culture, goals and metrics, and IT. Implementation is complex, with many interrelated issues to consider.

Change from the inside is difficult to achieve, so consider using outside help, at least in your first implementation. If you do not, then make sure that you have all the skills you need on your project team. Include people who understand the systemic nature of organizations, who have knowledge and skills in change management, who are able to consider information technology factors, and who also understand organization development.

If, after a while, you begin to see effects emerging in the organization perhaps even over and above those you had planned, such as new relationships developing inside and outside the company, new business practices being defined, and entrepreneurial and proactive behaviors emerging, then you will know you have been successful in achieving transformational change.

REFERENCE

1. Malone, T. W. and Rockart, J. F. [1991]. "Computers, Networks and the Corporation," *Scientific American*, vol. 265, no. 3.

BIOGRAPHIES

Peter Huckle is responsible for The Conference Group's operations in Europe. In addition to organizing the GroupWare Europe conferences, Peter is cochairman of the conference Advisory Board. Peter's technical specialty is the application of groupware—information technology which enables companies to make more effective use of their people and information resources.

Following academic studies in electronics and doctoral research in communications and computer sciences, Peter has held various marketing, strategic planning, and research and development appointments in the computer industry in both Europe and the United States for IBM, Motorola, and Digital Equipment Corporation.

Tracey Shearmon specializes in organization and group effectiveness. She has eight years experience as a consultant in the computer, telecommunications, and insurance industries. Prior to this, she worked in management development and operational personnel roles. She has worked at senior levels in organizations addressing strategic issues such as setting direction, organization design, and planning and managing change. The process Tracey uses facilitates client ownership and commitment to implementing decisions and changes.

Before starting Kingsgate, Tracey worked for Digital Equipment Corporation, British Telecom, and the Probation Service. Tracey has a B.Sc. in psychology specializing in organization, consumer, and clinical psychology.

Introduction to Chapter 18

Alexia Martin sits on the advisory board for the GroupWare Conferences that I run, as do several others that have written chapters for this book. However, while Frank Lancione, Ronnie Marshak, and Lesley Shneier write about technical issues, Alexia brings an organizational development perspective to both the book and the conferences. Her responsibility on the advisory board is to keep us up to date on the Organizational Development (OD) community and their interaction/ knowledge of groupware. Her contribution to this book is along the same lines.

We have been surprised to find that there isn't much synergy between these two disciplines, except where some visionaries like Peter and Trudy Johnson-Lenz of Awakening Technology have started their work. When asked, OD professionals prefer to focus on organizations and people rather than the technologies called "groupware." Technologists focus on the tools (i.e., software), and often forget the social and organizational implications of these tools. OD practitioners have critical knowledge about organizational change and change management that would be extremely valuable to the groupware community. There is some cross-pollination, but not as much as I would like to see.

The word "groupware" can be broken into "group," meaning people, and "ware," meaning software. In order to realize success, both parts must have equal emphasis. Therefore, I asked Alexia to write a chapter on the organizational aspects of groupware in the hope of getting some of the valuable OD information into a groupware book, and giving the OD people a reason for reading a groupware book and maybe thinking about crossing that line into the realm of groupware. While we do not have a track dedicated to OD in our GroupWare '9X conferences, we do have tracks on the organizational and cultural effects of groupware in an effort to look at the nontechnical problems facing groupware. I believe that these organizational challenges are harder to solve than the technical ones.

Alexia's practice spans OD and groupware, and she has done organizational research at SRI International. In her professional work, Alexia looks at groupware with a different eye than that of the technologists, vendors, consultants, and analysts who have written other chapters in this book. I have saved her chapter for last because it brings us full circle and answers some of the questions I asked in the introductory chapter.

Alexia also looks at total quality management (TQM) and groupware, groupware and business process redesign, and organizational learning and groupware. She examines ways in which groupware can be a tool for employee empowerment instead of merely a tool for downsizing. She also looks at some of the organizational pitfalls that result when groupware is introduced, and finally examines ten challenges organizations may run into on the path to reorganization.

Finally, Alexia explains OD and the role OD professionals play. This is not exactly groupware, but it is important for everyone dealing with groupware to understand these principles. She does link the OD roles to groupware in the final section of this chapter and illustrates her points with some excellent case studies.

Because this chapter discusses people, organizations, and technology, it is one of the most important chapters in the book. I recommend this chapter to business and technical people alike, and hope that some of the OD professionals who buy this book take a longer look at groupware, because just focusing on the people is as big a mistake as just focusing on the technology. It takes both to foster a successful collaboration, and collaboration is the way of the future for many business organizations.

CHAPTER 18

Possibilities, Pitfalls, and Partners

Alexia Martin
Co-Development International

With all the experience we have in implementing any kind of technology, just for the sake of introducing technology, we know *that* approach does not work. With groupware implementation we need to be engaged in nothing less than business transformation.

> At a major U.S. insurance company, the Information Technology group implements Lotus Notes as an experiment. The "techies" are enamored with the technology and set up a repository for the IT organization itself—department charters, short- and long-range goals, strategies, organizational charts, budgets, committee and task-force membership, and seminars and conferences available to staff—as well as about its customers—their business strategies, issues, and key projects. It's a great application for the IT group, but when they begin to roll Notes out to the rest of the organization, they fail. Staff in most groups refuse to input their information into the repository. Others continue to demand paper-based information—"it's worked for years, why change?" A key division manager criticizes the IT group for spending money on a Notes implementation and lobbies to reduce the IT budget, particularly for new technology experimentation. Eventually, Notes use dies off, even in the IT group.

> In a major European insurance company, management sees that groupware can play an enabling role as it shifts from a task- to a process-oriented focus. It understands it needs to take a team approach to delivering products and services to its customers. Change agents—both internal and external organization development (OD) specialists—are assigned to work hand-in-hand with

the IT group to develop a change strategy to implement a team-focused organization, supported by collaborative technologies—Notes, workflow, electronic meeting support, and so on. From experience, they know that people resist change and develop approaches to engage the workforce in the change initiative. Representatives from "user" groups are invited to participate in planning and to become part of a "performance support" team that will work to complete the groupware implementation. All members of the performance support team practice the art of giving "elevator speeches"—less-than-two-minute summaries of why the groupware implementation will support a person, team, or division manager in meeting company objectives. They develop benefit statements for individuals as well as the organization, knowing that a change must have value to each and every person, not just for the organization. A particularly good IT communicator is assigned responsibility to ensure that key executives are trained and supported to get up on the new technologies. The IT and OD team know that the implementation process will not be smooth and easy. They allow time to get issues on the table between management and employees and develop processes to address them in authentic ways. True to expectations, the implementation is not smooth, but the organization members are engaged in working through issues, learning about what works and what doesn't, and constantly making course corrections.

This chapter starts with possibilities for groupware implemented from the point of view that technology can be a catalyst and a support for significant organizational change. It includes a section on pitfalls to implementation. New implementation partners are needed, however, to ensure business transformation and avoid pitfalls. These partners are organization development professionals. The conclusion of the chapter details the roles and processes used by these very special change agents.

18.1 SEARCHING FOR SOLUTIONS

Business problems—an abysmal economy, global competitive pressures, fragmenting markets, and a changing work force—are compelling many enterprises to initiate major organizational changes. Trends in the environment, internal tasks, structures, and people are escalating the need for change. Downsizing, flattening hierarchies, team building, fostering communication and information sharing, total quality management, continuous process improvement, rethinking and redesigning business processes, organizational learning, employee empowerment, and capitalizing on cultural diversity are just a few of the change initiatives organizations engage in to reduce costs and time to market and provide competitive advantage.

In 1991, U.S. companies spent almost $14 billion on outside advice—up from $7 billion five years earlier. Managers buy countless how-to books, like this one, on improving business. Outside consultants offer very expensive training or facilitate managers and staff in experiential sessions to help them begin the journey toward putting their proposed concepts to work. For example,

Michael Hammer of Hammer and Associates urges companies to reorganize around process instead of by functional departments, to abandon most basic notions on which their organizations are founded, and to start from scratch to rethink end-to-end activities that create value for customers. Peter Senge, Director of the Massachusetts Institute of Technology's (MIT's) Systems Thinking and Organizational Learning program, encourages the development of a learning organization in which people learn through exercises and games that force them to think about the systemic causes of and potential solutions to business problems. Countless other consultants promote various change initiatives to address business problems. The challenge is how to put the change truly into operation.

18.2 COLLABORATIVE TECHNOLOGIES: AN OPTION

The information technology groups in some companies undergoing these change efforts have picked up the challenge and are implementing client-server architectures and relational databases to distribute information where and when needed. A few are engaged in introducing groupware, most notably workflow technology and organizational repositories such as Lotus Notes, to operationalize the change toward improved collaboration and other organizational change initiatives.

A year-long research project—Collaborative Technology Environments (CTE) by SRI International completed in 1993—focused on a subset of groupware, collaborative technologies. CTs, as defined in Table 18.1, include only those information systems and software applications that specifically and explicitly support collaborative work. *They specifically support two or more people in achieving common objectives.* One of the significant findings of this vendor-sponsored CTE market research was that organizations that implemented groupware from a "technology push," such as local workgroup experiments, had smaller implementations with less satisfied users than did companies that initiated some organization- or division-wide change such as implementing quality programs or re-engineering business processes. This finding is borne out by Professor N. Venkatraman, School of Management at Boston University, who posits that the benefits of information technology will be marginal as long as its deployment is confined to existing structures, processes, cultures, or strategies (see Figure 18.1).

The benefits achieved in those companies engaged in business scope redefinition included increased revenue and increased productivity—through reduced response times, quicker turnaround, reduced head count, eliminated meetings or shorter meetings, reduced travel costs, reduced write-offs, and more. In a study that Lotus Development Corp. commissioned about the impact of Notes on organizational productivity, Telesis, a division of Towers Perrin, reported an average return on investment over 100% and often as much as 500% or more. The average payback of the 23 quantifiable applications was within just three months.

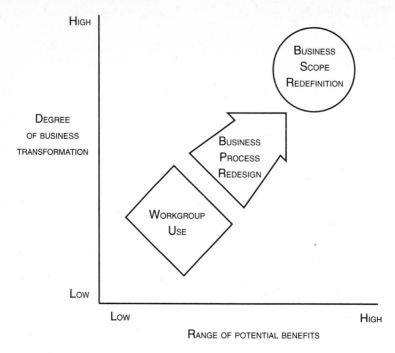

Fig. 18.1 Benefits for Level of Effort

Softer benefits identified in the SRI study included an enhanced ability to share intellectual capital, an ability to keep up with competitive pressures, improved customer satisfaction, reduced time to action, and improved quality of action.

18.3 POSSIBILITIES

In both the SRI research and in other engagements, we find the following organizational change initiatives supported by groupware.

18.3.1 Improved Collaboration

McKinsey & Co., Inc., a leading management consulting firm, has a goal to build a strong culture for knowledge, teamwork, and client services. Practice teams are the backbone of knowledge gathering and sharing, and client teams—cross-office, cross-functional, ad hoc groups—service clients. Both teams must interact. The practice teams collect and disseminate critical practice information through Lotus Notes, which serves as a repository for organizational information to the client service teams to use in their projects. A new level of worldwide collaboration is evolving from this collaboration between practice and client service teams, supported by the organizational repository.

Table 18.1 Collaborative Technologies

Technology	Definition	Uses
Collaboration Bases	These products exchange and update distributed information through a graphical user interface that makes their use logical to the way people work—by filling out forms, for example. They provide a repository for unstructured group and organizational information (unlike database management systems, which are repositories for highly structured data).	Improved business processes Organizational learning
Collaborative Workflow	These products support negotiating priorities, handling exceptions, or making judgments. They automate the actions or steps used in business processes.	Improved business processes Improved collaboration
Electronic Meeting Support Systems	These systems support face-to-face and distributed meetings with tools for such activities as brainstorming and categorization and evaluation of options. Some include visual mapping of ideas and concepts.	Improved collaboration Total quality management Improved business processes Organizational learning
Shared workspaces	This category encompasses several types of products for "live" collaboration across distance. Co-authoring/editing software provides a shared image of a document, drawing, or spreadsheet and enables multiple users to make changes. Screen-sharing software supports users in different locations viewing the same image on computers. Video-supported collaboration products combine desktop video conferencing with collaborative work tools such as shared drawing spaces or shared access to drawings.	Improved collaboration

As with all oil companies, British Petroleum has undergone significant downsizing. The resulting flatter organization distributes experts from various disciplines worldwide. They must collaborate about experiences and best practices to speed exploration, locate a new well site, or address crises such as oil spills, for example. BP is introducing groupware into its corporate culture of distributed experts with its Knowledge Networks project. The goal of this project is to support corporate-wide improvement of teamwork and information sharing among geographically distributed teams to increase BP's productivity and responsiveness to its changing markets. In an early prototype, petrophysical scientists in the United States and the United Kingdom share complex color images concurrently using Virtual Notebook System (VNS) from The ForeFront Group in order to select a well site. Being able to share information in real time, scientists in distributed locations can refer to the contents of their shared electronic notebook and make more informed decisions without having to travel.

18.3.2 Total Quality Management

The U.S. Air Force is undergoing massive restructuring, including downsizing, cost containment, and a strong focus on total quality and process improvement. Product and Process Improvement personnel are located worldwide at various bases and other facilities. Using a combination of Lotus Notes and Quality at Work from Quality Decision Management, this group of 200 people, among other activities, address process problems with the acquisition of fasteners, actuators, connectors, tools, and subsystems—FASTS, "the little stuff used in aircraft maintenance" that adds up to a significant expense in a worldwide fleet. Various team members working on a specific process improvement project may begin by evaluating the viability of a new product, and someone else may follow with a cost/benefit analysis. They store their results in a Notes repository. Some other member may access the information to support a go/no-go acquisition decision and record the rationale for their specific situation. Managers and members can track the acquisition processes. Using the new workflow engine from QAW, members are reminded of actions to take. Once an acquisition is complete, the Notes log and QAW process record serve as a permanent record of the overall process. The repository for all such projects can be used for reviewing best practices when a group member initiates another product acquisition process. Users of this system learn the total quality processes in doing their work.

A variety of other organizations, such as the U.S. Federal Aviation Authority, Bellcore, and Procter & Gamble, use electronic meeting support systems in their total quality activities. The processes of quality improvement—collecting and organizing ideas and evaluating alternatives—are natural for the tool set of these systems. The tool set, through structuring these processes, teaches total quality. Users learn and internalize quality improvement processes without formal training *while* doing the work.

18.3.3 Business Process Redesign

Young and Rubicam (Y&R), a leading advertising agency, is using an automated workflow system—ActionWorkflow from Action Technologies—to enable its advertising teams to deliver high-quality results while reducing charges for overtime and rush jobs. The workflow system standardizes the internal client-project/order process (the traffic system), a business process Y&R selected for re-engineering and subsequent automation because of its potential to improve productivity and demonstrate Y&R's commitment to quality to its clients. Benefits that Y&R achieved, in addition to improved quality of work, are increased customer satisfaction, higher productivity, less repetition of work, improved turnaround time, increased job satisfaction, and improved communication among the members of the account team. Advertising executives are freed from tracking the status of projects to be able to develop strategies, interface with clients, or come up with business-building ideas.

18.3.4 Organizational Learning

Learning expert Peter Senge makes the point that learning does not take place until a "state change" takes place in the body—a kind of physical "aha" that indicates the letting go of a rigidly held position or point of view. At Southern California Edison, a planning group was stuck trying to decide on the location for a new plant. Those participants with environmental concerns were in favor of a plant location strategy that would cause minimal environmental damage. The engineering members required adherence to the engineering specifications in the plant's development to the exclusion of all other concerns. The financial representatives required that any strategy adhere strictly to cost guidelines. The legal representatives insisted that the new site abide by covenants. Each constituency argued its point of view in each and every meeting. Using CM/1, a conversational structuring groupware system from Corporate Memory Systems, a skilled facilitator recorded the key issues of the plant site location, with solutions and pros and cons from each constituency, into a visual map. Once these groups had articulated their positions and shared their knowledge formally and visibly, they no longer had to defend their points of view or attack others. Letting go of their rigidly held positions, they could then move on to an objective examination leading to a mutually satisfying solution for all groups.

Maps and the issue analysis process support organic learning for the organization. They can be used to share knowledge with new group members. As issues are resolved, the concluding arguments can be recorded, and members are less likely to rehash the same issues because the map shows the ground the group has already covered. Maps serve as an organizational memory of the decision process—people remember the process and that it led to understanding, collaborative learning of the issues, and consensus. As participants learn to use the software, they improve their argumentation and thinking skills.

18.3.5 Employee Empowerment

After the devastating strike of air traffic controllers in the mid-1980s, the Federal Aviation Authority recognized the need to support organizational change in the interpersonal relationships between supervisors and subordinates. Specifically, management recognized that valuing the work force as never before, by treating individuals with the respect they deserve, was mandatory.

Use of GroupSystems V from Ventana Corp. is operationalizing this change by supporting peer assessments. Collectively, peer groups decide whom to choose for a new position, for example. Using a brainstorming tool, they develop a list of criteria by which to evaluate a candidate. They then use a voting tool to evaluate which criteria are most appropriate and a point-allocation tool to weight the criteria. Finally, they evaluate a candidate using the agreed-upon criteria and weighting. In these difficult sessions, everyone—staff and management alike—can anonymously enter evaluations. The result is that all levels of the organization have equal input in the evaluation process. GroupSystems V, and other meeting support systems, support an atmosphere where ideas flow freely. Because people can enter ideas and circulate them anonymously, the use of the system frees people to bounce ideas off one another or to criticize ideas without fear of rebuke from superiors or peers, and reduces the tendency for a few people to dominate a meeting.

18.4 PITFALLS

The examples in the last section described successful groupware implementations, primarily because of each organization's commitment to some organizational change to address its significant business problems. But implementation is not without its impediments. The SRI study documents the following pitfalls:

☞ *No quick fixes.* Business process re-engineering and other change initiatives themselves do not produce overnight solutions, let alone when technology is implemented to support them. The processes themselves may take several months if not years, and the results may not show up for considerably longer. Lexmark, a manufacturer of computer printers in Greenwich, Connecticut, which used to be a printer subsidiary for IBM, took two years to turn itself around through refocusing on customers, restructuring into teams and introducing communication technologies, focusing more attention on up-front design, eliminating management layers, and streamlining decision-making processes.

☞ *Difficulty in quantifying benefits.* The reports of direct hard-dollar benefits from Lotus are the exception; the hard-dollar benefits of other groupware are difficult to identify. And success has a dark side: Pitney Bowes Management Services reports that while re-engineering brings greater productivity, employees now fear their own job loss and report they are overburdened with work.

☞ *Lack of senior management's commitment, support, and participation.* Starting an organizational change effort and technology implementation in the trenches without executive buy-in is deadly. Unless executives actually use the technology to communicate and to share information, the implementation will be difficult. Managers and staff have a hard time, for example, taking electronic meeting support technology seriously unless their executives are hands-on users. At one aerospace company, meeting support technology lies idle, or at best is used only by the implementation team, because management was never convinced of its value and did not use it. Staff say, "We don't see them use, why should we?"

☞ *Need for new roles.* Even with technology such as electronic meeting support systems or Notes, facilitators are necessary to achieve benefits, at least until the work force becomes more competent in self-facilitation. However, adding new people or new roles in a time of downsizing is difficult to justify. A number of government agencies have had difficulty convincing themselves that electronic meeting support should be implemented because systems require a facilitator to be most effective.

☞ *Resistance to sharing information.* A work force that is accustomed to working individually will resist sharing information through repositories such as Notes. Knowledge is power in any company, and in knowledge companies, people use information to move ahead. In the CTE study, SRI found that people in the high-technology industry, banking, academia, and the military find sharing information particularly hard.

☞ *Competition among people.* At Price Waterhouse (PW), the real barrier to the Notes implementation was the competitive individualism of the work force. In her study of the organizational issues that arose after PW installed Notes, Wanda Orlikowski, Assistant Professor of Information Technologies at MIT's Sloan School of Management, reports that "that kind of mind-set reinforces individual effort and ability, and does not support cooperation or sharing of expertise." In addition, salespeople resist taking time to write up contact reports in order to share information because doing so takes away from their time in front of customers.

☞ *Information overload.* The use of groupware forces organizations and people to cope with the increased flow and handling of information. As access to information increases with broader participation in discussions, the possibility of being overwhelmed by irrelevant information also increases. And organizations do not necessarily have the right information. Any re-engineered organization has an abundance of data about its problems and issues, but lacks *operational* data to manage on a day-to-day basis to *fix* the processes.

☞ *A view that the technology is just a communication tool.* Professor Orlikowski also notes that at PW, the rapid pace of the implementation, driven by user demand, led users to view Notes as simply a new and better communications tool rather than as a "transforming technology" capable of supporting fundamentally redesigned work processes.

☞ *Technical incompatibilities.* For companies with sophisticated technology infrastructure, installing groupware will not be too difficult technically. However, in some cases, such companies will need to customize their groupware applications to fit their specific business environments. Few companies have invested in the required computer and network infrastructure. Systems that do exist are often incompatible between the departments or divisions that must collaborate. Personal computers may need upgrading, and additional operating systems and communication software must first be implemented.

☞ *Concern over negative impacts of technology on people.* Particularly with workflow technologies implemented to operationalize newly re-engineered business processes, workers worry that technology will change or eliminate the roles of people in the flow. See Table 18.2 for a complete list of potential negative impacts, with corresponding positive impacts.

The bottom line: Companies must manage change to reduce the pitfalls and possibility for negative impacts. The continuing proliferation of personal computing and networking is inexorable, and the transition must be managed properly to maximize the positive impacts. The key will be the extent to which all those involved can adopt a systemic, long-range perspective that emphasizes the value of workers and treats groupware, and any other information technologies, as

Table 18.2 Potential Impacts of Information Technologies

Negative Possibilities	Positive Possibilities
Deskilled or compartmentalized jobs offer fewer career paths	Establishment of work groups and team-building, along with cross-training of workers, ultimately expands skills and career options
Lack of commitment to deskilled jobs by workers results in discipline problems	Individual job satisfaction increases as workers are able to see the whole picture and how the job improves overall productivity, as they can with visual mapping or simulation technologies
Substituting computer judgment for human judgment, as with workflow technologies, trivializes human duties	Decision support systems, such as electronic meeting support systems, provide better understanding of available options in less time, allowing time to experiment with variables to reach improved decisions. Workflow technologies free people from administrivia to focus on strategic issues
Electronically mediated communications lack the richness of face-to-face communications	Automated support of routine work means more time for personal interactions; these systems expand the scope of communications, thereby enriching them
"Mae West" effect: heavy bottom level of low-level clerical workers, middle management is squeezed out, elite policy makers on top	Even with increased span of control, organizational structures are more productive and profitable, affecting the overall health of the economy such that new jobs are formed if workers reskill
Insulating information from experience and debate through use of computerized information systems reduces information quality	More egalitarian and free-spirited exchange is possible, supported by enhanced communication systems

tools to support and value people. Critical variables in successful implementation will include management's attitude toward change and addressing human resource issues such as job design, employee participation, and employee training or retraining.

18.5 PARTNERS

Back in the late '70s and early '80s, most large corporations began to implement office systems. Typically, an office automation task force was assigned to get the organization started. The makeup of this task force provides a lesson for today. Members included strategic planners, information technology folks (back then called MIS or data processing), financial analysts, representatives from the user community, and human resources personnel. Today, the shots are called by information technology (IT) groups working with the user community. Not bad, but perhaps not enough to ensure that the desired benefits are achieved. In just a few organizations, human resources personnel have been replaced by organization development (OD) professionals. I highly recommend that any organizational change initiative include OD professionals along with IT professionals.

18.5.1 What Is OD Anyway?

What is an OD professional? First of all, the term is not universally used. In some companies, the OD folks are viewed with suspicion—they introduce the next "flavor-of-the-month change initiative" (and the last effort they promoted is out of favor), "they're too soft," or "they have no content expertise—they say they deal in 'process' only." So, they may go by different names. In our work at Co-Development International, we from time to time are called some of the names in Table 18.3, which taken together begin to define what an OD professional is. Factions, or specialties, of OD are listed in Table 18.4.

Organization development, a term coined in the '60s, is a relatively young field. It involves consultants, both internal and external, who help clients improve their organizations by applying knowledge from the behavioral sciences—psychology, sociology, cultural anthropology, and related disciplines. Partnering with technology implementors, OD professionals focus more on the "people" and "organizational" issues, and less on the tools and technology. This is not to say that technology people do not also focus on these softer issues. A partnership between the two can only add value to any organizational change initiative.

OD is a process of organizational change that takes a system perspective. OD practice follows known pathways and steps for planning and implementing change in an organization. Three models are the underlying and guiding frames of reference for any OD effort: 1) the action research model—research is first conducted, and then action is taken as a direct result of what the research data are interpreted to indicate [French, 1969]; 2) Lewin's three-step model of system change—unfreezing, moving, and refreezing [Lewin, 1958]; and 3) phases

Table 18.3 Functions of Organization Development Professionals

Names for OD Professionals

Business process design/redesign/re-engineering specialist

Change agent

Coach

Conflict resolver

Facilitator

Human resource specialist

Management consultant

Mediator

Negotiator

Organizational learning consultant

Process consultant

Team developer

Trainer

---

of planned change as delineated by Lippitt, Watson, and Westley [1958]. These can be summarized as consisting of the following elements:

- ☞ An outside consultant or change agent is the catalyst.
- ☞ Information is gathered from the client system to understand the system and its problem areas, and reported back to the client so that action can be taken.
- ☞ The consultant and client engage in collaborative planning for the purpose of defining change (and the specific actions to be taken).
- ☞ Planned change is implemented based on the information, but as much as possible, conducted by the client with the continuing help of the change agent.
- ☞ The change is institutionalized and the expertise to engage in continuous improvement is transferred from the change agent to the client system.

18.5.2 OD Role in Groupware Implementation

In the previous chapter Dr. Peter R. Huckle and Tracey Shearmon recommend an implementation approach that follows well-proven change-management processes. It is a common-sense approach of knowing where you want to go—developing a vision of the ideal end state (such as improved collaboration among worldwide divisions in order to speed time to market)—selecting a pilot opportunity (one that moves the organization towards the desired end state),

Table 18.4 Factions of Organization Development

OD Specialties
Business process design/redesign/re-engineering
Culture building
Cultural diversity
Enterprise development
Executive development/leadership development
Group dynamics and team development
Large system change
Meeting planning/facilitation
Organization behavior
Organization diagnosis/analyses
Organization restructuring/Organizational transitioning
Process improvement/Total Quality
Sociotechnical systems design
Transformation OD (major shifts such as to a learning organization)
Values clarification
Visioning and strategic planning

analyzing the current situation, evaluating the differences between the current situation and the pilot opportunity, and developing a project plan to implement the changes necessary to bridge the gap. Following Huckle and Shearmon's recommendation, you are well on your way to a successful groupware implementation. At Co-Development International, we characterize this approach with our Enterprise Development Model (see Figure 18.2).

At Co-Development International, we have found that once the change plan is identified, the next questions become: Who does the work? How does it get done? How does work go from concept to action? The success or failure of implementation depends on the dynamic interplay between three essential alliances:

☞ *Leadership*—formal and informal leaders who authorize, sponsor, and encourage the enterprise to develop towards its desired future vision. Leaders must act as developers and coaches. They also have a huge symbolic importance to the stakeholders—members watch leaders to see if the leaders really encourage the changes taking place by participating themselves and "walking the talk."

☞ *Stakeholders*—employees, customers, suppliers, vendors, and anyone else who has a stake in the enterprise. Stakeholders enact or inhibit the imple-

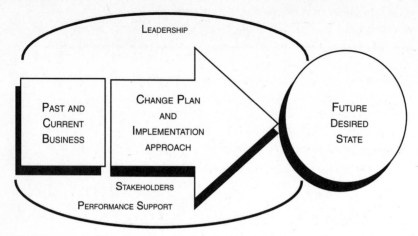

Fig. 18.2 Enterprise Development Model. Copyright 1990, Co-Development International.

mentation effort. They are the real owners—if they do not own the change, it does not happen.

☞ *Performance support*—advisors, coaches, consultants, and support personnel, from within and outside the organization, are the element of the enterprise that gives whatever support is necessary to enable stakeholders to actually perform to the desired future vision. Their job is to insure that stakeholders have the support and resources they need to change, step by step.

The notion of performance support is relatively new, but just as we have information technology specialists, we need development, or performance support, specialists to enable the organization to achieve new levels of *performance*. Our change efforts need ongoing performance support competencies to move forward. The performance support alliance competencies include:

☞ *Enterprise development:* They help leaders and stakeholders design, plan, implement, monitor, and communicate how any change will take place. They support leaders to think strategically, systematically, and developmentally.

☞ *Facilitate the shaping or creating of systems to support the new vision:* Typically, these people come from the stakeholder group and thus understand the current culture, while also keeping current with the latest social and technical tools and practices that enable change most rapidly and effectively. For example, they may have experience working with compensation specialists to ensure that the reward and recognition systems support organizational change such as improved collaboration, and thus provide new ways of thinking about this thorny issue.

☞ *Facilitate engagement, collaboration, and participation:* The performance

support alliance can support leaders or stakeholders in building key relationships. For example, they may work to involve groupware vendor participation in the success of an implementation—clarifying vision, schedules,
and commitments of all parties.

☞ *Coordination and project management:* The performance support alliance is
responsible for the overall coordination and project management and making sure that no one is left out of the process who needs to be involved.

☞ *Communication and visibility:* They keep the implementation process visible through visual maps, newsletters, white papers, briefings, and so on.

☞ *Enhance connections and help build networks:* They also serve as a clearing-
house for information and keeping everyone connected. They are a kind of
broker to outside resources such as best practices, advisors, and consultants. As such, they may need support themselves in getting on to new technology so they can share their information and networks using groupware.

☞ *Administrative logistics:* They coordinate and schedule key meetings, facilitate when necessary, arrange events and presentations, and help produce or
distribute materials.

☞ *Provide trustworthy emotional support through the change process:* When
change creates discomfort, such as people being moved out of roles they
have been in for their entire careers and into new roles with new skills or
new ways to work required, the performance support alliance provides emotional support. They are a sounding board for grievances or criticisms. They
provide clarity and support to guide people into the future vision.

☞ *Catch expected breakdowns and get the change process back on track:* Breakdowns will happen. Stakeholders will rebel, leaders will be recalcitrant
users. Performance support can work with both alliances.

18.5.3 Two Examples

One enterprise that recently reorganized to become flexible and able to
respond to market forces set up video teleconferences for the top leaders to
be able to "dialogue" with the workforce about the change process. However,
workers were resentful about the changes and did not trust the leaders. No
one asked questions in the teleconferences, so they were discontinued. In
one division where no performance support team had been installed, people
began an "underground" email dialogue in which they complained about the
teleconferences and other issues. The email correspondence was quite negative. The leaders in the division took an authoritarian stance and shut
down access to the email system to prevent further negativism. They set up
a system where input was no longer anonymous and where workers could
not access free bulletin board areas. The negative feelings and criticism
continued to grow in "backroom conversations."

In another division which had a performance support team, the same email phenomenon developed. The reaction made sense to the performance support team, because they, too, were part of the employee community and understood the distrust of leaders. They saw the email complaints as a sign of a vibrant and energetic group discussion and wanted to capture the energy for the implementation process. They designed a process to bring the leaders into the dialogue on email. The conversations took place anonymously, as they could not with the video teleconferences. It was not a smooth and easy process, but it got the issues on the table, and leaders and employees began to address them in authentic ways. Eventually, the tone of the email messages began to shift to a more positive stance, as more and more of the employees joined in the dialogue.

At Co-Development International we believe it is necessary to develop competence to address the "tests" that leadership, stakeholders, and performance support are hit with in any change process such as implementing groupware. What do we mean by tests? When the enterprise embarks on an implementation of any planned change, members engage in a number of testing behaviors to check for what will be required of them to function successfully in the desired future state. What behaviors will be validated and rewarded? What behaviors will not be allowed? What new responsibilities will be placed on people? What skills will be required? People will test and then watch for a response and will act on the message given in the response. For example, if the leaders announce that a new technology will support new processes and then do not use it when their role calls for it, the employees will not feel compelled to use it either. Stakeholders will model what they see and feel from their leaders.

Because this phenomenon of testing and modeling of responses is so powerful, it is important to expect these tests and be prepared for them. Each of the three alliances is tested around a specific theme related to their roles in the change, from our experience:

☞ *Leadership—tests of commitment.* Do leaders do as they want the employees to do? This test is tough because people wish to stay where they are—it's comfortable, and they fear the unknown, and so if the leaders do not change, they can continue to operate as they always have. On the other hand, we thrive on discovery and mastery of the unknown. Seeing commitment in action by our leaders engenders hope, commitment, and the courage to move toward the desired future state. This energy promotes breakthrough and true business transformation.

☞ *Stakeholders—tests of responsibility.* The test of the stakeholders—many of whom are the employees—is inward. Will they take personal and group responsibility for making change successful, or will they point fingers at each other and place blame? Can they question their own role in success? Will they act in ways that benefit themselves as individuals, or will they act in service of their departments, or can they act in service of the whole organization? Most complex change initiatives require responsibility at all levels and keeping them in balance. If the test of responsibility is responded to successfully, stakeholders can achieve a richness and new meaning to their work lives.

☞ *Performance support—tests of competence.* Performance support members are tested for their ability to promote necessary competence in the stakeholders. Workers need to feel confident that they can learn new skills and behaviors in order to let go of old ways of doing things. Workers need to know that support to deal with the emotions associated with change is available, and that they will be rewarded for their new behavior. To provide this assurance, competent, sensitive staff, committed to providing performance support, coming from the ranks or outside, is critical.

If it has not already done so, the information technology community must engage its organization development counterparts in groupware implementation. As someone with a foot on both sides, I feel strongly that a partnership between these two competencies enriches both each other and the organization. Whether groupware implementation takes place experimentally in a pilot effort, at a workgroup level, or in the enterprise as a whole, a partnership between IT and OD can ensure that the hoped-for benefits of technology investment are achieved. With the two competencies working collaboratively, the benefits of business transformation are highly likely.

REFERENCES

1. Burke, W. Warner, *Organization Development: Principles and Practices,* Little, Brown and Company, 1982.
2. French, W. L., "Organization Development: Objectives, Assumptions, and Strategies," *California Management Review,* Volume XII, 1969.
3. Friedman, Lisa and Gyr, Herman *et al, The Age of Enterprise: The Enterprise Development Reader,* unpublished manuscript from Co-Development International, September 1994.
4. Lewin, K., "Group Decision and Social Change." In *Readings in Social Psychology,* New York: Holt, Rinehart and Winston, 1958.
5. Lippitt, R., J. Watson, and B. Westley, *Dynamics of Planned Change.* New York: Harcourt, Brace, 1958.
6. Martin, Alexia, "Collaborative Technologies to Support Organizational Change," Business Intelligence Program, SRI International, October 1993.
7. Venkatraman, N., interviewed by Tom Lloyd in *Transformation, the International Publication of Gemini Consulting,* Summer 1994, Issue 3.

ACKNOWLEDGMENTS

The author wishes to acknowledge her colleagues at Co-Development International, specifically Dr. Lisa Friedman and Dr. Herman Gyr, developers of the Enterprise Development Model and related methodologies. Friedman and Gyr contribute two unique ideas to the body of change management theory: 1) The success or failure of implementation depends on the dynamic interplay among the alliance of leadership, stakeholders, and performance support personnel; and 2) Each of these alliance members are constantly tested around a specific theme related to their roles in the implementation.

BIOGRAPHY

Alexia Martin is director, technology solutions at Co-Development International in Saratoga, California, a management consulting firm. CDI's strategic focus is business transformation at the intersection of enterprise development, learning support, and technology solutions. Practices include strategic sourcing, business process re-engineering, and team and leadership development. Currently Ms. Martin's group is developing interactive, multimedia kiosks to give employees one-stop access to their personal records and a broad range of information and services from which they can make better informed choices for themselves, while simultaneously freeing human resources professionals to focus on more strategic services. Ms. Martin also provides facilitation services using electronic meeting support technology.

Additionally, Alexia continues as principal at her own firm, Intersections, in Los Gatos, California, a consulting group dedicated to developing opportunities at the intersections of people and technology, working and learning. Typically, Ms. Martin enables clients to take advantage of emerging technologies such as groupware or performance support systems.

Groupware
Resources

Appendices

The goal of this section is to provide reference information for those interested in groupware. This section covers vendors, events, paper and electronic news sources, user groups, and an extensive reading list. Every effort has been made to ensure accurate information; however, given the dynamic nature of the groupware market, maintaining up to the date information is difficult at best. This listing is accurate as of early 1995.

APPENDIX A: VENDORS

Calendaring and Scheduling

1Soft Corp.
Gregory Thorne
707 987 0256

Arabesque Software Inc.
Frank Coyle
206 867 3757

CE Software
Curtis Lee
515 221 1801

Campbell Services, Inc.
Ray Peabody
810 559 5955

Corporate Software, Inc.
David Gonzales
703 522 1310

CrossWind Technologies, Inc.
Kevin Colgate
408 335 5450

Experience in Software, Inc.
Carolyn Burd
510 644 0694

IBM, Software Solutions Division
800 IBM-CALL

International Project Management, Inc.
George Blackburn
508 529 4845

Microsystems Software, Inc.
Glenn Martyn
508 879 9000

Milum Corporation
Scott Hayes
512 469 2966

Now Software
Mike Sherwood
503 274 2800

Primavera Systems, Inc.
Kristy Tan
610 667 8600

Projectware Inc.
Sesh Srinivasan
408 773 8237

Russell Information Sciences
Alfred Lara
714 362 4000

Sarrus Software, Inc.
Liz Statmore
415 345 8950 or 800 995 1963

SuperTime, Inc.
Gary Babcock
905 764 3530

Thuridion
Evelyn O'Donnell
408 439 6983

Timephaser Corporation
J. Michael Mahon
619 490 3635

Trellis
Chip de Villafranca
508 485 7200

WorkFlow Designs
Joe Castro
214 991 3569

Electronic Mail

Alisa Systems Inc.
Don Cole
818 792 9474

Apple Computer, Inc.
800 SOS APPL

Artisoft, Inc.
Joe Stunkard
602 670 7100

Attachmate Canada Limited
Elaine Brill
416 979 1380

Baranof Software, Inc.
Peter Zimmer
617 783 0080

CE Software
Curtis Lee
515 221 1801

Clarify Software
Gwen Peterson
415 691 0320

Clark Development Co., Inc.
Steve Clark
801 261 1686

CompuServe
Michael Finney
614 457 8600

Corporate Software, Inc.
David Gonzales
703 522 1310

Datamedia Corporation
Fredric B. Gluck
603 886 1570

DaVinci Systems Support
919 881 4320

Daxtron Laboratories, Inc.
Kino H. Coursey
817 924 6707

Digital Equipment Corp.
Stephen F. Martin
603 881 6150

Enterprise Solutions Limited
Brenda Barnetson
818 597 8943

Futurus Corporation
Betsy Jinright
404 392 7979

Galacticomm, Inc.
Dihan Rosenburg
305 583 5990

Hewlett-Packard
Andrew Ransom
408 447 6214

IPD
Lenny Liebmann
908 291 8800

Infinite Technologies
Patty Lummis
410 363 1097

Lightspeed Software
Eric Schwocho
805 324 4291

LinkAge Inc.
Paul Saunders
613 594 9244

MCI
Mike Sutter
800 999 2096

MMB Development Corporation
Bob Baskerville
800 832 6022

MacLean, Pete
Pete MacLean
415 751 8336

Maxware Inc.
Helge Krogenes
203 226 2866

Microsoft
Dave Perry
503 245 0905

NetManage
Thomas Leuchtner
408 973 7171

Novell Inc.
Mark Ryan
408 577 7190

On Technology Corp.
Anne Beitel
617 374 1400

Oracle
David Michaud
415 506 3228

Radio Mail Corporation
Mark Elderkin
415 286 7839

Sarrus Software, Inc.
Liz Statmore
415 345 8950 or 800 995 1963

SkyTel
Jennifer Baily
408 451 3990

SoftArc Inc.
Dallas Kachan
905 415 7000

Sterling Software Network Services
Div.
David Winkler
614 793 7000

TEKNOW, Inc.
Laurie Parsons
602 266 7800

The Wollongong Group
Debbie Tjernagel
415 962 7100

Unipalm
Maria Porto
44 223 250 114

Verimation Inc.
Robert Cohen
201 391 2888

VoCal Telecommunications
Ron Emerling
818 447 9425

Wingra Technologies
Barb Kocher
608 238 4454

WordPerfect Corp.
Eldon Greenwood
801 222 3940

WorldTalk Corporation
Sherrie Maller
408 399 4000

Z-Code Software
Ken Burke
415 898 8649

Group Decision Support Systems

Corporate Memory Systems
Donna Jarrett
512 795 9999

Desktop Data
Brad Singer
800 255 3343

Don Barth Consulting
Don Barth
414 235 0294

Eden Systems Corporation
Richard P. Nashleanas
800 779 6338

Experience in Software, Inc.
Carolyn Burd
510 644 0694

Expert Choice Inc.
William L. Peace
412 682 3844

Global Consensus, Inc.
Wade Whitmer
214 446 1952

IBM, Software Solutions Division
800 IBM-CALL

Idea Fisher Systems, Inc.
Matt Engen
714 474 8111

McCall, Szerdy & Associates
Mike McCall
800 423 8890

Option Technologies, Inc.
Barbara Clark
612 450 1700

Pacer Software, Inc.
Peter Coppola
508 898 3300

Pangea Corporation
Marty Martel
703 256 6871

QSoft Solutions Corp.
Anita Pomerantz
716 264 9700

SMART Technologies Inc.
Natalie Young
403 245 0333

Show Business Software
Rachel Riley/Louise Darcy
1144 71 833 8041

Teamworker L.C.
Andrew Gear
801 943 0160

Trinzic Corp.
Lee Warner
603 427 0444

Ventana Corporation
Lynn Lyle
602 325 8228

Vidya Technologies
Kumar Nochur
617 497 7150

Group Editing

ConQuest Software
John McGrath
410 290 6290

On Technology Corp.
Anne Beitel
617 374 1400

Oracle
Product Inquiries
800 633 0596

STS Systems
Carolyn Mitchell
514 426 0822 x 2525

SoftSolutions
Jason Werner
801 226 6000

Uniplex
Shane Philips
800 356 8063

Verity, Inc.
Timothy Fogarty
415 960 7600

Visioneer
Customer Information Center
800 787 7007

Groupware Frameworks

Decathlon Data Systems, Inc.
Robert Williams
303 440 9000

Lotus Development Corporation
Bryan Simmons
617 577 8500

Softool Corporation
Jackie Webster
805 683 5777

TeamWARE Division, ICL Inc.
Shannon Hakesley
408 982 9146

Uniplex
Shane Philips
800 356 8063

Groupware Resources

Baseline Software
Karen Solomon
415 332 7763

Digital Media
Mitch Ratcliffe
415 575 3775

EDventure Holdings, Inc.
Daphne Kis
212 924 8800

Electronic Messaging Association
703 524 5550

Grantham & Nichols
Dr. Charles Grantham
510 834 1485

GroupTalk
David Coleman
415 282 9197

Groupware Report
Eileen Dennis
706 613 5348

IEEE Computer Society
Frieda L. Koester
714 821 8380

Morgan Kaufmann Publishers
Lisa Schneider
415 578 9911

Office Futures
Roger Whitehead
44 0883 713074

Patricia Seybold Group
Ronni T. Marshak
617 742 5200

Performance Resources Speakers
Phillip Knowlton
415 332 5211

The Conference Group
Bob Bierman
602 443 4090

WordPerfect Magazine
Kim Howard
801 227 3500

Groupware Services

Andersen Consulting
Gerald L. Mourey
312 507 8953

AnswerSet Corp.
Wendi Makuch
503 598 4500 x124

Awakening Technology
Peter & Trudy Johnson-Lenz
503 635 2615

BSG Corporation
Mike Alsup
713 965 9000

Bootstrap Institute
Douglas C. Engelbart
510 713 3550

Collaborative Strategies
David Coleman
415 282 9197

Consensus Development Corporation
Christopher Allen
415 647 6383

Corporate Software, Inc.
Jane Roach
617 440 1023

Creative Alternatives
Bernard Schwartz
708 488 0533

DPI Services, Inc.
Carol Martinez
408 629 3700

Dataquest, Inc.
Karl Wong
408 437 8213

Decision Dynamics Ltd.
Tony Gear
(44) 0942 522 030

Delfin Systems
Robert LaBrecque
703 758 0190 x 2173

EDM, Inc.
Mike Stackpoole
510 438 9651

Engecom S/A
Flavio Rossini
+55 11 535 1311

Frederick Computers Plus
John McNulty
301 815 8844

Frontiers
Peter Lloyd
(44) 081 449 3656

Gateway Group Inc.
David Waal
510 283 7900 x 204

Groupware Concepts, Inc.
Judi Mohler
214 233 7077

IBM, Software Solutions Division
800 IBM-CALL

ICM
201 535 3400

IPD
Lenny Liebmann
908 291 8800

JCJasik
Janus C. Jasik
508 877 9373

Kingsgate Applied Groupware
Peter Huckle
(44) 1962 860 670

Lante Corporation
Jeff Alvis
312 236 5100

Management Share Belgium
Marc Vanmaele
(32) 2 725 1890

McHale USConnect
Kevan Asadorian
216 498 3550

Optus
Max Schroeder
908 271 9568

Oracle Corporation
Kim Smith
703 708 6762

Resource Associates
Dale Taylor
805 899 4670

SRI International
Marcelo Hoffmann
415 859 3680

SWS Software, Ltd.
Euzen Varadinek
42 67 98 11 72

. Susanna Opper & Associates
Susanna Opper
413 528 6513

Teamworker L.C.
Andrew Gear
801 943 0160

Trillium Business Learning, Inc.
David Gendron
408 879 0111

Groupware Vertical Applications

Business Automation Incorporated
Robert C. Novy
714 998 6600/800 266 6385

Lysis Corp.
Deborah Fain
404 892 3301

Management Directions
David Joiner
901 761 5429

Market Power, Inc.
Todd Kingsley, III
916 265 5000

Pinnacle Business Systems, Inc.
Peter Hewtrey
800 932 6388

Premier One, Inc.
Clark Dircz
612 835 6179

QDM
Rosemarie Amodeo
508 688 8266

Repository Technologies, Inc.
Kathy Emerson
708 515 0780

Scopus Technology, Inc.
Aaron Omid
510 428 0500

Trellis
Chip de Villafranca
508 485 7200

US Connect/Real World Systems
Steve Plotkin
610 358 3245

Miscellaneous

Experience in Software, Inc.
Carolyn Burd
510 644 0694

Hybrid Networks, Inc.
Craig Struchman
408 725 3250

MDI
Michelle Davis
303 443 2706

Maxware Inc.
Helge Krogenes
203 226 2866

MultiLink, Inc.
Karyn A. Murphy
508 691 2100

Quarterdeck Office Systems
Stanton Kaye
310 392 9851

Simpact Associates, Inc.
Christie Aguilar
619 565 1865

Shared Memory Products

Chena Software, Inc.
Jennifer Hieter
610 770 1210

Collabra Software
David Jones
415 940 6400

Folio Corporation
Mike Judson
801 344 3671

Forefront Group, The
Dave Sikora
713 961 1101

JSoft Technologies
Joseph Jesson
708 356 6817

Odesta Systems Corp.
Ed Kriega
708 498 5615

Office Express Pty. Ltd.
Leah Bryant
61 2 389 4833

Quest Technologies Inc.
Lisa Handley
810 680 6653

The MESA Group, Inc.
Michel Yazbek
617 964 7400

Trax Softworks, Inc.
Anne Moriarty
800 367 8729

Trinzic Corp.
Eric Egertson
617 891 6500

Z/Max Computer Solutions, Inc.
Alan Lewis
315 635 1882

Shared Screen Products

Crosswise Corporation
Gary M. Gysin
800 747 9060

Farallon Computing, Inc.
Trudy Edelson
510 814 5307

Fujitsu Networks Industry, Inc.
Jim Zimmermann
203 326 2723

Group Logic, Inc.
Dimitri Korahais
800 476 8781

IBM
Max Alexander
404 238 6726

JSB Corporation
Tom Wallace
408 438 8300

LiveWorks
Denise Boucher
408 324 2200

RTZ Software
Seth Snyder
408 252 2946

Sun Solutions
John Quist
415 688 9852

Vis-a-Vis, Inc.
Wendy Sexsmith
 416 350 1418

Workstation Technologies
Tim Dubes
714 250 8980

Workflow

AT&T Global Information Solutions
Jim Davis
513 445 7257

Action Technologies
Mark Thorp
510 521 6190

Bull Worldwide Information Systems
Gary E. Olin
508 294 4911

D&B Software
Lorretta Gasper
404 239 3658

Delrina Corporation
Randy Busch
416 441 3676 x 2191

Digital Tools
Ritta Merilainen
408 366 6920

Edge Software, Inc.
Sales
510 462 0543

Edge Systems Inc.
Ken Concon
703 525 EDGE

Edify Corporation
William Matlock
408 982 2920

FileNet Corp.
Cathy M. Subatch
714 966 3496

G.E. Information Services
Egan Skinner
301 340 4536

Hewlett-Packard
Andrew Ransom
408 447 6214

IBM
Don DeMark
301 803 3169

IBM, Software Solutions Division
800 IBM-CALL

IMARA Research Corp.
Linda Gardner
416 581 1740

Intelligent Systems Group
Philip A. Mongelluzzo
203 876 6199

JetForm Corp.
Fred Lucici
617 647 7700

Keyfile Corporation
Patricia Hopper
603 883 3800 x 390

Meta Software Corp.
Louis J. Zand
617 576 6920

PC Docs Inc.
Lisa Bliss
904 942 3627

Portfolio Technologies
Eric Chin
510 226 5635

President Software, Inc.
Susan Mazur
408 985 1824

QDM
Rosemarie Amodeo
508 688 8266

Reach Software
Kim Pyser
408 733 8685

Recognition International Inc.
Grace Sechnick
214 579 6000

RightFAX
Julie Howard
602 327 1357

Saros Corporation
Kathryn Siewert
800 82-SAROS

Soft Solutions
Jason Werner
801 226 6000

Staffware Corp.
Chris Fletcher
617 239 8221

Synapsis S.A.
Oscar Lopez T.
562 632 1240

Workflow, Inc.
Terry Shore
610 459 9487

Xerox/XSoft
Mary Spollen
617 499 4487

Workgroup Products and Utilities

ASD Software Inc.
Francine Dubois
909 624 2594

Aegis Software Inc.
Eli Horowitz
516 374 0800

Apple Computer, Inc.
800 SOS APPL

Axxis Corporation
Steven Schwartz
407 696 4200

Baseline Software
Karen Solomon
415 332 7763

Cadre Technologies Inc.
TeleProfessional Services
401 351 5950/800 743 2273

Corporate Software, Inc.
David Gonzales
703 522 1310

DSSI
Ken Norwood
818 991 0200

Digital Equipment Corp.
Stephen F. Martin
603 881 6150

ELF Technologies, Inc.
Cynthia S. Lavoie
206 232 7808

Groupware Concepts, Inc.
Judi Mohler
214 233 7077

IBM Corp.
Fred G. Castaneda
512 838 4725

Norton-Lambert Corp.
Melissa Bloom
805 964 6767 x 5920

Oracle
Product Inquiries
800 633 0596

Percussion Software
Audrey J. Augun
617 267 6700

Popular Programs, Inc.
Douglas G. Morgan
713 530 1195

PowerSoft Corp.
Doug Miller
508 287 1500

SandPoint Company
Ellen P. Slaby
617 868 4442

Softool Corporation
Cartee Bales/Jackie Webster
805 683 5777

Visible Systems Corporation
Don Sherwood
617 890 2273

The following section contains non-vendor information including a reading list covering groupware books, technical articles, academic journals, computer trade magazines, and the business press. It also includes information on: events, newsletters, and other groupware information services.

APPENDIX B: BOOKS

Even though there is intense interest in groupware, not many books are on the market yet. The listing below covers many of the better volumes and also includes books on related subjects such as re-engineering and tools for business change.

Currid, Cheryl. *Re-engineering Toolkit: 15 Tools and Technologies for Re-engineering Your Organization,* Prima Publishing, 1994.

Davenport, Thomas. *Process Innovation, Re-engineering Work Through Information Technology*, Harvard Business School Press, 1993.

Davidow, William H. and Malone, Michael S. *The Virtual Corporation: Structuring and Revitalizing the Corporation for the 21st Century*, Harper Business, 1992.

Dekoven, Bernard. *The Connected Executive,* Institute for Better Meetings, 1990.

Gewirtz, David. *Lotus Notes 3 Revealed, Your Guide to Managing Information and Improving Communication Throughout Your Organization*, Prima Publishing, 1994.

Grief, Irene. *Computer-Supported Cooperative Work: A Book of Readings,* Morgan Kaufman Publishers, (800) 745-7323, 1988.

Hammer, Michael and Champy, James. *Re-engineering the Corporation: A Manifesto for Business Revolution,* Harper Business, 1993.

Johansen, Robert, Sibbet, David, Benson, Suzyn, Martin, Alexia, Mittman, Robert, Saffo, Paul. *Leading Business Teams; How Teams Can Use Technology and Group Process Tools to Enhance Performance*, Addison Wesley, 1991.

Kaye, Anthony R. *Collaborative Learning Through Computer Conferencing, The Najaden Papers,* Institute of Educational Technology, Open University, U.K.

Lloyd, Peter. *Groupware in the 21st Century, Computer Supported Cooperative Working Toward the Millennium,* Adamantine Press Ltd., 1994.

Marca, David and Bock, Geoffrey. *Groupware: Software for Computer Supported Cooperative Work*, IEEE Computer Press, 1992.

Moore, Geoffrey. *Crossing the Chasm, Marketing and Selling Technology Products to Mainstream Customers,* Harper Business, 1991

Morton, Michael S. Scott. *the Corporation of the 1990's: Information Technology and Organizational Transformation*, Oxford University Press, 1991.

Olson, G. M., Olson, J. S., Mack, L. A., Cornell, P., and Luchetti, R. *Computer Augmented Teamwork, Chapter 10*, "Flexible Facilities for Electronic Meetings." Bostrom, Watson, and Kinney, Eds. Van Nostrand Reinhold, 1993.

Opper, Susanna and Fersko-Weiss, Henry. *Technology for Teams: Enhancing Productivity in Networked Organizations*, Van Nostrand Reinhold, 1992.

Gavriel Salvendy. *Handbook of Human Factors*, Wiley Modules, 1987.

Schrage, Michael. *Shared Minds: The New Technologies of Collaboration*, New York: Random House, 1990.

Tapscott, Don and Caston, Art. *Paradigm Shift: The New Promise of Information Technology*, McGraw-Hill, 1993.

Toffler, Alvin. *Powershift*, Bantam Books, 1990.

White, Thomas and Fischer, Layna. *The Workflow Paradigm: The Impact of Information Technology on Business Process Re-engineering*, Future Strategies, Inc., 1994.

Wilson, Paul. *Computer Supported Cooperative Work*, Intellect Books, 1991.

The following list was compiled by Karen Takle Quinn from "GSS Stepping Stones," an annotated reading and resource list of group support systems.

Bostrom, Robert P., Watson, Richard T., and Kinney, Susan T., Eds. *Computer Augmented Teamwork: A Guided Tour*, Van Nostrand Reinhold, 1992.

Galegher, J. Kraut, R.E. and Egido, C. *Intellectual Teamwork: Social and Technological Foundations of Cooperative Work*, Lawrence Erlbaum Associates, 1990.

Grantham, Charles E. and Nichols, Larry D. *The Digital Workplace: Designing Groupware Platforms*, Van Nostrand Reinhold, 1993.

Jessup, Leonard M. and Valacick, Joseph. *Group Support Systems: New Perspectives*, Macmillan, 1993.

Johansen, R. *Groupware: Computer Support for Business Teams*, Macmillan, 1988.

Keen, Peter G. W. and Cummins, J. Michael. *Networks in Action: Business Choices and Telecommunications Decisions*, Wadsworth Publishing, 1994.

Keen, Peter G. W. and Knapp, Ellen M. *Every Manager's Guide to Business Processes: Quality, Learning, Re-engineering, Logistics*, Harvard Business School Press, 1995.

Keen, Peter G. W. and Knapp, Ellen M. *Process Payoffs: Building Value Through Business Process Investment*, Harvard Business School Press, 1995.

Mallach, Efrem G. *Understanding Decision Support Systems and Expert Systems*, Dow/Irwin, 1993.

Olson, M. H. *Technological Support for Work Group Collaboration*, Lawrence Erlbaum Associates, 1989.

Taylor, James C. and Felton, David. *Performance by Decision*. Prentice Hall, 1993.

Turban, E. *Decision Support Systems and Expert Systems (3rd Ed.)*, Macmillan, 1993.

Lotus Notes Books

Barnes, Kate. *10 Minute Guide to Lotus Notes Release 3*, Alpha Books.

Helliwell, John. *HELP! Lotus Notes 3.0*, Ziff-Davis, 1994.

Lotus Notes Application Developer's Reference (*Release* 3), Lotus Publishing, 1994.

Pyle, Lisa. *Creating Lotus Notes Applications*, Que Publishing, 1993.

Schulman, Mark. *Using Lotus Notes*, Que Publishing, 1993.

Conference, Symposium, and Academic Proceedings

Baecker and Buxton. *Readings in HCI*, 1987.

BCS-HCI: People and Computers, Cambridge, 1985–1991.

CHI: Human Factors in Computing Systems, ACM, 1982–1992.

Coleman, David and Collaborative Strategies. *Conference Proceedings Groupware '93, '94 & '95*, The Conference Group, (800) 247-0262, 1993, 1994, 1995.

Coleman, David and Huckle, Peter. *Groupware '94 Europe, Groupware '94 Boston*, The Conference Group, (800) 247-0262, 1994.

CSCW: Computer-Supported Cooperative Work, ACM, 1988–1990.

CSCW '88 & '90 Proceedings, Association for Computing Machinery (ACM), 1990.

Global Networks: Computers and International Communication, MIT Press, 1993.

Helander. *Handbook of HCI*, Elsevier/North-Holland, 1988.

Hendriks, Paul. *GroupWare '91 Proceedings*, Software Engineering Research Centre, Netherlands.

Mantei, M., *Capturing the Caputer Lab Concepts: A Case Study in the Design of Computer Supported Meeting Environments*, CSCW, 1988.

Marshak, Ronni. *Workflow '94 (Boston and San Jose)*, The Conference Group, (800) 247-0262, 1994.

Martz, W. B., Chappell, D. A., Roberts, E. E., and Nunamaker, J. F. "Designing Integrated Information Facilities to Support Electronic Meetings," *HICSS Proceedings*, 1991.

Product Catalogs

Coleman, David. *The Groupware Product and Services Catalog*, Collaborative Strategies and Creative Networks, published annually, 1994.

Lotus Development Corporation. *The Lotus Notes Guide*, Affinity Publishing Co., 1994.

APPENDIX C: JOURNALS

Academy of Management Journal

Accounting, Management and Information Technologies

ACM Transactions on Computer-Human Interaction

ACM Transactions on Office Information Systems

Behaviour and Information Technology

British Journal of Management

Collaborative Computing

Communications of the ACM

Concurrent Engineering: Research & Applications

Decision Support in Public Admin.

Decision Systems

Group Decision and Negotiation

Harvard Business Review

IEEE Transactions on Systems, Man, and Cybernetics

Information Systems

Interacting with Computers

International Journal of Man Machine Studies

International Journal on Intelligent and Cooperative Information Systems

Journal of Applied Psychology

Journal of MIS

Management Science

MIS Quarterly

PRESENCE

Technical/Trade Publications

Byte	*Info World*
Communications Week	*Network World*
ComputerWorld	*PC Magazine*
Datamation	*PCWeek*
InformationWeek	*Scientific American*

Business Publications

Business Week	*Inc.*
Fortune	*The New York Times*
Forbes	*The Wall Street Journal*

APPENDIX D: CONFERENCES/EVENTS

LotusSphere	January	Orlando, FL	(800) 655-6887
Principles of Process	January	San Francisco, CA	(510) 642-6117
Management & Re-engineering WebWorld	January	Orlando, FL	(508) 470-3880
Networld	February	Boston, MA	(800) 829-3976
Client/Server Conference & Exposition	February	San Jose, CA	(800) 808-3976
GroupWare '95	March	Boston, MA	(800) 247-0262
Workflow '95	March	Boston, MA	(800) 247-0262
WebWorld	April	Orlando, FL	(508) 470-3880
AIIM	April	San Francisco, CA	(800) 477-2446
DeskCon II	May	San Jose, CA	(800) 829-3400
VRWorld '95	May	San Jose, CA	(800) 632-5537
GroupWare '95	June	London	(800) 247-0262
Workflow	June	San Francisco, CA	(617) 247-1025
Database & Client Server World, The Second Generation	June	Boston, MA	(508) 470-3880
GroupWare '95	August	San Jose, CA	(800) 247-0262
Workflow '95	August	San Jose, CA	(800) 247-0262
NetWorld + Interop	September	Las Vegas, NV	(800) 488-2883
National BPR Conference	September	Arlington, VA	(703) 708-9050
Telecom XIV	October	Anaheim, CA	(800) 829-3400
EMA Messaging and Leadership	October	Washington, DC	(703) 524-5550

E-MAIL World/Internet Expo	November	Boston, MA	(508) 470-3880
Comdex	November	Las Vegas, NV	
Workflow '95	December	Amsterdam	(800) 247-0262
Project World	December	Santa Clara, CA	(617) 431-9797
Database & Client Server World	December	Chicago, IL	(508) 470-3880

APPENDIX E: ORGANIZATIONS

WARIA (Workflow and Re-engineering International Association)
Layna Fischer
Chair
Future Strategies, Inc.
3640 North Federal Highway
Lighthouse Point, FL 33064
Phone (305) 782-3376, FAX 305-782-6363 E-mail; waria@gate.net

WALNUT (Worldwide Notes Users Group)
Gary Clare
President
Coopers & Lybrand
1251 Avenue of the Americas, New York, NY 10020
Phone (212) 536-3010, FAX (212) 536-2021

APPENDIX F: ELECTRONIC RESOURCES/SITES

The Internet newsgroup "comp.groupware" is the best place for information and discussions on groupware, and is read by about 28,000 people monthly from all over the world.

Other internet newsgroups that also have groupware information include:
biz.comp.services
biz.comp.software
ca.seminars
comp.client-server
comp.human-factors
comp.infosystems
comp.mail.misc
comp.newprod
comp.org.acm
comp.org.eff.news
comp.org.ieee
comp.os.ms-windows.apps
ieee.announce

Lotus Notes discussions (miscellaneous)
Profesional conference announcements and calls for papers

Business Process Redesign List   The name of the list is BPR, and to join it send the following one-line message to mailbase@mailbase.ac.uk: join BPR <your first name> <your last name>. If you require any further information on the BPR discussion list, contact the list owner, Gerard Burke (a.g.burke@cranfield.ac.uk).

Business Process Redesign Mailing List   The newsgroup BPR-L has been created on Internet, accessible through regular mail from any platform. To subscribe, send an email message to listserv@is.twi.tudelft.nl or to listserv@zxduticai.twi.tudelft.nl with one line of text.

Other Information Resources on Groupware

GroupTalk (The Newsletter of Workgroup Computing)
David Coleman, Editor
Collaborative Strategies
1470 DeHaro Street, San Francisco, CA 94107
For subscription information, contact Abby Kutner
Phone (415) 282-9197, FAX (415) 550-8556 or E-mail; grouptalk@collobora
Possible electronic publication in late 1995. $395 annually, $449 overseas

GroupWare News
Roger Whitehead, Editor; Office Futures
14 Amy Road
SURREY RH8OPX UK
Phone 44 (88) 371-3074, FAX 883-716793, E-mail; rwhitehead@cix.com-pulink.co.uk.
250£/year, 275£ outside Europe

Workgroup Computing Report
Ronni Marshak, Editor
The Patricia Seybold Group
148 State Street, 7th Floor
Boston, MA 02109
Phone (617) 742-5200, E-mail; Rmarshak@mcimail.Com

Ferris Newsletter
David Ferris, Editor
Ferris Networks
353 Sacramento St.
San Francisco, CA 94111
Phone (415) 986-1414, FAX (617) 742-1028

MacGroupware Yellow Pages
ftp://netcom.com/pub/consensus/groupware

LNOTES-L A mailing list created to exchange information bet
Lotus Notes users. This list will supplement comp.groupware (a Usenet
group) in aiding Lotus Notes users and prospective users in many is
including, but not limited to, technical support, bug reports and workarou
configuration information, recommendations for future versions of Notes.
general talk about Lotus Notes development, implementation, administra
and so forth. Please note that this list is in no way connected with Lotus Co
ration or any of its subsidiaries. To subscribe to this list, send a messag
lnotes-l-request@wums.wustl.edu. In the body of the letter, enter SUBSCF
LNOTES-L. You will then be automatically added to the list.